CALIFORNIA PERSONAL INJURY PROOF

CALIFORNIA CONTINUING EDUCATION OF THE BAR

CALIFORNIA PRACTICE BOOK NO. 48

By
ELMER LOW

in association with

PAUL I. PEYRAT
Chief Legal Editor

MARY C. FISHER, MELVIN S. WITT
Legal Editors

Library of Congress Catalog Card No 71-630382

© 1970 by The Regents of the University of California
Printed in the United States of America

CALIFORNIA CONTINUING EDUCATION OF THE BAR

The State Bar of California, guided by its Committee on Continuing Education of the Bar, which is assisted by the Advisory Committee of Deans of Accredited Law Schools, offers educational programs for the benefit of practicing lawyers through the facilities of University of California Extension and in conjunction with local bar associations.

Practice books are published to accompany the various programs. Authors are given full opportunity to express their individual legal interpretations and opinions, and these obviously are not intended to reflect any position of the State Bar of California or of University Extension. Chapters written by employees of state or federal agencies are not to be considered statements of governmental policies.

State Bar Committee for 1969-1970

E. DEAN PRICE, Modesto, Chairman
JOHN M. CRANSTON, San Diego, Vice Chairman
VINCENT CULLINAN, San Francisco, Liaison Governor
THOMAS M. JENKINS, San Francisco, Liaison Governor
FORREST A. PLANT, Sacramento, Liaison Governor
JOHN T. WILLIAMS, Oakland, Liaison Governor
EDWARD J. ALLEN, Red Bluff
D. CAMERON BAKER, JR., San Francisco
WILLIAM J. BETTS, Concord
ARTHUR H. BREDENBECK, Burlingame
LOUIS M. BROWN, Los Angeles
SAMUEL L. KURLAND, Los Angeles
RONALD H. MAAS, San Jose
EUGENE A. MASH, Merced
DONALD E. OREN, Fresno
VARNUM PAUL, San Francisco
ISADORE PRINZMETAL, Los Angeles
ROBERT L. RISLEY, Santa Ana
WILLIAM T. SELBY, Ventura
JAMES C. SOPER, Oakland
BORIS S. WOOLLEY, Torrance
KENNETH B. WRIGHT, Los Angeles
BERTON J. BALLARD, San Francisco, Secretary

Advisory Committee of Law School Deans

Dean J. LANI BADER, Golden Gate College
Dean EDWARD L. BARRETT, JR., University of California (Davis)
Dean ROBERT K. CASTETTER, California Western University
Dean EDWARD C. HALBACH, JR., University of California (Berkeley)
Dean BAYLESS MANNING, Stanford University
Dean J. P. MCFARLAND, San Francisco Law School
Dean DOROTHY W. NELSON, University of Southern California
Dean LEO O'BRIEN, Loyola University
Dean ARTHUR M. SAMMIS, Hastings College of the Law
Dean GORDON D. SCHABER, McGeorge School of Law, University of the Pacific
Dean MURRAY A. SCHWARTZ, University of California (Los Angeles)
Dean JOSEPH A. SINCLITICO, JR., University of San Diego
Acting Dean GEORGE A. STRONG, University of Santa Clara School of Law
Dean FRANCIS R. WALSH, University of San Francisco
Dean PAUL W. WILDMAN, Southwestern University

> *It is a rare law graduate who knows how to ask questions — simple single questions, one at a time, in order to develop facts in evidence, either in interviewing a witness or examining him in court.*
>
> Chief Justice Warren E. Burger
> 92d annual meeting of the
> American Bar Association

Preface

To assist attorneys in developing evidence in a personal injury case, the California Continuing Education of the Bar has prepared this practice book with contributions from many members of the bar.

Elmer Low of Los Angeles and Pasadena provided the original manuscript, continuing consultation, and a final review of the edited manuscript. Mr. Low has practiced personal injury and trial law for nearly 30 years. He received a B.S. degree from the City College of New York, an LL.B. from Fordham University, and a J.S.D. from New York University. He is a member of the American, Western, California, and Los Angeles Trial Lawyers Associations, has held offices in a number of lawyer's groups, and is currently President of the Pasadena Bar Association. Mr. Low is also the author of How to Prepare and Try a Negligence Case (1957) and numerous articles and papers on trial practice. He is a frequent and informative speaker at meetings of trial lawyers.

In preparing the original manuscript, Mr. Low was aided by Clyde Lockwood of the Los Angeles bar, and the draft was edited and augmented by Continuing Education of the Bar attorneys.

Valuable technical information was supplied by:

Daniel J. O'Connell, Supervising Inspector, California Highway Patrol, Sacramento; and

Ernest S. Starkman, Professor of Engineering, University of California, Berkeley.

Leading plaintiff and defense trial practitioners from throughout California read parts of the manuscript and contributed comments and suggestions that have been incorporated in the text. They are: C. Richard Bartalini, Alameda; James K. Norman, Auburn; Warren C. Deutsch, Beverly Hills; David R. Fuller, Chico; Clifford B. Mitchell, Eureka; Truman F. Campbell, Robert E. Coyle, Harold D. Sandell, and Robert E. Sears, Fresno; George W. Humphries, Glendale; Eugene McClosky, Hollywood; Ingall W. Bull, Jr., Harold J. Hunter, Jr., John T. La Follette, Malcolm H.

PREFACE

Mackey, John A. McCaskey, Jr., Donald C. Petersen, Richard F. Runkle, and John D. St. Pierre, Los Angeles; Wm. Shannon Parrish, Thomas F. Schrag, and John F. Van De Poel, Oakland; David C. Rust, Sacramento; Nat A. Agliano, Salinas; Albert R. Abramson, Thomas M. Carnes, R. Jay Engel, Vernon L. Goodin, L. F. Haeberle, III, Desmond G. Kelly, Michael Kennedy, Eugene N. Rosenberg, Richard Saveri, and C. Gordon Taylor, San Francisco; Francis J. Stillman, San Mateo; Richard Belcher, Nat Brown, Jr., and Claude H. Smart, Jr., Stockton; David Jay Morgan, South San Francisco; J. Clinton Peterson, Vallejo; and Lawrence Weitzer, Wilmington.

The index was prepared by Dorothea A. Flaherty. Production editing was handled by Loralee Windsor Lowe with the assistance of Robyn Brode.

WILLIAM A. CARROLL
Assistant Administrator

Contents

Introduction xi

PART I Witnesses

1. Examining Witnesses 1
2. Impeachment 37
3. Plaintiff 59
4. Police Officers 87
5. Technical Experts 143
6. Medical Experts 175
7. Other Witnesses on Damages 239

PART II Exhibits and Demonstrations

8. Handling Exhibits and Demonstrations 253
9. Police Accident Reports 287
10. Discovery Documents 301
11. Business Records 319
12. Official Records 337
13. Hospital and Medical Records 343
14. Medical Bills 379
15. Photographs 391
16. X-Ray Films 407
17. Motion Pictures 423
18. Models 441
19. Maps and Diagrams 451

PART III Judicial Notice

20. Judicial Notice 467

References Cited in Text 495
Table of Statutes 497
Index 507

Proof is the establishment by evidence of a requisite degree of belief concerning a fact in the mind of the trier of fact. Evidence Code §190.

Introduction

This book deals with the presentation, introduction, and use of evidence in personal injury trials. It shows how to qualify the witnesses who are commonly called, how to elicit the kinds of testimony typically given, how to lay the foundation for the introduction of exhibits in evidence, and how to interpret and explain them to the jury. Chapters 1 (Examining Witnesses), 2 (Impeachment), 8 (Handling Exhibits and Demonstrations), and 20 (Judicial Notice) round out the coverage of procedures for using evidence to convince the trier of fact.

The question-answer dialogues used throughout the book serve as a basis for witness examination or at least as examples of testimony that can be expected. They are not intended to be followed verbatim by lawyer and witness. In using these dialogues, the lawyer must fill in the facts of his case, and should not hesitate to use his own time-tested variations as long as they satisfy Evidence Code requirements. The dialogues have been edited to be grammatical, coherent, succinct, and generally applicable, while retaining some courtroom flavor. Words enclosed by brackets [ ] are optional or alternate phrasings or examples of matter that might be stated in a typical question or answer.

This book is not a substitute for careful witness preparation. No witness can be counted on to deliver a complete or effective answer merely because he is asked a particular question. Similarly, although questions have been designed to avoid successful objection, no one can guarantee that an opponent will not object, or that the trial judge will not sustain the objection.

Discussions of the admissibility of evidence usually start with specific sections of applicable California statutes, particularly the Evidence Code (as amended through 1969). This practice book does not undertake exhaustive analysis of case law, but refers the reader to the extended discussions and case analyses in Witkin publications, particularly Witkin, CALIFORNIA EVIDENCE (2d ed, 1966). Further references are made to CALIFORNIA TRIAL OBJECTIONS (Cal CEB 1967) and Johns, CALIFORNIA DAMAGES (1969). The decisional law cited has been checked through 71 C2d and 276 CA2d (the final volumes in the second series of these reports).

INTRODUCTION

This book concentrates on procedures for introducing evidence at a personal injury trial; it does not cover the proof of particular facts. For the latter, see the multi-volume set AMERICAN JURISPRUDENCE, PROOF OF FACTS. On medical proof, see also Houts, LAWYER'S GUIDE TO MEDICAL PROOF (1966).

PAUL I. PEYRAT
Chief Editor

PART I
Witnesses

1

Examining Witnesses

I. General Considerations

A. [§1.1] Preparing Witness for Direct Examination
1. [§1.2] Attendance; Dress; Behavior
2. [§1.3] How To Answer Questions
3. [§1.4] Testimony on Time, Speed, Distance
B. Direct Examination Techniques
1. [§1.5] Style and Sequence
2. [§1.6] Phrasing Questions
3. [§1.7] Semantics
4. [§1.8] Addressing and Referring to Parties and Witnesses
C. Using Questions Objectionable in Form
1. [§1.9] Calling for Narrative Answers
2. [§1.10] Leading
   a. [§1.11] Preliminary and Foundational Matters
   b. [§1.12] Experts

II. Lay Witnesses

A. Qualifications
1. [§1.13] Credibility
2. [§1.14] Competency; Capacity
3. [§1.15] Personal Knowledge
B. [§1.16] Lay Opinion Testimony
1. [§1.17] Subject Matter
2. [§1.18] Foundation

III. Expert Witnesses

A. [§1.19] Special Qualifications
1. [§1.20] Reasons for Showing
2. [§1.21] Sufficiency

            3. [§1.22] Offers To Concede
            4. [§1.23] Arguing Comparative Qualifications
        B. [§1.24] Expert Opinion Testimony
            1. [§1.25] Subject Matter
            2. [§1.26] Bases for Opinions
            3. [§1.27] Stating Reasons and Bases
        C. [§1.28] Using Hypothetical Questions
            1. [§1.29] On Direct Examination
            2. [§1.30] On Cross-Examination

    IV. [§1.31] Refreshing Memory
        A. [§1.32] Types of Writings Used To Refresh
        B. Before Testimony
            1. [§1.33] Writings
            2. [§1.34] Suggestion
        C. During Testimony
            1. [§1.35] Writing Handed to Witness
            2. [§1.36] Writing Carried to Stand
            3. [§1.37] Leading Questions
        D. [§1.38] Adverse Party's Rights
        E. [§1.39] Request for Production as Discovery Device

    V. Tactics Against Cross-Examination
        A. [§1.40] Preparing the Witness
        B. [§1.41] Objecting
        C. [§1.42] Eliciting Unfavorable Matter on Direct

    VI. Redirect Examination
        A. [§1.43] Purposes; Limitations
        B. [§1.44] Showing Prior Consistent Statements

    VII. [§1.45] Rebuttal

I. GENERAL CONSIDERATIONS

A. [§1.1] *Preparing Witness for Direct Examination*

A trial lawyer's primary opportunity to prove his client's case is during the direct examination of favorable witnesses. The lawyer should therefore prepare each witness he intends to call, not only to testify fully and accurately, but also to be a person whom the trier of fact will listen to, understand, remember, and believe.

Methods for preparing witnesses vary from lawyer to lawyer and depend on such factors as the witness's importance to the case, age,

EXAMINING WITNESSES §1.2

status, and experience in court. Witness preparation techniques are discussed in the tape recording *Preparing and Examining Witnesses* (Cal CEB 1968). See also CALIFORNIA CIVIL PROCEDURE DURING TRIAL §§2.33, 10.7–10.10, 19.20 (Cal CEB 1960). Sections 1.2–1.4 of this book list a number of the instructions on courtroom demeanor and direct testimony that lawyers commonly give to their witnesses. Further instructions to prepare a witness for cross-examination are given in §1.40.

Occasionally, a lawyer encounters a witness who defies preparation or would make a bad impression no matter how much time was devoted to preparing him. Without revealing this difficulty to his adversaries, the lawyer can sometimes obtain a stipulation that a fact or facts are true or that a witness, if called, would testify to a particular fact. See CCP §283; *Palmer v Long Beach* (1948) 33 C2d 134, 199 P2d 952; *O'Hare v Peacock Dairies, Inc.* (1941) 42 CA2d 788, 793, 110 P2d 90, 93; BAJI No 1.02. The request for a stipulation should be made outside the presence of the jury. *Romeo v Jumbo Mkt.* (1967) 247 CA2d 817, 56 CR 26.

1. [§1.2] Attendance; Dress; Behavior

A lawyer often gives many of the following instructions when preparing a witness to testify on direct examination:

> You will be served with a subpena to appear as a witness in the [Superior/Municipal] Court. The courtroom is Room ...... on the ...... floor of the County Courthouse which is at .... Get there no later than ...... o'clock. My office will call you if there is any change in the time.

Comment: See CCP §1985.1 on the use of agreements to appear at another time than that specified in the subpena.

> Come right into the courtroom and sit in one of the spectators' benches. Don't sit next to the [plaintiff/defendant] or anyone you know. Avoid talking with anyone, even during a recess.
>
> You will probably have to wait a little before your name is called. This will give you a chance to watch other witnesses testifying.
>
> If there's anything you think you should tell me before you start testifying, write it down on a piece of paper and ask the bailiff to bring it to me. He will be in uniform.
>
> When your name is called, walk straight through the gate to where the clerk will swear you in, then go to the witness chair and sit down.

I will ask you questions, then one or more other attorneys will. The judge or one of the attorneys will tell you when you are excused.

When you leave the stand, walk directly out of the courtroom [and return to your job]. Don't nod or stop to talk to me or the [plaintiff/defendant]. If you do, or stay around the courtroom after you have finished testifying, jurors might get the idea that you have a financial interest in the case.

(Men)

Wear [a conservative suitcoat and tie/your uniform/your workclothes].

(Women)

Wear [a conservative suit or dress/your uniform]. You'll probably want to wear nylons, very little make-up, and not much jewelry.

The idea is to look neat and dignified, but not too stylish.

While I'm asking you questions, or while you are answering, one of the other lawyers may interrupt with an objection. These are mostly on technicalities that you don't need to worry about. Just listen closely to the next question and answer it as precisely as you can.

Be respectful to court personnel and lawyers, but not too friendly; jurors may get the idea that you appear in court often.

Please don't drink any alcohol or take tranquilizers before you come to court; it won't really make you less nervous and may cause you to sound confused.

I notice that you [chew gum/tap your foot/talk with your hand over your mouth/etc.]; that can distract jurors and they may not hear everything you have to say.

I can tell from talking to you that you know your facts, and you're going to be a fine, strong witness who comes across as a sincere and dignified person.

2. [§1.3] How To Answer Questions

Advice to a witness on how to answer questions on direct examination could be stated as follows:

Don't try to memorize your story or any particular answers. Just listen carefully to each question I ask and answer it as directly and truthfully as you can.

Don't guess at the answer. There's nothing wrong with saying you don't understand the question, don't know, or don't remember. If I think you should know the answer, I'll ask another question or hand you something to refresh your memory.

It's usually best to be as brief as possible; I can always ask another question if I want more information. If you volunteer information that goes beyond the question, jurors may think you are biased in favor of [Mr. ....] and lose faith in your testimony.

Also, if I ask a question that calls for information you think might hurt [Mr. ....], don't try to hold it back or you may sound biased. Just answer my question in a truthful and straightforward way.

3. [§1.4] Testimony on Time, Speed, Distance

Lay witnesses often testify about time, speed, and distance in numerical terms that are patently incorrect. For example: "When I first saw him a minute before he hit me he was about 30 feet away, going 45 miles an hour." A lawyer who is preparing a witness to testify should look for these misconceptions and help the witness to correct them.

The witness can be encouraged to use conceptual terms and avoid numbers on direct examination. For example, "It happened almost instantly," "It was only a brief time," "He was going faster than I was," "I was moving with the flow of traffic," "He was quite close," "He was at least half a block away," and so forth. Lay witnesses are permitted to give testimony on these matters in opinion form. See §1.17.

Of course, cross-examiners often press witnesses for precise numercial estimates, hoping for misstatements that can be exploited to discredit the witness and counsel's theory of the case.

B. Direct Examination Techniques

1. [§1.5] Style and Sequence

The lawyer should plan each direct examination in advance so that he can ask questions clearly and smoothly. His own assured and professional attitude may help to calm nervous witnesses and engender confidence in the lawyer. By using a conversational tone that is loud enough for all to hear, he encourages the witness to speak out. Some lawyers try to sit or stand near the jury to make sure that the witness speaks toward the jury loudly enough to be heard. By contrast, a lawyer who pauses to formulate each question, stumbles over phrasing, shuffles papers, and moves from place to place in the courtroom, can upset an already anxious witness and distract jurors from the testimony.

Some lawyers carry an outline of topics or questions for each witness in their trial notebooks. Others write out questions verbatim. Verbatim questions can be useful when the phrasing must be precise to avoid an objection. However, reading questions verbatim may bore jurors, the witness's answers may sound rehearsed and unconvincing, and the lawyer may have trouble phrasing additional questions if the one he asks does not get the expected answer.

Some trial lawyers strive to begin and end each direct examination on a strong point, feeling that jurors at those times are most attentive and receptive. Other lawyers adhere to a strict chronological development, or to the sequence in which the issues in the case will be argued. There is no "correct" order; the lawyer should outline what seems to him the best sequence for each examination.

2. [§1.6] Phrasing Questions

Questions asked on direct examination should be short and direct, requiring a single, specific answer. They should be proper in form and not call for inadmissible matter. No lawyer can prevent adverse counsel from objecting, but proper phrasing can reduce the chances that objections will be sustained and discourage opponents from constantly interrupting. There are occasions when lawyers ask questions that are technically objectionable in form in order to speed up the examination and give greater impact to the testimony. See §§1.9–1.12. For extensive discussion of objections to the form of questions, see CALIFORNIA TRIAL OBJECTIONS chaps 7–16 (Cal CEB 1967).

3. [§1.7] Semantics

Direct examiners should avoid unusual words and legal jargon. Many witnesses and jurors do not understand words like "prior," "subsequent," "plaintiff," "deposition," "interrogatories," and "statement." Nor should the examiner lapse into the jargon of the witness, especially one testifying as an expert. The lawyer must not let his own self-satisfaction at understanding what the witness is saying distract him from his main purpose, to inform and convince the trier of fact.

The words a lawyer uses not only contribute to the clarity of his questions, but can also subtly influence the thinking of judges and jurors. For example, a plaintiff's lawyer often refers to the injuries that his client "suffered"; a defense attorney speaks of injuries "experienced," "sustained," or "incurred."

EXAMINING WITNESSES §1.9

Some lawyers avoid the word "opinion" when examining their own witnesses. They feel that a stronger impression is made when they ask their expert about his "conclusion," "judgment," "determination," or "diagnosis." Of course, the conclusions of opposing experts can be dismissed as "mere opinions."

4. [§1.8] Addressing and Referring to Parties and Witnesses

A lawyer usually refers to and addresses the party he represents by name. Constantly, but unobtrusively, he reinforces the idea that his client is a person who deserves the jury's sympathy and support. He refers to adverse parties, on the other hand, in depersonalized terms: "the plaintiff," "the defendant."

Lawyers address their own witnesses by name so that jurors will be more likely to remember them and their testimony. Titles such as "Doctor" and "Officer" are used to suggest competence or authority.

For example, a plaintiff's lawyer, questioning his own medical witness, might ask:

Q. Dr. Smith, did Miss Jones tell you what injuries she suffered in the accident of ...., 19......?

A defense attorney cross-examining an adverse medical witness might ask:

Q. Sir, did the plantiff tell you whether she incurred any injury in the alleged accident of ...., 19......?

Comment: Many of the question-answer dialogues set out in this book may be used by a lawyer representing either plaintiff or defendant. Thus, references to the plaintiff in these dialogues are given as "[Mr. ..../plaintiff]" to suggest that a plaintiff's lawyer would usually use his client's name while a defense attorney would more often use "plaintiff."

C. *Using Questions Objectionable in Form*

1. [§1.9] Calling for Narrative Answers

A narrative answer is one in which the witness responds at length to a general question, rather than stating individual facts in answer to a series of specific questions. The witness tells his story in his own words and sequence, uninterrupted by the lawyer. If a witness is favorable, and can express himself clearly and logically, little is gained by keeping a close question-answer rein on him. Specific questions can later be asked to direct the witness to any points he failed to mention or emphasize.

Adverse attorneys rarely object on the ground that a question is too general or calls for a narrative answer. For discussion of this objection, see CALIFORNIA TRIAL OBJECTIONS §10.4 (Cal CEB 1967); Witkin, CALIFORNIA EVIDENCE §1154 (2d ed, 1966). The trial judge, as part of his exercise of control over the mode of interrogation (Evid C §765), can permit narrative answers. Nevertheless, the direct examiner should be prepared to ask specific questions in case an objection is made and sustained.

Narrative answers are not always advantageous. Asking a general question gives adverse counsel a chance to interrupt. If the witness is nervous or his thoughts not well organized, a narrative answer can be rambling and confusing. He might utter unexpected harmful testimony, use phraseology that conveys a wrong impression, or state inadmissible matter that causes the interruption and confusion of an objection or motion to strike. If the witness's narrative answer lacks detail, the examiner must follow up with specific questions, and jurors are more likely to feel that the witness is being coached than if specific questions had been asked in the first place.

Lawyers who use "takeoff questions" usually tell the witness in advance when the question will be asked and what the witness should do. For example:

> Now when I reach this point I'm going to ask you ["What did you see then?"]. I want you to tell the jury [what you saw] just like you told the story to me. I won't interrupt you unless I think you're getting off the track, or there is some specific point that should be cleared up. Don't try to memorize or rehearse what you're going to say. Just think about [what you saw], and fix in your mind the way it happened, then tell the jury about it in your own words. But there is one thing—if you remember anything between now and the time you are called to the witness stand that you haven't told me about, please let me know right away.

2. [§1.10] Leading

A leading question suggests to the witness the answer desired by the examiner. Evid C §764. It is improper to ask a leading question on direct or redirect examination except under certain special circumstances. Evid C §767. For a listing and discussion of exceptions, see CALIFORNIA TRIAL OBJECTIONS §§13.4–13.11 (Cal CEB 1967); Witkin, CALIFORNIA EVIDENCE §1157 (2d ed, 1966).

Lawyers sometimes intentionally ask leading questions in order to keep the flow of testimony smooth and interesting, and to help the witness keep his answers relevant, responsive, complete, and free of

EXAMINING WITNESSES §1.12

inadmissible matter. Adverse attorneys usually do not object to questions that are only mildly or technically leading, and most judges will permit some leading. But a question should not appear patently designed to suggest an answer the witness would not otherwise give, or to give him the words in which his answer is to be phrased.

A direct examiner's problem is to ask questions specific enough to control the witness, but not so specific that opposing counsel is moved to object. Questions should suggest the subject and scope of the answer but not its substance or content.

A question is not leading simply because it can be answered "yes" or "no." It is leading if it suggests that the answer is "yes" rather than "no," or vice versa. Nor is an otherwise leading question automatically converted into nonleading form by such words as, "State whether or not . . . ," "if any," or "if at all," although these words may save a few questions from objection.

a. [§1.11] Preliminary and Foundational Matters

Leading questions are properly used to elicit background information from a witness in order to bring him "to the point to which he is expected to testify" (*Bruce v Western Pipe & Steel Co.* (1917) 177 C 25, 27, 169 P 660, 661), or to "lead the witness more quickly to matters which are material to the issues" (*People v Orona* (1947) 79 CA2d 820, 827, 180 P2d 694, 698). See also CALIFORNIA TRIAL OBJECTIONS §13.5 (Cal CEB 1967); Witkin, CALIFORNIA EVIDENCE §1157 (2d ed, 1966). A preliminary question like the following would usually be allowed:

Q. Mr. ...., did you witness an automobile accident at the intersection of .... and .... Streets at about ......m. on ...., 19......?

Comment: A trial judge also has discretion to permit leading questions to be asked of a witness in connection with the identification of exhibits. *People v Wilson* (1941) 46 CA2d 218, 224, 115 P2d 598, 601. Judges may also permit leading questions in connection with the authentication of writings and for other foundational purposes.

b. [§1.12] Experts

Questions that suggest the desired answer can legitimately be asked of expert witnesses. See *People v Campbell* (1965) 233 CA2d 38, 44, 43 CR 237, 241; *Chula v Superior Court* (1952) 109 CA2d 24, 38, 240 P2d 398, 407; Official Comment to Evidence Code §767. This exception to the leading question prohibition is made on the theory that experts are not as suggestible as lay witnesses, at least in the field of their competence, and that the examiner can often help an expert tell the trier of fact what he knows by suggesting alternatives to the expert's technical language.

It is not always wise to ask leading questions of experts. An opponent can interpose objections, and even though they are overruled, the process interrupts the testimony and can cause confusion. Even if no objections are made, jurors may form the impression that the lawyer rather than the witness is testifying, or conclude that improper questions are being used.

II. LAY WITNESSES

A. *Qualifications*

1. [§1.13] Credibility

A lay witness is any witness who is not testifying as an expert. See Evid C §800. When lawyers talk of "qualifying" a lay witness, they usually mean bringing out his general character, background, and impartiality. This is "qualification" in a broad sense of the term, and emphasizes the witness's credibility, rather than his competency or capacity to testify (see §1.14).

Evidence about the credibility of a witness is relevant evidence (Evid C §210), and the credibility of a witness may be supported by any party, including the party calling him (Evid C §785). However, evidence of good character is inadmissible to support credibility unless evidence of bad character has been admitted to attack credibility. Evid C §790. The judge may also exclude credibility testimony if he decides that its admission would take too much time, cause undue prejudice, confuse the issues, or mislead the jury. Evid C §352.

The factors of a witness's general background that incline jurors to heed his testimony vary from witness to witness and operate in conjunction with his general appearance, demeanor, and manner of testifying. The witness's name not only identifies him as an individual, but may connect him with a locally respected national group. A residence address in a good neighborhood, home ownership, and the fact that he has lived in the community for a number of years can suggest that he is a person of substance. His occupation, academic or honorary titles, and other accomplishments may help identify him as an experienced and intelligent individual, even though there is no thought of qualifying him as an expert witness. His acquaintance with the party for whom he testifies can show his opportunity to observe the matter about which he testifies; his lack of acquaintance indicates his dis-

EXAMINING WITNESSES §1.15

interestedness in the outcome. Some lawyers even bring out that the witness is testifying in response to a subpena on the theory that this suggests impartiality.

2. [§1.14] Competency; Capacity

"Qualification" in a narrow sense means the competency or capacity to be a witness. A person is qualified to testify as a witness unless the trial judge determines that he (a) cannot be understood, even with the help of an interpreter; (b) cannot understand his duty to tell the truth; or (c) is specifically disqualified by a statute. Evid C §§700–701.

The party that calls the witness does not need to make a preliminary showing that the person is competent to be a witness. The burden is on the opposing party to prove his lack of capacity. Official Comment to Evidence Code §405. See also CALIFORNIA TRIAL OBJECTIONS §18.5 (Cal CEB 1967); Witkin, CALIFORNIA EVIDENCE §768 (2d ed, 1966). The matter is usually determined following a voir dire examination conducted by the judge or opposing counsel. See Witkin, EVIDENCE §773.

3. [§1.15] Personal Knowledge

"'Personal knowledge' means a present recollection of an impression derived from the exercise of the witness' own senses. . . ." Official Comment to Evidence Code §702. Personal knowledge depends on the capacity of the witness to perceive and recollect. See Official Comment to Evidence Code §701. See also Evid C §170 (perceive means to acquire knowledge through one's senses).

Except for experts testifying in opinion form (see Evid C §§801–802; §§1.24–1.27), the testimony of a witness concerning a particular matter is inadmissible unless he has personal knowledge of that matter. Evid C §702(a). See Witkin, CALIFORNIA EVIDENCE §771 (2d ed, 1966).

The party that calls a witness does not need to show that the witness has personal knowledge of the matter about which he is to testify unless another party objects. For grounds of objection, see CALIFORNIA TRIAL OBJECTIONS §§18.24–18.29 (witness incompetent), 21.5, 21.20 (insufficient foundation to show that witness has personal knowledge) (Cal CEB 1967).

When an objection is made, personal knowledge must be shown before the witness may testify further concerning the matter. Evid C §702(a). The party that called the witness must produce evidence sufficient to sustain a finding of the witness's personal knowledge. See Official Comment to Evidence Code §403. Personal knowledge can be shown by the witness's own testimony, which is the usual case, or by any other admissible evidence. Evid C §702(b).

Even though the examiner is not required to show his witness's personal knowledge, he often wants to bring out the witness's opportunity and capacity to perceive and recollect to support his credibility. See Evid C §780(c), (d). For a discussion of impeachment by showing faulty perception or recollection, see §2.4.

B. [§1.16] *Lay Opinion Testimony*

Any competent lay witness can testify in the form of an opinion if it relates to certain subjects (see §1.17), or is rationally based on his perception, and would be helpful to a clear understanding of his testimony. Evid C §800. See generally CALIFORNIA TRIAL OBJECTIONS §§20.1–20.2 (Cal CEB 1967); Witkin, CALIFORNIA EVIDENCE §391 (2d ed, 1966).

Testimony in the form of an opinion expresses an inference, conclusion, or other subjective statement of the witness. See Official Comment preceding Evidence Code §800. Opinion testimony is often contrasted with "factual" testimony—testimony about conditions and events perceived by the witness. In practice, it is sometimes difficult to distinguish fact from opinion. Much "factual" testimony contains some inference, opinion, or subjective statement.

A direct examiner who is met with the objection that his question or the testimony calls for, or is, inadmissible opinion can argue that:

(1) the testimony is essentially factual, although it appears to contain some measure of inference, judgment, or subjective interpretation;

(2) the testimony is on a subject about which lay opinion testimony is permitted by law without further foundation (see §1.17); or

(3) the opinion is rationally based on the witness's perception, and would help the jury understand his testimony (see §1.18).

Failing these three approaches, the lawyer could try to establish that the witness is qualified to testify as an expert on the particular subject, and that the opinion is a proper one for expert testimony and is based on proper matter. See §§1.19, 1.25–1.26.

1. [§1.17] *Subject Matter*

A lay witness is "permitted by law" to testify in opinion form on certain subjects even though he makes no foundational showing that the opinion is rationally based on his perception or helps to make his testimony clear. Official Comment to Evidence Code §800. Included in this group of subjects are the following, which are discussed in the indicated sections of Witkin, CALIFORNIA EVIDENCE (2d ed, 1966):

Subject	Witkin
Sanity of a person (see also Evid C §870)	§393
Witness's own intent, motive, or knowledge	§394
Value of witness's services	§402
Value of witness's property	§403

Lay opinion testimony on the following subjects can be received, although the proponent may be required to show that the opinion is rationally based on the witness's perception and would help to make his testimony clear:

Subject	Witkin
Identity of a person	§392
Speed, distance, size, etc.	§396
Appearance or demeanor of a person	§397
Intoxication	§398
State of health, prior illness or injury	§399
Age, parentage	§400
Ownership or possession of property	§401
Character for honesty, veracity, etc. (see also Evid C §§780(e), 790, 1100)	§1241

2. [§1.18] Foundation

A lawyer drawing opinion testimony from a lay witness does not need to elicit foundational testimony until an opponent objects that the testimony is, or would be, inadmissible opinion. He may wish to do so, however, both to avoid an objection, and because foundational testimony tends to add weight to opinion. To establish that an opinion is (a) rationally based on the witness's perception and (b) helpful to a clear understanding of his testimony, the lawyer can examine the witness on such matters as: his opportunity to observe the matter to which his opinion relates; his training, skill, or experience in forming judgments of that kind; any specific facts or information he remembers taking into account; and his inability to convey fairly his impressions or describe his observations other than in terms of a conclusion.

A lay witness may state on direct examination the reasons for his opinion and the matter on which it is based; the judge can even require him to do so before he testifies to his opinion. Evid C §802. Unlike some expert opinion testimony (see §1.26), lay opinions should not be based on the statements or opinions of other persons, or on otherwise irrelevant, speculative, or inadmissible matter.

III. EXPERT WITNESSES

A. [§1.19] Special Qualifications

A lawyer "qualifies" a witness to testify as an expert by eliciting testimony, usually from the witness himself, to show his special knowledge, skill, experience, training, and education in the subject on which he is to testify. A witness "testifies as an expert" when he:

(1) testifies in the form of an opinion on a subject that is beyond common experience (see Evid C §801);

(2) states the reasons for his opinion and the matter on which it is based (see Evid C §802), which may include matter not personally known to him and otherwise inadmissible (see Evid C §801(b));

(3) testifies about facts that nonexperts would be incapable of perceiving, comprehending, or describing (see Witkin, CALIFORNIA EVIDENCE §407 (2d ed, 1966)).

A person who is otherwise competent to be a witness (see §1.14) is qualified to testify as an expert on a particular subject unless the judge determines that the person does not have sufficient special knowledge, skill, experience, training, and education to qualify him as an expert on that subject. See Evid C §720.

The lawyer who calls a witness to testify as an expert need not show the witness's special qualifications unless another party requires it. The proponent can ask questions that call for expert testimony until the adversary objects that the witness is not competent to give the testimony asked for, or that a sufficient foundation has not been laid showing that the witness is qualified as an expert. See CALIFORNIA TRIAL OBJECTIONS §§20.6, 20.12, 21.8 (Cal CEB 1967). Special qualifications can be shown by the witness's own testimony or any other admissible evidence. Evid C §720(b).

1. [§1.20] Reasons for Showing

The reasons for bringing out a witness's special qualifications on direct examination include:

(a) To qualify him to testify as an expert (see Evid C §720);

(b) To show part of the matter on which his opinion testimony is based (see Evid C §802);

(c) To support his credibility (see §1.13);

(d) To provide a factual basis for arguing the superiority of his qualifications over those of adverse experts (see §1.23);

EXAMINING WITNESSES §1.22

(e) To show qualifications in a favorable light before the witness is cross-examined on qualifications under Evid C §721(a) (see §2.15).

Qualifications are frequently brought out on direct examination even when the lawyer does not anticipate an objection to the witness's testifying as an expert.

2. [§1.21] Sufficiency

The Evidence Code does not prescribe what kinds or quantities of special knowledge, skill, experience, training, or education must be shown to qualify a witness to testify as an expert. The trial judge must determine in each case whether the special qualifications shown are sufficient to justify permitting the witness to testify as an expert on the particular subject. The judge's determination is binding on the jury although the jury can consider the witness's special qualifications in determining the weight to be given the testimony. See Official Comment to Evidence Code §720; Evid C §405. See also Witkin, CALIFORNIA EVIDENCE §1175 (2d ed, 1966).

Holding a professional license or a college degree does not necessarily qualify a witness to testify as an expert, nor does the lack of a license, degree, or formal education automatically disqualify him. See CALIFORNIA TRIAL OBJECTIONS §20.6 (Cal CEB 1967); Witkin, EVIDENCE §411.

The lawyer who wants to qualify the witness as an expert must bring out those particular aspects of his training, experience, and achievements that will convince the judge to permit him to testify, and the jurors that he should be believed. Qualifying particular expert witnesses to testify is discussed in chaps 4–6, and §7.11.

3. [§1.22] Offers To Concede

When a lawyer begins to elicit an expert witness's special qualifications, the adverse attorney may offer to "waive the testimony as to qualifications" or "concede that the witness is qualified to testify as an expert." He does this when he has no reason to believe he can persuade the trial judge that the adverse expert is not qualified and his testimony should be excluded. He hopes that jurors will view his offer as a magnanimous gesture to speed up the trial and spare them from listening to uninteresting preliminary testimony. He also hopes that jurors will forget, or give less weight to, the testimony of an expert whose qualifications were not shown.

The lawyer who calls an expert witness often declines to accept a concession offer. He usually wants to ask questions about special qualifications for the reasons listed in §1.20. The adverse attorney may object that further showing of special qualifications is irrelevant since he has conceded that the witness is qualified to testify as an expert. The proponent of the testimony can rejoin that the evidence is relevant to show part of the basis for the witness's opinions (see Evid C §802) and to support his credibility (see Evid C §§210, 785).

An offer to concede may be countered with a statement like:

Proponent. Your Honor, we appreciate counsel's offer to concede [Mr./Dr./Professor/etc.] ....'s qualifications, but it is pertinent to an evaluation of his testimony to bring out some of the highlights of his background and accomplishments. [It is necessary to present his qualifications to enable the jury more fairly and justly to evaluate his testimony.]

The attorney can sometimes bring out a witness's qualifications while appearing to accept a concession:

Proponent. Your Honor, we appreciate counsel's offer to let us skip over a lengthy recital of [Mr./etc.] ....'s education, experience, training, skills, honors, and other accomplishments, and I'll just have him mention one or two things that will help the jury get to know him.

Sometimes concessions can be accepted advantageously. The witness whose qualifications are meager or lackluster compared to those of other experts in the case may make a better impression on the jury because his qualifications have been conceded by the other side. In accepting a concession of qualification, counsel can still convey the idea that the witness is a fully qualified expert. For example:

Proponent. As I understand it, Your Honor, counsel is conceding that [Mr./etc.] .... has the special knowledge, skill, training, experience, and education to qualify him to testify as an expert witness in this case. With that understanding I will forgo examining him on his background and accomplishments and proceed directly to the substance of his testimony.

4. [§1.23] Arguing Comparative Qualifications

Juries are commonly instructed to consider (a) the qualifications of expert witnesses in determining the weight to be given their opinions and (b) the relative qualifications of opposing experts in resolving conflicts in their testimony. See BAJI Nos 2.40–2.41. An attorney who has elicited testimony from an expert witness that shows his background and accomplishments can argue that he is better qualified than opposing experts, that any conflicts in expert testimony should therefore be resolved in favor of the party that called him, and that his testimony outweighs any contrary evidence or inferences.

B. [§1.24] Expert Opinion Testimony

An expert witness can testify in the form of an opinion if the opinion is (1) related to a subject that is sufficiently beyond common experience that an expert's opinion would assist the trier of fact (see §1.25) and (2) based on proper matter (see §1.26). Evid C §801.

The opinion testimony of any witness must be a judgment or conclusion that he himself has formed or reached. An expert can base his opinion, in part, on the opinions of other experts. See *Kelley v Bailey* (1961) 189 CA2d 728, 737, 11 CR 448, 455. But he cannot simply repeat another's opinion as his own on no other basis than reliance on the other person's judgment. Nor can he give an opinion that is nothing more than the consensus of a committee, group, or "experts in the field." See *Frampton v Hartzell* (1960) 179 CA2d 771, 4 CR 427.

1. [§1.25] Subject Matter

Expert opinion testimony is limited to subjects that are beyond the competence of persons of common experience, training, and education. Official Comment to Evidence Code §801. A witness could be prevented from testifying in opinion form as an expert if the subject were one of such common knowledge that men of ordinary education could reach the conclusion as well as the witness; the trier of fact would not then be assisted by the expert. See *People v Cole* (1956) 47 C2d 99, 103, 301 P2d 854, 856. As a practical matter, however, there are few topics in which some persons are not better educated and more experienced than most people. And, of course, the witness might be able to give the same testimony as lay opinion. See §§1.16–1.18.

Among the subjects that are proper for expert opinion testimony are the following, which are discussed in the indicated sections of Witkin, CALIFORNIA EVIDENCE (2d ed, 1966):

Subject	Witkin
Medical diagnosis, causation, prognosis	§413
Mental condition	§415
Vehicle accident points of impact, speed (from skid marks), causation	§418
Mechanical conditions, defects, etc.	§419
Safety and operating standards and practices	§420
Value of services	§422
Value of property	§423

2. [§1.26] Bases for Opinions

The opinion of a witness testifying as an expert must be based on matter (a) of a type that reasonably may be relied on by an expert in forming an opinion on the subject to which his testimony relates and (b) that an expert is not precluded by law from using as a basis for his opinion. Evid C §801(b).

"Matter" includes any conceivable basis for an opinion: facts, data, the witness's knowledge and experience, and other intangibles. Official Comment preceding Evidence Code §800. Matter need not be independently admissible. An expert can base an opinion on matter made known to the witness at or before the trial, as well as on matter perceived by or personally known to him. Evid C §801(b).

Evidence Code §801(b) requires a case by case determination of whether particular opinions are based on proper matter. For example, it is reasonable for a doctor to rely on a report given him by another doctor, but it is not reasonable for an accident investigator determining a point of impact to rely solely on the statements of bystanders. See Official Comment to Evidence Code §801. Both statements are hearsay: One is a proper basis for opinion testimony while the other is not. Similarly, expert opinion testimony cannot be based on irrelevant or speculative matter, not because those matters are inadmissible, but because it is not reasonable for experts to rely on them.

3. [§1.27] Stating Reasons and Bases

A witness testifying in the form of an opinion may "state on direct examination the reasons for his opinion and the matter . . . upon which it is based . . . ." Evid C §802. There does not seem to be any practical distinction between "reasons" and "matter." Taken together, they permit the witness to testify about the sources from which he derived the facts, data, and other information on which he based his opinion; the particular facts and information that influenced his conclusion; and his thought processes, including the application of analysis, logic, and judgment to the facts and information he considers.

Detailed testimony from an expert witness about the matter on which his opinions are based, and the reasons for them, tends to support, explain, and give impact to his opinion testimony. Sometimes it can also forestall an objection to the opinion testimony under Evid C §803, which requires the exclusion of an opinion based in whole or significant part on improper matter.

The direct examiner does not need to question his expert witness about the reasons or bases for his opinions unless the trial judge exercises his discretion under Evid C §802 to require the witness to be so examined before he testifies in opinion form. Under §802, the judge might even permit an adverse attorney to examine the witness about reasons and bases on voir dire before permitting the opinion testimony. In addition, the witness can be fully cross-examined about reasons and bases. Evid C §721(a)(3).

C. [§1.28] *Using Hypothetical Questions*

Hypothetical questions recite facts and other matter on which an expert witness is asked to base his opinion testimony. The witness is asked to assume, for the purposes of his answer, that the matter recited in the question is true, whether or not he has any knowledge of that matter, and even though he may believe it untrue. The matter on which his opinion is based is thus "made known" to him during the trial. See Evid C §801(b).

The use of hypothetical questions has been much criticized, but they are not abolished by the Evidence Code and are still employed by lawyers to elicit and test expert opinion testimony. See generally CALIFORNIA TRIAL OBJECTIONS §20.9 (Cal CEB 1967); Witkin, CALIFORNIA EVIDENCE §§1179–1181 (2d ed, 1966). When a hypothetical question is used, the jury can be instructed what it is and how to deal with it. See BAJI No 2.42.

Each fact or other item of information recited in a hypothetical question must be supported by evidence. The question cannot assume a fact not in evidence (except when the question is asked solely to test the credibility of a witness rather than to elicit his opinion testimony). *People v Busch* (1961) 56 C2d 868, 874, 16 CR 898, 901. See also Witkin, EVIDENCE §§1179–1180.

A fact recited in a hypothetical question need not be undisputed. The question is proper if there is some evidence to sustain the recited fact, the fact is reasonably inferrable from the evidence, or it is within the possible or probable range of the evidence. See *Guardianship of Jacobson* (1947) 30 C2d 312, 324, 182 P2d 537, 544; *Hutter v Hommel* (1931) 213 C 677, 680, 3 P2d 554, 556; *Sullivan v San Francisco* (1950) 95 CA2d 745, 762, 214 P2d 82, 92; *People v Becker* (1949) 94 CA2d 434, 444, 210 P2d 871, 877.

In formulating a hypothetical question, a lawyer has considerable latitude to select the facts in evidence that support his theory of the case and to omit the facts that favor his opponent. See *People v Wilson* (1944) 25 C2d 341, 349, 153 P2d 720, 724; *Hutter v Hommel, supra; Perkins v Sunset Tel. & Tel. Co.* (1909) 155 C 712, 716, 103 P 190, 192. However, the trial judge can exclude a question when an adverse attorney objects that it is so selective that it is unfair or misleading, it assumes a fact not in evidence, or the assumed facts conflict with undisputed and unimpeachable evidence. See Evid C §352; *Estate of Gould* (1922) 188 C 353, 356, 205 P 457, 458; *Estate of Dolbeer* (1906) 149 C 227, 243, 86 P 695, 702. See also Trial Objections §20.9.

An objection to a hypothetical question should point out specific deficiencies and should be made in time to give the examiner an opportunity to correct the question. See *Waller v Southern Pac. Co.* (1967) 66 C2d 201, 210, 57 CR 353, 360.

1. [§1.29] On Direct Examination

Hypothetical questions are used on direct examination (a) to supply information to an expert witness who does not have personal knowledge of the event, instrumentality, or person about whom he is to testify; and (b) as a convenient means of summarizing and restating all the favorable matter that supports the opinion to be delivered by the witness.

The Evidence Code permits an expert witness to state the matter on which his opinion is based (Evid C §802), either before or after he states his opinion. That matter can include information that is neither perceived by nor personally known to him. Thus, the use of a hypothetical question is necessary only to supply the witness with information that he did not learn from his own observations or from his study of reliable information concerning the subject. For example, facts developed through other witnesses at the trial, or information that became unavailable after the time he last investigated or examined the subject may be brought out in hypothetical questions.

Hypothetical questions asked of a party's own witness should usually be as balanced and broad as possible. The witness can often tell the lawyer in advance what unfavorable facts can be included in the question and considered by him without changing his conclusion. Generally, the more balanced the question, the fairer the examiner seems to be in presenting both favorable and unfavorable facts, the less vulnerable the question is to attack, and the less likely jurors are to reject the witness's opinion in resistance to a one-sided version of the facts.

It is good practice to write out a hypothetical question in advance and give a copy of it to the witness before he is called. This permits him to study it so that his answer does not come as a snap judgment. In many situations the witness should be asked to help formulate the question so that his answer can best serve the needs of the case.

It can be advantageous to give a copy of the question to opposing counsel and the judge and work out objections or changes in chambers. This can avoid arguments, interruptions, and stalemates before the jury.

The following dialogue shows one of the ways in which a hypothetical question could be used on direct examination:

Q. Please answer your next questions on the basis of the following facts: [Recite all facts.] Did you familiarize yourself with these facts and this information before coming here today?
A. Yes, I did.
Q. Based on those facts, have you [concluded/reached a judgment/formed an opinion/etc.] whether ....?
A. I have.
Q. Please state your conclusion.
A. ....
Q. What are the reasons for your conclusion?
A. [Witness gives his analysis and synthesis of the information, and points out matters of particular significance.]

2. [§1.30] On Cross-Examination

Hypothetical questions can be used on cross-examination (a) to gain favorable opinion testimony from an adverse expert; (b) to gain an admission that his opinion would be different if he were to base it on different assumptions; and (c) to test his accuracy, competency, or credibility.

The matter recited in a hypothetical question used on cross-examination must be within the limits of the evidence, except when the purpose of the question is to test the credibility, accuracy, or competency of the expert witness. *People v Busch* (1961) 56 C2d 868, 874, 16 CR 898, 901.

In constructing a hypothetical question to ask an adverse expert, the cross-examiner should draw from the evidence a set of facts that will force a fair-minded expert to give an answer consistent with the cross-examiner's theory. The witness can be told to assume these facts for purposes of answering the question, even though he might not believe they are true and has already given a contrary opinion based on different or contradictory matter. The cross-examiner should avoid using data that the trier of fact is unlikely to believe. The best situation is often the one in which the expert can continue to accept all the matter that his original opinion was based on, but is also asked to consider new information supplied by the cross-examiner that the witness did not know about or consider previously. If the cross-examiner can convince the trier of fact that the facts recited in his hypothetical question are more complete and accurate, the opinion given by the expert on cross-examination may prevail over the opinion he gave on direct examination.

For example, cross-examination of a defense medical doctor by a plaintiff's lawyer might proceed as follows:

Q. Sir, I would like you to assume that [eight weeks after the accident, Mr. .... was still suffering severe headaches in the occipital region]. Assuming that, would your opinion that [he had recovered from his injuries in two or three weeks] still be the same?
A. Well, I don't believe that [he still had occipital headaches at that time].
Q. I didn't ask you to believe it. I asked you to assume it. [It is a fact in evidence, testified to by a witness under oath, just like the facts you have testified to in giving the reasons and bases for your opinion.] Now, assuming those facts, would your opinion be the same?
A. No. [If he still had the headaches, he had not recovered.]

Comment: If the witness continues to resist or obstinately sticks to his opinion no matter what facts he is asked to assume, jurors can get the impression that he is more an advocate for the side that called him than a disinterested expert.

Q. Now, assuming [those headaches, and a marked tenderness over the area of the cervical spine eight weeks after the accident], wouldn't that be consistent with [a severe cervical sprain or whiplash-type injury to the neck] rather than the [mild strain that you say you diagnosed]?
A. Well, perhaps that is so, if you assume those things.
Q. Now, if you also assume that [X-ray films of his neck region made ten weeks after the accident showed a "marked straightening of the lordotic curve"], would your opinion still be [that he suffered a mild strain that cleared up in two or three weeks]?
A. No.
Q. Those [occipital headaches, tenderness over the spine, and X-ray findings] are consistent with [a severe cervical strain], aren't they?
A. Yes.
Q. [In fact, sir, if you saw a private patient, unconnected with any litigation, and he gave you a history of ...., and complained of ...., and you made X-ray films that showed ...., your diagnosis would be ...., would it not?]
A. ....

IV. [§1.31] REFRESHING MEMORY

"Refreshing memory" is the process of restoring to a witness a present recollection of matters he once knew so that he is able to testify about those matters fully and accurately from his memory of them. Memory can be revived by showing the witness a writing or by oral suggestion, and before as well as during testimony.

Refreshing a witness's memory with a writing (Evid C §771) differs from reading it into evidence as past recollection recorded (Evid C §1237). In refreshing memory, the writing is used to revive the witness's memory and to enable him to testify fully and accurately about what he once observed. The witness's testimony is the evidence, not the writing. In past recollection recorded, the witness's memory is not revived by showing him the writing, but he is able to testify that the writing accurately records what he previously observed. The writing can then be read to the trier of fact as evidence. See §§8.25–8.32.

Ordinarily, a witness who has no actual present memory of the events, but knows only what has been shown or suggested to him in the attempt to revive his memory, should not testify as if his memory has been refreshed. Lawyers should avoid any refreshment technique that amounts only to feeding the witness information, then convincing him he remembers it. Cross-examination can often expose this kind of pseudo-memory, destroying the witness's, and sometimes the lawyer's, credibility.

A cross-examiner can try to refresh the memory of an adverse witness in order to obtain accurate testimony. However, a cross-examiner sometimes uses the words "refresh your memory" when his real purpose is to attack the credibility of the witness by confronting him with contradictory evidence or an inconsistent statement. The cross-examiner hopes the witness will admit that his direct testimony was incorrect or that he is less certain about what he said, but at least the contradictory matter comes before the trier of fact.

A. [§1.32] *Types of Writings Used To Refresh*

A writing can be used to refresh memory either before or during the witness's testimony. Evid C §771(a). See generally, Witkin, CALIFORNIA EVIDENCE §§1167–1169 (2d ed, 1966). "Writing" includes photographs, sound recordings, drawings, and "any form of . . . words, pictures, sounds, or symbols" recorded on "any tangible thing." Evid C §250. (The use of tape recordings to refresh memory was noted in *People v Superior Court* (1969) 70 C2d 123, 74 CR 294.)

Any writing can be used to refresh memory. It need not have been prepared by the witness or under his direction, and it need not have been made near the time the recorded events occurred. In short, it need not conform to the requirements applied to writings read into evidence as past recollection recorded.

The accuracy of a witness's testimony can be attacked on the basis of deficiencies in the writing used to refresh his memory. For example, the adverse attorney can point out, in cross-examination and argument, that the writing was contradicted by other evidence, made by an untrustworthy person, made at a time remote from the event recorded, too lacking in detail to truly refresh the witness, contrary to the witness's testimony, or unsupportive of his supposed memory. These grounds for attacking the credibility of testimony are not grounds for preventing the witness from using the writing to refresh his memory, or for striking testimony based on the writing.

Writings commonly used to refresh memory in personal injury cases include statements to an investigator (see §2.12), depositions and answers to interrogatories (see §10.22), transcripts of prior testimony, police vehicle accident reports (see §4.22), doctors' examination reports (see §6.28), and hospital and other medical records (see §13.1).

B. Before Testimony

1. [§1.33] Writings

Some lawyers have a witness read over all his previous statements and depositions, examine all photographs and diagrams in the lawyer's file, and read the written statements and depositions of other witnesses. This not only refreshes the witness about what he observed, but also shows him what he has said on prior occasions and what others have observed and said. The witness has a chance to consider how his testimony can be reconciled, if at all, with his prior statements and with other evidence.

A potential disadvantage of this approach is that each writing seen by the witness is subject to a request for production by an adverse party when the witness takes the stand. See §§1.38–1.39. The lawyer may thus wish to limit his witness to those wirtings that can be produced with equanimity for his adversaries.

It is sometimes helpful to ask a witness on direct examination whether he refreshed his memory before trial with a writing or writings. This will explain to jurors how the witness is able to remember past events so well. On the other hand, bringing the fact out on direct may inform the adverse party of a writing that he did not know about.

EXAMINING WITNESSES §1.35

2. [§1.34] Suggestion

A lawyer can refresh the witness's memory before trial by suggestion, without showing him a writing. Perhaps the simplest way to help the witness remember conditions and events is to tell the witness to (a) try to recall what he observed; (b) give some thought to each detail he recalls, so that by association other facts will come to mind; and (c) think of a logical order in which to describe what he observed, so that it will come back to him more readily in court. The lawyer can also ask the witness specific or leading questions that help him fill in the details. He can point out inconsistencies and help adjust the witness's memory to known physical facts and to testimony that will be given by other witnesses.

There is a question about what use the lawyer himself can make of writings when he is trying to refresh the memory of a witness before trial. For example, if the lawyer reads a witness's prior statement to him, the witness has used the writing to refresh his memory just as if he had read it himself. The writing may thus become a "writing used by the witness," subject to production under Evid C §771. See §§1.38–1.39. Rather than read the writing to the witness, the lawyer might read it himself, then make suggestions to the witness based on what he has read.

If the lawyer uses his own handwritten notes to prepare the witness, do those notes become a writing used by the witness that is subject to production? In this situation there is a conflict between preserving the privacy of an attorney's work product (see CCP §2016(g)), and giving cross-examiners a full opportunity to see the writings on which testimony is based (Evid C §771).

C. During Testimony

1. [§1.35] Writing Handed to Witness

Even though a witness has been thoroughly prepared to testify and has had his memory refreshed before trial, he may forget a fact or give an incorrect answer on the stand. One way to refresh the witness's memory at this point is to hand him a writing. The witness should not read directly from the writing but should look at it when he needs to, then set it aside and answer the question from his refreshed memory.

It is probably not necessary to establish that the witness does not have a present recollection before showing him a writing to refresh his memory. For example:

Q. Mr. ...., how many northbound traffic lanes are there on .... Street?

§1.36 EXAMINING WITNESSES

A. [I just don't remember./I really don't know./Three, I think.]

Examining lawyer. Your Honor, with your permission I'd like to show the witness this [statement that he made on ...., 19......./deposition/photograph/diagram/etc.] in order to refresh his memory on this point.

Comment: At this point, adverse counsel is entitled to ask to inspect the writing well enough to formulate objections to testimony made from it. After the witness has testified, adverse counsel can inspect the writing, cross-examine the witness about it, and introduce pertinent portions in evidence. See Evid C §771(b). See also §1.38.

Q. Mr. ...., please [read that to yourself/examine that]. Does that refresh your memory as to how many northbound traffic lanes there are?

A. [Yes, of course, there are four traffic lanes in each direction.]

2. [§1.36] Writing Carried to Stand

The lawyer may prefer that a witness, especially one who needs his memory continually refreshed, carry a writing to the witness stand. Policemen, for example, often testify with the aid of vehicle accident reports (see §§4.21–4.23), and doctors use medical and hospital records and reports (see §§6.27–6.28). The use of writings by these witnesses actually adds to the clarity and credibility of their testimony. Not only can they testify in greater detail and in logical sequence, but jurors can have greater confidence in the accuracy and completeness of testimony when the witness does not depend entirely on memory.

Although technically a witness is supposed to testify from his own memory refreshed by a writing, many police officers and doctors have no independent recollection of the facts contained in their reports. In effect, they read their reports as past recollection recorded (see §§8.25–8.32), although they are usually permitted to testify as if from refreshed memory.

It can be helpful to ask a few questions at the outset to inform the jury what the witness is doing with the writing and that it is proper for him to use it. For example:

Q. At the time you carried out this [investigation/examination/etc.] did you prepare a [memo/report/etc.] of [what you observed/your findings/etc.]?

A. Yes, I did.

Q. Did you bring that with you today?

A. Yes.

EXAMINING WITNESSES §1.38

Examining lawyer to adverse counsel. You have a copy of that, don't you?
Adverse lawyer. Yes, I do.
Q. Would consulting that [memo/report/etc.] help you to remember more accurately and completely what you observed and found?
A. Yes, it would.

Comment: Further questions could be asked to establish the circumstances under which the refreshing writing was prepared and its accuracy.

3. [§1.37] Leading Questions

Leading questions may be asked on direct or redirect examination to refresh a witness's memory. Official Comment to Evidence Code §767. See also Witkin, CALIFORNIA EVIDENCE §1157 (2d ed, 1966). It is usually better not to ask a leading question until the witness has said he does not remember. There may still be an objection to the question, but at least the direct examiner will not appear to be using improper procedure. For example:

Q. What was the make and model of that car?
A. [I know what it was, but I just can't remember.]
Q. Was it a [Ford two-door hardtop]?
Adverse lawyer. I object, Your Honor. That question is leading and suggestive.
Examining lawyer. Your Honor, the witness has said that he doesn't remember, and a leading question may be used to refresh the witness's memory.

Comment: If the witness gives an incorrect answer, the question may suggest the correct answer. For example:

Q. What was the make and model of that car?
A. It was a [Chevrolet two-door hardtop].
Q. Excuse me, Mr. ...., are you sure it was a [Chevrolet, or was it a Ford]?
A. Of course, it was a [Ford two-door hardtop].

D. [§1.38] *Adverse Party's Rights*

An adverse lawyer can request the witness or the party that called him to produce any writing used by the witness to refresh his memory — whether before or during testimony. Evid C §771(a). If the writing is not produced on request, the witness's testimony about it shall be stricken, unless production is excused because the witness and the

§1.39 EXAMINING WITNESSES

party that called him do not possess or control the writing and cannot reasonably procure it by subpena or otherwise. Evid C §771(c). If the writing is produced, the adverse attorney may inspect it, cross-examine the witness about it, and introduce into evidence those portions that are pertinent to the witness's testimony. Evid C §771(b).

Evidence Code §771 does not say when the request for production of the writing can be made. If the witness carries the writing to the stand, or it is handed to him, adverse counsel could ask to see it, or a copy of it, immediately. Counsel could support this request by pointing out that if he can follow the writing while the witness testifies he can formulate his cross-examination on the writing, if any, with less delay. If the witness testifies without the aid of a writing, most attorneys wait until cross-examination to ask the witness whether he used a writing to refresh his memory. If the writing is produced at that time, the attorney could ask the court for a five- or ten-minute continuance to inspect the writing and determine whether and how to use it. Theoretically, nothing prevents adverse counsel from interrupting a witness's direct examination after the first question or two, asking to examine the witness on voir dire to determine whether he used a writing to refresh his memory, and requesting that the writing be produced. If there is no valid excuse for not producing the writing, the witness can be prevented from testifying about the matters on which the writing refreshed his memory.

E. [§1.39] *Request for Production as Discovery Device*

The right to have a writing produced extends to all writings the witness used to refresh his memory, apparently no matter how long before the trial. See Evid C §771. Thus, some lawyers have used the procedure as a discovery device. The lawyer asks the witness on voir dire or cross-examination (1) whether he has seen writings, such as papers or photographs, or heard recordings relating to the facts at any time since the accident or events in question, and (2) whether they aided his memory. If the cross-examiner can establish that the witness used a writing, he requests that it be produced, whether or not it is discoverable or admissible. If the writings are not produced, he moves that the witness be prevented from testifying or that his testimony be stricken.

In *Kerns Constr. Co. v Superior Court* (1968) 266 CA2d 405, 72 CR 74, a gas company foreman filled out an accident report that was, according to its printed title, "Confidential" and "Made Out for the Use of the Company's Attorneys." Before the foreman's deposition was taken by an adverse party, he read over his report, which was

EXAMINING WITNESSES §1.40

furnished to him by the gas company's attorney. The court required the gas company to furnish the report to the adverse party. The company was said to have waived any attorney-client, or work product, privilege it may have had when it furnished the report to the foreman and permitted him to testify refreshed by it.

V. TACTICS AGAINST CROSS-EXAMINATION

A. [§1.40] *Preparing the Witness*

Preparing a witness includes preparing him to be cross-examined. Witnesses worry that trick questions will make them say the wrong thing or that they will be made to look foolish.

The lawyer might convey the following instructions to a typical witness:

> After I have finished questioning you, the other lawyers get a chance to ask you questions. Don't worry about this part of your testimony; there is no way they can trick you or embarrass you as long as you answer their questions honestly and straightforwardly.
>
> Don't exaggerate, or try to withhold information that you might think is unfavorable to our side. Listen to the questions carefully and answer them directly; don't volunteer information. If you can, answer the questions with "yes" or "no"; if you cannot, say so and go on to give your answer.
>
> If you don't know the answer or don't remember, just say so; don't guess at the answer. Tell what you saw or know, but don't try to fill in the gaps with what you think must have happened.
>
> Don't give opinions or estimates unless you are asked for them.
>
> Don't repeat what someone else told you unless you are asked to do so.
>
> If you don't understand the question, say so, and let the cross-examiner ask it again. If you think you understand it, but aren't sure, you can even rephrase it yourself. For example, you might say, "If you mean such and such, then my answer is thus and so." But don't give the impression that you are sparring with the cross-examiner or trying to avoid answering a legitimate question.
>
> Let me do the objecting. If the question is not proper, I will object to it.
>
> Wait until the lawyer finishes his question, answer it, then stop.
>
> He may appear to be waiting for you to say more, but if he wants to know more, let him ask another question.

If the answers you give are correct, don't worry too much that they might be incomplete or misinterpreted by the jury. I get a chance after the cross-examination to ask you further questions that will clear matters up.

Usually lawyers only badger a witness if it appears he is not telling the truth. If a cross-examiner does try to needle you, don't argue with him, but keep calm and hold your temper. That will make him look foolish.

The other lawyer may ask you whether you have talked to any attorneys about your testimony. Of course, your answer will be "yes," won't it? We are discussing your testimony right now, and it's entirely proper that we do so.

Another common question is, "How much are you being paid for your testimony?" The answer is that you aren't being paid anything for your testimony, but you are getting the witness fee provided by law, [and Mr. .... (party) has agreed to compensate you for the pay you will miss when you come to court.]

B. [§1.41] *Objecting*

The lawyer whose witness is being cross-examined must often exercise restraint. If he interrupts without cause, he may alert the trier of fact to the damage being done to his case. In the face of damaging cross-examination, it is often best to project an image of unconcern, general confidence, or preoccupation with more important matters.

Of course, the lawyer should not permit the cross-examination to exceed proper bounds. He should be thoroughly familiar with the objections that can be asserted against cross-examination questions and use those objections to protect the witness from improper questioning, preserve the witness's credibility, and keep out improper matter.

Generally, objections that can be asserted against questions and testimony on direct examination can also be used in cross-examination. See generally CALIFORNIA TRIAL OBJECTIONS (Cal CEB 1967). Leading questions are usually permitted on cross-examination but may be objected to if the witness appears biased in favor of the cross-examiner, or unduly influenced by questions that suggest the desired answers. See Evid C §767. Cross-examination for other than impeachment purposes can be objected to if it exceeds the scope of the direct examination. Evid C §773. See TRIAL OBJECTIONS chap 27. Cross-examination to attack the witness's credibility can be ob-

EXAMINING WITNESSES   §1.43

jected to if it involves improper impeachment. See TRIAL OBJECTIONS chap 22. An objection can also be made if the cross-examiner's manner and questioning unduly harass or embarrass the witness. Evid C §765.

C. [§1.42] Eliciting Unfavorable Matter on Direct

It is sometimes a good tactic to bring out unfavorable matter during direct examination. In the benign context of direct examination, the negative material is likely to receive less attention and have less impact. Jurors may even admire the apparent fairness of a direct examiner who shows the bad along with the good. Of course, these advantages must be weighed against the danger that adverse attorneys did not know about or plan to explore the unfavorable matters, and the direct examiner will have unnecessarily hurt his case by bringing them to the jury's attention.

VI. REDIRECT EXAMINATION

A. [§1.43] Purposes; Limitations

Redirect examination is conducted by the direct examiner subsequent to cross- or recross-examination of the witness. Evid C §762. If another party does not cross-examine the witness, there can be no redirect examination of him. Any matters not covered in the direct examination will have to be brought out in the testimony of other witnesses, or on rebuttal. See §1.45 for a discussion of rebuttal.

The principle purposes of redirect examination are: (1) to rebut unfavorable evidence and inferences raised during cross-examination; (2) to correct any errors or misimpressions conveyed by the witness or cross-examiner; (3) to explain apparent inconsistencies and clarify ambiguities in the witness's testimony; and (4) to rehabilitate the witness, *i.e.,* to support his credibility after attempts were made on cross-examination to impeach him.

Redirect examination should not be used merely to repeat or recapitulate matter covered in the direct examination. See Evid C §774 (a witness once examined cannot be reexamined on the same matter without leave of court). Of course, some reference to the same matter may be necessary, and should be permitted.

Direct examiners sometimes use redirect examination to bring out testimony they failed for some reason to elicit on direct examination. The trial judge has discretion to permit this. Evid C §772(c). However, it also appears that the trial judge has discretion under Evid C §774: (a) to limit redirect examination to new matter that was raised on cross-examination or (b) to decide that the matter sought to be raised is actually the same as that testified to on direct examination.

Generally, the rules for excluding evidence during examination also apply to redirect examination. See CALIFORNIA TRIAL OBJECTIONS §23.3 (Cal CEB 1967). This includes the rule limiting the use of leading questions. Evid C §767; see §1.10. However, a certain amount of leading may be necessary to accomplish the corrective and rehabilitative functions of redirect examination. Unless a leading question is asked, the witness may remain unaware of an inadvertent error, ambiguity, or unintended and unfavorable implication in his testimony.

Some lawyers avoid redirect examination, fearing that it only reemphasizes inconsistent and damaging material elicited during cross-examination and gives adverse counsel another chance to cross-examine. However, if the witness's testimony is sound and believable, redirect examination gives him an opportunity to correct inadvertent mistakes and to explain apparent inconsistencies. If the witness is a party, his failure to explain or deny unfavorable facts or evidence may be considered by the trier of fact in determining what inferences to draw against him. Evid C §413.

B. [§1.44] *Showing Prior Consistent Statements*

Prior statements of the witness that are consistent with his testimony at the trial can be shown on redirect examination to support his credibility only if (a) evidence of an intervening inconsistent statement was admitted to attack his credibility or (b) there was a charge, express or implied, that his testimony at trial was fabricated or influenced by bias or improper motive arising after the prior consistent statement was made. Evid C §791. Evidence of these prior consistent statements is not made inadmissible by the hearsay rule. Evid C §1236.

It is doubtful that a witness would be permitted to testify about a prior consistent statement on redirect examination if all the cross-examiner had done was to ask him about a prior inconsistent statement, and he denied making it. In these instances, it could hardly be said that "evidence" of an inconsistent statement had been "admitted." On the other hand, it could be argued that the cross-examiner, merely by asking about an inconsistent statement, was making an "implied charge" that the witness's testimony was "recently fabricated." See Evid C §791(b). Perhaps the determining factor would be how far the cross-examiner went in asking the witness about the prior inconsistent statement, *i.e.,* whether his questioning created an implication

EXAMINING WITNESS §1.45

that he had evidence that an inconsistent statement had been made.

In a situation in which a witness admits on cross-examination that he has made a prior inconsistent statement, redirect examination to show an even earlier consistent statement might go as follows:

Q. Mr. ...., you testified on direct examination [that you were not unconscious following the accident], is that correct?
A. Yes.
Q. And then on cross-examination you said that you told [their investigator that you were uncertain whether you were unconscious or conscious after the accident], is that right?
A. Yes.
Q. Now, before you said anything to [their investigator], did you ever tell anyone [that you were not unconscious after the accident]?
A. Yes, I certainly did.
Q. Who did you tell?
A. [The doctor who examined me at the hospital.]
Q. When was it that you told him, and what were the circumstances?
A. [It was when I first arrived at the hospital, and he was asking what had happened to me.]
Q. Can you tell us why you made the opposite statement to [the investigator]?
A. Yes. [It was the way he asked me. He said, "You can't be absolutely sure of that, can you?" And I guess I agreed with him that I couldn't be absolutely sure.]

Comment: Instead of having the witness testify about the prior consistent statement on redirect examination, counsel could have him, or a person who heard the statement, testify about it on rebuttal, or introduce an exhibit that embodied the statement.

VII. [§1.45] REBUTTAL

Rebuttal is the presentation of evidence after each other party has presented his original case. CCP §607. The right to offer evidence in rebuttal without undue restriction is constitutionally guaranteed. See *Pence v IAC* (1965) 63 C2d 48, 50, 45 CR 12, 14.

Evidence can be presented in rebuttal to refute or oppose the evidence offered by other parties, or its implications. Rebuttal can also be used to rehabilitate a witness, or to explain ambiguities and inconsistencies in his testimony that were developed during cross-examination. A prior consistent statement can be shown to rebut intervening evidence of an inconsistent statement. See §1.44. The trial judge may even permit, "for good reason, in the furtherance of justice," evidence on the party's original case. CCP §607(b). However, merely cumulative evidence is usually not permitted. See Witkin, CALIFORNIA EVIDENCE §1097 (2d ed, 1966).

Rebuttal evidence may be given by a new witness or by a witness who has already testified, although the latter may not be reexamined on the same matter he testified about on direct examination without leave of court. Evid C §774. For example, a defense doctor's testimony that he had examined the plaintiff thoroughly, but had found no objective signs of injury and heard no complaints of pain, could be met by testimony on rebuttal from plaintiff and his spouse that the examination lasted only ten minutes, and that the plaintiff told the doctor about headaches and other symptoms. The plaintiff could also testify that he in fact had headaches at that time and was taking drugs for them. However, the plaintiff would not be permitted to rehash his direct testimony about the nature and extent of his injuries.

2

Impeachment

I. [§2.1] Defined

II. Grounds for Impeachment

   A. [§2.2] Bias; Interest; Motive
   B. [§2.3] Prior Settlement with Adversary
   C. [§2.4] Faulty Perception or Recollection
   D. [§2.5] Bad Character for Veracity
   E. [§2.6] Prior Felony Conviction
   F. [§2.7] Prior Inconsistent Statement
      1. [§2.8] Pinning Down Testimony
      2. [§2.9] Not Confronting Witness with Statement
      3. [§2.10] Confronting Witness with Statement
      4. [§2.11] Pressing for Admission
      5. [§2.12] Introducing Extrinsic Evidence
   G. [§2.13] Contradictory Facts; Introducing Otherwise Inadmissible Matter

III. [§2.14] Impeaching Experts

   A. [§2.15] Qualifications
   B. [§2.16] Fees and Court Appearances
   C. [§2.17] Subject of Testimony
   D. [§2.18] Reasons and Bases for Opinion
   E. [§2.19] Technical and Medical Publications

I. [§2.1] DEFINED

To impeach a witness is to attack his credibility: either his believability as a person, or the believability of some part of his testimony. When a lawyer says that he impeached a witness, he may mean merely that he attacked the witness's credibility, without claiming that the attack was successful. Or, he may mean that he so discredited the witness that the trier of fact did not believe the witness's testimony.

Lawyers usually impeach adverse witnesses in the course of cross-examining them, but a witness can also be impeached by introducing exhibits and testimony from other witnesses that contradict or discredit the witness. A lawyer can also attack the credibility of a witness that he himself has called. Evid C §785. This does not mean that the lawyer can cross-examine his own witness. Impeachment on direct or redirect examination must conform to rules applicable to direct examination; leading questions can be asked only with concurrence of the trial judge. Evid C §767.

Grounds for attacking a witness's credibility are discussed in §§2.2–2.19. See also Evid C §§780, 721–722; BAJI No 2.20; Witkin, CALIFORNIA EVIDENCE §§1223–1275 (2d ed, 1966). For discussion of the limitations on impeachment, see CALIFORNIA TRIAL OBJECTIONS §§22.8–22.9 (Cal CEB 1967).

II. GROUNDS FOR IMPEACHMENT

A. [§2.2] *Bias; Interest; Motive*

To determine the credibility of a witness, the judge or jury may consider evidence of his bias, interest, or other motive. Evid C §780(f). A witness may be biased for the adverse party or against the impeaching party.

The lawyer can ask a witness about, and introduce extrinsic evidence to show, such matters as (1) family, social, or employment relationships with the other party; (2) acceptance of gifts, favors, an additional witness fee, lunch, or even a free drink or two; and (3) statements to representatives of the other party, visits to the adverse attorney's offices, or refusal to talk to representatives of the party. See generally Witkin, CALIFORNIA EVIDENCE §§1229–1235 (2d ed, 1966).

The fact that a witness is or was employed by defendant's insurer can be brought out to attack his credibility, even though evidence that the defendant was insured is inadmissible to prove negligence or other wrongdoing. See Evid C §1155; *Causey v Cornelius* (1958) 164 CA2d 269, 280, 330 P2d 468, 475; *Moniz v Bettencourt* (1938) 24 CA2d 718, 76 P2d 13; Witkin, EVIDENCE §§374–375.

B. [§2.3] *Prior Settlement with Adversary*

The credibility of an unfavorable witness can sometimes be attacked by showing that the witness was involved in the same accident

IMPEACHMENT §2.3

and had previously settled a claim by, or against, an adverse party. See BAJI No 2.28. However, evidence of a prior settlement is not automatically admissible. The judge, on his own motion if adverse counsel fails to object, can require the impeaching lawyer first to convince the judge that (1) the proposed evidence is relevant on the issue of credibility, and the jury could reasonably be affected by it (whether or not the judge is so affected); and (2) the proposed evidence would not be unduly prejudicial, confusing, or time consuming (see Evid C §352). *Granville v Parsons* (1968) 259 CA2d 298, 304, 66 CR 149, 153.

A lawyer wanting to ask an adverse witness on cross-examination about his prior involvement in the case, and his settlement with the adverse party, might proceed as follows:

Q. You are testifying here as a witness for [name of adverse party], are you not?
A. I am.

Comment: If the cross-examiner knows that the witness was not subpenaed, he can ask, "Were you subpenaed by [name of adverse party] to testify here today?" When the witness answers, "No," the attorney can ask rhetorically, "Then you are appearing here voluntarily as a witness for [name of adverse party], are you not?"

Q. Isn't it true that at one time you [asserted/alleged/swore] that [name of adverse party] was negligent and caused this accident?
A. [I don't know what you mean.]
Q. Didn't you file a complaint in this case against him?
A. [I don't know what my lawyer did.]
Q. Well, are you the [name] described as the plaintiff in this complaint dated ...., 19......, which I now show you?
A. Yes.
Q. Is this your signature at the end?
A. Yes.
Q. Would you please read paragraphs ...... and ...... of that complaint?
A. [Reads allegation of negligence.]
Q. So you did once allege that he was negligent, didn't you?
A. I guess I did.
Q. Now, didn't you settle your claim against him?
A. Yes.
Q. For how much?
A. $...............

Q. And in return for that $..............., you released him from any further claim of liability, did you not?
A. I did.
Q. Do you have any further claims against him?
A. No.
Q. And it was after you settled that claim with him that you decided to testify on his behalf in this action, right?
A. That's right.

Comment: In this situation, the adverse party is entitled to an instruction that this testimony was received only on the issue of the witness's credibility, not as evidence of the adverse party's liability. See Evid C §§355, 1152; BAJI No 2.28; *Granville v Parsons, supra.*

C. [§2.4] *Faulty Perception or Recollection*

In determining the credibility of the witness, the judge or jury can consider the extent of his capacity and opportunity to perceive and recollect the matter about which he testifies. Evid C §780(c), (d). Even though the judge has ruled that the witness is competent in that he had personal knowledge (see generally §1.15), a cross-examiner can attack his credibility by showing that he may not have observed as well or as thoroughly as his direct examination suggests.

A cross-examiner can suggest that perception was distorted by showing that the witness was under the influence of liquor or drugs. See generally Witkin, CALIFORNIA EVIDENCE §1228 (2d ed, 1966). Cross-examination can also show that the witness "filled in" what he did not actually observe with what he imagined must have happened. For example, when the witness claims to have seen an automobile collision:

Q. Did you say that you were standing on the [northwest] corner of the intersection when this collision happened?
A. Yes.
Q. And you were [waiting to cross .... Street], is that right?
A. Yes.
Q. And you had no expectation or inkling that an accident would occur at that time and place, did you?
A. Of course not.
Q. There was no reason in the world for you to expect it, right?
A. That's right.
Q. So you weren't paying particular attention to the two automobiles that later collided as they approached this intersection, were you?

IMPEACHMENT §2.5

A. No, I guess I wasn't.
Q. As a matter of fact, the first thing about the accident that caught your attention was the screech of brakes, correct?
A. Yes.
Q. And that was just an instant before you heard the impact, right?
A. That's right.
Q. Well, that split second between the time you heard the brakes and turned your head, and focused your eyes on the collision, didn't give you much time to observe the speed of those cars and their positions and distance from each other, did it?
A. No, it did not.
Q. And your estimate of the speed of the [white Ford] was made during that split second, correct?
A. Yes.
Q. There was quite a loud bang when they hit, wasn't there?
A. Yes, there was.
Q. Now, thinking back, and trying to be fair, didn't you get the idea that the speed was great because the noise of that impact was so great?
A. ....

D. [§2.5] *Bad Character for Veracity*

The credibility of a witness can be attacked by showing his bad character for honesty or veracity. Evid C §780(e). See also CALIFORNIA TRIAL OBJECTIONS §22.9 (Cal CEB 1967); Witkin, CALIFORNIA EVIDENCE §§1236–1242 (2d ed, 1966). In personal injury cases, lawyers rarely feel that this kind of attack is effective enough, or that the testimony of an adverse witness is important enough, to warrant calling a witness whose sole function is to testify to the bad character of the adverse witness.

To show an adverse witness's bad character for honesty or veracity, a witness must testify either that (1) he knows the general *reputation* (excepted from the hearsay rule (see Evid C §1324)) of the adverse witness for truth, honesty, and integrity in the community, or in a business or other group to which the adverse witness belongs, and the reputation is bad; or (2) he is acquainted with the adverse witness, and on the basis of that acquaintance, holds the *opinion* that the witness is untruthful or dishonest. Reputation or opinion testimony must relate to honesty or veracity. Evid C §786. Evidence of other character traits, such as immorality, unchastity, or carelessness, is inadmissible to attack credibility. Specific instances of conduct cannot be shown to prove bad character for honesty or veracity (Evid C §787), except that a prior felony conviction can be shown (Evid C §788; see §2.6).

The impeaching witness can give both reputation and opinion testimony. For example:

Q. Mr. ...., do you know [name of adverse witness]?
A. Yes, I do.
Q. Please tell us how long you have known him, and under what circumstances.
A. ....
Q. Does he have a general reputation among those who know him in [specify locale, business, or other group] with relation to his truthfulness, honesty, or integrity?
A. Yes, he does.
Q. Do you know what that reputation is?
A. Yes.
Q. What is it?
A. It is a bad reputation. He [can't be trusted/is dishonest/etc.].
Q. Now, on the basis of your own acquaintance with him, and what you personally know about him [without regard to his reputation], have you reached your own conclusion about his honesty and truthfulness?
A. I have.
Q. What is that conclusion?
A. That he is not truthful.
Q. Is he a person you would believe under oath?
A. No.

Comment: The last question, while not strictly relevant, might be allowed as another way of getting the witness to state his opinion. See Witkin, EVIDENCE §1240(2).

E. [§2.6] *Prior Felony Conviction*

Prior felony convictions of witnesses are rarely brought out in civil cases. Jurors usually see little connection between the prior conviction and whether the witness has testified truthfully. They may even be sympathetic to a witness whose past has been dredged up unnecessarily.

The prior conviction can be proved by introducing a record of the judgment of conviction without asking the witness about it, or by obtaining the witness's admission of it on cross-examination. Evid C §788. See also BAJI No 2.24. For example:

IMPEACHMENT §2.7

Q. Were you ever convicted of a felony?
A. Yes.
Q. What was that felony?
A. ....
Q. What was the date of conviction?
A. ...., 19.......

Comment: If the witness denies the conviction, and it is then proved by introducing a record of the judgment, the witness is doubly impeached: (1) by the conviction, and (2) by denying it under oath. If the witness admits the conviction, however, he gains sympathy, and the judge could sustain an objection on the grounds that introducing the record is cumulative, or that its introduction would unduly consume time (Evid C §352).

Proponent. Your Honor, I have here a certified true copy of the judgment [of/on the verdict in a trial held in] the Court of .... County, State of ...., dated ...., 19......, showing the conviction of one ...., residing at ...., of the crime of ....
Q. Are you the [name] described in this record?
A. Yes.
Q. Did you reside at .... at that time?
A. Yes.

Comment: The court should take judicial notice of the record if the proper procedure for obtaining judicial notice is followed. See Evid C §§452(d), 453. See also §§20.13–20.25. If the witness denies that he was the person convicted, further proof may be required.

F. [§2.7] *Prior Inconsistent Statement*

In determining the credibility of a witness, the court or jury may consider evidence of a statement made by him that is inconsistent with any part of his testimony at the hearing. Evid C §780(h). "Statement" means both oral and written verbal expression, and nonverbal conduct intended as a substitute for verbal expression. Evid C §225.

A statement is inconsistent if a true contradiction exists between the testimony and the statement, although the inconsistency may be implied rather than express. See Witkin, CALIFORNIA EVIDENCE §1254 (2d ed, 1966). The inconsistent statement used to impeach a witness is usually one he made before he testifies, but a subsequent statement could also be used. See Witkin, EVIDENCE §1253(2).

The lawyer should check all possible sources for statements previously made by probable adverse witnesses that are favorable to his theory of the case. These statements can usually be introduced as inconsistent with some part of the witness's testimony. Even relatively minor inconsistencies on peripheral matters can have a cumulative effect causing jurors to lose confidence in the veracity of the witness. And jurors are often more inclined to believe the truth of a prior statement than the truth of the testimony with which it is inconsistent. The inconsistent statement can be received in evidence not only to impeach the witness, but also as substantive evidence of the truth of the matter stated; evidence of the statement is not made inadmissible by the hearsay rule. Evid C §1235. Note that *People v Johnson* (1968) 68 C2d 646, 68 CR 599, holds Evid C §1235 unconstitutional in criminal cases. See also BAJI No 2.25 (extrajudicial admissions to be viewed with caution).

There are several ways to impeach a witness with his prior inconsistent statement. In one approach, the witness is not questioned at all about his prior statement (see §2.9), and the statement is later proved by extrinsic evidence (see §2.12). In another, the witness is asked whether he made a particular statement at a particular time and place to certain persons (see §2.10), and if he denies it, the statement is later proved by extrinsic evidence (see §2.12). In a third, the witness is not only asked whether he made the statement; he is pressed to admit that he did make it and that it was true (see §2.11). Unless the witness unequivocally admits making the inconsistent statement, the impeaching lawyer can prove it by extrinsic evidence (see §2.12). Whichever technique is employed, it can be helpful to begin by pinning down the witness to testimony that is clearly inconsistent with the statement (see §2.8).

1. [§2.8] Pinning Down Testimony

A lawyer who wants to introduce a witness's prior statement to impeach him should be sure that some part of the witness's testimony is clearly inconsistent with the statement. This sometimes requires asking questions on cross-examination that clarify and heighten the inconsistency, and increase the witness's commitment to his testimony. If, for example, an adverse witness testified on direct examination that Mr. .... did not appear intoxicated after the accident, and the witness had previously told an investigator that Mr. .... "looked drunk," the witness could be pinned down to his testimony as follows:

IMPEACHMENT §2.10

Q. Sir, you testified that you saw Mr. .... at the scene of the accident and that he did not appear intoxicated. Is that right?
A. Yes.
Q. By intoxicated, you mean the same as "drunk" or "under the influence of alcohol or a drug." Is that right?
A. That's right.
Q. Your present recollection, then, is that Mr. .... did not appear to be drunk or under the influence at the scene of the accident. Is that correct?
A. Yes, that's correct.
Q. And that is your testimony, right?
A. Right.

2. [§2.9] Not Confronting Witness with Statement

The lawyer need not show a prior inconsistent statement to the witness, disclose to him any information about it, or give him any opportunity during cross-examination to explain or deny it. Evid C §§768–770. As long as the witness has not been excused from giving further testimony in the case, the lawyer can later introduce extrinsic evidence of the statement to impeach the witness. Evid C §770(b). This nonconfrontational approach saves the impeaching lawyer from tipping his hand before other witnesses have been examined and cross-examined. See Official Comment to Evidence Code §770.

After the impeaching lawyer completes his cross-examination, he could make a statement such as the following for the record:

Cross-examiner. I have no [further] questions at this time, your Honor, but I request that the witness be instructed that he is not excused from giving testimony in this case, and he should keep himself available to be recalled as a witness at a later stage of this action.

Comment: Some lawyers use the phrase, "excused subject to recall," although ordinarily when a witness is "excused" he cannot be recalled without leave of court. Evid C §778. Saying "not excused" seems a safer way to preserve the right later to introduce extrinsic evidence of the witness's prior inconsistent statement.

3. [§2.10] Confronting Witness with Statement

The advantages of confronting a witness with his prior statement during cross-examination include:

(a) If the witness unequivocally admits making the statement, the impeaching lawyer does not have to call an impeaching witness or put on extrinsic evidence of the statement. Indeed, extrinsic evidence would be irrelevant and cumulative. See Witkin, CALIFORNIA EVIDENCE §1257 (2d ed, 1966).

(b) If the witness denies making the statement, and the lawyer later convinces the trier of fact that he made it, the witness is doubly impeached: by the statement (Evid C §780(h)) and by the denial of a fact (Evid C §780(i)).

(c) Giving the witness an opportunity to explain or deny the statement permits the impeaching lawyer later to introduce extrinsic evidence of the statement even though the witness has been excused (Evid C §770).

An adverse witness who has been pinned down to testimony that, for example, "Mr. .... did not appear intoxicated after the accident" (see example in §2.8), could be cross-examined as follows:

Q. Did you ever tell anyone that Mr. .... looked like he was drunk or under the influence right after the accident?
A. [No, sir, not that I recall.]

Comment: This kind of unspecific question usually does not alert the witness to a particular prior statement, and may elicit a denial that makes it more difficult for him to justify the conflict between his testimony and the statement.

Q. Sir, did you talk about this accident with [Mr. ..../my investigator] on ...., 19......, at [your house]?
A. ....
Q. On that occasion, didn't you tell him that Mr. .... looked like he was drunk at the scene of the accident?
A. ....
Q. Are you now testifying that you [did/did not] make that statement [or one substantially similar to it] to Mr. .... on ...., 19......, at about .... o'clock?
A. [Well, I guess I am.]

Comment: These questions show the time, place, and to whom the prior statement was made, and the substance of what the witness is claimed to have said. For an oral statement, they "give him an opportunity to explain or to deny the statement," then and there or on redirect examination. Evid C §770(a). See also Witkin, EVIDENCE §§1250 (2), 1257(b).

4. [§2.11] Pressing for Admission

If the witness admits making a prior statement, the cross-examiner

IMPEACHMENT §2.11

can stop there or ask him further questions to pin down the circumstances and the substance of the statement.

If the witness denies or equivocates, the lawyer can abandon the inquiry and later introduce extrinsic evidence of the statement (see §2.12), leaving the witness to explain or deny on rebuttal. Or the cross-examiner can continue to press the witness for an admission that the statement was made. Even if the witness does not admit it, the cross-examination can create such a strong suggestion that the statement was made that the witness will be discredited to some degree, even if no later evidence of the statement is introduced. For example:

Q. Well, you do remember that [Mr. ..../my investigator] came to your house, don't you?
A. Yes.
Q. And he identified himself as an investigator who wanted to talk to you about the events you [observed/were involved in] on ...., 19......, did he not?
A. I guess so.
Q. And you did [invite him in, sit down with him in your living room, and talk with him], didn't you?
A. Yes.
Q. [And while you were talking, you saw him making notes on a form that he had brought with him, correct?]
A. Yes.

Comment: If the investigator did make notes, and the witness refused or failed to sign them, a question such as, "And you didn't read over his notes or sign them, did you?" can sometimes forestall the witness from saying that he did not sign because the notes were inaccurate or slanted.

Q. And while you may not remember the exact date you talked to that investigator, you have no reason to believe that it was not ...., 19......, do you?
A. No.
Q. Now I want to show you this paper [which has been marked for identification as (plaintiff's/defendant's) exhibit ......], and I want you to read it.

Comment: At this point, the writing must be given to all other parties for inspection before the witness can be questioned about it. Evid C §768(b).

Q. Now does that refresh your memory about what you told [Mr.

.............../my investigator] on ...., 19......, about Mr. ....'s condition following the accident?

A. ....

Comment: If the witness answers "No," the attorney will probably have to abandon the inquiry, and later call the investigator as a witness. If the witness answers "Yes," the attorney can continue the questioning.

Q. You did tell him that Mr. .... looked drunk after the accident, didn't you?
A. [Yes./That's what it says here.]

Comment: Even a "Yes" answer to this question is not evidence that the person in question looked drunk after the accident. For that evidence the cross-examiner must get an affirmative answer to another question:

Q. And what you told [Mr. ..../my investigator] was true, wasn't it? Mr. .... did look drunk after the accident, didn't he?
A. Yes.

5. [§2.12] Introducing Extrinsic Evidence

An impeaching witness can be called to the stand whenever the attorney next has a chance to present evidence. If the witness is testifying about an oral statement, the lawyer usually takes some care to show his background and impartiality, for it is often a question of the word of the impeaching witness against the denial of the declarant. For example:

Q. What is your name and occupation?
A. My name is ...., and I am a private investigator.
Q. How long have you been in that business?
A. For ...... years.
Q. Have you been employed by attorneys representing both plaintiffs and defendants in personal injury cases?
A. Yes.
Q. Approximately how many cases have you investigated in which you have been called on to interview witnesses or persons involved in accidents?
A. ....
Q. Who employed you to investigate in this case?
A. [You did.]

IMPEACHMENT   §2.12

Q. How many different witnesses did you interview and take statements from in this case?
A. ....
Q. Did you, in the course of your investigation of this case, interview [name of declarant]? [By the way, if your notes would help you to refresh your memory on these matters, please feel free to consult them.]
A. I did.

Comment: The witness should testify to the time and place the statement was made and tell who was present. See Witkin, CALIFORNIA EVIDENCE §1256(b). The witness often seems more credible if these bare facts are followed with a few specific details about the occasion. The lawyer might also ask if the declarant asked to see his credentials, asked whom he represented, invited him in, gave him a cup of coffee, etc.

Q. When did you interview him?
A. On ...., 19......, from ...... to ....m.
Q. Where did this interview take place?
A. [At his residence at ....]
Q. Who was present besides Mr. .... and you?
A. [No one/Mrs. ..../etc.]

Comment: The witness should also describe the format of the interview, *i.e.*, whether the investigator asked for a narration or asked specific questions; whether the declarant wrote out his statement or recorded it; whether the witness paraphrased the statement on a form interview sheet; etc. If the investigator wrote down what the witness said, but the witness did not sign the writing, this should be explained. For example:

Q. Did you write down what he said?
A. Yes. [Right on the interview sheet.]
Q. Did he look at what you had written?
A. [Yes, I handed the sheet to him and asked him to read it over and correct any errors or misstatements.]
Q. Did he make any corrections or question anything?
A. No.
Q. Did you ask him to sign it?
A. Yes.
Q. Did he?
A. No.

Q. Did he give any reason for not signing?
A. [Just that he did not like to sign things.]

Comment: A leading question is often used to ask the impeaching witness about the statement made by the declarant. Broad questions like "What did he say?" or "What did he say with regard to Mr. ....'s condition following the accident?" could possibly elicit answers that are inadmissible hearsay because they are not inconsistent with anything said by the witness in testimony. The leading question is more precise and limits the evidence to matter that is inconsistent with the testimony. See Evid C §1235. For example:

Q. On that occasion did Mr. .... say that Mr. .... looked drunk after the accident?
A. Yes, he did.

Comment: If the declarant was asked about the statement when he was cross-examined, the question asked of the impeaching witness should use the same wording.

G. [§2.13] *Contradictory Facts; Introducing Otherwise Inadmissible Matter*

If a witness testifies to a fact, evidence to disprove it can be introduced to impeach the witness. See Evid C §780(i). This permits lawyers to introduce otherwise inadmissible evidence for the limited purpose (see Evid C §355; BAJI No 2.05) of attacking the credibility of the witness, unless the probable prejudice would substantially outweigh the probative value of the evidence (see Evid C §352(b)).

For example, if a witness denied that he owned a particular automobile, it could be shown that he purchased insurance for it or contracted to have it repaired, even though insurance (Evid C §1155) and subsequent remedial conduct (Evid C §1151) are not admissible to prove negligence.

Again, if a witness testifies that a thing or place was safe or well maintained, evidence that subsequent repairs or improvements were made can be introduced, not to show that the thing or place was unsafe or not well maintained, but to disprove a fact testified to by the witness. Evidence of subsequent improvements does not necessarily contradict testimony that a place was safe. Therefore, the cross-examiner often tries to get the witness to testify that the thing was the "safest design," or "most modern equipment," so that evidence of an improvement is more clearly contradictory.

IMPEACHMENT   §2.15

III. [§2.14] IMPEACHING EXPERTS

The credibility of an expert witness can be attacked on the same grounds and with the same techniques used to impeach any other witness. See §§2.1–2.13. In addition, an expert witness who gives opinion testimony exposes himself to cross-examination on the matters discussed in §§2.15–2.19. See Evid C §§721–722; *Hope v Arrowhead & Puritas Waters, Inc.* (1959) 174 CA2d 222, 230, 344 P2d 428, 433. See generally CALIFORNIA TRIAL OBJECTIONS §§20.12–20.13, 22.9(c) (Cal CEB 1967); Witkin, CALIFORNIA EVIDENCE §§1217–1222 (2d ed, 1966).

A. [§2.15] *Qualifications*

Evidence Code §721(a)(1) permits an expert witness to be fully cross-examined about his qualifications. Deficiencies in an expert's qualifications can be brought out (a) to disqualify the witness from testifying as an expert on a particular subject (see §§1.19, 1.21), and (b) to attack the credibility of the witness even though he is permitted to testify (see §1.23).

After an adverse expert has given direct testimony about his qualifications, a lawyer can object to further testimony by the witness on the ground that he has not been shown to be qualified as an expert on the subject. See CALIFORNIA TRIAL OBJECTIONS §§20.6, 20.20 (Cal CEB 1967). Or the lawyer can request permission to question the witness on his qualifications before he testifies further (to "take him on voir dire"), then decide whether to object. See Witkin, CALIFORNIA EVIDENCE §1174 (2d ed, 1966). In either situation, the lawyer may prefer not to make the objection unless he feels reasonably certain the judge will sustain it. Jurors may misinterpret the overruling of the objection as an endorsement of the witness's credibility rather than just his qualification to testify as an expert. On the other hand, a witness's apparent qualifications may be illusory. For example, a physicist may testify at length about his education and teaching experience in the field of motion, force, and momentum; but a probing voir dire examination can point up his lack of training and experience in vehicle accident reconstruction, and convince the judge that he should not be permitted to give an opinion on the speed of vehicles based only on his observation of the damage sustained by each.

Both voir dire and regular cross-examination can be used to bring out gaps and weaknesses in a witness's qualifications that will serve as a basis for argument that the witness's opinions should be given

§2.15   IMPEACHMENT

little weight. See §1.23 on arguing qualifications in connection with instructions such as BAJI Nos 2.40, 2.41.

If an adverse witness's direct testimony about his qualifications is brief, superficial, or lackluster, the lawyer may want to forgo cross-examination to avoid uncovering qualifications not mentioned by the witness on direct. If an adverse expert testifies at length about his qualifications on direct examination, the lawyer should listen for gaps, such as accomplishments the witness would have mentioned if he had them. For example, the cross-examination of an adverse medical witness might contain the following dialogue:

Q. You did not say what degree you received when you graduated from .... School. What was the actual degree conferred on you at the time you graduated?
A. At that time it was a D.O. or Doctor of Osteopathy.
Q. And you call yourself an M.D. today because all you osteopaths were permitted to do so by an act of the legislature in 1965, is that correct?
A. Well, the degrees are considered equivalent and no new osteopaths will be licensed as such in California.
Q. But you can call yourself an M.D. because of that legislative act, not because you earned that degree in medical school, isn't that correct?
A. [Well, yes, but the degree I earned is equivalent to an M.D.]
Q. Now you say you specialize in [surgery]. Are you a member or diplomate of [the American Board of Surgery]?
A. No.
Q. And [the American Board of Surgery] is a body that passes on the qualifications of those who seek certification as specialists in that field, isn't that right?
A. [Well, yes, but you don't have to be board-certified to be a specialist.]
Q. In order to be a board-certified specialist, a doctor has to take special training, and then pass certain examinations, isn't that correct?
A. Yes.
Q. And is it not also true that no first-rate hospital in this area has on its [surgical] staff any doctor who is not certified by [the American Board of Surgery]?
A. ....
Q. Just how many [cervical disc operations] have you performed?
A. ....

IMPEACHMENT §2.16

Q. On how many of those have you been "the surgeon" instead of assistant surgeon or something else?
A. ....

B. [§2.16] *Fees and Court Appearances*

The amount of the compensation and expenses paid, or to be paid, to an expert witness is relevant to his credibility and may be brought out by an adverse party. Evid C §722(b). Some cross-examiners routinely ask each adverse expert about fees, the frequency of his court appearances and legal consultations, and whether he is more often called by plaintiffs or by defendants. The lawyer seeks to cast doubt on the witness's impartiality and to suggest that the content of his testimony is influenced by his financial interest. Other lawyers cross-examine on these matters only when they are reasonably certain that the witness's fee will substantially exceed those charged by other experts in the case, or know that the expert testifies often and may appear to be a "professional witness," or that he usually testifies for the same side. For example:

Q. When was the last time you appeared in court as a witness?
A. ....
Q. Well, how often do you appear in the course of a year?
A. ....
Q. You also prepare reports for lawyers, don't you?
A. Yes.
Q. So a substantial part of your [practice/professional activity/etc.] involves work that you are asked to do by lawyers?
A. Yes.
Q. And a substantial part of your income, too, right?
A. Yes.
Q. How much are you being paid for your testimony in this case?

Comment: An experienced or well-prepared witness can often parry questions or give innocuous answers that make the cross-examiner appear argumentative and petty. For example:

A. [I'm not being paid anything for my testimony, although I (will be/have been) compensated for the time I have spent learning the facts, forming my conclusions, preparing the report I sent to Mr. ...., waiting to testify, and testifying here on the witness stand. My fee will depend on how long you keep me here, away from my practice.]

Q. Well, isn't it true that you are [almost] invariably called to testify by attorneys who represent [plaintiffs/defendants] in personal injury lawsuits?
A. ....

C. [§2.17] *Subject of Testimony*

A witness testifying as an expert can be fully cross-examined on "the subject to which his expert testimony relates." Evid C §721(a)(2).

Inquiry into the subject of the witness's testimony might reveal that it is not "sufficiently beyond common experience that the opinion of an expert would assist the trier of fact." Evid C §801(a). An adverse expert can also be asked questions, including hypothetical questions, to test his accuracy, competency, and credibility. See *People v Busch* (1961) 56 C2d 868, 16 CR 898. See also §1.30.

The questions asked probably need not be limited to the particular facts or opinions that the witness testified about, but may include matter perceived by or made known to him in the course of preparing to testify, and perhaps even his general knowledge of the area or subject in which he claims to be an expert. For example, a police officer who testified that a vehicle had been traveling 55 miles per hour because it had skidded 150 feet on a dry concrete road could be asked about the effect of the weight of the vehicle, the age of the concrete, the wear on the tire, and even about the formula used to determine a coefficient of friction. Such an inquiry might convince the trial judge that the witness was not qualified because his knowledge of the subject was deficient (see §2.15) or that he based his opinion on insufficient data (see §2.18). Even if the judge did not act to exclude the testimony or order it stricken, the witness might become so confused and inconclusive in his testimony that jurors would give it no weight.

D. [§2.18] *Reasons and Bases for Opinion*

Cross-examination about the matter on which an expert's opinions are based and the reasons for his opinions (permitted by Evid C §721(a)(3)) can sometimes reveal that the opinion was based on improper matter or that the expert did not consider or give appropriate weight to certain proper matter.

The opinion testimony of an expert can be excluded if it is based in whole or in part on improper matter. Evid C §803. For example, a police officer's opinion on point of impact would probably be excluded

IMPEACHMENT §2.19

if based solely on statements made to him by bystanders. See §4.53.

Even if there remains sufficient proper matter after the improper matter has been excluded from consideration, the weight of the opinion is compromised. If the matter is technically proper, but the witness does not have direct or personal knowledge of it, the attorney can argue that the opinion should be given less weight. For example, a doctor can probably rely on a history taken from the patient by a medical assistant or nurse, but the fact that the doctor did not record the history himself weakens his opinions.

An expert's opinion testimony can be attacked by showing that he did not gather all the information he should have. For example, a doctor's opinion that a patient suffered (or did not suffer) a brain injury is less convincing if he is made to admit on cross-examination that he did not order an electroencephalograph—although it is a standard diagnostic procedure in such cases—and did not send the patient to a neurologist for consultation—although he, the witness, is not a specialist.

Hypothetical questions can be used to inform an expert of data and information not known to him when he formed his opinion, or to require him to state an opinion based on a set of facts favorable to the cross-examiner. See §§1.28, 1.30.

Cross-examination can also reveal that the expert disregarded or did not give proper weight to matter that was known to him. For example, a defense doctor may testify on direct examination that when he examined the plaintiff he found no objective basis for the claimed injuries, and formed the opinion that the injuries were minor and had cleared up. The plaintiff's attorney on cross-examination can elicit testimony that (1) the patient did describe symptoms and subjective complaints to the doctor; (2) in medical practice diagnoses are often based primarily on subjective complaints; (3) pain, dizziness, forgetfulness, inability to concentrate, and similar symptoms can be real even though they cannot be detected by available physical examination techniques, tests, or special procedures; and (4) there was nothing about the demeanor of the patient to indicate that he was making up the symptoms, lying, acting in bad faith, or not cooperating during the examination.

E. [§2.19] *Technical and Medical Publications*

Some lawyers prepare for the technical and medical aspects of a case by reading the same scientific books and journals that are read by professionals and practitioners in those fields (as distinguished from books on technical subjects written for lawyers or laymen).

§2.19 IMPEACHMENT

These lawyers then note and copy passages and statements that support their theories of liability and recovery. Other lawyers ask their own experts to collect for them favorable references and quotations from the literature of the particular field.

Passages from technical literature are the out-of-court statements of their authors and cannot be introduced as evidence of the truth of the matter stated unless adverse parties agree to their admission, or fail to object. See Evid C §1200. There are, however, several ways in which scientific, technical, and professional books, articles, and journals can be used to impeach an expert witness:

(1) If the witness wrote the book or treatise, passages from it can be read into evidence as prior inconsistent statements. See §§2.7–2.12.

(2) If the witness admits that he referred to, considered, or relied on a publication by some other author, he can be cross-examined about its content or tenor. The cross-examiner can read a passage from the publication to him, then ask him whether he agrees with it and to explain any disagreement. See Evid C §721(b). See also CALIFORNIA TRIAL OBJECTIONS §22.9(c) (Cal CEB 1967); Witkin, CALIFORNIA EVIDENCE §1222 (2d ed, 1966).

(3) If the witness denies having read important sounding books and articles, the lawyer can argue that the witness is uninformed and does not keep up with developments in the field, especially if other witnesses identify them as standard authorities.

The cross-examination of an adverse expert on the content of a technical or medical book might proceed as follows:

Q. Sir, you keep up with the literature in your field, don't you?
A. Yes.
Q. And in reaching your opinions [on this admittedly complex problem], I'm sure that you referred to or considered certain standard works and treatises in your field, isn't that right?
A. Yes.

Comment: Should the witness answer "No," the cross-examiner can act surprised and still ask about specific publications. For example: "Don't you have a copy of [title of publication] by [name of author] in your office?" "Didn't you refer to it?" "Did you just make a judgment off the top of your head, without referring to anything?"

Q. Did you refer to, consider, or rely on [title of publication] by [name of author]?
A. Yes.

IMPEACHMENT §2.19

Comment: Again, if the witness answers "No," the cross-examiner can continue to name publications until he gets a "Yes," or has collected sufficient "No's" to argue that the witness is uninformed.

Note that the phrase "in reaching [your] opinions" was not used in the question that named a particular publication. This may keep the witness from quibbling over whether he consulted the book "in forming his opinion," or read it merely as part of his general education. In this same vein, some lawyers would substitute "did you look at" or "did you read" for the statutory words "refer to, consider, or rely on" (Evid C §721(b)(1)).

Q. And [name of author] is an eminent authority on [subject], isn't he?
A. Yes.
Q. This [book/article/etc.] is a reliable source of information on [subject], isn't it?
A. Yes.
Q. In fact, in forming your opinion you relied to some extent on the information in this [book/article/etc.], didn't you?

Comment: The witness can be examined on the publication even though he did not rely on it. He need only to have referred to or considered it (Evid C §721(b)(1)), although some trial judges say that "considered" means "favorably considered." If the witness says he relied on the book, the cross-examiner can show that the witness's opinion was not supported, even in one of his stated sources.

Q. Well, do you agree with this statement on page ......, that "................" [read passage]?
A. ....

Comment: Further questions would depend on the degree to which the passage contradicts the witness.

3

Plaintiff

I. Extent of Testimony

    A. [§3.1] Direct Examination
    B. [§3.2] Cross-Examination

II. [§3.3] Personal Background

    A. [§3.4] Name; Age; Birthplace; Residence
    B. [§3.5] Family Status
    C. [§3.6] Occupation and Work History
    D. [§3.7] Financial Status; Need To Return to Work

III. [§3.8] Liability Testimony

    A. [§3.9] Plaintiff's Condition and Appearance Before Accident
    B. [§3.10] Destination; Route; Purpose
    C. [§3.11] Vehicle
    D. [§3.12] Scene of Accident; Time of Day; Weather
    E. Chronology of Accident
        1. [§3.13] Plaintiff's and Defendant's Conduct Before Impact
        2. [§3.14] Impact
        3. [§3.15] Conditions After Impact
    F. [§3.16] Defendant's Admissions; Insurance
    G. [§3.17] Habit or Custom
    H. [§3.18] Plaintiff's Other Accidents

IV. [§3.19] Injury Testimony

    A. Health Before Accident
        1. [§3.20] Good Health
        2. [§3.21] Prior Conditions

3. [§3.22] Aggravation of Prior Condition; Predisposition to Injury
B. [§3.23] Mechanics of Injury
C. [§3.24] Description of Injuries and Treatment
D. [§3.25] Pain
E. [§3.26] Disability Generally; Impairment of Normal Life
1. [§3.27] Workers
2. [§3.28] Housewives
F. [§3.29] Mental Suffering

V. [§3.30] Impaired Earning Capacity

A. [§3.31] Checklist
B. [§3.32] Plaintiff's Testimony on Loss of Earnings

I. EXTENT OF TESTIMONY

A. [§3.1] Direct Examination

Plaintiff's lawyers often use the injured plaintiff as their primary witness. They examine him thoroughly on how the accident occurred and his injuries. Other witnesses are used to corroborate the plaintiff, fill in gaps, and supply expert testimony. The plaintiff is often the first major witness called.

There are cases, however, in which the plaintiff knows or remembers nothing of the circumstances in which he was injured, or has personally perceived few symptoms of injury in himself. In these cases, plaintiffs' lawyers may have to rely on other witnesses to establish both liability and damages. Of course, plaintiffs' lawyers usually try to find and use independent, disinterested witnesses who can verify and even go beyond the plaintiff's testimony on all major matters.

There are a few cases in which the plaintiff would be such a bad witness—so given to self-justification, self-pity, exaggeration, and contradiction—that his lawyer would prefer not to call him, or would question him only on highlights or on facts that cannot be supplied by other evidence. Or, other evidence may be so strong that it would be a good tactic to inquire only briefly into the plaintiff's background and the effects of his injury on his daily life, then let the cross-examiner decide how much additional matter to open up. A lawyer who obviously intends to hurry his client off the stand should be able to give a good reason for doing so. Otherwise jurors may get the impression that the lawyer has little faith in the client or his case.

B. [§3.2] *Cross-Examination*

Defense lawyers are faced with a dilemma in choosing whether to conduct a minimal or a detailed cross-examination of the plaintiff. If the plaintiff's direct testimony did not produce very damaging evidence, a brief cross-examination, or none at all, may convey the impression that the plaintiff's testimony was of little probative value. Too vigorous a cross-examination can evoke sympathy toward the plaintiff and may reinforce what he has said, or worse, elicit testimony favorable to the plaintiff that becomes more forceful because it is stated for the first time on cross-examination. On the other hand, a defense attorney who does not cross-examine loses a chance to develop defense evidence from the plaintiff's own testimony or to impair his credibility by bringing out inconsistencies.

Defense counsel's first opportunity to examine the plaintiff is usually on cross-examination after his direct testimony. In the rare cases in which the plaintiff is not called as a witness or testifies only briefly and cross-examination is restricted on the ground that it cannot exceed the scope of direct (see Evid C §773(a)), the defendant can later call him as an adverse witness and examine him as if on cross-examination (Evid C §776).

II. [§3.3] PERSONAL BACKGROUND

The plaintiff's lawyer wants to create the impression that his client is not only a believable witness, but also a person deserving of the jury's help. It is helpful to satisfy the jurors' natural curiosity about the plaintiff's life. Jurors are more willing to help a person they know than one about whose personal characteristics they must speculate and who remains for them an abstraction—"the plaintiff"—rather than a fellow human being.

Since the plaintiff's lawyer wants to show more than his client's mere credibility, the direct examination of a plaintiff on his background tends to be more extensive than that of other lay witnesses. Of course, the background evidence must be relevant. A deliberate attempt to appeal to the social or economic prejudices of the jury is misconduct unless the evidence sought is relevant to some issue in the case. See *Hoffman v Brandt* (1966) 65 C2d 549, 55 CR 417.

The plaintiff should usually be present in the courtroom throughout the trial. If he is not, his absence should be explained lest the jurors take it to indicate lack of interest in the outcome. He should be instructed to avoid exaggerated expressions of disbelief at the testimony of adverse witnesses. What is said about the dress and demeanor of witnesses generally (§§1.2–1.3) applies with particular force to plaintiffs.

A. [§3.4] *Name; Age; Birthplace; Residence*

Jurors will have heard the plaintiff's name pronounced as part of the name of the action and when the plaintiff is called to the witness stand. The lawyer may also ask the plaintiff to state his own name, pronouncing it correctly, spelling it, and, if it is unusual, indicating its national derivation. Plaintiff's lawyer usually addresses and refers to his client by name (for reasons, see §1.8) and as "Mr.," "Mrs.," or "Miss."

Defense attorneys often refer to the plaintiff as "the plaintiff" and do not address him by name (see §1.8). Or they may use an adult plaintiff's first name to suggest contempt or to provoke the witness. Any emphasis on plaintiff's name or national origin could be improper as an appeal to jurors' social prejudices.

The plaintiff's age is usually relevant on a damages issue (susceptibility to injury, chances for future employment, life expectancy, etc.), and stating it helps jurors form a picture of the plaintiff. The plaintiff should be prepared to state his or her age or date of birth naturally, accurately, and without coyness or hesitation.

A plaintiff's lawyer likes to establish, when he can, that his client resides in the community and has done so for some time, but they do not usually ask about prior residences if the plaintiff has moved many times. If the witness speaks with an accent, the jurors' curiosity should be satisfied, and their speculation stopped by asking him where he was born or raised.

If the plaintiff owns or is buying his home, that can be brought out. Although home ownership, is of questionable relevance, it could be argued that it tends to show stability, a stake in the community, and, therefore, credibility.

The direct examination of a plaintiff by his lawyer might begin as follows:

Q. Could you pronounce your last name again, please, and spell it for the jury?
A. ....
Q. When [and where] were you born?
A. On ...., 19...... [in ...., ...].
Q. And how old are you now?
A. ....
Q. Where do you reside at this time, Mr. ....?
A. ....

PLAINTIFF   §3.5

Q. How long have you lived there?
A. ....
Q. Is that a house or an apartment?
A. ....
Q. Do you own it or are you renting?
A. ....

B. [§3.5] *Family Status*

A plaintiff's lawyer can ask his client whether he is married, for how long, the names and ages of children, and the names and relationship of others living with him. These are usually regarded as harmless background questions and do not draw relevance objections. Compare, however, *Smith v Atchison, T. & S. F. Ry.* (1919) 179 C 611, 178 P 501 (nonreversible error to permit plaintiff to testify to number and ages of children to show reason for additional mental anguish over injuries). It can be argued that testimony about family status gives jurors a picture of the plaintiff's stability and responsibilities and is therefore relevant on the issue of the plaintiff's credibility. The evidence would also be relevant to show damages if the injury interfered in any way with the plaintiff's normal family relations. See §3.26.

The direct examination of the plaintiff might proceed as follows:

Q. Are you presently married, [Mr./Mrs.] ....?
A. [Yes/No.] I'm [single/a widow/a widower].
Q. What is your [wife's/husband's] name?
A. ....
Q. Is [he/she] here today?
A. Yes. [Sitting right over there.]
Q. How long have you been married?
A. ....
Q. Do you have children?
A. Yes.
Q. What are their names and ages?
A. ....
Q. Are they living at home with you?
A. ....
Q. Is anyone else living with you in your home?
A. ....

Comment: Questions by defense counsel about the birthdate or age of a child conceived before marriage are usually objectionable as calling for irrelevant evidence, as are questions about a plaintiff's prior marriages. Nor can defense counsel ask about the remarriage or the probability of remarriage of a widowed plaintiff. See *Cherrigan v San Francisco* (1968) 262 CA2d 643, 69 CR 42. See also Anno, 87 ALR2d 252 (1963). In fact, if there are prior or subsequent marriages, plaintiff's lawyer should make a motion ad limine: ask the judge in chambers before trial to instruct defense counsel not to refer to other marriages, and if a woman has remarried, to refer to her at all times by her name at the time of the accident. See *Cherrigan v San Francisco, supra.* On the propriety of motions ad limine, see *Sacramento & San Joaquin Drainage Dist. v Reed* (1963) 215 CA2d 60, 66, 29 CR 847, 851.

C. [§3.6] *Occupation and Work History*

The plaintiff's general character and stability can be shown by bringing out a history of long, steady, and increasingly responsible employment. The plaintiff's employment at the time of injury and at the time of trial is also relevant in showing loss of earnings and diminished earning capacity. See §§3.30–3.32.

If no damages for impaired earning capacity are claimed, direct examination on employment might proceed as follows:

Q. Were you employed at the time of the accident?
A. Yes.
Q. By whom?
A. ....
Q. What kind of work were you doing?
A. ....
Q. At the time of the accident, how long had you been [working for ..../doing that kind of work]?
A. ....
Q. What did you do before that?
A. ....

Comment: Other questions may be asked to show upgrading in job status and the plaintiff's present status. If the plaintiff lost earnings or his job, or was demoted or put on lighter work after the accident, this would be shown in connection with his injuries and damages.

D. [§3.7] *Financial Status; Need To Return to Work*

Showing that the plaintiff is in bad financial straits, when the only purpose is to gain jury sympathy, is improper. *Nakamura v Los*

PLAINTIFF §3.8

Angeles Gas & Elec. Corp. (1934) 137 CA 487, 30 P2d 1022. The wealth or poverty of the parties is not usually relevant in a personal injury case, and it can be misconduct to introduce evidence on these matters. See *Hoffman v Brandt* (1966) 65 C2d 549, 55 CR 417; 2 Witkin, CALIFORNIA PROCEDURE 1737 (1954). Thus, it would not be proper for defense counsel to contrast plaintiff's wealth with defendant's poverty in an attempt to hold down the amount of a verdict or to suggest that a working wife does not really need the money because her husband could support her.

In some cases, a plaintiff can show financial difficulties to justify returning to work even though he had not fully recovered from his injuries. There is little question that this would be proper on redirect examination or rebuttal after the defendant has suggested that the plaintiff returned to work because the disability or pain had terminated. It should also be proper on direct examination; the plaintiff is only anticipating the defense argument.

The direct examination of the plaintiff on these matters might proceed as follows:

Q. When did you return to work after the accident?
A. ....
Q. Did you miss any time after that date due to your injuries?
A. ....
Q. Had you recovered from your injuries when you resumed work?
A. No.
Q. Can you explain why you returned to work before you recovered from these injuries?
A. [I had no money coming in, my sick leave had run out, and I had to work so that my wife and kids could eat.]
Q. Did you have any source of income at that time other than your earnings on that job?
A. ....
Q. Did your wife work, Mr. ...., either before or after you were injured?
A. [No, she took care of the house and the kids.]

Comment: The meager financial status of the plaintiff might also be relevant on the issue of anxiety suffered by him from his loss of earnings, job, and future employment. See §3.29.

III. [§3.8] LIABILITY TESTIMONY

The following sections do not attempt to list or outline the facts that will establish a defendant's liability in any individual case. They do list categories of facts commonly touched on by a plaintiff in his direct testimony and discuss their applicability in common cases.

A. [§3.9] *Plaintiff's Condition and Appearance Before Accident*

The plaintiff's physical condition before the accident—his acuity, mobility, reflexes, etc.—can be relevant on the issues of liability and damages. For a discussion of damages, see §3.19.

A plaintiff's lawyer might want to elicit testimony that plaintiff's vision, hearing, balance, reactions, and so forth, were normal at the time of the accident to counter in advance any suggestion that the accident occurred because the plaintiff was somehow handicapped. If the plaintiff did suffer from some handicap, his lawyer would want him to explain it and perhaps describe the extra care he customarily took because of it. An eyeglass wearer, for example, can testify that he was wearing his glasses; or if he was not, the extent of his vision without them.

If the plaintiff was handicapped, a defense lawyer can suggest that (1) he was negligent in not using a corrective device; (2) he was negligent in getting into the position in which he was injured and did not exercise a level of care consistent with his known handicap; and (3) the accident was the unfortunate consequence of the plaintiff's own handicap rather than any negligence on the part of the defendant.

In a medical malpractice case, it is relevant to show how bad the plaintiff's health was when he received the treatment that injured him. If injury follows a grave illness, the jury is more likely to believe the doctor did the best he could in the circumstances or that any residual complaints were caused by the original illness rather than the doctor's treatment.

Defense counsel who have information that plaintiff had taken a drug or alcohol may ask about it or introduce evidence of it. The plaintiff's lawyer may anticipate this by frank inquiry into these matters on direct examination. The plaintiff can testify that neither he nor his reactions were impaired in any way. The fact that plaintiff had gone without sleep for a long time before the accident can be handled in similar fashion.

The clothing the plaintiff was wearing can also have a bearing on liability. A pedestrian wearing light clothing at night is more visible to approaching vehicle drivers. A person who slipped or tripped and fell can describe the style and condition of his shoes and if possible bring them to court.

PLAINTIFF   §3.12

B. [§3.10] *Destination; Route; Purpose*

The plaintiff's statement of where he was coming from and where and for what purpose he was going when injured can sometimes give plausibility to his version of the accident. Jurors like to know these facts even if they are not strictly relevant; they feel better oriented when they know some of the circumstances surrounding the accident.

The time plaintiff set out from his point of origin and his purpose may support testimony about whether he was hurrying at the time of the accident.

C. [§3.11] *Vehicle*

If the plaintiff was driving or riding in a vehicle, he should describe it and its mechanical condition before the accident. Testimony about the year, make, model, and color of the vehicle helps jurors form a mental picture of it and may assist them in understanding later testimony. That it was relatively new and undamaged before the accident helps to establish a basis for damages for repair costs. Its weight, compared to that of defendant's vehicle may help explain the forces and momentum involved.

The fact that lights, brakes, and other mechanical parts were in good operating condition helps to eliminate the plaintiff or his vehicle as a factor contributing to the accident. If the plaintiff's vehicle was struck from the rear, for example, the plaintiff will want to give any evidence he can that the brake lights were working properly, especially if the lights were broken by the impact and could not be tested after the accident. In rare cases, a plaintiff might be able to testify that he saw the reflection of the brake lights on his garage wall, or saw the lights working as the car was driven by another family member, although jurors might well be skeptical of the testimony. That the lights were working can also be inferred from plaintiff's testimony that he recently bought the car, or that he had driven it regularly in traffic and no one had told him his brake lights were not functioning.

D. [§3.12] *Scene of Accident; Time of Day; Weather*

The plaintiff should describe the place where the accident occurred unless a previous witness has done so, or a diagram or photographs have been introduced. In a vehicle collision or pedestrian knockdown case, for example, the plaintiff could give testimony on such matters as the location of the intersection or stretch of road; the number of traffic lanes; the angle of intersection or curve; grades and slopes;

traffic signs, signals, and markings painted on the road; whether the road surface was concrete or some other material; whether it was dry, wet, icy, smooth, bumpy, or broken; the location of trees, buildings, or other obstructions to lines of sight; the time of day and whether dusk, darkness, rain, fog, or smoke diminished visibility; and the presence and positions of other vehicles and people. The plaintiff should usually state distances in general terms, perhaps pointing out positions on a scale diagram and letting the attorney or someone else calculate the number of feet. See §1.4.

In a trip or slip and fall case the plaintiff could state the location of the defective or slippery spot; the composition of the walking surface; whether there were warning signs, sights or objects that distracted his attention from where he was walking, or obstructions to his vision; the level of lighting at the spot; and so forth.

The plaintiff can state on direct examination whether or how often he had been at the scene of the accident before the day he was injured. If the fact is brought out on cross-examination, defense counsel may be able to suggest either that the plaintiff should have been more careful since he was in an unfamiliar place, or that he was not paying attention since he was familiar with the place.

E. Chronology of Accident

1. [§3.13] Plaintiff's and Defendant's Conduct Before Impact

When a plaintiff describes how an accident occurred, he usually states, in roughly chronological order, what he did, if and when he saw the defendant, and what the defendant did. He may also state what he thought the defendant was doing or what he expected him to do, *e.g.,* "He looked like he was slowing down to let me pass." The plaintiff can also explain any steps he took to avoid or lessen his injury, such as wearing a seatbelt, bracing himself, or trying to get out of the way.

The following is an abstract of this kind of testimony as it might be given by a plaintiff whose car had been struck from the rear:

A. I saw the light changing; I put on my brakes and came to a gradual stop; I heard the squeal of tires and looked up to the mirror just as he hit me. He pushed my car forward into the car ahead of me.

Comment: If the plaintiff was stopped before the defendant hit him, he should say, in general terms, for how long (a moment or two, a few seconds, etc.). The defense lawyer may ask the plaintiff whether he had his foot on the brake when he was hit. If the plaintiff answers "Yes," but there was no evidence that the plaintiff's tires left skid marks after the impact, his testimony appears untrue. A "No" answer is evidence that the brake lights were not on at the time of the collision. Defense counsel may also ask whether the plaintiff had any warning of the collision. If the plaintiff says "No" there is an implication that he was not paying attention to his rear view mirror. If the plaintiff says "Yes," he may furnish a basis for arguing that he could have avoided the collision or mitigated its consequences (*e.g.*, by bracing himself).

The following is an abstract of a pedestrian's testimony about his and a driver's conduct:

A. I looked both ways and didn't see any cars close enough to be a danger. I stepped off the curb and started across the road. I was walking at a normal pace. I'm not sure when I first saw the defendant's car coming. I was looking at the cars coming from both directions. When I left the curb, no car looked close enough to be a hazard; I was sure he saw me and would let me cross. I guess I must have looked the other direction for a moment; when I looked back, he was coming fast right at me. I tried to jump back, but he hit me.

2. [§3.14] Impact

A plaintiff who testifies on direct examination about the physical forces in operation at the time of impact should do so to show both how the accident occurred and how the particular injuries were produced. Thus, a plaintiff can describe the position and movement of both his vehicle and his body at the moment of impact; the point, angle, and force of each impact on his vehicle and his body; his movements immediately following impact; and the nature of the surfaces and objects struck. For further discussion of the mechanics of injury, see §3.23.

For example, in a rearend collision case, the plaintiff's testimony might be:

A. [He/Defendant] smashed right into the back of my car; my head snapped back, then it must have gone forward, because I remember hitting the steering wheel with my chest. I don't know how fast he was going, but he knocked my car at least a car length into the car ahead of me. He hit just to the right of center. I was in the driver's seat, my seat belt was fastened, and my head was turned a little to look in the rearview mirror.

In a slip and fall case, the plaintiff's testimony might be:

A. My leg just went right out from under me. I reached to grab the counter but just banged my wrist as I came down on my right hip. My elbow and head also hit the floor.

3. [§3.15] Conditions After Impact

The plaintiff's description of his own injuries immediately after the impact can help to show how they were incurred. His description of vehicle damage can help to show the force and direction of impact. The presence and location of skid and gouge marks and debris on the roadway can show speed, directions, and point of impact.

A plaintiff who slipped and fell might testify about mud or liquid on his clothing or a substance observed on his shoes or the floor immediately after the fall.

F. [§3.16] *Defendant's Admissions; Insurance*

A plaintiff can testify to any nonprivileged statement he heard made or saw adopted by the defendant (Evid C §§1220–1221) or made by a person the defendant authorized to speak on that subject matter (Evid C §1222) or on whose liability, obligation, or duty the defendant's liability is based (Evid C §1224).

Occasionally, a defendant will make a statement that mentions his own insurance coverage. Although Evid C §1155 generally precludes testimony about liability insurance, evidence of a statement, such as "Don't worry, I'm insured," may be received in evidence if the statement amounts to an admission of fault and the mention of insurance is integral to that admission. See *Menefee v Williams* (1968) 259 CA2d 56, 66 CR 108; Witkin, CALIFORNIA EVIDENCE §§500, 374–375 (2d ed, 1966). However, if the admission of fault would stand alone without the mention of insurance, the judge could exclude the latter. For example, in the statement "It was all my fault, but don't worry, I'm insured," the judge might permit evidence only of the first clause, holding that the probative value of "but don't worry, I'm insured" is outweighed by the danger of prejudice. See Evid C §352.

In addition, not all statements that mention insurance are admissions of fault. In *Menefee v Williams, supra,* the statement "Don't worry, . . . if your insurance doesn't cover it, mine will" was held properly excluded because it contained no admission of fault.

G. [§3.17] *Habit or Custom*

A plaintiff can testify to his habit or custom—his regular response to a repeated specific situation—as evidence of his conduct at the time of the accident. Evid C §1105. See also Witkin, CALIFORNIA

EVIDENCE §§336–339 (2d ed, 1966). This evidence can be particularly useful when the plaintiff, perhaps because of his injuries, cannot remember the events leading up to the accident.

In a pedestrian knockdown case, for example, a plaintiff could testify that he always followed the same course, which included using the crosswalk at a given intersection, in order to reach the destination for which he was headed when hit. Of course, it might be even more effective if an independent witness testified that he had observed the plaintiff cross the street a number of times before the date of the accident and that plaintiff had always stayed in the crosswalk.

H. [§3.18] *Plaintiff's Other Accidents*

The plaintiff's involvement in accidents before or after the accident sued on is not relevant on the issue of his negligence; the evidence is too remote and likely to be unduly prejudicial. See *Shmatovich v New Sonoma Creamery* (1960) 187 CA2d 342, 9 CR 630; Witkin, CALIFORNIA EVIDENCE §323 (2d ed, 1966); Anno, 20 ALR2d 1210 (1951). However, if the plaintiff was injured in the other accident, and the injury is related to the one sued on, defense counsel could ask about details that would help to establish the severity of the trauma to plaintiff's body in the other accident and the nature and extent of the other injury. See *Prichard v Veterans Cab Co.* (1965) 63 C2d 727, 47 CR 904.

The plaintiff's lawyer can, in some cases, blunt the effect of cross-examination on other injuries and accidents by bringing them out on direct examination. See §§3.21–3.22.

IV. [§3.19] INJURY TESTIMONY

The plaintiff can testify about his physical condition before and after an accident to show the effects of injury on his body and mind. *Latky v Wolfe* (1927) 85 CA 332, 343, 259 P 470, 475. Even though the plaintiff is not a medical expert, he can describe conditions and sensations personally known to him (Evid C §702) and express opinions rationally based on his perceptions and helpful to an understanding of his testimony (Evid C §800). See *Bowman v Motor Transit Co.* (1930) 208 C 652, 284 P 443; *Boa v San Francisco-Oakland Terminal Rys.* (1920) 182 C 93, 187 P 2; *Whaley v Fowler* (1957) 152 CA2d 379, 384, 313 P2d 97, 100. See §7.1 on lay injury testimony generally.

Most plaintiff's lawyers do not rely on the plaintiff alone to testify about injuries; they also call medical experts and use medical exhibits. However, the lawyer must still decide how extensive the plaintiff's injury testimony should be. Some lawyers have the plaintiff describe every scratch and bruise from head to toe and every pain, minute by minute, hour by hour, and day by day. At the other extreme, some lawyers confine the plaintiff to a brief description of the effects of the injury on his daily life, leaving it to other, less partial witnesses, and to the trier of fact, to fill in the details.

Even though a plaintiff's lawyer plans to take only limited injury testimony from his client, both the lawyer and the plaintiff should be thoroughly prepared on the medical aspects of the case. By the time of trial—indeed, by the time of the plaintiff's deposition—the lawyer should know more about his client's injuries than any doctor in the case. This knowledge is gained from a detailed questioning of the client, a close reading of all medical records and reports, and from the lawyer's own observations of the client's appearance and movements.

During preparation of the case, the lawyer should ask his client about all prior and subsequent accidents, diseases, and injuries and all cuts, bruises, pains, and other signs and symptoms arising from the accident sued on. The plaintiff should be reminded of all aspects of his medical history, how he was injured, and every injury and symptom. Defense counsel may ask about these matters during a deposition or at trial, and if the plaintiff's answers are confused or contrary to his medical records, he can be impeached.

A. Health Before Accident

1. [§3.20] Good Health

The previous good health of a plaintiff who was essentially symptom-free and without physical limitations before the accident can be contrasted with his limitations and poor health after injury.

A plaintiff's testimony about his good health and capabilities before injury is usually brought out in connection with testimony about limitations resulting from the accident. See §3.26.

2. [§3.21] Prior Conditions

A defense lawyer often asks the plaintiff about preaccident injuries and physical limitations to ensure that only injuries caused by the accident are considered in determining damages and to suggest that some of the plaintiff's symptoms were due to preexisting conditions. A plaintiff's lawyer can counter any suggestion that he was trying to collect for an unrelated injury by asking the plaintiff about prior injuries on direct examination. For example:

PLAINTIFF §3.22

Q. Before this accident, had you ever received an injury to your [knee]?
A. Yes.
Q. When did you have that injury?
A. ....
Q. What sort of injury was it?
A. ....
Q. Did you see a doctor for it?
A. ....
Q. What treatment did you take for it?
A. ....
Q. Were you operated on?
A. ....
Q. Were you disabled?
A. [Yes, I was in bed for ...... days, and I couldn't go back to work for ...... days after that.]
Q. Did your [knee] heal?
A. Yes.
Q. When did you consider it healed?
A. ...., 19.......
Q. When did you last see a doctor for that injury?
A. ...., 19.......
Q. At the time of [defendant's collision with your car], was your [knee] troubling you in any way?
A. No.
Q. Was there any [limitation of motion/swelling/pain/etc.]?
A. No.

3. [§3.22] Aggravation of Prior Condition; Predisposition to Injury

A plaintiff is entitled to damages for the defendant's tortious aggravation of a preexisting physical or mental condition. See generally Johns, CALIFORNIA DAMAGES 70–72 (1969); 2 Witkin, SUMMARY OF CALIFORNIA LAW 1615 (7th ed, 1960). See also BAJI No 14.65.

The plaintiff's lawyer can ask him about prior conditions not only to anticipate cross-examination and to show what part of the plaintiff's present condition the defendant is responsible for, but also to show the extent to which the plaintiff was predisposed to the type of injury that resulted from the accident. The latter is particularly important when a dramatic injury or disability has resulted from a relatively minor trauma.

For example, a plaintiff with a preexisting heart condition can suffer a coronary occlusion following a blow to the chest or even the stress of being in an accident. Jurors would be unlikely to believe that the heart attack resulted from the relatively minor trauma of the accident unless they were also shown that the trauma was acting on already weakened tissue.

Although medical records and expert testimony should be used when available to show preexisting conditions, the plaintiff can also testify about prior episodes and symptoms. The plaintiff's testimony is particularly useful to show symptoms for which he did not seek medical attention. He can also testify that by the time of the accident he was symptom-free, or he can establish the level of his disability and pain at that time.

B. [§3.23] *Mechanics of Injury*

A plaintiff's testimony about the chronology of the accident should describe how he was injured as well as how the accident occurred. See §3.14.

If jurors are to be convinced that particular claimed injuries resulted from an accident caused by the defendant, they must be shown the connection between the forces to which the plaintiff was subjected and the results. There may be a fatal gap in such testimony as:

Q. [What happened then?]
A. [I was hit a terrific blow from the rear.]
Q. [And then what happened?]
A. [I got out of my car. My back hurt and I went to Dr. .... for treatment.]

The mechanics of injury can be especially important when there is a soft tissue injury with no objective signs to support the plaintiff's complaints or when the claimed injury was an unusual result from the trauma involved.

A plaintiff should be prepared to give a coherent description of the mechanics of injury even at his deposition. A common defense deposition question is: "What happened to your body inside that car at the time of impact?" If the plaintiff guesses at an answer or gets confused, his description may not fit established principles of physics, and he can be impeached at trial.

C. [§3.24] *Description of Injuries and Treatment*

A plaintiff can testify to each of the signs of injury that he perceived in himself and the symptoms, including pain, that he felt. See

PLAINTIFF §3.24

generally §3.19. He can also describe the medical treatment he sought and received for each injury. This testimony can be given in chronological order from the time of injury to the time of trial, and body area by body area.

Medical records and reports should be used before plaintiff testifies to remind him when he was seen by medical personnel, what he complained of on each of those occasions, and what treatment was given him. For example, an unprepared plaintiff asked what treatment he received in a hospital might reply, "They just kept me in bed." The hospital record will remind him of diagnostic tests, medications, and other procedures, as well as his own day to day complaints.

A plaintiff's description of treatment received can sometimes have greater impact than the testimony of the treating doctor. For example, a doctor might say, "an electroencephalogram was run." A plaintiff asked what tests were run, might answer:

A. There was one in which they laid me out on a table. Then they put this metal cap on my head that had wires running from it to a machine. They'd tell me to breathe deeply or to hold my breath. The operator sat there and turned dials on the machine.

Comment: Testimony about particular injuries should be straightforward without exaggeration or self-pity. Jurors are more receptive when the lawyer stresses the plaintiff's injuries and suffering in argument. For example, testimony about a facial laceration might proceed as follows:

Q. Did you receive any injury in the area of your face?
A. Yes, I did. [I had a cut over my left eye.]
Q. When did you first realize you had that injury?
A. Right away, I guess.
Q. How did you discover it?
A. [The first thing was that I couldn't see out of my left eye. I put my hand up to my eye and it came away covered with blood.]
Q. Did it hurt?
A. It sure did.

Comment: Although in this example pain is not a significant factor in diagnosing the laceration (compare dialogue, §3.25), it is brought out as an element of the detriment suffered by the plaintiff.

Q. What kind of pain was it?
A. [Kind of a dull ache at first.]
Q. Did you get any treatment for the cut at the scene?

75

A. Yes. [Somebody put a cloth over it and tied it with a handkerchief or something.]
Q. Did that have any effect?
A. Yes. It slowed down the bleeding.
Q. How did it affect the pain?
A. It didn't help that. In fact, when I got the blood out of my eye and could see again, there seemed to be more pain from the cut.

Comment: The lawyer could at this point bring out testimony about other injuries, signs, and symptoms perceived at the scene. Further testimony about the facial laceration might proceed as follows:

Q. Did you get further treatment for the cut?
A. Yes. I was taken to the hospital where they stitched it up.

Comment: If the injury is a significant basis for damages, the plaintiff's lawyer might well want more detail than "they stitched it up." For example:

Q. Just to go back a little, were you examined by a doctor at the hospital?
A. Yes.
Q. Was anything done about that bandage on your head?
A. Oh, yes. The doctor pulled it off. I remember that the cloth was stuck in the wound and it hurt.
Q. Did he give you an anesthetic or something to relieve the pain?
A. Yes. He sprayed something on the cut before he sewed it up.

Comment: The lawyer could continue with questions in this vein concerning the debridement, suturing, and dressing of the wound; pain after the anesthetic wore off; the removal of the stitches; the healing process; etc.

Q. Did that cut leave a scar?
A. Yes, it did.
Q. Would you please step down in front of the jury so that they can see it?
A. Yes.

Comment: It is helpful to have jurors see scars, lumps, and tissue loss firsthand. The plaintiff can remove clothing when that is necessary to show the injury, although injuries in genital and adjacent areas should usually be shown by photograph. A doctor, during his testimony, can also point out the plaintiff's disfigurement, limitations of motion, and other defects. See §8.36.

PLAINTIFF   §3.25

Even though jurors have seen a scar, the attorney may make a statement describing it for the record. For example:

Proponent. Let the record show that there is a four-inch scar running from above the outer end of his left eyebrow, through the eyebrow and across the bridge of his nose, about one-eighth to three-sixteenths inches wide, and that it is blanched.

D. [§3.25] Pain

Pain is both a symptom of underlying tissue injury or abnormality and a form of detriment for which damages may be sought. See generally Johns, CALIFORNIA DAMAGES 125–139 (1969); 2 Witkin, SUMMARY OF CALIFORNIA LAW 1613 (7th ed, 1960). See also BAJI No 14.13. Pain is sometimes called "physical pain" to distinguish it from "mental suffering," which includes fright, embarrassment, anxiety, and the like (see §3.29).

The plaintiff can testify about his pain (see generally §3.19) specifying the time of onset, location, duration, persistence, severity, and character of each area of pain he has experienced; what events or activities brought it on or aggravated it; what treatment he sought and received; and what effects (*e.g.,* nausea) the pain had on him. This description of pain can be tied in with the plaintiff's testimony about other signs and symptoms of injury. See §3.24. The testimony can detail pain at all stages from the moment of injury, through treatment, to the time the testimony is given, and according to each body area.

In cases in which there are no objective signs of injury, those aspects of the nature and cause of pain that are diagnostically significant can be brought out at the same time that the intensity and duration of the plaintiff's suffering is shown. For example:

Q. Did you suffer any pain [in your head] after the accident?
A. Yes.
Q. Where, exactly, was the pain located when you first noticed it?
A. Right here. [Indicates.]
Q. When did you first become aware of the pain [at the back of your head]?
A. When I got home.
Q. How long after the accident was that?
A. About ...... hours.

Comment: The plaintiff can state the time each area of pain was first felt. If the onset of pain was delayed, the delay should be explained, especially if the plaintiff stated at the scene of the accident that he was

§3.25 PLAINTIFF

not hurt, or declined to be taken to a hospital. The lawyer should determine from a medical expert whether the onset of pain is normally delayed for the injury involved or whether the physiological aspects of pain can exist even though the patient does not realize it, because he is unconscious or preoccupied. The plaintiff may have been "dazed," "numb," or "in a state of shock," and may not have become fully aware that he had been injured and was in pain until later.

Q. As time went on, did the pain stay [at the back of your head]?
A. [No, it seemed to go into my neck and shoulders and down my arms.]
Q. How long did that process take after you first noticed the pains?
A. Two or three hours.
Q. Can you describe the nature of that pain [in your head], please?
A. ....
Q. Had you ever had a pain like that before?
A. ....

Comment: While no one can truly communicate to another what his pain was like, the plaintiff should try to describe the nature and severity of his pain in terms that will remind jurors of pain they have suffered or can imagine. A pain can be described as "sharp," "dull," "deep," "throbbing," "shooting," "splitting," "like a toothache," etc. Phrases such as "it was horrible," "I kept hoping I would pass out," "I wanted to die," and the like, sound exaggerated unless the injury was serious. Doctors sometimes use such expressions as "lancinating pain," "exquisite pain," and "fulgurant pain," but these should be avoided by laymen.

The plaintiff can also describe whether the pain was constant, intermittent, or associated with factors like movement, fatigue, damp weather, etc.

Q. Can you describe the pain in your [neck, shoulders, and arms]?
A. [It was more a dull aching pain in the neck and shoulders and a numbness in the arms. Of course, if I turned my head or moved my arms, I would get a sharp twinge that really hurt.]
Q. Did you do anything about the pain?
A. Yes. [At first, when I thought it was just a headache, I took some aspirin.]
Q. Did that help?
A. [No. The pain got worse as time went on.]
Q. Did you do anything else?
A. Yes. [I called Dr. .... and went to his office.]

PLAINTIFF §3.25

Comment: Testimony about severe pain should be supported by testimony about the treatment sought for it. Did the plaintiff see a doctor? In the hospital, did he call the nurses for help? What drugs or therapy did he receive? Did they help? Did they have adverse side effects?

Testimony about treatment can be tied in with testimony about how long the pain continued and at what levels of severity and constancy. In addition, the plaintiff can testify about the effects of the pain on his life. For example:

Q. Did Dr. .... do anything for the pain?
A. Yes. He gave me some capsules called .... and a prescription to get more.
Q. How often did you take them?
A. At first, one every ...... hours; after .... days I cut down to ...... per day.
Q. How long did you take the drug at that dosage?
A. About ...... weeks.
Q. Did you have pain in your head and neck after seeing Dr. ....?
A. Yes.
Q. Please describe it and tell us when it occurred?
A. ....
Q. What did you do for it?
A. I would take those capsules I mentioned and lie down.
Q. How long did those daily headaches continue?
A. Well, they gradually tapered off over the next ...... weeks.
Q. Were there any changes in your activities after the accident?
A. Yes, I didn't go to work for ...... weeks.
Q. Did you do things around the house?
A. Well, I tried to, but any work or exercise seemed to bring on the headaches.
Q. When did you return to work?
A. ...., 19.......
Q. Did you work full-time?
A. Well, I was there full-time, but I had to stop often to rest or to keep the headaches from getting too bad. The other fellows had to carry part of my load.
Q. Do you still have pain in your head?
A. Yes.

Comment: The lawyer can continue with questions about the nature, frequency, and effects of the pain. However, he must keep in mind that the jury can be antagonized if testimony on pain is overdone.

E. [§3.26] *Disability Generally; Impairment of Normal Life*

The physical and mental disability that results from injuries suffered by the plaintiff in an accident can be shown to support his claim for lost wages and impaired earning capacity. See generally §3.30. In addition, the detriment for which a plaintiff may recover damages includes impairment of his capacity to enjoy life and of his ability to live a normal life and to continue his customary activities. See Johns, CALIFORNIA DAMAGES 140–142 (1969).

The plaintiff's disabilities and the limitations on his activities after the accident can be contrasted with what he could do before he was injured. For example:

(1) What was his occupation? What duties did he have on the job? Exactly what physical acitvities did he perform in carrying out those duties? Did he ever have any difficulty in performing them before the accident?

(2) What other income-producing or money-saving activities did he pursue? Did he wash, maintain, or repair his automobile? Did he paint, maintain, repair, remodel, or enlarge his house?

(3) What were his leisure time activities? Did he hunt, garden, play golf, swim, play cards, do handicrafts?

(4) What family activities did he engage in? Did he do routine chores around the house? Did he take his wife dancing, play ball with his children, or take his family hiking and camping?

(5) What civic, church, and social activities did he engage in?

In addition to interference with voluntary activities, the plaintiff can testify about the effects of the injury on normal daily activities. For example:

(1) Was it more difficult to sleep, dress, tie his shoes, drive his car, or ride the bus?

(2) Did he lose his ability to enjoy food or sexual relations?

Disabilities that interfere with these activities include those resulting from loss or damage to tissue and from pain or abnormal fatigue.

1. [§3.27] Workers

A manual worker's injury can make him unable to do the lifting, twisting, or stooping required by his job. The injury may force him to use tortuous methods and expend extra energy to accomplish what he could once do easily. An office worker may find that he cannot concentrate as he once did, that headaches keep him from working normal hours at normal efficiency, and that he must take work home. These workers may not lose wages as a result of their injuries, but they suffer detriment in the form of impairment of their capacity and ability to lead a normal life.

2. [§3.28] Housewives

It is usually not enough for a disabled housewife to say only, "I just can't do the things around the house I used to." She should testify how her injury affects her in lifting, holding, and caring for her children; standing in the kitchen or at the ironing board; pushing the vacuum cleaner; kneeling to scrub; driving to the store or school; lifting the laundry; and so forth. She may do these things despite the pain and added effort because she must. The effort to accomplish basic chores may prevent her from making clothes for the family, helping with homework, or pursuing civic and social activities. A housewife's disability can be tied in with the need to hire help to accomplish her functions, or the imposition of those burdens on other family members. Jurors might otherwise feel that she benefited from being relieved of household chores.

F. [§3.29] *Mental Suffering*

The pain and suffering for which a plaintiff may recover damages includes mental reactions to the accident and his injuries, such as fright, shock, and indignity at the time of the accident and subsequent nervousness, grief, emotional upset, embarrassment, shame, mortification, humiliation, worry, anxiety, and fear. See generally Johns, CALIFORNIA DAMAGES 127–130 (1969); 2 Witkin, SUMMARY OF CALIFORNIA LAW 1614 (7th ed, 1960).

The plaintiff is the person who knows his own mental and emotional reactions best. However, the plaintiff's testimony on these matters is not always necessary. Other witnesses can testify that he appeared shocked, humiliated, or worried; experts can testify to the medical basis for emotional distress; and jurors can infer mental suffering from the nature and extent of the injuries and their idea of his character. If the plaintiff testifies about these matters, he should not seem to be exaggerating his injuries or whining about them.

A plaintiff who describes the accident in which he was involved (see §3.23) can testify about his own emotional reaction to it. Was he frightened; did he "freeze"; was he shocked, numb, or immobile; was he incontinent or in disarray? Plaintiff's counsel should be concerned, however, that testimony about fright and shock brought out as an element of damages does not run counter to establishing that the plaintiff was a reasonable person acting in a reasonable manner at the time of the accident.

A plaintiff who testifies about the nature of his injuries and the treatment he received (see §3.24), and the physical pain he experienced at various stages of recovery (see §3.25), can similarly describe the anguish and worry that he experienced during that period, as well as the anxiety he presently experiences.

(1) Was he, and is he, worried about losing his job or being unable to conduct his business, not being able to support himself or his family, being unable to find work, being passed over for promotion, or being the first to be laid off?

(2) Was he, and is he, worried that further surgery or treatment will be required or that his injuries have left him vulnerable to reinjury, made him susceptible to other injuries or disease, or put him in a position where another injury could totally disable him?

(3) Has the accident left him nervous, irritable, "jumpy," or abnormally fearful of high places (after a fall) or of riding in an automobile (after a collision)?

A disfigured or disabled plaintiff may be able to testify that he or she no longer participates in social and recreational activities formerly enjoyed; that people seem to stare and then look away; and that he receives fewer invitations and declines others. This shows a basis for damages for feelings of embarrassment, anguish, and humiliation over injuries and, particularly if a young woman, anxiety and despair at prospects of ever marrying or leading a satisfying social life.

The plaintiff's fright, embarrassment, anxiety, or fear need not be rational so long as it actually results from the accident or injury and affects the plaintiff's life. For example, a plaintiff who received a burn injury could experience a very real and possibly disabling fear of developing cancer at the burn site, although the fear may proceed primarily from the chance remark of a doctor or even a lay person. See Anno, 71 ALR2d 338, 343 at §5 (1960).

V. [§3.30] IMPAIRED EARNING CAPACITY

An injured plaintiff is entitled to damages for any impairment of his capacity to earn money caused by the defendant's wrongful conduct. The plaintiff is not limited to money actually lost or reasonably certain to be lost in the future; he can recover for his lost or impaired capacity to earn even though he was not working at the time of the accident or received collateral compensation for work time missed. See generally Johns, CALIFORNIA DAMAGES 94–124 (1969); 2 Witkin, SUMMARY OF CALIFORNIA LAW 1611–1612 (7th ed, 1960). See also BAJI Nos 14.11–14.12.

The plaintiff's impaired earning capacity can be proved through

PLAINTIFF   §3.31

the business records of his employer (see chap 11); and through the testimony of an employer, supervisor, or personnel manager; a fellow worker or partner; another person in the same occupation; or an economist or "appraiser of impaired earning capacity" (see §7.9). The lawyer can also question the plaintiff to elicit testimony on the difference between his capacity to earn before and after the accident. See §§3.31–3.32.

If the plaintiff was the proprietor of a business and his personal efforts were the principal factor in determining the income of that business, he could testify to, and introduce business records to show, a decline of profits in the business following his injury. The degree to which profits declined would be evidence of the impairment of his earning capacity. See *Johns* 107–111; 2 Witkin, SUMMARY 1611.

A. [§3.31] Checklist

·The testimony of a plaintiff who was employed at a salary or wages at the time of the accident, and had returned to work before the trial, might cover such matters as:

1. His occupation, job title, and place of employment when injured.
2. Any secondary jobs for remuneration.
3. His duties and activities in his occupation(s).
4. The effect of his injuries on his ability to carry out those duties and activities (*i.e.*, how he was disabled from working (see also §3.26)).
5. The number of hours normally worked at the time of the injury including overtime and secondary jobs.
6. His rate of earning at the time of injury including wages, salary, tips, bonuses, and overtime pay (could be supported by W-2 Forms, tax returns, and employment records (see chap 11)).
7. Time missed from work (or unable to work) because of the injuries.
8. Fringe benefits lost including loss of seniority, bonuses, commissions, holidays, vacations, insurance coverages, and retirement and profit-sharing benefits.
9. Loss or delay of increases in earnings because of time missed.

If the plaintiff was not gainfully employed at the time of the accident or was for some reason not paid commensurate with his earning capacity, he could testify about:

1. Circumstances explaining his unemployment, or why he was earning below capacity.
2. His educational attainments and any special vocational training.
3. His strength and health before the injury.
4. His motivation to work steadily and to advance himself (*e.g.*, personal and family obligations).

5. Work experience before injury (time in that industry, and with the same employer; progress toward qualifying for higher-paying positions).

6. His individual skill, competence, business acumen, or goodwill.

If the plaintiff seeks damages for impairment of future earning capacity, in addition to the foregoing matters, he could testify about:

1. His present occupation, job title, employment, and rate of earning.

2. His occupational and employment goals at the time of the accident and at present.

3. His assessment of his prospects for employment in the future.

4. His willingness to take reasonable employment to the extent that he is capable of it.

(If damages for permanent impairment are sought)

5. His age and the prospective duration of his working career (*i.e.*, his life expectancy or time until retirement).

B. [§3.32] *Plaintiff's Testimony on Loss of Earnings*

Impairment of earning capacity can sometimes be shown through a plaintiff's testimony about the number of work days he missed because of his injuries and his rate of pay for that period. For example, if the plaintiff's only earnings were from a salary or wages, the only effect of the injuries was to keep him from working for a number of days, and he had returned to work by the time of trial without interruption to rate of advancement or loss of any fringe benefits, his testimony might proceed as follows:

Q. What was your position at the time of the accident?
A. ....
Q. What were your duties on that job?
A. ....
Q. What was your rate of pay at that time?
A. ...... dollars per [month/week/day/hour].

Comment: If there is likely to be any question about the truth of plaintiff's testimony about his rate of pay, the lawyer could support the plaintiff's testimony by offering plaintiff's "W-2 Form" or income tax return for the year preceding the year of injury or a statement of earnings or testimony from his employer.

Q. What effect did the injuries you suffered in this accident have on your working?
A. I couldn't go to work for ...... days.

PLAINTIFF §3.32

Q. Have you computed, from your rate of earning, which was ......
dollars per [month/hour/etc.], what your earnings for those ......
days that you missed should have been?
A. Yes. They should have been ...... dollars.

Comment: Plaintiff is entitled to recover his regular compensation for the time missed even though money was actually paid him as vacation or sick leave pay or gratuitously by his employer (see *Lewis v Contra Costa* (1955) 130 CA2d 176, 178, 278 P2d 756, 758). See generally *De Cruz v Reid* (1968) 69 C2d 217, 223, 70 CR 550, 554; Johns, CALIFORNIA DAMAGES 156–157 (1969); 2 Witkin, SUMMARY OF CALIFORNIA LAW 1609 (7th ed, 1960).

4

Police Officers

I. Preparation

A. [§4.1] Value as Witness
B. [§4.2] Reviewing Accident Report
  1. [§4.3] Sample California Highway Patrol Vehicle Accident Report
  2. [§4.4] Code for Interpreting California Highway Patrol Vehicle Accident Reports
C. [§4.5] Identifying the Officer
D. Interviewing the Officer
  1. [§4.6] Purpose
  2. [§4.7] Arranging Time and Place
  3. [§4.8] Compensation
  4. [§4.9] Checklist of Questions
  5. [§4.10] Evaluating Officer as Witness: Checklist
E. [§4.11] Officer's Deposition
F. Compelling Attendance at Trial
  1. [§4.12] Using Subpena
  2. [§4.13] Range of Subpena
  3. [§4.14] Depositing Fees; Reimbursing Police Agency
  4. [§4.15] Form: Clause in Subpena Showing Deposit of Fees
G. [§4.16] Courthouse Interview

II. [§4.17] Qualifying the Officer

A. [§4.18] Police and Investigative Background
B. [§4.19] Impartiality
C. [§4.20] Investigative Procedure

III. [§4.21] Using Report To Aid Testimony

A. [§4.22] Refreshing Memory

POLICE OFFICERS

    B. [§4.23] Past Recollection Recorded

IV. Activities and Observations at Accident Scene

    A. [§4.24] Time of Arrival
    B. [§4.25] Aiding Victims; Clearing Traffic
    C. The Roadway
        1. [§4.26] Using Diagram
        2. [§4.27] Layout; Contour; Surface
        3. [§4.28] Obstructions
    D. Vehicles
        1. [§4.29] Identity
        2. [§4.30] Point of Rest
        3. [§4.31] Damage
        4. [§4.32] Mechanical Condition
    E. Drivers; Passengers; Pedestrians
        1. [§4.33] Possession of License
        2. [§4.34] Identity; Position in Vehicle
        3. [§4.35] Injuries
        4. [§4.36] Intoxication
    F. [§4.37] Skid Marks; Debris
    G. [§4.38] Traffic Controls
    H. [§4.39] Weather
    I. [§4.40] Visibility
    J. [§4.41] Citations; Arrests

V. Statements of Parties and Witnesses

    A. [§4.42] Admissibility Under Hearsay Exceptions
        1. [§4.43] Party's Admissions
        2. [§4.44] Adoptive Admissions
        3. [§4.45] Driver's Statement To Show Liability of Employer or Owner
        4. [§4.46] Spontaneous Statements
    B. [§4.47] Statements About Liability Insurance
    C. [§4.48] Conviction; Plea of Guilty or Nolo Contendere

VI. [§4.49] Officer as Expert

    A. [§4.50] Deciding Whether To Use Officer
    B. [§4.51] Special Qualifications
    C. [§4.52] Attacking Qualifications
    D. Subjects of Expert Testimony
        1. [§4.53] Point of Impact

POLICE OFFICERS §4.3

    2. [§4.54] Vehicle's Mechanical Condition
    3. [§4.55] Loading of Truck
    4. [§4.56] Safe Speed Under the Conditions
    5. [§4.57] Speed Before Collision
    6. [§4.58] Influence of Narcotics

  VII. [§4.59] Eliciting Unfavorable Matter on Direct

I. PREPARATION

A. [§4.1] *Value as Witness*

California Highway Patrol and local police officers routinely investigate motor vehicle accidents. The investigating officer usually arrives on the scene promptly and observes physical facts, such as the position of vehicles, location of skid marks, and condition of the parties, as they exist immediately after the accident. He interviews witnesses while events are fresh in their minds and before they have formulated exculpatory stories. He is generally a trained observer, and the findings of his investigation, which are recorded in his accident report, are contemporaneous and comprehensive.

By the time a case comes to trial, the investigating officer usually cannot testify about his investigation on the basis of present, unassisted memory. But by using the accident report to refresh his memory or as his past recollection recorded (see §§4.21–4.23), he is able to testify on a broad range of subjects relating to his investigation.

B. [§4.2] *Reviewing Accident Report*

The lawyer should review the accident report immediately to determine the facts of the accident and the identity of witnesses to be interviewed. The report indicates what testimony can be expected from the officer, and it identifies other potential witnesses. For discussion of the uses of police accident reports, see §9.2. The accident report is rarely admissible in evidence as an exhibit. If the officer who conducted the investigation is not available as a witness and has not been deposed, the lawyer's ability to present the case can be seriously prejudiced.

The procedure for obtaining a copy of the report during the investigative stage of the case is discussed in §§9.3–9.5.

§4.3 POLICE OFFICERS

1. **[§4.3] Sample California Highway Patrol Vehicle Accident Report**

Most California police agencies use vehicle accident reports that duplicate or are based on the form used by the California Highway Patrol.

Following this discussion is a sample accident report, using the current CHP form, filled in with the facts describing a hypothetical collision. Code numbers are used at various points on pages one and two of the report; the CHP code sheet (which is not a part of an individual accident report) appears in §4.4.

Abbreviations appearing in the report may be standard, such as "N/B" and "S/B" for northbound and southbound, "p.o.i." for point of impact, etc. Others may be used locally or by the particular officer, such as "t.c." for traffic collision, "tlr" for trailer, and "veh" for vehicle. "N.I.P." is used on page one of the sample report to indicate that Driver No. 2's license was "not in [her] possession." Traffic lanes are identified throughout California as N-1 for the northbound lane nearest the center, N-2 for the northbound lane next from the center, etc. Southbound, eastbound, and westbound lanes appear as S-1, E-1, W-1, etc.

The officer's interview and investigation summary is at page three of the CHP form; additional summary pages are used if necessary. Highway Patrol investigators ordinarily begin their summaries with a statement entitled "Facts," but the lawyer must be alert for opinion (*e.g.,* an officer's conclusions on a driver's sobriety, actions before the collision, etc.), and for information that he did not perceive, but heard from others. For example, the lawyer could inquire whether the officer's statement, "There were no visible skid marks at the scene" was based on his own investigation or that of an assisting officer. Accident reports by CHP officers normally include the names of assisting officers following the "Facts" portion of the summary.

Statements of parties and witnesses are often summaries, in the officer's words, of what a person said. In some instances questions and answers that purport to be literal are included. Supplemental statements, such as those taken later at a hospital, are attached to the accident report; the officer who took the statement is identified at the bottom of the sheet.

In his "Recommendations" the investigating officer indicates whether violations occurred and whether citations were issued or

POLICE OFFICERS §4.3

arrests made. In the sample report the officer recommends that his report be considered "preliminary" (and it is so marked at the top of page one) until a statement can be taken of one of the victims. The lawyer should inquire to determine if further investigation was made, or if this preliminary report is final.

(Form begins on p 92)
(Code sheet for interpreting form begins on p 103)

STATE OF CALIFORNIA
CALIFORNIA HIGHWAY PATROL
TRAFFIC ACCIDENT REPORT

SPECIAL NOTE
PRELIMINARY

ARREST OR CITATION

No. _____ (DRIVER) (CITATION NUMBER) (SECTIONS)
No. _____
No. _____

ACCIDENT OCCURRED ON (ROUTE NO., SECTION, OR ROAD, STREET, ALLEY) Rt 101
3/10 mi North 101 (HIGHWAY, ROAD, STREET, ALLEY)
AT INTERSECTION WITH _____
1/2 mi feet (DISTANCE) OTHER DESCRIPTION of Centerville Road (NEAREST STREET, MARKER, OR LANDMARK)
(DIRECTION)

County: Monterey
City: Unic — Centerville
Area: 465 (JUDICIAL DISTRICT) 5 (BEAT)
(MILE POST) 89

CODING BOXES

2	3	4-5	6-7	8-9	10-11-12-13	14-15	16	17	18	19-20	21-22-23-24	25

465-4-66-13 (ACCIDENT NUMBER)

DAY OF WEEK Friday | 26
DATE April 1, 1966 | 27-28
TIME 1905 A.M. **P.M.** | 29-30
TOTAL KILLED 1 | TOTAL INJURED 2 | 31-32
37-38 33-36

MOTOR VEHICLE INVOLVED WITH
1. ☐ PEDESTRIAN
2. ☐ OTHER MOTOR VEH. IN TRAFFIC
3. ☐ PARKED MOTOR VEHICLE
4. ☐ TRAIN
5. ☐ BICYCLIST
6. ☐ ANIMAL
7. ☐ OTHER OBJECT
8. ☐ FIXED OBJECT
9. ☐ RAN OFF ROAD
10. ☐ OVERTURNED IN ROAD
11. ☐ OTHER NON-COLLISION

VEHICLE NO. 1

DRIVEN BY John Doe _____ RES. PHONE 678-1234
(NAME) (ADDRESS) 10 Main St., Centerville (CITY)
EMPLOYER _____ OCCUPATION Draftsman
(NAME OF PERSON, COMPANY OR ORGANIZATION) (ADDRESS) (CITY)
DESC. 24 M Brn Blu 5'10" 161 1-13-42 DR. LIC. P96412 CLASS 3 Calif TYPE Reg.
(AGE) (SEX) (HAIR) (EYES) (HT.) (WT.) (BIRTHDATE) (NUMBER) (TYPE CODE) (STATE) (REG. RESTR. TEMP.)
VEHICLE 64 Ford 4dr sedan Blk 01 VEH. LIC. ABC-123X11212 66 Calif
(YEAR) (MAKE) (MODEL OR TYPE—INCLUDE TRAILERS) (COLOR) (NUMBERS) (YEAR) (STATE)
PRESENT OWNER Driver pulling 2 ax tlr
GOING North on Rt 101 PARTS DAMAGED Left front side EXTENT: ☐ MINOR ☒ MAJOR
(DIRECTION) (STREET OR HIGHWAY) (BY FENDER, BR DOOR, FRONT, ETC.) ☐ MODERATE ☐ TOTAL
USES ROAD OR STREET ☐ FREQUENTLY ☐ RARELY ☐ NEVER BEFORE DATE DRIVER LAST USED ROAD Monthly (PRIOR TO ACCIDENT)
VEH. MOVED TO XYZ Towing, Centerville ON ORDERS OF CHP
(LOCATION) (CHP, POLICE, DRIVER, OR OWNER—IF OTHER, GIVE NAME AND ADDRESS)

DRIV. EXP. 6 (YEARS) | 39

50	51	52	53-54	55	56

VEHICLE NO. 2

(ALSO LIST) ☐ PEDESTRIAN ☐ BICYCLIST ☐ ENGINEER ☐ OTHER—WHEN INVOLVED
DRIVEN BY Mary Roe _____ RES. PHONE NTP
(NAME) (ADDRESS) 123 High St., Laketown (CITY)
EMPLOYER _____ OCCUPATION _____
(NAME OF PERSON, COMPANY OR ORGANIZATION) (ADDRESS) (CITY) (PHONE)
DESC. 28 F Brn DR. LIC. _____ CLASS _____ TYPE

DRIV. EXP. (YEARS) | 59-60 | 61

VEHICLE

VEHICLE 63 (YEAR) Chev. 2dr. sedan (MAKE) (MODEL OR TYPE—INCLUDE TRAILERS) White (COLOR) 01 (TYPE CODE) VEH. LIC. 66 (YEAR) PQR-456-Z44511 (NUMBERS) Calif (STATE) | 51

PRESENT OWNER Richard Roe (NAME) 123 High St. (ADDRESS) Laketown (CITY) | 52

GOING ___ (DIRECTION) ACROSS (PED.) ON Rt. 101 (STREET OR HIGHWAY) PARTS DAMAGED Total Rt. side (IF FENDER, RR DOOR, FRONT, ETC.) EXTENT: ☐ MINOR ☐ MODERATE ☐ MAJOR ☒ TOTAL | 53-54

USES ROAD OR STREET ☐ FREQUENTLY ☐ RARELY ☐ NEVER BEFORE DATE DRIVER LAST USED ROAD _____ (PRIOR TO ACCIDENT)

VEH. MOVED TO XYZ Towing, Centerville (LOCATION) ON ORDERS OF CHP (CHP, POLICE, DRIVER, OR OWNER—IF OTHER, GIVE NAME AND ADDRESS) | 55

PROPERTY DAMAGED OTHER THAN VEHICLES

OWNED BY _____ (NAME) _____ (DESCRIBE) _____ (ADDRESS) _____ (CITY) NOTIFIED? ☐ YES ☐ NO | 56

WITNESSES

1. Helen Gray (NAME) 18 (AGE) 9999 Market St. (ADDRESS) San Francisco (CITY) _____ (PHONE) | 57-58
2. | 59-60
3. | 61

VICTIMS

NO.	AGE 71-72	SEX 73	74 1. Killed	EXTENT OF INJURY (CHECK ONE ONLY)				VICTIM WAS (CHECK ONE ONLY) 75					IN VEHICLE 76		EJECTED BY IMPACT 79	STAT.
				2. SEVERE WOUND, DISTORTED MEMBER, OR HAD TO BE CARRIED AWAY	3. OTHER VISIBLE INJURIES, AS BRUISES, ABRASIONS, SWELLING, LIMPING, ETC.	4. MOMENTARY UN- CONSCIOUSNESS, COMPLAINT OF PAIN		1. PED.	2. DRIVER	3. PASS.	4. BICYC.	5. OTHER	VEHICLE NUMBER	POSITION (LR, RF, ETC.)		
1.	24	M		☒					☒				1	LF	☐ YES ☒ NO	DIST. ENG.
NAME Driver #1 TAKEN TO Monterey Co. Hosp. ADDRESS BY ABC Ambulance																
2.	23	F		☒						☒			1	RF	☐ YES ☒ NO	ROAD DEPT.
NAME Jane Doe TAKEN TO Monterey Co. Hosp. ADDRESS 10 Main St. Centerville BY ABC Ambulance																
3.	28	F	☒						☒				2	LF	☐ YES ☒ NO	MIL.
NAME Driver #2 TAKEN TO Monterey Co. Hosp. ADDRESS BY ABC Ambulance																
4.															☐ YES ☐ NO	D.A.
NAME _____ TAKEN TO _____ ADDRESS _____ BY _____																

REPORT MADE BY John Smith (OFFICERS) 5555 (I.D. NUMBERS) | CORONER | P.D.

CHP Form 110 (Rev 5-68)   ⊙ △ OSP   PAGE 1

TRAFFIC ACCIDENT REPORT
STATISTICAL DATA AND DIAGRAM

465-4-66-13
(ACCIDENT NUMBER)

COL.	CODE	ACCIDENT CHARACTERISTICS		COL.	DR. 1	DR. 2	DR. 3	DR. 4	DRIVERS AND VEHICLES
40	7	TRAFFIC CONTROL		62	50	65			POSTED SPEED LIMIT
41	5	CONTROL CONDITION		63-64	28				DRIVER'S VIOLATION
42	3	WEATHER		65-66	00	00			VISION OBSCUREMENTS
43	2	LIGHTING		67	7				DRIVER'S PHYSICAL CONDITION
44	5	LOCALITY		68	4				DRIVER'S SOBRIETY
45	3	ROAD CHARACTER		69	0				VEHICLE CONDITION
46	2	ROAD SURFACE		70	5				SPEED BEFORE ACCIDENT
47		HIGHWAY CONDITION		COL.	PED. 1	PED. 2	PED. 3	PED. 4	PEDESTRIANS
48-49		DIRECTIONAL ANALYSIS		77-78					PEDESTRIAN'S ACTION

PEDESTRIAN WAS: (Check one in each column)

			COL.						
STANDING		IN MARKED CROSSWALK	79						PEDESTRIAN'S CONDITION
WALKING		IN UNMARKED CROSSWALK							
RUNNING		NOT IN CROSSWALK	80						PEDESTRIAN'S SOBRIETY

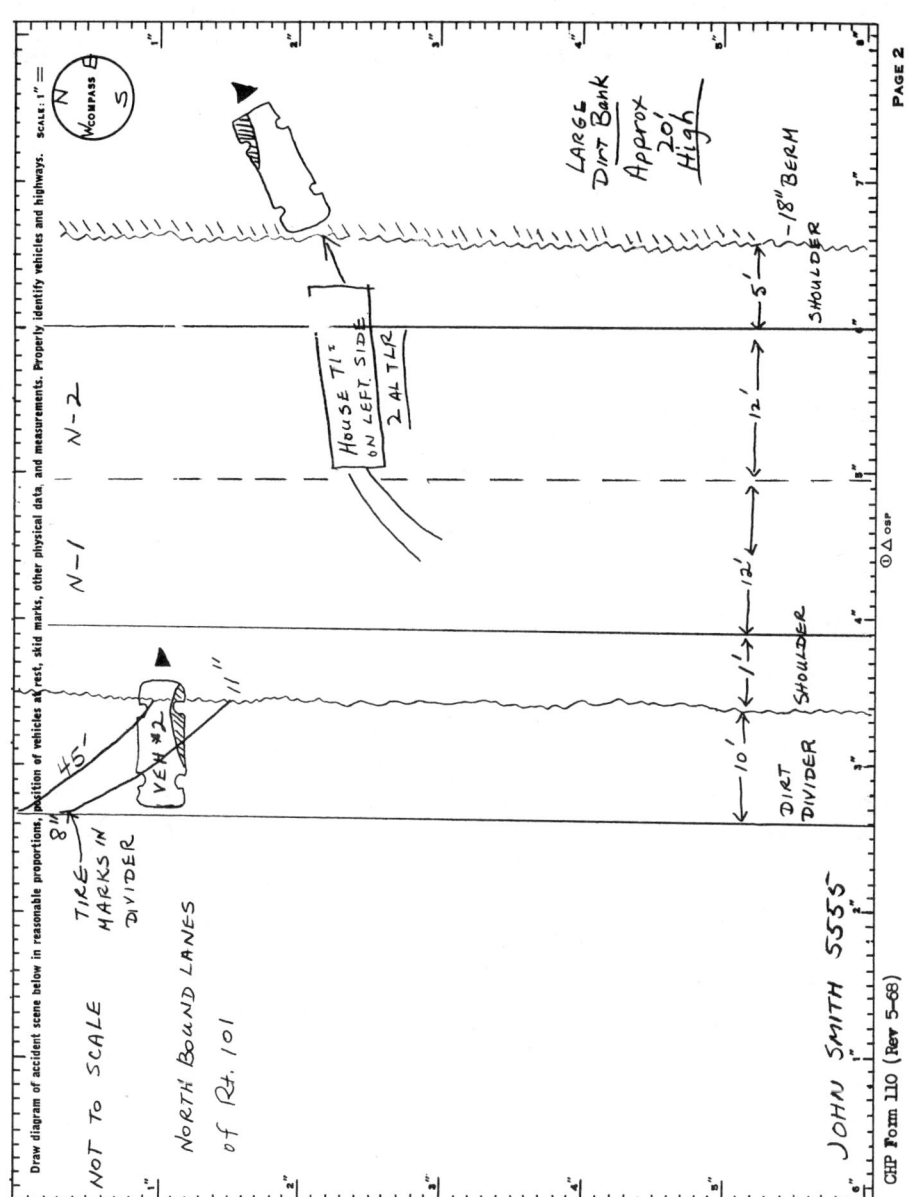

TRAFFIC ACCIDENT REPORT
INTERVIEW AND INVESTIGATION SUMMARY

ACCIDENT NUMBER   465-4-66-13

Give description of accident scene, factual data, statements, and officer's opinions, conclusions, and recommendations below:

FACTS - Called - advised by passing motorist 1908. Arrived 1912. This is a two-way roadway with 4 lanes divided. The northbound lanes are both approx. 12' in width. The east shoulder is improved and approx. 5' wide. At the east edge of the shoulder there is an 18" berm, then a dirt bank approx. 20' high. This bank is very steep. The west shoulder is approx. 1' wide, improved. The center divider is dirt and approx. 10' wide. The roadway at this point is straight with a downgrade to the north. Just north of this point the roadway has a curve to the east. The roadway at this time was wet and it was raining.

Veh #1 Veh #1 was facing east, lying partially on its left side. The rear wheels were on the berm at the east side of the roadway. Veh #1 had major damage to the left side - mostly in the front portion. The tlr. that veh #1 was pulling was still attached to the veh. The tlr.

was lying on its left side in the N-2 lane facing east and rear to west. Tlr. had total damage.

Veh #2 Veh #2 was facing east sitting in the center divider strip. Veh #2 was approx. 8' north of veh #1. Veh #2 had total damage with major portion to the right side in the front.

SKIDS There were no visible skid marks at the scene. There were some tire marks in the center divider strip. They were approx. 45' in length. These marks were made prior to traffic being diverted through center strip. These marks were approx. 8" wide at the east shoulder of the S-1 lane and 11" wide at the west shoulder of the N-1 lane.

DEBRIS There was debris in the complete area of the T.C. This included parts of vehs and tire dirt, glass, etc.

PHOTOS BY CHP _____ (NUMBER) _____ PHOTOS BY _____ (NAME) _____

NOTIFIED OF ACCIDENT—DATE _____ TIME _____ (ADDRESS)

BY WHOM _____

INVESTIGATED BY _John Smith_ 5555
 (OFFICERS) (I.D. NOS.)

| INVESTIGATION TIME | TOTAL TIME | REPORTS AT STATION | TOTAL TIME |
| FROM   TO | | FROM   TO | |

REPORT TYPED _____ BY _____
         (DATE)   (INITIALS)

APPROVED BY _____ (SUPERVISOR)

⊕ △ OSP

PAGE 3

TRAFFIC ACCIDENT REPORT
INTERVIEW AND INVESTIGATION
SUMMARY

ACCIDENT NUMBER 465-4-66-13

Give description of accident scene, factual data, statements, and officer's opinions, conclusions, and recommendations below:

GOUGES There were fresh gouges in the pavement starting in the N-2 lane 4' east of center lane and ending under the tlr being towed by veh #1. There were approx. 12' in length.

ATTENDING OFFICERS Sgt. H. White was at scene - directing traffic and assistance.

STATEMENTS See attached.

CONCLUSIONS Veh #1 was n/B traveling approx. 45 mph. Veh #2 was S/B and for some unknown reason veh #2 crossed center divider and entered N/B lanes, crossways in both lanes. I believe that veh #2 was S/B for the following reasons: (1) There were tire marks across the center divider. (See diagram & facts) which indicated that a S/B veh had slid across divider in a partial broad slide.
(2) Driver #1 stated he saw white car heading toward him before impact.

P.O.I. The P.O.I. was in the N-2 lane approx. 4' west of the east shoulder and 3/10 mile north 101 mon 99 (or) 1/2 mile north of Centerville

Rd. This was determined by the gouge marks (see facts) that were found at the scene and the location of veh #1.

RECOMMENDA-
TIONS   Driver #1 had been drinking but has no violations. Driver #2 was on the wrong side of the road but no citations issued as it is not known what caused Driver 2 to cross into the wrong lane.

PHOTOS BY CHP __6__ (NUMBER)   PHOTOS BY __Sgt. H. White__ (NAME)

NOTIFIED OF ACCIDENT—DATE __4-1-66__   TIME __1908__

BY WHOM __Passing Motorist__

INVESTIGATED BY __John Smith__ (OFFICERS)   I.D. NOS. __5555__

INVESTIGATION TIME FROM __1912__ TO __2150__   TOTAL TIME __238__

REPORTS AT STATION FROM __2215__ TO ____   TOTAL TIME ____

(ADDRESS)

REPORT TYPED ____ (DATE) BY ____ (INITIALS)

APPROVED BY ____ (SUPERVISOR)

PAGE 3

TRAFFIC ACCIDENT REPORT
INTERVIEW AND INVESTIGATION SUMMARY

ACCIDENT NUMBER 465-4-66-13

Give description of accident scene, factual data, statements, and officer's opinions, conclusions, and recommendations below:

STATEMENTS:

WITNESS   Grey stated she was sitting in the middle front, they were in the right hand lane (N#2) going about 60 m.p.h. They caught up to a N/B veh. towing a house trailer, she guessed it was going about 50 m.p.h., it was swaying very badly from side to side. When she first noticed it, it was using both N/B lanes. Suddenly the car turned to the right and hit the bank at the right edge of the road, the trailer whipped to the left and overturned, hitting a white car. The wind was blowing and it was raining very, very hard. Accident occurred on U.S. 101 at approx. 1905 hrs.

DRIVER #1 Stated he was driving north on 101 pulling 2 axle trailer. It was raining heavily and was windy. He had about 75' visibility. He was going about 45. He suddenly saw white sedan coming toward him from his left and swerved to right. He remembers no more until after collision.

Q. "Was your trailer whipping at all in the wind?"

A. "No. It was riding well. I was having no trouble with it."

PHOTOS BY CHP ....(NUMBER)....	PHOTOS BY ....(NAME)....	TIME		(ADDRESS)		
NOTIFIED OF ACCIDENT—DATE			INVESTIGATION TIME	TOTAL TIME	REPORTS AT STATION	TOTAL TIME
BY WHOM			FROM TO		FROM TO	
INVESTIGATED BY *John Smith* (OFFICERS)	*5555* (I.D. NOS.)		REPORT TYPED BY ...... (DATE) (INITIALS)		APPROVED BY *J. Brown* (SUPERVISOR)	
			① △ OSP			PAGE 3

STATE OF CALIFORNIA
CALIFORNIA HIGHWAY PATROL
SUPPLEMENTAL TRAFFIC ACCIDENT REPORT

LOCATION Rt 101 3/10 mi north 101   Original Accident No. 465-4-66-13
(Give name of city street, county road, or state route number and section letter)
City Unic   County Monterey
(Only if accident occurred within an incorporated city)
Area Code 465   Date of Accident 4-1-66   Time of Accident 1905

List Changes or Additions to Original Report:

Statement of Jane Doe
              10 Main Street
              Centerville
Taken at Monterey County Hospital on 4-4-66

We were going north on US 101 about 45 miles an hour when all of a sudden my husband swerved to the right. I don't believe it was raining heavy at time although some people had their lights on. The next thing I remember was my husband saying, "get her off me". I didn't remember anything else after the accident.

POLICE OFFICERS §4.4

2. [§4.4] Code for Interpreting California Highway Patrol Vehicle Accident Reports

ENTER ON PAGE ONE

17 Type of Roadway
1. Two-way roadway
2. Two-way roadway connection
3. One-way street
4. Off-center laned
5. Expressway
6. Expressway connection
7. Full freeway
8. Full freeway connection
9. Other

18 Number of Lanes
1. One lane
2. Two lanes
3. Three lanes
4. Four lanes
5. Four lane divided
6. Six lanes
7. Six lanes divided
8. Other undivided
9. Other divided

ENTER ON PAGE TWO

40 Traffic Controls
1. R.R. crossing gates
2. R.R. automatic signal
3. Officer or watchman
4. Traffic signals
5. Traffic signals (flashing)
6. Stop sign
7. Warning sign
8. Warning light (flashing)
9. No control present

41 Control Condition
1. Controls functioning
2. Controls not functioning
3. Controls turned off
4. Controls obscured
5. No control present

42 Weather
1. Clear
2. Cloudy
3. Raining
4. Snowing
5. Fog
6. Other

43 Lighting
1. Daylight
2. Dusk or dawn
3. Dark—no street lights
4. Dark—street lights

44 Locality
1. Mfg. or industrial
2. Shopping or business
3. Residential
4. School or playground
5. Open area
6. Other

45 Road Character
1. Straight road—level
2. Straight road—hillcrest
3. Straight road—on grade
4. Sharp curve or turn—level
5. Sharp curve or turn—hillcrest
6. Sharp curve or turn—on grade
7. Other curve—level
8. Other curve—hillcrest
9. Other curve—on grade

46 Road Surface
1. Dry
2. Wet
3. Muddy, slippery
4. Snowy, icy

§4.4 POLICE OFFICERS

47 Highway Condition
1. Holes, deep ruts
2. Loose material on surface
3. Obstruction, no lights, night
4. Obstruction, no warning, day
5. Construction or repair
6. Obstruction, previous accidents
7. Defective shoulder
8. Reduced road width
9. Other defects
0. No defects

48–49 Directional Analysis
A. Pedestrian Accidents
At Intersection
01. Car going straight
02. Car turning right
03. Car turning left
04. Car backing
05. All others
Not at Intersection
06. Car going straight
07. Car turning right
08. Car turning left
09. Car backing
10. All others

B. Intersection Accidents
Two or More Vehicles
11. Entering at angle
12. Same direction — both going straight
13. Same — one turn, one straight
14. Same — one stopped
15. Same — all others
16. Opposite direction — both going straight
17. Same — one left, one straight
18. Same — all others

C. Non-Intersection Accidents
Two or More Vehicles
19. Opposite direction — both moving
20. Same direction — both moving
21. One car parked
22. One car stopped in traffic
23. One car entering parked position
24. One car leaving parked position
25. One car entering alley or driveway
26. One car leaving alley or driveway
27. All others

D. All Other Accidents
28. Collision with non-motor vehicle: train, bicycle, etc. — at intersection
29. Same — not at intersection
30. Collision with fixed object in roadway at intersection
31. Same — not at intersection
32. Overturned in roadway — at intersection
33. Same — not at intersection
34. Left road at intersection
35. Left road at curve
36. Left road — straight road
37. Fell from moving vehicle
38. All others

62 Speed Zone
Insert Actual Speed Limit Applicable
15 30 45 60
20 35 50 65
25 40 55 70

63–64 Drivers' Violations
01. Under influence of alcohol (If not in 2 to 27 below)
02. Exceeding stated speed limit
03. Exceeding safe speed — but not stated limit
04. Did not grant right of way to pedestrian
05. Did not grant right of way to vehicle

POLICE OFFICERS §4.4

63–64 Drivers' Violations — cont.
06. Following too closely
07. Drove through safety zone
08. Passing standing street car
09. Passing on hill
10. Passing on curve
11. Cutting in
12. Other improper passing
13. On wrong side of road — not in passing
14. Failure to signal or improper signal
15. Improper turn — wide right turn
16. Same — cut corner on left turn
17. Same — turned from wrong lane
18. Other improper turning
19. Disregarded police officer
20. Disregarded stop and go light
21. Disregarded stop sign or signal
22. Disregarded warning sign or signal
23. Disregarded other traffic control device
24. Improper starting from parked position
25. Improper parking location
26. Failed to turn on lights
27. Other violations (hazardous)
28. No violation

65–66 Vision Obscurements
01. Rain, snow, etc., on windshield
02. Windshield otherwise obscured
03. Vision obscured by load
04. Trees, bushes, etc.
05. Building
06. Embankment
07. Signboards
08. Hillcrest
09. Parked vehicles
10. Moving vehicles
11. Blinded by headlights
12. Blinded by sunglare
13. Other obscurements
00. No obscurements

67 or 79 Physical Condition
1. Eyesight defective — uncorrected
2. Hearing defective — uncorrected
3. Other bodily defects
4. Ill
5. Fatigued
6. Apparently asleep
7. No apparent defects

68 or 80 Sobriety
1. Had been drinking — obviously drunk
2. HBD — ability impaired
3. HBD — ability not impaired
4. HBD — not known if ability impaired
5. Had not been drinking
6. Parked car or hit and run

69 Vehicle Condition
1. Defective brakes
2. Headlights insufficient or out
3. Headlights glaring
4. Rear light insufficient or out
5. Other lights or reflectors defective
6. Steering mechanism defective
7. Puncture or blowout
8. Worn or smooth tires
9. Other defects
0. No defects

70 Speed Before Accident
0. Legally parked
1. 1–10 miles per hour
2. 11–20 miles per hour
3. 21–30 miles per hour
4. 31–40 miles per hour
5. 41–50 miles per hour
6. 51–60 miles per hour
7. 61–70 miles per hour
8. 71 miles per hour and over
9. Standing still

§4.5   POLICE OFFICERS

77–78 Pedestrian's Action

01. Crossing or entering roadway at intersection
02. Same — not at intersection
03. Walking in roadway — with traffic
04. Same — against traffic
05. Standing in roadway
06. Getting on or off vehicle
07. Pushing or working on vehicle in roadway
08. Other working in roadway
09. Playing in roadway
10. Other in roadway
11. Not in roadway

C. [§4.5] Identifying the Officer

The attorney must determine from the accident report which officer or officers to interview, and from interviews, which to call as witnesses. His primary interest is in calling an officer who actually observed the facts and talked to the witnesses. This may not be the officer who filled out or signed the report. If he calls an officer who did not perceive the facts included in the report, the officer's testimony may be excluded as hearsay. And such an officer would not be able to lay a foundation for reading the report as past recollection recorded. See §§4.21–4.23.

The attorney begins by contacting the officer who signed the report as the investigator (not as the supervisor); he will know whether there were other officers at the scene and what was done by each. Sometimes, the first officer at an accident scene aids the injured, calls ambulances, clears vehicles and debris from the roadway, and directs traffic. He may or may not participate in the investigation. He may not even be mentioned in the accident report. If two officers are dispatched to conduct the investigation, one may examine the vehicles and measure distances while the other interviews witnesses. Either or both may prepare the report or parts of it. Even if one officer is dispatched to investigate and prepare the report, other officers at the scene may give him information, take photographs, record witness statements, etc. Furthermore, if a witness cannot be interviewed at the scene, the investigating officer or another may record his statement later at the hospital. The supervisor who signs the report rarely participates in the investigation; his function is to review the investigator's decisions on citations, arrests, and the need for further investigation.

The attorney should try to determine from the investigating officer and his supervisor whether a followup investigation was made. The California Highway Patrol, for example, has several accident units that investigate selected accidents. They are comprised of men who have specialized training and experience in accident reconstruction, automobile mechanics, truck loading, etc. Reports of their investigations are delivered to the primary investigating officer and he includes

POLICE OFFICERS §4.9

their information in his report or files a supplementary one. The accident report may not disclose whether any followup investigations were made, and, if so, who made them.

D. Interviewing the Officer

1. [§4.6] Purpose

Police officers who were at the accident scene or who investigated the accident are interviewed early in the investigation of the case to (a) determine what they can testify to, including matter not mentioned in the accident report, (b) assess their probable value and effectiveness as witnesses, (c) learn the basis for statements made in the report, and (d) obtain leads for further investigation.

The lawyer also wants to determine the extent to which the officer's testimony will be favorable so that he can decide whether to call him as a witness or to prepare to cross-examine him if he is called by an adversary.

2. [§4.7] Arranging Time and Place

An interview with a California Highway Patrol officer is arranged by contacting the area commander at his headquarters. The area commander sets an appointment for the officer at the area office, normally at the beginning or end of the officer's shift. Procedures for arranging interviews with officers of local police departments vary.

3. [§4.8] Compensation

California Highway Patrol regulations prohibit its officers from accepting remuneration for interviews. Interviews are thus scheduled during duty hours. Local police agencies may have similar policies, but in some localities the officer will expect to be compensated for the interview.

Some lawyers prefer to use a private investigator to interview police officers. His bill to the lawyer for investigative expense is often not itemized and the lawyer does not know whether the officer was paid or not. Other lawyers instruct the investigator to itemize all payments to officers, fearing the embarrassment of being accused in court of having given consideration for the statement and subsequent testimony.

4. [§4.9] Checklist of Questions

The interviewer must determine whether the officer's recollection of the facts differs from the accident report. Often he reviews the report, entry by entry, with the officer. In the process he also covers the following subjects:

a. How much does the officer presently remember of the accident? Does the report refresh his memory? Can it be used as past recollection recorded? See §§4.21–4.23.
b. How soon did he arrive on the scene? Had conditions changed prior to his arrival? See §4.24.
c. Did he investigate the accident with other officers? Who were they, and what did each do in the investigation? See §4.5.
d. Did he or any other officer make notes or photographs? Where are they? See §9.7 on subpena duces tecum.
e. Were any statements made that are not recorded in the accident report? What were they and who made them?
f. Was any followup investigation made? By whom? See §4.5.
g. Who is the custodian of the original accident report? See §§9.7–9.8 on subpena duces tecum.

5. [§4.10] Evaluating Officer as Witness: Checklist

An investigating officer is usually a good witness. He does not normally volunteer, qualify answers, or evade. When a question calls for a "Yes" or "No" answer, he replies accordingly. He usually appears in uniform, gives a businesslike presentation, and knows what he is talking about. All of this lends authority to what he says.

However, the most experienced and articulate officer can be ineffective if he did not arrive on the scene until long after the accident, or cannot distinguish it in his mind from the many others he has investigated, particularly if the case is not brought to trial for a long time. An individual officer may not have sufficient training, experience, skill, or interest to observe and record accurately and thoroughly. Occasionally, he is a biased or pugnacious witness, or his manner is flippant, halting, monotonous, or otherwise ineffective. Some officers are simply not good investigators; some are not good witnesses; and some are neither.

The interviewer, as he questions the officer about the information contained in his accident report, can form an impression of his value and impact as a witness or how he can be cross-examined if called by the other side. Some factors to consider are:

a. Will his testimony about the facts be favorable or unfavorable?
b. Is he articulate, confident, unlikely to be shaken on cross-examination?
c. Does he limit his answer to the question asked?
d. Does he appear to know what he is talking about?
e. Does he appear bored or resentful for being drawn into the lawsuit?

POLICE OFFICERS §4.13

f. Does he have any prejudices against plaintiff, defendant, or their lawyers?

g. Does he know or has he had business dealings with any of the parties, witnesses, or opposing counsel?

h. Has he made any value judgments about the parties, the witnesses, or any phase of liability (*e.g.,* speed, inattention, intoxication)?

i. How well qualified is he to make the judgments he has made?

j. Can he be qualified and should he be called to testify as an expert? If so, on what subjects? See §§4.49–4.51.

E. [§4.11] *Officer's Deposition*

If the officer is an important and favorable witness, the lawyer frequently takes his deposition in the early stages of trial preparation. If no deposition is taken and the officer dies, or moves beyond subpena range (see §4.13) before the trial, there may be no way of getting his findings into evidence since it is often impossible to introduce his accident report in evidence. See §9.9.

F. Compelling Attendance at Trial

1. [§4.12] Using Subpena

The officer who is called to testify in a civil case is always subpenaed either by serving him personally, or serving his immediate superior. See Govt C §68097.1. The party calling him is required to reimburse his agency for the time he spends at trial (see §4.14) and his agency would probably not permit him to appear voluntarily. The officer may agree with the subpenaeing lawyer to appear at a time other than that specified in the subpena. Govt C §68097.9. But if the officer is ordered to return to court an additional day the party that called him must deposit an additional fee to reimburse his agency (Govt C §68097.5), unless relieved of that duty by the court for "good cause shown" (Govt C §68097.55).

2. [§4.13] Range of Subpena

A California Highway Patrol officer can be subpenaed to appear as a witness "before any court located in this State, in any civil action or proceeding in connection with a matter regarding an event or transaction which he has perceived or investigated in the course of his duties . . . ." Govt C §68097.3. A local police officer, like other witnesses, can not be compelled to attend a trial if it is held out of the county in which he resides unless the place of trial is less than 150 miles from his place of residence. CCP §1989.

3. [§4.14] Depositing Fees; Reimbursing Police Agency

A subpena directed to a California Highway Patrol officer, sheriff, deputy sheriff, or city policeman must include a statement that the party calling him has deposited with the court clerk the fees required by Govt C §§68097.2, 68097.4. The deposit currently required is $45, and the party must reimburse the police agency $45 for each day that the officer attends in response to the subpena. Govt C §68097.2. If a highway patrolman is subpenaed under Govt C §68097.3 (see §4.13) the party calling him must reimburse the state for his salary while in attendance and for his "actual, necessary and reasonable" travel expenses. Govt C §68097.4.

4. [§4.15] Form: Clause in Subpena Showing Deposit of Fees

Some counties have special subpena forms for policemen with a recital of the deposit printed on it. If a special form is not available, a statement such as the following is typed or stamped on the front of the subpena, below the clerk's signature. The allegation recites that the sum has been deposited and lines are provided for a second signature of the clerk, acknowledging the deposit.

In accordance with the requirements of Government Code section .... $............... has been deposited with the Clerk of this
68097.2/68097.4
Court. Receipt No. ....

Dated: ....

_____, Clerk

By_____
            Deputy Clerk

G. [§4.16] *Courthouse Interview*

Usually the lawyer or his private investigator will have interviewed the officer during the investigative phase of the case. See §§4.6–4.10. Whether or not this was done, the lawyer interviews the officer at the courthouse before he calls him to the stand. If an investigator made the previous interview, the lawyer will want to make his own determination of the officer's probable testimony and demeanor as a witness. If the lawyer interviewed the officer during pretrial investigation, the courthouse interview permits a fresh appraisal of his testimony and effectiveness. At the courthouse interview the lawyer determines the extent to which the officer will rely on the accident report in giving his testimony, and whether the officer has brought the

POLICE OFFICERS §4.18

original or a copy with him, or will need to use the lawyer's copy. See §§4.21–4.23, 9.6.

II. [§4.17] QUALIFYING THE OFFICER

The lawyer usually begins his examination of a police officer by showing his police and investigative experience and training, his impartiality, and his personal knowledge of the accident. This testimony supports his competency to testify (see §§1.13–1.15 on the qualifications of lay witnesses) and his credibility. Counsel should gear his examination to the officer's particular training and experience, as determined in a prior interview. See §§4.6, 4.16.

California Highway Patrol officers usually qualify well. Many have college degrees. Most officers have attended a 16-week course at the California Highway Patrol Academy in Sacramento, where they receive instruction in the theory, techniques, and procedures of accident investigation, and are given practice investigating mock accidents. Following this the officer receives 30 to 90 days of on-the-job training with a training officer or sergeant; he is then assigned to work with an experienced officer until it is determined that he is equipped to work alone. He may also periodically attend brushup courses or take specialized training for membership in special units that make followup investigations in certain types of accident cases. See §4.5.

A local police officer generally has less formal training. The lawyer should inquire whether he received accident investigation training in his department, was selected for assignment to the Highway Patrol Academy, or attended courses in police work such as those given at Northwestern University. If the officer lacks formal training, the lawyer must concentrate on his practical, on-the-job experience.

A. [§4.18] *Police and Investigative Background*

The mere fact that the witness is a police officer may be enough to convince jurors that testimony about his observations at the accident scene is accurate and reliable. But if the officer has training and experience in accident investigation, the lawyer often brings it out to enhance his credibility, even though he does not intend to qualify the officer to testify as an expert.

If the lawyer wants to qualify the officer as an expert, his inquiry into special training and experience can be made at the beginning of the officer's testimony, or reserved until he reaches the subjects of the expert testimony. See §4.51.

§4.19   POLICE OFFICERS

   The examination of a police officer might begin as follows:
Q. What is your name?
A. ....
Q. What is your present occupation?
A. [California Highway Patrol/Police] officer.
Q. Where do you live, Officer ....?
A. ....
Q. How long have you been a [highway patrolman/police officer]?
A. ...... years.
Q. What is your rank?
A. ....

Comment: The officer seldom has a superior rank in his police agency, but if he does, this should be brought out in examination. For example, "When were you promoted to sergeant?"

Q. What was your duty assignment on ...., 19 ......, the date of the accident in this case?
A. ....
Q. Did your duties include the investigation of motor vehicle accidents?
A. They did.
Q. Could you estimate the number of accidents you have investigated during your years in the department?
A. Yes. More than ....
Q. About how many have you investigated since ...., 19 ...... [date of the accident]?
A. ....

Comment: The number of accidents investigated since the accident helps explain to jurors why the officer needs to use the accident report to aid his memory. See §§4.21–4.23.

Q. Have you received training in accident investigation?
A. Yes.

Comment: See §4.51 for additional testimony to qualify the officer as an expert.

B. [§4.19] *Impartiality*

   Jurors often regard police officers testifying in civil cases as impartial public employees who have no reason not to tell the truth. The lawyer will wish to establish that the officer's investigation was made in the course of his official duties, before any litigation, and with no

POLICE OFFICERS §4.21

reason to favor one side or the other. See Veh C §§2408 (duty of highway patrolman to investigate causes and control of highway accidents) and 2412 (duty to gather evidence to prosecute law violations). Many lawyers like to bring out that the officer was subpenaed because they believe it helps establish impartiality.

Q. Did you investigate the motor vehicle accident on ...., 19......, at [location] involving [persons involved]?
A. Yes, I did.
Q. Was this investigation made in the course of your official duties?
A. Yes, it was.
Q. Were you subpenaed to appear here today?
A. Yes, I was.

C. [§4.20] *Investigative Procedure*

The lawyer usually wants to show that the accident investigation was carefully and comprehensively performed. The standard accident report forms are prepared so that the investigating officer follows a systematic procedure for inserting the information called for. It is often helpful for the officer to explain how he completes the form:

Q. Do you have a set procedure for conducting your accident investigation?
A. Yes.
Q. Did you follow that procedure in this case?
A. Yes.
Q. What did you do?
A. [I filled out an accident report form that asks for a great deal of information. When I was finished, I had a complete report of the accident.]

III. [§4.21] USING REPORT TO AID TESTIMONY

A police officer who makes investigations in the course of his duties soon forgets the details of particular accidents. By the time of trial he normally has little or no recollection of the facts that he observed, opinions he formed, or statements that were made to him in the course of his investigation. Fortunately, most, if not all, of this information is recorded in the police accident report, and it is customary for the officer to use the report to help him testify fully and accurately about the accident.

The lawyer should determine, by interviewing the officer before he takes the stand, whether his memory is refreshed by the report and he can testify about the accident from that memory. If looking at the report revives the officer's memory of the details of his investigation and findings, the lawyer can examine him about the accident, and the officer can use the report on the stand to refresh his memory. See §4.22. However, if the officer's memory is not revived, and he has no independent recollection of the details of the accident, the attorney may (a) question the officer as if the report refreshed his memory (see §4.22) or (b) have the officer lay a foundation for reading the report as past recollection recorded (see §4.23).

The copy of the report that the officer uses on the stand is often one that he has brought with him, either on his own initiative or at the request of the lawyer who subpenaed him. The lawyer who wants to be sure that the original report is produced in court can serve a subpena duces tecum on the departmental records custodian or on the investigating officer. See §§9.6–9.8. The officer can also use a copy of the report that the lawyer had previously obtained at the investigation stage. See §§9.3–9.5.

A. [§4.22] *Refreshing Memory*

A police officer can use an accident report to refresh his memory. (*Robinson v Cable* (1961) 55 C2d 425, 11 CR 377; *Fernandez v Di Salvo Appliance Co.* (1960) 179 CA2d 240, 3 CR 709) as long as it in fact refreshes his memory. He need not have participated in its preparation, made the statements recorded in it, or signed it. See §1.32 for a general discussion of writings used to refresh memory. The officer usually carries the report with him when he takes the stand. See generally §1.36.

Theoretically, the officer who is testifying from memory should refer to the accident report when necessary, then lay it aside and answer questions in his own words. In practice, the officer's testimony often amounts to little more than reading or paraphrasing the report. This testimony is hearsay since it is evidence of a statement (the report) made other than by a witness at a hearing. Evid C §1200. However, an adverse attorney will usually permit an officer to testify this way unless he feels that by objecting he can keep out unfavorable testimony from an officer who can neither remember nor lay a foundation for reading the report as past recollection recorded.

It is good practice to let the jury know that the officer is using the report to refresh his memory. For example, after the officer has testified about his qualifications, about the number of accidents he has investigated before and since, and how the accident investigation is conducted (see §4.20), he could be asked:

Q. Officer ...., did you bring with you to court today [the/

POLICE OFFICERS §4.23

    a copy of the] vehicle accident report relating to that accident?
A. Yes, I did.
Q. Would it help to refresh your memory about the details of the accident to refer to the report as you testify?
A. It would.

Comment: In some cases it is helpful to ask the officer whether he participated in preparing the report and where he got the copy he is using to refresh his memory.

B. [§4.23] *Past Recollection Recorded*

    The attorney may be forced to lay the foundation for reading the accident report as past recollection recorded if the officer cannot testify on refreshed memory and the opponent's objection is sustained.

    The foundation that must be laid under Evid C §1237 is discussed generally in §§8.27–8.31. The appropriate officer to lay this foundation is the one who perceived the facts recorded in the accident report, *i.e.,* the officer who made the observations and measurements, or interviewed the witnesses, even though another officer actually wrote up the report. If two officers investigated the accident, it may be necessary to call both as witnesses to lay the foundation for the parts of the report based on the observations of each.

    Assuming that the officer has already testified about the number of accidents he has investigated before and since (see §4.18), and how the investigation was conducted, his examination might continue as follows:

Q. At this time do you remember the details of your investigation?
A. No.
Q. Do you have a sufficient present recollection of your investigation to be able to testify fully and accurately about it?
A. No.
Q. Did you [prepare/help prepare] a report of your investigation?
A. Yes.

Comment: If the officer was working alone, he will have made the observations and written the report. If he was working with another officer, the latter may have written down the officer's statements about the matters recorded. Even though the officer does not remember the investigation, he may be able to tell from the placement of signatures on the report that he was the one who gathered the information.

    If another officer wrote up the report, the witness should be asked whether he did so at the witness's direction, or for the purpose of recording the witness's statement. See Evid C §1237(a)(2).

§4.24 POLICE OFFICERS

Q. Do you have [a copy of] the report with you?
A. Yes.
Q. Whose signature is this at the bottom of the first page?
A. Mine.
Q. Have you read the report over recently?
A. Yes.
Q. Can you tell us whether it is [the report you made/the report of your investigation written up by Officer ....]?
A. Yes, it is.
Q. When was the report prepared?
A. On ...., 19.......
Q. How long after the accident was that?
A. [At the end of my shift that same day.]
Q. How do you know that?
A. [We are required by department rules to turn in reports at that time. My supervisor's signature is on the report, dated ...., 19.......]
Q. Were the statements that you [wrote down in this report/made to Officer ....] true statements of the facts?
A. Yes.
Q. Is this [copy of the] report an accurate record of those statements?
A. Yes.

IV. ACTIVITIES AND OBSERVATIONS AT ACCIDENT SCENE

A. [§4.24] *Time of Arrival*

It is often important to establish how long after the accident the officer arrived at the scene, and whether victims, vehicles, and debris had been moved, or road and weather conditions changed.

The question, "How soon after the accident did you arrive at the scene?" would be subject to objection as calling for hearsay or opinion. Thus, the officer is usually asked when and how he was notified of the accident and how long it took him to reach the scene. For example (see sample accident report in §4.3):

Q. How were you notified of the accident?
A. A passing motorist told me and a few minutes later I got a call on the radio from my dispatcher.
Q. What time did the motorist tell you about it?
A. At eight minutes past seven; the dispatcher called a minute or two later.

POLICE OFFICERS §4.25

Q. How far were you from the scene?
A. About a mile away.
Q. Did you go there directly?
A. Yes.
Q. How long did it take you to get there?
A. Just a few minutes.
Q. Can you be more specific?
A. I got there at ....
Q. Did you see anything at the scene to indicate how long before you got there the accident had occurred?
A. ....

Comment: The officer may have noted such details as whether water was still draining from a damaged radiator, and traffic was not yet backed up, or that victims and vehicles had been moved, engines were cold, etc.

B. [§4.25] *Aiding Victims; Clearing Traffic*

When the officer arrives on the scene promptly, he first clears traffic and makes arrangements for the care of anyone who has been injured. The manner in which traffic is diverted from the accident scene may be important to show whether skid marks, debris, and other evidence have been obscured. In addition, the amount of time devoted to diverting traffic may indicate that the officer's interviews with parties and witnesses were delayed. This can have a bearing on counsel's ability to show that a statement made to the officer was a "spontaneous statement" under the Evid C §1240 exception to the hearsay rule. See §4.46. For example:

Q. What was the first thing you did when you arrived at the scene?
A. I checked with each of the injured people and radioed for ambulances.
Q. Did you regulate traffic?
A. Yes.
Q. What did you do?
A. I set up flares and saw to it that there would be room for ambulances. Almost immediately Sergeant White arrived to handle the traffic that had piled up; the dispatcher had sent him to assist.
Q. Then about how long after you arrived was it before you began to conduct your investigation?
A. About ...... minutes. I spent the first few minutes helping to remove the victims from the cars.

C. The Roadway

1. [§4.26] Using Diagram

The accident report usually contains a diagram of the accident scene. The officer looks at this diagram to refresh his memory; the facts reflected in it can also be the subject of his testimony as past recollection recorded.

In addition, the officer is often asked to draw a diagram on the courtroom blackboard, or to point out positions and locations on a diagram previously prepared. See chap 9 on the use of maps and diagrams. For example (see sample accident report in §4.3):

Q. Did you draw a diagram of the scene as a part of your accident report?
A. Yes.

Comment: Usually the officer does not draw the diagram to scale. If it is to scale, however, the lawyer should also inquire what the scale is.

Q. Is it to scale?
A. Yes it is.
Q. What is the scale?
A. It is ....
Q. When did you draw the diagram?
A. I did most of it at the scene, but I may have made a clean copy afterwards before I filed the accident report.
Q. If you wish to refer to your diagram, feel free to do so, and tell us what you observed of the scene. Please move to the diagram on the bulletin board and show us what Route 101 looks like at the point where this accident occurred. You may take your diagram with you if you like.
A. [Officer moves to courtroom diagram.]
Q. Now, in what direction does Route 101 lie?
A. It goes north and south.
Q. How many lanes are there?
A. There are two northbound and two southbound lanes.
Q. Would you mark the lanes for us on the diagram, showing which is the N-1 lane, the N-2 lane, etc.?
A. Yes. This is the N-1 lane [marking northbound lane nearest center divider], this is the N-2 lane [marking northbound lane nearest shoulder].
Q. Is there a divider strip at this location?
A. Yes, a dirt divider separates the northbound from the southbound lanes.

POLICE OFFICERS §4.28

Q. Would you mark the location of the dirt divider on the diagram?
A. [Officer does so.]
Q. Did you measure the divider?
A. Yes.
Q. How wide is it?
A. It is ten feet wide.
Q. Are the northbound lanes marked in any way?
A. Yes, they are separated by a broken white line.
Q. Did you measure the width of the northbound lanes?
A. Yes. They are each 12 feet wide.
Q. Is there a shoulder next to the N-2 lane?
A. Yes, there is.
Q. How wide is it?
A. Five feet wide.

Comment: To the extent they are relevant, the lawyer has the officer locate divider strips, curbs, shoulders, parking lanes, driveways, etc., on the diagram and show their measurements.

2. [§4.27] Layout; Contour; Surface

An officer is often asked to describe the physical area of the accident (referring to the sample accident report in §4.3):

Q. Is Route 101 flat or on a grade at this location?
A. It is on a slight grade downward toward the north.
Q. Does it curve at all, or is it straight?
A. It is straight.
Q. What construction material is the road made of?
A. It is concrete.
Q. Was the road surface dry or wet?
A. It was wet; it had been raining for some time.

3. [§4.28] Obstructions

An investigating officer can usually answer questions about the general condition of the accident site (referring to the sample accident report in §4.3):

Q. When you arrived at the scene did you see anything on or near the roadway that would have obscured or interfered with the vision or progress of a northbound motorist?
A. No, I did not.
Q. Did you see anything that would have obstructed or interfered with a motorist driving southward at this location?
A. No, I did not.

§4.29 POLICE OFFICERS

Q. Were there any chuckholes or other breaks or bumps in either the northbound or southbound lanes?
A. No. The road in all four lanes was in very good condition.

D. Vehicles

1. [§4.29] Identity

An officer might begin his testimony about the vehicles at the accident scene as follows (referring to the sample accident report in §4.3):

Q. When you arrived at the scene, how many vehicles appeared to have been involved in the collision?
A. Two. One of them was pulling a house trailer.
Q. What were the makes and colors of those vehicles?
A. Vehicle No. 1, driven by Mr. Doe, was pulling the house trailer; it was a black Ford—a 1966 four-door sedan. Vehicle No. 2, in which Mrs. Roe was found, was a white two-door Chevrolet sedan.

3. [§4.30] Point of Rest

Unless the vehicles were moved before he arrived, the officer can state where they came to rest after the collision. For example (referring to the sample accident report in §4.3):

Q. Where was Mrs. Roe's vehicle when you arrived?
A. It was eight feet north of the Doe vehicle, facing east in the center divider strip.
Q. Will you draw that on the diagram please?
A. [Officer does so.]
Q. Was there any indication that it had been moved after it came to rest following the collision?
A. No.
Q. And where was Vehicle No. 1, the black Ford, when you arrived?
A. It was facing east and was partially on its left side; its rear wheels were on the berm at the east side of the roadway. The trailer was on its left side in the N-2 lane and was still attached to the Ford.
Q. Would you mark their positions on the diagram?
A. [Officer does so.]

3. [§4.31] Damage

The officer can describe vehicle damage. This testimony is valuable in laying the foundation for later expert opinion testimony on point of impact (see §4.53), or possibly on speed (see §4.57), and on monetary

POLICE OFFICERS §4.33

damages. For example (referring to the sample accident report in §4.3):

Q. Did you examine the two vehicles for damage?
A. Yes, I did.
Q. What did you find?
A. There was total damage to the Chevrolet—the worst damage was on the right side in front. The Ford had major damage to its left front side; its trailer was totaled.
Q. Could you tell whether the damage to the two cars was fresh?
A. Yes. It was fresh damage to both cars.
Q. How could you tell?
A. There were paint transfers from each vehicle to the other vehicle.

   4. [§4.32] Mechanical Condition

The investigating officer usually notes any mechanical defects he observes in the vehicles. He may also see facts from which it can be inferred whether a defect existed at the time of an accident, and perhaps caused it, or resulted from it. For example, he may be able to testify that tires were in good condition, or were worn, flat, punctured, or blown out; that lights were on, or were off, not working, dim, or improperly aimed; that a windshield was smeared, or the wipers not functioning; that the brake pedal went to the floor, or there was no fluid, or the drums were hot; etc. See §4.54 on opinion testimony on mechanical condition.

E. *Drivers; Passengers; Pedestrians*

   1. [§4.33] Possession of License

The investigating officer routinely asks each driver involved in an accident to show his driver's license. The accident report reflects whether the driver had a license in his possession or not. (See accident report at §4.3 where Driver No. 2 did not have a license in her possession, as shown by the entry "NIP.") The accident report shows the state granting the license, its expiration date, and whether it contains any qualifications on use (*e.g.,* requiring that the driver wear glasses, limiting the weight of the vehicle that can be driven by the licensee, etc.).

Failure to have a driver's license, or to have a license for a particular class of vehicle, has been held immaterial, and the lawyer does not question the officer about it unless some causal relationship is shown between the injuries and the failure to have a license. *Armenta v Churchill* (1954) 42 C2d 448, 458, 267 P2d 303, 309. If there is a causal relationship, the lawyer may ask the officer if a license was shown to him on demand. Further testimony on the contents of the license may be subject to objection on the basis of the best evidence rule.

2. [§4.34] Identity; Position in Vehicle

An officer's determination of who was driving each vehicle and where passengers were sitting is often based on what these people tell him at the scene, *i.e.,* on hearsay. If there is a dispute about who was driving, or where someone was riding, the lawyer should phrase questions carefully, and bring out any observations of the officer that bear on the matter. For example (referring to the sample accident report in §4.3):

Q. Did you determine who was driving the white Chevrolet?
A. Yes. Mrs. Roe was the driver.
Q. How did you determine that?
A. She was alone in the car when I got there. She was behind the wheel and it didn't look like she could move due to her injuries. Also, she told me she was the driver.
Q. Did anyone at the scene identify himself to you as the driver of the black Ford?
A. Yes.
Q. Did he show you a driver's license?
A. Yes.
Q. What was the name and address he gave you?
A. ....
Q. Were there others in his car at the time of the collision?
A. Yes.
Q. Who were they?
A. There was a lady in the car who said she was Mrs. Doe.

3. [§4.35] Injuries

An officer can describe injuries he observed. For example (referring to the sample accident report in §4.3):

Q. Did you see any injured persons at the scene when you arrived?
A. Yes, I did.
Q. Who appeared to be injured?
A. Mrs. Roe was badly injured inside her car. Mr. and Mrs. Doe were also badly injured.
Q. Where was Mr. Doe when you arrived?
A. He was pinned under the steering wheel.

POLICE OFFICERS §4.36

Q. And his wife?
A. She was still inside the car.
Q. What led you to believe that Mr. Doe was injured?
A. His leg was bleeding, he had several large cuts on his face, he was moaning and holding his arm, and he appeared to be suffering.
Q. What was done for the injured?
A. Mr. Doe and his wife were removed to the Monterey County Hospital after I radioed for an ambulance. Mrs. Roe was also removed to the hospital.

Comment: A lay witness can testify to his observations of the nature, extent, and effect of a person's injuries, stating those observations in opinion form, and to the person's exclamations, manifestations, and statements of present pain. See §§7.1–7.2.

4. [§4.36] Intoxication

A police officer may express a nonexpert opinion that a person was under the influence of alcohol or was "intoxicated." See Evid C §800; *People v Ravey* (1954) 122 CA2d 699, 702, 265 P2d 154, 156. See also Witkin, CALIFORNIA EVIDENCE §398 (2d ed, 1966). Compare §4.58 on narcotics. This kind of testimony must be based on the officer's own perceptions of the person and not on what someone else told him. *Stuart v Dotts* (1949) 89 CA2d 683, 201 P2d 820. The attorney must be sure that the officer does not testify about any arrest or citation. See §4.41. For example (referring to the sample accident report in §4.3):

Q. Did you observe anything with respect to Mr. Doe's sobriety?
A. Yes, I did.
Q. What was his condition?
A. He had been drinking.

Comment: If an officer believed that a driver had been drinking or was under the influence of alcohol, the following dialogue would be appropriate:

Q. What led you to that conclusion?
A. His speech was thick, he had poor balance, and I saw several open beer cans in his car.

Comment: If tests had been performed to determine intoxication the lawyer might ask:

Q. Did you perform any test to determine his equilibrium?
A. Yes.

§4.37   POLICE OFFICERS

Q. How did you do this?
A. ....
Q. What happened when Mr. .... attempted to perform this test?
A. ....

F. [§4.37] *Skid Marks; Debris*

The officer normally takes measurements of the location of all skid marks, tire marks, gouge and brush marks, vehicle parts, caked mud, and other debris, and records them in his accident report. His testimony on these observations can help lay a foundation for later expert opinion on point of impact (see §4.53) or perhaps speed (see §4.57). For example (referring to the sample accident report in §4.3):

Q. Did you see any skid marks?
A. No.
Q. Did you see any tire marks?
A. Yes.
Q. What is the difference?
A. ....
Q. Please mark on the diagram where the tire marks were located.
A. There were two tire marks in the center of the divider strip about 45 feet long. They were approximately eight inches wide at the east shoulder of the S-1 lane and 11 inches wide at the west shoulder of the N-1 lane.
Q. Did these tire marks extend into lane N-1 or N-2?
A. No.
Q. Did you measure the distance between the two marks?
A. No, I did not. They appeared to be the normal distance of two tire marks of a vehicle.
Q. Of what sort of vehicle?
A. A passenger car.
Q. Did they appear to widen as they moved to the east?
A. Yes, they did. They spread out and were wider at the 11-inch end.
Q. Was there any glass and debris in the area?
A. Yes, I found a great deal of broken glass, chrome, and caked mud.
Q. Where was it located?
A. In the vicinity of the trailer.
Q. Please mark the location on the diagram.
A. [Officer does so.]
Q. Did you find any other marks in the northbound portion of the highway?
A. Yes, I found gouge marks in the pavement starting in the N-2 lane,

POLICE OFFICERS §4.40

four feet east of the line dividing the two northbound lanes; they traveled in an arc, ended under the trailer, and were about 12 feet long.
Q. Were they parallel to one another?
A. I found one big mark and several smaller ones, but I would not say that they ran parallel to each other.
Q. Where were the little ones located with relation to the larger one?
A. They were on the right side, heading north.
Q. Were these fresh gouge marks?
A. Yes.
Q. How can you tell?
A. Old ones get discolored and dark after a period of time.

G. [§4.38] Traffic Controls

The accident report (see §4.3) contains a description of the traffic controls at the accident scene:
Q. Were there any traffic controls at this location?
A. Drivers in the northbound lanes were in a reduced speed zone; there were signs reducing the speed to 50 miles per hour.

Comment: Similarly, the officer can be questioned on his observations of any traffic lights, directional or other traffic warning signs, railroad crossings, crosswalks, etc. For instance, if traffic lights controlled the area, he might be asked: "When you arrived were the lights working?" and "Did you notice any defects in their operation?"

H. [§4.39] Weather

The investigating officer must describe weather conditions in the accident report (see §4.3):
Q. What was the weather like when you arrived?
A. It was raining, and had been for several hours.

Comment: The weather conditions when the officer arrived are relevant to show weather conditions at the time of the accident only if he arrived promptly, before they had changed.

Q. Did the weather affect the condition of the road surface where this accident occurred?
A. The road was wet.

I. [§4.40] Visibility

A police officer can testify about visibility conditions that he perceived at the accident scene and may give his opinion, as a nonexpert,

125

of the approximate distance that people or objects could be seen. See Evid C §800. His testimony on these subjects is objectionable as irrelevant, however, unless he was at the scene promptly after the accident, before conditions had changed. In *Bettencourt v Direct Transp. Co.* (1962) 210 CA2d 405, 407, 26 CR 623, 625, the officer's conclusions about visibility, and a driver's ability to see a dangerous situation, were held to be inadmissible as they were based on tests made at a different time and under different conditions from those prevailing at the time of the accident. See also *Schauf v Southern Cal. Edison Co.* (1966) 243 CA2d 450, 455, 52 CR 518, 521.

The examination of the officer should be cast in terms of what he himself perceived on his arrival at the accident scene:

Q. You testified that you arrived at the scene at 7:12, is that correct?
A. Yes.
Q. What were the light conditions at that time?
A. It was dusk, and as I mentioned, it was raining.
Q. From what distance did you see other cars in front of you?
A. ....

J. [§4.41] *Citations; Arrests*

One of the purposes of the accident investigation is to determine whether anyone violated the law. In examining the officer about his investigation, the lawyer should not seek to have him testify whether he did or did not arrest or issue a citation to anyone. This is irrelevant evidence and its admission can be cause for reversal, whether it is done on direct or cross-examination. *Ungefug v D'Ambrosia* (1967) 250 CA2d 61, 69, 58 CR 223, 228. See §4.48 on admissibility of admissions and effect of guilty and nolo contendere pleas.

V. STATEMENTS OF PARTIES AND WITNESSES

A. [§4.42] *Admissibility Under Hearsay Exceptions*

The police officer interviews drivers, passengers, and pedestrians who were involved in the accident, and witnesses who may have information on how it happened. He then records their statements in his accident report, often using his own words to summarize what is said. Witnesses at the scene tend to be more candid, less guarded, and less equivocal than when they are asked later about the events. Parties' statements may even amount to admissions of negligence.

Testimony by a witness of what someone else said to him is hearsay evidence if it is offered as proof of the matter stated. Evid C §1200.

POLICE OFFICERS §4.43

A statement made to the officer during the course of his investigation cannot, therefore, be the subject of that officer's testimony unless the statement can be received under an exception to the hearsay rule. See Evid C §§1220–1252.

The exceptions generally applicable to an officer's testimony about statements of others include admissions of a party (Evid C §1220), adoptive admissions by a party (Evid C §1221), statements by the deceased in wrongful death actions (Evid C §1227), declarations against interest (Evid C §1230), prior inconsistent statements (Evid C §1235), spontaneous statements (Evid C §1240), or dying declarations (Evid C §1242).

1. [§4.43] Party's Admissions

The hearsay rule does not preclude an officer from testifying about a statement made by a party to the action, as long as the statement is offered against that party in either his individual or his representative capacity. Evid C §1220. Typical of statements falling into this category are those (a) by a driver (to show his negligence) and (b) by an injured passenger or pedestrian (to show contributory negligence or last clear chance).

Since an admission can be offered only against a person who is a party to the action at the time of trial, attorneys should exercise care in omitting or dismissing parties; their presence in the lawsuit may affect the admissibility of their statements.

An officer could be asked about an adverse party's statement as follows:

Q. In the course of your investigation did you ask the [plaintiff/defendant] how the accident happened?
A. Yes, I did.
Q. When did this take place?
A. Within a few minutes after I arrived at the scene.
Q. Did he appear to understand your questions?
A. He did.
Q. Did he appear to have any difficulty in answering them?
A. No.
Q. Did he appear to be coherent and responsive to your inquiries?
A. Yes.
Q. Did he make a statement about how the accident happened?
A. He did.
Q. [Referring to your report if necessary,] please tell us what he said to you.
A. ....

2. [§4.44] Adoptive Admissions

A statement may also be admissible, despite the hearsay rule, if the party against whom it is offered "by words or other conduct manifested his adoption or his belief in its truth." Evid C §1221. The manifestation can be in the form of silence in circumstances where a reasonable man would have disassociated himself from the statement. Evidence Code §1221 requires that the party against whom the statement is offered have "knowledge of the content" of the statement. This requirement may present an obstacle to admissibility when the statement was made in the excitement of an automobile accident, particularly when the party was injured. In *Fisch v Los Angeles Metropolitan Transit Authority* (1963) 219 CA2d 537, 540, 33 CR 298, 300, an officer testified that the plaintiff pedestrian failed to deny a driver's statement that the plaintiff ran into the driver's car. On appeal this was held inadmissible because the extent of plaintiff's injuries made it unlikely that he heard and understood the statement.

3. [§4.45] Driver's Statement To Show Liability of Employer or Owner

Lawyers often wish to have the officer testify about a driver's statements to establish the vicarious liability of his employer (under respondeat superior) or the owner of the vehicle he was driving (under Veh C §17150). If the driver is an adverse party, the officer's testimony can be received as the driver's admission to show his liability. Evid C §1220. Sometimes a driver's statement can be received as a declaration against interest (Evid C §1230) or a spontaneous statement (Evid C §1240).

In addition, Evid C §1224 seems to provide that testimony about a driver's statement can be received against an employer or owner even though the driver has not been made a party. However, in *Markley v Beagle* (1967) 66 C2d 951, 59 CR 809, an employee's statement was inadmissible to show an employer's respondeat superior liability despite the language of Evid C §1224. (Note that *Markley v Beagle* was not a motor vehicle case and the employee's statement in that case in no way admitted liability on his own part.)

If the admission of a driver-defendant does not qualify as a spontaneous statement or declaration against interest, counsel should consider carefully before dismissing him from the action. Whatever the restrictions under the *Markley* rule, if the driver is joined, his statement may at least be offered against him personally as an admission of a party. Evid C §1220.

4. [§4.46] Spontaneous Statements

Evidence Code §1240 provides that evidence of a "spontaneous statement" is not made inadmissible by the hearsay rule when two conditions are met:

(1) The statement must purport to "narrate, describe or explain an act, condition or event perceived by the declarant." Evid C §1240(a). This requirement rarely offers a problem when the statement is made by a person who was involved in the accident. When the statement was made by someone else, however, counsel must establish that he witnessed the "act, condition or event." Direct proof is not required but there must at least be "a persuasive inference" that the declarant witnessed it. *Ungefug v D'Ambrosia* (1967) 250 CA2d 61, 68, 58 CR 223, 228.

(2) The statement must have been made "while the declarant was under the stress of excitement caused by such perception." Evid C §1240(b). Res gestae cases decided before the Evidence Code was adopted offer examples of the degree of excitement and spontaneity traditionally required. In *Wiley v Easter* (1962) 203 CA2d 845, 854, 21 CR 905, 911, the district court of appeal held:

> A statement resulting from a question and answer interview of a motorist involved in an accident, especially when conducted by a police officer, suggests at once lack of spontaneity and on the contrary points to deliberation upon the facts engendered by an instinct of self-protection against claims of liability, civil or criminal. . . .

This does not mean that a statement made to a police officer following an accident is never "spontaneous" within the meaning of Evid C §1240. See *People v Costa* (1953) 40 C2d 160, 168, 252 P2d 1, 6, where a statement in reply to a police officer's question, "What happened?" was held properly admitted; the court noted that the question was not part of an extended interrogation.

Wiley suggests that when the police officer is testifying, it is particularly important to establish that the statement was indeed a spontaneous one and not merely a narrative of events given when the declarant was enough in control of himself to deliberate in his answers. For example:

Q. Did you talk to the [plaintiff/defendant] at the scene?
A. Yes, I did.
Q. How soon after you arrived was this?
A. ....
Q. What was his emotional condition when you saw him?
A. He was very upset.

Comment: The officer may give his opinion on emotional state, *i.e.,* that a person acted calm or excited, rational or irrational, hesitant or aggressive, composed or angered, etc. *Holland v Zollner* (1894) 102 C 633, 639, 36 P 930, 932. See also *People v Deacon* (1953) 117 CA2d 206, 210, 255 P2d 98, 101 (nonexpert testimony that voices in another room sounded angry).

Q. On what do you base your opinion that he was upset?
A. He was [crying/wringing his hands].
Q. Did he appear to be excited?
A. Yes, he did. He was [talking very excitedly and moving his hands in an excited fashion].
Q. Did he say anything to you?
A. Yes.
Q. What did he say?
A. ....

B. [§4.47] *Statements About Liability Insurance*

Parties to an accident sometimes make statements about their insurance coverage, voluntarily or in response to questions by another party or an officer. The officer's testimony about statements relating to liability insurance coverage is not admissible to prove negligence or other wrongdoing. Evid C §1155. However, when insurance is mentioned as an integral part of an admission of fault, evidence of the statement may be received. See discussion in §3.16. See also Witkin, CALIFORNIA EVIDENCE §375 (2d ed, 1966).

C. [§4.48] *Conviction; Plea of Guilty or Nolo Contendere*

A judgment of conviction for violation of the Vehicle Code or a local ordinance on motor vehicle operation "shall not" be res judicata, or constitute grounds for collateral estoppel in a later civil action. Veh C §40834. On the other hand, a plea of guilty may be admissible as an admission, but it is not conclusive. *Teitelbaum Furs, Inc. v Dominion Ins. Co. Ltd.* (1962) 58 C2d 601, 605, 25 CR 559, 561. A plea of nolo contendere, however, is not admissible in evidence as an admission of guilt. Pen C §1016; *In re Hallinan* (1954) 43 C2d 243, 247, 272 P2d 768, 771.

See §4.41 on inadmissibility of evidence of arrests and citations, and §2.6 on the admissibility of prior felony convictions to impeach a witness.

VI. [§4.49] OFFICER AS EXPERT

In the course of his investigation, the officer often forms opinions about how the accident happened. He may conclude that the point of impact was at a certain location and, from this, that one driver was passing another. He may conclude from skid marks that a driver was speeding or slow to react to danger.

The officer, as a lay witness, can express many of his observations in opinion form. These include distances and sizes, the speed of vehicles he has observed, and whether a person was ill, injured, or intoxicated. See §§1.16–1.18 on lay opinion testimony.

Officers can sometimes be qualified to testify as experts on such matters as point of impact and speed before impact. See §§4.53, 4.57. These are subjects that are sufficiently beyond common experience that the opinion of an expert would assist the trier of fact (Evid C §801(a)), and officers may have sufficient special knowledge, skill, experience, training, or education to satisfy a trial judge that they are qualified to testify as experts on these subjects. See §§1.24–1.27 on expert opinion testimony generally.

A. [§4.50] *Deciding Whether To Use Officer*

Lawyers are reluctant to rely on a police officer as an expert witness when (1) there is a question whether the trial judge will permit the officer to testify as an expert, or (2) the opponent is expected to call an expert with more impressive academic qualifications (*e.g.,* an engineer, chemist, physicist, etc.). Before deciding to call the investigating officer as an expert witness, the lawyer should interview him to determine the extent of his training and experience in accident investigation and reconstruction, discover whom his opponent intends to call on the same subject matter, and, if possible, learn the attitude of trial judges in his area on police officers as experts.

If an adverse attorney proposes to call the investigating officer and elicit expert opinion testimony from him, the lawyer can (1) call his own expert witness, (2) design a voir dire examination to show gaps in the officer's qualifications and convince the judge he is not qualified to testify as an expert, and (3) prepare a cross-examination to minimize the weight of the officer's testimony.

B. [§4.51] *Special Qualifications*

Many judges are hesitant to approve a policeman's qualifications as an expert, and it is important to impress on the court that the officer's training and experience justify using him for this purpose. When the

§4.51 POLICE OFFICERS

officer is first called as a witness he is introduced to the court and jury by having him identify himself, his place of duty and residence, and the police agency with which he is associated. In addition, he is questioned to establish his professional competence and impartiality. See §§4.18–4.19 for dialogue. The lawyer usually waits until he reaches the subject on which he wishes the officer to give his opinion, then questions the officer carefully and thoroughly about his qualifications to testify as an expert.

The direct examination on qualifications should be based on what the officer has told the lawyer are his particular accomplishments. For example:

Q. Officer, you earlier told us that you have been with the [Highway Patrol] for ...... years. I would like to ask you a few more questions about your experience in accident investigation. Before joining the [Highway Patrol] did you serve with any other police agency?
A. Yes, I was with the ....
Q. How long did you serve with the ....?
A. ....
Q. Have you been in the military service?
A. Yes, I was in the [Navy] from .... to ....
Q. What was your rank in the [Navy]?
A. ....
Q. And did your duties in the [Navy] include any investigative work?
A. Yes. I served with the [Shore Patrol] for ...... years.
Q. Have you attended any courses in accident investigation while you have been with the [Highway Patrol]?
A. Yes. I attended a ......-week course on motor vehicle accident investigation in 19........
Q. Please describe the subjects that were covered in that course.
A. ....

Comment: Training with any other police department, in the military, or at a specialized school, such as the recruit training, brushup courses, or specialized training given at the California Highway Patrol Academy, or a course given at Northwestern University (see §4.18) may be brought out at this point.

Q. Does your police department provide on-the-job training in accident investigation?
A. Yes, it does.
Q. And did you receive on-the-job training?
A. Yes.

132

POLICE OFFICERS §4.52

Q. When was this?
A. ....
Q. Would you describe your duties during this on-the-job training period?
A. ....
Q. Have you ever supervised other officers in accident investigation work?
A. Yes. [I have had new officers assigned to me and we have worked in pairs while I supervised their on-the-job training in accident investigation.]
Q. Have you ever conducted any accident investigation training courses?
A. Yes, I have.
Q. What was the content of those courses?
A. ....
Q. Have you prepared any written instruction materials or articles in the area of accident investigation or prevention?
A. Yes. I wrote ....
Q. Have you received any medals, awards, or citations during your career as a police officer?
A. ....

C. [§4.52] *Attacking Qualifications*

If a lawyer anticipates that the opinion testimony of an investigating officer called by an opponent will be unfavorable, he usually examines him on voir dire in an attempt to show that the officer should not be permitted to give expert testimony on the subject. If sufficient doubt is cast on the officer's qualifications the judge will rule that he may not give his opinion. Even if the judge permits the officer to testify as an expert, the examination on voir dire alerts the jurors to weaknesses in his qualifications and they may respond by giving his opinion testimony less weight.

The following is sample voir dire examination of a local policeman whom the opponent wishes to use as an expert to establish a vehicle's speed before the collision.

Q. You testified that you have been a member of the .... Police Department since 1962. Is that correct?
A. Yes.
Q. Did you have any investigative experience before joining the department?
A. No, I didn't.

§4.52

Q. You also testified that you graduated from high school. When was that?
A. In 19.......
Q. Was that in June, 19......?
A. That's right.
Q. Then this was your first full-time job?
A. Yes.
Q. Have you attended college?
A. No.
Q. You have taken no college level courses?
A. No, I haven't.
Q. What science courses did you have in high school?
A. General science and chemistry.
Q. What year in school was the general science course?
A. My freshman year.
Q. Then you were how old at that time? About 14?
A. 14 or 15.
Q. And when did you have chemistry?
A. My junior year.
Q. You were about 16 or 17 when you had it?
A. Yes.
Q. What mathematics did you study?
A. I had two years of algebra; in my first and second years of high school.
Q. When you were about 15 years old?
A. Yes.
Q. Am I correct, then, that you have not studied any science or mathematics in any school since you were about 15 or 16 years old?
A. That's right.
Q. And how old are you now?
A. ....
Q. Now, when you joined the .... Police Department you received some training?
A. Yes, I did.
Q. How long a course was that?
A. ...... weeks.
Q. I suppose you covered a variety of subjects dealing with the Penal Code, the law of arrest, procedures in criminal cases, and so forth?
A. Yes.
Q. With all of that, how much time was given over to motor vehicle accident investigation?

POLICE OFFICERS §4.52

A. I would estimate about ...... hours.
Q. What was your first assignment after you finished recruit training?
A. I was assigned to the .... Station as a patrolman.
Q. You were not assigned to motor vehicle accident investigation during this tour of duty?
A. No.
Q. How long were you on this tour of duty at .... Station?
A. Three years.
Q. And were you then assigned to the accident investigation unit?
A. Yes, I was.
Q. And that was when?
A. In 19.......
Q. What month?
A. In September.
Q. And the accident in this case occurred in February of the next year?
A. That's right.
Q. When you were assigned to the accident investigation unit, did you receive any further training in accident investigation?
A. Yes, a ......-week course.
Q. That would have been in September or October, 19.......
A. Yes.
Q. And then where were you assigned?
A. To an accident investigation crew as a working partner.
Q. Was your partner a man of some experience?
A. Yes, he was.
Q. And his duties included supervising you to some extent, am I correct?
A. Yes.
Q. So on the date of the accident you had only been actively investigating accidents for about four months and most of that time you were still under your partner's supervision?
A. Yes.
Q. Was your supervising partner with you when the accident investigation was made in this case?
A. No, I had been transferred to another car by then.
Q. On another subject, Officer, just how much of this accident investigation do you remember now, without referring to the accident report?
A. Very little, if anything.
Q. Therefore, any opinion that you have on the speed that the parties were driving before the accident is based entirely on what you saw, and thought, and wrote on the accident report form?

135

A. Yes, that's right.
Q. And you made that report in February, 19......, when you had been investigating accidents for only a few months?
A. That's correct.
Adverse attorney. Your Honor, I object to any use of Officer .... as an expert witness on speed before impact on the ground that the proper foundation has not been laid. He lacks the requisite formal education or training in accident investigation. He lacks sufficient experience to form the opinions on which his testimony now would be based.
Court. ....

D. Subjects of Expert Testimony

1. [§4.53] Point of Impact

A properly qualified officer can testify to his opinion of the point at which two vehicles collided on the basis of his observations of such matters as the positions in which the vehicles came to rest, the damage to each, and skid marks, gouges, and debris on the roadway.

After an officer has described his general qualifications and what he observed, testimony could proceed as follows (referring to the sample accident report in §4.3):

Q. Did you receive instruction in the use of skid marks, tire marks, debris, and vehicle damage to determine a vehicle's course of travel before and after a collision?
A. Yes.
Q. Have you ever testified in court as an expert witness to give your opinion on the point of vehicle impact in accident cases?
A. Yes, I have on many occasions.
Q. Have you formed an opinion about which vehicle made the two tire marks in the divider strip?

Comment: See §4.37 for prior factual testimony on these marks.

A. Yes. I believe they were made by Vehicle No. 2, the Chevrolet.
Q. Did you come to a conclusion about the course of travel of the car that made these marks?
A. Yes. In my opinion the vehicle that made these tire marks was in the process of going into a broadside skid.
Q. What is your basis for that opinion?
A. The difference of the widths of the marks. When a tire is traveling straight ahead the marking maintains an exact width at all times; but if the car turns sideways, the mark becomes wider.

POLICE OFFICERS §4.55

Q. What is the significance of the fact that the distance between the two tracks widens out?
A. This means to me that the vehicle was in the process of turning.
Q. What vehicle made these marks and what was its direction?
A. I believe that the marks were made by the passenger car, Vehicle No. 2, and that it was traveling in a southerly direction and skidded, turning to the east and passing onto and over the divider strip.
Q. Officer, where do you believe these two vehicles came into contact?
A. At this point in Lane N-2. [Indicates on diagram.]
Q. Would you mark that on the diagram?
A. [Officer does so.]
Q. How do you account for the fact that the vehicles were not found at the point that you have marked as the point of impact?
A. The force of the collision threw them into their final positions.
Q. What is the basis for your opinion that the point of impact was at the location you marked on the diagram?
A. The debris is all located near this spot, and in addition, the gouge marks made by the truck trailer and the location and extent of the damage on both vehicles indicate that the collision occurred there.

Comment: The officer cannot base his opinion of point of impact on statements of witnesses unless the declarant testifies to the same effect at the trial. *Kastner v Los Angeles Metropolitan Transit Authority* (1965) 63 C2d 52, 45 CR 129.

2. [§4.54] Vehicle's Mechanical Condition

Occasionally the investigating officer qualifies as an expert who can give opinion evidence that a vehicle was or was not mechanically defective before the accident. Usually, however, an engineer or mechanic is used for this purpose. An officer with the requisite qualifications should be permitted to testify that he tested brake pedals or the steering mechanism and to describe their condition. He may in some circumstances have sufficient expertise to give his opinion whether the condition was preexisting or was caused by the collision.

3. [§4.55] Loading of Truck

Some police officers have sufficient experience in observing and inspecting trucks to testify as experts that a truck was, or was not, properly loaded. *Risley v Lenwell* (1954) 129 CA2d 608, 631, 277 P2d 897, 914. In most cases technical experts, such as mechanical engineers, physicists, or trucking line supervisors are used on this

§4.56   POLICE OFFICERS

subject. See chap 5. If the officer has the necessary qualifications, however, he is examined thus:

Q. Officer, in your ...... years with the [Highway Patrol] have you gained any experience in the proper loading of trucks?
A. Yes, I have.
Q. Would you tell us what that experience was?
A. [Part of my duties for the past ...... years has been to inspect trucks to see if they conform to state truckloading requirements.]
Q. What was the truck carrying?
A. ....
Q. How was the load [secured/placed] in the truck?
A. ....
Q. Are you familiar with the California Highway Patrol regulations governing the loading of trucks?
A. Yes, I am.
Q. Your Honor, I ask that the Court take judicial notice of Title ......, Subchapter ......, Article ......, Sections ...... of the California Administrative Code.

Comment: The court is required to notice these regulations judicially. Evid C §451; see §20.36. Counsel should have copies of the regulations for the court and opposing counsel.

Q. Officer, would you read section ......?
A. [Officer reads section aloud.]
Q. Was the load that the truck in this case was carrying secured in conformity with the provisions of this regulation?
A. ....
Q. What is the basis for your answer?
A. ....
Q. Does the way in which a truck is loaded have any bearing on its tendency to sway or not to sway?
A. ....
Q. Do you have any opinion whether the way in which the truck was loaded would have caused it to sway or not to sway?
A. ....

   4. [§4.56] Safe Speed Under the Conditions

A trial judge may permit an officer to state his opinion of what was a safe speed for each driver under the conditions prevailing at the time of the collision. See *Norman v Tully* (1957) 149 CA2d 530, 533, 308 P2d 875, 878. The officer can base his opinion on such factors as

POLICE OFFICERS §4.59

his investigation of other accidents at the same place or under similar conditions and his own driving experience under comparable conditions.

5. [§4.57] Speed Before Collision

An expert witness may give his opinion of a vehicle's speed before impact, based on the length of skid marks, the nature and condition of the road, the make and condition of the vehicle, and any "other relevant factors." *Ungefug v D'Ambrosia* (1967) 250 CA2d 61, 65, 58 CR 223, 226. These other factors generally require a good knowledge of coefficients of friction and other principles of physics. An opinion on speed based on the characteristics of skid marks and on vehicle damage has been held to be admissible in a nonjury case. See *Hoffman v Slocum* (1963) 219 CA2d 100, 104, 32 CR 635, 638.

For a discussion of the training and experience needed by an officer to testify about speed on the basis of skid marks, see *Crooks v Pirrone* (1964) 228 CA2d 549, 552, 39 CR 622, 623 (affirming trial judge's exercise of discretion in excluding officer's testimony).

6. [§4.58] Influence of Narcotics

Although a witness may give a nonexpert opinion that someone is intoxicated (see §4.36), only an expert who is specially qualified may testify that in his opinion a person he observed was under the influence of narcotics. Traffic accident investigators seldom qualify as experts on this subject.

The reported California decisions that permit expert opinion on this subject are criminal cases in which the police officer was assigned to the narcotics detail of his department. See *People v Smith* (1967) 253 CA2d 711, 61 CR 557 (voir dire printed in opinion); *People v Gurrola* (1963) 218 CA2d 349, 32 CR 368. There is no reason, however, why an officer who has the necessary qualifications should not be permitted to give expert testimony on narcotics in a civil case.

Counsel should advise the officer not to testify about any arrest or citation. See §4.41.

VII. [§4.59] ELICITING UNFAVORABLE MATTER ON DIRECT

If the officer's testimony has both good and bad aspects, counsel may call him and elicit the favorable testimony. He may then bring out the unfavorable testimony, attempting by carefully framed questions to minimize its significance. The credibility of a witness may be

§4.59   POLICE OFFICERS

attacked by the lawyer who calls him on direct examination (Evid C §785) to show that he is mistaken or that he has an insufficient foundation for an unfavorable opinion that he has expressed.

For example, the sample accident report at §4.3 shows by the use of code number "4" in column 67 on page 1, that Driver No. 1 had been drinking but that it was not known whether it affected his driving (see §4.36). Counsel knows that his opponent will bring out this information. He may therefore question the officer and attempt on direct examination to impeach him on this unfavorable subject while not affecting his credibility on the favorable matters on which he has already testified. For example (referring to the sample accident report in §4.3):

Q. Officer, you have testified that you talked to my client, Mr. Doe, at the scene. Is that correct?
A. Yes, I did.
Q. Did you form an opinion whether he had been drinking?
A. Yes, I did.
Q. What was your opinion?
A. That he had been drinking.
Q. What was the basis for this opinion?
A. His speech was thick, there were opened beer cans in the car, and he was unsteady on his feet.
Q. Officer, did you make any notation of this in your accident report?
A. Yes, I wrote that he had been drinking in my investigation summary.
Q. Is that your only reference to this subject in your report?
A. No. I also noted it under the statistical data portion of the report on page 2.
Q. What does the report say on page 2?
A. Well, we use code numbers to answer certain questions, and I inserted the code number "4" where it asks whether Driver No. 1 had been drinking.
Q. What does the code number "4" mean?
A. It means that he had been drinking, but I could not determine whether it impaired his driving or not.
Q. What other code numbers relate to this section of the report on sobriety?
A. There are six in all. Number "1" means he was obviously drunk, "2" that he had been drinking and his ability to drive was impaired, "3" that he had been drinking but his ability was not impaired, "5" that he had not been drinking, and "6" that he was in a parked car or that it was a hit and run accident.

POLICE OFFICERS §4.59

Q. Then you did not believe that he was obviously drunk or that he had been drinking to the point that his driving ability was impaired. Is that correct?
A. No. I believed that he had been drinking, but I did not know if it had impaired his ability to drive.
Q. Does your report show that Mr. Doe was injured as a result of this collision?
A. Oh yes. He was badly injured.
Q. Where on his body did you see injuries?
A. On his chest, arms, and head.
Q. What injuries did you see on his head?
A. His face was bleeding and he had several scalp injuries.
Q. Dr. .... testified that Mr. Doe had suffered a severe cerebral concussion, among other injuries, in this accident. Were you aware that he had suffered a concussion when you formed your opinion that he had been drinking?
A. No.
Q. Do you know from your training that a person with a cerebral concussion sometimes has thick speech and may appear to be incoherent?
A. Yes.
Q. If you had known that Mr. Doe was suffering from a cerebral concussion, would you have been so sure that he had been drinking?
A. No, I don't suppose I would have been; I was merely acting on his appearance and the presence of the beer cans in the car.
Q. Do you know that Mr. Doe had been drinking from those beer cans before the accident?
A. No, I do not.

5

Technical Experts

I. **Reasons for Using**

    A. [§5.1] Before and at Trial
    B. [§5.2] Examples in Personal Injury Cases

II. **[§5.3] Determining Appropriate Specialty: Checklists**

    A. [§5.4] Vehicle and Carrier Accidents
    B. [§5.5] Slip and Fall
    C. [§5.6] Premises; Buildings; Construction Sites
    D. [§5.7] Chemicals; Foods; Drugs; Explosions

III. **Descriptions of Specialties**

    A. [§5.8] Ceramic Engineers
    B. [§5.9] Chemical Engineers
    C. [§5.10] Chemists
    D. [§5.11] Civil Engineers
    E. [§5.12] Climatologists; Meteorologists
    F. [§5.13] Electrical Engineers
    G. [§5.14] Health Chemistry Engineers
    H. [§5.15] Industrial Engineers
    I. [§5.16] Mechanical Engineers
    J. [§5.17] Metallurgical Engineers
    K. [§5.18] Nonprofessional Experts
    L. [§5.19] Pharmacologists
    M. [§5.20] Physicists
    N. [§5.21] Toxicologists

IV. **[§5.22] Criteria for Selecting Expert**

    A. [§5.23] Knowledge of Subject
    B. [§5.24] Credibility

C. [§5.25] Personality and Manner of Expression
D. [§5.26] Locality of Trial
E. [§5.27] Cost
F. [§5.28] Using More Than One Expert

V. **Locating Experts**

A. [§5.29] Through Other Lawyers and Court Decisions
B. [§5.30] Through Client
C. [§5.31] Universities
D. [§5.32] Articles; Books; Research Services

VI. **Preparing To Examine**

A. [§5.33] When To Employ Expert; Discovery Considerations
B. [§5.34] Testing Expert's Hypothesis
C. [§5.35] Determining Form of Questions

VII. **Qualifications**

A. Sufficiency
 1. [§5.36] To Permit Admission of Opinion Testimony
 2. [§5.37] To Gain Jurors' Confidence
B. [§5.38] Handling Offers To Concede Qualifications
C. [§5.39] Particular Items: Checklist
 1. [§5.40] Name; Address; Occupation
 2. [§5.41] Registration and Licenses
 3. Education and Degrees
  a. [§5.42] Professionals
  b. [§5.43] Nonprofessionals
 4. Present Employment
  a. [§5.44] Professor
  b. [§5.45] Officer of Research or Consulting Firm
  c. [§5.46] Employee of Defendant Company
  d. [§5.47] Nonprofessional
 5. Specialization
  a. [§5.48] Professional
  b. [§5.49] Nonprofessional
 6. [§5.50] Previous Employment
 7. [§5.51] Military Service
 8. [§5.52] Professional Societies
 9. [§5.53] Lecturing and Teaching
 10. [§5.54] Authorship
 11. [§5.55] Patents
 12. [§5.56] Consultation Experience in Other Cases
 13. [§5.57] Knowledge of Subject in Issue

TECHNICAL EXPERTS §5.2

VIII. **Eliciting Opinion Testimony**
  A. [§5.58] Admissibility
  B. [§5.59] Showing Subject of Opinion
  C. [§5.60] Stating Bases of Opinions
   1. [§5.61] Facts in Evidence
   2. [§5.62] Expert's Perceptions; Tests; Analyses
   3. [§5.63] Expert's Special Qualifications
   4. [§5.64] Books; Treatises; Other Literature
   5. [§5.65] Community and Industry Standards
   6. [§5.66] Standards Set by Statute and Official Regulation
  D. [§5.67] Expressing Opinion
  E. [§5.68] Stating Reasons for Opinion

I. REASONS FOR USING

A. [§5.1] *Before and at Trial*

Technical experts can be invaluable in helping the lawyer develop the proper theory for a personal injury lawsuit. They use scientific procedures to analyze and supply facts and information, and they may suggest new avenues of discovery. From their analysis of these facts and assumptions they construct a theory of liability or nonliability. At trial, effective expert witnesses reduce these complex matters to terms that jurors can understand, express their conclusions on relevant matters of liability, and demonstrate the validity of their analyses and conclusions. In so doing, they are instruments by which the client's case is stated, explained, and supported by scientific proof.

This chapter deals with persons who can testify as experts on the liability phases of a personal injury case. For a general discussion of expert testimony, see §§1.19–1.30. See also chap 4 on police officers as experts, chap 6 on medical experts, and chap 7 on economists and other experts on damages.

B. [§5.2] *Examples in Personal Injury Cases*

The following are examples of some of the ways in which technical experts can advance or rebut theories of liability in personal injury cases.

In motor vehicle collision cases, engineers and physicists can often locate the point of impact, thereby establishing liability in divider line and intersection cases. (See §4.53 on the police officer's expert testimony on point of impact.) They may be able to establish a driver's speed or course of travel before a collision; his ability to see dangerous conditions, other vehicles, or pedestrians; and his ability to hear warning signals. They often determine a driver's or a pedestrian's reaction time and thus support or rebut claims of last clear chance or contributory negligence. They have been used to testify on the likely effect of impact had seatbelts been worn. *Truman v Vargas* (1969) 275 CA2d___, ___, 80 CR 373, 377. See also *Mortensen v Southern Pac. Co.* (1966) 245 CA2d 241, 53 CR 851.

Some experts can determine who had the right of way at a controlled intersection by reconstructing a driver's route and computing his travel time and traffic light phases.

In slip and fall cases experts analyze the flooring, carpeting, pavement, stairway, etc., and its condition at the time of the accident. They study the shoes worn by the plaintiff and perform experiments to determine the coefficient of friction. They study lighting and maintenance conditions that might have created a hazard. They apply their knowledge of standards of planning, construction, and maintenance of the walking surface and of local ordinances and building standards governing construction and maintenance.

Experts are used in most product liability cases to testify on defective design or construction of vehicles, equipment, containers, etc. Only an expert can determine the effect of pressure, temperature, vibration, friction, and other stresses to which it is exposed.

In explosion cases experts determine and explain the physical forces that created the hazard and the standard of care that would have avoided it.

II. [§5.3] DETERMINING APPROPRIATE SPECIALTY: CHECKLISTS

Sections 5.4–5.7 contain checklists of particular technical problems that may arise in personal injury cases, and show the areas of technical specialization in which they traditionally are handled. These areas are then described (in alphabetical order) in §§5.8–5.21. In some instances men in more than one specialty can handle a problem or some aspect of it. And one specialist may have the necessary training and experience to testify on matters traditionally handled in another specialty. The following lists are, therefore, only general guidelines that suggest where the lawyer may start his search for an expert witness. The person originally contacted often directs him to another man with the qualifications for the precise problem in the case.

A. [§5.4] *Vehicle and Carrier Accidents*

Accident reconstruction: Mechanical Engineer, Physicist, Civil Engineer

TECHNICAL EXPERTS §5.4

Acoustics: Mechanical Engineer
Aircraft design and construction: Mechanical Engineer
Aircraft maintenance: Mechanical Engineer, Mechanic
Airport runways: Civil Engineer, Mechanical Engineer
Airport design: Civil Engineer, Mechanical Engineer
Blood alcohol tests: Toxicologist, Chemist
Bridge construction: Civil Engineer
Bulldozer design and construction: Mechanical Engineer
Bulldozer maintenance: Mechanical Engineer, Mechanic
Corrosion (metal): Mechanical Engineer, Metallurgical Engineer, Mechanic
Electricity (engines/power): Electrical Engineer
Fibers and Fabrics (synthetic): Chemical Engineer, Chemist
Fire; Explosions: Chemist, Chemical Engineer, Mechanical Engineer
Fireresistant materials: Civil Engineer
Gasoline: Chemical Engineer, Mechanical Engineer, Chemist
Glass: Ceramic Engineer, Chemist
Headlights: Electrical Engineer, Mechanical Engineer, Physicist, Ceramic Engineer
Highway construction: Civil Engineer
Illumination: Electrical Engineer, Physicist
Impact (vehicle): Mechanical Engineer, Physicist
Internal combustion machines: Mechanical Engineer
Intoxication: Toxicologist, Chemist
Lighting: Electrical Engineer, Physicist
Lubrication: Mechanical Engineer, Mechanic
Machine design and construction: Mechanical Engineer
Machine maintenance: Mechanical Engineer, Mechanic
Metals (strength, stresses, corrosion, resistance to temperature): Mechanical Engineer, Metallurgical Engineer
Nuclear Power: Chemical Engineer, Physicist
Point of Impact: Mechanical Engineer, Physicist
Power (electrical): Electrical Engineer
Power (machine): Mechanical Engineer
Power (nuclear): Chemical Engineer, Physicist
Paint: Chemist, Chemical Engineer, Civil Engineer
Pavement: Civil Engineer
Petroleum: Chemical Engineer, Mechanical Engineer
Plastics: Chemist
Pumps (hydraulic): Civil Engineer, Mechanical Engineer
Pumps (mechanical): Mechanical Engineer
Railroads: Mechanical Engineer
Railroad terminals: Civil Engineer
Rubber: Chemical Engineer, Chemist
Seatbelts: Mechanical Engineer, Physicist
Ship design and construction: Mechanical Engineer

§5.5   TECHNICAL EXPERTS

Sidewalks: Civil Engineer, Physicist
Speed: Mechanical Engineer, Physicist
Tires: Mechanical Engineer, Civil Engineer, Chemical Engineer, Chemist
Tractor design and construction: Mechanical Engineer
Tractor maintenance: Mechanical Engineer, Mechanic
Truck loading: Mechanical Engineer, Physicist, Trucker
Tunnels: Civil Engineer, Mechanical Engineer
Visibility: Civil Engineer, Physicist
Wheels: Mechanical Engineer, Metallurgical Engineer
Windshields: Civil Engineer, Ceramic Engineer

B. [§5.5] *Slip and Fall*

Building construction: Civil Engineer
Drugs: Toxicologist, Chemist
Illumination: Electrical Engineer, Physicist
Intoxication: Toxicologist, Chemist
Lighting: Electrical Engineer, Physicist
Metal stresses: Mechanical Engineer, Metallurgical Engineer
Mud: Civil Engineer, Chemist
Paint: Chemical Engineer, Chemist
Pavement: Civil Engineer
Rubber: Chemical Engineer, Chemist
Shoes: Mechanical Engineer, Physicist
Sidewalks: Civil Engineer, Physicist
Stairs: Civil Engineer, Physicist
Wax: Chemist
Wood (stresses, expansion with moisture, etc.): Civil Engineer

C. [§5.6] *Premises; Buildings; Construction Sites*

For most of the following subjects, see also §5.15 on the industrial engineer.

Acoustics: Mechanical Engineer
Air conditioning: Mechanical Engineer
Boilers: Mechanical Engineer, Metallurgical Engineer
Building materials (concrete etc.): Civil Engineer
Crane design and construction: Mechanical Engineer
Crane maintenance: Mechanical Engineer, Mechanic
Concrete: Civil Engineer
Conveyor design and construction: Mechanical Engineer
Conveyor maintenance: Mechanical Engineer, Mechanic
Dams: Civil Engineer
Electricity (equipment and engines): Electrical Engineer, Electrician
Elevators (electric): Electrical Engineer
Fire: Civil Engineer, Mechanical Engineer

TECHNICAL EXPERTS §5.7

Flooding: Civil Engineer
Geology: Civil Engineer
Harbors: Civil Engineer
Heating: Mechanical Engineer
Hoists: Mechanical Engineer
Illumination (lighting): Electrical Engineer, Physicist
Metals (stresses etc): Mechanical Engineer, Metallurgical Engineer
Paint: Chemist, Chemical Engineer
Pipes: Mechanical Engineer
Poisons: Toxicologist
Pumps: Mechanical Engineer
Rivers: Civil Engineer
Sanitation: Civil Engineer, Chemist
Sidewalks: Civil Engineer, Architect
Soils: Civil Engineer
Stairways: Civil Engineer, Architect
Structures (buildings): Civil Engineer, Architect
Swimming Pools (electrical shock): Electrical Engineer
Tractors: Mechanical Engineer
Trucks: Mechanical Engineer
Tunnels: Civil Engineer, Mechanical Engineer
Ventilation: Mechanical Engineer
Water flooding and control: Civil Engineer
Water heaters: Mechanical Engineer

D. [§5.7] *Chemicals; Foods; Drugs; Explosions*

Air pollution: Civil Engineer, Mechanical Engineer
Caustic substances: Chemist
Chemical contamination: Chemical Engineer, Chemist, Toxicologist
Chemical reactions: Chemist
Chemicals (manufacture and control): Chemical Engineer
Cleansing agents: Chemist
Corrosion (metal): Mechanical Engineer, Metallurgical Engineer
Drugs: Toxicologist, Pharmacologist, Chemist
Explosives: Chemical Engineer, Civil Engineer
Fertilizers: Chemist
Fabrics and Fibers (synthetic): Chemical Engineer
Fire: Chemist, Chemical Engineer
Food processing: Chemical Engineer, Chemist
Glass: Chemist, Ceramic Engineer
Paint: Chemist, Chemical Engineer
Pesticides: Chemist, Toxicologist
Poisons: Chemist, Toxicologist
Radiation: Chemical Engineer, Health Engineer
Ventilation: Mechanical Engineer

III. DESCRIPTIONS OF SPECIALTIES

A. [§5.8] Ceramic Engineers

The work of ceramic engineers is similar to that of metallurgical engineers, except that they work with nonmetallic solids rather than metals.

B. [§5.9] Chemical Engineers

Chemical engineers work on the development, manufacture, and control of chemical products; raw materials (natural and synthetic) processing; petroleum refining; rubber production; chemical contamination; chemical corrosion; and food processing. They are concerned with the physical plant that is used to process materials (pipes, boilers, pressure vessels, etc.), while chemists, whose work is often closely related, are more concerned with chemical reactions.

C. [§5.10] Chemists

Chemists deal with chemical reactions. They study the composition of various kinds of matter in its different states (gaseous, liquid, solid, solution, and colloidal), the changes in composition that they undergo, and the accompanying energy phenomena. Inorganic chemists study the properties and behavior of chemical elements and their inorganic compounds with a view to their application in research and industry. Organic chemists deal with carbon containing substances, biochemists with processes and products of living organisms, and agricultural chemists with such subjects as soils, fertilizers, and insect pests.

D. [§5.11] Civil Engineers

Civil engineers are responsible for the planning, design, and construction of buildings, airports, terminals, power plants, etc. They also work in hydrology—the control of water, water resources, flood control, and river and harbor development. They specialize in sanitation (air and water pollution; liquid, solid, and gaseous waste control) and in radiological health problems. They work with soils and earthquake damage and handle geological problems. They also plan and construct highways, bridges, dams, tunnels, airport runways, and railroad rights of way, and they work in traffic engineering.

Subspecialties of civil engineering include structural, sanitation, or transportation engineering.

TECHNICAL EXPERTS §5.16

E. [§5.12] *Climatologists: Meteorologists*

Climatologists and meteorologists study temperature, humidity, snow, rain, sunshine, clouds, and other weather phenomena. They can also give data on times of sunrise and sunset.

F. [§5.13] *Electrical Engineers*

Electrical engineers develop electrical machinery and power systems. They also work on problems related to electrical radiation, communications, computers, illumination, and electrical shock.

G. [§5.14] *Health Chemistry Engineers*

Health chemistry engineering is a relatively new field and is concerned with radiation dangers from the health viewpoint. It encompasses safety aspects of radiation much as industrial or safety engineering deals with more general safety problems.

H. [§5.15] *Industrial Engineers*

Industrial engineers are concerned primarily with organizing and conducting the technical aspects of manufacturing operations—the design of manufacturing systems and the prediction, control, and evaluation of the results obtained. Very often they are responsible for creating a safe environment for workers and protecting them against industrial accidents and diseases. They advise in the design, layout, and construction of plants and their equipment. They also attend to safety procedures in the production process (developing rules and procedures for handling toxic substances, assuring proper ventilation, providing safety clothing and equipment, etc.).

I. [§5.16] *Mechanical Engineers*

Mechanical engineers design and construct machines, vehicles (automotive, aeronautical, and maritime), propulsion systems, and a variety of mechanical equipment (cranes, pipes, pumps, etc.). They work on heating, ventilation and air conditioning, air pollution, combustion and fires, vibration, friction, corrosion, lubrication, welding, power generation, and acoustical problems. Automotive, petroleum, and aeronautical engineering are some of the subspecialties of mechanical engineering.

J. [§5.17] *Metallurgical Engineers*

Metallurgical engineers specialize in the extraction of metals from ores, refining, and alloying. They work with the chemical composition of metals and alloys; welding problems; and problems related to metal stress, fatigue, strength, and resistance to temperature.

K. [§5.18] *Nonprofessional Experts*

A "nonprofessional expert" as the term is used in this book is a person qualified by training and experience to serve as an expert on a particular subject who does not, however, have a professional degree or professional training at a university (*e.g.,* mechanics, truck drivers, equipment operators, lighting installers, plumbers, and electricians). A nonprofessional expert is helpful when the problem is practical rather than theoretical. For example, an automobile mechanic's opinion can be very effective in establishing whether a vehicle part was properly installed or lubricated or whether it showed signs of pre-existing wear.

It is often less costly to hire a nonprofessional as an expert witness (see §5.27), and often the lawyer will prefer a well-qualified local nonprofessional in preference to a professional who is unknown locally. See §5.26. In all cases, however, the lawyer must be sure that the nonprofessional has sufficient experience and practical qualifications to qualify him as an expert on the precise problem in the case. See §§5.23, 5.36–5.37. He must also take into account the qualifications of the expert his opponent proposes to call. If he fears that the jury will be impressed with the opposing expert's educational qualifications, he may decide to use a professional instead of or in addition to his nonprofessional. See §5.28 on the use of more than one expert.

L. [§5.19] *Pharmacologists*

Pharmacologists study the changes produced in living animals (from micro-organisms to humans) by chemical substances other than food. They study the action of drugs and other agents used to treat disease and in many respects their work is closely related to that of toxicologists. Pharmacologists are not to be confused with pharmacists, who attend to the preparation of drugs on prescription.

M. [§5.20] *Physicists*

Physics is the study of the structure and behavior of matter, energy, forces, and radiation. Physicists conduct experiments and formulate theories about electricity, light, atoms, heat, and mechanical forces.

Their work is the theoretical foundation of all branches of engineering. Physicists are found in industrial laboratories and factories, universities, and government.

Biophysicists develop and apply techniques of physics to the diagnosis and prevention of diseases in plants and animals. Geophysicists apply principles of physics to geology, petroleum, mining, and the study of earthquakes. Optical physicists work with cameras, microscopes, spectroscopes, and infrared and ultraviolet rays; more recently they have been instrumental in the development and application of the laser.

Chemical physicists consider the effect of extreme temperature or pressure on chemical substances. More specifically, they often work on the mechanical, electrical, and thermal properties of plastics, rubber, and metals.

Solid state physicists work on the optical, acoustical, electronic, and other properties of all kinds of solid matter. They were largely responsible for the development and application of transistors and diodes.

Atomic, nuclear, and particles physicists deal with the properties of atoms, nuclei, and particles (electrons etc.). Most legal problems relating to their work, except problems of radiation, are normally handled by electrical engineers. Health problems related to radiation are generally handled by health chemistry engineers.

N. [§5.21] *Toxicologists*

Toxicologists work with the chemistry, effects, antidotes, and detection of poisons.

IV. [§5.22] CRITERIA FOR SELECTING EXPERT

For a witness to testify as an expert, the subject on which he testifies must be "sufficiently beyond common experience that the opinion of an expert would assist the trier of fact." Evid C §801(a). In many cases, success or failure is determined by the lawyer's ability to choose the right man to present expert testimony.

If the technical problem in the case is one that is frequently seen (*e.g.*, reconstructing the point of impact in a vehicle collision), the lawyer often has less difficulty locating an expert within the proper specialty than finding the best man among the many who may be available.

The lawyer whose case presents a unique problem must use his imagination and ingenuity to locate proper expert assistance. For example, a lawyer defending the product liability case of a claimed

§5.23 TECHNICAL EXPERTS

defect in the design of a vehicle used in construction work recently used a civil engineer who specialized in photogrammetry to help prepare the case and then called him as an expert witness. Using photographs of the construction area (a hill since leveled), the photogrammetrist constructed a three-dimensional model of its configuration at the time of the accident. He also determined the position of the equipment's grading blade at the time of the accident.

A. [§5.23] *Knowledge of Subject*

If the expert witness's analysis of the problem is incorrect or superficial, it can jeopardize the entire case. The lawyer's primary aim in selecting an expert is to find one whose analysis of the problem will be accurate and whose opinion testimony will stand up under cross-examination.

Some problems require a theoretical approach and can be handled only by an expert with extensive academic experience. Others are best handled by a person of practical experience. More than one product liability case, for example, has been lost when a brilliant theoretical justification of equipment design has been contradicted by a mechanic (with a high school education) who testified that the equipment was faulty, gave examples from his own experience, and then demonstrated the fault to the jury.

B. [§5.24] *Credibility*

The attorney should be careful to investigate the purported expert's qualifications before he is hired. Some experts testify so often that they have gained a reputation among lawyers as "professional experts." In some cases they are used frequently because they have superior qualifications; but frequent use is not an assurance of good qualifications. For example, some men who hold themselves out as professional "safety experts" are well qualified, but others lack training and experience and are vulnerable on cross-examination. Some experts tend to accommodate their expert opinion to support the client's position regardless of its merit, thus diminishing their credibility.

The lawyer should therefore determine whether the expert has consistently testified for either plaintiffs or defendants, or whether he has been available to both. If it is brought out on voir dire or cross-examination that the expert has restricted himself to one side or the other, it may suggest to the jury that his opinion testimony is manufactured to accommodate his client.

See generally §§2.14–2.19 on attacking the credibility of experts.

TECHNICAL EXPERTS §5.28

C. [§5.25] Personality and Manner of Expression

An expert with the highest professional qualifications can be an ineffective, or even destructive, witness if he antagonizes the jury through behavior that is arrogant, impatient, or otherwise annoying. His personality must not be abrasive, he must project well, and he must be convincing in his presentation. An effective expert expresses himself well without patronizing the jurors or talking over their heads.

D. [§5.26] Locality of Trial

The place of trial may suggest the value of selecting a local man as the expert witness. In rural and mountain areas, particularly, juries often pay more heed to a man they know personally or by reputation than to an outsider. As an example, illumination problems in slip and fall cases are often handled by electrical engineers or physicists, who are ordinarily found only in urban areas. In the proper case, a lighting contractor may have the requisite experience to give expert testimony on the subject, and the lawyer may choose to use him because he is from the jurors' locality, is highly respected for his honesty, and is accepted in the community as knowledgeable.

E. [§5.27] Cost

The potential worth of a civil case normally determines the economic feasibility of hiring an expert and, if one is hired, the extent of his investigation.

Experts are normally employed by private agreement; they may charge a flat fee or by the hour for pretrial investigation with daily fees for court attendance. If they prepare diagrams, photographs, models, etc., there is an additional charge that may be substantial. Some experts are available for informal assistance, such as telephone consultation, as part of their over-all fee; others make additional charges for these services. The lawyer should determine the fee and the scope of the work to be performed before finally retaining the expert.

Expert witnesses are not employed on a contingent fee basis; it is improper to condition the fee, or its amount, on the success of the litigation. *Von Kesler v Baker* (1933) 131 CA 654, 656, 21 P2d 1017, 1019. Experts may be examined on their fee arrangements and the amounts of their fees. Evid C §722(b). See generally §2.16.

F. [§5.28] Using More Than One Expert

If his case permits the expense, an attorney may use more than one

§5.29   TECHNICAL EXPERTS

expert. For example, in a vehicle product liability case a mechanical engineer might be called to testify about scientific tests made on the vehicle part; in addition, a qualified mechanic or operator who worked with the part might be called to testify on its day by day use and its capacity (or lack of capacity) to perform in practice. The trial judge may, however, limit the number of expert witnesses a party may call. Evid C §723.

In big cases, a second expert can be used as a rebuttal witness or to check an expert's tests and evaluations and to assure that his opinion is valid. He may also be a "silent expert" — one who is hired to advise on case preparation but not to testify.

V. LOCATING EXPERTS

A. [§5.29] *Through Other Lawyers and Court Decisions*

The first and most reliable source of information on locating qualified experts is other lawyers. The new lawyer, or one with a novel problem, can usually get the best advice on locating the appropriate expert from his colleagues. It is often possible to get good advice from law firms that specialize in plaintiff's or defendant's work, and who have actually used expert witnesses in a variety of fields.

Judges in their opinions often identify the expert used in the case and describe the technical problem about which he testified. Even when the reported opinion does not include the expert's name, his identity can be obtained either from the attorney who called him in the case, or from the court files at the clerk's office.

B. [§5.30] *Through Client*

A client often has good information on the location of an expert. This is particularly true in product liability defense work, where a defendant often employs knowledgeable experts or knows of reliable and honest men in the industry. See §5.46.

C. [§5.31] *Universities*

The lawyer who seeks information from a university on the identity of experts on its faculty may, or may not, be successful in obtaining the best man as an expert. Much depends on perseverance. The inquiry is often handled by a clerical staff member who has no reason to know who, if anyone, has testified as an expert witness before. The lawyer should persist until he finds someone who knows the faculty and their specialties. Since the lawyer is often merely directed to a staff member who is known to be experienced in the subject matter,

TECHNICAL EXPERTS §5.32

it is essential that he define the problem as specifically as possible. If two or more disciplines are concerned with his problem (*e.g.,* electrical engineering and physics) inquiries can be directed to both departments.

While no general rule can be applied, a lawyer may look first to universities (rather than to industry) when he needs a physicist as an expert witness. Physicists in industry often work in such specialized fields that they are not well equipped to discuss the basic rules of physics in which the lawyer is usually interested. The university physicist, used to dealing with students on all levels, is generally better equipped to explain his subject in language that jurors can understand.

All major universities and colleges in California have chemistry and physics departments and the following California universities and colleges have engineering programs that are presently accredited by the Engineer's Council for Professional Development:

California Institute of Technology (Pasadena)
California State College at Long Beach
California State College at Los Angeles
Fresno State College
Harvey Mudd College (Claremont)
Loyola University (Los Angeles)
Sacramento State College
San Diego State College
San Fernando Valley State College (Northridge)
San Jose State College
Santa Clara University
Stanford University (Palo Alto)
University of California at Berkeley
University of California at Davis
University of California at Los Angeles
University of California at Santa Barbara
University of Southern California (Los Angeles)

D. [§5.32] *Articles; Books; Research Services*

Lawyers sometimes locate their experts from those who have written books or articles on the particular subject. In addition, there are services that provide information on expert witnesses.

The LAWYER'S DESK REFERENCE by Robb, Philo & Goodman (1968) contains lists of technical experts by name, address, and subject of specialty. The list is not separated by states and the reader must locate California experts from the general list. In some specialties the authors also include names of professional societies from which additional names can be obtained.

Jury Verdicts Weekly, a pamphlet published by E. N. Raymond & Associates, 231 Franklin Street, San Francisco 94102 (telephone 863-6963), is another useful publication. It contains descriptions of jury cases showing parties, counsel, judge, and the names of medical and other experts. This is followed by a brief description of the facts, testimony, injuries, damages, settlement demands, and the amount (and vote on) the verdict. The description is sufficient to identify the expert and the subject of his testimony. Subscriptions for the weekly issues presently cost $5 a month. A semiannual index is also available, to subscribers and nonsubscribers, at $20 a copy. It lists expert witnesses by specialty (*e.g.*, "mechanical engineer"), but reference to the weekly editions is normally necessary to identify the precise subjects on which they testified. As an additional service, the publisher prepares compilations of information either by problem (*e.g.*, brake failure) or by name of expert, by extracting pertinent case reports from the weekly editions. On request, these compilations may be used by subscribers or nonsubscribers for $50.

VI. PREPARING TO EXAMINE

A. [§5.33] When To Employ Expert; Discovery Considerations

In some cases the lawyer is so familiar with the problem that he does not need an expert's assistance in case preparation and therefore does not hire one until shortly before trial, if at all. In most instances, however, the expert should be hired early in the preparation of the case so that he can equip himself to testify, aid the lawyer in investigating the facts, and suggest topics for exploration in discovery procedures. On the other hand, once he is hired it is likely that the opposing lawyer will try to take his deposition.

The degree to which an expert's factual knowledge and opinion is subject to discovery is not entirely settled in California. See generally Witkin, CALIFORNIA EVIDENCE §§817–820 (2d ed, 1966); Louisell, MODERN CALIFORNIA DISCOVERY, 1968 Supp, §§10.11–11.03. A few generalizations can be made on the basis of California courts of appeal opinions:

(1) The name and address of an employed expert is discoverable by interrogatory, whether he is hired to assist in case preparation, to testify as an expert witness, or both. *Kenney v Superior Court* (1967) 255 CA2d 106, 112, 63 CR 84, 89.

(2) If he was hired solely in an advisory capacity, the product of his investigation is protected under the work product rule (CCP

TECHNICAL EXPERTS   §5.35

§2016), but if he was hired as a prospective witness, discovery is permitted of the "information and opinion" on the subject "about which he is a prospective witness." *Scotsman Mfg. Co. v Superior Court* (1966) 242 CA2d 527, 531, 51 CR 511, 514.

(3) Even after the witness has been identified as a potential witness, information supplied to him by either the lawyer hiring him or the lawyer's client, is protected by the attorney-client privilege. *Kenney v Superior Court, supra.*

(4) An expert's written report is discoverable if it is restricted to "information and opinion." If it contains advisory or unfavorable information, the court may protect it from production. See *Scotsman Mfg. Co. v Superior Court, supra.* The report can be inspected if it is shown that the expert has refreshed his memory by referring to it in preparation for a deposition. Evid C §771(a); *Kerns Constr. Co. v Superior Court* (1968) 266 CA2d 405, 72 CR 74; see §1.39. Similarly, during trial a lawyer can see a report that the expert has used to refresh his memory either before or during testimony. Evid C §771(a); see §§1.38–1.39.

The uncertainty in knowing whether discovery will or will not be allowed under CCP §2016 leads some lawyers to instruct their experts to submit no written reports until shortly before trial. In some cases, however, a written report is helpful during settlement discussions.

B. [§5.34] Testing Expert's Hypothesis

The lawyer who calls an expert as his witness should have a working understanding of the technical subject on which the expert is to testify. If necessary, he should use the expert as his instructor so that he is thoroughly familiar with the facts, the analysis, and the technical reasons for the expert's conclusions. He should write out the expert's hypothesis before trial and study it carefully for weaknesses. If the case permits the expense, he should hire a second (nonwitness) expert to check the expert witness's tests and opinion. In any event, he should be certain that the expert witness has dealt honestly and fully with the opponent's probable theory and evidence; no expert should be put on the witness stand who has not done this.

C. [§5.35] Determining Form of Questions

The advisability of using questions that call for narrative rather than specific answers is discussed in §1.9. The lawyer is sometimes confident that the expert is equipped to testify in narrative form. A sample of this kind of examination appears at §5.62.

VII. QUALIFICATIONS

A. Sufficiency

1. [§5.36] To Permit Admission of Opinion Testimony

The lawyer who calls an expert witness must be prepared to demonstrate to the trial judge that the witness has the requisite skill, experience, training, or education in the subject about which he is testifying. Evid C §720(a). See generally §1.19. The judge may require these special qualifications to be established before the expert is allowed to state his opinion (Evid C §§720(b), 802), and the judge's ruling on the sufficiency of qualifications and the subjects on which the expert can give opinion testimony will not be disturbed on appeal absent an abuse of discretion (*People v Haeussler* (1953) 41 C2d 252, 261, 260 P2d 8, 13).

University degrees are helpful in establishing expertise, but they are not indispensable. Nonprofessionals with sufficient practical experience are used as experts (see, *e.g., People v Smith* (1956) 142 CA2d 287, 292, 298 P2d 540, 543 (laboratory technician to identify blood and compare rug fibers); *Risley v Lenwell* (1954) 129 CA2d 608, 631, 277 P2d 897, 913 (police officer to show proper truck loading practice); *Robinson v Kelly* (1949) 95 CA2d 320, 325, 212 P2d 921, 924 (private investigator on significance of gouge marks in road); *Lemley v Doak Gas Engine Co.* (1919) 40 CA 146, 151, 180 P 671, 674 (machinist who had worked extensively on type of engine in question).

If the proposed expert lacks formal educational qualifications, the lawyer must demonstrate clearly that his practical experience permits him to speak authoritatively on the subject.

2. [§5.37] To Gain Jurors' Confidence

The lawyer elicits a witness's qualifications for the benefit of the jurors as well as the judge (§5.36). Although the court's ruling that a witness qualifies as an expert is binding on the jurors, they may consider his qualifications in determining the weight to be given his testimony. Official Comment to Evidence Code §720; *Pfingsten v Westenhaver* (1952) 39 C2d 12, 244 P2d 395. There is no doubt that the better a witness is shown to be qualified in his field, the better he will command the respect and confidence of the jurors. But the lawyer must maintain a proper perspective. An overelaborate examination on qualifications may bore jurors before the substance is reached or lead them to suspect that the emphasis on qualifications is intended to cover weaknesses in the client's case.

TECHNICAL EXPERTS §5.39

B. [§5.38] *Handling Offers To Concede Qualifications*

It is seldom to the benefit of the lawyer calling an expert witness to forgo examining him on his qualifications. Offers by the opposing attorney to concede must therefore be anticipated. See generally §1.22.

C. [§5.39] *Particular Items: Checklist*

Before counsel calls his expert to the witness stand he should acquaint himself thoroughly with the witness's background so that he can elicit from him the facts that lend stature to his opinion. This section contains a checklist that can be used in interviewing the expert and planning an effective presentation of his qualifications. (Sections 5.40–5.57 contain sample question-answer dialogues covering these items.)

1. Name
2. Business address
3. Length of local residence or employment
4. Profession or occupation — define and explain
5. Professional registration or license
6. Education and degrees
   a. Professional man: university attended, earned and honorary degrees
   b. Nonprofessional: level of schooling attained, technical training (civilian and military)
7. Specialization within profession or occupation — define and explain
8. Present employment:
   a. By whom employed
   b. How long
   c. Where
   d. Capacity
   e. Duties
      (1) Consultant: projects undertaken, significant clients, geographic location of work, amount of consultative work, and if with large firm, number of partners, associates, technicians employed, etc.
      (2) Professor: university, position on faculty, subjects taught, research conducted, laboratories supervised, major fellowships or lectureships, nature and amount of practical experience and consultation work, etc.
      (3) Nonprofessional: nature and variety of work performed, specialization experience, training and experience with relevant equipment or operation, etc.
9. Previous professional or occupational experience (as in 8 above)
10. Professional experience while in military (as in 8 above)
11. Professional society memberships; offices held
12. Lecturing or teaching
13. Authorship (books, articles, professional papers at conventions, etc.)

§5.40 TECHNICAL EXPERTS

14. Patents
15. Consultation experience
16. Knowledge of condition, substance, equipment, or operation in issue

1. [§5.40] Name; Address; Occupation

Q. State your name and address, please.
A. ....
Q. What is your business address?
A. ....
Q. How long have you [lived/practiced your profession] in this area?
A. ....
Q. What is your profession?
A. ....
Q. What is a [mechanical engineer]?
A. ....

Comment: See §§5.8–5.21 for descriptions of specialties.

2. [§5.41] Registration and Licenses

Q. Are you a registered [mechanical engineer] in California?
A. Yes, I am.

Comment: The Business and Professions Code contains statutes regulating the registration and licensing of, among others, pharmacists (§4000 et seq), architects (§5500 et seq), professional engineers (§6700 et seq), contractors (§7000 et seq), geologists (§7800 et seq), and land surveyors (§8700 et seq).

Professional engineers are registered in the categories of chemical, civil, industrial, mechanical, metallurgical, petroleum, and structural engineers. Unless a man is registered by the California State Board of Registration for Professional Engineers he may not hold himself out as a "professional engineer," "consulting engineer," or as an engineer of any of the listed branches ("civil engineer" etc.). Bus & P C §§6704, 6787. A "structural engineer" is a registered civil engineer who has been found qualified by the board as a structural engineer. Bus & P C §§5501, 6736.

3. Education and Degrees

    a. [§5.42] Professionals

Q. Would you tell the jury something of your educational background?
A. I attended [the University of ....] and received a [Bachelor of Science] degree in [mechanical engineering] in 19.......

TECHNICAL EXPERTS   §5.44

[I received my Masters degree from the University of ....
in 19......, and my Ph.D. from the University of .... in
19......]

Comment: If the witness is in private business, rather than at a university, it is often helpful to show that he has kept current in his specialization. For example:

Q. Have you had any further education in the field of ....
   since you received your [Ph.D.]?
A. [I make it a practice to keep current by attending seminars given
   by various professional societies in my field; I would estimate that
   I attend ...... a year. In addition, I keep up with all the current
   literature; I do a great deal of reading.]

Comment: On the danger of referring to specific publications, see §5.64.

b. [§5.43] Nonprofessionals

If the expert witness is a mechanic, machinist, driver, equipment operator, etc., and has not had any higher education, the attorney can be brief.

Q. You graduated from high school?
A. Yes, I did.

Comment: See §5.51 on training received in the military.

4. Present Employment

a. [§5.44] Professor

Q. Where are you presently employed?
A. I am on the faculty of the [............... School at the University
   of ....].
Q. What is your rank?
A. [Professor.]
Q. How long have you been on the faculty?
A. For ...... years; since 19 ....
Q. What are your duties on the faculty?
A. [I teach courses in the department, supervise graduate and post-
   graduate students, and I supervise the research done by the
   .... Research Institute at the University.]
Q. [What sort of problems are handled by the institute?]
A. ....

b. [§5.45] Officer of Research or Consulting Firm

Q. Where are you presently employed?
A. I am the [president] of [name of corporation/laboratory/etc.].
Q. What does your [company/laboratory] do?
A. [We test and develop various chemicals used in research and industry.]
Q. How many employees does your [company/laboratory] have?
A. There are ...... chemists, ... technicians, and about ...... other employees; about ...... altogether.
Q. You mentioned that you are the [president] of the [company/laboratory]. Are you an active [president]?
A. [Yes, I am the head administrative officer.]
Q. Is the work of your [company/laboratory] limited to California?
A. No, we have clients [in all western states/throughout the country/in this country and in Europe.]

c. [§5.46] Employee of Defendant Company

Many attorneys believe that it is advisable to tell the jury immediately if the witness is associated with the company that is a party to the lawsuit. If his other qualifications are discussed first and his association with the defendant is not brought out immediately, it may appear that counsel is attempting to hide or gloss over his association.

Q. Are you employed by the .... Company?
A. Yes, I am.
Q. What is your position?
A. I am [chief engineer of the Department of Field Engineering].
Q. What are your duties in this position?
A. [It is a consulting and advisory position; I supervise a staff of engineers who advise our various field offices on engineering problems as they arise.]
Q. When did you join the .... Company?
A. In 19.......
Q. What was your position at that time?
A. I was employed as [an associate engineer, designing and developing ....]
Q. What other positions have you held with the company?
A. ....

d. [§5.47] Nonprofessional

Q. By whom are you employed?
A. The .... Company.

TECHNICAL EXPERTS §5.51

Q. How long have you been with the .... Company?
A. For ...... years.
Q. What type of work do you do?
A. ....

5. Specialization

a. [§5.48] Professional

Q. Do you have any specialty within your field?
A. Yes, I specialize in [automotive engineering].
Q. What does [an automotive engineer] do?
A. ....

b. [§5.49] Nonprofessional

Q. How long have you been [operating cranes]?
A. ...... years.
Q. Have you worked with a variety of [cranes]?
A. Yes.
Q. How many different types?
A. About ....
Q. What sort of work do [these cranes] perform?
A. ....
Q. Have you ever supervised other [crane operators]?
A. Yes.
Q. When was that?
A. [From 19...... until now; I often supervise other men now.]

6. [§5.50] Previous Employment

Q. Would you tell the jury what employment you had before you assumed your present position?
A. ....

7. [§5.51] Military Service

Q. Were you in the service?
A. Yes. [I was in the Army from 19...... to 19.......]
Q. And did your work in the [Army] involve [chemistry]?
A. Yes. [I was assigned to the chemical warfare division of the Corps of Engineers.]
Q. What were your duties?
A. [I supervised men in the uses of various chemicals and handled the logistics of chemicals and their storage.]

Comment: Any relevant training received in the service should be brought out if the witness's educational qualifications are weak.

8. [§5.52] Professional Societies

Q. Do you belong to any professional [engineering] societies?
A. Yes, I am a member of the [American Society of Mechanical Engineers].
Q. What is the [American Society of Mechanical Engineers]?
A. ....
Q. How is membership obtained?
A. ....
Q. Have you held any offices in these societies?
A. Yes. [I am presently vice-president of ....]

9. [§5.53] Lecturing and Teaching

If the witness is a professor this material has already been covered in his description of his employment duties. See §5.44.

Q. Have you done any lecturing?
A. Yes, [I have delivered papers to the national convention of the American Society of Chemical Engineers].
Q. Have you done any teaching?
A. [When I first received my doctorate I taught at the .... University for about three years; since then I have had to resign from the faculty because of the demands of the laboratory.]

10. [§5.54] Authorship

Q. Have you published any books or articles?
A. Yes, I have published [a book on the subject of ...., and I have written several articles that have appeared in the Journal of .... and the Journal of ....]
Q. Did your book have more than one edition?
A. Yes, it is in its ...... edition.
Q. Has it been translated?
A. Yes, into [French/etc.].
Q. Is it used as a textbook?
A. Yes, it is.
Q. And is it used by [consulting engineers]?
A. Yes, it is.

11. [§5.55] Patents

Q. Do you hold any patents in the field of [chemical engineering]?

TECHNICAL EXPERTS §5.57

A. Yes.
Q. How many?
A. .... [And there are some pending.]

12. [§5.56] Consultation Experience in Other Cases

Q. Have you served as a consultant [in motor vehicle accident cases/on chemical engineering problems/etc.]?
A. Yes, I have.
Q. Can you estimate the number of times you have done so?
A. About ...... times.
Q. How long have you been doing this type of consultation?
A. For about ...... years; since 19.......
Q. Have you ever served as a consultant for plaintiffs in court cases?
A. Yes, I have.
Q. And for defendants also?
A. Yes.
Q. Then you do not specialize in either plaintiff's work or defense work?
A. No, I do not.

Comment: Counsel may then show that the witness has worked for people or companies of the same character as the opponent. For instance, if he were called by the plaintiff, with a trucking company as the defendant, counsel would ask:

Q. Have you ever been retained by a trucking company to make an accident investigation for it?
A. Yes, I have.
Q. More than once?
A. Yes, on several occasions.
Q. Could you name trucking firms you have had as clients?
A. Yes. .... and ....

13. [§5.57] Knowledge of Subject in Issue

As a final step in stating his qualifications, the expert witness may relate his training and experience to the particular product, substance, condition, equipment, or operation in issue. For example, a chemist who is to give an opinion on the effects of a certain cleaning fluid on humans might testify as follows:

Q. [Dr./Professor/Mr.] ...., have you done any [medical or drug research]?

§5.57   TECHNICAL EXPERTS

A. Yes, I have.
Q. What have you done in this field?
A. My [laboratory] has had contracts with the [National Cancer Institute] relating to the problem of .... We also have had contracts with .... to do research related to the effects of [certain drugs on the heart], and with [pharmaceutical houses] on [toxicity and the nervous system].
Q. Are you acquainted with the [chemical composition] of [the cleaning product called ....]?
A. Yes, I am.
Q. Did you investigate it at my request?
A. That's right.
Q. What are the [principal ingredients of this product]?
A. [Sodium hydroxide and ....]
Q. Would it be fair to say that [sodium hydroxide] is the main active ingredient?
A. Yes. In fact it says so on the label.
Q. Have you had occasion to use [sodium hydroxide]?
A. Many times.
Q. In your laboratory?
A. Yes.
Q. In industry?
A. Yes.
Q. In reactions?
A. Yes.
Q. Did you use it [when you taught chemistry]?
A. Yes, of course.
Q. Have you had occasion to read about [sodium hydroxide] in writings of professional articles that you have referred to?
A. Yes.
Q. Have you purchased [sodium hydroxide] for your laboratory or for the university or for the various companies you have worked with?
A. Yes, I have.
Q. [Doctor], have you had occasion when working in your field as a chemist to supervise the safety of people handling [sodium hydroxide]?
A. Yes, I have.
Q. Could you tell us the circumstances of that?
A. For about a five-year period when I was employed by .... Research Laboratory I was on the safety committee. We monitored the over-all company safety programs in terms of a research

TECHNICAL EXPERTS §5.59

laboratory. We instructed personnel in the handling of [sodium hydroxide] and other chemicals.
Q. When you were associated with the staff at .... University, did you have any responsibility for supervising the safety of people who worked in the laboratory?
A. Yes, I did.
Q. Who were those people?
A. Other faculty members, graduate students, undergraduates, and technicians.
Q. Are there hazards to human beings associated with the handling of these chemicals?
A. Yes, there are.
Q. And are you acquainted with the nature of these hazards?
A. Yes.
Q. And you know what precautions are usually taken in laboratories and in industry?
A. Yes.

VIII. ELICITING OPINION TESTIMONY

A. [§5.58] Admissibility

The word "opinion," as used in the Evidence Code, includes "all opinions, inferences, conclusions and other subjective statements made by a witness." Official Comment preceding Evidence Code §800. An expert witness's opinion testimony is limited to subjects that are "sufficiently beyond common experience" that the opinion of an expert would assist the trier of fact. Evid C §801(a). See §1.24 for general discussion of statutory requirements and §1.25 on subjects of opinion testimony.

In addition, the expert's opinion must be based on matter contemplated by Evid C §801(b). See §§1.26–1.27 for general discussion of bases of opinion testimony and on stating the bases and reasons for opinion. See also §§5.60–5.66 on bases of technical experts' opinions.

If the expert's opinion is otherwise admissible, it is not objectionable on the ground that it "embraces the ultimate issue to be decided by the trier of fact." Evid C §805.

B. [§5.59] Showing Subject of Opinion

In the process of qualifying the witness to testify as an expert, the lawyer has usually made the jury aware of the subject on which the expert has been called to testify. The lawyer can also define the problem specifically as he asks the expert witness whether he has an opinion on the particular problem at hand. For example:

Q. [Professor/Dr./Mr.] ...., have you formed an opinion on whether [the brakes on (defendant's/plaintiff's) automobile were in good working condition at the time of the accident]?
A. Yes, I have.

C. [§5.60] *Stating Bases of Opinions*

An expert may state on direct examination the reasons for his opinion and the matter on which it is based; and in some cases the trial judge may require him to do so before he states his opinion. Evid C §802. See generally §1.27. Common bases for technical opinions are discussed in §§5.61–5.66.

1. [§5.61] Facts in Evidence

An expert can base opinion testimony on facts that he perceived for himself or on facts that were "made known to him at or before the hearing" (Evid C §801); *Rosenberg v Goldstein* (1966) 247 CA2d 25, 30, 55 CR 306, 309. Witnesses may have testified about facts earlier in the trial or they may have been placed in evidence in the pleadings, stipulations, depositions, or answers to interrogatories or requests for admission. The lawyer calling him usually wants to ensure that any necessary facts not generated by the expert's own investigation have already been introduced through testimony, exhibits, or other means. He may then (a) ask the expert to state the facts and assumptions on which he proceeded in forming his opinion, or (b) propose hypothetical questions (see §1.28) to the expert.

For example, the examination of a brake expert in a case of allegedly defective brake design would be made after other evidence had been produced during trial, such as the weather on the day in question, the terrain, the age of the car, the history of its maintenance, etc. The expert could then testify about the weight and structure of the particular vehicle, the characteristics of its braking system, the type of brake fluid used, etc.

In some cases the lawyer cannot schedule his witnesses to ensure that there is already evidence to support all of the facts. If an objection is raised that a proper foundation has not been shown for the expert's opinion testimony, the lawyer calling him can ask the court's permission to connect the testimony by proving the omitted fact later.

TECHNICAL EXPERTS §5.63

2. [§5.62] Expert's Perceptions; Tests; Analyses

An expert, like any other witness, can testify about relevant matters that he perceived for himself, including tests and analyses that he performed. These matters are "perceived by or personally known to the witness" (Evid C §801), and he may rely on them in forming his opinion.

In the following dialogue the expert testifies on his examination of a car's brakes and the tests he performed. This dialogue uses general questions that call for narrative answers; with other witnesses the lawyer might choose to ask more detailed questions that require specific and shorter answers. See §§1.9–1.12 on the form of questions.

Q. Did you make an examination of the braking system on the defendant's car?
A. I did.
Q. Will you describe that examination to us?
A. ....
Q. Did you perform any further inspections?
A. No, that was the extent of my inspection.
Q. Did you perform any tests?
A. Yes, I did.
Q. Will you describe them, please?
A. ....
Q. Are there ways of determining how fast a vehicle can stop at a specific speed?

Comment: The attorney is, in effect, asking the witness to state if he relied on scientifically proved assumptions or mathematical formulas in making his determinations.

A. Yes. To do this I computed, mathematically, by the use of various formulas, the ratio of braking area to weight to determine what the stopping distance would normally be at various speeds.

3. [§5.63] Expert's Special Qualifications

An expert's special knowledge, skill, experience, training, and education are expressly made proper bases of his opinion. Evid C §801(b). This is true whether he is a professional (*e.g.,* an engineer) or a nonprofessional. For example, a truck mechanic who qualifies as an expert can properly rely on his years of experience maintaining and repairing the type of truck in question.

§5.64 TECHNICAL EXPERTS

An example of testimony that assumes this experience and knowledge is the following statement by a brake expert:

Q. Could there have been any loss of hydraulic fluid from the braking system?
A. No.
Q. How did you determine this?
A. The master cylinder was full and I found no leaks there or in the brake lines. My experience is that if there had been any leakage at the wheel cylinders, there would have been traces of hydraulic fluid on the brake linings, but here the linings were not stained or glazed. Further, my tests of the fluid, showed that it did not vaporize until heated to temperatures much higher than the temperatures that we find in the operation of automobile braking systems.

4. [§5.64] Books; Treatises; Other Literature

In qualifying an expert, lawyers can bring out that he reads current literature to maintain his knowledge in his specialty. See §5.42. The lawyer must use caution making this inquiry. If the expert testifies that in forming his opinion he referred to, considered, or relied on a particular "scientific, technical, or professional text, treatise, journal or similar publication," he may be cross-examined on its content or tenor. Evid C §721(b). Even the best prepared expert witness can be embarrassed by detailed questioning on the contents of a treatise. See generally §2.19. Therefore, in most situations lawyers attempt to avoid having their experts express any reliance on these materials. An exception to this is in a case where the expert must base his opinion, at least in part, on technical manuals issued in connection with a specific piece of equipment. In these instances, the expert must be warned before trial that he may encounter thorough cross-examination on the publications and should prepare himself accordingly.

An expert testifying about alleged defects in the brakes of a motor vehicle, for example, might be questioned as follows about his reliance on technical publications:

Q. In reaching your conclusion did you consider any printed materials?
A. Yes. I consulted the literature put out by the automobile manufacturer about the schematic construction of the braking system. I also considered literature put out by the brake fluid manufacturer about its qualities at high temperatures.

TECHNICAL EXPERTS §5.67

5. [§5.65] Community and Industry Standards

The technical expert often uses customs and practices in the pertinent industry in forming his opinion about whether the equipment was defective, sufficient safety was provided, etc. Experts may give testimony on the recognized and accepted operating standards and practices in their profession or business. See, *e.g., Rosenberg v Goldstein* (1966) 247 CA2d 25, 29, 55 CR 306, 309 (standards and practice in lawn sprinkler installation business); *Reynolds v National Gas Equip., Inc.* (1960) 184 CA2d 724, 738, 7 CR 879, 888 (accepted engineering practice in gas burner design); *Blinkinsop v Weber* (1948) 85 CA2d 276, 283, 193 P2d 96, 100 (accepted construction and architectural practice).

For example, when brake design is alleged to be defective in a motor vehicle case, a brake expert's testimony that he made tests and analyses and studied schematic drawings and other instructional literature put out by the manufacturer of the brake system (see §5.64) can be followed by his testimony about the practice of brake manufacturers in general.

Q. Did you compare these brakes against standards for design of brakes in the brake industry?
A. Yes.
Q. What did you do?
A. I mathematically checked the design factors [and found the design of these brakes to be in accordance with the standard design of braking systems commonly used on vehicles of this weight and type].

6. [§5.66] Standards Set by Statute and Official Regulation

In forming his opinion, the technical expert may also rely on statutory and official administrative regulations in effect when the accident occurred. He may testify on relevant safety orders, construction standards, etc. See *Alber v Owens* (1967) 66 C2d 790, 800, 59 CR 117, 124 (safe place to work case under Lab C §6400; testimony on construction and safety orders (8 Cal Adm C).

See §§20.34–20.37 on judicial notice of statutes, ordinances, and official rules and regulations.

D. [§5.67] *Expressing Opinion*

After the expert has testified about the facts and other bases on

§5.68 TECHNICAL EXPERTS

which he proceeded (see §§5.61–5.65), he states his conclusion on the particular question.

Q. Based on [your examination of the parts of the braking system that you have made and the tests and analysis that you have described], have you reached an opinion about whether the [brakes on the (plaintiff's/defendant's) automobile were in good working condition at the time of the accident]?
A. Yes, I have.
Q. What is your opinion?
A. My opinion is that the [brakes on (plaintiff's/defendant's) car were in good working order].

E. [§5.68] *Stating Reasons for Opinion*

An expert opinion is only as good as the reasoning behind it, and the jury considers the basis for the expert's conclusions when weighing its validity. Frequently the basis for the opinion is apparent from the witness's testimony about the facts that he relied on, the tests that he performed, and the analysis that he made. By asking the witness to state the reasons for the opinion he has just expressed, the expert is given the opportunity to sum up all the scientific evidence supporting his conclusion. For example:

Q. What are the reasons for your opinion that [these brakes were not defective]?
A. [I examined the car thoroughly and made a minute inspection of the brakes and the entire braking system. I tested the braking system using greater pressure than would ever be applied in operating it on the road, and I found that the brakes operated well; there were no leaks in the brake fluid. I checked the design factors mathematically and found the design to be in accordance with industry standards in vehicles of this weight and type. I tested the vehicle by driving it over the same territory for the same period that the [plaintiff/defendant] testified [in his deposition] that he traveled. I was able to uncover nothing in my examination and in all of my tests indicating there was anything at all wrong with these brakes.]

6

Medical Experts

I. [§6.1] Reasons for Calling Medical Experts

II. [§6.2] Content and Sequence of Testimony

III. Evidentiary Privileges
   A. [§6.3] Attorney-Client
   B. [§6.4] Physician-Patient; Patient-Litigant Exception

IV. [§6.5] Qualifications
   A. Sufficiency
      1. [§6.6] Licensed Doctors
      2. [§6.7] Nondoctors
   B. Form of Questions
      1. [§6.8] General
      2. [§6.9] Specific
   C. [§6.10] Particular Items
      1. [§6.11] Name; Profession; Office Address
      2. [§6.12] License
      3. [§6.13] Education and Degrees
      4. [§6.14] Internship and Residency
      5. [§6.15] Military Service
      6. [§6.16] Private Practice: Entry; Duration
      7. Nature of Practice
         a. [§6.17] General
         b. [§6.18] Specialty: Orthopedic Surgery
            (1) [§6.19] Training and Experience
            (2) [§6.20] Board Certification
      8. [§6.21] Medical Society Memberships
      9. [§6.22] Teaching and Lecturing
      10. [§6.23] Hospital Staff Memberships

MEDICAL EXPERTS

11. [§6.24] Authorship
12. [§6.25] Familiarity with Medical Literature
13. [§6.26] Honors; Prizes; Special Recognition

V. Using Medical Records, Reports, and Exhibits

A. [§6.27] Types
B. [§6.28] Refreshing Memory

VI. [§6.29] Occasion for Seeing Patient: Professional Relationship

A. [§6.30] Personal or Family Physician
B. [§6.31] Medical-Legal Examiner

VII. [§6.32] Patient's Medical History

A. [§6.33] Admissibility
   1. [§6.34] Under Hearsay Rule Exceptions
   2. [§6.35] Solely To Show Basis of Opinion
B. [§6.36] Nature and Diagnostic Importance
C. [§6.37] Symptoms; Subjective Signs
D. [§6.38] Circumstances of Accident
E. [§6.39] Preaccident History

VIII. [§6.40] Physical Examination and Findings

A. [§6.41] Admissibility
B. [§6.42] Using Specific Questions
C. [§6.43] Character and Type of Examination
D. [§6.44] General Appearance and Mental Status
E. [§6.45] Explaining Medical Terms and Injuries
F. [§6.46] Connecting Findings to Injuries
G. [§6.47] Findings as Injuries
H. [§6.48] Clinical Tests and Manipulations
I. [§6.49] Absent and Negative Findings
J. [§6.50] Explaining Failure To Make Observation or Test

IX. [§6.51] Special Diagnostic Procedures

A. [§6.52] Admissibility
B. [§6.53] Extent of Testimony

X. [§6.54] Reports from Other Examiners

A. [§6.55] Determining Whether To Call Outside Consultant
B. Admissibility
   1. [§6.56] To Show Basis of Referring Doctor's Opinions

MEDICAL EXPERTS §6.1

      2. [§6.57] Extent of Showing
   C. [§6.58] Identity and Reliability of Tester or Examiner
   D. [§6.59] Referral as Customary Medical Practice
   E. [§6.60] Reasons for Test or Examination
   F. [§6.61] Return and Identity of Results and Report
   G. [§6.62] Witness's Reliance
   H. [§6.63] Contents

  XI. Medical Opinion Testimony
   A. [§6.64] Admissibility
     1. [§6.65] Proper Bases
     2. [§6.66] Improper Bases
     3. [§6.67] Procedures for Showing Bases and Reasons
   B. [§6.68] Diagnosis: Nature and Extent of Injuries
     1. [§6.69] Admissibility
     2. [§6.70] Relating Diagnoses to Injuries
   C. [§6.71] Cause of Injuries
     1. [§6.72] Value of Causation Testimony
     2. [§6.73] Admissibility
     3. [§6.74] Form of Testimony
   D. [§6.75] Prognosis: Continuing, Permanent, and Future Injuries
     1. [§6.76] Admissibility
     2. [§6.77] Reasonable Medical Certainty
     3. [§6.78] Continuing Conditions; Permanency
     4. [§6.79] Future Conditions

I. [§6.1] REASONS FOR CALLING MEDICAL EXPERTS

    There is a definite correlation between the size of personal injury verdicts and the effectiveness of testimony by medical experts. Well-prepared and well-presented medical testimony carries weight and convinces triers of fact. Although television and popular books have made today's judges and jurors more sophisticated about medical terminology and concepts, they still depend on the testimony of medical doctors for a clear and authoritative picture of the plaintiff's injuries and their effect on his life.

    Plaintiff's lawyers use medical experts to show (a) the existence, nature, and extent of injuries; (b) the causal connection between the claimed injuries and the accident; (c) the duration and degree of disability and suffering and their probably future course; (d) the necessity for past and probable future treatment; and (e) the amount and reasonableness of charges for treatment. In medical malpractice cases, expert medical testimony is also used to establish that a defendant's conduct failed to meet the applicable medical standard.

Defendants use medical witnesses to (a) refute false, exaggerated, and unsound claims of injury; (b) show the absence of a causal connection between claimed injuries and defendant's alleged misconduct; (c) point up the probabilities for rehabilitation; and (d) provide a more conservative assessment of plaintiff's medical needs.

Expert medical testimony is not required in all personal injury cases, although it is nearly always valuable. The plaintiff and other lay witnesses often can adequately describe the nature and extent of plaintiff's injuries, and hospital records and medical reports can be used to supply medical evidence. However, most experienced trial lawyers consider it unwise to try personal injury cases without calling a medical expert.

II. [§6.2] CONTENT AND SEQUENCE OF TESTIMONY

Medical experts testify about conditions they personally have perceived (Evid C §702), state their opinion testimony (Evid C §801), and state the reasons and bases for their opinions (Evid C §802). See §§1.19–1.30 for a general discussion of expert testimony. The lawyer should plan in advance the order in which to elicit this mixture of observed facts, opinions, and other matter to gain and keep the attention of the trier of fact and to emphasize favorable evidence.

Doctors often testify more comfortably when they follow a standard sequence that parallels the general order of clinical examinations and medical report forms. A medical witness usually begins by stating his qualifications and his reason for seeing the patient. He continues by recounting what the patient or other persons told him about the onset, progress, and apparent causes of the injuries (medical history) and what he learned from the patient's medical records. He describes what he observed when he examined the patient and tells what he learned from laboratory, electrographic, and other special reports and procedures and from other doctors to whom the patient was referred. He may describe the treatment given and the patient's response to it. The foregoing testimony establishes the bases of the doctor's opinions, and parts of it are direct evidence of the plaintiff's injuries. The witness usually concludes by stating his opinions and the reasons for them.

Attorneys can vary this standard sequence to give the medical testimony greater impact. Sometimes it is more effective to have the doctor first state one or more opinions, then describe the history, examination, etc., to show the reasons for his conclusions. Or, as a

MEDICAL EXPERTS §6.4

doctor describes his examination and findings, counsel may elicit the doctor's conclusions from each separate piece of information. In other cases, an attorney might question a doctor about each separate item of injury, showing the nature, causes, and probable duration of each injury and the information that led to those determinations.

III. EVIDENTIARY PRIVILEGES

A. [§6.3] *Attorney-Client*

When a medical expert has seen a patient for the purpose of transmitting information from and about the patient to the patient's lawyer, or to help the lawyer evaluate the patient's condition, the attorney-client privilege can be invoked to prevent the expert from disclosing or testifying about the patient's physical and mental condition. Evid C §§952–954; *San Francisco v Superior Court* (1951) 37 C2d 227, 234, 231 P2d 26, 29. See also CALIFORNIA TRIAL OBJECTIONS §35.5 (Cal CEB 1967); Witkin, CALIFORNIA EVIDENCE §§806, 810–811 (2d ed, 1966).

The "confidential communications" protected by the privilege include (1) what the patient told the doctor about his condition and how his injuries were incurred; (2) what the doctor learned by examining the patient and from laboratory tests and other special procedures; and (3) the doctor's opinions, advice, and reports. The attorney-client privilege cannot be used, however, to prevent a doctor from testifying about information he obtained other than while examining the patient as the lawyer's agent. Nor can a lawyer cause a doctor's knowledge or opinions to become privileged by having the doctor conduct a medical-legal examination or prepare a medical-legal report. *San Francisco Unified School Dist. v Superior Court* (1961) 55 C2d 451, 11 CR 373; see Witkin, EVIDENCE §810.

B. [§6.4] *Physician-Patient; Patient-Litigant Exception*

There is a patient-litigant exception to the physician-patient and psychotherapist-patient privileges in personal injury and wrongful death cases. Evid C §§996, 1016; *San Francisco v Superior Court* (1951) 37 C2d 227, 232, 231 P2d 26, 28. See also CALIFORNIA TRIAL OBJECTIONS §§36.8, 37.8 (Cal CEB 1967); Witkin, CALIFORNIA EVIDENCE §§852, 859 (2d ed, 1966). The exception prevents a plaintiff from tendering the issue of his own condition, or that of his child or decedent, and then claiming a privilege on doctors' information and opinions about that condition.

Defendants sued for negligence, however, can use the physician-patient privilege to prevent the introduction of medical evidence of their own physical or mental condition or that of a person to whom they entrusted their vehicle. The patient-litigant exception to the privilege does not apply, because the defendant did not tender the issue of his negligence merely by filing an answer denying negligence. *Carlton v Superior Court* (1968) 261 C2d 282, 67 CR 568; TRIAL OBJECTIONS §36.8.

There is a question whether a plaintiff can invoke the physician-patient privilege to prevent a doctor from testifying about, for example, the plaintiff's bad eyesight or intoxication when the accident occurred. Some lawyers argue that the patient-litigant exception permits disclosure of medical information relating to the liability issues as well as to the damages issues. See TRIAL OBJECTIONS §36.8. Other attorneys argue that eye trouble and intoxication are not issues the plaintiff has tendered. Just as a defendant does not tender the issue of his liability by denying allegations of negligence, the plaintiff does not tender the issue of his negligence by filing a complaint.

In certain circumstances, doctors can invoke a patient's privilege. See Evid C §§994–995, 1014–1015. However, doctors do not have a personal privilege to refrain from testifying as expert witnesses even in cases in which they are not paid an expert witness fee in excess of the ordinary witness fee. *San Francisco v Superior Court, supra,* 37 C2d at 233, 231 P2d at 29. Like any other witness giving information relevant to the issues, they must testify about their knowledge of special facts about the patient. The doctor is probably also required to testify in the form of an opinion, especially since the passage of Govt C §68092.5, which provides for the payment of a court-determined fee to a nonparty witness who is required to give expert opinion testimony.

IV. [§6.5] QUALIFICATIONS

A medical witness's qualifications are his special knowledge, skill, experience, training, and education in medicine or that branch of medical knowledge to which his testimony relates. For a general discussion of the qualifications of expert witnesses, see §§1.19–1.23.

There is no need to show a witness's special qualifications unless another party objects to his testifying as an expert. See Evid C §720. See also §1.19. However, for the reasons listed in §1.20, the qualifications of medical witnesses are frequently shown even though opposing counsel have offered to concede them. See §1.22 on handling offers to concede qualifications.

MEDICAL EXPERTS   §6.7

A. *Sufficiency*

1. [§6.6] Licensed Doctors

Holding a medical degree or a license to practice medicine in California does not automatically qualify a person to testify as a medical expert. Trial judges usually accept licensed physicians and surgeons as experts on the nature, extent, and causes of personal injuries, whether they are general practitioners or specialists, and even if they have not had special training or experience in areas related to the injuries in issue. See, *e.g., Rash v San Francisco* (1962) 200 CA2d 199, 206, 19 CR 266, 270 (surgeon can testify about nature and causes of brain injuries; he need not be neurologist). See also *Thompson v Long Beach* (1953) 41 C2d 235, 241, 259 P2d 649, 652 (general practitioners can testify about impaired vision, and their testimony may be accepted over that of eye specialists); *People v Haney* (1967) 249 CA2d 810, 817, 58 CR 36, 41 (general practitioner-autopsy surgeon can testify about sperm survival; he need not be expert on infertility); *Estate of Gore* (1953) 119 CA2d 796, 260 P2d 859 (eye, ear, nose, and throat specialist can testify about mental condition (testamentary capacity); he need not specialize in psychiatry).

In malpractice cases, however, physicians and surgeons testifying about the standard of practice in a special field of medicine should have some occupational experience in that field. See *Huffman v Lindquist* (1951) 37 C2d 465, 476, 234 P2d 34, 41; Witkin, CALIFORNIA EVIDENCE §§ 1176–1178 (2d ed, 1966).

2. [§6.7] Nondoctors

Nothing in the Evidence Code prohibits a person from testifying as an expert in a field related to medicine even though he does not hold a license to practice medicine or even an M.D. degree. See Witkin, CALIFORNIA EVIDENCE §411 (2d ed, 1966).

Physiologists, psychotherapists, chemists, and certain technicians are sometimes better trained and more experienced in limited areas of medical knowledge than physicians and surgeons. See, *e.g.,* Anno, 70 ALR2d 1029 (1960) (chemists can testify about effects of poisons on human body).

Further, such persons as nurses and chiropractors can be qualified to give opinion testimony. See *Longuy v La Societé Francaise de Bienfaisance Mutelle* (1921) 52 CA 370, 376, 198 P 1011, 1013 (nurse can testify on cause of death of child under nursing care); *People v Thompson* (1911) 16 CA 748, 753, 117 P 1033, 1035 (nurse can testify that tissue she saw was placental tissue); *Johnston v Peairs*

(1931) 117 CA 208, 216, 3 P2d 617, 620 (chiropractor can testify about injuries and their causes); Anno, 52 ALR2d 1384 (1957) (chiropractors as expert witnesses).

B. *Form of Questions*

1. [§6.8] General

Trial lawyers sometimes elicit testimony from a doctor about his qualifications by asking a general question such as: "Doctor, will you please turn to the jury and, without any undue modesty, tell them about your medical background, education, experience, and accomplishments?" The lawyer can then supplement the doctor's recital of his background by asking specific questions to bring out anything the doctor might have omitted and to highlight outstanding honors, skills, and achievements.

The use of a general question to elicit qualifications is particularly effective when the doctor is an experienced witness who can recite his background concisely, logically, and in an interesting manner. Since there is very little chance that the doctor's testimony about his qualifications will contain any inadmissible matter, opposing counsel should have no reason to object to a general question on grounds that it is too general, or calls for a narrative answer. See CALIFORNIA TRIAL OBJECTIONS §§9.2, 10.2 (Cal CEB 1967). See generally §1.9.

2. [§6.9] Specific

Some attorneys prefer to use specific questions to elicit each particular item of qualification. This approach is especially helpful with doctors who either are not comfortable on the witness stand or might give a dull or disjointed statement of their qualifications. The lawyer should avoid asking a question that might elicit a negative answer or show a deficiency in his qualifications. Thus, it is advisable either to ask questions from a written biographical statement supplied by the doctor or to go over proposed questions with him in advance.

C. [§6.10] *Particular Items*

The lawyer must decide how extensive his inquiry into the witness's special qualifications should be. He must bring out enough to qualify the witness to testify as an expert, and to serve the other purposes listed in §1.20. But he must avoid losing jury attention before the substance of the testimony is reached.

Sections 6.11–6.26 set forth questions that can be asked to qualify a medical doctor. The lawyer can choose from them the questions

MEDICAL EXPERTS §6.14

best asked of his medical witness, and add others to develop any additional achievements.

1. [§6.11] Name; Profession; Office Address

Q. Please state your name and profession.
A. My name is Dr. .... I am a physician and surgeon.

Comment: If the doctor practices locally, showing his office address can help identify him to the jury.

Q. Where do you practice, Doctor?
A. My office is at ...., here in ....

2. [§6.12] License

Q. Do you hold a license to practice medicine in California?
A. Yes.
Q. How long have you been licensed in this state?
A. .... years.
Q. Are you licensed to practice in any other states?
A. Yes, in ....
Q. When and where were you first licensed to practice medicine?
A. In 19...... in the state of ....

3. [§6.13] Education and Degrees

Q. Please tell us your college and medical school, when you graduated, and what degrees you received.
A. I received a Bachelor of [Arts/Science] degree from .... College in 19......, and my Doctor of Medicine degree from the medical school at .... University in 19.......
Q. Is that medical school accredited by the Council on Medical Education and Hospitals of the American Medical Association?
A. Yes.

4. [§6.14] Internship and Residency

Q. Did you serve an internship?
A. Yes.
Q. Where?
A. At .... Hospital in ....
Q. For how long?
A. ...... months.
Q. What residencies have you held?

§6.15 MEDICAL EXPERTS

A. I was a resident in [state specialty] at the .... Hospital in .... for a period of ...... years.

5. [§6.15] Military Service

Q. Dr. ...., please outline your medical experience in the armed forces.
A. [I was commissioned a Captain in the United States Army Medical Corps in 19...... and served as head of the .... Department at .... Army Hospital in .... for ...... years.]

6. [§6.16] Private Practice: Entry; Duration

Q. Did you enter private practice [after finishing your residency/after you were discharged from the armed forces]?
A. Yes.
Q. When was that?
A. ...., 19.......
Q. Have you been in private practice since that date?
A. Yes [except for (describe periods of special training or other experience)].
Q. How many years then have you been practicing medicine?
A. ......years.

7. Nature of Practice

a. [§6.17] General

Counsel should not seem to apologize for offering a general practitioner as an expert witness, even in trials in which testimony will be in the field of a medical specialty and specialists will also testify. Whenever possible, the doctor's special knowledge, training, and experience in situations like the one involved in the case should be shown.

Q. What is the nature of your practice?
A. I am in the general practice of medicine in ....
Q. Doctor, in the course of your practice, have you had occasion to diagnose and treat cases of ....?
A. Yes.
Q. Approximately how many of these cases have you seen?
A. During my residency, I saw as many as ......, and perhaps ...... more during my military service. Since I have been in private practice, I have seen an average of ...... of these cases every year.

MEDICAL EXPERTS §6.18

Q. Do you handle these cases yourself, or do you refer them to other doctors?
A. I handle them myself [except for a few, perhaps ...... a year, that present unusual complications; these I handle with the assistance of a consulting orthopedic surgeon].
Q. Have you done any postgraduate study or participated in any workshops or seminars dealing with the care and treatment of ....?
A. Yes.
Q. Please describe those briefly for us.
A. ....

b. [§6.18] Specialty: Orthopedic Surgery

A doctor calling himself a specialist is not necessarily more expert or knowledgeable in that specialty than any other doctor, but most doctors who engage in a specialty practice can show education, training, and experience in their specialty beyond that of nonspecialists. Jurors, at any rate, generally believe that specialists are more learned and skilled in their specialties than nonspecialists and often give greater weight to their testimony.

There are about 20 recognized medical specialties and a number of recognized subspecialties. In the following dialogues, specialty qualifications are shown as they might be elicited from an orthopedic surgeon. For question-answer dialogues illustrating the qualifications of other specialists, see 9 AM JUR PROOF OF FACTS 241–353 (1961).

Q. Dr. ...., do you specialize in your medical practice?
A. Yes.
Q. What is your specialty?
A. I am an orthopedic surgeon.
Q. Would you briefly describe the nature of your specialty?
A. An orthopedic surgeon deals with the corrective treatment of diseases and deformities in muscles, joints, and bones, including the spine.
Q. Do [ruptures of cervical intervertebral discs] fall within the province of orthopedic surgery?
A. Yes.
Q. And within your specialty of orthopedic surgery, do you practice a subspecialty?
A. [I try to limit my practice to cases involving injuries to the cervical spine, and I take referrals from other doctors only when they involve disease or injury in the cervical spine. However, that is

not a recognized subspecialty; there is no board or association of doctors who limit their practice to that extent.]

(1) [§6.19] Training and Experience

Q. What special training have you had in the field of orthopedic surgery?
A. [I participated in a program of resident orthopedic training at the .... Hospital for ...... years following a ......-year residency in general surgery at .... Hospital. In addition, I did a year of postgraduate study in the field of .... at the .... University Medical School.]
Q. In addition to that formal training, have you had practical experience in the field of orthopedic surgery?
A. Yes. [In 19......, I entered private practice as a specialist in orthopedic surgery, and I have practiced that specialty ever since.]
Q. In your practice have you seen cases of [describe injuries in issue]?
A. Yes.
Q. Approximately how many have you seen in your professional career?
A. During my residency in orthopedics, I probably saw ...... or more, and another ...... during my military service. In my practice I have seen an average of ...... per year.
Q. How do these patients come into your care?
A. Some contact me directly, but most are referred by other doctors.

(2) [§6.20] Board Certification

There are a score of specialty boards, organized by doctors for the purpose of elevating the standards of practice in given specialty areas. These boards certify, as fellows or diplomates, doctors who have met their standards of training and experience and have passed their written and oral examinations. Board certification is an indication of achievement, although it is not an infallible indicator of the ability or knowledge of a particular medical witness. A doctor may be a very knowledgeable and competent medical specialist without having obtained board certification.

Q. Are you certified as a specialist in orthopedic surgery by the American Board of Orthopaedic Surgery?
A. Yes.
Q. How long have you been certified?
A. Since 19........

MEDICAL EXPERTS §6.22

Q. What is the function of certification by a specialty board such as the American Board of Orthopaedic Surgery?
A. Certification shows that a doctor has met the board's requirements for training, skill, and experience in the specialty beyond what is required of physicians and surgeons generally.
Q. Do you have to be certified by the board in order to practice orthopedics?
A. No, any M.D. may practice orthopedics and call himself a specialist in orthopedics without being board-certified.
Q. Is certification by the American Board of Orthopaedic Surgery recognized by doctors, hospitals, and medical societies throughout the country as an indication of additional professional competence in the field of orthopedics?
A. It is.
Q. What requirements must you meet in order to be certified?
A. You must meet the board's requirements for postgraduate study and for residency in the specialty, and you must pass two examinations given by the board, one after two years of residency, and the other after two years of private practice.

8. [§6.21] Medical Society Memberships

Q. Do you belong to any medical societies or groups?
A. Yes. [I belong to the American Medical Association, the .... County Medical Society, and the Western Orthopaedic Association, and I am a Fellow of the American College of Surgeons.]
Q. Have you held offices in any of these organizations?
A. Yes.
Q. What offices?
A. ....

9. [§6.22] Teaching and Lecturing

Q. Have you done any teaching?
A. Yes. I am presently [an associate professor in orthopedics] at .... Medical School.
Q. How long have you held that position?
A. For ...... years.
Q. Any other teaching or lecturing?
A. Yes. [In 19......, I delivered a series of lectures to The .... Medical Society on the subject: .... In the summer of

§6.23   MEDICAL EXPERTS

19......, I was a staff consultant for a conference-workshop program held at the .... University Hospital on the treatment of ....]

Q. Who attended those programs?

A. [The lectures were attended by over ...... orthopedists from around the country, and there were ...... participants from the United States and many other countries at the conference-workshop.]

10. [§6.23] Hospital Staff Memberships

Q. Dr. ...., are you a member of the staff at any hospital?

A. Yes.

Q. What hospital or hospitals?

A. ....

Q. What is the significance of being on a hospital staff?

A. It means that I can admit my patients to these hospitals.

Q. What about a doctor who is not on a staff?

A. He cannot admit his patients, although if he already has a patient there, he may be allowed to treat that patient.

Q. Have you held any offices in connection with your staff membership at these hospitals?

A. Yes. [I was Chief of Staff at the .... Hospital from 19...... to 19....... I am presently Chief of Staff at .... Hospital; and I am Visiting Consulting Orthopedic Physician on the staff of .... and .... Hospitals.]

11. [§6.24] Authorship

Q. Dr. ...., have you written any books or articles [on the subjects of ....]?

A. Yes.

Q. Please tell us the titles of your books and articles, the dates they were published, and perhaps give us a brief idea of their subject matter.

A. ....

Q. Have you delivered papers before professional groups?

A. Yes. I have delivered more than ...... papers before various medical societies on topics related to ....

12. [§6.25] Familiarity with Medical Literature

To show that a doctor is well-read in the standard sources and keeps up with current medical literature, counsel may ask on direct examination what medical books and journals the witness regularly reads

MEDICAL EXPERTS §6.27

or consults. Often the very names of the publications are impressive. Further, having the doctor name a number of books and journals on direct examination can reduce the effect of the kind of cross-examination discussed in §2.19 in which the cross-examiner asks the doctor whether he has considered various texts and articles, hoping that a series of denials will make the doctor appear uninformed, and his medical knowledge limited and out of date. On the other hand, some lawyers feel that asking a doctor what books he has read furnishes adversaries with a list of publications that can be used in cross-examining the doctor. See §2.19.

A relevance objection to testimony about familiarity with medical literature is normally overruled. The testimony can be received to show part of the doctor's qualifications, *i.e.*, his continuing education.

Q. Dr. ...., in the course of your medical practice, do you regularly read and study various books and journals in the field of [orthopedics]?
A. I do.
Q. Do you do this on a regular basis?
A. Yes.
Q. Why do you look at these publications?
A. I look at some because they are the standard textbooks or reference works in the field. Others keep me up to date on new developments and the latest techniques.
Q. Please name some of the more important books and journals that you read.
A. ....

13. [§6.26] Honors; Prizes; Special Recognition

Before trial, the lawyer should determine whether the doctor has any accomplishments not covered by the preceding questions. If he has received honors, prizes, or special recognition for his work, questions eliciting these facts will put a finishing touch on his qualifications.

V. USING MEDICAL RECORDS, REPORTS, AND EXHIBITS

A. [§6.27] *Types*

In preparing to take testimony from a doctor, the lawyer should review all medical records and reports that relate to the patient. These include the records of each hospital or clinic to which he was admitted, the office records of each doctor who treated him, and the reports and notes of each doctor or technician to whom he was sent for examination or testing.

Some of these documents can be used during the doctor's testimony. A treating doctor can refresh his memory from his office records or hospital records, and a consultant can use his report or notes. See §6.28. A medical witness can testify from and about the reports he received from other doctors and from technicians to show part of the basis for his opinions. See §§6.54–6.63. A doctor can also interpret and explain to the trier of fact the contents of a hospital or medical record that has been received in evidence. See §§13.20–13.40.

The lawyer should also consider whether the doctor's testimony can be made clearer by the use of exhibits such as X-rays and medical diagrams and models and appliances. See generally chaps 16, 18, 19.

B. [§6.28] *Refreshing Memory*

A doctor can use any writing, before trial or while he is testifying, to refresh his memory. Evid C §771; see generally §1.32. Commonly the writing used will be a report that the doctor has prepared or his office medical records for the patient. A doctor who treated the patient in a hospital can use the hospital record.

It is often a good tactic to have the doctor refer to a report or record while he is testifying. The doctor will be more comfortable and is more likely to testify in the sequence, phraseology, and detail that the lawyer has worked out with him before the trial. A doctor who appears to remember details about one of his many patients looks more like a professional witness than a practicing physician, and jurors often have greater faith in the accuracy of testimony that they can see is drawn directly from a report. The lawyer should ask a few questions to establish what record the doctor is referring to. For example:

Q. Dr. ……………, did you bring with you a copy of [your office medical records/the examination report you made] relating to [Mr. ……………/plaintiff]?
A. Yes, I did.
Q. When did you prepare that [record/report]?
A. [I made an entry in the file each time I saw him, and I put all the papers and reports I received about him in the file as they reached me./I made notes as I examined him, and dictated the report later that same day./Etc.]
Q. Would it assist you in testifying about your [treatment/evaluation] of [Mr. ……………/plaintiff] to refer to that [record/report]?
A. Yes, it would.

MEDICAL EXPERTS §6.30

Comment: Counsel can then question the witness directly, and the witness can answer, after referring to the writing, as if testifying from memory. It would be improper to ask the doctor, "What do your records say about . . . ?" unless the writing qualified as past recollection recorded. See §8.25. On the other hand, no harm is done if counsel occasionally says, for example, "Now, referring to your report, Doctor, tell us what findings you made when you examined his lumbar spine."

Adverse counsel is entitled (1) to inspect any writing the doctor uses, or has used, to refresh his memory; (2) to cross-examine the witness about it; and (3) to introduce pertinent portions in evidence. See §1.38.

VI. [§6.29] OCCASION FOR SEEING PATIENT: PROFESSIONAL RELATIONSHIP

It is helpful to show the professional capacity in which each medical witness saw the patient and the times and places of each examination or contact. Counsel should establish whether the witness was the patient's personal or family physician; a doctor on duty at a hospital emergency room or other treatment facility; a doctor to whom the patient went or was sent for treatment; a consultant to the treating doctor; a doctor to whom the patient was sent by his own or an adverse lawyer for a medical-legal examination and evaluation; or even a doctor who never examined the patient but is to testify on the basis of hypothetical facts.

The professional relationship between doctor and patient should be brought out in a positive way on direct examination, to enhance the doctor's testimony and forestall certain types of cross-examination. The times of examinations can be related to the date of the accident. See §§6.30–6.31 for two examples of showing professional relationship and occasion for seeing the patient.

A. [§6.30] *Personal or Family Physician*

If the medical witness is the patient's personal or family physician, his contacts over the years with the patient and his knowledge of his health and character can be emphasized. Even when the doctor is not a specialist in injuries of the type involved in the case, the jury can be shown why he is particularly qualified to testify about the patient.

Q. Dr. ...., how long have you been seeing [Mr. ..../ plaintiff] professionally?
A. Since 19.......

Q. Aside from the injuries he sustained in the accident that is involved in this lawsuit, how often would you say you have examined and treated him during that period?
A. ....
Q. Can you tell us briefly why you saw him on each of those occasions?
A. Yes. [I gave him a general physical examination on ...., 19......; prescribed for bronchitis on ...., 19......, etc.]
Q. When did you last see [Mr. ..../plaintiff] before ...., 19......, the date of the accident?
A. On ...., 19.......
Q. What was the state of his health on that date?
A. ....

Comment: If plaintiff did have medical problems before the accident, counsel may wish to go into greater detail about his prior health, especially conditions similar to those claimed to have resulted from the accident.

Q. When did you first see [Mr. ..../plaintiff] after ...., 19......?
A. On ...., 19.......
Q. What was the occasion for seeing him then?
A. [He called me from his home complaining of .... and requesting that I see him, and I made a house call at his home early that evening.]
Q. Did you examine [Mr. ..../plaintiff] on that occasion?
A. Yes.

B. [§6.31] *Medical-Legal Examiner*

When the medical witness is a doctor who examined the patient at the request of an attorney, an adverse lawyer can attack the witness's credibility and the weight of his testimony by raising a number of points, including: (1) The witness saw the patient only once; (2) he examined the patient for a brief period; (3) he examined the patient to prepare a report for a lawyer and to prepare to testify, rather than to treat the patient's injuries; (4) he is paid a fee for his report and for his court appearance; (5) he relies on referrals from lawyers for part of his income; (6) he is more a professional witness than a practicing physician; and (7) he testifies more for one side than another. See also §2.16 for a discussion of cross-examination under Evid C §722(b) on the compensation and expenses paid or to be paid an expert witness by the party who called him.

MEDICAL EXPERTS §6.31

Lawyers who call medical-legal examiners as witnesses sometimes try to anticipate these attacks by having the doctor frankly state the nature of his practice and his professional relationship to the patient. Some lawyers even try to build up a medical-legal examiner as an expert in forensic medicine, *i.e.,* a doctor particularly competent to probe and assess litigants' claimed injuries and to testify about them, uninfluenced by the friendship or compassion a treating doctor might feel for his patient.

Testimony about a doctor's practice, the fees he charges, and his professional relationship with a patient are relevant to his credibility but not to the medical issues in the case. The trial judge may think it improper on direct examination to bring out evidence of these matters to support credibility before credibility has been attacked. However, an adverse attorney raising the objection could lose favor with the trier of fact if he later tried to raise the same matters in cross-examination or argument.

Q. Dr. ...., when did you first see [Mr. ..../the plaintiff]?
A. ...., 19.......
Q. At whose request did you see him?
A. At your request.
Q. What was the purpose of your seeing him?
A. [To examine him, to hear his complaints, to determine the state of his health, and to prepare a report of my findings and conclusions from that examination.]

Comment: The following questions might be asked of a doctor a substantial part of whose practice is devoted to medical-legal examinations. The purpose is to reduce the effect of cross-examination on the same matters.

Q. Does the making of such examinations and the preparation of such reports form a regular part of your medical practice?
A. Yes, it does.
Q. About how many of these examinations do you do in the course of an average [year/month]?
A. Approximately ....
Q. What percentage of your practice do these examinations comprise?
A. About ...... percent.
Q. And can you give us an estimate of how often you have testified as a medical expert?
A. Yes. ....
Q. Doctor, have you made examinations, prepared reports, and

§6.31   MEDICAL EXPERTS

    testified in law suits at the request of attorneys representing injured persons as well as attorneys representing defendants?
A. Yes, I have.

Comment: The next questions relate to the doctor's fee, although they do not call for the amount. Many lawyers would ask no questions about fees on direct examination unless they were reasonably certain that the cross-examiner would raise the question anyway (under Evid C §722(b)), and in those situations some lawyers might even bring out the amount.

Q. Do you have a regular rate or fee that you charge for an examination and report and an additional rate when you take time from your practice to appear and testify in court?
A. Yes.
Q. Is your fee in this case in any way dependant on the outcome of this lawsuit?
A. No.
Q. How long did this examination of [Mr. ..../plaintiff] take?
A. About ...... minutes.
Q. Is that about the time that you customarily spend on these examinations?
A. Yes.

Comment: An adverse attorney sometimes attacks a medical-legal examiner on the basis that he saw the patient only once, and then for a short time.

Q. Dr. ...., in the course of your practice, are patients referred to you by other doctors for your examination, evaluation, and conclusions as a consultant?
A. They are.
Q. Is that a common medical practice even in cases in which no litigation is involved?
A. Yes.
Q. In those cases, do you make an examination and a report for the other doctor?
A. Yes.
Q. Have you seen [Mr. ..../plaintiff] professionally or examined him on any other occasions?
A. Not to my knowledge.

MEDICAL EXPERTS §6.34

VII. [§6.32] PATIENT'S MEDICAL HISTORY

A medical history is a patient's account of his past and present health and the symptoms of his disease. Taking a history is considered an important part of every clinical examination; if the patient is unable to give a history, the doctor will try to obtain the information from someone else. The doctor wants to know the patient's present complaints, how he incurred his injuries, what treatment he has received, and what other illnesses and injuries he has experienced. He may also ask about illnesses experienced by the patient's parents and family. The information gained is sometimes the principal or sole basis for the doctor's diagnosis, for there may be no determinative physical findings or laboratory test results.

Testimony about medical histories is elicited by both plaintiffs' and defendants' attorneys to show part of the basis for the opinions of their medical witnesses. Defense lawyers also look to medical histories given by plaintiffs for admissions about the extent of their injuries and how they were incurred. Conversely, plaintiffs' attorneys are often eager to have history testimony from medical witnesses that confirms or recapitulates the plaintiff's testimony about the nature and causes of his injuries.

A. [§6.33] *Admissibility*

A medical history is a statement the doctor hears from the patient (or some other person). A doctor may not give evidence about what the patient told him unless (1) the evidence can be received under some exception to the hearsay rule; (2) it is offered for some purpose other than to prove the truth of the matter stated; or (3) there is no objection to its admission. See Evid C §1200; CALIFORNIA TRIAL OBJECTIONS §§4.7, 19.4 (Cal CEB 1967).

1. [§6.34] Under Hearsay Rule Exceptions

When defense counsel elicits evidence of the plaintiff's medical history, the evidence can be received under the hearsay rule exception for admissions of a party. Evid C §1220. This exception does not apply if the history was given to the doctor by some person other than the plaintiff, except when the plaintiff is charged with the statement of another (*e.g.*, a parent suing for injury to a minor child under CCP §376 or an heir or representative suing for wrongful death under CCP §377). See Evid C §§1226–1227.

The part of the history comprising the patient's statements to the doctor of his present complaints and symptoms is usually received, even when offered by the plaintiff, under the exception for statements of existing mental or physical state. See Evid C §§1250, 1252; §6.37.

Other statutory exceptions to the hearsay rule that may apply under particular circumstances include spontaneous statement (Evid C §1240), dying declaration (Evid C §1242), and statement of declarant's previously existing mental or physical state (Evid C §§1251–1252; see §6.39).

2. [§6.35] Solely To Show Basis of Opinion

A medical witness can testify about a patient's medical history even though the statements by the patient or other person are not admissible under any hearsay rule exception. Under Evid C §802 an expert may state on direct examination the matter on which his opinion is based, and it is proper to base a medical opinion on a patient's statements concerning the history of his condition. See Official Comment to Evidence Code §801; *People v Wilson* (1944) 25 C2d 341, 348, 153 P2d 720, 724. However, the evidence is received only for the limited purpose of showing part of the basis for the doctor's opinions and conclusions, not to establish the truth of the matter stated. *People v Brown* (1958) 49 C2d 577, 585, 320 P2d 5, 10; *Johnson v Aetna Life Ins. Co.* (1963) 221 CA2d 247, 252, 34 CR 484, 487.

For foundation, it should be sufficient under Evid C §§801(b) and 802 for the doctor to testify that (a) the patient's history contributed to the formation of the doctor's diagnosis or other opinion, and (b) it is reasonable, or a customary medical practice, for doctors to rely on medical histories in forming medical opinions.

California decisions that predate the Evidence Code seem to say that a doctor can testify about what a patient stated to him only when he also declares that (a) the patient's statements were *necessary* to enable him to form an opinion about the nature and extent of the patient's disease or injury, and (b) the history actually constituted part of the basis for his opinions. See *People v Shattuck* (1895) 109 C 673, 678, 42 P 315, 316; *Johnson v Aetna Life Ins. Co., supra; Willoughby v Zylstra* (1935) 5 CA2d 297, 300, 42 P2d 685, 686. However, although the cases use the word "necessary," they do not directly hold that the doctor must use it, and trial judges should admit medical history testimony from a doctor who testifies, for example, that the history contributed to his opinions although he could have reached them without it.

Counsel for the opposing party is entitled to an instruction that the

MEDICAL EXPERTS §6.36

matter is admitted only for the limited purpose of showing the information on which the doctor based his opinions, and not as evidence of their own truth. See Evid C §355; BAJI No 2.43. If opposing counsel does not request the instruction, however, he may not complain on appeal. *Tierney v Charles Nelson Co.* (1937) 19 CA2d 34, 38, 64 P2d 1150, 1152.

A doctor can testify about a medical history even if it was given by someone other than the patient—especially if the patient was unconscious, a child, or otherwise unable to give a history, and the person giving it was relating facts perceived by or known to him. See *People v Powell* (1949) 34 C2d 196, 204, 208 P2d 974, 979; *People v Terrell* (1955) 138 CA2d 35, 57, 291 P2d 155, 168; Comment, 35 So Cal L Rev 193 (1961). The person who gave the history can be called and cross-examined by the adverse party. Evid C §804. The doctor can also testify about a history that was taken and recorded by a paramedical employee, nurse, intern, or other doctor, under such circumstances that the testifying doctor reasonably could rely on it in forming his opinions. See Evid C §801; Witkin, California Evidence §§409–410 (2d ed, 1966).

B. [§6.36] *Nature and Diagnostic Importance*

Trial lawyers often elicit medical history testimony simply by asking a doctor to state the history or to read his notes or record of it. In other cases, a lawyer may first ask the doctor to explain how the history was taken and of what importance it was to him and continue with specific questions about particular parts of the history (see §§6.37–6.39). If the medical history is of prime importance in the case, *e.g.*, in establishing a disputed diagnosis, background testimony can be elaborate. For an example of rather detailed testimony about the nature and importance of a medical history, see Houts, Lawyers Guide to Medical Proof §4.09 (1966).

Q. Dr. ...., as a part of your examination of [Mr. ..../ plaintiff], did you obtain his medical history?
A. Yes.
Q. What procedure did you follow to get his history?
A. [At the beginning of the examination, I asked him questions and noted the answers that I considered significant. As the examination progressed, I asked more particular questions.]
Q. What information were you seeking?
A. I wanted to know what his present complaints were, what symptoms he felt, how he had been injured, what treatment he had received, and what his past medical history was.

Q. Did you record what he told you as he went along?
A. Yes. [I made notes on my examination form from which I dictated the history as it appears on my examination report.]
Q. Do you take a medical history as a part of every clinical examination?
A. Yes [unless the patient's condition prevents it].
Q. Is it the customary medical practice to do so?
A. It is.
Q. What is your objective in obtaining a patient's medical history?
A. [To get information from the patient—sometimes information that only he can furnish—that will assist me in diagnosing his condition.]
Q. How valuable is information supplied by a patient to you in reaching medical conclusions about him?
A. [The information is almost always useful, and sometimes a medical history furnishes the entire basis for a diagnosis; there may be no significant clinical findings or laboratory test results.]

Comment: While showing the nature and importance of the medical history, a lawyer can also elicit testimony that lays a foundation for admission of the history to show part of the basis for the doctor's opinions. See §6.35. Even when the lawyer anticipates no objection to the doctor's recounting of the medical history, foundational testimony can further highlight its importance.

Q. And is it considered a reasonable and sound medical practice for doctors to rely on the patient's statements of his own symptoms and how his injuries were incurred as part of the basis for medical conclusions about his condition?
A. Yes.
Q. Did the things that [Mr. ..../plaintiff] told you as part of his medical history constitute part of the basis for your conclusions about his condition now and in the future?
A. Yes, they did.
Q. Were his statements necessary to enable you to arrive at the opinions you did about his condition and his future?
A. They were.

C. [§6.37] *Symptoms; Subjective Signs*

Symptoms are manifestations of disease or injury that are recognized or complained of by the patient. "Symptom" is sometimes used in a narrow sense as equivalent to "subjective sign," something felt or sensed by the patient, but not perceptible to another. Symptoms and

MEDICAL EXPERTS §6.37

subjective signs are thus distinguished from objective signs, which are phenomena that can be observed by a doctor or detected by X rays or laboratory equipment. Subjective symptoms nonetheless exist and are well-recognized aids to doctors in diagnosing injuries.

Since a patient's statements of his present symptoms are statements of his then existing mental or physical state, the doctor may normally testify to these statements under an exception to the hearsay rule. Evid C §§1250, 1252; *Bloomberg v Laventhal* (1919) 179 C 616, 619, 178 P 496, 497; *Willoughby v Zylstra* (1935) 5 CA2d 297, 300, 42 P2d 685, 686. See also Witkin, CALIFORNIA EVIDENCE §554 (2d ed, 1966).

Complaints or symptoms that were experienced after the accident but did not persist to the time of the doctor's examination probably do not qualify for admission as statements of present mental or physical state, although they are admissible on other grounds (see §§6.34–6.35).

Q. What were [Mr. ....'s/plaintiff's] chief complaints when you took his medical history?
A. ....
Q. Did he report any additional symptoms to you?
A. Yes.
Q. What were they?
A. ....
Q. Are these complaints of [headache/radiating pain down the left arm/dizziness] what you call symptoms or subjective signs?
A. That is correct.
Q. From the standpoint of medical terminology, Doctor, is there a distinction between subjective signs and objective signs?
A. Yes, there is.
Q. Please tell us what that distinction is.
A. [A subjective sign is something that is felt or sensed by the patient, although it may not be observable by the doctor. An objective sign is an indication of disease or injury that the doctor can detect, perhaps with the aid of some instrument, but without any statement from the patient.]

Comment: Lawyers for plaintiff frequently want to establish that subjective symptoms are medically significant and credible indicators of injury. This anticipates defense attacks on the reliability of the symptoms related by the patient-plaintiff.

Q. In the regular course of medical practice, Doctor, do subjective

§6.37 MEDICAL EXPERTS

signs play an important part in helping a doctor arrive at a diagnosis?
A. Yes, they do. [They are often more important than objective signs, X-ray films, or test results.]
Q. In this case, did you rely in part on the subjective symptoms related to you by Mr. .... in arriving at your diagnosis of his condition?
A. Yes.
Q. Were the symptoms he related entirely consistent with your clinical findings, the X-ray films, and the laboratory test results?
A. Yes, they were.
Q. Did you observe anything in examining Mr. .... that led you to believe that he might be exaggerating or falsifying the symptoms and complaints that he related to you?
A. No.

Comment: Defense lawyers frequently want to elicit medical testimony that subjective symptoms cannot be confirmed by the doctor, and that any conclusions based on them are only as valid as the veracity of the patient. This testimony can serve as the basis for an attack, not only on plaintiff's doctor's opinions, but also on damage claims for pain and other subjective complaints. The following group of questions might be asked by a defense lawyer:

Q. Dr. ...., with regard to plaintiff's complaints of [state subjective symptoms], was there any objective test or examination that a doctor could have performed to determine whether or not he was actually experiencing those symptoms?
A. No.
Q. Do you have to rely, then, on the truthfulness of what the patient says about these subjective complaints rather than on anything you are able to observe objectively?
A. That is correct.
Q. A patient could exaggerate or even falsify these subjective complaints, could he not?
A. Yes.
Q. Do you consider this plaintiff's subjective complaints consistent with the objective findings that you made?
A. No.
Q. Please explain the inconsistencies.
A. ....
Q. Did you find any objective basis for his subjective complaints?
A. No.

MEDICAL EXPERTS §6.38

Comment: Unpleasant symptoms, *e.g.,* pain, nausea, and vertigo, are elements of detriment that can be emphasized by a plaintiff's lawyer in the course of showing their relationship to the doctor's diagnosis.

Q. Dr. ...., was the ["intermittent pain" that Mr. .... complained of as radiating from his neck down his right arm] a symptom that was consistent with your eventual diagnosis of [a herniated cervical disc]?
A. Yes.
Q. What is the relationship between the symptom and the injury?
A. [Herniated disc material pressing on the fifth cervical nerve root would cause sharp pain down the median nerve to the hand as he moved his head and neck.]

Comment: The time and character of the onset of symptoms may be important to the diagnosis. Plaintiff's attorney is also interested in having delayed symptoms explained medically lest jurors believe that they were fabricated when plaintiff began to think of recovering damages.

Q. Dr. ...., according to his history, when did [Mr. ..../plaintiff] first begin to feel symptoms after the accident?
A. ....
Q. When did he [first seek medical assistance/take to his bed/come home from work/call you] because of these pains and symptoms?
A. ....
Q. Is this delay of ...... [hours/days] from the time of the accident until the time symptoms were felt consistent with your eventual diagnosis of ....?
A. Yes.
Q. What are the medical explanations, if any, for this delayed reaction?
A. ....

D. [§6.38] Circumstances of Accident

In the course of taking a medical history, the doctor usually asks the patient how the injuries were incurred, or what were the apparent causes of his condition. Knowing the circumstances of the accident, *e.g.,* the patient's activity, the speed and direction of forces, and the composition of surfaces struck, can help the doctor to diagnose the nature and extent of injuries. However, doctors do not always know in advance what will be diagnostically significant, and they sometimes

§6.39 MEDICAL EXPERTS

note details in the history that are of no medical importance but have a bearing on the liability issues in the case.

Anything a patient tells a doctor about the cause of his injuries can be put in evidence by the defense as plaintiff's admission. See §6.34. The plaintiff, however, can bring out only those aspects of the medical history relating to the circumstances of the accident that can be shown to have contributed to the doctor's diagnosis or other medical opinion. See §6.35. The plaintiff may want the doctor to give foundational testimony to establish that the parts of the history relating to the cause of his injuries constituted part of the basis for the doctor's opinions. See *Johnson v Aetna Life Ins. Co.* (1963) 221 CA2d 247, 252, 34 CR 484, 487; *Tierney v Charles Nelson Co.* (1937) 19 CA2d 34, 37, 64 P2d 1150, 1152; *Losleben v California State Life Ins. Co.* (1932) 119 CA 556, 560, 6 P2d 1012, 1013. For a discussion of the admissibility of opinion testimony about medical causation, see §§6.71–6.74.

Q. As part of his medical history did [Mr. ..../plaintiff] tell you [how he incurred his injuries/what seemed to trigger his symptoms]?
A. Yes.
Q. Did the information he gave you contribute to your diagnosis of his condition?
A. Yes [part of it was helpful].
Q. What history did [Mr. ..../plaintiff] give about how he incurred his injuries?
A. ....

E. [§6.39] Preaccident History

Doctors often ask patients for a past history, *i.e.*, a statement of diseases, injuries, and general health experienced before the accident. Defense lawyers question medical witnesses about the past history to develop evidence that at least part of the plaintiff's present condition is not attributable to the accident sued on. The patient's statements to the doctor can usually be introduced by the defense under the hearsay rule exception for admissions. See §6.34. In addition, if a plaintiff's medical witness denies on cross-examination that he asked the patient about his preaccident history, it can be argued that his examination of the patient was incomplete and that his opinions are therefore suspect. If he admits that he knew of significant prior injuries that he did not mention on direct examination, he may then appear biased in plaintiff's favor. If he denies that the plaintiff told him of some prior condition, about which the defendant is able to

MEDICAL EXPERTS §6.39

introduce evidence, the plaintiff appears less than frank in his dealings with the doctor, and the doctor's opinions, formed without consideration of important parts of the past history, are without basis or, at least, less credible.

A plaintiff's attorney wants past medical history brought out on direct examination to show the relationship between prior disease or disability and the effects of the accident, to establish that the patient's prior health was fully considered by the witness in forming his medical opinions, and to prevent a cross-examiner from being the first to bring out testimony about the prior injuries or conditions.

A doctor can testify for the plaintiff about a patient's statements of his preaccident medical history to show part of the basis for the doctor's medical opinions. *Groat v Walkup Drayage & Warehouse Co.* (1936) 14 CA2d 350, 357, 58 P2d 200, 203; *Willoughby v Zylstra* (1935) 5 CA2d 297, 300, 42 P2d 685, 686. See generally §6.35. It is also possible that statements about past mental or physical state may be admitted as evidence of the truth of the matter stated, if the declarant is not available as a witness. Evid C §§1251–1252.

Medical records are sometimes introduced to prove or corroborate testimony about past medical history.

Q. Dr. ...., did you ask [Mr. ..../plaintiff] about his past medical history up to the time of the accident on ...., 19......?
A. Yes, I did.
Q. What history of prior diseases and injuries did he give you?
A. ....
Q. Is there any relationship between these prior conditions, the injuries he suffered on ...., 19......, and the symptoms and disabilities he has experienced since then?
A. Yes.
Q. What is that relationship?
A. ....

Comment: Many lawyers do not rely on the patient to tell, or the doctor to inquire, about all prior conditions. Plaintiff's counsel are particularly careful to ensure that their medical witnesses know and testify about all relevant prior injuries.

Q. Did you ask [Mr. ..../plaintiff] particularly about [prior injury or blows to his back, or any prior pain or stiffness in that region]?
A. Yes.
Q. And what history, if any, did he give you of [prior back injury]?

§6.40   MEDICAL EXPERTS

A. ....
Q. Do you see any connection, Doctor, between these prior [symptoms/injuries] and the pain and disability that he has experienced [in that area] since the accident on ...., 19......?
A. ....
Q. Did you determine from him whether, during the period before the accident, he was experiencing any symptoms [in his back] or was symptom-free?
A. Yes.
Q. What did he say?
A. ....
Q. As far as you know, then, what was the state of his health immediately before the accident on ...., 19......?
A. ....

VIII. [§6.40] PHYSICAL EXAMINATION AND FINDINGS

The part of a clinical examination in which the doctor makes his own systematic inspection of the patient can be called the "physical examination." It is distinguished from the taking of a medical history and the performance of X-ray, electrographic, laboratory, and other special diagnostic procedures. In the physical examination the doctor makes his observations of the patient's physical status and reactions to stimuli and manipulations by using his own senses and instruments that extend his senses, such as the stethoscope and ophthalmoscope. The medical facts directly perceived by the doctor are called "signs," "objective signs," or "findings" and are distinguished from the symptoms, complaints, and opinions related to the doctor by the patient and other persons.

Physical examinations usually follow a standard and systematic pattern. In a general physical examination, the doctor (a) records his observations of the patient's general appearance and mental status; (b) notes measurements, such as height, weight, body temperature, pulse count, and blood pressure; and (c) proceeds through a systematic evaluation of each of the following areas and systems: head (external), neck, eyes, ears, nose, mouth, throat, teeth, chest, lungs, cardiovascular, abdomen, lymphatics, genitalia, rectum, prostate, hernia, back, extremities, skin, and neurological. Specialized examinations, such as orthopedic examinations, go into greater detail in a particular area or system.

Examining doctors usually make an effort to keep physical examinations both objective (confined to what the doctor perceives him-

MEDICAL EXPERTS §6.43

self) and comprehensive (all organs and systems are examined despite the apparent importance of obvious or early discovered signs).

A. [§6.41] *Admissibility*

Testimony by an examining doctor about medical facts observed during a physical examination is admitted both as personally perceived evidence of plaintiff's physical condition (see Evid C §702) and to show part of the basis for the witness's opinions (see Evid C §802; *Inskeep v Busby* (1962) 207 CA2d 848, 851, 24 CR 819, 820).

Testimony about how an examination was conducted and how objective findings were perceived or obtained should be admissible to support the validity and accuracy of the findings and to give the jury a better idea of their significance. This evidence can be said to be relevant to the credibility of the witness. See Evid C §210.

B. [§6.42] *Using Specific Questions*

The very objectivity and completeness of a physical examination can act to dilute the doctor's testimony about his findings. Even experienced witnesses, when asked by counsel merely to "state their findings," tend to drone on through a long list of findings: some positive, some negative; some irrelevant, others unimportant; many stated in terms incomprehensible to the jury. Significant findings are recited like the rest, without proper emphasis or background.

Thus, trial lawyers commonly ask specific questions to elicit particular significant findings. They follow clear and dramatic order of presentation and the witness explains medical terms as they are used. They try to bring out the connection between each finding and its medical cause; explain the procedure used by the doctor in arriving at a finding, especially when it involved a test or manipulation; and omit or explain unimportant, ambiguous, absent, and negative findings (see §6.49).

C. [§6.43] *Character and Type of Examination*

Some attorneys question medical witnesses at length about the nature and importance of the physical examination and findings. For an example, see Houts, Lawyer's Guide to Medical Proof §§504(2)–504(4) (1966). Others ask few, if any, background questions, on the assumption that building up the physical examination might devalue the history or risk the loss of jury attention before the actual findings are reached.

§6.44 **MEDICAL EXPERTS**

Q. Dr. ...., in addition to taking [Mr. ....'s/plaintiff's] medical history, did you also make a direct physical examination?
A. Yes.
Q. Did you observe objective signs, and make findings during this physical examination?
A. Yes.
Q. Are the terms "signs," "objective signs," and "findings" used interchangeably by doctors?
A. Yes, they are.
Q. And is it correct to say that an objective sign is something that you observe directly during your examination rather than a symptom or complaint that is related to you by the plaintiff or someone else?
A. That is correct.

Comment: The examination may have been general, specialized (*e.g.*, orthopedic or neurological), limited to one area or system, or terminated early (*e.g.*, because of the patient's need for immediate life-saving procedures). If the examination was other than a general physical, this can be explained in direct testimony.

Q. Did you do a general physical examination, or some type of specialized or limited examination?
A. ....
                        (If specialized)
Q. How does [an orthopedic] examination differ from a general physical examination?
A. ....
                        (If limited)
Q. Why didn't you do a complete general physical examination at that time?
A. [The patient was in such pain that I could not.]

Comment: Any pain or discomfort (see §6.48), or mental distress caused by the examination itself can be shown.

Q. Did [Mr. ..../plaintiff] disrobe for this examination?
A. Yes.

D. [§6.44] *General Appearance and Mental Status*

Examining doctors usually make some notation of the patient's general appearance (at least the familiar "well-developed, well-

MEDICAL EXPERTS §6.44

nourished Caucasian male") and of any significant abnormalities of appearance and mental status. It is sometimes effective to ask a doctor to describe his first impression of the patient. Emergency room doctors, for example, see dramatic acute conditions: Bleeding, coma, stupor, open wounds with protruding bones, and the like. Doctors who conduct medical-legal examinations months after an accident may observe scars, limping, muscle spasm, and similar conditions. Defense examiners may catch the plaintiff in movements or attitudes inconsistent with claimed injuries.

Q. Dr. ...., what was the first thing you noticed about [Mr. ..../plaintiff] as he came into your [office/examining room]?
A. ....
Q. What was the significance of that?
A. ....
Q. What else did you observe about his general appearance?
A. [I noted that he was a young, well-developed, well-nourished Caucasian male.]

Comment: Counsel should also be sure that the doctor's standard "well-developed, well-nourished" note does not mask an observation he made, but did not record, perhaps because it seemed too obvious, as when plaintiff had an arm in a cast or walked with a limp.

A general question that draws such a general answer might better be omitted, for it tells the jurors no more than they can see themselves. Specific questions are more likely to elicit the answers counsel seeks. For example, in a head injury case, the testimony might proceed as follows:

Q. Did you make any observations about how he moved during the examination?
A. Yes. [He moved slowly and hesitantly, with great care to avoid sudden movement. He was reluctant to lie down when I asked or, once down, to get up again.]
Q. What was the significance of these signs?
A. [These are signs commonly exhibited by persons who have recently experienced severe headaches. They move slowly and are reluctant to turn or bend at the neck in order to protect themselves from any change in blood flow that might cause further pain.]

Comment: The foregoing answer is an example of an observation the doctor may not have noted in his examination form or report, for he undoubtedly observed more diagnostically significant evidence of brain injury than the way plaintiff moved. Plaintiff's counsel brings it out not so much because of its diagnostic significance, but because the observation is evidence of the nature and extent of injuries.

Q. What were your observations of his general mental status?
A. [Among other things, I observed during the examination that he was subject to outbursts of irritability, about which he quickly became very apologetic.]
Q. How did this finding fit in with your other findings and with your diagnosis?
A. [It was quite consistent. It is typical for a patient who has incurred a brain injury to exhibit irritability over which he seems to have no conscious control.]

Comment: Depending on its importance in the total injury picture, each finding may be explored in greater depth. In this illustration, a plaintiff's lawyer could go on to elicit testimony that the plaintiff could not control his irritability; that this was disturbing to him; and that it might have an organic basis in changed cerebral cell structure or electrical patterns, or a psychological basis in plaintiff's fear that his mental abilities were affected by the injury.

E. [§6.45] *Explaining Medical Terms and Injuries*

Lawyers generally tell doctors to use terminology the jury will understand, and most doctors try hard to comply. They may even overdo it at the beginning. But as their testimony proceeds, they tend to lapse into medical jargon. Lawyers who have studied the medical aspects of their cases and have learned the medical terminology must therefore be alert to the danger that testimony they have no difficulty understanding may be incomprehensible to jurors.

In addition, a plaintiff's lawyer can work toward helping jurors visualize the injuries and conditions being described by the doctor.

For example, in a head injury case, the testimony might proceed as follows:

Q. What were your findings when you examined [Mr. ....'s/ plaintiff's] head?
A. I palpated four depressions where trephine holes had been made over the pterion and posterior parietal areas bilaterally.
Q. Can you break that down to be sure that we all understand you? First, what does "palpate" mean?
A. That means to feel with my fingers.
Q. And "bilaterally"?
A. That means on both sides.

MEDICAL EXPERTS §6.45

Q. And can you point out on your own head the "pterion" and "posterior parietal" areas?
A. Yes. The pterion is here [indicates] and the posterior parietal area is here [indicates].
Q. So, with your fingers, you felt four depressions in his skull, one on each side of his face at the temples, about half way between the corners of his eyes and his ears [indicates], and two in the back of his head a little below the top [indicates]?
A. That is right.
Q. Were the depressions in the bone of the skull?
A. Yes.
Q. How deep in the bone were each of these depressions when you felt them?
A. About five millimeters.
Q. Isn't five millimeters a little more than three-sixteenths of an inch, or about as deep as the eraser on this pencil?
A. That is right.
Q. What diameter were the depressions?
A. Thumbnail size.
Q. Do you mean an average thumbnail of about three-quarters of an inch in diameter?
A. Well, one half to three quarters of an inch.

Comment: In addition to verbal descriptions, it is helpful to use models, drawings, gestures, and other demonstrative materials to help the jurors visualize what the doctor is talking about.

Q. You said you found the depressions where trephine holes had been made. What is a "trephine"?
A. A trephine is a circular bone saw. It is used to drill out a disk of bone from the skull.

Comment: Even doctors sometimes use medical language loosely, both in written reports and on the witness stand. The lawyer may have to elicit an explanation of an imprecise usage to conform the doctor's testimony to other medical evidence and to spare him an attack on cross-examination.

Q. Technically, is there a difference between a trephine hole and a burr hole?
A. Yes, the trephine actually takes out a circular disk of bone, while a burr just drills a hole without preserving the disk of bone.
Q. When you said "trephine hole," were you just using that as a general term for a hole drilled in the skull, or did you mean to

draw the technical distinction between a trephine hole and a burr hole?
A. I was just using it as a general term. When I saw Mr. ...., what mattered to me was the nature of the depressions in his skull at that time, not how they had been made.

F. [§6.46] *Connecting Findings to Injuries*

Some objective signs are observed in areas remote from the lesions or injuries that produce them. The well-known Babinski reflex in the foot, for example, is an indicator of abnormality in the brain stem or spinal cord (see §6.48). A plaintiff's lawyer should have the doctor connect these remote findings to the pathological conditions that produce them.

For example, in a case involving injury to the cervical spine, the testimony might proceed as follows:

Q. Did you observe any objective signs of injury in examining [Mr. ....'s/plaintiff's] arms and hands?
A. Yes. I found diminished sensation to pain, temperature, and touch on the radial or thumb side of his right hand and forearm.

Comment: Testimony about how the doctor arrived at this finding and how he assured himself that the patient was not malingering has been omitted from this example.

Q. Did the nature and pattern of this diminished sensation, or numbness, indicate to you the nature of [Mr. ....'s/plaintiff's] injury?
A. Yes, it did.
Q. What did it indicate?
A. First, the diminished sensation indicated some interference with the transmission of nerve impulses from his hand and forearm to his brain. Since there were no injuries in the arm or shoulder, it further indicated the probability that the injury was in the area where the nerve roots leave the spinal cord, between the fourth and fifth cervical vertebrae.
Q. Where are the fourth and fifth cervical vertebrae located?
A. Up here [indicates] in the neck.
Q. What sort of interference with the transmission of nerve impulses was there?
A. In this case, pressure on the nerve roots.

MEDICAL EXPERTS §6.48

Q. How would pressure on the nerve roots up in the neck have anything to do with numbness or diminished sensation in the hand?
A. The sensory nerve fibers that have their endings in these areas of the hand and forearm pass through the spinal column between the fourth and fifth cervical vertebrae and from there to the brain as part of the spinal cord. Pressure on the nerve roots in this area blocks the return of nerve impulses from the thumb and forearm.
Q. Can pressure on the nerve root at this point be caused by a herniated disc?
A. It can.
Q. Does your finding of diminished sensation in the area of the thumb and forearm corroborate a diagnosis of a herniated disc between the fourth and fifth cervical vertebrae?
A. It does.
Q. Was the numbness in his hand and arm caused by that injury to the intervertebral disc in his neck?
A. It was.

G. [§6.47] *Findings as Injuries*

Treating doctors are interested in objective signs primarily for their aid in establishing a diagnosis so that treatment can be given. However, many clinical findings have an additional legal significance; they are themselves direct evidence of the plaintiff's injuries.

The preceding section, for example, contained illustrative testimony about diminished sensation in the thumb as an indicator of cervical disc injury. Counsel might well want to go on from that point to ask the doctor about the effects of the diminished sensation on plaintiff's normal activities. Did it interfere with the usefulness of his hand, leave him more susceptible to further injury, and so on?

H. [§6.48] *Clinical Tests and Manipulations*

In addition to looking at (inspection), listening to (auscultation), and feeling (palpation) the patient, doctors scratch, tap, and manipulate body areas in order to elicit objective signs of injury. These clinical (distinguished from laboratory or electrographic) tests and manipulations include the familiar tapping on tendons with a rubber mallet to determine the presence and force of reflexes and the raising and bending of legs to elicit pain indicative of low back and sciatic nerve injuries. (See *Comment* below.)

Medical witnesses are often asked to explain how and why these clinical tests were performed. Instead of merely having the doctor say, "he showed a positive Babinski, indicating possible pyramidal tract lesion," the line of questioning might proceed as follows:

Q. Did you test [Mr. ..../plaintiff] for a Babinski reflex?
A. Yes.
Q. How is that test performed?
A. The patient lies on his back with shoes and socks removed. The doctor draws a sharp object, like the point of a pencil, across the sole of the foot from the heel toward the ball of the foot and observes the reaction of the big toe.
Q. What reaction is normal, and what reaction is abnormal in a person of plaintiff's age?
A. In an adult, the normal reaction is for the toe to flex, to curl down toward the sole of the foot. When the toe points up in the direction of the top of the foot, the reaction is abnormal, and we say "the sign is positive" or "he has a positive Babinski."
Q. What does a positive Babinski test indicate?
A. It is an indicator of organic damage or deficiency of the upper motor neurons in the area of the pyramidal tract.
Q. Where is the pyramidal tract located?
A. At the base of the brain, where the spinal cord passes through the skull.
Q. And motor neurons are nerve fibers that connect with muscles, is that correct?
A. Yes.
Q. Did [Mr. ..../plaintiff] show a positive or negative Babinski sign?
A. ....

Comment: Some important tests and manipulations cause pain to the patient. Indeed, pain may be the response that makes the test diagnostically significant. Medical testimony about the pain and discomfort experienced by patient in the course of the examination can support additional damages. For example, after the doctor has described the procedure and results of a straight-leg raising test, a plaintiff's attorney might ask:

Q. Dr. ...., is this a test that causes discomfort to the patient?
A. Yes.
Q. What is the nature of that discomfort?
A. [When the test is positive, the patient feels a sharp pain in his lower back.]
Q. Is this pain a necessary part of the test?
A. Yes. [Pain produced by raising his leg is the sign that indicates sciatic nerve involvement.]

MEDICAL EXPERTS §6.49

I. [§6.49] *Absent and Negative Findings*

In a typical personal injury case, most areas and systems of a patient's body show no signs of disease or injury, and the doctor's examination form, if he used one, contains such entries as "WNL" (within normal limits), "neg" (negative), "benign throat," "lungs clear," and the like. As to these areas the examination was "essentially negative," *i.e.,* nothing significant was found, nor was the absence of findings significant. For problems that arise when a doctor does not record a notation for areas and systems found normal, see §6.50.

Doctors testifying for the defense can sometimes cite the absence of positive signs or even a particular sign as evidence that the plaintiff did not suffer a claimed injury. Further, defense attorneys sometimes make use of the absence of positive findings by asking, on cross-examination, a question like: "Now, if he had [state claimed injury] wouldn't you expect to find [describe signs]?

A plaintiff's lawyer questioning his medical witness may pass quickly over absent, ambiguous, and unimportant findings in order to keep the testimony interesting. It is wise, however, to have the doctor say that the absence of findings was not significant, so that the question of absent findings is not raised for the first time on cross-examination. This is particularly true in cases in which the witness saw no positive objective signs and based his diagnosis entirely on the patient's symptoms and history. In these cases, the lawyer would have the doctor testify in greater detail about the importance of subjective signs (see §6.36) and explain why there were no objective signs when the patient was examined.

Q. Dr. ...., [in addition to the areas you have mentioned] did you also examine the plaintiff's other bodily areas and systems?
A. I did.
Q. Did you find any objective signs of injury or disease [in these areas]?
A. No.
Q. Was the absence of signs [in these areas] consistent with the diagnosis that you reached?
A. Yes.
Q. From a diagnostic standpoint, was it significant that you did not see any objective signs?
A. No.
Q. Please tell us why that is so.
A. ....

Comment: In some cases, negative findings are diagnostically significant in ruling out possible causes of injury. For example:

Q. In your report you state that [no Kernig or Brudzinski signs were elicited]. Without going into how you test for these signs, what is their significance?
A. [They are both indicators of meningitis when the signs are positive.]
Q. Does their absence [rule out meningitis]?
A. Their absence is a definite indication that there is [no inflammatory involvement of the meninges].

J. [§6.50] Explaining Failure To Make Observation or Test

Even though physical examinations are systematic, doctors rarely complete all the clinical tests and observations that could conceivably be performed on the patient. When they are called as witnesses, however, they should be prepared to explain why they omitted a particular test. A lawyer who knows that an opposing medical witness made and relied on a test his witness omitted, can ask his own witness to testify about its value and his reasons for not performing it.

A problem can arise with doctors who do not routinely make a note of absent or negative findings in their examination forms or reports. On the witness stand they are sometimes unable to remember whether they did not examine the area or simply failed to record the results. Jurors may assume they did not perform a thorough examination, and their testimony may be less effective.

To avoid these problems, a lawyer can prepare the witness by suggesting that he (1) think of all the tests, manipulations, and investigations he could have performed in examining the patient; (2) try to recall all those he actually did perform, whether noted on his examination report or not; and (3) try to recall the reasons he had for not performing tests he might have performed. The lawyer can then choose those tests and findings that were particularly significant for discussion on direct examination, and the doctor avoids possible embarrassment on cross-examination.

IX. [§6.51] SPECIAL DIAGNOSTIC PROCEDURES

Examining doctors sometimes administer special diagnostic tests and procedures to gain information about a patient's internal anatomy and function. These procedures include: radiographic (X-ray) examinations, which show the condition and relationships of internal

MEDICAL EXPERTS   §6.52

organs and structures; electrographic procedures, such as electroencephalography (EEG), which give graphic representations of electrical activity in living tissues; and laboratory tests and analyses such as biopsies, blood counts, and urinalyses, which show the chemical and cellular makeup of tissues and fluids.

The equipment and techniques used for these special diagnostic procedures distinguish them from the usual clinical or physical examination in which the doctor relies on direct observation (see §6.40). Special diagnostic procedures convert bodily phenomena that the doctor cannot observe into a form that can be perceived by an expert. The trustworthiness of a doctor's testimony about clinical findings depends on his observational skills and his ability to interpret what he observed. The trustworthiness of his testimony about findings from special procedures depends, in addition, on the reliability of the techniques and equipment used and the care and skill of the person who conducted the procedure.

A. [§6.52] *Admissibility*

Testimony about recognized medical tests and procedures is admissible. See Witkin, CALIFORNIA EVIDENCE §652 (2d ed, 1966). A doctor who personally conducted a special diagnostic procedure should be permitted to testify about it and his findings from it just as he is permitted to testify about clinical tests and findings. See §6.41.

There is a question whether testimony about findings from a special procedure is received (1) as matter personally known to the doctor (see Evid C §702), in which case it is factual testimony, or (2) as matter on which it is reasonable for an expert to rely (see Evid C §801(b)), in which case it is opinion testimony. The doctor does not directly see the fracture or narrowed disc space represented by lines and shadows on an X-ray film. He does not hear or feel the irregular brain waves shown by wavy lines on an electroencephalogram. However, if counsel can establish the reliability of the process used to convert these bodily phenomena to a film or graphic representation, he can argue that the doctor should be permitted to testify as if he perceived the internal phenomena with his own senses.

A doctor should also be permitted to testify about a special procedure conducted by an assistant under his supervision. In these cases, the doctor delegates only the mechanics of administering the procedure; he remains responsible for its medical validity, the reliability of the technique and equipment, the competence of his assistant, and any findings based on the result. A different case is presented if the doctor sends the patient out to an independent doctor or technician for a special procedure. In these cases, the doctor can testify about the outside examination and findings only to show part of the basis for his own opinions. See §6.56.

B. [§6.53] *Extent of Testimony*

A doctor's testimony about a special procedure can be brief, for example: "I ran an EEG to check electrical activity in the brain and found minimal abnormal discharges."

If a foundation is required before the testimony will be received, the doctor can be asked to testify about the scientific validity and medical acceptance of the procedure; the reliability and accuracy of the equipment and technique used; and the skill, training, and experience of the operator. See Witkin, CALIFORNIA EVIDENCE §§641, 652 (2d ed, 1966).

If the lawyer wants more extensive testimony about a special procedure, he can also ask the doctor to state its purpose; the medical need or indication for it; the steps followed by the operator; the position and activity of the patient; the form (films, graphs, etc.) of the results; the data or information the doctor sees in the film or graph; his interpretation of the lines, shadows, etc.; the diagnostic significance of his findings; and so forth.

Plaintiff's lawyers can also bring out medical testimony about any danger to the patient and pain, anxiety, and discomfort involved in the procedure. A defense lawyer can question the medical need for a risky, painful, or expensive procedure and argue that it was done, not for a diagnostic purpose, but solely to build up the damages.

X. [§6.54] REPORTS FROM OTHER EXAMINERS

Examining physicians often send patients, or samples of patients' tissues and fluids, to other doctors and technicians for consultative clinical examinations and special diagnostic tests and procedures. The results of these outside examinations are reported to the referring doctor in the form of X-ray films, graphs (electrocardiograms etc.), numerical totals or percentages (blood counts, urinalyses, etc.), and oral and written reports interpreting the data and commenting on the patient and his physical status. The referring doctor can base his own conclusions about his patient partly on the facts and opinions obtained from these outside tests and examinations.

MEDICAL EXPERTS §6.56

A. [§6.55] Determining Whether To Call Outside Consultant

If the results of the outside test or examination are important, perhaps because diagnosis is in dispute, the lawyer should consider calling as a witness the outside consultant in addition to the referring doctor who is usually the principal medical witness. This consultant can explain in detail how the examination was carried out, what findings were made, and what conclusions he reached about the patient. He can also authenticate for admission any X-ray films, graphs, or written reports (see chap 16), and verify that the referring doctor was relying on the correct films, graphs, and reports in forming his opinions. By calling the doctor or technician who actually performed the test or examination, the lawyer reduces the possibility that adverse counsel will convince the judge and jury that the films or graphs relied on by the referring doctor were improperly made or did not represent the plaintiff at all. When a consultant doctor or technician is called as a witness, he is qualified and led through his testimony like any other medical witness, although usually his testimony is more limited than that of the principal medical witness.

On the other hand, when a lawyer feels that it is not worth the expense or time to call additional medical witnesses, he can have a referring doctor testify about the outside examinations and the reports returned to him by consultants to show part of the basis for his own opinions. The following sections discuss admissibility and presentation of testimony by a referring doctor about the results of outside examinations and tests.

B. Admissibility

1. [§6.56] To Show Basis of Referring Doctor's Opinions

Testimony by a doctor about reports, evaluations, and analyses sent him by other doctors and technicians is hearsay if offered to prove the truth of the matter stated therein. See Evid C §1200; *Frampton v Hartzell* (1960) 179 CA2d 771, 4 CR 427 (doctor permitted to give own opinion, but not those of other doctors who participated in conference about patient). Therefore, if an adverse attorney raises the hearsay objection, the witness can testify about the information and opinions given him by other doctors and technicians only to show part of the basis for his own opinions. See Evid C §802; *Kelley v Bailey* (1961) 189 CA2d 728, 738, 11 CR 448, 455; *Hope v Arrowhead & Puritas Waters, Inc.* (1959) 174 CA2d 222, 230, 344 P2d 428, 433; *Christiansen v Hollings* (1941) 44 CA2d 332, 347, 112 P2d 723, 731.

If he asks for it, the opposing party can obtain an instruction (similar to BAJI No 2.43) that the evidence of the test and examination results and reports is admitted only for the limited purpose of showing the information on which the doctor based his opinions, and not as evidence of their own truth. See Evid C §355; *Kelley v Bailey, supra*. The opposing party is also entitled to subpena and cross-examine the doctors and technicians who made the outside examinations, if those persons are available. Evid C §804(a).

2. [§6.57] Extent of Showing

Evidence Code §802 permits an expert witness to "state on direct examination the reasons for his opinion and the matter . . . upon which it is based," "Matter" includes facts, data, and other intangibles. Official Comment preceding Evidence Code §800. Thus, the referring doctor should be permitted to testify to the information he sees in the films or graphs and to opinions in the reports sent to him by the outside consultants. Nothing in the language of Evid C §802 limits the referring doctor's testimony to (a) the fact that he sent the patient to a certain doctor for tests, (b) the fact that he received results and a report on which he relied in reaching his diagnosis, and (c) what his diagnosis is.

The trial judge has discretion under Evid C §§352 and 802 to limit the extent of the testimony the witness can give about the bases of his opinions. By the same token, it would appear that the trial judge has discretion to permit the referring doctor to read portions of written reports to the jury and to point out things on films and graphs even though they have not been received in evidence. The judge could even admit as exhibits the films, graphs, and reports relied on by the witness.

In *Kelley v Bailey* (1961) 189 CA2d 728, 11 CR 448, the testifying doctor was permitted to read to the jury portions of a medical report sent to him by a doctor who was not called as a witness. It could be argued that there is no essential difference between reading another doctor's report to the jury and pointing out signs in films and graphs or receiving reports, films, and graphs in evidence. But see *Kostick v Swain* (1953) 116 CA2d 187, 196, 253 P2d 531, 537 (medical report of absent doctor not admissible without foundation to qualify it as business record even though testifying doctor was "no doubt . . . influenced by the report in shaping his testimony for trial").

Thus, the extent of the testimony sought from the referring doctor about the results and contents of outside tests and examinations depends both on the time the lawyer wants to invest in making the showing and on what the adverse lawyer and the trial judge will permit.

MEDICAL EXPERTS   §6.59

C. [§6.58] *Identity and Reliability of Tester or Examiner*

When a referring doctor is testifying he usually does not attempt to state the qualifications of the doctor, technician, or laboratory that performed the procedure or examination in the detail that he states his own qualifications. If the qualifications of the tester or examiner were that important, it would be an indication that he should have been called as a witness. It is appropriate, however, for the testifying doctor to say a few words about the ability, reliability, and reputation of the person to whom he referred the patient for examination or testing. For example, if the witness referred the patient to a radiologist:

Q. Dr. ...., as a part of your examination of [Mr. ..../ plaintiff] did you send him out to have X-ray pictures made of [his neck]?
A. I did.
Q. To whom did you send him?
A. To Dr. ....
Q. Does Dr. .... have a specialty?
A. Yes. He is a radiologist.
Q. Is it your understanding that he is certified as a specialist in radiology by the American Board of Radiology?
A. Yes.
Q. As far as you know, is his principal medical practice one of making X-ray examinations at the request of other doctors?
A. Yes, it is.
Q. Do you know his reputation as a radiologist among doctors in your area?
A. Yes, I do. [It is excellent.]

D. [§6.59] *Referral as Customary Medical Practice*

Q. Is it the customary medical practice for [an orthopedist] like yourself to send patients with [neck complaints] to a [radiologist] for this type of examination?
A. It is.
Q. Was this examination one you could have performed yourself in your own office?
A. No.
Q. Why is that?
A. [I do not have the equipment to do it.]
Q. Is it also regular medical practice for doctors who refer patients

for this kind of examination to rely on the results of these examinations and the conclusions of the doctors who perform them in forming their own diagnoses of the patient's condition?
A. Yes, it is.

E. [§6.60] Reasons for Test or Examination

It is well to have the witness state the medical reasons or indications for wanting a particular test or examination performed. This better enables the jury to understand the doctor's testimony about how he reached his diagnosis. It also works to defeat suggestions by opposing counsel that medical expenses claimed by the injured person were unnecessary, excessive, or not attributable to the accident.

Q. What information were you seeking to obtain from this examination?
A. [I wanted to rule out the possibility that any of the vertebrae were fractured and also to look at the alignment and spacing of the bones.]
Q. Were these matters that could have been determined by you in clinical examination?
A. No.
Q. Did you expect that having the examination made would contribute to the accuracy and certainty of your diagnosis?
A. Yes.

Comment: Even examinations that show no signs of injury can contribute to the accuracy of diagnosis by ruling out possible causes of pain and disability. If films or test results are negative, counsel may go on to have the doctor explain the value to him of the absence of signs.

F. [§6.61] Return and Identity of Results and Report

In the course of showing the manner in which the doctor received the results of the examination, counsel may seek to forestall any suggestion that there might have been a mixup, or that the films, graphs, and reports examined by the witness might have depicted some other patient.

Q. Did Dr. .... report back to you the results of his examination of [Mr. ..../plaintiff]?
A. He did.
Q. What did he send you?
A. [Four radiographic views of Mr. ....'s cervical spine

MEDICAL EXPERTS §6.63

and a written report of his procedure and what he saw in the developed films.]
Q. Did the written report refer to [Mr. ..../plaintiff] by name?
A. Yes.
Q. Were the [X-ray films] also identified as being of [Mr. ..../plaintiff]?
A. Yes. [Each film was numbered and the numbers were those referred to by Dr. .... in his written report.]

G. [§6.62] *Witness's Reliance*

Q. Did you examine these [films] sent you by Dr. ....?
A. Yes, I did.
Q. Did your analysis of what they showed form part of the basis for your diagnosis?
A. It did.
Q. Did you also read and rely on the written report that Dr. .... sent you along with them?
A. Yes.
Q. Doctor, if you examined and analyzed [the films] yourself, what additional aid did you receive by reading Dr. ....'s report?
A. [As a specialist in radiology, Dr. .... is sometimes able to identify things in the films that I might miss, and, of course, it is always helpful to have an additional opinion on the interpretation, even if it only confirms what I see in them.]
Q. Did [these films and] this report by Dr. .... constitute part of the basis for your diagnosis and conclusions about [Mr. ..../plaintiff]?
A. Yes, they did.

H. [§6.63] *Contents*

Having established that the witness sent the patient out for radiography, received films and a report, and relied on them in reaching a diagnosis and other conclusions, counsel must consider whether, and in what manner, the informational content of the films and report should be presented to the jury. If permitted by the court, the testifying doctor might (1) state the facts and opinions he read in the films, graphs, and accompanying report that contributed to his diagnosis; (2) use the films in court, pointing out on them what he saw; and (3) read the report to the jury. Counsel might also offer the films and the report in evidence as exhibits.

§6.64 MEDICAL EXPERTS

Q. Dr. ...., please tell us what you see in these [X-ray films].
A. ....
Q. And what was Dr. ....'s analysis?
A. ....
Q. What is the significance of these findings to your diagnosis of [Mr. ....'s/plaintiff's] condition?
A. ....

XI. MEDICAL OPINION TESTIMONY

A. [§6.64] Admissibility

Medical opinions about the nature and extent of injuries (diagnosis), their causes, their probable future course (prognosis), the necessity for and reasonable value of medical services (see §§14.5–14.9), and other medical subjects, are often the principle determinants of damage awards in personal injury cases. Medical doctors are generally qualified to testify as experts on these subjects, and the subjects themselves are sufficiently beyond common experience that the opinion of an expert would assist the trier of fact (see Evid C §801(a)). For a general discussion of the admissibility of expert opinion testimony, see §§1.19–1.30.

Preceding sections of this chapter have discussed the admissibility of certain testimony and exhibits on the ground that the offered evidence formed part of the basis for a medical witness's opinions. The reverse of this coin is that opinion testimony is admissible in evidence over objection only if it is based on proper matter. See §§6.65–6.66.

1. [§6.65] Proper Bases

A medical expert can base his opinion on any matter that reasonably may be relied on by a doctor in forming a medical opinion, unless some statute or decision precludes the use of that matter. Evid C §801(b). For a general discussion of the proper bases for expert opinion testimony, see §1.26. In forming an opinion, a medical expert is not confined to his own experience or to facts personally known to or observed by him. *Hope v Arrowhead & Puritas Waters, Inc.* (1959) 174 CA2d 222, 230, 344 P2d 428, 433.

The matter on which a doctor can base his medical opinion testimony includes:

(a) His own special knowledge, skill, experience, training, and education (Evid C §§801–802);

MEDICAL EXPERTS   §6.66

(b) The products of his education and study of his profession (*Hope v Arrowhead & Puritas Waters, Inc., supra*);

(c) Medical and scientific books and medical cases on record (*Healy v Visalia & Tulare R.R.* (1894) 101 C 585, 591, 36 P 125, 126);

(d) Statements made to him by the patient concerning the history of his condition (*People v Wilson* (1944) 25 C2d 341, 348, 153 P2d 720, 724);

(e) His personal observations of the patient (*Inskeep v Busby* (1962) 207 CA2d 848, 24 CR 819);

(f) Reports of other doctors (*Kelley v Bailey* (1961) 189 CA2d 728, 738, 11 CR 448, 455);

(g) The results of tests made by himself or other experts (*Christiansen v Hollings* (1941) 44 CA2d 332, 347, 112 P2d 723, 731); and

(h) Facts and opinions contained in hospital records (*Gillett v Gillett* (1959) 168 CA2d 102, 107, 335 P2d 736, 739; see §13.41).

2. [§6.66] Improper Bases

Few reported decisions have held medical opinion testimony inadmissible on the ground that it was based on matter that the witness was precluded by law from considering as a basis for his opinion. See, however, *People v Luis* (1910) 158 C 185, 195, 110 P 580, 584 (diagnosis of feeblemindedness based solely on person's exterior appearance properly excluded). Generally, irrelevant or speculative matters are not a proper basis for a doctor's opinion. See Official Comment to Evidence Code §801. See also CALIFORNIA TRIAL OBJECTIONS §§20.8, 20.20 (Cal CEB 1967) (objection that opinion testimony is based on improper matter).

It has been said that the opinion of an expert may not be predicated on the opinion of another expert. *Hope v Arrowhead & Puritas Waters, Inc.* (1959) 174 CA2d 222, 230, 344 P2d 428, 433; *Christiansen v Hollings* (1941) 44 CA2d 332, 347, 112 P2d 723, 731. However, this rule seems to preclude opinion testimony only if the witness had no other basis for his opinion than another doctor's opinion. (*E.g.,* "Dr. X told me he diagnosed a concussion; I trust his skill and judgment; therefore it is my opinion that the patient suffered a concussion.") If the testifying doctor has any basis in addition to the other opinion, such as a history, findings, or test results made by himself or someone else, he can consider the other opinion as part of the basis for his own opinion. *Kelley v Bailey* (1961) 189 CA2d 728, 737, 11 CR 448, 455; *Hope v Arrowhead & Puritas Waters, Inc., supra; Christiansen v Hollings, supra.*

3. [§6.67] Procedures for Showing Bases and Reasons

A medical expert may state on direct examination the "reasons for his opinion" and the "matter on which it is based." Evid C §802. For a general discussion of showing reasons and bases, see §1.27. Evidence Code §802 permits a doctor to testify about the sources of his knowledge of the patient (medical history, physical examination, reports, etc.), the particular medical facts and information derived by the doctor from those sources, and his own processes of analysis and judgment in applying medical principles to his information about the patient.

Unless the trial judge requires the medical witness to be examined about the matter on which his opinion is based before he gives that opinion (see Evid C §802), a lawyer could simply ask the doctor for his opinion and leave it to adverse counsel to inquire into the bases and reasons for it. However, it is usually advantageous to introduce the matter on which the opinion is based on direct examination to support, explain, and give weight to the opinion testimony. In addition, showing reasons and bases, as is permitted by Evid C §802, furnishes a convenient way to introduce evidence, albeit for a limited purpose, that corroborates other parts of the case. There are several methods that can be used to introduce evidence of the reasons and bases for a medical expert's opinions.

If the medical witness lacks knowledge of the patient, perhaps because he did not examine him or see pertinent medical records, a hypothetical question can be used to furnish him (and the trier of fact) with a recital of the matter on which the opinions are to be based. See §§1.28–1.29 for a discussion and the form of the question.

If the doctor did examine the patient, the lawyer can take him through detailed testimony about the history he obtained, the examination he made, the records and reports he considered, and so forth (as illustrated in preceding sections), before asking for his opinions. When this approach is followed, the sources of the doctor's information can be recapitulated in the question that asks for his opinion. For example:

Q. Dr. ...., based on [your examination of this man and your findings, the medical history you obtained, the hospital records that you read and considered, the X-ray report you got from Dr. ...., and your experience in this field] do you have an opinion whether ....?
A. Yes.

MEDICAL EXPERTS §6.67

Comment: Some lawyers believe that words like "Have you [formed/arrived at/reached] a medical [judgment/conclusion]" are more forceful than "do you have an opinion?" See §1.7.

If the lawyer is asking about an opinion arrived at previously, while the doctor was treating the patient, the question can end with words like "did you [arrive at a diagnosis of/reach a determination whether/form a conclusion about] ....?"

Q. What is that opinion?
A. ....

Comment: Again, it is usually more forceful to phrase this question in terms of the substance of the opinion sought, for example: "What caused these injuries?", "Did the accident cause these injuries?", and so forth.

Q. What specific facts from those sources contributed to your conclusion?
A. ....

Comment: Another approach that can be used when there has not previously been extensive testimony about the history, examination, etc., is to ask the doctor for his opinion and follow with questions that elicit the reasons and bases for it. For example:

Q. Without going into detail, Dr. ...., please tell us what sources of information you relied on in reaching this [conclusion/determination/diagnosis/opinion]?
A. [I relied on the findings of my physical examination of plaintiff on ...., 19......, the medical history I obtained from him at that time, and the X-rays and report I received from Dr. ....]
Q. Did you also take into account [his records from .... Hospital and the records of Dr. ...., who had been treating him from ...., 19......, through ...., 19......]?
A. Yes, I considered those.
Q. Doctor, earlier you described for us your long experience and intensive training in the field of [orthopedics]. Can you tell us whether the knowledge and skill you gained during this experience and training formed part of the basis for your conclusions about [plaintiff's condition]?
A. Of course, those factors contribute to any medical opinion that I arrive at.

Q. Is it the customary and regular medical practice for [doctors/orthopedists/etc.] like yourself to base your conclusions on the factors and matters that we have just discussed?
A. It is.
Q. Now, Dr. ...., what specific findings did you make when you examined [Mr. ..../plaintiff] that led you to conclude [state opinion]?
A. ....
Q. What, if anything, was the significance of [state specific medical fact]?
A. ....
Q. How did you get from [state facts] to [state opinion]?
A. ....

Comment: The lawyer can continue in the same manner through the medical history, test results, and so forth.

B. [§6.68] *Diagnosis: Nature and Extent of Injuries*

A diagnosis is a doctor's determination and description of a patient's disease or injury. Diagnoses recorded in medical records are often brief labels: capsule categorizations in standardized medical terminology. They are formulated by doctors to classify their patients' conditions and to provide themselves and other medical personnel with a framework for prescribing treatment and predicting future developments. In addition, diagnoses are usually called for in the medical report forms doctors are often required to fill out.

A patient can have a separate diagnosis applied to him and recorded each time he is seen by a doctor. Differences between diagnoses result from differences of opinion among doctors, actual changes in the patient's condition, and changes in opinion as doctors receive additional information about the patient and see his response to treatment.

Trial lawyers are usually more concerned with establishing the nature and extent of the plaintiff's injuries than with the capsule diagnosis itself. Indeed, lawyers sometimes use the word "diagnosis" in this broader sense, to indicate all of the doctor's opinions about the nature, extent, origins, and effects of plaintiff's injuries.

1. [§6.69] Admissibility

Medical diagnoses and descriptions of the nature and extent of injuries are opinions that are a proper subject of expert testimony, because the true nature of plaintiff's physical status is sufficiently

MEDICAL EXPERTS §6.70

beyond common experience that the opinion of a doctor would assist the trier of fact. See Evid C §801(a); Witkin, CALIFORNIA EVIDENCE §413 (2d ed, 1966). A medical witness can thus testify about his own diagnosis. He can also testify about diagnoses made by other doctors when he does so to show part of the basis for his own opinions. See *Kelley v Bailey* (1961) 189 CA2d 728, 737, 11 CR 448, 455; §6.56. The witness may also explain changes in his diagnosis and differences with those of other doctors.

Opinions about the nature and extent of injuries may be based on the same kinds of matter and reasons that support other medical opinions. See Evid C §801(b); §6.65.

2. [§6.70] Relating Diagnoses to Injuries

Opinion testimony about the nature and extent of injuries can be elicited from a medical witness without ever asking him to state his, or anyone's, diagnosis. However, many doctors feel more comfortable testifying about injuries and their effect on plaintiff's life when it is done in the course of explaining and expanding on the succinct medical terminology of a diagnosis. Further, jurors can be impressed by the very words of a capsule diagnosis. It fulfills their expectations of what a doctor would say, and they may more readily accept injury testimony when it comes as explanation of a diagnosis.

Plaintiff's lawyers often use a brief diagnosis as a starting point for testimony about the nature and extent of injuries. (Defense lawyers, on the other hand, are often quite happy with a succinct and unexplained statement of plaintiff's injuries.) For example, in a head injury case, the direct examination of a plaintiff's doctor might proceed as follows:

Q. Dr. ...., when you examined [Mr. ..../plaintiff] on ...., 19......, did you diagnose his condition at that time?
A. Yes.
Q. What was your diagnosis?
A. My diagnosis at that time was "postconcussion syndrome."

Comment: Diagnoses usually describe the patient's condition when he is examined. Diagnoses like the one above also reflect the nature of the original injury, and the causes of the patient's present status.

Q. Was it your conclusion that he had previously suffered a cerebral concussion?
A. Yes.

§6.70

Q. Could you determine when the concussion had been suffered?
A. [Not precisely.]
Q. On the basis of what you observed, could it have occurred on [Give date of accident]?
A. Yes.
Q. What is a cerebral concussion, Doctor?
A. That is a jarring or shaking of the brain.
Q. If a person receives a sharp blow to his head, does his brain move or bounce against one side of the skull and then the other?
A. Yes.
Q. Can this happen even though the blow does not cause a fracture of the skull or even a laceration of the scalp?
A. Yes.
Q. From what you have said, Doctor, a diagnosis of cerebral concussion indicates the manner in which the brain is injured, that is, shaken or jarred?
A. That's correct.
Q. Does "cerebral concussion" as a diagnosis also refer to a physical status or condition?
A. Yes.
Q. What is the condition covered by that diagnosis?
A. It is a condition of unconsciousness, feeble pulse, cold skin, and pallor, followed later by partial stupor, headache, retrograde amnesia, and sometimes vomiting.

Comment: Even though the doctor has already testified about the medical history, physical examination, and test results, particular symptoms and findings can be related to the diagnosis to show part of the basis for it. See §6.67. This testimony can be extensive in cases in which the accuracy of the witness's diagnosis seems likely to be challenged. Further, testimony at this point about symptoms of pain and discomfort reinforces other testimony about the detriment suffered by the plaintiff.

Q. Did his history [as you learned it from him and his medical records] reflect the signs and symptoms that commonly follow a cerebral concussion?
A. Yes.
Q. What particular matters confirmed that diagnosis?
A. [The hospital records show that he was unconscious when he was brought into the emergency receiving room.]
Q. Now, Dr. ...., what is postconcussion syndrome?
A. The term refers to a group of symptoms that commonly follow

MEDICAL EXPERTS §6.70

concussions, including headaches, dizziness, irritability, and so forth.
Q. When you examined Mr. .... on ...., 19......, what particular findings, symptoms, and other matter contributed to your diagnosis of postconcussion syndrome?
A. ....
Q. Did your diagnosis also cover [the forgetfulness and inability to concentrate] that Mr. .... told you about?
A. Yes.
Q. Are these all symptoms that are commonly experienced by persons who have suffered concussions?
A. Yes.

Comment: The existence of symptoms and signs at the time of the examination can indicate the nature and severity of the original injury as well as showing the patient's condition at the time of the examination.

Q. Assuming that Mr. .... suffered a concussion on ...., 19......, and based on the residuals and aftereffects that you found and he told you about when you examined him on ...., 19......, did you reach a conclusion about the severity of his concussion?
A. Yes.
Q. How severe a concussion was it?
A. ....

Comment: A diagnosis made at an examination done shortly before trial can often be projected by the doctor into testimony about his condition at the time of trial and in the future.

Q. How long after a concussion are these residuals and aftereffects expected to last?
A. [It is difficult to give a specific time; it varies from person to person and according to the severity of the original injury.]
Q. Is it medically consistent with your conclusions about Mr. ....'s original injury and his condition that when you examined him on ...., 19......, he was still suffering from the same aftereffects?
A. Yes.
Q. Assuming that he is still suffering from these residuals, does your diagnosis of postconcussion syndrome still apply to him as he sits here today in this courtroom?
A. It does.

Comment: From this point, plaintiff's counsel would usually pursue in greater detail each of the plaintiff's symptoms and disabilities, show their effects on his life, and proceed to explore the probable future course of the injury.

C. [§6.71] Cause of Injuries

Doctors often form opinions about the etiology (medical cause) of a patient's condition. Doctors usually ask for information about causation when taking medical histories, because knowing the probable causes of a disease or injury often helps the doctor arrive at a diagnosis and decide on a course of treatment. See §6.38.

A plaintiff is entitled to recover damages only for the detriment proximately caused by defendant's breach of duty. CC §3333. In personal injury cases, establishing proximate cause can require proof that (1) defendant's wrongful conduct resulted in trauma to the plaintiff (*i.e.*, the action of forces or agents on him); and (2) the forces and agents resulted in the particular injuries or detriment for which the plaintiff claims damages. The first is not a medical question, but the second is an appropriate area for medical testimony.

Medical opinion testimony is not always needed to establish causation. In many cases, the trier of fact can infer the connection from other evidence. However, expert medical testimony is practically essential when (1) signs and symptoms are remote in time and bodily area from the forces claimed to have caused them; (2) extensive injuries are claimed to have resulted from relatively small forces; (3) plaintiff had a preexisting condition, not connected with the accident, that could have caused the detriment for which damages are claimed or could have caused the accident; or (4) a disease or injury incurred after the accident, but not because of it, could have produced the detriment for which damages are claimed. See examples in §6.72.

1. [§6.72] Value of Causation Testimony

The value of medical opinion testimony in establishing causation is illustrated by the following cases. Verdicts for plaintiffs have been sustained on the basis of medical testimony that:

(a) Trauma fracturing a hip was a contributing cause to death five months later from myocardial infarction due to coronary arteriosclerosis. *Robison v Leigh* (1957) 153 CA2d 730, 315 P2d 42.

(b) A fall on an iron bar caused a hernia requiring surgical repair that resulted in death from an embolism. *Muzzy v Supreme Lodge of the Fraternal Bhd.* (1933) 129 CA 1, 18 P2d 107.

MEDICAL EXPERTS §6.73

(c) A fall on a sidewalk precipitated cancer that resulted in a spontaneous fracture of the femur eight months later. *Shaw v Owl Drug Co.* (1935) 4 CA2d 191, 40 P2d 588.

(d) A fall in a hole could result in a stroke and hemiplegia. *Perkins v Sunset Tel. & Tel. Co.* (1909) 155 C 712, 103 P 190.

(e) Plaintiff's back complaints resulted from a disc injury suffered in an automobile accident rather than from preexisting Parkinson's disease and encephalitis. *Inskeep v Busby* (1962) 207 CA2d 848, 24 CR 819.

(f) Plaintiff's insanity was caused by a whiplash injury to the neck when her car was struck from the rear. *Frampton v Hartzell* (1960) 179 CA2d 771, 4 CR 427.

(g) A fall on a stairway triggered latent schizophrenia resulting in disabling mental illness. *DiMare v Cresci* (1962) 58 C2d 292, 23 CR 772.

(h) Sulphur smog "lighted up" preexisting cancer requiring complete removal of the larynx and, in another plaintiff, aggravated a preexisting heart condition. *Hagy v Allied Chem. & Dye Corp.* (1953) 122 CA2d 361, 265 P2d 86.

(i) Lead poisoning facilitated meningitis that caused death. *Travelers Ins. Co. v IAC* (1949) 33 C2d 685, 203 P2d 747.

In few of the foregoing cases could a trier of fact have connected the trauma caused by defendants' wrongful acts and the eventual injury or death without the medical expert opinion testimony. Even in cases in which the connection or absence of connection between the accident and the injuries seems self-evident, the medical witness can be asked for his opinion whether the accident caused, or could have caused, the injuries seen in the plaintiff. See, *e.g., Dow v Oroville* (1913) 22 CA 215, 226, 134 P 197, 202 (proper for doctor to testify that plaintiff's rib fractures and bruises could have been produced by fall into trench).

Defendants use medical testimony about causation to rebut plaintiffs' testimony that links the claimed injuries to the accident and to show that the injuries claimed by the plaintiff were probably caused by disease or trauma for which the defendant was not responsible.

2. [§6.73] Admissibility

Medical causation is a subject sufficiently beyond common experience that the opinion of a doctor would assist the trier of fact. See Evid C §801(a). It is proper for a medical expert to give his opinion on the causal connection between an accident and an injury and whether a certain agency, means, or instrument might have produced

§6.74   MEDICAL EXPERTS

a particular injury. *Perkins v Sunset Tel. & Tel. Co.* (1909) 155 C 712, 715, 103 P 190, 192; *Inskeep v Busby* (1962) 207 CA2d 848, 851, 24 CR 819, 820; Witkin, CALIFORNIA EVIDENCE §413 (2d ed, 1966). Medical opinions of the manner in which, or means by which, a person may have received physical injuries are proper subjects of expert testimony. *Dow v Oroville* (1913) 22 CA 215, 226, 134 P 197, 202.

An opinion about the causal connection between particular injuries and the forces or agencies for which defendant is responsible may be based on the same kinds of matter and reasons that properly support other medical opinions. See §6.65. This includes the medical history given by the patient. See *Muzzy v Supreme Lodge of the Fraternal Bhd.* (1933) 129 CA 1, 9, 18 P2d 107, 110; §9.38.

A medical witness need not testify positively to support a finding of proximate cause; his opinion of the probabilities is sufficient. *Robison v Leigh* (1957) 153 CA2d 730, 732, 315 P2d 42, 44. Further, expert evidence of a medical possibility taken with other evidence of a nonexpert character may be sufficient to support an inference of medical probability. *Hagy v Allied Chem. & Dye Corp.* (1953) 122 CA2d 361, 374, 265 P2d 86, 95. Thus, a doctor's opinion testimony about medical causation should be received in evidence whether he says that the trauma incurred in the accident "did" (or did not) cause the injuries, "probably" caused the injuries, or "could have" caused the injuries. However, the latter testimony, in that it expresses only a possibility, would not alone sustain a recovery. See *Francis v Sauve* (1963) 222 CA2d 102, 118, 34 CR 754, 762.

3. [§6.74] Form of Testimony

Trial lawyers want their medical witnesses to testify in positive terms when stating opinions about causal connection. For example: "The accident caused these injuries" or "His present symptoms are the direct result of the injuries he received in the accident." Or, for the defense: "All his present symptoms are due to his preexisting arthritis, which was not aggravated by the accident," "His heart attack occurred before the collision, not as a result of it," or "The congenital defect is causing his back pain."

Doctors, however, usually prefer to speak of possible causes and hesitate to commit themselves to positive opinions about the cause of a patient's condition. In these cases, lawyers seek testimony that the connection between the accident or other cause and the claimed injuries is probable or that there is a "reasonable medical probability" that the injuries resulted from the accident or other cause.

MEDICAL EXPERTS §6.74

Q. Dr. ...., have you concluded whether [the accident you learned about in taking his medical history/the congenital defect you found/etc.] caused the [injuries/symptoms/disabilities] that [Mr. ..../plaintiff] described to you when you examined him?
A. Yes, I have.
Q. What caused these symptoms and disabilities?
A. ....

Comment: Sometimes a plaintiff's doctor is unwilling to say more than: "These injuries could have resulted from the accident." This testimony gives the defense a chance to get the witness to "admit" on cross-examination that the stated causal relationship was merely a possibility and to argue that the plaintiff has thus failed to establish that the claimed injuries were proximately caused by the accident. If a plaintiff's lawyer feels he must use such a medical witness, he can either ask the doctor to explain his answer, hoping that the explanation might contain statements indicating probability, or he can be sure that he has other evidence that, taken together with the doctor's statement of medical possibility, can support an inference of medical probability. See §6.73.

Similarly, defense medical testimony that some factor for which the defendant is not responsible "could have caused" the plaintiff's present symptoms and disabilities provides plaintiff's attorney with an opportunity to object that the testimony is speculative and to argue that the defendant is merely raising a cloud of possibilities in an attempt to confuse the jury and defeat a meritorious claim.

Q. Dr. ...., could the injuries that [Mr. ..../plaintiff] described to you have resulted from [a fall into a trench six feet deep/a preexisting heart condition/etc.]?
A. Yes, that could have been the cause.
Q. Were there any indications in your findings or the history you received, or any other source, that his injuries resulted from some other cause?
A. No.

Comment: If preexisting or subsequently developing conditions independent of the accident are involved in the case, testimony about medical causation must be tailored to the particular facts of the case.

In all cases it is appropriate for counsel to bring out the reasons for the doctor's conclusions about causation and the matter on which his opinions are based. See §6.67.

D. [§6.75] *Prognosis: Continuing, Permanent, and Future Injuries*

A prognosis is a doctor's prediction of the probable future course of injuries or disease. It is a forecast that can be stated in terms of the likely duration or permanency of symptoms currently experienced; the possibility of, or increased susceptibility to, the later development of detrimental conditions not yet manifest; and the prospects for recovery and return to a normal life.

The prognoses that are stated in medical records are often general, brief, and conclusory (*e.g.,* "excellent," "fair," "serious," "good if epilepsy does not develop," etc.). Some doctors avoid venturing any prognosis for a patient, preferring to diagnose, treat, and wait to see how he responds. Their prognoses tend to be stated in optimistic terms to encourage the patient toward recovery or adjustment to his condition. Thus, while a plaintiff's probable future condition can be the principal determinant of verdict size, doctors' statements of prognoses are often of little aid to trial lawyers, except as a starting point for testimony about the future consequences of plaintiff's injuries.

Defense lawyers are often content with the prognoses stated in the medical records or by their medical witnesses. The very brevity, generality, optimism, and emphasis on prospects for recovery and adjustment that characterize many prognoses are favorable to the defense point of view.

Plaintiff's attorneys are more likely to use stated prognoses as starting points for detailed testimony about the future consequences of injury. Sometimes they even bypass a stated prognosis to ask a medical witness directly whether plaintiff's symptoms and disabilities are likely to continue beyond the date of the trial, whether any of his injuries will be permanent, and whether the plaintiff can expect to suffer new symptoms or reinjury in the future.

1. [§6.76] Admissibility

Medical prognoses are a proper subject of medical opinion testimony; the probable future course of plaintiff's injuries is sufficiently beyond common experience that the opinion of a doctor would assist the trier of fact. See Evid C §801(a); Witkin, CALIFORNIA EVIDENCE §413 (2d ed, 1966). A medical witness can testify about his own prognosis and about the prognoses of other doctors that were relied on by him as part of the basis for his conclusions. See *Kelley v Bailey* (1961) 189 CA2d 728, 737, 11 CR 448, 455; §6.56. He should be permitted to state and explain any prior prognoses he made and the differences between his current predictions and those of other doctors.

Opinions about the future course of injuries are based on the same

MEDICAL EXPERTS §6.77

kinds of matter and reasons that properly support other medical opinions. See Evid C §801(b); §6.65.

2. [§6.77] Reasonable Medical Certainty

Under CC §3283, a plaintiff may recover damages for detriment suffered through the time of trial, and for detriment "certain to result in the future." Before a jury may allow a recovery for prospective damages, the evidence must show with reasonable certainty that the future detriment will follow. *Bauman v San Francisco* (1940) 42 CA2d 144, 163, 108 P2d 989, 1000.

However, the law does not require a doctor to testify that future results are "reasonably certain" to occur before his testimony is admissible. Testimony in less certain terms is admissible, as long as it is not conjecture that merely establishes a possibility of future trouble. See *Cordiner v Los Angeles Traction Co.* (1907) 5 CA 400, 404, 91 P 436, 437. The jury is to determine from all the evidence, including any expert medical testimony, whether the future detriment is reasonably certain to occur. *Paolini v San Francisco* (1946) 72 CA2d 579, 589, 164 P2d 916, 922.

Jurors are commonly instructed to award damages for detriment that plaintiff is "reasonably certain to suffer in the future." See BAJI Nos 14.10, 14.12, 14.13. Thus, it is to plaintiff's advantage to obtain medical testimony stated in terms of "reasonable certainty."

If the witness is reluctant to use the words "reasonably certain," counsel should seek as strong a statement as the doctor is willing to make. Examples of testimony that has been received include "Medical experience (or my experience) in these cases is that this result will follow"; "medical statistics show that in the majority of these cases the result is"; "this result will probably occur"; "my experience is that we can expect this result in this case"; "I would not be surprised if it occurred"; and even "it might occur." See *Carrasco v Bankoff* (1963) 220 CA2d 230, 33 CR 673; *Mendoza v Rudolf* (1956) 140 CA2d 633, 295 P2d 445; *Paolini v San Francisco, supra; Ostertag v Bethlehem Shipbuilding Corp.* (1944) 65 CA2d 795, 151 P2d 647; *Bauman v San Francisco, supra; Riggs v Gasser Motors* (1937) 22 CA2d 636, 72 P2d 172; *Cordiner v Los Angeles Traction Co., supra.* It is usually better to have the doctor testify about "threats" and "dangers" than "possibilities" and what "might follow."

Trial lawyers sometimes find it helpful to discuss with a medical witness before trial the question: How certain is "reasonably certain"? Some attorneys tell doctors that an injury is reasonably certain to continue or result if it is more likely than not to do so, even if there is as little as a 51-percent likelihood that it will. It is also said that the certainty requirement of CC §3283 cannot be strictly applied when prospective damages are sought, since probabilities are really the basis for the award. See 2 Witkin, SUMMARY OF CALIFORNIA LAW 1597 (7th ed, 1960).

Suppose that a plaintiff's doctor testifies: "One person in ten with his injury and his progress to date can be expected to suffer grand mal seizures in the future." Would this testimony be stricken as speculative under CC §3283 since it does not show that the epilepsy is "certain to result in the future"? A plaintiff's attorney might argue that

(a) The testimony shows that the trauma created a greater susceptibility to the future development of epilepsy, and this susceptibility or weakened physical status is a present detriment for which damages can be awarded.

(b) The testimony should at least be received to show the basis for the plaintiff's present anxiety and mental suffering about his future health.

3. [§6.78] Continuing Conditions; Permanency

When there is evidence that plaintiff is still experiencing injuries and disabilities at the time of trial, it is appropriate to have a medical witness state how long the signs and symptoms can be expected to continue. If possible, the medical testimony should fix probable duration with certainty. However, even if a plaintiff's medical testimony falls short of this, evidence that plaintiff is currently experiencing symptoms that inferentially will continue after the trial tends to prove future damages and justifies an instruction on future damages. See *Loper v Morrison* (1944) 23 C2d 600, 611, 145 P2d 1, 6; *Mendoza v Rudolf* (1956) 140 CA2d 633, 295 P2d 445.

Medical opinion testimony can also be used to establish whether plaintiff's injuries are permanent. See *Guerra v Balestrieri* (1954) 127 CA2d 511, 519, 274 P2d 443, 447.

Q. Dr. ...., as a part of your examination of [Mr. ..../ plaintiff], did you arrive at a prognosis of his injuries?
A. I did.
Q. By the way, Doctor, what is a prognosis?
A. It is a medical prediction of the probable future course of a patient's disease or condition.
Q. What was the prognosis with regard to [state specific injuries]?
A. [I would say good.]
Q. Can you be a little more specific, Doctor? How long do you

MEDICAL EXPERTS §6.79

   expect [Mr. ..../plaintiff] to be troubled by [list symptoms and disabilities]?
A. ....
Q. Are these effects reasonably certain to continue for that period?
A. Yes.
Q. With regard to [specify other injuries], what is the prognosis for those injuries?
A. ....
Q. Can these injuries be characterized as permanent?
A. Yes, they can.
Q. From a medical standpoint, Doctor, are these injuries reasonably certain to be permanent?
A. Yes, they are.
Q. Please tell us the facts and the reasons that are the basis for your conclusion that these injuries are permanent.
A. ....

Comment: A plaintiff's lawyer will continue to bring out the relationship of the continuing and permanent injuries to plaintiff's life and activities.

Q. Will [Mr. ..../plaintiff] ever be able to [state activity]?
A. ....

4. [§6.79] Future Conditions

Doctors can sometimes predict with reasonable certainty that a patient will in the future experience difficulties that are greater or different from any injuries or disabilities currently exhibited. For example, a patient may appear to have made a good recovery from a skull fracture, yet his doctor might consider him a likely candidate for future epileptic seizures. See *Bauman v San Francisco* (1940) 42 CA2d 144, 108 P2d 989; *Cordiner v Los Angeles Traction Co.* (1907) 5 CA 400, 91 P 436.

Q. Dr. ...., from a medical standpoint, what does the future hold for [Mr. ..../plaintiff]?
A. [I don't think anyone can say positively what the future holds for him, although we certainly hope that he will have a good recovery.]
Q. I agree, Doctor, that we all hope for a good recovery, but in view of the severity of his injury, as you have described it to us, what consequences of his injury constitute a threat to him in the future?
A. ....
Q. Considering [state facts showing severity of injury] and all that you know about [Mr. ..../plaintiff], is he more likely

§6.79 MEDICAL EXPERTS

than not or less likely than not, to develop [state condition] at some later time in his life?

A. ....

Q. Based on your long experience in this type of case, and your reading of medical literature about cases of this type, what are the statistical probabilities for the development of [state condition] following injuries of the severity that [Mr. ..../plaintiff] suffered?

A. ....

Q. Is there a reasonable medical certainty that [Mr. ..../plaintiff] will suffer [state condition] at some time in the future?

A. ....

Comment: See §6.77 for a discussion of the kinds of testimony that can be developed if the doctor does not testify in terms of reasonable certainty.

7
Other Witnesses on Damages

I. [§7.1] Lay Witnesses Generally

    A. [§7.2] Bystanders at Accident Scene
    B. [§7.3] Nurses; Medical Personnel
    C. Family Members
        1. [§7.4] Suffering and Disability
        2. [§7.5] Nursing Services
    D. [§7.6] Fellow Workers; Supervisors
    E. [§7.7] Acquaintances; Neighbors

II. [§7.8] Employer; Personnel Manager

III. [§7.9] Economists; Statisticians; Appraisers of Impaired Earning Capacity

    A. [§7.10] Basis of Testimony
    B. [§7.11] Qualifications: Checklist
    C. [§7.12] Topics of Testimony

I. [§7.1] LAY WITNESSES GENERALLY

Both plaintiffs' and defendants' lawyers look to lay witnesses for valuable supplementary testimony on injuries and damages. When medical expert testimony is in conflict or is difficult to understand, jurors tend to accept the version most consistent with the facts observed by lay persons who saw the plaintiff over a long period of time and in unguarded moments. Jurors are often skeptical of a plaintiff's testimony about his suffering and disability, but they are more willing to trust the testimony of impartial observers.

§7.2 OTHER WITNESSES ON DAMAGES

Lay witnesses can testify to the plaintiff's exclamations or statements of present pain or bodily condition. See Evid C §§1250, 1252; *Bloomberg v Laventhal* (1919) 179 C 616, 619, 178 P 496, 497. This includes both outcrys, grimaces, and the like that are manifestations of pain and more deliberate statements by the declarant of his existing mental or physical state. See generally Witkin, CALIFORNIA EVIDENCE §554 (2d ed, 1966).

A lay witness can testify to his observations of the nature, extent, and effect of a plaintiff's injuries and of the condition of his health. See *Jordan v Great W. Motorways* (1931) 213 C 606, 612, 2 P2d 786, 789; *Latky v Wolfe* (1927) 85 CA 332, 345, 259 P 470, 476. Lay testimony about the apparent health or physical condition of a person he knows can be stated in opinion form. See Evid C §800; *Robinson v Exempt Fire Co.* (1894) 103 C 1, 5, 36 P 955, 956; Witkin, EVIDENCE §399. See generally §§1.16–1.18.

A lay witness can also testify about a person's physical condition before injury (*Lowenthal v Mortimer* (1954) 125 CA2d 636, 640, 270 P2d 942, 945) and his capacity for work before and after injury (*Majors v Connor* (1912) 162 C 131, 136, 121 P 371, 374).

Lay witnesses testifying about the plaintiff's physical condition usually begin with testimony to establish their own credibility (see §1.13), proceed to describe their opportunity to observe the plaintiff, and then tell what they have seen and heard.

A. [§7.2] Bystanders at Accident Scene

In his concern to establish fault, the lawyer should not overlook persons who saw the accident and its aftermath as witnesses on injuries and damage. See, *e.g., Kline v Santa Barbara Consol. Ry.* (1907) 150 C 741, 749, 90 P 125, 128, in which a bystander testified that the plaintiff was unable to stand and suffered intensely following a collision.

A witness who saw the plaintiff immediately after an accident could testify to such matters as: He was unconscious, dazed, incoherent, or "in a fog"; he was bleeding, bruised, limping, or holding his neck; he uttered cries or showed expressions or other manifestations of pain; his clothing was torn and his glasses or watch broken; he asked for help, for a doctor, or for painkillers; he received first aid; etc. If the witness also saw the plaintiff just before the accident, he could compare the plaintiff's appearance then with his postaccident condition.

A witness who saw the accident may be able to testify about the speed and condition of the vehicles, the nature of the surfaces the plaintiff struck, whether the plaintiff was pinned in the wreckage, the proximity of other injured or dead persons, and the like. This testimony can be relevant on the nature and extent of injuries even though liability has been admitted. See *Sumrall v Butler* (1951) 102 CA2d 515, 520, 227 P2d 881, 885.

B. [§7.3] *Nurses; Medical Personnel*

Nurses are competent to testify to the extent of a patient's suffering and to his involuntary declarations and exclamations of pain and suffering. See *Kimball v Northern Elec. Co.* (1911) 159 C 225, 231, 113 P 156, 159; *Green v Pacific Lumber Co.* (1900) 130 C 435, 440, 62 P 747, 748. Like other lay witnesses, a nurse can often express her observations in opinion form, but she is not usually qualified to give medical opinion testimony as an expert. See *Hutton v Brookside Hosp.* (1963) 213 CA2d 350, 355, 28 CR 774, 777.

Nurses, whether in the hospital or in the home, see the patient more frequently than doctors see him. They can testify that the patient cried out or moaned, called for analgesics, and thrashed about. On the other hand, they may testify that he slept well, watched television, and seemed in good spirits.

A private duty nurse can also testify about what services she provided the plaintiff, his apparent need for those services, and her charge for providing them. To show the reasonableness of this item of medical expense, the nurse can also relate her charge in this case with her usual charge and with the rate charged by other nurses. See chap 14 on introduction of medical bills.

Other medical personnel, such as ambulance drivers, hospital orderlies, and technicians are often able to furnish helpful injury testimony. And the lawyer should not overlook the possibility of using the plaintiff's fellow patients and hospital room or ward mates as lay witnesses.

C. *Family Members*

1. [§7.4] Suffering and Disability

Members of the plaintiff's family can testify to manifestations of suffering and can compare the plaintiff's condition and activities before and after injury. See, *e.g., Kline v Santa Barbara Consol. Ry.* (1907) 150 C 741, 749, 90 P 125, 128 (daughter testified that mother was unable to walk, suffered intensely for days, and could not be moved); *Walter v England* (1933) 133 CA 676, 689, 24 P2d 930, 935 (husband testified that plaintiff was in good health mentally and physically before the accident, but afterward woke him in the night crying in pain); *Latky v Wolfe* (1927) 85 CA 332, 345, 259 P 470, 476 (husband testified about nature, extent, and effects of wife's injuries); *Jones v Southern Pac. Co.* (1925) 74 CA 10, 37, 239 P 429, 439 (relatives testified about appearance and bodily health of decedent before and after injury that lead to death).

2. [§7.5] Nursing Services

In addition to the medical services provided by independent doctors and nurses (see chap 14), a plaintiff is entitled to compensation for the reasonable value of necessary nursing services provided by family members. *Kimball v Northern Elec. Co.* (1911) 159 C 225, 231, 113 P 156, 159 (plaintiff's mother was registered nurse); *Ciriniconi v Green* (1959) 175 CA2d 812, 816, 346 P2d 867, 869 (daughter was vocational or practical nurse). See generally Johns, CALIFORNIA DAMAGES 86–87, 154–156, 204–205 (1969). See also §14.2. Even if the family member who provides the services is not trained as a nurse, the plaintiff is entitled to the reasonable value of the nursing services rendered. *Large v Williams* (1957) 154 CA2d 315, 320, 315 P2d 919, 923 (mother); *Seedborg v Lakewood Gardens Civic Ass'n* (1951) 105 CA2d 449, 454, 233 P2d 943, 946 (sister-in-law and husband).

The testimony of a wife who, although not a trained nurse, provided nursing services to her husband, might proceed as follows:

Q. Mrs. ...., what was your occupation at the time Mr. .... [was injured/returned from the hospital]?
A. ....

Comment: If the wife was employed other than as a housewife, it can be shown that she missed work or had to quit to provide the care. However, the reasonable value of nursing services provided is the measure of damages, not the amount of earnings she lost. See *Seedborg v Lakewood Gardens Civic Ass'n, supra.*

Q. Did you have a discussion with Dr. .... about the care that your husband would require while he was recuperating at home?
A. Yes.
Q. When did that discussion take place?
A. [About a week before he was brought home from the hospital.]
Q. Did you discuss hiring a private nurse to provide that care?
A. Yes, we did.

OTHER WITNESSES ON DAMAGES §7.5

Q. Did you decide to hire a private nurse?
A. No.
Q. Please tell us why not.
A. [We just couldn't afford it. The cost of a nurse for ...... hours a day would have been $...... every day. It was better for me to [quit my job and] take care of him myself.]

Comment: If the wife is a trained nurse, she can testify about the cost of nursing services. Otherwise a medical witness can testify about the nature and extent of services needed and their reasonable value. See §§14.5–14.6. Or the wife might be permitted to state the going rate for nursing services as she learned it in investigating the cost of hiring a nurse. Further, the wife could describe the services rendered, and the jurors would be entitled to draw on their own judgment and experience in determining the reasonable value of those services. *Seedborg v Lakewood Gardens Civic Ass'n, supra.*

Q. Did Dr. .... instruct you in the care to give your husband?
A. Yes.
Q. Please describe the services you provided.
A. [I bathed him in bed, gave him alcohol rubs, brought him his medicine, took his temperature and his pulse every ...... hours, and kept a hospital-type chart for the doctor.]
Q. Did you also apply traction to his [neck]?
A. Yes.
Q. Did Dr. .... show you how to do that?
A. Yes.
Q. Please tell us how you did that, and how often.
A. ....
Q. Do you know how many hours a day you devoted to providing this nursing care to your husband?
A. [Yes. About ...... hours per day.]
Q. How long did you provide care at this rate?
A. ....
Q. Did you report to Dr. .... about the care you were giving and your husband's progress?
A. Yes.
Q. Did you receive further instructions from him?
A. Yes.

Comment: Periods of less intensive care, including any care being provided at the time of trial, can also be shown.

If there has been evidence of the going rate for nursing services of the kind the wife rendered, she may be permitted on that basis to state the reasonable value of her services. For example:

Q. Based on the going rate for private nursing services, which [you have/Dr. .... has] testified was $...... per day, and the time you spent caring for your husband, can you give us your assessment of the reasonable value of the nursing services you provided him?
A. Yes. At $...... per day for ...... days my nursing services were worth $.......

D. [§7.6] *Fellow Workers; Supervisors*

A plaintiff's fellow workers are in a position to observe his apparent condition, personality, and ability to work both before and after injury. See, *e.g., Majors v Connor* (1912) 162 C 131, 136, 121 P 371, 374, in which the son of a mason, himself a mason, testified that he worked with his father both before and after the accident and that afterward the father could not "do near the work" he had been able to do before. Similarly, a plaintiff's job supervisor may assess his pre and postaccident capabilities and prospects for advancement.

If the plaintiff was self-employed, other persons in the same or similar fields can testify about his potential earnings in that field. For example, in *Connolly v Pre-Mixed Concrete Co.* (1957) 49 C2d 483, 489, 319 P2d 343, 346, a tennis promoter, a tennis writer (both former players), and a broadcasting system sports director testified about plaintiff's earning potential as a professional tennis player, although at the time of injury she was still an amateur.

E. [§7.7] *Acquaintances; Neighbors*

Plaintiff's acquaintances and neighbors observe him in his ordinary daily activities over a period of time, and in unguarded moments. They see him working around his house and on his car, and in his leisure time activities. They are often not so closely associated with the plaintiff that their testimony is colored by sympathy.

For example, a neighbor might testify as follows:

Q. Are you a neighbor of Mr. ....?
A. Yes. [I live next door/on the same street/etc.]
Q. How long have you known him?
A. Since 19.......
Q. Do you still [live next door to him]?
A. Yes.

OTHER WITNESSES ON DAMAGES §7.7

Q. How often did you see him over the years before ...., 19......, the date of the accident he was in?
A. ....
Q. In what circumstances did you see him?
A. [We went golfing together many times; my wife and I went to their house to play bridge and for parties, and they came to our house; we served on committees together in church; etc.]
Q. Did you work together on home repairs?
A. Yes. [He has helped me many times, and I have helped him.]
Q. Have you had occasion to observe his activities around the house?
A. Yes.
Q. What were some of the things he did before the accident?
A. [He used to paint his house every three years; he worked on his car, waxing it and fixing the motor; he mowed the grass and worked in his garden; etc.]
Q. Did he ever exhibit any weakness or difficulty before the accident in doing those things?
A. No. [He was always strong and active.]
Q. Have you seen him since he returned from the hospital on ...., 19......?
A. Yes.
Q. How often?
A. ....
Q. What were the occasions?
A. ....
Q. Please describe what you have observed of his physical and mental condition from that time to the present.
A. ....
Q. Did he ever say anything to you about his condition at those times?
A. Yes.

Comment: There is an exception to the hearsay rule for a person's statements of his then existing mental or physical state. See Evid C §§1250, 1252.

Q. What did he say?
A. ....
Q. What was his appearance at those times?
A. ....
Q. Have you seen him paint his house since the accident?
A. No.
Q. Has his house been painted?
A. Yes.

Q. By whom?
A. [He hired a professional painter to do it in 19......, and last year I saw his wife out touching up some of the trim.]
Q. Have you played golf with him since the accident?
A. [We tried to once on ...., 19......, but he quit after ...... holes. He said his back hurt too much to go on.]
Q. Could you describe his personality before and after the accident?
A. ....

Comment: The dialogue can continue with other observations of pain and disability.

II. [§7.8] EMPLOYER; PERSONNEL MANAGER

The plaintiff's employer or his employer's personnel manager can often give valuable testimony on the issue of impaired earning capacity. He can state the plaintiff's position, wage or salary, competence, prospects for advancement before and after injury, and the extent to which fringe benefits were lost or reduced. For example:

Q. Mr. ...., what is your occupation?
A. [President/Personnel Manager/etc.] of .... Company.
Q. Did your company employ Mr. ...., the plaintiff in this action, on ...., 19...... [date of injury]?
A. Yes.

Comment: If business records of the company have been received in evidence (see chap 11) the witness can refer to them for facts about the plaintiff.

Q. When was he first employed?
A. ...., 19.......
Q. In what capacity?
A. ....
Q. What was his job title on the day he was injured?
A. ....
Q. What were his duties?
A. ....
Q. [Did you have occasion to observe his capabilities?/Do your records contain ratings of his efficiency?]
A. Yes.
Q. How was he performing?
A. ....

OTHER WITNESSES ON DAMAGES §7.10

Q. Based on his performance, what were his prospects in your company?
A. ....

Comment: While the foregoing question calls for a degree of speculation, the witness because of his position may be qualified to predict with reasonable certainty plaintiff's probable employment future.

Further questions can be asked to determine whether or when the plaintiff returned to work; the amount of earnings lost; whether he missed raises in pay or overtime pay because of his absence from work; whether he returned to the same job; whether he was capable of doing the same work; and whether his prospects for advancement or probable duration of employment were affected by his injury. The witness may also be able to testify about the plaintiff's loss of such fringe benefits as bonuses, pension and profit-sharing rights, and insurance coverage.

The collateral source rule generally prevents a defendant—unless it is a public entity—from putting on evidence that the plaintiff received sick leave pay, insurance, union welfare, or other benefits. See *De Cruz v Reid* (1968) 69 C2d 217, 223, 70 CR 550, 554. See generally Johns, CALIFORNIA DAMAGES 152–161 (1969); 2 Witkin, SUMMARY OF CALIFORNIA LAW 1609 (7th ed, 1960).

III. [§7.9] ECONOMISTS; STATISTICIANS; APPRAISERS OF IMPAIRED EARNING CAPACITY

In cases of major injury or the death of a wage earner, an economist or similarly qualified witness can testify as an expert on the amount of future damages. The economist analyzes past economic performance (such as the earning capacity of an individual or of persons of similar characteristics) and makes a prediction of probable future performance.

For an extended discussion of the proof of lost earning capacity and of future expenses, see 16 AM JUR PROOF OF FACTS 701 (1965).

A. [§7.10] *Basis of Testimony*

The testimony of an economist or statistician must usually be based on facts put in evidence through exhibits and the testimony of other witnesses.

The plaintiff, or plaintiff's heirs, can testify to his capabilities and aspirations before the injury, his age and health at the time of the injury, and the extent of his disability after the injury.

A doctor can show the extent of his disability, its probable duration or permanence, the nature of the medical care he will require in the future, and the present cost of that kind of care.

The plaintiff's employer, using his employment records, can show his pre and postaccident position, abilities, compensation, and prospects.

A personnel, vocational, or rehabilitation expert can relate plaintiff's disability to his employment prospects.

A home economist can show the value of the domestic services and work around the home that the plaintiff provided before injury.

The court can take judicial notice of such matters as life expectancy (see BAJI No 14.69 and Appendix A) and the present cash value of future loss (see BAJI No 14.70 and Appendix B). See also §20.41.

B. [§7.11] Qualifications: Checklist

To be qualified to testify about the kinds of future expectancies noted in §7.12, the witness should have training and experience in the fields of economics and statistics. See generally §§1.19–1.23 on qualifying expert witnesses. The lawyer qualifying an economist can bring out such matters as

1. Name, address, and occupation.
2. Education and degrees.
3. Training in economics and statistics.
4. That economics is a science concerned with the production, distribution, and consumption of goods, money, and services.
5. That statistics is a science concerned with the collection, analysis, and use of numerical data.
6. Employment experience (*i.e.,* work as an economist or statistician for governmental or private agencies).
7. Teaching experience.
8. Private practice: duration, location, nature.
9. Special consultation work or the preparation of studies for government and industry, especially as related to the injured or deceased person's occupation or industry or to the particular future expectancies problem in the case.
10. Professional affiliations (*e.g.,* American Economic Association, American Statistical Association, American Society of Econometric Appraisers, Associated Appraisers of Earning Capacity).
11. Authorship (books, articles, and papers delivered to professional societies).
12. Previous experience in evaluating impaired earning capacity, value of household services, future medical expenses, etc., in connection with civil litigation.
13. Previous testimony in other cases.

C. [§7.12] *Topics of Testimony*

In personal injury cases, economists are often able to testify to such matters as

(1) The plaintiff's capacity to earn at the time he was injured (based on evidence of his probable life or work life expectancy, education, skills, and past earnings record (or the average earning capacity of persons of similar intelligence, sex, skills, etc.), price and earnings trends, and the probable employment market for a person of his capabilities, motivation, and diligence);

(2) The plaintiff's capacity to earn following his injury (based on evidence of the extent and permanence of his disability and the employment market for a person of such disability);

(3) The present value of the monetary difference between his earning capacities before and after the injury;

(4) The present value of lost benefits, such as health and welfare, pension and profit-sharing, and social security rights.

(5) The value of his capacity to perform unpaid, but money-saving duties in the maintenance of home and family (which is a part of earning capacity);

(6) The projected personal expenditures of a deceased person for his own maintenance (to be deducted from his lost earning capacity); and

(7) The present value of medical expenses reasonably certain to be incurred in the future (based on evidence of the kinds and duration of medical care required, the present cost of the care, and reliable statistics on medical cost trends).

PART II
Exhibits and Demonstrations

8

Handling Exhibits and Demonstrations

I. [§8.1] Terminology

II. [§8.2] Value; Uses

III. [§8.3] Offering Exhibits in Evidence: Checklist
- A. [§8.4] Bringing to Court; When To Use
- B. [§8.5] Keeping Track; Using Indexes and Duplicates
- C. [§8.6] Custody; Release to Owner: Form
- D. [§8.7] Inspection by Adverse Counsel
- E. [§8.8] Marking for Identification
- F. [§8.9] Laying Foundation
    1. [§8.10] Relevance
    2. [§8.11] Authentication
    3. [§8.12] Best Evidence Exception
    4. [§8.13] Hearsay Exception
- G. [§8.14] Formal Offer
- H. [§8.15] Receiving and Marking in Evidence
- I. Presenting to Jury
    1. [§8.16] Passing to Jurors
    2. [§8.17] Explaining; Interpreting; Reading
    3. [§8.18] Using Viewing Aids

IV. [§8.19] Sending Exhibits to Jury Room

V. [§8.20] Admission by Agreement
- A. [§8.21] Written Stipulation: Form
- B. [§8.22] Request for Admission: Form
- C. [§8.23] Pretrial Order: Form
- D. [§8.24] Oral Stipulation

§8.1 EXHIBITS AND DEMONSTRATIONS

   VI. [§8.25] Writings as Past Recollection Recorded
      A. [§8.26] Distinguished from Writings Used To Refresh Memory
      B. [§8.27] Laying Foundation: Checklist
        1. [§8.28] Witness's Writing
        2. [§8.29] Another's Writing
          a. [§8.30] Declarant's Testimony
          b. [§8.31] Writer's Testimony
      C. [§8.32] Reading into Evidence
      D. [§8.33] Adverse Parties' Rights

   VII. [§8.34] Using Things Not in Evidence To Help Witnesses Testify

   VIII. [§8.35] Viewing Scenes and Objects Outside Courtroom

   IX. [§8.36] Demonstrations and Experiments

I. [§8.1] TERMINOLOGY

The Evidence Code does not define the terms "exhibit" and "demonstration." It is convenient, however, to use "exhibits" to refer to tangible things, such as writings and material objects brought to the attention of the trier of fact, and "demonstrations" to refer to sights, sounds, odors, movements, and the like. This usage is consistent with the code definition of "evidence" as (a) testimony, (b) writings and material objects, and (c) other things presented to the senses that are offered to prove the existence or nonexistence of a fact. Evid C §140.

The categories "testimony," "exhibits," and "demonstrations" sometimes overlap. A written transcript of prior testimony, for example, is an exhibit since it is a tangible object. Its content, however, is testimony and is subject to the rules that govern testimony.

When a testifying doctor manipulates a plaintiff's arm and points to scars and indentations on his bared back, the doctor is conducting a demonstration of the plaintiff's loss of motion and tissue. The doctor's verbal description of what he is doing and what he sees is his testimony.

When a witness writes a series of numbers on the courtroom blackboard and totals them, he is putting on a demonstration. The numbers are his testimony, even though written rather than spoken, and the blackboard with the figures on it is an exhibit. The blackboard would not ordinarily be offered or marked in evidence, although a photo-

EXHIBITS AND DEMONSTRATIONS §8.2

graph of it could be. If the witness writes on a large sheet of paper instead of a blackboard, the paper can be offered and marked as an exhibit.

The terms "exhibits" and "demonstrations" are used in this book in preference to the familiar "demonstrative evidence" for greater precision and to avoid conflict with the definition of "evidence" in Evid C §140. Similarly, "writing," which is defined in Evid C §250, is preferred to "documentary evidence." The term "real evidence" is reserved for those exhibits that are relevant because their own appearance or condition is in issue. Real evidence includes, for example, the brake cylinder claimed to have been defective, the carpet on which plaintiff says he tripped, etc. Thus, real evidence is distinguished from representations or reproductions, *e.g.,* most photographs, models, and drawings.

II. [§8.2] VALUE; USES

Exhibits and demonstrations are used in personal injury trials to inform and persuade judges and jurors. They complement and supplement testimony and are a welcome relief from witnesses' and lawyers' words. Properly presented, exhibits and demonstrations have an influence that can exceed their actual informational content. Evidence that can be seen or touched attracts attention, is better remembered, and is more readily believed.

However, the jurors can be bored by the use of too many exhibits or offended by distasteful ones. They may overlook important exhibits in a mass of others and react negatively to exhibits that strike them as disgusting or unnecessary. An adverse attorney can argue that the lawyer who has presented a welter of exhibits is trying to distract attention from a weak case.

An exhibit becomes "evidence" (as defined in Evid C §140) when it is offered in evidence, even though it is not technically admissible and is not received. However, the exhibit cannot properly be considered by a trier of fact in determining the existence or nonexistence of a disputed fact until it has been admitted in evidence.

An exhibit used solely to aid a witness in testifying need not be offered in evidence. There are exhibits used to illustrate, support, and otherwise lend credence to testimony that are not offered in evidence, since the testimony thus supported is sufficient to prove the facts. For a discussion of these exhibits, see §8.34. Of course it would be improper, and could be misconduct, to expose the jury to an exhibit or demonstration that is patently inadmissible and has no legitimate use as an aid to testimony.

III. [§8.3] OFFERING EXHIBITS IN EVIDENCE: CHECKLIST

Before the trial starts, the lawyer should plan when and how to introduce or use each of his exhibits. He will then be able to handle exhibits properly and smoothly, impressing jurors with his competence, enhancing the effectiveness of his proof, and ensuring a proper record in the event of an appeal.

The following are steps a lawyer can take in offering an exhibit in evidence (see discussion in §§8.4–8.15):

a. Show exhibit to adverse counsel.
b. Request that it be marked for identification.
c. Hand it to clerk to be marked for identification.
d. Record identification number in exhibit index.
e. Elicit foundational testimony.
f. State that exhibit is offered in evidence.
g. Show it to adverse counsel again.
h. Hand it to judge if he wants to see it.
i. Hand it to clerk to be marked in evidence.
j. State for record that exhibit has been received.
k. Record "in evidence" number in exhibit index.

Not all of these steps need to be taken with every exhibit. For example, some lawyers never ask that an exhibit be marked for identification unless it has been offered in evidence and rejected. If the exhibit is shown to adverse counsel, and they voice no objection to its admission, laying a foundation can be dispensed with. See §8.24. In addition, there are some writings and material objects used in court that are never offered in evidence. See §8.34.

A. [§8.4] Bringing to Court; When To Use

Each exhibit should be presented in the courtroom at the propitious moment. Some are brought in early so that the jury can be exposed to them from the outset and witnesses can refer to them while testifying. Other exhibits are kept under cover until the moment they are to be used so that their production comes as a surprise to adverse witnesses and attorneys. (Some exhibits should not be produced in court until they have been shown to adverse counsel in chambers. See §8.7.) Keeping exhibits under cover can also prevent adverse counsel from thumbing through them on the counsel table, using them in cross-examining the proponent's witnesses, or even introducing them out of order and having them marked as his own exhibits.

Writings and small exhibits can be brought to court in a briefcase at

EXHIBITS AND DEMONSTRATIONS §8.6

the beginning of the trial. Sometimes a good opportunity to use an exhibit occurs sooner than the attorney anticipates. Bulky exhibits, on the other hand, are kept in the office until the day they are to be introduced; bringing them too soon may mean carrying them away again at the end of the court day.

B. [§8.5] *Keeping Track; Using Indexes and Duplicates*

Most trial lawyers use some system to assure that each exhibit comes readily to hand when it is needed. They do not waste jury time or give an impression of disorganization by fumbling through a briefcase or stalling while an assistant hurries back to the office. Writings and photographs can be kept in a file folder in the lawyer's briefcase. Exhibits can be filed in the order in which they are to be produced, grouped in categories or according to the witness first expected to testify from or about them, or tabbed so they can be located as needed.

Many lawyers keep in their trial notebooks an exhibit index, like the one the court clerk uses. On it they list every exhibit they anticipate using. And they may record on a separate sheet each exhibit used by other counsel. If an exhibit is marked for identification, the identification number is recorded on the sheet. When the exhibit is received in evidence, the name of the authenticating witness and the exhibit number are also recorded. The exhibit index can be checked from time to time against the one kept by the clerk. It tells the lawyer, at a glance, which of his potential exhibits have been received in evidence and which have been marked for identification but not formally admitted. To be sure that all crucial exhibits have been received, the lawyer should check his exhibit index against the clerk's before he closes his presentation of evidence. An attorney who keeps an exhibit index can also ask the clerk to "find number 15 [for identification/in evidence]," rather than having to shuffle through a stack of exhibits himself to find the one he wants.

Some lawyers keep at the counsel table a photocopy or duplicate of each exhibit, and mark it with the same number that the clerk has given the original. The lawyer can then refer to the duplicate while a witness uses the original or without having to ask the clerk to locate it. As a courtesy, and to save time, the lawyer may also provide other counsel with duplicates for their use.

C. [§8.6] *Custody; Release to Owner: Form*

A writing or material object remains in the custody of the lawyer until it is marked for identification or in evidence. At that point, physical custody and the responsibility for keeping the exhibit safe

§8.6   EXHIBITS AND DEMONSTRATIONS

and unaltered pass to the clerk. An exhibit that has been marked by the clerk remains a part of the record in the case unless the court orders it released. An order for release would be made only if all parties agreed, or on motion of one party after the time for appeal has expired. See CCP §§1952, 1952.2; CAL RULES OF CT 243, 531.

An exhibit that has been received in evidence, or offered but rejected, can be made part of the record on appeal. See CALIFORNIA CIVIL APPELLATE PRACTICE §11.8 (Cal CEB 1966). A problem may arise when the owner of a valuable exhibit or the custodian of an original hospital or business record wants it returned immediately, or at the close of the trial, and asks the parties to so stipulate. Often a copy or photograph of the exhibit will serve for purposes of an appeal, and the copy can be substituted for the original. Otherwise the lawyer should not agree to release the exhibit.

The clerk of the court in which the exhibit was received may have printed forms for the release of exhibits pursuant to CCP §1952.2 and CAL RULES OF CT 243 or 531. If not, the following form can be used:

Copies: Original to file; one copy for each other attorney; one office copy.

                                   (Title of Court)

                                     No. ....
                                     STIPULATION, ORDER, AND
(Title of Case)   RECEIPT FOR RELEASE OF
                                     EXHIBIT(S)

                                     STIPULATION

The undersigned hereby stipulate that the following exhibits shall be released to the following persons:

1. .... to ....
    (Description of exhibit)   (Name of person)

2. (List additional exhibits and persons.)

                                 _____
                                       (Signature of attorney)
                                       (Typed name of attorney)

                    Attorney for ....

                                 _____
                                     (Signature of attorney)
                                     (Typed name of attorney)

                    Attorney for ....

EXHIBITS AND DEMONSTRATIONS §8.7

ORDER

The clerk shall return the described exhibits pursuant to the stipulation above.

Dated: ....

                                    Judge of the .... Court

RECEIPT

Received:

1. .... by   (Signature)
    (Description of exhibit)   (Typed name)

Dated: ....
                                            (Title)

2. (Continue)

D. [§8.7] Inspection by Adverse Counsel

A lawyer should hand the exhibit, or offer to show it, to adverse counsel both (1) when he asks that it be marked for identification (if he does) or first uses it in examining a witness and (2) when he formally offers it in evidence. (A writing used to refresh the memory of a witness need not be shown to adverse counsel unless he asks to see it. Evid C §771. See also §1.38. A writing to be read into evidence as past recollection recorded must be shown to all parties before it is read or any question concerning it is asked. Evid C §768. See also §8.33. A writing that embodies a prior inconsistent statement of a witness need not be shown to the witness, but if it is shown to him, it must be shown to all parties. Evid C §768. See also §§2.9, 2.11.)

The showing of an exhibit to adverse counsel at the time of marking for identification can be brief. At this point, adverse counsel should be limited to objections that would prevent the exhibit from being seen by the jury or discussed by any witness — for example, that the exhibit is inflammatory, unduly prejudicial, or confusing or that laying the foundation for it would consume undue time. See Evid C §352. Adversaries will have a full opportunity to inspect for other objectionable features if the exhibit is offered in evidence.

There are some exhibits that ought to be shown to adverse counsel in chambers before they are shown in the courtroom or to jurors. These are exhibits whose very existence or appearance might be inflammatory or unduly prejudicial. Of course, some lawyers routinely produce these exhibits in open court hoping that surprised opponents will not object, but this could constitute misconduct or elicit a reprimand. The exhibits should be produced in chambers first for a decision on their admissibility. See CALIFORNIA TRIAL OBJECTIONS

§28.2 (Cal CEB 1967); Witkin, CALIFORNIA EVIDENCE §§633–634 (2d ed, 1966).

It can also be good practice to show a lengthy or detailed exhibit to adverse counsel before trial or in chambers or to give them a copy when the exhibit is marked for identification or shown to a witness. This gives adversaries additional time to study it and can save jury time, avoid interruption of the pace of the trial, and allow objections or deletions from the exhibit to be decided without unduly arousing juror curiosity.

E. [§8.8] *Marking for Identification*

Marking an exhibit for identification means having the clerk give it an identifying number or letter before it is offered in evidence or after it is offered and rejected. The exhibit can then be referred to by its identification number until it is received and marked in evidence.

Most exhibits do not need to be marked for identification. The lawyer simply refers to the exhibit by description while eliciting foundational testimony, then offers it in evidence. If the exhibit is received, it is "marked in evidence," and can be referred to by that number. Therefore, many lawyers do not ask that an exhibit be marked for identification except when (a) there are many exhibits and confusion would be avoided by having each numbered at the outset or as it is produced; (b) there is likely to be extensive foundational or other testimony about the exhibit, perhaps from more than one witness, before it is offered; (c) the lawyer intends to use the exhibit but not formally offer it in evidence (see §8.34); or (d) the exhibit is offered but not received or marked in evidence. An adverse attorney might request that an exhibit be marked for identification because references have been made to it, or he might later want to offer it in evidence himself.

Generally, even an irrelevant, unauthenticated, or otherwise objectionable exhibit can be marked for identification, unless it is patently inflammatory, prejudicial, or inadmissible or there is a strong suspicion that counsel seeks to have it marked for identification as his only means of calling it to the attention of the trier of fact.

When several exhibits are presented for marking at the same time, the proponent informs the court that he wants them marked, offers to show them briefly to the other lawyers (and the judge), then hands each to the clerk to affix or write on the identification number. It is a good idea for the proponent to say a few words to identify each exhibit for the record. For example:

EXHIBITS AND DEMONSTRATIONS §8.9

Proponent. At this time Your Honor, I ask that the following exhibits be marked for identification as [plaintiff's/defendant's] exhibits ...... through ....

Exhibit one is a transcript of the deposition of ....

Two is a scale drawing of the intersection of .... and .... Streets.

Three through seven are photographs of plaintiff's automobile.

Eight is a sheet of paper with four photographs on it, lettered A, B, C, and D, that show plaintiff in the hospital.

Nine is the shirt that plaintiff was wearing at the time of the accident.

Comment: When a single exhibit is to be marked for identification during the course of testimony, the proponent can interrupt his examination to say:

Proponent. Your Honor, I ask that this [map] be marked for identification as [plaintiff's/defendant's] exhibit ....

Comment: Again, the proponent shows the exhibit to each attorney (and the judge) and hands it to the clerk to be marked. There is usually no need to describe the exhibit, since a further description and a foundation for its admission can be elicited from the witness.

The trial judge may instruct the clerk to mark the exhibit for identification (*e.g.,* "Let it be marked [plaintiff's/defendant's] [exhibit ....../next in order] for identification") although this is not necessary as long as the clerk does in fact give it a number, and counsel records that number on his own exhibit index (if he uses one).

F. [§8.9] Laying Foundation

Laying the foundation for an exhibit means proving the existence of the preliminary facts on which the admission of that exhibit depends. See Evid C §§400–401. (Some lawyers refer to this as "authenticating" the exhibit, but "authentication" as defined in Evid C §1400 may be only one aspect of laying the foundation for a writing. See §8.11.)

Preliminary facts are usually proved through the testimony of a witness, who may be termed the "foundational" (or "authenticating") witness. In some cases, foundational proof is derived from the appearance of the exhibit itself, from other exhibits, or from the testimony of several witnesses. A trial judge can require that foundational testimony be heard outside the presence of the jury. Evid C §402.

§8.10 EXHIBITS AND DEMONSTRATIONS

There is no need to lay a foundation for an exhibit if all other parties agree to its admission in evidence. Thus, the proponent of an exhibit can offer it in evidence without attempting to prove preliminary facts if he has obtained a stipulation or does not expect that adverse counsel will object. See §8.20. On the other hand, the lawyer may want to elicit foundational testimony even though the exhibit could be received by stipulation. This testimony identifies the exhibit and enhances its probative value by showing how it was prepared, where it came from, and that it was safely kept and not altered.

The particular preliminary facts to be proved vary from exhibit to exhibit (see chaps 9–19). Sections 8.10–8.13 list the common foundational requirements.

1. [§8.10] Relevance

Only relevant evidence is admissible. Evid C §350. A first step in laying the foundation for an exhibit is to show that it is relevant, *i.e.*, that it has a "tendency in reason to prove or disprove [a] fact that is of consequence to the determination of the action" (Evid C §210). The trial judge must also be satisfied that the probative value of the exhibit is not substantially outweighed by a probability that its admission would (a) require undue consumption of time or (b) create a substantial danger of undue prejudice, of confusing the issues, or of misleading the jury. Evid C §352.

Showing the relevance of an exhibit often begins by having a witness identify it. For example, if the exhibit is a material object, the lawyer may begin by asking "What is this?" Further questions might include: Has the witness seen it before; where did it come from; who had custody of it from the date of the accident until trial; has it been altered in any way since that time; and what conditions or defects does the witness see in it? The witness thus relates the exhibit's present condition to its condition at the time of the accident and shows its bearing on the issues.

2. [§8.11] Authentication

If the exhibit is a writing, it must be authenticated before it, or secondary evidence of its content, may be received in evidence. Evid C §1401. "Authentication" means introducing evidence sufficient to sustain a finding that a writing is in fact the writing that the proponent claims it to be. Evid C §1400. "Writing" includes pictures, sounds, symbols, and photographs as well as handwriting, typewriting, and printing. Evid C §250. See generally Witkin, CALIFORNIA EVIDENCE

EXHIBITS AND DEMONSTRATIONS §8.14

§§672–687 (2d ed, 1966); CALIFORNIA TRIAL OBJECTIONS §21.6 (Cal CEB 1967).

Authenticating a writing usually means showing who made or signed it or what file or source it came from. If the writing is a depiction (a photograph, diagram, etc.) it must be shown that it is a correct representation of what it purports to depict.

3. [§8.12] Best Evidence Exception

If the exhibit is offered to prove the content of a writing, the proponent should be prepared to show that it is the original writing, or that it is a copy of the writing that can be received under an exception to the best evidence rule. Evid C §1500. See generally Witkin, CALIFORNIA EVIDENCE §§688–711 (2d ed, 1966); CALIFORNIA TRIAL OBJECTIONS §§25.1–25.17 (Cal CEB 1967).

4. [§8.13] Hearsay Exception

If the exhibit is or embodies a statement made by a person other than while testifying at the hearing, and the exhibit is offered to prove the truth of the matter stated, the proponent should be prepared to show that it is admissible under an exception to the hearsay rule. See Evid C §1200. A "statement" is (a) oral or written verbal expression or (b) nonverbal conduct intended as a substitute for verbal expression. Evid C §225. See generally Witkin, CALIFORNIA EVIDENCE chap VII (2d ed, 1966); CALIFORNIA TRIAL OBJECTIONS chap 19 (Cal CEB 1967).

G. [§8.14] Formal Offer

The proponent of an exhibit who wants that exhibit considered by the trier of fact in reaching a finding or verdict must formally offer it in evidence. See *Spanfelner v Meyer* (1942) 51 CA2d 390, 124 P2d 862.

An offer in evidence can be made at any stage of the trial, although it is usually done at the conclusion of a witness's foundational testimony or as a final step, after all the lawyer's case-in-chief witnesses have testified. The offer may be made in open court or in chambers, but the lawyer should be sure that the record shows that it was made. If the exhibit is not received in evidence the first time it is offered, it can be marked for identification, and the lawyer can offer it again, perhaps after eliciting further foundational testimony.

§8.15   EXHIBITS AND DEMONSTRATIONS

The offer of an exhibit in evidence can be stated in words such as the following:

Proponent. Your Honor, at this time [plaintiff/defendant] offers in evidence this [photograph/document/etc.], [which has been marked ...... for identification,] as [plaintiff's/defendant's] exhibit ...... in evidence.

Comment: The exhibit is then held out to adverse counsel who can examine it closely to determine whether it is objectionable, question the foundational witness to develop facts on which an objection might be based, and object to its admission in evidence.

If no objection to the exhibit is made, or objections are overruled, the proponent should offer to hand the exhibit to the judge and then to the clerk to be marked in evidence.

H. [§8.15] *Receiving and Marking in Evidence*

The proponent of an exhibit should assure himself that the trial judge has indicated for the record that the exhibit has been received in evidence, and that the clerk has given the exhibit a number.

After an exhibit has been offered, if there is no objection, or objections were overruled, the judge will usually say something like:

Judge. Let it be marked [plaintiff's/defendant's] exhibit ....

If the judge says nothing, the proponent can request a ruling. For example:

Proponent. Your Honor, may I have a ruling on that?

If the judge's demeanor indicates that the exhibit has been received in evidence, but the judge has not said so, the proponent should make a statement for the record. For example:

Proponent. May the record show that the evidence is received and marked as [plaintiff's/defendant's] exhibit ...... in evidence?

If the judge does not indicate what exhibit number the exhibit is to receive (if he says "Let it be marked plaintiff's next in order," for example), the proponent should make a statement for the record, such as:

Proponent. Thank you, Your Honor. Mr. [clerk] does that come in as [plaintiff's/defendant's] exhibit ...... in evidence?

The proponent must be certain that the clerk actually marks the exhibit in evidence, and records it on his exhibit sheet. Since some

EXHIBITS AND DEMONSTRATIONS §8.17

exhibits offered are never marked for identification, while some marked for identification are never offered or are offered in a different order, the "in evidence" number may differ from the "for identification" number.

I. *Presenting to Jury*

1. [§8.16] Passing to Jurors

After an exhibit has been received and marked in evidence, the proponent can ask that it be passed to the jury, using such words as:

Proponent. Your Honor, may I [request that the clerk] hand that exhibit to the jury and request that they pass it down each row so that each juror can [read it/look at it more closely/etc.].

There are drawbacks to passing exhibits. Jurors are distracted from the testimony that is being presented while they are passing and examining an exhibit. If the exhibit is detailed or lengthy, jurors will gain little from the brief look they can get while it is passed, and the look they do get may be more misleading than helpful. Further, an exhibit of several parts can get shuffled, and a delicate exhibit may be damaged. If too many exhibits are passed, the impact of crucial exhibits is minimized.

An exhibit usually should not be passed to jurors unless a witness has explained exactly what it shows. If an exhibit is simply passed, the jurors may overlook or misinterpret what the attorney wants them to see.

Sometimes the problems of passing an exhibit can be overcome by making a copy for each juror to examine while a witness is testifying from the original or the copy that has been marked in evidence. The witness can then describe or read portions of the exhibit, and the jurors can follow on their own copies.

If there is only one copy of the exhibit, the witness can be asked to step near the jury box and point out important features so that jurors can see them before the exhibit is passed to them.

2. [§8.17] Explaining; Interpreting; Reading

Most exhibits should be explained or interpreted to the trier of fact by a witness. The explanation can be brief (*e.g.*, "this photograph shows the left front door, and here at the bottom you can see that the lower hinge was broken"), or it can be detailed and extensive (see, *e.g.*, §§13.20–13.40 on interpreting and explaining the contents of a hospital record).

The exhibit can help the witness to testify, and the testimony about the exhibit increases its probative value. For example, if a doctor has relied on an X-ray film in forming his opinions, interpreting the film in court helps him to state his opinions and the basis for them, and the interpretation qualifies the film for admission in evidence (see §16.5).

Although lawyers do not ordinarily testify about exhibits, they sometimes call the jury's attention to significant features. For example, as the exhibit is marked in evidence, the attorney might say: "Your Honor, may I pass to the members of the jury this photograph of the left front door of ....'s car that shows the lower hinge."

After a written document is received in evidence, the lawyer can ask a witness to read it, or parts of it, to the jury. This is usually a better way of presenting its contents than simply passing it to jurors to read themselves. The witness can focus on important passages or those that jurors might otherwise skim over, and if the witness reads well, his intonations and emphasis will aid juror understanding. However, reading more than a few short passages from a document may bore jurors and cause confusion. It is better for a witness to intersperse short passages with testimony discussing and explaining the significance of what is read.

Similar principles apply when a lawyer reads from an exhibit. Reading a short passage can emphasize and clarify the meaning of the exhibit. However, if the attorney wants to read more, he should probably wait until closing argument when he can relate the parts he reads to the points he is making.

3. [§8.18] Using Viewing Aids

Viewing aids are used to help jurors see exhibits better. These aids—magnifying glasses, light boxes, projectors and screens, etc.—are not themselves exhibits and need not be marked for identification or in evidence. (The use of viewers and projectors for slides and motion pictures and light boxes for X-ray films is discussed in §§15.19, 16.18, and 17.26.) "Overhead" or "opaque" projectors can project enlarged images of book pages and other exhibits of similar size on a screen.

In a case in which the lawyer wanted jurors to see nicks in a sickle blade, to help establish that the sickle had been used to hack through a cable, he passed a magnifying glass to jurors along with the sickle. An alternative would have been to make a photograph of the blade through a microscope or enlarging lens, and introduce the enlarged photograph as a separate exhibit along with the sickle.

In addition to photographs made through enlarging lenses, photographs of ordinary objects can be enlarged to become display exhibits. Thus, a photograph of a page of a hospital record—perhaps showing the day a certain drug was administered—can be enlarged to display size (*e.g.*, three by four feet) so that the entry can be seen by all jurors as the witness testifies about it.

IV. [§8.19] SENDING EXHIBITS TO JURY ROOM

When jurors retire to deliberate, they may take with them "all papers which have been received as evidence . . . except depositions," and "any exhibits which the court may deem proper." CCP §612. See generally CALIFORNIA CIVIL PROCEDURE DURING TRIAL §18.19 (Cal CEB 1960); 2 Witkin, CALIFORNIA PROCEDURE 1803 (1954). Normally, a trial judge permits all exhibits that have been received and marked in evidence to be sent to the jury room, except when there is a danger of misinterpretation, as with hospital records and X-ray films.

Each lawyer who wants particular exhibits to be sent with the jury should ask the judge whether he will permit it. This request can be made in chambers or at the bench before the lawyer begins his final argument. Then, if the judge refuses to permit a particular exhibit to go with the jury, the lawyer can read it, display it, and discuss it more fully in his argument. The request might be stated as follows:

Proponent. Your Honor, before I begin I would like to know if the following exhibits will be sent with the jury when it retires, as provided by CCP §612: [List exhibits, *e.g.*, plaintiff's exhibits one through six, and nine in evidence.]

Occasionally a lawyer wants to send with the jury an exhibit that was not formally received in evidence, perhaps a diagram or model used by a witness as an aid in testifying that would also help jurors to understand the evidence. The lawyer can argue that this is permitted by CCP §612 when it states that the jury may take with them "any exhibits which the court may deem proper," in addition to "papers which have been received as evidence."

A lawyer who does not want an opponent's exhibit to go to the jury room can argue that the trial judge can and should keep from the jury exhibits that might be unduly prejudicial, confusing, or misleading. This power is suggested by CCP §612, and is analogous to the judge's power to exclude evidence under Evid C §352. If one side's crucial evidence was mostly testimony, which jurors must remember while deliberating, it can also be argued that it would be unfair and prejudicial for them to have before them the other side's exhibits.

Further, jurors might misinterpret an exhibit or perform an experiment, the results of which the parties have no opportunity to meet, answer, or explain. See *Higgins v Los Angeles Gas & Elec. Co.* (1911) 159 C 651, 115 P 313. See generally Leavitt, *The Jury at Work,* 13 HASTINGS LJ 415, 420 (1962).

V. [§8.20] ADMISSION BY AGREEMENT

Any exhibit can be received in evidence if all parties agree to its admission. An attorney has authority to stipulate to the admission of an exhibit even though it might be objectionable. See CCP §283; *People v Mathews* (1958) 163 CA2d 795, 801, 329 P2d 983, 986; *Morgan v Morgan* (1956) 139 CA2d 704, 294 P2d 45. See also 1 Witkin, CALIFORNIA PROCEDURE 62, 67 (1954).

An opponent's failure to object to offered evidence can be regarded by the trial judge as an agreement to its admission. Trial judges rarely exclude exhibits on their own motion, although they may remind counsel of objections that could be raised. Further, the trial judge who admits an exhibit in evidence does not commit reversible error unless an attorney has made a timely objection or motion to exclude or strike that states a clear, specific, and proper ground for excluding the exhibit. Evid C §353. See also CALIFORNIA TRIAL OBJECTIONS §4.7 (Cal CEB 1967).

The advantages of obtaining advance agreement to the admission of an exhibit include: (a) Witnesses whose only function would be to provide foundational testimony need not be called: (b) the pace of the trial need not be interrupted, nor jurors bored, with preliminary testimony; and (c) the lawyer spares himself the time and expense of preparing foundational witnesses and uncertainty about whether his foundational evidence will be sufficient and the exhibit received. Sometimes lawyers agree in advance to share the cost of having exhibits such as diagrams or aerial photographs prepared for the use of both sides.

The disadvantages of seeking advance agreement include: (a) The exhibit must be revealed to opponents before trial; (b) the lawyer must ask a favor (the agreement) of opposing counsel and may then feel obligated to grant a favor in return; and (c) the lawyer loses an opportunity to emphasize the significance of the exhibit through foundational testimony about it. Also, the procedure for obtaining advance agreement (preparing and circulating a written stipulation form etc.) may be more trouble than having a witness give foundational testimony.

EXHIBITS AND DEMONSTRATIONS §8.21

The advantages of seeking agreement begin to outweigh the disadvantages in a particular case when, for example, no authenticating witness is readily available at a reasonable fee; the opponent has discovered or otherwise already seen the exhibit; the opponent has already asked a favor and will agree to admission of the exhibit in return; or there are many exhibits to be offered and substantial trial time can be saved by agreement.

A. [§8.21] Written Stipulation: Form

A lawyer with exhibits to offer in evidence can circulate a written stipulation form to be signed by attorneys for other parties. This is rarely done in personal injury cases where the introduction of exhibits is often routine, and circulating a stipulation before trial would not be worth the effort. It could be useful and timesaving in special cases, however.

If a written stipulation is used it should be circulated well before trial so that alternate methods can be pursued if an adversary declines to sign. Agreement often can be encouraged by attaching a copy of the exhibit to the stipulation form and by supplying a separate copy for the use of each other attorney.

Copies: An original to be signed and filed; a copy for each other attorney; one office copy.

(Title of Court)

(Title of Cause)

No. ....
STIPULATION FOR ADMISSION OF EXHIBITS

The undersigned parties hereby stipulate that the following exhibits, copies of which are attached, shall be admitted in evidence as exhibits for .... without further foundation:
    plaintiff/defendant

1. ....
2. ....

_____
(Signature of attorney)
(Typed name of attorney)

Attorney for ....

_____
(Signature of attorney)
(Typed name of attorney)

Attorney for ....

Comment: The original, signed by all attorneys, should be filed with the clerk of court so that it will bind the parties. See CCP §283.

Some stipulation forms state in greater detail the foundational objections that are waived or state that the right to object to particular entries or parts is reserved. See, *e.g.,* §13.13.

Rather than a formal stipulation form, some attorneys simply send a letter asking for agreement to the admission of specified exhibits.

B. [§8.22] *Request for Admission: Form*

A request for admission (CCP §2033) is a device that could be used to secure agreement to the admission of exhibits in evidence, although it is rarely used in personal injury cases. The request served on adverse parties asks them to admit the genuineness of documents and the truth of the preliminary facts on which the admissibility of the exhibits rests. An adversary can also be asked to admit the facts that the exhibit would prove; admission of those facts would eliminate the need for the exhibit.

Serving a request for admission has several advantages over circulating a written stipulation form. The proponent is not asking adverse parties for a favor. Inaction by the adverse party is deemed an admission of facts. The adverse party cannot simply decline to agree, but must decide whether to deny the facts or to state reasons for neither admitting nor denying. And if the adverse party denies without sufficient reason to do so, he can be made to pay the costs of proving the facts.

The "genuineness" of a document appears to be the equivalent of its authenticity: The writing is what it purports to be. However, an admission of the genuineness of a written exhibit does not automatically qualify it for admission in evidence. Additional admissions of fact may be necessary to establish that the exhibit is relevant and within exceptions to the hearsay, best evidence, and other exclusionary rules. The difficulty of stating these additional facts is a drawback to the use of requests for admissions.

The following form can be used to request admissions.

Copies: Original to be filed with proof of service; one copy to be served on adverse party; one office copy.

(Title of Court)

No. ....

(Title of Cause)   REQUEST FOR ADMISSION

To .... and his attorney:
　　(Name of party)

EXHIBITS AND DEMONSTRATIONS §8.23

.................................., ..., requests that you admit, for the
   Plaintiff/Defendant   (Name)

purposes of this action, within .... days from the date
                                     (E.g.) not less than 20

of the service of this request on you, the following:

That each of the following described documents, of which the attached exhibits are copies, is genuine:

    Exhibit 1, ...
                                (Describe document)

    Exhibit 2, ...
                                (Describe document)

That each of the following facts is true:

1. ....
                       (Set forth foundational facts)

2. ....
                       (Set forth foundational facts)

Dated: ....

                                             _____
                                             (Signature of attorney)
                                             (Typed name of attorney)

                                Attorney for ....

Comment: Copies of the documents described in the request must be served with it, unless copies have already been furnished the party, and on request the originals must be made available for inspection. For related forms, see 1 CALIFORNIA CIVIL PROCEDURE FORMS MANUAL 242–254 (Cal CEB 1966). For discussion, see Witkin, CALIFORNIA EVIDENCE §§1004–1010 (2d ed, 1966).

C. [§8.23] *Pretrial Order: Form*

If a pretrial conference is held, a lawyer can ask adverse counsel for agreement to the admission of exhibits in evidence. The pretrial order can then list the exhibits (a) marked in evidence, (b) "authenticated by consent of the parties," and (c) marked for identification. CAL RULES OF CT 214(a)(1)(ii). For a general discussion of exhibits at pretrial and for pretrial statement and order forms, see CALIFORNIA PRETRIAL AND SETTLEMENT PROCEDURES §§8.26, 8.37, 8.48–8.49, 9.52, 10.11, 10.19–10.20 (Cal CEB 1963). Note that the admission of exhibits can also be discussed at a trial setting conference (CALIFORNIA PRETRIAL AND SETTLEMENT PROCEDURES SUPPLEMENT §11.50 (Cal CEB 1967)), but since no order is made listing agreed on exhibits, a separate written stipulation may be used.

§8.24   EXHIBITS AND DEMONSTRATIONS

If adverse counsel agree to the admission of exhibits in evidence without qualification, the pretrial order can list them as "marked in evidence." If, for some exhibits, they agree only to a waiver of foundational objections or some form of qualified admission, those exhibits can be listed separately. If adverse counsel decline to agree to the admission of some exhibits these can, if the proponent wishes, at least be listed as "marked for identification."

(Insert in Pretrial Order. For form of order, see
2 CALIFORNIA CIVIL PROCEDURE FORMS MANUAL 303 (Cal CEB 1966)
or PRETRIAL AND SETTLEMENT §10.19.)

Exhibits

A. The following exhibits shall be received and marked in evidence at the trial:

1. A ....
(*E.g.*) scale diagram of the intersection of ....
............................., as .... exhibit ....
and .... Streets   plaintiff's/defendant's

(Continue to list and describe exhibits,
giving number or letter designations)

B. The following exhibits shall be received in evidence without further foundation, but subject to all other objections:

(List, describe, and designate as above)

C. The following exhibits are marked for identification as follows:

(List, describe, and designate as above)

D. [§8.24] *Oral Stipulation*

Oral agreement to the admission of an exhibit can be sought before trial. This saves having to prepare a written stipulation or other paper. However, it gives less assurance that adverse counsel will not object to the exhibit when it is offered at trial. They may forget that they agreed or think that the exhibit offered is not the same as the one to which they agreed. It can be helpful to give them a copy of the exhibit for their own files and send a letter acknowledging their agreement.

The proponent can also wait until trial before asking adverse counsel to stipulate to admission of the exhibit. Of course, the lawyer should not ask for a stipulation in the hearing of the jury (see *Romeo v Jumbo Mkt.* (1967) 247 CA2d 817, 56 CR 26); he could be reprimanded for unfairly creating a situation that makes adverse counsel appear to be depriving the jury of evidence or forcing the proponent to comply with a technicality. The drawback of waiting until trial to ask for a stipulation is that the proponent must either (a) prepare a

EXHIBITS AND DEMONSTRATIONS §8.25

foundational witness and have him ready to appear or (b) run the risk that the adversary will decline to stipulate and it will be too late to get the exhibit admitted at a favorable time or at all.

The lawyer who has obtained a prior agreement to admission of an exhibit should state for the record that it is being received by stipulation. This will satisfy the requirement of CCP §283 that stipulations be entered in the minutes of the court, and can enhance the weight of the exhibit. For example:

Proponent. Your Honor, at this time the [plaintiff/defendant] offers in evidence, as [plaintiff's/defendant's] exhibit ......, this [describe exhibit].

[All parties have stipulated, Your Honor, that this exhibit is a true and correct copy of an authentic business record of .... and that no further foundation for its admission need be laid.]

[Of course, all parties reserve the right to make any other objection to it or to particular parts of it.]

Comment: Some lawyers simply offer an exhibit in evidence during the trial in the hope that no one will object. However, an adverse party can resist the admission of an exhibit presented this way without appearing to be an obstructionist by saying:

Adverse lawyer. Your Honor, I haven't had a chance to look this over yet. Perhaps I can review it during the next recess, and we can consider it then.

(Or)

Adverse lawyer. Your Honor, I would have no objection to counsel using it, but I think it might violate [section ...... of] the Evidence Code to let it be received in evidence. Maybe we can discuss it further [at the bench/in chambers/at the next recess].

Comment: The latter statement leaves the implication that the proponent either does not know the law, or is trying to circumvent it. If the offered exhibit is inadmissible, the proponent risks being admonished by the judge for trying to introduce it without laying a foundation or asking other counsel.

VI. [§8.25] WRITINGS AS PAST RECOLLECTION RECORDED

Certain writings can be read into evidence as the recorded past recollection of a witness. Evid C §1237. These are writings that contain an earlier statement of the witness about matters he no longer recalls well enough to testify about fully and accurately.

Succinct and forceful prior statements are sometimes more effective evidence than a witness's testimony on the same matters. Even if his memory were refreshed, cross-examination at trial might reveal gaps, inconsistencies, and uncertainties. Thus the lawyer might prefer to leave the witness's memory unrefreshed and prepare him only to lay a foundation for the writing. On the other hand, jurors may be suspicious of a witness who testifies that he made a statement that was true but claims that his memory of the facts is not sufficiently refreshed by reading it to testify and be cross-examined about the facts.

Police officers and examining physicians are witnesses who frequently have no independent recollection of the events recorded in their reports and whose memories are not refreshed by reading them, because so many other cases have intervened. Yet officers (see §4.22) and doctors (see §6.28) often testify from their reports as if their memories were refreshed even though their testimony may actually be little more than a paraphrase of the content of their reports.

A writing for which a proper foundation has been laid under Evid C §1237 (or waived) can be "read into evidence," but may not be received in evidence as an exhibit unless offered by an adverse party. A sound recording of the witness's voice is a "writing." Evid C §250. The judge should permit a recording to be played for the trier of fact even though the code speaks of "reading" it, and even though permitting it to be played is, in a sense, "receiving" it in evidence.

A written statement can be read into evidence to the extent that it "would have been admissible if made by [the witness] while testifying." Evid C §1237(a). Thus, the "matter" or "fact" that may be read apparently includes opinions to which the witness could have testified as well as perceptions of conditions and events.

A. [§8.26] *Distinguished from Writings Used To Refresh Memory*

Reading a writing into evidence as past recollection recorded (Evid C §1237) differs from using a writing to refresh memory (Evid C §771). In the former, the witness is able to testify that the writing accurately records a true statement previously made by him about certain facts but he has no independent recollection of those facts; he knows what occurred only because the writing tells him what he said about it then. The writing is the evidence of the facts.

On the other hand, if the writing refreshes the witness's memory so

EXHIBITS AND DEMONSTRATIONS §8.28

that he has an independent recollection of the facts and can testify about them fully and accurately from memory, the writing is not read to the trier of fact, and the witness's testimony is the evidence.

B. [§8.27] Laying Foundation: Checklist

Certain preliminary facts must be established before a writing can be read into evidence as past recollection recorded. See Evid C §1237. It must be shown that:

1. The witness once perceived or knew facts (conditions, events, conclusions) relevant to the lawsuit;
2. He has insufficient present recollection of that matter to enable him to testify fully and accurately about it;
3. He made a statement concerning the matter when it occurred or was fresh in his memory;
4. The statement was recorded when it was made by (a) the witness himself, (b) a person acting under the witness's direction, or (c) a person acting for the purpose of recording the witness's statement;
5. The statement made by the witness was true (the person who made the statement must himself testify to this);
6. The writing is an accurate record of the statement.

1. [§8.28] Witness's Writing

If the witness himself wrote down his observations of an event, the writing is his statement and the foundation for it might be laid as follows:

Q. Mr. ...., did you [witness an automobile accident at the intersection of .... and .... Streets on ...., 19......]?
A. Yes.

Comment: The witness's memory can usually be sufficiently refreshed before he takes the stand to enable him to answer "yes" to this preliminary question. The question may be asked in leading form. See §1.11.

Q. Do you remember [the details of that accident/the color of the vehicles that were involved/etc.]?
A. No. [I remember seeing it, but not much else.]

Comment: The lawyer who wants to have the writing read in evidence should phrase the question in terms best calculated to elicit a "no" answer. He wants to show that the witness does not remember the matter "fully and accurately." Probably any significant loss of memory or uncertainty about the facts should justify the reading of his statement.

Q. Do you recall whether you wrote down any notes or made any record of what you saw?
A. Yes, I did.
Q. Did you bring that record with you today?
A. Yes, I have it here.

Comment: The lawyer may have the writing marked for identification, but should not offer it in evidence. Since the writing is shown to the witness, all parties must be given a chance to inspect it before the witness is questioned about it. Evid C §768.

Q. Have you read it over before coming to court today?
A. Yes.
Q. Can you identify the record as one that you personally made?
A. Yes.
Q. How?
A. [I recognize my handwriting and my signature at the end.]
Q. Is it a record of your description of the accident we are talking about?
A. It is.
Q. When did you write down the statement?
A. ...., 19.......
Q. Were the events and conditions you saw fresh in your memory then?
A. They were.
Q. Was your statement a true statement of what you observed?
A. Yes.
Q. Is this document an accurate record of your description on ...., 19......, of that accident?
A. Yes.

Comment: Adverse counsel can examine the witness on voir dire to test the foundational evidence. The proponent can then ask questions about the content of the statement, have the witness read it to the jury, or read it himself. See §8.32.

2. [§8.29] Another's Writing

A writing made by another person can be read as the witness's past recollection recorded if the person who made it was acting (a) under the witness's direction, or (b) for the purpose of recording the witness's statement. See Evid C §1237(a)(2).

EXHIBITS AND DEMONSTRATIONS §8.31

a. [§8.30] Declarant's Testimony

The person who made a prior statement can usually lay the foundation for it to be read even though the statement was written down by another. The declarant can testify directly that he observed certain facts, does not have sufficient present recollection of the matter to be able to testify fully and accurately about it, and made a true statement about it when it was fresh in his memory. See checklist items 1, 2, 3, and 5 in §8.27 and dialogue in §8.28. In addition, he can testify that he directed some other person to record his statement (§8.27, item 4(b)), or he can testify to circumstances from which it can be inferred that the writing was made by a person "for the purpose of recording the witness's statement" (see §8.27, item 4(c)). The declarant may remember, for example, that an investigator, police officer, or newsman asked him about the accident and wrote down his responses. Even though the witness did not make the writing himself and does not remember the matter it records, he can still testify that it is an accurate record of his statement (see §8.27, item 6), based on his recollection that he read it over at the time and thought it accurate or that he signed it, initialed its pages, or made changes in it in his own handwriting.

b. [§8.31] Writer's Testimony

The testimony of the person who made the writing may be necessary to lay the foundation for reading it into evidence. This person can testify that he made the writing at the direction of the declarant (see §8.27, item 4(b)), or for the purpose of recording the declarant's statement (see §8.27, item 4(c)), and that the writing is an accurate record of that statement (see §8.27, item 6).

An investigator who took a statement from a person who witnessed an accident might, for example, testify:

Q. Did you [at my request] interview Mr. .... about the accident of ...., 19......?
A. I did.
Q. When and where did you do that?
A. On ...., 19......, at ....
Q. In what manner did you go about getting information from him?
A. [Well, I asked him to tell me what he had seen. Then I asked specific questions to fill in some of the details he missed and to get his statement in order.]
Q. At that time did he appear to have a good memory for the details of the accident?
A. Yes, he did. [He told the story and answered my questions confidently. The facts seemed to be fresh in his memory.]

Comment: The answers to the foregoing questions corroborate the testimony of the declarant. However, since Evid C §1237(a)(3) specifies that the witness must testify that the statement he made was true, it is doubtful that the testimony of the person who recorded it could alone constitute a foundation for reading it into evidence.

Q. Did you write down what he told you?
A. I did.
Q. Did you write it down for the purpose of recording his statement [about the accident]?
A. I did.
Q. Do you have the writing with you today?
A. Yes. I have it right here.
Q. Is the writing an accurate record of the statement he made to you?
A. It is.

Comment: The witness can also be asked to point out such features as the declarant's signature or initials on the writing, or any changes he personally made in the wording.

Adverse counsel can examine the witness on voir dire to test the foundational evidence.

C. [§8.32] Reading into Evidence

Evidence Code §1237(b) states that the writing may be "read into evidence," but does not say how or by whom. After the witness has completed his foundational testimony, the lawyer could simply ask him to read the document to the jury. Or, the lawyer could take the writing from the witness and ask the court's permission to read it.

A third alternative, which is often the best, is to leave the writing in the witness's hands and ask a series of questions about its content. For example:

Q. Please just read from that document and tell us what [you/he] said about [the directions in which the vehicles were moving.]
A. ["I saw a blue car moving north on Main Street and a red car headed west on First."]
Q. [What was the speed of the blue car?]
A. ["About 45 miles per hour."]

D. [§8.33] Adverse Parties' Rights

Whenever it appears that a writing is to be used as a witness's past recollection recorded, adverse counsel is entitled to inspect it before the witness is asked any questions about it. See Evid C §768. He can

EXHIBITS AND DEMONSTRATIONS §8.33

ask to use it in questioning the witness on either voir dire or cross-examination either to keep the writing from being read or to cast doubt on its value as evidence. He can also inspect it for matter that would not be admissible if stated by the witness while testifying. See Evid C §1237.

If a proponent of the evidence were to offer the writing in evidence, or begin to read it without having laid a foundation, an adverse lawyer could object that the evidence is hearsay. If the proponent attempted to lay a foundation, and one of the elements was clearly missing, the objection could be renewed. If there was no patent gap in the foundation, the adverse lawyer could still question the witness on voir dire in an attempt to show, through the witness's testimony, that a foundational element was missing. For example:

Adverse counsel. Your Honor, may I [interrupt at this point and] take the witness on voir dire as to the foundation?
Trial judge. You may.
Q. Isn't it true, Mr. ...., that that document does refresh your memory about that accident?
A. ....
Q. And you could testify accurately and fully about it if you used it to refresh your memory, couldn't you?
A. ....
Q. You didn't write it yourself did you?
A. ....
Q. Mr. .... wasn't acting under your direction when he wrote it, was he?
A. ....
Q. And you don't know of your own knowledge why he was writing it, do you?
A. ....
Q. If you don't remember the accident, you can't really be sure that your statement about it way back on ...., 19......, was a true statement of the facts, can you?
A. ....
Q. Since you don't remember what you said at that time, you don't really know whether this is an accurate record of your statement, do you?
A. ....
Q. Did you sign that statement?
A. No.
Q. Were you asked to sign it?
A. Yes.

Q. And you didn't sign it because it was not what you said, isn't that right?
A. ....

Comment: Unless the attorney feels he can get a response that will keep the writing from being read, it is usually better not to challenge on voir dire but to save questions like the foregoing for later cross-examination.

VII. [§8.34] USING THINGS NOT IN EVIDENCE TO HELP WITNESSES TESTIFY

There are several ways in which writings and material objects can be used at trial even though they are not offered or received in evidence. For example, writings can be used to refresh memory (see §§1.31–1.39), as past recollection recorded (see §§8.25–8.32), and as prior inconsistent and consistent statements (see §§1.44, 2.7–2.12).

In addition there are writings and objects that are brought into the courtroom, used and pointed to by witnesses, and seen by the trier of fact, but never offered in evidence. These things are "exhibits" in the broad sense of the term and may help a witness to convey information and the lawyer to persuade. An attorney may choose not to offer an exhibit when he feels that formal admission would not enhance its probative value enough to justify the time and trouble needed to lay a foundation and have it received and marked in evidence. The value of such an exhibit is in its use by a witness rather than in its being formally received in evidence, passed among jurors, or sent to the jury room.

The lawyer who wants to use an exhibit in the courtroom but does not intend to lay a foundation for it or offer it in evidence, may be charged with using an improper tactic or subterfuge to expose the jury to inadmissible matter. To avoid this, the lawyer should (a) clear the intended use of the exhibit in advance, (b) be prepared to show that a foundation could be laid if required, or (c) argue that the exhibit is being used solely to help a witness testify clearly and accurately. Trial judges can permit witnesses to use unadmitted, even inadmissible, exhibits to illustrate their testimony or to help them convey information and ideas.

For example, a witness might use two pencils or toy cars to show the angle at which vehicles collided. The demonstration gives jurors a clearer picture than the witness's words could. A mechanic is helped to testify how a brake cylinder works if he can hold one and move its parts while he describes it.

EXHIBITS AND DEMONSTRATIONS §8.35

The witness who uses an unadmitted exhibit as a testimonial aid should be prepared to identify it and vouch for its usefulness. For example:

Q. Dr. ...., you say you inserted a Smith-Petersen's Nail in his femur. Can you show us what one looks like?
A. Yes. I brought one with me.
Q. Would using that nail help you to describe the operation you performed on [Mr. ..../the plaintiff]?
A. It would.
Q. How does this appliance you have in your hand compare in size, shape, and appearance to the one you put in his leg?
A. It is a duplicate.
Q. Could you describe that nail for the record, please?
A. ....

VIII. [§8.35] VIEWING SCENES AND OBJECTS OUTSIDE COURTROOM

The trial judge can order the jury to be conducted in a body to the place where a material fact occurred. CCP §610. See generally Witkin, CALIFORNIA EVIDENCE §§643–645 (2d ed, 1966). The lawyer should be prepared to convince the judge that a jury view of the scene or instrumentality would be a sufficiently greater aid to juror understanding than verbal descriptions, photographs, or diagrams to justify the disruption, inconvenience, and time needed to take them there. See Evid C §352.

The statutory reference to the "place" where any material fact occurred should be interpreted broadly enough to allow taking the jury outside the courtroom to view exhibits that are too large to be brought inside, such as vehicles, construction equipment, and the like. Mobile equipment can be driven to the courthouse and viewed out the window or on the street, although it is sometimes less expensive to transport the jury to the place where a piece of machinery is in use than to bring the machinery to the courthouse.

The scenes and objects to which jurors are conducted are evidence (see Evid C §140), and the knowledge jurors gain by viewing them may be considered along with other evidence in the case. See *Neel v Mannings, Inc.* (1942) 19 C2d 647, 654, 122 P2d 576, 580. See also Witkin, EVIDENCE §645. The lawyer can ask that the jury be so instructed.

Code of Civil Procedure §610 contemplates that the trial judge will appoint a person to "show" the place to the jury. No other person is supposed to speak to them during the trip on any matter connected

§8.35   EXHIBITS AND DEMONSTRATIONS

with the trial. "Showing" the place, however, can go beyond the mere pointing out of pertinent facts. See, *e.g., Haley v Bay Cities Transit Co.* (1947) 82 CA2d 950, 187 P2d 850, in which several demonstrations were conducted at the scene. See generally Witkin, EVIDENCE §644. As a practical matter, it is often helpful to have a witness describe changes in the scene between the time of the accident and the time of the visit, the operation of the machinery being viewed, where he was standing or what he or some other person was doing, and so forth. If the judge, the attorneys for all parties, and the court reporter are all present, there seems to be no error in taking testimony at the scene: Court is being conducted at the scene rather than in a courtroom. Even if no testimony is taken, the trial judge should be present. See *Rau v Redwood City Woman's Club* (1952) 111 CA2d 546, 245 P2d 12, 17; *Haley v Bay Cities Transit Co., supra.* The court reporter should also go to record anything said by the person appointed to show the scene (or anyone else) and questions asked by jurors.

The lawyer who wants the trier of fact to view a scene or object outside the courtroom should usually make his motion at the beginning of the trial. This allows the view to be scheduled at a convenient time, or before testimony and exhibits are received so that they can be better understood by jurors. Also, if the motion is denied, counsel will have time to prepare other means of informing the jury of the matters to be viewed. Of course, in some cases, the desirability of a jury view comes to light only after witnesses have tried to describe the scene.

A motion for a jury view is usually made in chambers and accompanied by an offer to arrange or pay for transportation to the scene. It can also specify a person to show the scene or indicate whether the lawyer wants testimony to be taken there. An oral motion might be made as follows:

Proponent. Your Honor, the [plaintiff/defendant] feels that the jury would be greatly aided in understanding the evidence and issues in this case if they see firsthand [the place where this accident took place/the machinery involved in this accident].

Therefore, I move for an order that the jury be conducted to [specify place] to view [specify scene, operation, etc.]. I further request that at the scene Mr. .... be permitted to describe pertinent facts and demonstrate [how he operated his vehicle/how that machine works/etc.] and that the reporter be present to record that testimony.

I have arranged to have [a bus/limousines/etc.] available at [specify time and date], if that would be convenient, to transport you, the

EXHIBITS AND DEMONSTRATIONS §8.36

jury, the bailiff, the reporter, adverse counsel, Mr. ...., and me to the scene. The whole process should take about ...... hours.

IX. [§8.36] DEMONSTRATIONS AND EXPERIMENTS

A demonstration is any activity or event conducted by a witness or lawyer during testimony or argument. What the witness does can convey information to the trier of fact as well as his words and the appearance of exhibits. And "evidence" includes sights and sounds as well as testimony and exhibits. See Official Comment to Evidence Code §140.

An experiment is an activity carried out, often with the aid of elaborate apparatus and materials, to test a hypothesis or establish what results occur under certain controlled conditions. An experiment conducted before the jury is a form of demonstration. The jurors gain information from what takes place as well as by the testimony of the witness about what he is doing, what is happening, and what it proves. A witness can also conduct an experiment outside the presence of the jury, then testify about it and the results achieved.

Permission to conduct a courtroom experiment and the admissibility of testimony about an experiment depend on such factors as relevance, the similarity of conditions, the experimenter's qualifications, the accuracy of his observation, and the tendency to clarify rather than confuse. *Schauf v Southern Cal. Edison Co.* (1966) 243 CA2d 450, 455, 52 CR 518, 521. See also Witkin, CALIFORNIA EVIDENCE §§648, 650–651 (2d ed, 1966).

Demonstrations can clarify, illustrate, reinforce, and replace testimony. Jurors are often more impressed by what they see or think they see than by mere verbal descriptions. However, a demonstration or experiment that goes wrong is worse than useless. For this reason, many experiments are performed before trial, and their results are communicated by testimony, exhibits, or motion pictures (see §17.23). Experiments conducted at trial should be foolproof, should not be difficult or time consuming to set up, and should not expose the witness to a lengthy voir dire or cross-examination.

Demonstrations are usually permitted during a trial unless the judge feels that their relevance is marginal—they have little tendency in reason to prove or disprove a disputed fact (see Evid C §§210, 350)—or that their probable probative value is outweighed by the time needed to present them or the danger of undue prejudice, of confusing the issues, or of misleading the jury (see Evid C §352). See generally Witkin, EVIDENCE §649. If apparatus is to be brought into court and

§8.36 EXHIBITS AND DEMONSTRATIONS

set up, the lawyer should secure the judge's permission in advance. Otherwise, the lawyer can simply go ahead with each demonstration. For example:

Q. At what angle did those vehicles collide?
A. About 60 degrees.
Q. Can you show us the angle with [your hands/these two pencils/these toy cars/etc.]?
A. Yes. They hit like this. [Witness demonstrates.]

Comment: The lawyer can also ask the witness to use exhibits that have been received in evidence. For example:

Q. Now Mr. ...., would you please step over to that [scale diagram/terrain model/etc.], which is [plaintiff's/defendant's] exhibit ...... in evidence, and place these model cars in the positions the vehicles were in at the moment of impact?
A. Here and here. [Witness demonstrates.]
Q. For the record, are you indicating that [the point of impact was in the right hand northbound lane of .... Street, and that the angle between the cars was about 60 degrees]?
A. That's right.

Comment: The lawyer may also state for the record matters spontaneously demonstrated by the witness. For example:

Q. How high can you lift your right arm now?
A. No higher than this. [Witness demonstrates.]
Q. Up to about the level of your shoulder, is that it?
A. That's right.

Comment: A doctor can point out scars, atrophy, and other results of injury that he can see on plaintiff's body but that jurors might not otherwise notice. See Witkin, EVIDENCE §647(d). He can also manipulate the plaintiff's limbs to show the extent of motion or stick pins in him to show absence of sensation.

Q. Dr. ...., I'm going to ask [Mr. ..../the plaintiff] to step up in front of the jury box and remove his shirt. Would you please come down [from the witness chair] and point out on his back the scars and atrophy that you have testified about?
A. Certainly. [Witness points to, describes, and explains pertinent physical facts.]
Q. Thank you, Doctor. Now can you show us the extent of motion he has in his left arm?

A. Yes. [Witness moves plaintiff's arm and explains results.]
Q. Thank you. Is there a way that you can demonstrate to us the absence of sensation that he claims to have in his left arm and hand?
A. Yes. I can prick him with a needle or hold a burning match to his skin and we can observe his reaction.
Q. Mr. .... has given his consent that you carry out this experiment, Doctor, so please proceed and explain to us what you are doing as you go along.
A. I have sterilized this needle in alcohol and I am now pressing it into his skin as firmly as I can without drawing blood. You can see that there is no reaction of withdrawal or expression of distress or crying out in pain. He is insensitive to the needle.
Q. Doctor, is there any way you can tell whether he is feeling pain but masking it?
A. Yes. The pupils of the eyes contract when pain is felt, and the person has no control over it. He cannot mask that because it is an involuntary reflex like the heartbeat.
Q. Have you been observing plaintiff's eyes during this experiment?
A. I have.
Q. What did you see?
A. There was no contraction; he did not feel the pain.

Comment: In the foregoing demonstration the jury observes one result directly (no grimace or outcry), and the doctor reports another result to them that they cannot see (no pupillary contraction).

9

Police Accident Reports

I. Value

  A. [§9.1] Contents
  B. [§9.2] Uses

II. Obtaining Report

  A. [§9.3] For Investigative Use
   1. [§9.4] Request and Declaration: Form
   2. [§9.5] Authorization: Form
  B. [§9.6] For Use at Trial
   1. [§9.7] Subpena Duces Tecum
   2. [§9.8] Form: Declaration for Subpena Duces Tecum

III. Admission as Exhibit

  A. [§9.9] Admissibility
  B. [§9.10] By Stipulation
  C. Objections to Admission
   1. [§9.11] Privilege
   2. [§9.12] Hearsay
   3. [§9.13] Authentication
   4. [§9.14] Best Evidence
  D. [§9.15] Offering Report in Evidence

IV. Using Report To Show Prior Statement of Witness

  A. [§9.16] Prior Inconsistent Statement
  B. [§9.17] Prior Consistent Statement

I. VALUE

A. [§9.1] Contents

A police motor vehicle accident report is a comprehensive and contemporaneous record of facts, statements, and opinions about an accident. It records the investigating police officer's observations of people, vehicles, and the scene, including the contour and condition of the road and the location of traffic controls, skidmarks, debris, etc. It contains the officer's record of statements made to him by drivers, injured persons, and other witnesses. In addition, police reports often contain the investigating officer's conclusions on such matters as point of impact, vehicles' speeds, and the sobriety of drivers.

A sample California Highway Patrol report is reproduced in §4.3. Chapter 4 of this book discusses and illustrates the testimony that an officer can give using a report as a memory aid.

B. [§9.2] Uses

The attorney usually examines a copy of the police report early in the litigation. He learns what facts and opinions the investigating officer can testify to if called as a witness, and what statements his client and other persons made to the officer at the scene or shortly after the accident. The report can also give the lawyer leads on witnesses to interview and on the need for expert testimony.

At the trial (or at the officer's deposition, if he is deposed), the report can be used to refresh the officer's memory (see §§4.21-4.22) or as his past recollection recorded (see §4.23). The report can also refresh the memory of a person who was involved in or witnessed the accident (see generally §§1.31-1.39), and it is sometimes possible to lay a foundation for reading a witness's statement recorded in the report as his past recollection (see generally §§8.25-8.33).

Witnesses can be confronted with statements recorded in a police report that are inconsistent with their testimony at trial (see §9.16). A report can also sometimes be used as a prior consistent statement to rehabilitate a witness. See §9.17.

On rare occasions, a police report, or parts of it, can be received in evidence as an exhibit. See §§9.9-9.15.

II. OBTAINING REPORT

A. [§9.3] For Investigative Use

One of the first steps taken by an attorney in a motor vehicle accident case is to obtain and study a copy of the police accident report.

POLICE ACCIDENT REPORTS §9.4

He may do this even before agreeing to represent a prospective client.

The enforcement agency that has the report is required to disclose its entire contents to any person who has a proper interest in it, including: a driver who was involved in the accident, his legal guardian, his parent, if a minor, or his authorized representative; a person injured in the accident; the owner of a damaged vehicle or property; a person who may incur civil liability arising out of the accident; and an attorney who represents any of these persons. Veh C §20012. Most agencies will give a copy of the report to any authorized person who pays a fee (usually two or three dollars).

Some prospective clients or their insurers will have already obtained a copy of the report that the lawyer can use, or the lawyer can ask them to do so. More often, the lawyer himself presents or mails a request for the report to the agency, together with the required fee, and either (1) a declaration under penalty of perjury showing that he represents a person entitled to see the report, or (2) an authorization signed by such a person. The lawyer can determine by telephone which agency, and which office in that agency, has the report, the amount of the required fee, and any additional local requirements.

1. [§9.4] Request and Declaration: Form

The lawyer who represents a person entitled to see a police accident report (see §9.3) can obtain a copy of the report by requesting it and presenting a declaration under penalty of perjury that he represents a person so entitled. Veh C §20012. The request and declaration can be in the following form.

Copies: Original to present to police agency; one office copy.

To: ....
     (Name of enforcement agency)
Please .... to the undersigned a copy of your vehicle accident
         give/mail
report for the accident described below.

DECLARATION

I am an attorney at law .... I represent
                        licensed to practice in California
........................, who ....
(Name of client)   (E.g.) was a driver involved in/owns one of the vehicles
.... an accident on ....,
damaged in/may incur civil liability arising from
19......., at ....
             (Location)

Executed on ...., 19......, at ...., California.
I declare under penalty of perjury that the foregoing is true and correct.

_____
(Signature of attorney)
(Typed name of attorney)

....
(Address)

2. [§9.5] Authorization: Form

Whether or not the lawyer has agreed to represent a person entitled to see a police accident report (see §9.3), he can obtain a copy of the report by requesting it and presenting an authorization signed by the person. Printed authorization forms are available from legal stationers, or the following form can be used.

Copies: Original to present to police agency; one office copy.

AUTHORIZATION

The undersigned ....
 (E.g.) was a driver involved in/was injured in/owns one of the
.... a vehicle accident in-
vehicles damaged in/may incur civil liability arising from
vestigated by your department on ...., 19......, at ....,
 (Location)

involving ....
 (Names of one or more drivers or other persons)

I hereby authorize .... to see and make or re-
 (Name of attorney or firm)
ceive copies of any reports, diagrams, photographs, or other information you have about that accident.

Dated: ....

_____
(Signature)
(Typed name)

B. [§9.6] *For Use at Trial*

Attorneys who want to use a police accident report at trial should decide whether to use the original report or a copy. The original report may be preferred when it shows an erasure or subsequent addition or when the report is to be received as an exhibit and an original might be more impressive. The lawyer who wants an original can subpena it (see §9.7) or ask a subpenaed officer to bring the original rather than a copy. Some agencies may be reluctant to release an original even to an officer except in response to a subpena duces tecum.

POLICE ACCIDENT REPORTS §9.7

The lawyer who is content to use a copy at trial can often use a copy already in his file, *e.g.*, one that he previously obtained for investigative purposes. The copy used should be relatively free of extraneous marks such as the lawyer's marginal notations or underlining. If a markedup copy were used to refresh a witness's memory, for example, adverse counsel could argue that the witness's testimony was based on an unfair writing. See §1.32 on writings used to refresh memory.

A police officer subpenaed to testify frequently brings to court a copy of the report, sometimes even the original, and the lawyer can ask an officer to do so. The officer uses the report to refresh his own memory and may permit an attorney to use it in examining other witnesses, or to have it read as past recollection recorded. The officer may be under an obligation, however, to return to police files an unsubpenaed original report that he "checked out" for his own use.

The lawyer should subpena the report if he does not have a clean copy of his own to use or does not want to rely on a simple request to the officer to bring a copy, or wants the original report rather than a copy.

1. [§9.7] Subpena Duces Tecum

A subpena duces tecum for a police accident report can be directed to the custodian of the record. The custodian of California Highway Patrol reports is the area commander of the area in which the accident occurred. The name of the custodian can be determined by telephoning or writing the department or local police agency.

A subpena duces tecum for the report can also be served on the investigating officer. Under the rules and practice of many departments, the officer can take an original report from the files to court. Thus, the report is "under his control" as required by CCP §1985.

The issuance and service of subpenas duces tecum for the production of business records is discussed generally in §11.9. (Police records probably can be subpenaed as are other business or official records, although they may not be business or official records for purposes of the hearsay rule exceptions stated in Evid C §§1271, 1280. See §9.12.) The lawyer can use a printed subpena duces tecum form available from the court clerk, or type a subpena based on the Judicial Council form. See 2 CIVIL PROCEDURE FORMS MANUAL 351–352 (Cal CEB 1966).

A subpena duces tecum directed to a highway patrolman, deputy sheriff, marshal, or police officer should contain a statement that the required fees have been paid into court. Govt C §68097.2. For the wording of that statement, see §4.15.

The lawyer who wants to assure that the subpenaed officer or custodian attends in person with the original record should add to the subpena the clause set forth in Evid C §1564. See §11.15 for the wording of this clause.

2. [§9.8] Form: Declaration for Subpena Duces Tecum

A subpena duces tecum is invalid unless there is also served an affidavit (or declaration under penalty of perjury (see CCP §2015.5)) in the form prescribed by CCP §1985. CCP §1987.5. For a general discussion of the contents of a declaration for a subpena duces tecum, see §11.10. The following declaration can be used to support a subpena duces tecum for a police accident report.

Copies: Original to file with the clerk of the issuing court; one copy for the witness; one office copy.

(Title of Court)

(Title of Cause)

No. ....
DECLARATION FOR SUBPENA DUCES TECUM

.... declares:
(Name)

1. I am an attorney for the .... in this action.
   plaintiff/defendant

2. This cause has been set for trial on ...., 19......., at ....m., in Department .... of this court.

3. .... has in his possession or under his control
   (Name of witness)
records and documents relating to an accident that occurred on ...., 19......., at ...., involving ....
                              (Location)   (Names of one or more
.... and including ....
drivers, injured persons, etc.)   (Specify records sought, e.g.)
....
official vehicle accident reports, diagrams, statements, photographs, notes, and memoranda
....

4. These records and things are material to the issues in this case and admissible in evidence, and there is good cause for their production be-

cause they contain facts and information relating to the aforementioned accident, and this is an action for ....
personal injuries to/the wrongful death of

....
(Name of plaintiff or decedent)   alleged to have been

suffered in that accident.

5. The pleadings, records, and files in this action are here incorporated by this reference.

Executed on ...., 19......., at ...., California.

I declare under penalty of perjury that the foregoing is true and correct.

_____
(Signature of declarant)
(Typed name of declarant)

Attorney for ....
Plaintiff/Defendant

III. ADMISSION AS EXHIBIT

A. [§9.9] Admissibility

Most California trial attorneys and judges believe that police accident reports cannot be introduced in evidence as exhibits except by stipulation. See J. Title, *Police Accident Reports* 43 CAL SBJ 711 (1968); Letter from Kenneth G. Nellis in 44 CAL SBJ 243 (1969). Judges exclude reports on grounds that they are privileged (Veh C §20013) and that they are hearsay (Evid C §1200).

When a lawyer takes testimony from an investigating officer, the contents of his report comes into evidence as his testimony if he uses the report to refresh his memory (see §4.22) or as his past recollection recorded (see §4.23). However, the attorney who wants to introduce the report itself in evidence faces a serious problem. He must either (1) obtain the agreement of adverse counsel (see §9.10), or (2) convince the trial judge that the portions of the report offered are not privileged (see §9.11), then lay a foundation to satisfy hearsay, best evidence, and authentication requirements (see §§9.12–9.14). Stipulations are not readily given, and judges feel bound to exclude police reports by appellate decisions that have held them inadmissible.

A lawyer who wants badly to introduce a police report—perhaps because the officer was not deposed and is no longer available to testify—can try to bargain for a stipulation (see §9.10) or to use the arguments noted in §§9.11–9.12 to convince the judge that at least parts of the report can be received.

B. [§9.10] By Stipulation

If the attorneys for all parties agree, a police accident report can be received in evidence by stipulation. See CCP §283. In *Morgan v Morgan* (1956) 139 CA2d 704, 294 P2d 45, otherwise inadmissible probation reports were received by stipulation. See generally 1 Witkin, CALIFORNIA PROCEDURE 63, 67 (1954). Although Veh C §20013 says that no driver's report "shall be used as evidence in any trial," this creates a privilege which the driver, by stipulation, can waive.

A stipulation for the admission of a police report is often difficult to obtain. Since adverse lawyers can usually block the admission of the record by objecting that it is privileged (see §9.11) or hearsay (see §9.12), they generally refuse to stipulate to its admission unless they receive a substantial concession in return. Thus, the lawyer who seeks a stipulation should be ready to offer a concession, or perhaps withhold his request until the opponent has asked for a favor. He should not wait until trial to request a stipulation unless he knows he can compel the officer's attendance if the request is refused.

The attorney should not ask for a stipulation within the jury's hearing. See *Romeo v Jumbo Mkt.* (1967) 247 CA2d 817, 56 CR 26. To do so could constitute misconduct. See *Robinson v Cable* (1961) 55 C2d 425, 11 CR 377, in which the court admonished counsel not to attempt to introduce a police report or refer to it as an "official report" before the jury.

If all attorneys agree to the admission of the report in evidence, the stipulation, if oral, should be stated in open court and entered in the court minutes, or, if written, filed with the clerk. See CCP §283. See generally §8.24.

C. Objections to Admission

1. [§9.11] Privilege

An attempt to introduce a police accident report into evidence as an exhibit may be met with an objection that it is privileged by statute. Vehicle Code §20008 requires motorists in certain personal injury accidents to make, or cause to be made, a written report of the accident to the California Highway Patrol or city police department. Vehicle Code §20013 states that "no such accident report shall be used as evidence in any trial, civil or criminal, arising out of an accident . . . ."

Decisions conflict on whether Veh C §20013 (or its predecessor, former Veh C §488) precludes the use as evidence of vehicle accident reports prepared by highway patrol and police officers. Cases stating that the section does not apply to reports prepared by officers include:

POLICE ACCIDENT REPORTS §9.12

Hodges v Severns (1962) 201 CA2d 99, 20 CR 129; *Kelliher v Ray* (1941) 43 CA2d 252, 110 P2d 712; *Inouye v McCall* (1939) 35 CA2d 634, 96 P2d 386. See also *Ellison v Lang Transp. Co.* (1938) 12 C2d 355, 84 P2d 510 (court found no reversible error in any of trial court's rulings, one of which was admission in evidence of police report); *Dwelly v McReynolds* (1936) 6 C2d 128, 56 P2d 1232.

Cases stating that reports prepared by officers are excluded by the statute include: *Kramer v Barnes* (1963) 212 CA2d 440, 27 CR 895; *Summers v Burdick* (1961) 191 CA2d 464, 13 CR 68; *Fernandez v Di Salvo Appliance Co.* (1960) 179 CA2d 240, 3 CR 609; *Morales v Thompson* (1959) 171 CA2d 405, 340 P2d 700.

Most motorists do not make the separate written report of their accidents contemplated by Veh C §20008. They "cause one to be made" by orally giving the required information to the investigating officer at the scene, and the officer's written report satisfies the driver's duty to report. From this, an attorney opposing admission of a police report can argue that the officer's report is therefore privileged under Veh C §20013 since it is in effect the report required of the driver by Veh C §20008.

On the other hand, an attorney who wants to offer a police report in evidence can argue that the Veh C §20013 privilege, if it applies to the officer's report at all, applies only to that portion of the report that embodies the motorist's statements to the officer.

Robinson v Cable (1961) 55 C2d 425, 429, 11 CR 377, 379, does not resolve this conflict. Although the court admonished counsel for his persistent reference to the police accident report as the "official report," and then stated that on retrial he should "refrain from such conduct and from his attempts to introduce the report into evidence," it is not certain that the court's admonition was based on an unexpressed assumption of privilege under Veh C §20013. The court may have been concerned with the hearsay quality of the report (see §9.12) or merely with the particular course of conduct by counsel in the case.

2. [§9.12] Hearsay

A police accident report offered in evidence is hearsay: It is a statement made by the officer other than while testifying at a hearing. Evid C §1200. In addition, parts of the report are hearsay at another level because they record statements made to the officer by drivers and other witnesses.

An attorney who wants to introduce a police report in evidence as an exhibit, and who can convince the judge that the report is not excluded by Veh C §20013 (see §9.11), can try to qualify it under the business or official records exceptions to the hearsay rule. Evid C §§1270–1271, 1280. See generally CALIFORNIA TRIAL OBJECTIONS §§19.19–19.20 (Cal CEB 1967). See also chaps 11 and 12. The lawyer can try to lay a foundation for the report through the affidavit (see §11.12) or testimony (see §§11.17–11.20) of the custodian of records that the report was prepared by police personnel in the ordinary course of business at or near the time of the acts, conditions, and events recorded. See Evid C §§1271, 1280, 1561.

California courts have refused to admit police accident reports as business or official records on grounds that they are largely based on information given to the officer by persons who are under no business duty to report to the police, and are records, not of the officer's observations of acts, conditions, and events, but of hearsay and opinion. See *MacLean v San Francisco* (1957) 151 CA2d 133, 143, 311 P2d 158, 164; *Hoel v Los Angeles* (1955) 136 CA2d 295, 309, 288 P2d 989, 997. See also *Behr v Santa Cruz* (1959) 172 CA2d 697, 705, 342 P2d 987, 992 (fire ranger's official report). The courts state that the sources of the information in the report are not "such as to indicate its trustworthiness" (Evid C §§1271(d), 1280(c)).

However, a police report can be received under the business records exception if its contents are based on the observations of an officer or public official whose job it is to know the facts recorded. See *Taylor v Centennial Bowl, Inc.* (1966) 65 C2d 114, 126, 56 CR 561, 568.

Thus, an attorney who wants to introduce a police report can argue that the judge should admit at least those portions of the report that record the investigating officer's personal observations. In addition, if a witness's statement recorded by the officer could be received under some hearsay exception (*e.g.,* spontaneous declaration, admission, declaration against interest), that part of the report should also be admitted. And, some entries in opinion form may also be admissible if the opinions are of the type the officer could give without being qualified as an expert. See Evid C §800. See generally §1.16.

3. [§9.13] Authentication

Because the accident report is a writing, it must be authenticated before it is received in evidence. Evid C §1401. This means that someone must testify that it is the accident report for this particular accident. Authentication testimony may be given by the officer who prepared the report, by anyone who saw it prepared (Evid C §1413), or by the custodian (Evid C §1530(a)(2)). It may also be done by stipulation or by any other means provided by law. Evid C §1400(b).

If a copy of the accident report is used, it may be argued that attes-

POLICE ACCIDENT REPORTS   §9.16

tation or certification in compliance with Evid C §1530(a) is sufficient authentication under Evid C §1401. See Official Comment to Evidence Code §§1401, 1530. The safer approach is to authenticate the attested or certified copy the same way that an original is authenticated.

4. [§9.14] Best Evidence

The best evidence rule (Evid C §1500) normally presents no problem with police accident reports. In California nothing prevents an attorney from subpenaing an original report. See §9.6.

Evidence Code §1530 provides that "a purported copy of a writing in the custody of a public entity, or of an entry in such a writing, is prima facie evidence of the existence and content of such writing or entry if . . . the copy is attested or certified as a correct copy of the writing or entry" by the public custodian. The attestation (with seal) or certificate (no seal) "must state in substance that the copy is a correct copy of the original, or of a specified part thereof, as the case may be." Evid C §1531. There is no reason why an attested or certified copy of a police report would not qualify for admission under this exception to the best evidence rule.

See CALIFORNIA TRIAL OBJECTIONS chap 25 (Cal CEB 1967) on the best evidence rule generally.

D. [§9.15] *Offering Report in Evidence*

An attorney who wants to offer a police accident report in evidence as an exhibit should state his intention and make his offer in chambers, not before the jury. This gives the parties a chance to work out what parts, if any, can be received despite Veh C §20013 (see §9.11) and under the business records exception to the hearsay rule (see §9.12). It may be improper for a lawyer to offer the report in evidence for the first time before the jury. See *Robinson v Cable* (1961) 55 C2d 425, 429, 11 CR 377, 379.

If a police report is received in evidence, there are several ways to call its contents to the attention of the jury. These methods are discussed generally in §§8.16–8.19.

IV. USING REPORT TO SHOW PRIOR STATEMENT OF WITNESS

A. [§9.16] *Prior Inconsistent Statement*

The investigating officer frequently records in his report statements he has taken from drivers, injured persons, and other witnesses of the accident. These statements, made soon after the accident, tend to be more positive and reactive than later statements, which may be equivocal or reflective.

If an adverse witness says something at trial that is inconsistent with what he told the officer at the scene, the lawyer can use evidence of his prior statement to impeach him. For a discussion of impeachment with a prior inconsistent statement, see §2.7. The lawyer should, however, be prepared to meet an objection that the statement to the officer, particularly if made by a driver, is privileged under Veh C §20013. See §9.11. An answer to this objection might be that Veh C §20013 forbids the use of the report "as evidence," and that counsel proposes to use evidence of the statement solely as impeaching matter, not as evidence. Another answer is that the report itself is not "used as evidence." The evidence is either (a) the officer's testimony about what the declarant told him (the officer's memory having been refreshed by reading the report), or (b) the witness's admission on being shown the report that he had made the prior inconsistent statement. The latter use of the report is illustrated by the following dialogue:

Q. You have testified here today that the pedestrian was 20 feet away when you first saw him, is that correct?
A. Yes.
Q. Do you recall telling a police officer about the facts of this accident?
A. Yes.
Q. Was that at the scene of the accident?
A. It was.
Q. Was that while the events of the accident were fresh in your memory?
A. Yes.
Q. Did you want to tell the police officer all that you knew of the accident?
A. Yes.
Q. And you knew that what you were telling him was important and was being used in the police investigation of the accident, correct?
A. Yes.
Q. And what you told him was true, wasn't it?
A. Yes.
Q. Did you see the officer write down what you told him?
A. I don't remember that.
Q. But you did know he was investigating the accident and that he would prepare a report of his investigation, didn't you?
A. Yes.
Q. I now show you this document, and ask you to read paragraph ......

on page ......; does that refresh your recollection of what you told the officer at that time?
A. Yes.
Q. What did you tell him?
A. That the pedestrian was about three feet away when I first saw him.

Comment: If the witness denies that he made the statement, or that the report correctly records what he said, the lawyer can call the officer as an impeaching witness or attempt to introduce the report.

B. [§9.17] *Prior Consistent Statement*

A witness cannot read from a police report, nor can it be introduced in evidence, on the sole justification that it is being used only to show a prior consistent statement to rehabilitate the witness. See *Fernandez v Di Salvo Appliance Co.* (1960) 179 CA2d 240, 3 CR 609; *Morales v Thompson* (1959) 171 CA2d 405, 340 P2d 700. For a general discussion of rehabilitation through the use of prior consistent statements under Evid C §791, see §1.44.

A witness can, however, use a police report to refresh his memory. Either the declarant or the officer can be called to testify about a statement made to the officer, and either can use the report as a memory aid. See *Fernandez v Di Salvo Appliance Co., supra.* See also §4.22 on the officer's use of the report to refresh his memory.

10

Discovery Documents

I. [§10.1] Value

II. [§10.2] Depositions
   A. Uses at Trial
      1. [§10.3] To Refresh Memory
         a. [§10.4] Of Own Witness
         b. [§10.5] Of Adverse Witness
      2. To Show Prior Inconsistent Statement
         a. [§10.6] By Own Witness
         b. [§10.7] By Adverse Witness
         c. [§10.8] When Deponent Becomes Own Witness
      3. To Show Prior Consistent Statement
         a. [§10.9] By Own Witness
         b. [§10.10] By Adverse Witness
      4. [§10.11] As Past Recollection Recorded
         a. [§10.12] By Own Witness
         b. [§10.13] By Adverse Witness
      5. [§10.14] As Substitute Testimony
         a. [§10.15] When Witness Unavailable
         b. [§10.16] In Interests of Justice
         c. [§10.17] When Deposition Is of Adverse Party, Agent, or Witness
   B. [§10.18] Objections to Admission
   C. [§10.19] Substitution of Parties and Supplemental Proceedings
   D. [§10.20] Presentation at Trial
   E. [§10.21] Availability to Jury During Deliberations

III. Interrogatories
   A. [§10.22] Uses
   B. [§10.23] Restrictions on Use

IV. Other Discovery Documents
  A. [§10.24] Request for Admission
  B. [§10.25] Motions for Production and Inspection and for Examination by Physicians

I. [§10.1] VALUE

Lawyers use discovery methods before trial to search out facts, ascertain the opponents' case, develop their own case, preserve testimony, and decide whether to settle or try the case. Discovery proceedings reduce surprise and concealment in litigation and help get at the truth. The discovery act was intended "to take the 'game' element out of trial preparation while yet retaining the adversary nature of the trial itself." *Greyhound Corp. v Superior Court* (1961) 56 C2d 355, 376, 15 CR 90, 99.

During trial, discovery documents are used to refresh memory, impeach credibility by showing prior inconsistent statements, support credibility by showing prior consistent statements, substitute as testimony in proof of material facts, and make the final argument to the jury.

II. [§10.2] DEPOSITIONS

Lawyers use the term "deposition" to refer both to the hearing before trial at which a witness's testimony is taken, and to the reporter's transcript of that testimony. The deposition is the most common tool of discovery in personal injury cases. The following sections deal with use of depositions at trial and their admission in evidence; it does not cover preparation for and taking of depositions. For coverage of those subjects, see Witkin, CALIFORNIA EVIDENCE §§947–977 (1966); Louisell, MODERN CALIFORNIA DISCOVERY 44–118 (1963).

A. Uses at Trial

1. [§10.3] To Refresh Memory

A deposition transcript is a writing that may be used to refresh the memory of a witness. Evid C §771; Witkin, CALIFORNIA EVIDENCE §1167 (1966). When used to refresh memory, the deposition must be produced at the hearing at the request of an adverse party or the testimony will be stricken. Evid C §771. See generally §1.38.

When the prospective witness is friendly, the lawyer should show the witness his deposition before the trial and have him read it to refresh his memory. The witness's forthright testimony on the stand is more likely to impress the jury than if he has to have his memory refreshed by his deposition.

a. [§10.4] Of Own Witness

The deposition may be used by the lawyer to refresh the memory of his client who is on the stand and cannot recall the answer to a question. Evid C §771. It may also be used to refresh the memory of a client who gives a wrong answer, *i.e.,* contrary to the known facts and to his answer in the deposition. CCP §2016(d)(1).

Unless the requirements are waived, a deposition used in trial must have been signed by the witness (CCP §2019(e)) and filed in court (CCP §2019(f)(1)). The deposition can then be used as follows to refresh the memory of the witness who cannot remember a particular fact testified to in his deposition:

Q. [What was your destination at the time of the accident]?
A. I can't remember.
Q. Do you recall having your deposition taken on ...., 19......?
A. Yes.
Q. Were you under oath during the deposition?
A. Yes.
Q. Do you think your memory was clearer at the time regarding the details surrounding the accident than it is now, ... months later?
A. Yes, it was clearer then.
Q. I show you a copy of your deposition and ask you to read page ......, lines ...... to ....
A. [Witness complies.]
Q. Does that refresh your memory of [what your destination was at the time of the accident]?
A. It does. Now I remember that [I was on my way to the theater].

Comment: Opposing counsel is entitled to inspect the writing, cross-examine the witness about it, and introduce pertinent portions in evidence. Evid C §771(b). If a portion of a deposition is to be read to the jury, counsel commonly ask the judge to explain what a deposition is. See BAJI No 2.06. Most judges will make the explanation or allow the lawyer to make it.

If, during the examination, the witness gives an answer contrary to the deposition, his memory can be refreshed as follows:

Q. [What was the color of the car that forced you to swerve?]
A. [Blue.]

Q. Do you recall having your deposition taken on ...., 19......?
A. Yes.
Q. Were you under oath during the deposition?
A. Yes.
Q. Do you think your memory was clearer at the time regarding the details surrounding the accident than it is now, ... months later?
A. Yes, it was clearer then.
Q. I show you a copy of your deposition and ask you to read page ......, lines ...... to ....
A. [Witness complies.]
Q. Does that refresh your memory of [the color of the car]?
A. Yes. [Now I remember that it was red].

Comment: The deposition of a nonparty witness may also be used to refresh his memory on the stand. The rules, authorities, and foundational questions are essentially the same as for the witness who is a party.

b. [§10.5] Of Adverse Witness

If an adverse party or witness is being questioned under cross-examination or Evid C §776, his deposition may be used not only to refresh his memory (Evid C §771) but also to contradict or to impeach his testimony (CCP §2016(d)(1)). See §10.7 on the use of a prior inconsistent statement to impeach an adverse party.

If the adverse party or witness answers a question on the stand contrary to the answer he gave in his deposition, the cross-examining lawyer should use the deposition to impeach as well as to refresh memory. A risk exists, however, that the witness will, in the face of an impeaching technique, stand on the answer given at trial and, if the jury believes him, he is neither impeached successfully nor is his memory refreshed.

2. To Show Prior Inconsistent Statement

a. [§10.6] By Own Witness

If the lawyer's own witness gives testimony inconsistent with a favorable statement in his deposition, the lawyer will first try to refresh the witness's memory with the deposition. See §§10.3–10.4. However, if the witness's memory is not refreshed, and does not change his testimony to conform to the deposition, the lawyer may have to use the deposition as a prior inconsistent statement of the witness. Evidence Code §1235 permits an inconsistent statement to be used as substantive evidence. Technically, the lawyer is impeaching his own witness (permitted by Evid C §785), but he usually tries to bring out the single inconsistency without affecting the witness's credibility on other matters.

b. [§10.7] By Adverse Witness

Probably the most common use of a deposition is to impeach an adverse party or witness by showing his prior inconsistent statement. The deposition is evidence of the matter stated as well as a means of attacking credibility. See Evid C §1235.

At the trial, part or all of a deposition may be used against any party to contradict or impeach the testimony of the deponent as a witness (CCP §2016(d)(1)), provided that the party was present or represented at the taking of the deposition or had due notice of it (CCP §2016(d)). The witness need not be shown the deposition in examining him about a prior inconsistent statement (Evid C §768(a)) or given any information concerning the statement (Evid C §769). If the deposition is shown to the witness, all parties may inspect it before the questioning begins. Evid C §768(b). For further discussion of impeachment with prior inconsistent statements, see §§2.7–2.12.

A cross-examination might proceed as follows:

Q. You testified on direct examination that [your car did not leave any skid marks]. Is that right?
A. Yes.
Q. Are you sure of that?
A. Yes.
Q. Do you recall ever making a statement that [your car did leave skid marks]?
A. No. I don't recall it.
Q. Are you sure?
A. Quite sure.
Q. Did you appear with your attorney, at .... Street on Wednesday, ..., 19......, at ....m., to be examined about your knowledge of the facts in this case?
A. Yes.
Q. Were you sworn as a witness?
A. Yes.
Q. Were you then asked questions by me, and did you answer those questions?
A. Yes.
Q. That was about ...... months after the accident, wasn't it?

§10.7   DISCOVERY DOCUMENTS

A. Yes.
Q. Your recollection of the accident was fresher then than today, isn't that correct?
A. Yes.
Q. Were the questions and your answers taken down by a reporter and later transcribed?
A. Yes.

Comment: The following three questions would be asked only if the witness did read and sign his deposition.

Q. Did you then read over and correct the transcript of your testimony?
A. Yes.
Q. Was this done in your attorney's office?
A. Yes.
Q. Did you then sign the transcript?
A. Yes.
Q. I show you a document that purports to be the original transcript of your signed deposition, and ask you if that is your signature?
A. It is.
Q. Will you now please read to yourself lines ...... through ...... on page ......? [Hand deposition to witness.] Were you asked ["Did your car leave skid marks?"] and did you answer ["Yes."]?
A. Yes.
Q. And that was the truth, wasn't it; [your car did leave skid marks]?
A. Yes.

Comment: The above approach uses the time, place, and circumstances of taking the deposition to emphasize the contradiction. The lawyer may choose, however, not to lay a foundation of time, place, and circumstances. Evid C §§768–769. The following is permissible under the Evidence Code:

Q. Did your car leave any skid marks at the scene of the accident?
A. No.
Q. Did you ever tell anyone at any time, at any place, and under any circumstances that your car left skid marks?
A. I did not.
Q. Didn't you state under oath before this trial that your car did leave skid marks?
A. [I did not./I can't remember.]
Q. I will read to you from the transcript of your testimony in your deposition at page ......, lines ...... through .... ["Question.

DISCOVERY DOCUMENTS §10.8

Did your car leave skid marks at the scene of the accident? Answer. Yes, it did."]

Comment: Laying a detailed foundation of time, place, and circumstances of the prior inconsistent statement may better persuade the jury to question the witness's integrity.

After the testimony in the deposition has been read, some lawyers ask:

Q. Now, which is true, what you testified to in your deposition or what you are testifying to now?

Comment: Some courts disallow this question on the ground that it is argumentative. However, the jury has two versions of the same fact from the witness and should know which one the witness now believes to be correct.

The cross-examiner should also consider whether he wishes merely to show the conflict in the witness's testimony or also to seek to establish that the version in the deposition is correct. If he simply shows the conflict, he may leave the witness looking suspect in the eyes of the jury. But this approach permits the witness's attorney to bring out on redirect examination the version that the witness believes to be correct, which may not be the version in the deposition. While re-cross-examination may then be used to discredit the testimony, the effect on the jury is greater when it is done during the cross-examination.

Before using a deposition to impeach, counsel should consider whether the point is worthwhile. Impeaching a witness on minor matters, if overdone, can make the lawyer appear to be too attentive to small details and arouse sympathy for the witness in the jury. See BAJI No 2.21.

Use of a deposition against an adverse, nonparty witness to show his prior inconsistent statement is essentially the same as against an adverse party. The deposition of a nonparty witness may be used by any party to contradict or impeach his testimony on the stand. In addition, the deposition of anyone who at the time of taking the deposition was an officer, director, superintendent, member, agent, employee, or managing agent of a party may be used by an adverse party for any purpose. CCP §2016(d)(2). The same is true of an officer, director, etc., of a person for whose immediate benefit an action or proceeding is prosecuted or defended. CCP §2016(d)(2).

c. [§10.8] When Deponent Becomes Own Witness

A party does not make a person his own witness for any purpose simply by taking his deposition. CCP §2016(f). Under CCP §2016(f), however, if a deposition is introduced in evidence, the deponent is deemed to be the witness of the party that introduces it unless (1) the deponent is an adverse party, or a person for whose immediate benefit the action is prosecuted, or an officer, director, agent, etc., of the party or person; (2) the deposition is introduced to contradict or impeach the deponent; or (3) the deposition is introduced to explain or clarify portions already introduced by an adverse party. CCP §2016(f). Any party may rebut any relevant evidence in a deposition whether introduced by him or by another party.

3. To Show Prior Consistent Statement

   a. [§10.9] By Own Witness

A deposition can be used on direct or redirect examination to show a prior consistent statement of a witness or party when (1) a prior inconsistent statement has been admitted to attack his credibility, and the prior consistent statement in the deposition was made before the alleged inconsistent statement (Evid C §791(a)); or (2) an express or implied charge is made that his testimony at the trial is recently fabricated or is influenced by bias or other improper motive, and the prior consistent statement was made before the improper motive allegedly arose (Evid C §791(b)). See generally §1.44.

Thus, if the party has testified that his car left no skid marks and evidence is introduced to show an earlier out-of-court statement that his car did leave skid marks, a still earlier consistent statement in the deposition can be introduced. Evid C §791(a).

The following is a sample foundation for use of a deposition to show a prior consistent statement:

Q. You testified earlier in this trial that [your car left no skid marks], isn't that correct?
A. Yes.
Q. Did you hear the testimony of Mr. .... that on ...., 19......, you told him [your car did leave skid marks]?
A. Yes.
Q. Do you recall your deposition being taken on ...., 19......?
A. Yes.
Q. Was that before the date Mr. .... thinks you told him that [your car did leave skid marks]?
A. Yes.

DISCOVERY DOCUMENTS §10.10

Q. At the deposition were you sworn as a witness?
A. Yes.
Q. Were you then asked questions by Mr. ...., the attorney for the other side?
A. Yes.
Q. Did you answer those questions?
A. Yes.
Q. Were the questions and your answers taken down by a reporter and later transcribed?
A. Yes.
Q. Did you then sign the deposition?
A. Yes.
Q. I show you a document which purports to be the original transcript of your signed deposition. Is that your signature?
A. Yes, it is.
Q. Will you now please read to yourself lines ...... through ...... on page ......? [Hand deposition to witness who reads it.] Were you asked ["Did your car leave skid marks?"], and did you answer ["Yes."]?
A. Yes.

Comment: If the witness denies that he made the inconsistent statement, he can so testify. If he admits making it, he might want to explain why, *e.g.,* "It was the way he asked me. He said, 'You can't be absolutely sure of that, can you?' and I suppose I agreed with him that I couldn't be absolutely sure. Before testifying in this trial I read over the deposition and it refreshed my memory about the skid marks."

b. [§10.10] By Adverse Witness

In the rare situation when the opposing attorney tries to impeach his witness through use of a prior inconsistent statement (Evid C §791(a)) or charge of improper motive (Evid C §791(b)), a deposition can be used by the other side to show a prior statement consistent with the testimony of the adverse party at the trial. Evid C §791. The credibility of a witness may be attacked by the party calling him (Evid C §785), and the objection that an attorney cannot "impeach his own witness" is no longer a valid ground for objection. Evid C §785; see CALIFORNIA TRIAL OBJECTIONS §22.3 (Cal CEB 1967).

Ordinarily the lawyer will limit his attack to the offending portion of the testimony rather than making a larger attack on his witness's credibility. He will use the prior inconsistent statement as a means of refreshing memory rather than impeaching. Nevertheless, credibility has been attacked within the meaning of Evid C §791, and evidence of a prior consistent statement in the deposition is admissible. For foundational questions, see §10.9.

4. [§10.11] As Past Recollection Recorded

A deposition is a writing that may be read to the trier of fact as the past recollection recorded of a witness if a proper foundation is laid. See Evid C §1237. See generally §§8.25–8.33. Introducing the contents of a writing in evidence as past recollection recorded differs from refreshing a witness's memory with a writing. In refreshing memory, the writing revives the witness's memory so that his testimony rather than the writing is the evidence. In past recollection recorded, the writing does not revive the witness's memory; he testifies that the writing accurately records what he previously observed. The writing then can be read to the court as evidence, but only the adverse party can offer the writing as an exhibit. Evid C §1237(b).

a. [§10.12] By Own Witness

If, during direct or redirect examination, a party on the stand is unable to testify to a particular fact from memory, his deposition may be used to refresh his memory. See §10.4. If the deposition does not refresh his memory but he is able to testify that the deposition accurately records what he previously observed, the deposition can be read to the trier of fact as evidence. Before using a deposition as his witness's past recollection recorded, the lawyer must show that it meets the requirements of Evid C §1237. See §8.27.

A sample foundation for admission of the deposition to show past recollection recorded follows.

Q. Did you [witness an automobile accident on ...., 19......]?
A. Yes.
Q. [What time of day did it occur]?
A. I don't recall.
Q. Do you remember [the make or color of vehicles involved or other details of the accident]?
A. No.
Q. Do you recall your deposition being taken at [my office] on ...., 19......?
A. Yes.
Q. Do you recall answering questions at that time about the details of the accident?
A. Yes.

DISCOVERY DOCUMENTS §10.14

Q. Were the events of the accident still fresh in your mind at that time?
A. Yes.
Q. Did you see a court reporter writing down the questions and answers as you testified at that deposition?
A. Yes.
Q. I now show you this transcript of your deposition. Is this your signature at the end?
A. Yes.
Q. Was your testimony at that deposition a true statement of what you observed?
A. Yes.

Comment: Adverse counsel will usually stipulate that the deposition transcript is an accurate record of what the witness said. Otherwise, the reporter may be called to state that it is accurate, or the judge may find accuracy from the reporter's certification.

The lawyer can then ask permission to read the deposition. He might read the questions, while the witness or an associate reads the answers.

b. [§10.13] By Adverse Witness

When an adverse witness is on the stand for cross-examination or is called under Evid C §776, the opposing party may use his deposition to show past recollection recorded if the witness cannot remember the answer to a question he answered at the deposition. Evid C §1237. The foundation is essentially the same as for the lawyer's own party. See §10.12. The deposition may be received in evidence since it is offered by the adverse party. Evid C §1237(b).

However, if an adverse witness claims not to remember facts that he testified to at his deposition, the lawyer is unlikely to be able to lay a foundation for reading the deposition as past recollection recorded. The deposition is more readily used to show his prior inconsistent statements (see §10.7).

5. [§10.14] As Substitute Testimony

There are circumstances in which the contents of a deposition can be introduced in evidence in lieu of calling the witness to testify. See §§10.15–10.17. Ordinarily it is preferred that a witness testify orally at the trial rather than introduce his evidence by way of deposition, because in most instances oral testimony is more persuasive to the jury than a deposition. See *Allstate Ins. Co. v King* (1967) 252 CA2d 698, 710, 60 CR 892, 898, in which an insurance policy cooperation clause was held to have been breached to the insurer's prejudice by defendant's disappearance before trial. Under the circumstances of the case, the defendant's deposition was not an adequate substitute for his live testimony. Nevertheless, a witness's deposition may be used as a substitute for his testimony in certain instances.

    a. [§10.15] When Witness Unavailable

If a witness is unavailable, the deposition of that witness, whether or not a party, may be used by any party for any purpose. CCP §2016(d)(3). Evidence Code §240(a) defines an unavailable witness as one who is

(1) Exempted or precluded on the ground of privilege from testifying about the matter to which his statement is relevant.

(2) Disqualified from testifying to the matter. (A witness is disqualified who is either unable to communicate well enough to be understood or who does not understand the duty of a witness to tell the truth. Evid C §701.)

(3) Dead or unable to attend or to testify because of physical or mental illness or infirmity. (Proof of death can be made by introduction of a certified copy of the death certificate, testimony of the attending doctor, or testimony of a surviving spouse or other member of the family. Proof of illness or infirmity can be made by testimony of the attending physician or by a witness having personal knowledge of the illness. See 4 AM JUR PROOF OF FACTS 446–450 (1960) for laying of foundation.)

(4) Absent and not subject to court process. (Proof can be made either by testimony of the process server who unsuccessfully tried to locate the witness or by testimony of a witness who has personal knowledge that the person is absent from the area.)

(5) Absent and the party wishing to use his deposition cannot procure the witness's attendance despite the exercise of reasonable diligence. (Proof includes a showing of the efforts made to procure attendance as well as evidence regarding the deponent's whereabouts. See 4 AM JUR PROOF OF FACTS 435–446 (1960) for laying of foundation.)

If the party offering the deposition caused the disqualification, death, inability, or absence of the deponent to prevent him from testifying the deponent's deposition cannot be used. Evid C §240(b).

    b. [§10.16] In Interests of Justice

Use of the deposition will be allowed as a substitute for testimony if the court finds, after application and notice, that exceptional circumstances make the use desirable in the interests of justice, due regard being given to the importance of presenting oral testimony of witnesses. CCP §2016(d)(3)(ii). An example is the situation in which a doctor's deposition was taken, but he is called away on an emergency case at time of trial. If the doctor's evidence is crucial, the court might permit the introduction of his deposition as a substitute for his testimony. The adverse party may, however, oppose use of the deposition on the ground that the importance of the doctor's evidence warrants his testimony in court or that its cross-examination of the doctor at the taking of the deposition was not complete.

c. [§10.17] When Deposition Is of Adverse Party, Agent, or Witness

Under CCP §2016(d)(2) the deposition of a party or officer, director, superintendent, member, agent, employee, or managing agent of the party or person may be used by an adverse party for any purpose. It may be used to establish any material fact, a prima facie case, or even to prove the whole case. *Mayhood v LaRosa* (1962) 58 C2d 498, 24 CR 837. The deposition of an adverse party may be used as substantive evidence as well as to contradict or impeach. *Alvarez v Felker Mfg. Co.* (1964) 230 CA2d 987, 1002, 41 CR 514, 523; Witkin, CALIFORNIA EVIDENCE §1146 (2d ed, 1966).

No showing need be made of exceptional circumstances or of the unavailability of an adverse party (or officer, etc.) before his deposition is used as a substitute for testimony. Thus, if he does not appear at the hearing, his deposition may be introduced without any showing of reasons for the absence or efforts to procure attendance.

The plaintiff can begin his case by introducing the defendant's deposition in evidence and reading questions and answers damaging to the defendant's case. This use of a deposition may be more effective than attempting to impeach or contradict the witness on the stand with his deposition. It can be used in this manner even though the adverse party is present and could be called under Evid C §776.

B. [§10.18] Objections to Admission

The lawyer who plans to use a deposition at trial must be familiar with objections that can be made to admission of the deposition. The basic rule is that objections may be made at the trial to receiving in evidence all or part of a deposition, just as if the witness were present and testifying on the stand. CCP §2016(e).

Objections can be waived, however, by failure to object at the deposition to the form of questions or answers or to errors of any kind that might have been eliminated if promptly presented. CCP

§2021(c)(2). For example, objections that the questions are leading, ambiguous, etc., are waived unless made when the questions were originally asked.

Objections to the competency of a witness or to the relevancy, competency, or materiality of testimony can be waived if the ground of the objection might have been obviated or removed if presented at the deposition. CCP §2021(c)(1). For example, if a deponent gives a summary of the contents of a document in his possession, an objection on the ground that the document itself is the best evidence of its contents (see Evid C §1500) may be waived unless made at the deposition, since a seasonable objection might have resulted in admission of the document itself.

A stipulation reserving all objections to the time of hearing will prevent operation of the waiver provisions of CCP §2021(c). See, e.g., *Johnson v Nicholson* (1958) 159 CA2d 395, 412, 324 P2d 307, 317 (trial court properly granted motion made at trial to strike non-responsive answer when all objections except as to form of questions reserved when deposition taken).

A deposition cannot be admitted over objection if the deponent dies without reading and signing it. CCP §2019(e); *Voorheis v Hawthorne-Michaels Co.* (1957) 151 CA2d 688, 312 P2d 51. However, the reading and signing requirements are sometimes waived by stipulation, and the signature may also be waived if the deponent is ill, cannot be found, or refuses to sign. CCP §2019(e).

C. [§10.19] Substitution of Parties and Supplemental Proceedings

Substitution of parties does not affect the right to use depositions previously taken, and when an action has been dismissed in any court of the United States or any state and another action on the same subject matter is later brought between the same parties, depositions taken in the former action may be used in the latter. CCP §2016(d)(4); Witkin, CALIFORNIA EVIDENCE §1147 (2d ed, 1966). See also CCP §§2017(a)(4), 2017(b) on the use of depositions originally taken to perpetuate testimony.

D. [§10.20] Presentation at Trial

If the judge does not permit a deposition to be read in evidence, the lawyer should have it marked for identification, and should ask to read relevant portions as an offer of proof to make it part of the record on appeal. To have all or part of a deposition admitted in evidence, the lawyer introducing it should read the questions and answers he wishes admitted. Introducing a deposition without reading it is improper when opposing counsel has objected. See *Estate of Doyle* (1932) 126 CA 446, 452, 14 P2d 909, 911 (admission of depositions held, however, not to be reversible error because objection was general rather than specific). See generally Witkin, CALIFORNIA EVIDENCE §1149 (2d ed, 1966).

As each question and answer is read, any objections and motions to strike must be made, and the court rules on each objection or motion as it comes up. The best procedure is to present the deposition to the trial judge and make the objections and motions to strike in the absence of the jury to prevent objectionable matter from reaching it. Witkin, EVIDENCE §1150. For example:

Proponent. Your Honor, we wish to offer portions of this witness's deposition in evidence.

Opponent. Your Honor, I want the questions and answers read so that I may make objections to certain questions and motions to strike certain answers. May we adjourn to chambers so that we can make our objections before the deposition is read to the jury?

Comment: After the court has ruled on the objections, the admitted portions of the deposition are read to the jury.

If a party offers part of a deposition in evidence, any party may then introduce any other parts. CCP §2016(d)(4). Formerly the rule was that a party could not offer selected parts of the deposition; it had to offer the entire deposition. Witkin, EVIDENCE §1151.

E. [§10.21] *Availability to Jury During Deliberations*

Depositions cannot be taken into the jury room. CCP §612. They contain all the questions and answers taken down at the deposition, many of which may be extraneous and some of which may have been ruled inadmissible. Also, the jury may give the transcribed testimony greater weight than the oral testimony. The selected portions of the testimony from the deposition are therefore read into evidence and the jury instructed to consider that testimony as if it had been given in court. BAJI No 2.06.

III. INTERROGATORIES

A. [§10.22] *Uses*

Interrogatories are a series of written questions to an adverse party that require answers under oath. Rules governing trial use of interrogatories and the answers are the same as for depositions. CCP

§2030(b). Accordingly, they may be used, like depositions, to show prior inconsistent statements (see §§10.6–10.8) and prior consistent statements (see §§10.9–10.10), to refresh memory (see §§10.3–10.5), as past recollection recorded (see §§10.11–10.13), and as a substitute for testimony (see §§10.14–10.17).

In general, the code distinguishes between use of any depositions (hence any interrogatories) for the limited purpose of impeachment and contradiction (CCP §2016(d)(1)) and use of certain depositions (hence certain interrogatories) for any purpose (CCP §2016(d)(2)–(3)).

Interrogatories have an advantage over depositions in that they can compel a party to obtain and disclose more detailed information. For example, a corporate defendant may be required to obtain information from numerous employees to answer the interrogatories. A weakness of interrogatories is that the adverse attorney usually drafts the answers artfully, thus limiting the possibilities of impeachment. Still, they are effective instruments for obtaining useful information in preparing and presenting a case.

B. [§10.23] Restrictions on Use

Any part or all of an interrogatory is admissible at the trial, or hearing of a motion (see *The 1880 Corp. v Superior Court* (1962) 57 C2d 840, 842, 22 CR 209, 210), or an interlocutory proceeding, subject to the rules of evidence. CCP §2016(d). Although questions may be permissible in interrogatories that call for answers inadmissible at trial (see *Greyhound Corp. v Superior Court* (1961) 56 C2d 355, 392, 15 CR 90, 109), the answers may not be used at the trial if proper objection is made. Thus, questions calling for hearsay, opinions, and conclusions are permissible although the answers may not be admitted in evidence if intended to have probative value. See *West Pico Furniture Co. v Superior Court* (1961) 56 C2d 407, 417, 15 CR 119, 123. The lawyer wishing to prevent interrogatories from being admitted in evidence should bear in mind the distinction between propriety of questions in interrogatories to obtain information leading to probative facts and use of the answers themselves at trial as probative evidence.

Interrogatories between two parties to an action are not admissible against a third party, nor are they usable in lieu of a deposition against the third party. See *Associates Discount Corp. v Tobb Co.* (1966) 241 CA2d 541, 552, 50 CR 738, 745. A reason for the exclusion is that the third party could not propose cross-interrogatories or request further response.

IV. OTHER DISCOVERY DOCUMENTS

A. [§10.24] *Request for Admission*

A request that the adverse party admit the genuineness of any relevant document or the truth of any relevant matter of fact (CCP §2033) is a little used but effective discovery device. Similarly, the answers to requests for admission are seldom used at trial. It should be borne in mind that if a party denies the genuineness of a document or the truth of a matter of fact in the request and that document or fact is proved at trial, the party may be assessed the cost of proof including attorney's fees. CCP §2034(c). For discussion and forms of request for admission, see §8.22.

B. [§10.25] *Motions for Production and Inspection and for Examination by Physicians*

A party may obtain a court order requiring any party to produce and permit the inspection of unprivileged books, papers, photographs, objects, or tangible things relevant to the subject matter. CCP §2031. In personal injury cases the device is used mainly to obtain inspection of machinery, equipment, and other physical objects involved in an accident.

On motion, the court may order a party to submit to a physical, mental, or blood examination by a physician. CCP §2032(a). The party examined is entitled, on request, to a copy of the written report. CCP §2032(b)(1).

Most of these matters are handled not by discovery methods but by stipulation of the parties, since it is burdensome and costly to go to court over matters allowed by the law. There are occasions, however, when a stipulation is not possible and the discovery devices must be used. They can be used in conjunction to obtain a desired result at trial.

11

Business Records

I. [§11.1] Defined; Uses at Trial

II. Admission in Evidence
    A. [§11.2] By Agreement
    B. [§11.3] By Laying Foundation
       1. [§11.4] Relevance
       2. [§11.5] Authentication
       3. [§11.6] Best Evidence
       4. [§11.7] Hearsay
    C. [§11.8] By Subpenaed Copy Delivered with Custodian's Affidavit
       1. [§11.9] Issuance and Service of Subpena
       2. [§11.10] Supporting Declaration: Form
       3. [§11.11] Notice Describing Procedure for Compliance: Form
       4. [§11.12] Custodian's Declaration
       5. [§11.13] Opening and Offering Copy in Evidence
    D. By Custodian's Testimony
       1. [§11.14] When Required: Checklist
       2. [§11.15] Clause Requiring Personal Attendance of Custodian with Original Records

III. [§11.16] Using Wage Record To Show Earnings Loss
    A. [§11.17] Identifying Witness
    B. [§11.18] Identifying Record and Mode of Preparation
    C. [§11.19] Record Made in Regular Course of Business
    D. [§11.20] Time of Preparation At or Near Time of Act, Condition, or Event
    E. [§11.21] Trustworthiness
    F. [§11.22] Content of Record

I. [§11.1] DEFINED; USES AT TRIAL

"Business records" are every kind of record maintained by every kind of business, governmental agency, profession, occupation, calling, or institution, whether carried on for profit or not. See Evid C §§1270, 1560(a).

The business records commonly used in personal injury cases include employment and earnings records of an employee before and after injury, profit and loss statements of a business in which the injured person was a participating owner, company rules and regulations, accident reports prepared by company employees, a doctor's office records of examination and treatment and hospital records (see chap 13), and the official records of public agencies (Witkin, CALIFORNIA EVIDENCE §576 (1966)). On police accident reports, see §9.12.

The introduction of business records at trial can spare the need to call and examine as witnesses the persons who made the entries, or observed the facts entered in them, and they are often a more efficient way of proving facts.

II. ADMISSION IN EVIDENCE

A. [§11.2] *By Agreement*

Adverse lawyers are sometimes willing to stipulate that a business record can be received in evidence as an exhibit without foundational testimony or affidavit. For a general discussion and forms of admission by agreement, request for admission, and pretrial order, see §§8.20–8.24.

If there is any question about the admissibility of particular items in a business record, the parties can decide before the record is offered whether those entries should be covered or deleted, or they can stipulate to foundational matters, and reserve objections to the admission of particular items. The proponent of a business record can state that it is being received by stipulation. For example:

Proponent. Your Honor, at this time, pursuant to stipulation of all parties, the [plaintiff/defendant] offers in evidence, as [plaintiff's/defendant's] exhibit ......, this copy of [describe record, *e.g.,* the wage and employment records for (name of employee)] from the business records of [name of business].

(Optional)

The parties have stipulated that this exhibit is a true and correct copy of an authentic business record of [name of business], and

BUSINESS RECORDS §11.5

that no further foundation need be laid [but all parties reserve the right to make any other objection, and to move to delete or strike any entries, statements, or other portions of the record that are not legally admissible].

Comment: The proponent should make sure that the stipulation is entered in the minutes of the court or that the court record clearly shows that the exhibit has been received in evidence. See CCP §283. See also §8.24 on oral stipulations.

B. [§11.3] By Laying Foundation

If foundational objections are made to the admission of business records in evidence, the records must be shown to be relevant (see §11.4), authentic (see §11.5), in compliance with the best evidence rule (see §11.6), and within an exception to the hearsay rule (see §11.7). The burden of proof is on the party producing the record. See *Bufano v San Francisco* (1965) 233 CA2d 61, 72, 43 CR 223, 230.

1. [§11.4] Relevance

Only relevant evidence is admissible (Evid C §350) so that business records, to be admissible, must tend to prove or disprove a disputed fact in the case (Evid C §210). See generally §8.10.

Even though the evidence is relevant, a trial judge has the power to exclude the business record on the ground that its probative value is substantially outweighed by the time needed to introduce it or by the danger that it would prejudice, confuse, or mislead. Evid C §352; see *Witt v Jackson* (1961) 57 C2d 57, 67, 17 CR 369, 375 (record must not confuse or mislead jury).

2. [§11.5] Authentication

A business record is a writing (see Evid C §250) and therefore must be authenticated before it, or a copy, can be received in evidence (Evid C §1401). The party offering the record must show that it is the writing the proponent claims it is, *i.e.,* the record, or a copy, from a particular business relating to its transactions, conduct, or affairs. See Evid C §1400. This authenticating evidence can be given by the record custodian or other qualified witness either through testimony or through the affidavit prescribed by Evid C §1561.

Authentication of the record as a whole should serve to authenticate its parts, but a specific entry can still be excluded by a showing that it is not what it purports to be, *e.g.,* that it was altered or a forgery or that some part is missing.

3. [§11.6] Best Evidence

The best evidence of the content of a writing is the original writing itself, and no evidence other than the original writing is admissible to prove its contents except as provided by statute. Evid C §1500. However, a statutory exception permits production of a true, legible, and durable copy of the business records in response to a subpena duces tecum (Evid C §1560) unless the original records are specifically requested (Evid C §1564). See §11.8. Certain types of copies are as admissible as the original writing itself if made and preserved as a part of the records of a business in the regular course of the business. Evid C §1550; Witkin, CALIFORNIA EVIDENCE §§575, 707 (1966).

4. [§11.7] Hearsay

Business records are statements made other than by a witness while testifying at the hearing. See Evid C §1200. They are, however, not made inadmissible by the hearsay rule if they (a) were made in the regular course of business; (b) were made at or near the time of the act, condition, or event; (c) were made in a manner that indicates their trustworthiness; and (d) are authenticated by the custodian or another qualified witness. Evid C §1271.

The business record statutes are based on the assumption that records kept in the general course of business are usually accurate and may be used as evidence of the matter recorded. See *Loper v Morrison* (1944) 23 C2d 600, 608, 145 P2d 1, 5. The object is to eliminate the need to call as a witness each person who made an entry. See 23 C2d at 609, 145 P2d at 5.

The trustworthiness of a business record can be shown to the trial judge through the testimony of the custodian or any other person who knows the facts about sources of information and method and time of preparation. If the judge finds the showing is insufficient, he can sustain the foundational hearsay objection and exclude the record. See *Luthringer v Moore* (1948) 31 C2d 489, 501, 190 P2d 1, 9 (records excluded when custodian testified only that they were "day to day" records and said nothing about mode of preparation). If the procedure prescribed in Evid C §§1560–1562 is followed, the affidavit (or declaration under penalty of perjury (CCP §2015.5)) of the records custodian or other qualified witness will supply the necessary evidence of trustworthiness. See §§11.8–11.12.

While the business records as a whole may be admissible in evidence under the Evid C §1271 exception to the hearsay rule, specific entries may still be excluded as hearsay if they record what some third person told the entrant. For example, transit company records might include an accident report signed by a bus driver stating, "I talked to a bystander. He told me the other driver wasn't looking where he was going." Even though the report might be admissible as a business record, a further hearsay objection could be made to the bystander's statement to the driver. The business record exception only provides a method of proving an admissible act, condition, or event; it does not make a record admissible when oral testimony of the same facts would be inadmissible. *McGowan v Los Angeles* (1950) 100 CA2d 386, 392, 223 P2d 862, 866 (record excluded when no proof that blood tested for alcohol level was decedent's blood).

If a record does not meet the requirements of Evid C §1271, it may still be received under other exceptions to the hearsay rule, such as admission of a party (*London v Guberman* (1963) 214 CA2d 215, 220, 29 CR 279, 283), a declaration against interest, or to refresh memory. See Witkin, CALIFORNIA EVIDENCE §574 (2d ed, 1966).

C. [§11.8] By Subpenaed Copy Delivered with Custodian's Affidavit

A lawyer who wants to introduce a business record in evidence, but does not care to solicit or rely on the agreement of adverse counsel, can follow the procedure prescribed in Evid C §§1560–1566. (Before amendment in 1969, this procedure applied only to hospital records. See REVIEW OF 1969 CODE LEGISLATION 112–113 (Cal CEB 1969).)

This procedure permits the lawyer to serve a subpena duces tecum on the custodian of the record or other qualified witness (see §11.9), along with the lawyer's affidavit or declaration for issuance of the subpena (see §11.10). If the custodian is eligible and chooses to do so, he can respond to the subpena by delivering a copy of the record to the court in the manner prescribed by Evid C §1560 (see §11.11), along with his affidavit or declaration as prescribed by Evid C §1561 (see §11.12). The lawyer can then offer in evidence the delivered copy of the record. See §11.13. The copy of the record is as admissible as the original would have been if the custodian had been present to testify to the matters stated in his affidavit. Evid C §1562. The statements in the custodian's affidavit ordinarily satisfy the best evidence and authentication requirements and the business records exception to the hearsay rule.

If the business is a party, a written notice to the party's attorney served at least 20 days before the trial may be used instead of a subpena. CCP §1987(c).

1. [§11.9] Issuance and Service of Subpena

Subpenas duces tecum are issued to parties who request them by the clerk of the court (or the judge if there is no clerk), signed and sealed, but otherwise in blank. CCP §1985. The attorney fills in the subpena before serving it. Of course, an attorney who has a supply of unsigned, unsealed subpena blanks on hand can fill them out before having them "issued" (*i.e.,* signed and sealed by the clerk).

Filling in the subpena form usually presents few problems. The attorney can learn, often through a telephone call, the name of the custodian of records (or other qualified witness) of the business whose records are to be subpenaed. The name on the subpena should be the same as that of the person declared to have possession or control of the records as shown on the affidavit or declaration served with the subpena. Since the affidavit or declaration must contain a description of the records sought and must be served along with the subpena, no purpose is served by describing the matters and things sought in the subpena itself. The blank in the subpena form that calls for a description can contain a reference to the affidavit, such as "described in the attached [declaration/affidavit] for subpena duces tecum."

A final consideration in filling out the subpena form is determining whether to add the statement in Evid C §1564 requiring the personal attendance of the custodian with the original records. See discussion in §11.15.

Service of the subpena is made in the usual way by delivering to the witness a copy of the subpena and a copy of the affidavit or declaration on which it is based and, if demanded, tendering witness fees. CCP §§1987, 1987.5. The subpena with proof of service can be filed with the court at the same time as the original affidavit or declaration, which should be filed before the time designated for the witness's appearance at trial. CCP §1987.5. When the subpena is served, the attorney may also give the custodian notice of how he may respond without attending in person with the original records (see §11.11), and a copy of the declaration for him to fill out and sign (see §11.12).

2. [§11.10] Supporting Declaration: Form

Service of a subpena duces tecum is invalid unless there is also served an affidavit (or declaration under penalty of perjury (see CCP

BUSINESS RECORDS §11.10

§2015.5)) that (a) specifies the exact matters or things desired to be produced, (b) states that the subpenaed witness has them in his possession or under his control, (c) shows good cause for their production, and (d) sets forth in full detail the materiality of the records to the issues in the case. CCP §§1985, 1987.5.

The description of the records subpenaed should be broad enough to specify all the records the attorney wants, but narrow enough to exclude records he has not seen, or does not want. The allegation of custody or control should be positive; one made on information and belief may not be sufficient. *Lewis v Superior Court* (1953) 118 CA2d 770, 258 P2d 1084.

The statements showing good cause and materiality must be statements of evidentiary fact, not based on information and belief. See generally CALIFORNIA CIVIL PROCEDURE DURING TRIAL §§3.22–3.27 (Cal CEB 1960). Statements that "there is good cause," "the records are material," and they "are admissible" are statements of legal conclusions that do not satisfy the requirements of CCP §1985. Usually the facts that show materiality also tend to show good cause, and these facts are often run together in the declaration.

Some court clerks supply printed forms of declarations for subpenas duces tecum, which lawyers can obtain and fill out. Otherwise, a form like the following can be used.

Copies: Original to file with the clerk of the issuing court; one copy for the witness; one office copy.

(Title of Court)

(Title of Cause)　　　　　No. ....
　　　　　　　　　　　　DECLARATION FOR
　　　　　　　　　　　　SUBPENA DUCES TECUM

.... declares:
　　(Name of declarant)

1. I am an attorney for .... in this action.
　　　　　　　　　　　　　　plaintiff/defendant

2. This cause has been set for trial on ...., 19......., at ....m., in Department .... of this Court.

3. .... is the custodian of records of ....
　　(Name of witness)　　　　　　　　　　　　　　　　　　　(Name of

.... and has the following matters or things in .... possession or under .... control:
business)　　　　　　　　　　　　　　　　　　　　　　his/her
　　　　　　　　　　　his/her

(Specify records sought, e.g.)

325

§11.11 BUSINESS RECORDS

    a. Employment and wage records of ....
(Name of employee)

    b. ....

(Continue)

  4. These records and things are material to the issues in this case and admissible in evidence, and there is good cause for their production, in that:

    a. This is an action for ....
personal injuries to/the wrongful death of

....
(Name of plaintiff or decedent)

    b. These records and things are, and contain, evidence of ....
(E.g.)

....
the earnings of the plaintiff before and after the accident of ...., 19......., ...
on which this action is based

Comment: Although the foregoing statements are usually sufficient to establish good cause and materiality, the lawyer may wish to state additional facts and to add statements such as the following:

    c. These records and things form part of the basis of, and reasons for, the opinions of expert and other witnesses who will testify at the trial of this case, are records of the past recollections of these witnesses, and will refresh their memories.

  5. The pleadings, records, and files in this action are incorporated by this reference.

  Executed on ...., 19......., at ...., California.

  I declare under penalty of perjury that the foregoing is true and correct.

_____
(Signature of attorney)
(Typed name of attorney)
Attorney for ....
Plaintiff/Defendant

Comment: A copy of the declaration or affidavit must be served at the same time as the subpena duces tecum, and the original should thereafter be filed with the court that issued the subpena before the time designated for the appearance of the witness and production of the records at trial. CCP §1987.5.

  3. [§11.11] Notice Describing Procedure for Compliance: Form

  A lawyer who prefers that the custodian deliver a copy of the business record to court, rather than attending in person with the original, can encourage him to do so by personal or telephone contact. The lawyer can also give the custodian a notice explaining the procedure established by Evid C §§1560–1566 for compliance with a subpena duces tecum and a blank declaration form (see §11.12) to fill in and sign. While there is no statutory requirement that counsel furnish these forms, it is a courtesy and helps to gain cooperation and encourage a prompt and appropriate response to the subpena.

The notice and declaration forms are usually attached to the copies handed to the custodian when the subpena is served. The subpena itself must be properly served; service of the notice and declaration forms alone do not compel production of a medical record.

Notice and declaration forms should not be given to a custodian if the lawyer desires his personal attendance or the original records (in which case he will also add to the subpena the clause called for by Evid C §1564) or if the business is a party or the place where a cause of action is alleged to have arisen. Evid C §1560.

The following form can be used to instruct the custodian on how to comply with Evid C §1560.

Copies: Original to attach to the copy of the subpena duces tecum delivered to the party served; one office copy.

NOTICE

To the person named in the attached Subpena Duces Tecum:

Evidence Code section 1560 permits you to avoid personal attendance in court with the original records described in the subpena if you complete the following steps:

1. Make a true, legible, and durable copy of each of the records described in the subpena.
2. Complete and sign the enclosed declaration.
3. Put the declaration, and the copy of the records, in a sealed envelope or wrapper.
4. Write the following information on the outside of that sealed envelope or wrapper:
    (a) Title of action: ....
    (b) Number of action: ....
    (c) Date of subpena: ....
    (d) Name of person who signed the declaration enclosed with the records.
5. Enclose the sealed envelope or wrapper in an outer envelope or wrapper and seal it.

§11.12   BUSINESS RECORDS

6. Mail or deliver the above to the following addressee: ....
(Name and address of court clerk, deposition officer, or other person designated in Evid C §1560(c))

7. To comply with Evidence Code section 1560, you must mail or deliver the above within five days after you receive the subpena.

IF YOU DO NOT COMPLETE THE ABOVE STEPS WITHIN FIVE DAYS AFTER YOU RECEIVE THE SUBPENA, YOU MUST ATTEND IN PERSON WITH THE ORIGINAL RECORDS AT THE TIME AND PLACE INDICATED IN THE SUBPENA.

If you have any questions concerning the foregoing, please do not hesitate to contact this office.

                                      Very truly yours,

                                        _____
                                        (Signature of attorney)
                                        (Typed name of attorney)

                                        ....
                                                (Address)

                                        ....
                                               (Telephone)

                          Attorney for ....
                                               (Name of party)

Comment: The attorney should fill in all blanks in this form.

4. [§11.12] Custodian's Declaration

Attorneys give custodians blank declaration (or affidavit) forms to fill out for the same reasons they give them the notice discussed in §11.11 (to gain cooperation etc.) and also to ensure that the custodian's declaration will be sufficient to qualify the records for admission in evidence. They are not required by statute to provide custodians with these forms.

A declaration by the custodian in the form prescribed by Evid C §1561 is usually sufficient to provide the foundation for admission of the records in evidence. Although the statements in the declaration are in part conclusional, they will usually satisfy the requirements of the authentication and best evidence rules and the business records exception to the hearsay rule.

The attorney wishing to have copies delivered with the custodian's declaration can furnish the following form of declaration.

BUSINESS RECORDS §11.13

Copies: Original to attach to the copy of the subpena duces tecum delivered to the party served; one office copy.

DECLARATION

(In compliance with Evidence Code section 1561
and Code of Civil Procedure section 2015.5)

Title of action: ....
Number of action: ....
Date of subpena: ....
Name of party obtaining subpena: ....
Name of business: ....

_____

The undersigned declares:
1. I am the duly authorized custodian of the records of the above-named business.
2. I have authority to certify those records.
3. (Check one of the following)

☐ The copies transmitted are true copies of all the original records described in the subpena.

☐ No copies or records are transmitted, because the business has none of the records described in the subpena.

☐ The copies transmitted are true copies of part of the original records described in the subpena. The business does not have any other of the described records.

4. The records referred to above were prepared by the personnel of the above-named business, in the ordinary course of business, at or near the time of the acts, conditions, or events recorded.

Executed on ...., 19......, at ...., California.

I declare under penalty of perjury that the foregoing is true and correct.

Sign here: _____
Print name: ....

Comment: The attorney should fill in the five items above the line in the form.

5. [§11.13] Opening and Offering Copy in Evidence

The sealed envelope delivered by the custodian, containing the copy of the business record and the custodian's affidavit or declaration, is filed by the clerk with the other files of the case. Unless the parties agree otherwise, the records remain sealed until trial, when they are opened on order of the judge in the presence of all parties who have appeared in person or by counsel. Evid C §1560(d).

Any attorney, not necessarily the one who subpenaed the records, can request that the judge direct the clerk to open the envelope and can offer the records in evidence. He can do this in chambers or in open court after the jury has been selected, or he may wish to wait until he calls the witness in connection with whose testimony the record is to be used. At that time, the offering attorney may also request permission to read the custodian's affidavit to the trier of fact and perhaps even to state briefly how the record was subpenaed, prepared, and delivered to court. It appears that no matter who first offers the record in evidence, it will be numbered as the exhibit of the party who subpenaed it.

The request for opening the records may be made as follows:

Proponent. Your Honor, the attorneys for all parties being present, [name of party] requests that you direct the clerk to open the sealed envelope containing the business records delivered by [name of custodian or other witness] to this court pursuant to a subpena duces tecum.

(Optional)

[Name of party] also requests that the attorneys for all parties examine the records and indicate any parts they consider inadmissible so that we can either agree to cover or delete those parts or can be heard on their admissibility.

Comment: The records may be offered in evidence as follows:

Proponent. Your Honor, at this time I would like to offer in evidence, as [plaintiff's/defendant's] exhibit ......, the business records of [name of business] relating to ....

(Optional)

Your Honor, these records were subpenaed by [name of party] on ...., 19......, and [name of custodian], who is the custodian of records of that business, made a copy of the records, put them in a sealed envelope, together with his [affidavit/declaration under penalty of perjury], wrote the name and number of this action and other identifying information on that envelope, and [mailed/delivered] the envelope directly to this court. [The sealed envelope was opened in chambers at the beginning of this trial in the presence of all parties./All parties or their attorneys being present, I ask the court to direct the clerk to open that envelope

BUSINESS RECORDS §11.15

so that the records may be received in evidence.] Of course, Your Honor, the records are received subject to any objections that may be properly made to any particular entries or pages.

(Optional)

Proponent. Your Honor, I also request permission to read to the jury the [affidavit/declaration under penalty of perjury] signed by the records custodian and delivered to this court with the records.

D. By Custodian's Testimony

1. [§11.14] When Required: Checklist

Foundational testimony from the custodian or other qualified witness must be elicited to introduce subpenaed business records when:

1. The subpena duces tecum commands personal attendance by containing the clause set forth in Evid C §1564 (see §11.15);
2. The custodian, although eligible to mail to court a copy of the records, chooses to attend in person and testify;
3. The "business" is a party to the action or is the place where the cause of action is alleged to have arisen (Evid C §1560(b));
4. The custodian is compelled to attend by subpena served on him by a party other than the party subpenaing the records.

2. [§11.15] Clause Requiring Personal Attendance of Custodian with Original Records

An attorney can require a records custodian to attend court in person with the original records and give foundational testimony for their admission in evidence. This is done by inserting in the subpena duces tecum the clause set forth in Evid C §1564.

Unless the continuity of the trial would be interrupted, the custodian's testimony can add weight and credibility to the evidence contained in the records, especially if the case is tried before a jury. In addition, original records may be more legible and may carry greater impact, with their varied inks and papers, than photocopies.

A subpena containing the Evid C §1564 clause takes precedence over subpenas without the clause, whatever the order of service. Thus, any attorney can force attendance of the custodian even though other attorneys in the case would prefer that the custodian simply deliver a copy of the records with his affidavit or declaration. The custodian is considered to be the witness of the first party to serve him with a subpena containing the clause. Evid C §1565.

The clause is usually typed into the subpena duces tecum form in the space following the description of the things and matters subpenaed, although it could be typed on a separate sheet attached to and incorporated by reference into the subpena.

The following is the clause required by Evid C §1564:

> The personal attendance of the custodian or other qualified witness and the production of the original records is required by this subpoena. The procedure authorized pursuant to subdivision (b) of Section 1560, and Sections 1561 and 1562, of the Evidence Code will not be deemed sufficient compliance with this subpoena.

III. [§11.16] USING WAGE RECORD TO SHOW EARNINGS LOSS

The plaintiff ordinarily will not submit the issue of earnings loss to the jury on his testimony alone, since jurors may be skeptical when considering damages claimed from lost earnings. Similarly, the defendant is not likely to submit the issue on plaintiff's testimony alone unless it is in accord with the payroll records of the business for which the plaintiff works or was working. Unless the amount of lost earnings can be stipulated, the actual payroll records should be brought to court and used as a basis for the testimony offered on the issue of earnings loss. They may be procured by a subpena duces tecum, and the proponent should consider whether he wishes the custodian or other qualified witness to appear and give testimony regarding authenticity and content. Testimony of the bookkeeper or other qualified custodian may result in greater weight being given to the loss of earnings shown. For example, the custodian can testify that the record is the basis for computing income tax withholding and social security amounts. Those items indicate acceptance of the record by the federal government, which helps to dispel any doubt about the record's accuracy. Testimony may not be required, however, because Evid C §1560 now permits the custodian or other qualified witness to comply with a subpena duces tecum for the production of business records by delivering a copy to the court within five days, together with an affidavit. See §11.8. For contents of the affidavit, see Evid C §1561 and §11.12. Personal appearance and production of the original record may still be required. Evid C §1564; see §11.15.

A. [§11.17] Identifying Witness

The authenticating witness must be the custodian of the business records or other qualified witness. Evid C §1271(c). Ordinarily the bookkeeper, the accountant, or another person closely associated with keeping of the records will appear in response to the subpena duces

BUSINESS RECORDS §11.18

tecum. The witness is qualified to give the necessary foundational testimony and to testify to what the records show regarding the plaintiff's wage record and may be qualified as follows:

Q. What is your occupation?
A. Bookkeeper.
Q. Where are you employed?
A. ....
Q. How long have you worked for this employer?
A. ...... years.
Q. What are your duties?
A. [I keep the wage records.]
Q. Do you keep the wage records of the company yourself?
A. Yes.

Comment: If the answer is no, further questioning should show that the witness is familiar with the wage record system and can identify the entries as correct. For example:

Q. Are you familiar with the payroll record system?
A. Yes.
Q. Describe how it works.
A. [I have two clerks who make the entries from time cards/etc.]
Q. Is there any supervising or checking that you do personally to ensure the accuracy of these entries?
A. Yes. [I personally review their work and am fully familiar with the payroll records.]

B. [§11.18] *Identifying Record and Mode of Preparation*

The custodian or other qualified witness must identify the record and show how it is made. Evid C §1271(c); see Witkin, CALIFORNIA EVIDENCE §588 (2d ed, 1966). The witness should have sufficient knowledge of the record to answer questions such as the following:

Q. I show you a card bearing the name of ...., the plaintiff in the case, which was part of the record you brought to court today. Can you identify it?
A. Yes, it is the payroll record of ...., the plaintiff.
Q. Is it the entire payroll record for him?
A. Yes, it is.
Q. Are you familiar with how it was made?
A. Yes, [I made it myself/it was made by a clerk under my supervision].
Q. Describe the mode of preparation.

§11.19   BUSINESS RECORDS

A. [We receive a time card showing the hours worked by the employee for the pay period. The card is made out by the employee and the information verified by his supervisor. We then enter into the payroll journal the number of hours worked, the hourly wage, the gross wage, and the net amount. In addition, that information is entered on a compensation record card for the employee.]

Q. Are the entries on plaintiff's payroll record correct?

A. Yes, they are.

C. [§11.19] Record Made in Regular Course of Business

A writing made as a record of and offered to prove an act, condition, or event must be made in the regular course of business in order to come within the exception to the hearsay rule. Evid C §1271. The requirement can be satisfied by the testimony of the custodian or qualified witness as follows:

Q. Do you have the payroll record of ...., the plaintiff in this case?

A. Yes, I do.

Q. What period does it cover?

A. [His entire work period for the company which covers from ...., 19......, to ...., 19.......]

Q. Was the record prepared in the ordinary course of business?

A. Yes.

Comment: Though the preceding question is routinely asked without objection, it is leading and calls for a conclusion of the witness. However, leading questions are permissible in establishing preliminary facts (see §1.11), and the question calls for a mixture of fact and conclusion. Further, the affidavit procedure in Evid C §1561 itself calls for the statement of the custodian or other qualified witness that the records were prepared in the ordinary course of business.

D. [§11.20] Time of Preparation At or Near Time of Act, Condition, or Event

The evidence must show that the writing was made at or near the time of the act, condition, or event. There should be no difficulty establishing that fact, because modern bookkeeping methods dictate regular and prompt entries to keep the record up to date. The witness is simply asked the question directly:

Q. Are the entries in the record made at or near the time when the work is done?

A. Yes.

BUSINESS RECORDS §11.22

Comment: See *Comment,* §11.19 on the objection that the question is leading. In the unlikely event that the objection is sustained, the proponent need only ask when the entries are made.

E. [§11.21] Trustworthiness

There must be a preliminary showing that the record is reliable or trustworthy. It is made by demonstrating that the sources of information and method and time of the record's preparation indicate its trustworthiness. Evid C §1271(d). Ordinarily the testimony of a qualified witness covering the requirements of Evid C §1271(a)–(c) will demonstrate whether the record is trustworthy. It is important not to overlook asking the witness whether the entries are correct.

F. [§11.22] Content of Record

To use a wage record to best advantage, the amount of time and wages lost should be spelled out for the jury. The attorneys may, after examining the subpenaed record, agree to the amount lost and so stipulate to the court. The record itself may contain a copy of a letter (usually in response to an inquiry from the plaintiff) stating what the loss of wages has been so that the parties have the company's own interpretation of what the payroll record shows. The defendant may object to receipt of the letter in evidence on the grounds that it is not truly a part of the business record because the company is not in the business of writing letters to attorneys regarding wage losses. The letter, however, appears to be as credible as regular entries, since it is prepared by a qualified person on the basis of the entries.

If the custodian or other qualified witness is present and the foundation has been laid for admission of the record, the witness should be asked to state what the record shows about the amount of time lost following the injury, the reason given for the time loss, the rate of pay, the total gross wages lost without regard to sick leave or other benefits received, and any loss of overtime pay, bonuses, or fringe benefits such as vacation and sick leave credit. This specific testimony will aid the trier of fact in determining the over-all damages from loss of time at work.

12

Official Records

I. [§12.1] Admissibility

    A. [§12.2] By Agreement
    B. [§12.3] By Custodian's Affidavit as Business Record
    C. [§12.4] By Judicial Notice and Independent Evidence of Trustworthiness
    D. [§12.5] By Foundational Testimony

II. Particular Records

    A. [§12.6] Laying Foundation for Plaintiff's Public School Records
    B. [§12.7] Vital Statistics
    C. [§12.8] Findings of Presumed Death; Missing Person Records

III. [§12.9] Absence of Public Record

I. [§12.1] ADMISSIBILITY

Official records are records kept by governmental agencies. They include death certificates, coroner's and autopsy reports, census results, vital statistics, and other records that may be used in personal injury cases. An official record can be received in evidence by agreement or on a showing that it is relevant, authentic, in compliance with the best evidence rule, and within an exception to the hearsay rule.

An official record is not made inadmissible by the hearsay rule if: (a) The writing was made by and within the scope of duty of a public employee; (b) it was made at or near the time of the act, condition, or event; and (c) the sources of information and method and time of preparation indicate its trustworthiness. Evid C §1280. Evidence Code §1280 requires the same showing of trustworthiness as that Evid C §1271 requires for business records. Official Comment to Evidence Code §1280; see *Behr v Santa Cruz* (1959) 172 CA2d 697, 705, 342 P2d 987, 992. Unlike the business records exception, however, the official records exception contains no express requirement that testimony by the custodian or other qualified witness be produced regarding identity and mode of preparation. See Evid C §1271(c).

Specific entries in the official record may still be excluded by the hearsay rule if they record what a third person told the entrant or contain the entrant's conclusions rather than evidence based on his personal observation of the facts. The official would not be permitted to testify to those matters on the stand, and they are usually excluded even though the record containing them is admitted. See *McGowan v Los Angeles* (1950) 100 CA2d 386, 392, 223 P2d 862, 866.

The writing offered in evidence as an official record may be a copy. The best evidence rule is satisfied if the copy is attested, certified, or accompanied by the custodian's affidavit or declaration. See Evid C §§1506–1508, 1530–1564. The attestation, certificate, or declaration is usually sufficient to authenticate the record as well.

A. [§12.2] *By Agreement*

Lawyers often agree to admit official records in evidence. This eliminates the need to lay a foundation for admission. For discussion and forms for written and oral stipulation, pretrial orders, and requests for admission, see §§8.20–8.24.

B. [§12.3] *By Custodian's Affidavit as Business Record*

Most official records are also business records since "business" includes governmental activity. See Evid C §§1270, 1560. Therefore, a lawyer can subpena an official record, and if the custodian of the record or other qualified witness complies with the subpena duces tecum by mailing or delivering a copy of the record to court, together with an affidavit reciting the foundational facts set forth in Evid C §1561, the copy can be received in evidence. See Evid C §§1560–1564. For a discussion and forms for this procedure, see §§11.8–11.13. The custodian's affidavit usually satisfies authentication, best evidence, and hearsay requirements.

OFFICIAL RECORDS §12.6

C. [§12.4] By Judicial Notice and Independent Evidence of Trustworthiness

Trial judges can admit an official record in evidence without a witness's testimony or a custodian's affidavit by taking judicial notice of statutes governing the preparation and keeping of the record, or by considering independent evidence that it was prepared in a manner assuring its trustworthiness. See Official Comment to Evidence Code §1280; *Vallejo N. R.R. v Reed Orchard Co.* (1915) 169 C 545, 571, 147 P 238, 250 (statistical report of state agency admitted, court judicially noticing statutory duty to prepare report). See generally chap 20 on judicial notice. This method of securing admission of an official record is generally less certain than calling a witness or subpenaing the records under Evid C §1560.

D. [§12.5] By Foundational Testimony

When a witness is called to lay the foundation for introduction of an official record, his testimony should cover (1) his identity; (2) the record's identity; (3) that the writing was made by and within the scope of duty of a public employee; (4) that the writing was made at or near the time of the act, condition, or event; and (5) the sources of information and method and time of preparation (to indicate trustworthiness of the record). See, *e.g.,* §12.6.

II. PARTICULAR RECORDS

A. [§12.6] Laying Foundation for Plaintiff's Public School Records

School records are used in personal injury cases to support or rebut a minor plaintiff's contention that an accident has caused brain damage, emotional disturbance, or some other interference with intellectual performance. An adult claiming that an accident has affected his emotional and intellectual capacity can use school records to show a normal intelligence and emotional capacity before the accident. Proper trial preparation necessitates obtaining these records well in advance of depositions and trial to avoid unintentional discrepancies between the testimony and the records regarding dates, courses, and grades.

The authenticating witness is ordinarily the custodian of the records or some person sufficiently familiar with the record-keeping system to lay a proper foundation. For example:

(Identity of witness)

Q. What is your name and occupation?

§12.6
OFFICIAL RECORDS

A. .... I am the custodian of records of [name of school/board of education/etc.].

(Identity of records)

Q. Are you here pursuant to a subpena?
A. Yes.
Q. Did that subpena direct you to bring the school records of [name of plaintiff]?
A. Yes, it did.
Q. Do you have them with you?
A. Yes.
Q. Please describe what the records consist of.
A. [The records show the activity of the plaintiff during the two years he spent in this school in the eighth and ninth grades. They show the results of four physical examinations of him by the school doctor; they show his marks in four different types of intelligence tests given to him; and they show his report cards kept by the teachers, together with their remarks about his abilities and personality.]

(Entries made by public employee)

Q. Were these records made in the regular course of school business?
A. Yes.
Q. Were they made of every student?
A. Yes.
Q. Who made the entries in the plaintiff's records?
A. They were made by [his teachers, the school doctor, and the departmental employee who regularly tests the students for intelligence and achievement.]
Q. Was it within the scope of their duties to make these entries?
A. Yes.

(When entries made)

Q. Do the records show when the entries were made?
A. Yes. [The findings on physical examinations were entered shortly after they occurred, the report cards were made out at the end of each period covered by them, and intelligence and achievement test results were entered shortly after the tests were given.]

Comment: The trial judge draws an inference of trustworthiness from the facts relating to sources of information and the method and time of preparation. The witness may also be asked if the entries were correctly made.

At this point, having laid the foundation, the proponent can offer the records in evidence. The adverse party can object that the founda-

OFFICIAL RECORDS §12.9

tion is insufficient, or that particular portions of the records should not be received because they contain the statements of persons other than a public employee or inadmissible opinions. See *Behr v Santa Cruz* (1959) 172 CA2d 697, 705, 342 P2d 987, 993; Witkin, CALIFORNIA EVIDENCE §591 (2d ed, 1966). Opinions of teachers, doctors, and test givers recorded in an official record could be admitted over objection on the ground that they are by experts who could testify to those matters on the stand. An opponent could argue, however, that the judge should not admit opinion evidence without giving opportunity for cross-examination of the expert on the bases of his opinions. See Evid C §§802–803. Entries of intelligence test scores, physical findings, report card grades, and absence reports should be admitted as factual data.

B. [§12.7] *Vital Statistics*

Records of birth, fetal death, death, or marriage are not made inadmissible by the hearsay rule if the maker was required by law to file the writing in a designated public office, and it was made and filed as required by law. Evid C §1281. Any such record (or certified copy) registered within one year of the event is prima facie evidence of the facts stated in it. Health & SC §10577. On proper objection, however, it would still have to be shown to be relevant (see §11.4) and authentic (see §11.5), but it would not be made inadmissible by the hearsay rule. Records from other jurisdictions are similarly admissible. Official Comment to Evidence Code §1281.

C. [§12.8] *Findings of Presumed Death; Missing Person Records*

A written finding of presumed death made by an authorized federal employee is admissible in any court as evidence of the death of the person presumed dead and of the date, circumstances, and place of his disappearance. Evid C §1282. Similarly, a written report by an authorized federal employee that a person is dead or alive; missing; missing in action; interned in a foreign country; captured, beleaguered, or besieged by a hostile force; or detained in a foreign country against his will is admissible in any court as evidence of the facts stated in the report. Evid C §1283.

III. [§12.9] ABSENCE OF PUBLIC RECORD

It is sometimes relevant to show the absence of a record of an act, condition, or event. A statutory exception to the hearsay rule has been made for a writing by an official stating that he has made a diligent search and failed to find a record. The writing is not made inadmissible by the hearsay rule when offered to prove the absence of a record in the custodian's office. Evid C §1284. The writing of course must be properly authenticated. See Evid C §§1401, 1453; Official Comment to Evidence Code §1284.

13
Hospital and Medical Records

I. [§13.1] Uses at Trial

II. [§13.2] Contents

III. [§13.3] Obtaining Copy of Client's Record Before Suit
    A. [§13.4] Form: Letter Requesting Medical Records
    B. [§13.5] Form: Authorization

IV. [§13.6] Admissibility
    A. Foundational Requirements
        1. [§13.7] Relevance
        2. [§13.8] Authentication
        3. [§13.9] Best Evidence
        4. [§13.10] Hearsay
        5. [§13.11] Physician-Patient Privilege
    B. [§13.12] Covering and Deleting Objectionable Items and Entries

V. Procedures for Securing Admission as Exhibit
    A. [§13.13] Stipulation
    B. [§13.14] Delivery of Subpenaed Copy with Custodian's Affidavit
        1. [§13.15] Form: Supporting Declaration
        2. [§13.16] Encouraging Delivery of Copy
        3. [§13.17] Offering Records in Evidence
    C. [§13.18] Personal Attendance of Custodian with Original Records
    D. [§13.19] Foundational Testimony

§13.1   HOSPITAL AND MEDICAL RECORDS

VI. **[§13.20] Particular Entries: Admissibility; Interpretation**
    A. [§13.21] Cover Sheet: Data and Diagnostic Summary
        1. [§13.22] Personal Data
        2. [§13.23] Insurance Coverage
    B. [§13.24] Narrative or Final Summary
    C. [§13.25] Medical History
        1. [§13.26] Circumstances of Accident
        2. [§13.27] Past and Family History
    D. [§13.28] Physical Examination Reports
    E. [§13.29] Vital Signs Chart
    F. [§13.30] Laboratory and Electrographic Reports
    G. [§13.31] Operation Report
    H. [§13.32] Doctors' Orders; Medication Sheet
    I. [§13.33] Doctors' Progress Notes
    J. [§13.34] Nurses' Notes
    K. [§13.35] Medical Opinions
        1. [§13.36] Diagnosis
        2. [§13.37] Causation
        3. [§13.38] Prognosis
    L. [§13.39] X-Ray Films and Reports
    M. [§13.40] Letters and Other Extraneous Matter

VII. **[§13.41] Using Record To Show Basis for Opinion Testimony**

VIII. **Using Record To Impeach**
    A. [§13.42] Prior Inconsistent Statement
        1. [§13.43] Confronting Witness
        2. [§13.44] Forgotten Statement
        3. [§13.45] Statement of Preaccident Health
        4. [§13.46] Absence of Complaints
    B. [§13.47] Confronting Adverse Expert with Contradictory Matter

I. [§13.1] USES AT TRIAL

Hospitals and clinics routinely maintain a record for each patient admitted or treated, and doctors maintain an office record for each patient they see. These medical records can be introduced in evidence as exhibits, medical witnesses can testify from them, and lawyers can refer to them in argument.

Jurors ordinarily give great credence to the facts and opinions contained in medical records. These records are prepared and compiled by persons whose interest is in caring for the patient rather than in any

HOSPITAL AND MEDICAL RECORDS §13.2

litigation. If the court permits the record to be taken to the jury room, jurors can be expected to study it carefully. However, medical records are often voluminous; barely legible; and replete with medical terminology, symbols, and abbreviations. Jurors permitted to read a record could overlook some entries and misinterpret others. Therefore, even though a record has been received in evidence as an exhibit, lawyers rarely rely solely on it for medical proof; they also introduce a doctor's testimony. Some lawyer may even request that it not be passed to the jury or sent to the jury room. And some judges do not permit jurors to see the record even if a lawyer requests it. See generally §§8.16, 8.19.

The most effective way to communicate information from a medical record to the trier of fact is usually to have a doctor read and explain parts of the record as he testifies. See §13.20. The use of the record supports and adds weight to the doctor's testimony, and the testimony enhances the value of the record.

In addition, a lawyer can bring a record's contents to the attention of the jury by having a medical witness state the matter as part of the basis for his opinions (see §13.41). Or he can confront an adverse doctor with medical information from the record that is inconsistent with his findings and conclusions (see §13.47). The contents of a record that has not been received in evidence can sometimes be put before the jury if the record is used to refresh a witness's memory or as past recollection recorded (see §6.28), or to show a prior inconsistent or consistent statement (see §13.42).

II. [§13.2] CONTENTS

Medical records are compilations of observed facts, opinions, and graphic or photographic depictions. These entries are added to the patient's file throughout the period of hospitalization or care. A typical record consists of a number of pages clipped together or kept in a file folder. Some of these pages are printed form sheets filled in by hand or typewriter. Others may be photocopies of reports, tracings on graph paper, etc., the originals of which have been filed elsewhere or destroyed. X-ray films are often filed separately, as are emergency room and outpatient records.

Some pages of a hospital record contain a number of individual entries, each made at a different time by a different doctor, nurse, or hospital employee. In a doctor's office record, most of the entries are made by the doctor who examined and treated the patient or one of his nurses, although reports from other doctors and technicians may be included.

III. [§13.3] OBTAINING COPY OF CLIENT'S RECORD BEFORE SUIT

Medical records can be used from the earliest stages of trial preparation as well as at trial. Even before an action is filed, a plaintiff's lawyer is entitled to inspect and copy his client's or decedent's medical records on presentation to the hospital or doctor of a written authorization signed by the patient or his parent, guardian, personal representative, or heir. Evid C §1158. Some lawyers employ a legal services firm to obtain copies of medical records. Others telephone the hospital or doctor's office to determine how to address a request for the records, then send a letter requesting copies (see §13.4) along with a signed authorization form (see §13.5).

A. [§13.4] *Form: Letter Requesting Medical Records*

(Name and address
of hospital, clinic,
or doctor's office)

...................................:
Gentlemen/Dear ....

This office represents .... in his claim for dam-
                        (Name of patient)
ages for the injuries he received in an accident on ...., 19........

Pursuant to Evidence Code section 1158, and the enclosed authorization, please send to this office a copy, which can be a photocopy, of all medical records in your possession pertaining to the care and treatment of ....
     (Name of patient)

               (If particular records desired, add)
, including, but not limited to ....
                        (Specify records desired)

Please send your bill for preparing the copy and we will immediately send our check.

                        Very truly yours,

                        _____
                        (Signature of attorney)
                        (Typed name of attorney)

B. [§13.5] *Form: Authorization*

AUTHORIZATION FOR MEDICAL INFORMATION

To: (Name of hospital,   Re: (Name of patient and other
        clinic, or doctor)   identifying information such
                                                  as address, date of birth,
                                                  medical number, etc.)

HOSPITAL AND MEDICAL RECORDS §13.6

This authorizes you to permit .... or ....
(Name of attorney or firm)   his/its
representative to inspect and copy all records under your custody or control relating to the above-named patient, and to furnish ....
him/it
with a legible and durable copy of those records.
Dated: ....

_____
(Signature of patient, parent, etc.)
(Typed name and capacity if not patient)

Comment: Printed authorization forms like the one above can be obtained from legal stationers. Lawyers often have their clients sign a number of printed blank authorization forms at the first interview. The forms can then be addressed and used as needed.

IV. [§13.6] ADMISSIBILITY

The admissibility of medical records in evidence can be considered in two steps:
 (1) The admissibility of the whole record as an exhibit; and
 (2) The admissibility of particular items and entries.

Hospital records are admissible in evidence as exhibits if a proper foundation is laid. *McDowd v Pig'n Whistle Corp.* (1945) 26 C2d 696, 700, 160 P2d 797, 799. The same rule should also apply to doctor's office records. But see *Horowitz v Fitch* (1963) 216 CA2d 303, 313, 30 CR 882, 888, in which such a record was held properly excluded, the court noting that no attempt had been made to qualify it as an admissible business record. See §§13.7–13.11 on foundational requirements and §§13.13–13.19 on procedures to satisfy those requirements.

The admission of a medical record in evidence, however, does not prevent any party from objecting to particular items or entries in the record. Inadmissible matter is not made admissible simply by inclusion in an admissible hospital or business record. As a general rule, only those portions of the record are admissible that would be admissible if testified to by the entrant. See *People v Salcido* (1966) 246 CA2d 450, 462, 54 CR 820, 828; *Johnson v Aetna Life Ins. Co.* (1963) 221 CA2d 247, 252, 34 CR 484, 487; *Hutton v Brookside Hosp.* (1963) 213 CA2d 350, 355, 28 CR 774, 777. The admissibility of particular items and entries commonly found in hospital records is discussed in §§13.20–13.40.

The presence of inadmissible matter in an otherwise admissible hospital record does not render the record inadmissible. *People v*

Gorgol (1953) 122 CA2d 281, 300, 265 P2d 69, 81. Inadmissible portions can be covered or deleted, or the judge may instruct the jury to disregard them. See *People v Terrell* (1955) 138 CA2d 35, 57, 291 P2d 155, 169; *People v King* (1951) 104 CA2d 298, 309, 231 P2d 156, 162. See generally §13.12.

Special rules apply to the discoverability and admissibility of the proceedings and records of hospital medical staff committees concerned with the reduction of morbidity and mortality and the evaluation and improvement of the quality of care. See Evid C §§1156–1157.

A. Foundational Requirements

1. [§13.7] Relevance

A medical record that was made at a time too remote to have any tendency in reason to prove or disprove a disputed fact in the case may be excluded as irrelevant. See Evid C §§210, 350; *People v Bjornsen* (1947) 79 CA2d 519, 532, 180 P2d 443, 451. A judge can also exclude a medical record on the ground that its probative value is substantially outweighed by the time needed to introduce it or that its admission would create a danger of undue prejudice or might confuse or mislead the jury. See Evid C §352.

2. [§13.8] Authentication

A medical record is a writing, as are each of its entries, pages, and parts, including charts, graphs, X-ray pictures, and photographs. See Evid C §250. If an adverse attorney objects to introduction of a record, a copy of it, or secondary evidence of its contents, on the ground that it has not been authenticated (see CALIFORNIA TRIAL OBJECTIONS §§21.6, 21.20 (Cal CEB 1967)), the lawyer offering the record should be prepared to establish that the record he offers is in fact from the hospital or office named, and that it relates to the care and treatment of the person named. See Evid C §§1400–1401. See generally §8.11. If required, this authenticating evidence can be given by the custodian of the records or other qualified witness, either through testimony (see §13.19), or the affidavit prescribed by Evid C §1561 (see §13.14).

Authentication of the whole record should authenticate each part, although an adverse attorney could try to establish that some entry in the record had been altered or entered erroneously or fraudulently or that some part of the record was missing.

3. [§13.9] Best Evidence

A special exception to the best evidence rule is provided for business records, including hospital and doctor's office records. Evid C

HOSPITAL AND MEDICAL RECORDS §13.10

§§1560–1562. If the prescribed procedure is followed, copies of these records are as admissible in evidence as originals. Evid C §1562. For procedure and forms, see §§13.14–13.17. A lawyer who wants to introduce a copy of a medical record instead of the original without following the procedure prescribed by Evid C §§1560–1562 must either secure the agreement of the other counsel, or introduce the copy under some other exception to the best evidence rule.

Often some pages of a medical record are actually copies of original sheets that were kept elsewhere or destroyed. Under Evid C §1562 it does not appear to matter that part of the record offered is a copy of a copy rather than a copy of an original.

4. [§13.10] Hearsay

Medical records, and the written entries in them, are statements made by persons other than while testifying. When a record or part of one is offered to prove the truth of the matter stated in it, it is hearsay evidence. Evid C §1200(a).

However, hospital records are business records. *Loper v Morrison* (1944) 23 C2d 600, 608, 145 P2d 1, 5; *Frampton v Hartzell* (1960) 179 CA2d 771, 774, 4 CR 427, 430. Doctor's office records also come within the definition of "business records." See Evid C §§1270, 1560; *Horowitz v Fitch* (1963) 216 CA2d 303, 313, 30 CR 882, 888. Thus, medical records are not made inadmissible by the hearsay rule if (a) they were made in the regular course of the hospital's or doctor's business; (b) they were made at or near the time of the acts, conditions, and events recorded; and (c) the sources of information and the method and time of preparation indicate their trustworthiness. Evid C §1271; *McDowd v Pig'n Whistle Corp.* (1945) 26 C2d 696, 700, 160 P2d 797, 799. See also Witkin, CALIFORNIA EVIDENCE §§578, 584 (2d ed, 1966).

The trustworthiness of a medical record can be shown through the testimony of the hospital records custodian or any other person who knows the facts about sources of information and method and time of preparation. See §13.19. Of course, if the judge thinks that the showing is insufficient, he can sustain the foundational hearsay objection and exclude the record. See *Luthringer v Moore* (1948) 31 C2d 489, 501, 190 P2d 1, 9 (records custodian said nothing about mode of preparation; only that they were "day to day" records).

The trustworthiness of medical records can also be shown by the affidavit of the records custodian or other qualified witness, if the procedure prescribed by Evid C §§1560–1562 is followed. Indeed, in prescribing what is to be stated in the affidavit, Evid C §1561 probably relaxes the showing that would otherwise be required by Evid C §1271. See Witkin, EVIDENCE §588.

Even though a medical record has been received in evidence as a business record over a hearsay objection, adverse counsel may direct a further hearsay objection against a particular entry that records what some third person told the person who made the entry.

5. [§13.11] Physician-Patient Privilege

The patient-litigant exception prevents use of the physician-patient and psychotherapist-patient privileges to exclude medical records relating to the care and treatment of the plaintiff, or a person for whose injury or death damages are sought. Evid C §§996, 1016. See discussion in §6.4.

Plaintiffs sometimes seek to introduce medical records relating to the physical or mental condition of the defendant or the person to whom the defendant entrusted his motor vehicle. In these situations, the defendant or other person has not tendered the issue of his own health. Therefore, he can invoke the physician-patient privilege against admission of the records. See *Carlton v Superior Court* (1968) 261 CA2d 282, 67 CR 568.

B. [§13.12] *Covering and Deleting Objectionable Items and Entries*

Even though a medical record is received in evidence as an exhibit, any party can object to particular items or entries and request that those items be kept from the jury. See §13.6. Failure to object to particular items when the record is offered (or to reserve the right to object later) may amount to a waiver.

Deletions from a record should be discussed and carried out in chambers. Sometimes one or more pages can be removed from the record without also removing useful and admissible information. Otherwise, inadmissible portions can be covered with paper or opaque tape, crossed out with opaque ink, or cut out. Of course, major deletions of this sort should not be performed on original medical records without the custodian's permission, since cutting or blotting out for evidentiary purposes could make the record misleading for medical purposes.

It is not usually necessary to cover or delete inadmissible matter if the record is not passed to the jury or sent to the jury room. A medical witness who reads and interprets the record can be instructed, out of the jury's hearing, not to refer to the inadmissible parts.

HOSPITAL AND MEDICAL RECORDS §13.13

Although jurors can be instructed to disregard certain matter in a medical record, this is not a very effective way to keep it from their consideration. Jurors have even been known to look under opaque tape. A judge sitting without a jury can receive the offered record and state that he will consider only admissible portions. See *People v Powell* (1949) 34 C2d 196, 204, 208 P2d 974, 979.

V. PROCEDURES FOR SECURING ADMISSION AS EXHIBIT

A. [§13.13] Stipulation

Lawyers are often willing to stipulate that medical records be admitted as exhibits without foundational affidavits or testimony. See, e.g., *Gillett v Gillett* (1959) 168 CA2d 102, 106, 335 P2d 736, 738; *Barr v Scott* (1955) 134 CA2d 823, 286 P2d 552. For a general discussion of admission by agreement and forms for written and oral stipulations, requests for admission, and pretrial orders, see §§8.20–8.24.

Counsel should also try to agree, before the record is admitted, on what parts should be covered or deleted (see §13.12), although the stipulation can reserve the right to object to particular entries. For example, in *Barr v Scott, supra,* the parties stipulated in advance that a hospital record might be introduced in evidence "subject to the right of [a party] to object, on proper grounds, to any item contained therein." 134 CA2d at 825, 286 P2d at 554.

If the agreement to the admission of a medical record is not in writing, a statement of it should be made for the record. For example:

Proponent. Your Honor, at this time the [plaintiff/defendant] offers evidence, as [plaintiff's/defendant's] exhibit ......, this copy of the records of [name of hospital/clinic/doctor] relating to the care and treatment of [name of patient].

(Optional)

The parties have stipulated that this exhibit is a true copy of an authentic business record of that [hospital/clinic/doctor] and that no further foundation need be laid. But all parties reserve the right to make any other objection to the record, and to move to delete, strike, or cover any entries, statements, or other portions of the record that are not legally admissible.

Comment: The proponent should be sure that the stipulation is entered in the minutes of the court or that the court record clearly shows that the exhibit has been received in evidence. See CCP §283.

§13.14   HOSPITAL AND MEDICAL RECORDS

B. [§13.14] *Delivery of Subpenaed Copy with Custodian's Affidavit*

The lawyer who does not care to solicit or rely on the agreement of adverse parties can usually secure the admission of a medical record in evidence by following the procedure prescribed in Evid C §§1560–1566. (This procedure originated in 1959 legislation designed to facilitate the production and admission of hospital records. It was amended in 1969 to cover all business records.)

The lawyer obtains a subpena duces tecum for the records and serves it along with a supporting declaration on the custodian of the record or other qualified witness. Usually the custodian is eligible to and does respond to the subpena by mailing or delivering a copy of the record to the court in the prescribed manner (see Evid C §1560), accompanied by his affidavit or declaration (see Evid C §1561). The delivered copy can then be offered in evidence without further foundation; it is as admissible as the original would have been had the custodian been present and testified to the matters stated in his affidavit. See Evid C §1562. See also §13.18 on occasions when the custodian must attend in person with the original records.

The issuance, service, and content of the subpena duces tecum is discussed in §11.9. The attorney's declaration, which must be served with the subpena, is discussed in §11.10, and a form of declaration supporting a subpena for medical records is set out in §13.15. The notice informing the custodian how to comply with a subpena and the custodian's declaration are discussed, with forms, in §§11.11–11.12.

1. [§13.15] Form: Supporting Declaration

The service of a subpena duces tecum is invalid unless at the same time there is served an affidavit or declaration under penalty of perjury (see CCP §2015.5) such as the following. CCP §1987.5. See generally §11.10.

Copies: Original to file with the clerk of the issuing court; one copy for the witness; one office copy.

(Title of Court)

(Title of Cause)

No. ....
DECLARATION FOR
SUBPENA DUCES TECUM

.... declares:
(Name of declarant)

1. I am an attorney for .... in this action.
   plaintiff/defendant

352

HOSPITAL AND MEDICAL RECORDS §13.15

    2. This cause has been set for trial on ...., 19......, at ....m., in Department .... of this Court.

    3. .... is the custodian of records of ....
              (Name of witness)   (Name of
.... and has the following matters or things in ....
hospital/clinic/doctor)   his/her
possession or under .... control:
                           his/her

Matters and Things To Be Produced

    a. Medical records relating to the care and treatment of ....
                                                                                          (Name of
............,
patient)

                             (Optional clauses)
                       (To exclude irrelevant records)

for the period ...., 19......, through ...., 19.......

                   (To help custodian locate desired records)

located in and filed with the records of ....
                                                              (Specify department, ward,
....
etc.)

                    (To suggest broad scope of subpena)

including admittance, emergency room and outpatient records, diagnoses, prognoses, medical histories, laboratory, examination and consultation results and reports, X-ray films, charts, tracings, and all other writings and depictions relating to the hospitalization, care, and treatment of ....
                  (Name of patient)

         (To assure inclusion of specific records that are
         sometimes not filed with main record, e.g.)

    b. The .... X-ray films of ....'s lumbar spine and
        (Number)   (Name of patient)
lower back, made from ...., 19......, through ...., 19......, and the records of the outpatient clinic of the hospital relating to the care and treatment of .... as an outpatient, from ....
                 (Name of patient)
................, 19......, through ...., 19.......

                         (To obtain bills)

    c. Bills and statements showing charges for hospitalization, diagnoses, care, and treatment of .... for the period ....
                         (Name of patient)
................, 19......, through ...., 19.......

                             (Continue)

4. These records and things are material to the issues in this case and admissible in evidence, and there is good cause for their production, in that:

a. This is an action for damages for .... personal injuries to/the wrongful death of .... (Name of patient)

b. These records and things are and contain evidence of .... (Name of patient) ....'s physical condition .... both before and after the accident of ...., 19......, on which this action is based, and of the nature, extent, and causes of .... his/her injuries/death and the detriment suffered by .... him/her/plaintiff(s)

5. The pleadings, records, and files in this action are incorporated by this reference.

Executed on ...., 19......, at ...., California.

I declare under penalty of perjury that the foregoing is true and correct.

          _____
          (Signature of attorney)
          (Typed name of attorney)

         Attorney for ....
              Plaintiff/Defendant

2. [§13.16] Encouraging Delivery of Copy

A lawyer may want to encourage the custodian or other witness to mail or deliver a copy of the subpenaed medical record to court, rather than attending in person with the original. Introducing a delivered copy avoids the time lost and disruption involved in taking foundational testimony. In many cases the lawyer can encourage the custodian to deliver a copy by telephoning him and giving him a notice (see form, §11.11) that explains how to comply with the subpena duces tecum without attending in person and a blank declaration form (see §11.12) for him to fill in and sign. The lawyer is not required to do this; it is done as a courtesy to gain cooperation, and to encourage a prompt and appropriate response to the subpena. The notice and declaration form can be attached to the papers handed the custodian when the subpena duces tecum is served.

3. [§13.17] Offering Records in Evidence

Even if medical records have been delivered to the court pursuant to Evid C §§1560–1561, they are not "in evidence" until they have

HOSPITAL AND MEDICAL RECORDS §13.19

been offered in evidence by an attorney during the trial, and the trial judge has indicated that they have been received. For a discussion of opening and offering business records delivered to court pursuant to subpena, see §11.13. On offering exhibits in evidence, see §8.3.

The lawyer may ask the trial judge to state for the record and the jury's benefit what they are, how they were procured, and that they are evidence in the case. See §11.13.

C. [§13.18] Personal Attendance of Custodian with Original Records

The personal attendance of a custodian, perhaps in uniform, can sometimes enhance the weight of the medical record, and the foundational testimony of the custodian highlights the exhibit more than a stipulation or custodian's affidavit. A lawyer can require a medical records custodian or other witness to attend court and bring the original records by serving on him a subpena duces tecum containing the clause set forth in Evid C §1564 (see §11.15).

In addition, a medical records custodian must attend in person with original records, and the lawyer must be prepared to take his foundational testimony (see §13.19), when (1) the hospital or doctor is a party in the action; or (2) the hospital or doctor's office is the place where a cause of action is alleged to have arisen. Evid C §1560.

Although not required, the Evid C §1564 clause can be inserted in a subpena duces tecum directed to a records custodian who is not eligible under Evid C §1560 merely to deliver a copy.

If another attorney in the case subpenaed medical records without requiring the witness's attendance, a lawyer can serve an additional subpena duces tecum on the witness in order to examine him on foundational matters, or at least to hear more foundational evidence than is likely to be contained in the affidavit.

The lawyer should also insert the Evid C §1564 clause when he wants to introduce or use original records rather than a copy even though he may not care whether the witness attends in person. Original medical records, with their varied inks and papers, can be more legible and have greater impact than photocopies, and may show places where the record was altered or augmented.

D. [§13.19] Foundational Testimony

If a medical record is not received in evidence by agreement or on the basis of the custodian's affidavit, the proponent must lay a foundation through the testimony of the custodian or other qualified witness. See generally §8.9.

Foundational testimony should establish that:

(1) The witness is qualified to testify about the identity and mode of preparation of the records;

(2) The records he has brought with him are all the records described in the subpena;

(3) The records were prepared by hospital or doctor's office personnel;

(4) The records were prepared in the regular course of hospital or doctor's business;

(5) Entries were made at or near the time of the acts, conditions, or events recorded; and

(6) The sources of information and method and time of preparation indicate the trustworthiness of the offered record.

See Evid C §1271.

For example, a hospital records custodian could be examined as follows:

Q. What is your occupation?
A. I am the custodian of medical records at .... Hospital.
Q. What are your duties as the hospital records custodian?
A. [Primarily, to file the records of each patient so that they can be located later if needed; to make sure that the records are not seen or taken by unauthorized persons; and also to see that all the essential parts of the record have been completed by the doctors, nurses, and other personnel of the hospital before the records are filed.]

Comment: If the witness is other than a custodian, the lawyer can ask additional questions to show the connection between the witness's duties and his ability to testify about the identity and mode of preparation of the records. See *People v Terrell* (1955) 138 CA2d 35, 57, 291 P2d 155, 168 (foundation for hospital record laid by resident doctor); *Poulsen v Oceanic S.S. Co.* (1961) 197 CA2d 69, 74, 17 CR 421, 425 (foundation for ship's medical log laid by second officer).

Q. Are you here in court today in response to a subpena duces tecum served on you as the custodian of records of .... Hospital?
A. Yes.
Q. What matters and things did the subpena require you to bring with you?
A. [The medical records of (state name of patient).]
Q. Do you have those records with you?
A. Yes, I do.
Q. Where did you get them?

HOSPITAL AND MEDICAL RECORDS   §13.20

A. [From the Medical Records Library at .... Hospital.]
Q. Is this the original record for Mr. .... as it is kept by the hospital, or is it a copy?
A. These are original records.
Q. Did you search for all the records that were described in the subpena?
A. Yes, I did.
Q. Are these all those records?
A. ....

Comment: If the custodian has not brought all the described records, he should specify those he did not bring and why.

A lawyer who anticipates a dispute over whether the records actually are those of the patient, or whether someone may have tampered with them, can ask additional questions to establish custody, identity, and accuracy. See, *e.g.,* 6 AM JUR PROOF OF FACTS 137 (1960).

Q. Are you familiar with the method by which these records were prepared?
A. Yes.
Q. Who prepares or writes the entries and the various pages that go to make up these records?
A. [Entries are made by various nurses and other hospital personnel, and by the staff physicians who see the patient.]
Q. Were those entries made at or near the time of the acts, conditions, and events recorded?
A. Yes, they were.
Q. Was this record prepared by those persons in the ordinary and regular course of hospital business?
A. Yes.

Comment: Again, if the lawyer anticipates a dispute, he can ask more particular questions about the method and time of preparation of the individual parts of the record.

VI. [§13.20] PARTICULAR ENTRIES: ADMISSIBILITY; INTERPRETATION

Sections 13.21–13.40 discuss the kinds of entries commonly found in hospital records, and their admissibility if objected to after the record as a whole has been received in evidence. Several of these sections also contain examples of the testimony a doctor might give in interpreting and explaining particular entries.

Testimony by a doctor that explains and interprets the entries in a hospital record can be justified on the grounds that the doctor is (a) clarifying the evidence contained in the exhibit so that the trier of fact can understand and appreciate its significance (*Gillett v Gillett* (1959) 168 CA2d 102, 107, 335 P2d 736, 739); or (b) showing part of the matter on which his opinion testimony is based (Evid C §802).

A medical witness can be asked about all the items in the record that support his opinions and the theories of the lawyer examining him. He can also translate and explain medical terminology and abbreviations. If the lawyer asks him specific questions that direct him to significant entries, the testimony can be kept lively and away from unimportant and inadmissible matter.

A. [§13.21] *Cover Sheet: Data and Diagnostic Summary*

The first page or section of a typical hospital record is variously called the "cover sheet," "front sheet," "admission record," "data and diagnostic summary," etc. It records the date and time of admission and discharge and personal data relating to the patient. It may also contain summaries of diagnoses, treatment, condition on discharge, and the probable causes of the patient's condition.

1. [§13.22] Personal Data

The personal data recorded on a cover sheet can help to identify and authenticate the hospital record as that of the person whose medical condition or death is in issue. See §13.8. The record usually gives the patient's name, home address, age, occupation, and the names of his doctor and closest relative or other person to contact in an emergency. In addition to this relatively innocuous and self-explanatory data there are sometimes entries that could be prejudicial and should be kept from the jury. These might include entries purporting to show the patient's religion or marital status.

2. [§13.23] Insurance Coverage

Cover sheets often carry a line recording the patient's hospitalization and medical insurance coverage, or the person responsible for paying the patient's account. Plaintiffs' lawyers can have this line covered or deleted as irrelevant under the collateral source rule. See §14.9.

In this connection, the entire hospital record should be examined for references to insurance, including copies of insurance application

HOSPITAL AND MEDICAL RECORDS §13.25

forms, references to "Blue Cross" or "SDI" (State Disability Insurance), and even a nurse's note that the patient was visited by an adjustor or claims representative.

B. [§13.24] Narrative or Final Summary

Hospital files sometimes contain a "narrative summary" or "final summary" of the data in the record. This entry may be filed near the beginning of the hospital record so that doctors looking at the file can read it and spare themselves reading the rest. It can cover the circumstances of admission, medical history, physical examinations, laboratory and test reports, operations, daily progress, treatment, condition on discharge, and prognosis.

These summaries should be checked for statements that conflict with the more detailed parts of the record. Further, a doctor sometimes includes in the summary certain facts and opinions known to him that did not get recorded in the more detailed, but structured, parts of the record.

A "final summary" covering history of injuries, patient's complaints, and treatment was read into evidence in *People v Gorgol* (1953) 122 CA2d 281, 265 P2d 69.

C. [§13.25] Medical History

Entries reflecting the patient's medical history can be found at various places in a hospital record. A history may be recorded on a separate printed sheet designed for the purpose, on a physical examination form, or even on the cover sheet under a heading such as "causative agent."

Since a medical history entry is a record of what the patient or some other person told the person who made the entry, it is hearsay. However, a medical history entry and testimony about it can often be received over a hearsay objection, either under an exception to the hearsay rule or for the limited purpose of showing part of the basis for a medical opinion. That is, evidence of a medical history recorded in a hospital or doctor's office record is admissible on the same grounds as a medical witness's testimony about the history given to him by a patient. See §§6.32–6.35.

A lawyer who wants to bring out a medical history recorded in a hospital record could simply ask the witness, "Was a medical history obtained from Mr. ....?" and "What history did he give?" Greater emphasis can be given to the history if questions such as the following are asked.

§13.26   HOSPITAL AND MEDICAL RECORDS

Q. Dr. ...., is there a medical history for [Mr. ..../plaintiff] in the hospital record?
A. Yes, there is.
Q. Can you tell from the record who made that entry?
A. [Yes, the history sheet is signed by Dr. ...., and the entry appears to be in the same handwriting as his signature.]
Q. Can you tell when the history was taken?
A. [Yes, the sheet is dated ...., 19......, and the time is given as ....]
Q. Does the entry indicate who gave the information to the doctor?
A. [Yes, it begins "Patient states . . . ," so it appears that the information came from Mr. ....]

Comment: If the history were particularly important, the lawyer could ask the doctor about the importance of the medical history to a proper evaluation of a patient's condition. See §6.36.

Q. What symptoms did [Mr. ..../plaintiff] complain of at that time?
A. ....

Comment: The patient's statement of his present symptoms, including physical sensation, mental feeling, pain, and bodily health, are generally admissible under a hearsay rule exception for statements of declarant's then existing mental or physical state. Evid C §§1250, 1252; *Bloomberg v Laventhal* (1919) 179 C 616, 178 P 496; see §6.37.

1. [§13.26] Circumstances of Accident

A defense lawyer can usually introduce, under a hearsay exception for admissions, a medical history entry about the circumstances of the accident and how the patient incurred his injuries. See Evid C §§1220, 1226–1227. See also §6.38. The entry can also be used as a prior inconsistent statement if the patient's testimony is inconsistent. See §13.42.

A plaintiff's attorney must either find some other applicable hearsay rule exception (see §6.34), or justify the admission of the medical history entry on the ground that it is to be received not to show the truth of the matter stated, but only to show part of the basis for a medical opinion. See discussion in §6.35.

The foundation for introducing an entry for the limited purpose of showing part of the basis for an expert's opinion can be laid by any medical expert witness. If there is no medical witness to so testify,

HOSPITAL AND MEDICAL RECORDS §13.28

the proponent of the evidence might argue that the diagnosis and prognosis recorded in the hospital file were based in part on the patient's history as it was recorded, and that the history entry should therefore be received to show part of the basis for those recorded opinions. But see *Johnson v Aetna Life Ins. Co.* (1963) 221 CA2d 247, 251, 34 CR 484, 486, in which an entry offered "for the purpose only of showing what information the doctors had in coming to the diagnosis appearing in the records," was excluded on the ground that the entry was irrelevant to any diagnosis in the hospital file.

2. [§13.27] Past and Family History

Entries recording the patient's past medical history and family medical history can contain information that is personally prejudicial to a patient-plaintiff without being relevant to any issues in the lawsuit. For example, a plaintiff's attorney might well move to cover or delete an entry, such as "father and mother, both deceased, were alcoholic," especially in a case where it is claimed that the patient had been drinking, or "venereal disease, cured."

D. [§13.28] *Physical Examination Reports*

Physical examination reports may be in a doctor's handwriting, or typed on forms from the doctor's handwritten or dictated notes. Insofar as they embody what the doctor observed while examining the patient, these entries are admissible as matter personally perceived by the examining doctor. See §6.41.

Physical examination reports may be filled with abbreviations and symbols that are meaningless to judges and jurors. The helpful information they contain should be pinpointed and explained by a medical witness. It is important to remember that the doctor's findings not only show part of the basis for diagnoses and other medical opinions, but also are direct evidence of injuries as observed by the examiner. See §6.47.

The attorney questioning a medical witness about a physical examination reported in a medical record might begin with a few preliminary questions. For example:

Q. Does the record show whether [Mr. ..../plaintiff] was given a physical examination?
A. Yes.
Q. Where is that in the file?
A. Here on pages ...... through ....
Q. Does the report show the time of the examination?

§13.29 HOSPITAL AND MEDICAL RECORDS

A. Yes, it was ....m. on ...., 19.......
Q. Does it indicate who conducted the examination and who filled out the report?
A. [Yes. The report is signed by Dr. ...., and it is in his handwriting.]

Comment: To avoid losing juror interest, a lawyer could skip these preliminary questions and ask about the findings immediately.

Q. What did [Dr. ..../the examining physician] observe of [Mr. ....'s/plaintiff's] general appearance and mental status?
A. ....
Q. What were his findings concerning the patient's head?
A. ....

Comment: Medical terms and symbols should be explained, especially if the record may later be seen by the jury.

Q. To be more specific, he wrote "normocephalic." What does that mean?
A. That the patient's skull was normal in size and shape.
Q. What is this symbol here at the bottom of page ...... that is followed by the word "laceration"?
A. That symbol is one that doctors use to mean "without." The symbol and the word mean that he found no lacerations or cuts on the patient's head.
Q. Are there any findings relating to the eyes, ears, nose, mouth, or throat?
A. No.
Q. Does that mean that the examining doctor did not look, or that he looked and did not find anything abnormal, or what?
A. This record indicates that in each case he looked, because he wrote "neg.," meaning "negative" in the place for reporting each one of those areas.

Comment: In each instance counsel can ask further questions to relate the findings, or absence of findings, to the diagnoses in the record and the witness's opinions.

E. [§13.29] *Vital Signs Chart*

At regular intervals during each day of a patient's hospitalization, nurses or other paramedical employees measure the patient's temperature, pulse rate, respiration rate, blood pressure, and food and liquid intake and output. These vital signs show fluctuations in the patient's

HOSPITAL AND MEDICAL RECORDS §13.30

condition and are used in the hospital to keep track of improvement or deterioration. The charts on which these observations are recorded are admissible as records of the direct, or instrument-aided, perceptions of the nurses and others who made the entries.

Ordinarily, little need be said in court about a vital signs chart; it is largely self-explanatory. However, if the patterns on the chart furnish diagnostic clues to the nature of the patient's condition, or the chart contains any other medically significant data, these can be interpreted by a witness.

F. [§13.30] *Laboratory and Electrographic Reports*

Hospital files frequently contain reports of laboratory analyses of fluids and tissue and graphs showing the electrical activity of the heart (electrocardiogram), brain (electroencephalogram), or other tissue. Sometimes small laboratory slips and graphs are photocopied on letter-size paper for easier filing.

These reports and graphs are as admissible as if they were supported by the technician or other person who ran the tests or recorded the results. See, *e.g., People v Gorgol* (1953) 122 CA2d 281, 292, 265 P2d 69, 76, in which an electroencephalographic report and an unidentified examiner's report were read into evidence.

These laboratory and electrographic reports are valuable when they support or contradict the opinions of medical witnesses, the opinions in the hospital record, or the plaintiff's claim of injury. A urinalysis showing the presence of blood in the patient's urine shortly after admission, for example, supports a claim of kidney injury. The absence of blood in a spinal fluid sample drawn and analyzed after admission tends to contradict a medical opinion that the plaintiff suffered a subdural hematoma.

The lawyer might begin asking about laboratory reports with a few preliminary questions. For example:

Q. Dr. ...., I see that page ...... of the record is entitled "laboratory reports" and that there are two slips of paper pasted on that page, one marked "hematology" and the other "urinalysis." What are these slips of paper?

A. They are laboratory reports of chemical analyses of the patient's blood, that is "hematology," and his urine.

Q. Does the record indicate who prepared these reports?

A. [The report is initialed, but I don't know whose initials they are; presumably a technician in the laboratory at the hospital.]

Q. Does it indicate who requested these analyses?

A. Yes. Dr. ....

§13.31   HOSPITAL AND MEDICAL RECORDS

Q. What was the date of the request?
A. ...., 19.......
Q. When were the analyses done?
A. Both slips are dated ...., 19.......

Comment: To avoid losing juror interest, many trial lawyers would skip the preliminary questions and ask about the laboratory findings immediately.

Q. Doctor, do the laboratory reports you find in that record show any abnormalities?
A. .....*..........
Q. Does the record show whether the patient's brainwave activity was tested while he was in the hospital?
A. Yes. It indicates that the tests were made on ...., 19......, and ...., 19.......
Q. Where is that in the record?
A. [Pages ...... and ...... are marked "Consultation Sheets; EEG Lab."]

Comment: The lawyer can continue in the usual way, asking what an electroencephalogram is, its diagnostic significance, who performed the procedure, the findings, and their relation to the patient's condition.

G. [§13.31] *Operation Report*

The surgeon in charge of each operation performed on a patient prepares a report giving the details of that procedure, including the anesthetic used, who was present, the indications for surgery, and a recital of the manual and mechanical steps taken. A plaintiff's lawyer might ask a medical witness to interpret this report to impress on the jury the seriousness of the plaintiff's condition.

A defense attorney could object to an operation report and move to exclude it on the ground that the details of the operation are irrelevant; what matters is the result. In response, a plaintiff's lawyer could argue that the report and testimony about it should be received to show the nature and extent of the plaintiff's injuries, the basis of his suffering and residual disability, the ordeal of treatment, and the reasonableness of medical expenses incurred.

Examination to explain an operation report might proceed as follows:

Q. Dr. ...., does the record indicate whether any operations were performed on [Mr. ..../plaintiff]?
A. Yes. Page ...... of the record is an operation report.

HOSPITAL AND MEDICAL RECORDS §13.32

Q. Who made out that report?
A. It is signed by Dr. ....
Q. What was the date of the operation?
A. ...., 19.......
Q. Who performed the operation?
A. Dr. .... is listed as the surgeon.
Q. Who else was present?
A. The assistant surgeon was Dr. ....; the anesthetist was Dr. ....; the surgical nurse was Miss ....; the instrument nurse was Miss ....
Q. What was the operation?
A. [A craniotomy.]
Q. And briefly, Doctor, what is the nature of that operation?
A. [In this case, four burr holes were drilled through the patient's skull.]
Q. Is that considered a major or a minor operation, Doctor?
A. [Major.]
Q. Did [Mr. ..../plaintiff] receive a general anesthetic or a local anesthetic?
A. ....
Q. What time did they start administering the anesthetic?
A. ....
Q. What time did the operation itself begin?
A. ....
Q. Is a preoperative diagnosis given in the report?
A. Yes. [It says "concussion; possible subdural hematoma," which would be a clot of blood under the layer of tissue that covers the brain.]
Q. What does the report show under "indications for surgery"?
A. ["Rule out or evacuate hematoma."]
Q. And did Dr. ...., the surgeon, describe in that report the procedure followed in the operation?
A. Yes.
Q. Would you read that part to us please?
A. ....

Comment: The lawyer can interrupt the witness's testimony about the operation to have him explain medical terms and notations and to clarify the description of the procedure.

H. [§13.32] *Doctors' Orders; Medication Sheet*

Whenever a doctor prescribes medication, tests, diagnostic procedures, or other forms of treatment for a hospitalized patient, the

365

§13.32 HOSPITAL AND MEDICAL RECORDS

orders are written down, signed by the doctor, and kept in the patient's hospital file in a section called "doctors' orders" and sometimes also on a separate "medication sheet." As each instruction is carried out by a nurse or other hospital employee, the order is checked off and initialed by that person.

Lawyers examine these doctors' orders entries for a day-by-day outline of the treatment given to the patient and for indications of his condition. An order for skull films, for example, indicates that the doctor suspected, or at least wanted to rule out, skull fracture as the cause of the patient's symptoms. An order for side rails and crash net shows that the patient needed to be protected from falling out of bed, perhaps because he was agitated and thrashing about. Prescriptions for analgesics support the inference that the patient was in pain. Indeed, a medication sheet showing the type, strength, amount, and frequency of drugs given the patient, together with nurses' notations of his distress, can be a plaintiff's most effective evidence of pain and suffering.

Testimony about doctors' orders should be admissible as a description of the acts of the doctors and hospital personnel. However, a trial judge might cut off a witness's testimony about the implications of certain orders on grounds that the testimony is based on speculation.

The witness might be questioned about doctors' orders entries as follows:

Q. According to the record, Dr. ...., what treatment and medication was prescribed for [Mr. ..../plaintiff] on ...., 19......?
A. ....
Q. Where do you find that information, Doctor?
A. Here on page ....
Q. What is that part of the record called?
A. "Doctors' orders."
Q. What is the purpose of that section of the record?
A. [The doctor who is in charge of the patient, or any doctor who is called to see him, writes out his orders for treating or managing the patient. When the orders are carried out by nurses or by other hospital personnel, the orders are checked off and initialed. That way everyone always knows exactly what has been prescribed and given.]
Q. Who prescribed the [Percodan] on ...., 19......?
A. That entry is signed by Dr. ....
Q. Is there an indication whether that order was carried out?

HOSPITAL AND MEDICAL RECORDS §13.34

A. Yes. [The initials of a nurse appear right here in this column on the doctors' orders sheet.]

Comment: The doctor can be asked additional questions about the nature of the drug or procedure, its purpose, how often it was given, what its use indicates about the patient's condition, whether it was an addictive medication or painful procedure, and so forth.

I. [§13.33] Doctors' Progress Notes

A section of the hospital record called "doctors' progress notes" contains further day-by-day information on the treatment given, the patient's response to treatment, and the patient's condition as observed by the various doctors who saw him. It contains statements of both the observations and the medical opinions of these doctors. If testimony about the opinions stated is objected to, the witness should be able to find facts to support those opinions in the record. See §13.35.

J. [§13.34] Nurses' Notes

Nurses record their observations of the patient in a part of the hospital record called "nurses' notes." Because the nurses generally see the patient more frequently than do the doctors, their notes can be extremely important. An entry in the nurses' notes is customarily made by each shift of nurses each day, and there will be additional notations if a doctor calls for the nurses to check the patient more frequently or the patient calls for assistance or otherwise attracts attention.

Just as doctors scan nurses' notes for medically significant information, lawyers should examine the notes closely for entries supporting their positions. For example, a plaintiff's claim of pain while in the hospital is supported by nurses' notes showing that he thrashed about, called for painkillers, moaned and cried, and so forth. On the other hand, claims of constant pain are refuted by entries that say the patient spent a quiet night, appeared in good spirits, or watched television. Defense lawyers are sometimes particularly aided by the nurses' full documentation of the pranks of an active child-patient.

Nurses' notes contain relevant evidence on the issue of the nature and extent of the plaintiff's injuries, and they are admissible as part of the business records of the hospital. See *Loper v Morrison* (1944) 23 C2d 600, 609, 145 P2d 1, 5. However, an adverse attorney can object to, and move to strike, an opinion that a nurse is not qualified to give. See *Hutton v Brookside Hosp.* (1963) 213 CA2d 350, 355, 28 CR 774, 777, in which a nurse's opinion that a patient "seemed too ill to be moved" was declared clearly objectionable.

K. [§13.35] *Medical Opinions*

Medical opinions are scattered throughout hospital records, and they do not always appear under such identifying headings as "diagnosis," "etiology," "causative agent," or "prognosis." The doctors and other persons who make entries in hospital records are rarely concerned about separating statements of what they have perceived from statements of their conclusions. Some diagnoses entered in a record (*e.g.,* "fractured femur") are actually statements of what the doctor saw when he examined the patient, or an X-ray film, rather than conclusions he reached based on findings, the patient's history, and other sources.

The admissibility of hospital record entries of medical opinions is not entirely clear under the Evidence Code. See 2 LA Super Ct Judges' Bull, Feb. 21, 1968. There is rarely any problem in receiving an opinion entry if a medical witness testifies that he based his own opinion on that entry. The witness can read or testify about the entry for the limited purpose of stating part of the matter on which his opinion is based. See Evid C §802; *Kelley v Bailey* (1961) 189 CA2d 728, 737, 11 CR 448, 454 (medical witness read to jury opinions from report of another doctor). There is a question, however, whether an opinion entry is admissible when offered as evidence of the patient's condition, its causes, or probable consequences.

An attorney who opposed admission of an opinion entry could argue that the doctor or other person who made the opinion entry in the record is not present in court to state, or be cross-examined on, his qualifications or the reasons and bases for his opinions (and he may be beyond subpena range). Opinion testimony that is based wholly or in significant part on improper matter must be excluded. See Evid C §803. But if the entry or testimony about it is received, the objecting attorney has no opportunity to ask the entrant about the matter on which his opinion was based to determine whether it was proper matter. Cases supporting exclusion of opinion entries include *Hutton v Brookside Hosp.* (1963) 213 CA2d 350, 355, 28 CR 774, 777; *People v Terrell* (1955) 138 CA2d 35, 57, 291 P2d 155, 169.

A lawyer who wanted an opinion entry to be received as evidence without limitation could argue that one of the purposes of the business records exceptions to the hearsay rule (Evid C §§1270–1272) and the best evidence rule (Evid C §§1560–1562) is to permit these

HOSPITAL AND MEDICAL RECORDS §13.36

records to be introduced without calling each of the persons who made an entry in them. The doctors who make opinion entries in hospital records could testify to the same opinions if called as witnesses. An opinion recorded in a medical record made in the regular course of business can be assumed to have been based on proper matter, because the doctor who made it was interested only in caring for the patient, not in litigation. Further, he wrote down his opinion where it was subject to the scrutiny of other doctors. The medical record itself can be scanned for the information that was available to the doctor when he formed his opinion. Cases that support the admissibility of opinion entries in hospital records include *McDowd v Pig'n Whistle Corp.* (1945) 26 C2d 696, 700, 160 P2d 797, 799 (diagnosis); *People v Salcido* (1966) 246 CA2d 450, 462, 54 CR 820, 828 (diagnosis); *Frampton v Hartzell* (1960) 179 CA2d 771, 4 CR 427 (causation); *People v Gorgol* (1953) 122 CA2d 281, 302, 265 P2d 69, 82 (opinion on patient's mental status).

1. [§13.36] Diagnosis

Diagnoses are entered at various points in hospital records under such headings as "admitting diagnosis," "clinical diagnosis," "diagnostic summary," "presenting diagnosis," "impression," "indication" (for surgery), or under no label at all. For evidentiary purposes, a diagnosis is any entry in a medical record that embodies a doctor's opinion of the nature, extent, or causes of the patient's disease or injury. Thus, an entry on the doctors' orders page such as "watch this patient, he may need psychiatric care" or, in the doctors' progress notes, "malingering?" can be viewed as a diagnostic statement.

The admission of a hospital record to show the diagnosis of the patient's condition and the nature and extent of his injuries was approved in *McDowd v Pig'n Whistle Corp.* (1945) 26 C2d 696, 700, 160 P2d 797, 799. The court regarded diagnostic entries as matter "customarily contained in such records" and therefore admissible when a proper foundation was laid for admission of the record. See also *People v Salcido* (1966) 246 CA2d 450, 462, 54 CR 820, 828. See generally §13.35. For a discussion of medical testimony about diagnoses, see §§6.68–6.70.

Testimony about a diagnosis entry might proceed as follows:

Q. Dr. ...., was a diagnosis of [Mr. ....'s/plaintiff's] condition made when he was admitted to the hospital?
A. Yes.
Q. Where do you find that?

A. [Here on the cover sheet under the heading "Admitting Diagnosis."]
Q. Who made that diagnosis?
A. [Dr. ...., who examined the man when he was brought in.]

Comment: It can be helpful if the testifying doctor can say a word or two about the qualifications of the doctor who made the diagnosis.

Q. Is Dr. .... a licensed medical doctor?
A. Yes. [He is a resident physician at the hospital. His duties at that time included examining and diagnosing incoming emergency cases.]
Q. What was that admitting diagnosis?
A. ....
Q. Do you find support for it in the findings Dr. .... made in examining the patient.
A. Yes.
Q. What particular findings support the diagnosis?
A. ....

Comment: If the diagnosis is one that conflicts with the attorney's position, he may be able to get testimony that: The diagnosis was made before the doctor received special diagnostic procedure test results; the doctor's examination was limited; admitting diagnoses are regarded by doctors as first impressions only; and so forth.

The witness can also be asked about later diagnoses that appear in the record, particularly the discharge diagnosis.

2. [§13.37] Causation

Hospital record entries embodying doctors' opinions about the connection between an automobile accident, a whiplash injury, and plaintiff's insanity were received in evidence in *Frampton v Hartzell* (1960) 179 CA2d 771, 4 CR 427. However, the objection raised in this case that no foundation had been laid was held not to raise the question of the admissibility of the opinion portions of the record. For a general discussion of the admission of opinion entries, see §13.35. For a discussion of opinion testimony on causation, see §§6.71–6.74.

3. [§13.38] Prognosis

Predictions of the probable future course of the patient's injuries are not commonly found in hospital records, although sometimes they appear on a cover sheet or in a final summary. In a personal injury case, the patient's future course is usually important enough to warrant

HOSPITAL AND MEDICAL RECORDS §13.40

calling a medical witness to testify about it, although a defense attorney might be happy to introduce and rely on a brief and perhaps optimistic prognosis entry. For a general discussion of the admission of opinion entries, see §13.35. For a discussion of medical testimony about prognoses, see §§6.75–6.79.

L. [§13.39] X-Ray Films and Reports

Hospital patients are often sent to the hospital's radiology department for X-ray examination. A staff radiologist's written report of an examination and the X-ray films themselves are part of the patient's hospital record, although the films are often filed separately from the main body of the record. To obtain production of the films, the lawyer may have to specify them separately when he subpenas them. See §13.15. He may also have to separately subpena films and reports made by an independent radiologist who used hospital facilities.

The reports of radiologists contain statements of what they see in the films and its significance. (What they "see" is often partly what they perceive and partly opinion.) An entry in a hospital record that embodies an X-ray examination report should thus be as admissible as reports of other diagnostic procedures (see §13.30) and other opinions (see §13.35).

X-ray films brought or delivered to court as part of a medical record should be received in evidence with the rest of the record. Any medical expert who testifies at the trial should then be able to interpret the films to the trier of fact and base his own opinion testimony on what he sees in them.

See chap 16 for a general discussion of the admissibility of X-ray films and reports and testimony about them.

M. [§13.40] Letters and Other Extraneous Matter

Some items are placed in hospital records simply because hospital personnel can think of no other convenient place to file them. In this category are letters to the hospital from the patient's relatives or from lawyers or insurance companies requesting information about his condition and copies of his records. Sometimes an arrest warrant or "police hold" finds its way into the hospital file.

These items rarely relate to the care and treatment of the patient; are not records of acts, conditions, or events; and are not prepared by the personnel of the hospital in the ordinary course of hospital business. Thus they are not qualified for admission under Evid C §§1270–1272 or §§1560–1562, and they should be removed from the record before it is offered or received in evidence.

VII. [§13.41] USING RECORD TO SHOW BASIS FOR OPINION TESTIMONY

A medical expert can base his opinion testimony on information he derives from a patient's hospital record. Evidence Code §801(b) requires that the matter on which opinion testimony is based be "of a type that reasonably may be relied upon by an expert in forming an opinion upon the subject." Doctors customarily and reasonably rely on hospital records in reaching medical opinions. See, *e.g., Gillett v Gillett* (1959) 168 CA2d 102, 107, 335 P2d 736, 739. Using a hospital record can enable a doctor who never personally examined the patient, or examined him long after the accident, to testify about the patient's condition, its causes, and its probable future course.

The following example illustrates how a defense doctor can use entries in a hospital record to show the basis of his opinion about the nature of a plaintiff's injuries.

Q. Dr. ...., did you examine the plaintiff in this case at my request?
A. Yes.
Q. When did you do that?
A. ...., 19.......
Q. What did you do at that time?
A. [I gave him a complete general physical and neurological examination, took his medical history, ran an EEG, and reviewed his hospital records.]
Q. In your examination of him, and in the tests you ran on him, were there any objective signs of [a head or brain injury]?
A. No.
Q. Did you reach a conclusion about the nature of the injury, if any, that he received in the accident of ...., 19......?
A. Yes.
Q. What is your conclusion?
A. [That at most he suffered a mild concussion.]
Q. Without going into detail yet, Doctor, can you tell us the sources of information that you relied on in reaching that conclusion?
A. I relied principally on information that I got from the man's hospital record.
Q. Doctor, I now hand you this file marked [for identification] [plaintiff's/defendant's] exhibit .... Is this the hospital record that you refer to?
A. Yes.
Q. Have you seen a copy of this record before?
A. Yes.

HOSPITAL AND MEDICAL RECORDS §13.41

Q. Can you tell us the circumstances?
A. Yes. [You sent a copy to me before I examined the man.]
Q. Have you familiarized yourself with the contents of this record?
A. Yes.

Comment: If the record has already been received in evidence, there is no need for the witness to identify it. If the record has not been received, a doctor able to identify it and testify about the mode of its preparation could lay a foundation for its admission with testimony similar to that usually given by a hospital records custodian. See §13.19.

Q. Doctor, is it a customary medical practice for doctors to rely on hospital records in diagnosing and treating patients?
A. It is.
Q. What are some of the reasons these records are relied on by doctors?
A. [They are comprehensive in that they cover all aspects of the patient's hospitalization and treatment; the entries are made by doctors and hospital personnel who are directly observing the patient and whose primary concern is treating the patient; and the entries are made with the expectation that they will be read and relied on by doctors.]

Comment: Testimony that the doctor relied on the record and that it is reasonable for doctors to rely on these records not only shows that the doctors' opinions were based on proper matter (see Evid C §§801(b), 803), but also provides a basis for showing the contents of the record as matter on which the doctors' opinions are based (see Evid C §802).

Q. What period of time does this record cover?
A. ...., 19......, through ...., 19.......
Q. How do you know that?
A. It says right here on the cover sheet, "Admitted: ...., 19......, at ....m." and "Discharged: ...., 19......."
Q. According to the record, what was the admitting diagnosis?
A. The doctor who filled in that entry wrote ["cerebral contusion"].
Q. Does that mean that the plaintiff had [a contusion]?
A. [Not necessarily. The admitting diagnosis is often just a first impression of what might be wrong with the patient; sometimes we call it just that, "the impression." It gives us an idea what we should be prepared for, but subsequent information may not bear it out.]

§13.41   HOSPITAL AND MEDICAL RECORDS

Q. Is there also an entry in the record indicating a final diagnosis?
A. Yes.
Q. Where is that, and what is it?
A. Here on page ......, in a part called "the diagnostic summary," under the heading "discharge diagnosis" we have ["cerebral concussion, mild"].
Q. Who made that diagnosis?
A. The sheet is signed by Dr. ...., who was the treating doctor.
Q. Aside from the opinions of Dr. ...., or any other doctor, what other information in the record contributed to your conclusion about the plaintiff's condition?
A. [First there was the medical history. The patient told the doctor that he did not think he had been unconscious for more than a few seconds. Also, since he told how the accident occurred, there was no retrograde amnesia of the type that is usually present in severe concussions.]
Q. Does the record show whether any physical examination was carried out?
A. Yes. Pages ...... through ...... of the record are a physical examination report form.
Q. When and by whom was the examination performed?
A. The form is dated ...., 19......, and is signed by Dr. ....
Q. Is there anything in that part that supports your conclusion?
A. Yes. [The doctor noted the patient's cuts and bruises, but the neurological part of the examination was essentially negative.]

Comment: The doctor can be asked in detail about specific signs that would have shown up if the injury had been severe.

Q. Were laboratory or electrographic tests run in the hospital?
A. Yes. There is an EEG report here on page ...... of the record.
Q. What is an EEG?
A. That is a recording on graph paper of the electrical activity of the patient's brain tissue.
Q. When was that test performed?
A. The morning after he was admitted to the hospital.
Q. What were the results?
A. The EEG was well within normal limits.
Q. What does the record show about drugs and medication?
A. The only medication was aspirin for the first two days, a tetanus innoculation, and antibiotics against any infection from his cuts.

HOSPITAL AND MEDICAL RECORDS §13.43

Q. Where do you find that?
A. In the section of the record called "doctors' orders."
Q. Is this treatment consistent with [a cerebral contusion or severe concussion]?
A. No.
Q. If [a contusion or severe concussion] had been suffered, would you expect the record to show other drugs being administered?
A. Yes. [At the very least I would expect the patient to have asked for, and been given, more powerful painkillers.]
Q. Do the nurses' notes show any such requests by the patient?
A. No. Right from the start they indicate that he was doing well and resting comfortably.

VIII. USING RECORD TO IMPEACH

A. [§13.42] Prior Inconsistent Statement

Medical records sometimes reflect statements made by a patient that are inconsistent with his testimony at trial. See, *e.g., Poulsen v Oceanic S.S. Co.* (1961) 197 CA2d 69, 75, 17 CR 421, 425 (seaman impeached by entry in ship's medical log). These statements can be found in medical history entries in which the patient states his symptoms and the causes of his condition (which often includes how the accident happened) and his own and his family's past medical history. Doctors' progress notes and nurses' notes may include statements made by the patient, *e.g.,* "Patient says headaches are gone." Similarly, an absence of entries reflecting complaints of pain can be used to refute testimony that complaints were made or pain experienced. Inconsistent statements can be called to the attention of the trier of fact in several ways. If the hospital record has been received in evidence, a medical witness can read them in the course of explaining and interpreting the record, and an attorney can read them during argument. Whether or not the record has been received, the witness can be confronted with statements that are inconsistent with his testimony. See §§2.7–2.12 for a discussion of the use of prior inconsistent statements.

1. [§13.43] Confronting Witness

Q. You were examined by a doctor when you arrived at the hospital, were you not?
A. Yes.
Q. You told him where you had pain, didn't you?
A. I guess so.

Q. Did you tell him [that you had no pain in your back or neck]?
A. ....

Comment: If the witness denies the statement, and the record has not yet been received in evidence, the lawyer should be prepared to lay a foundation for its admission or to call the doctor to whom the statement was made.

2. [§13.44] Forgotten Statement

Sometimes a lawyer will confront a witness with a prior inconsistent statement in the context of refreshing the memory of the witness. For example:

Q. You also told that doctor how you were injured and how the accident happened, didn't you?
A. Yes, I suppose I did.
Q. But you don't remember exactly what you told him, do you?
A. Of course not.
Q. Now I ask you to look at this entry here on page ...... of your hospital record from that hospital, and tell the jury whether that refreshes your recollection of what you told the doctor.
A. ....
Q. What did you tell him? [You can read that entry if you wish.]
A. ....

Comment: Again, if the witness denies that his memory is refreshed or that he said what is recorded in the hospital file, counsel should be prepared to lay a foundation for admission of the file in evidence, or to call the doctor to whom the statement was made.

3. [§13.45] Statement of Preaccident Health

Sometimes a patient's statement of past medical history can be used to impeach him. For example:

Q. You said that you were in good health before the accident, right?
A. Yes.
Q. Did you have any trouble with [your right knee] before the accident?
A. No.
Q. I am looking at page ...... of your hospital record; didn't you tell Dr. .... when you were admitted to the hospital that [you had arthritis in your right knee for ten years]?
A. ....

HOSPITAL AND MEDICAL RECORDS §13.47

4. [§13.46] Absence of Complaints

The absence of complaints by the patient can sometimes be shown to contradict his claims of pain and suffering. But see *Loper v Morrison* (1944) 23 C2d 600, 609, 145 P2d 1, 5, in which excluding the particular hospital record was not error because the nurses' notes did not, in fact, refute the plaintiff's testimony. For example:

Q. You have testified that you were in pain throughout the time you spent in the hospital, is that right?
A. Yes.
A. And that you couldn't sleep because of the pain and discomfort, correct?
A. That's right.
Q. Did you tell the nurses or the doctors you were in pain?
A. ....
Q. Did you ask for any drugs or painkillers?
A. ....
Q. Please look at pages ...... through ...... of this hospital record which are the doctor's progress notes for the period ...., 19......, through ...., 19......, and pages ...... through ......, which are the nurses' notes for the same period and tell the jury whether there are any entries that show that you were in pain and ask for drugs?
A. There aren't any.
Q. In fact, what do the entries for ......a.m. in the nurses' notes for each of those days say?
A. ["Patient says he spent a comfortable night."]

B. [§13.47] *Confronting Adverse Expert with Contradictory Matter*

A lawyer can often glean from medical records information that was not known to an adverse medical witness when he reached his opinions. This matter might support or even require a different opinion if the doctor were to give it appropriate consideration. A doctor confronted with this information on cross-examination can sometimes be led to modify his opinion testimony.

Of course, confronting the witness is not always the best strategy. Doctors can often explain away apparently contradictory matter if given a chance to do so. Thus a lawyer might prefer not to confront the adverse witness, but to introduce the medical records, have favorable witnesses explain the matter and its importance, then argue that the adverse doctor's opinions should be disregarded because he ignored the matter.

§ 13.47   HOSPITAL AND MEDICAL RECORDS

An example of how an adverse medical witness might be confronted with contradictory matter from a hospital record follows.

Q. Doctor, you testified that in your opinion [Mr. ..../plaintiff] had [a herniated disc in his lower spine], is that right?
A. Yes.
A. And you based that opinion primarily on [your clinical examination of him], right?
A. Yes. [And on some X-ray films I had made.]
Q. Did you know about [the myelographic examination] that was performed at .... Hospital?
A. Yes.
Q. You didn't disregard the results of that examination in forming your opinion, did you?
A. No. I took them into consideration along with the other things.

Comment: At this point the lawyer might ask additional questions to gain admissions from the doctor that the hospital is a good one (perhaps a teaching hospital, or one connected with a university) and that the doctor or technician who performed the procedure was competent (perhaps a recognized expert in his field). Testimony about the nature of the procedure could also be elicited if it would help the jury to understand the results and their significance.

Q. Now, Doctor, let me direct your attention to [the myelographic examination report] on page ...... of [Mr. ....'s/plaintiff's] records from .... Hospital. Do you find that?
A. Yes.
Q. What does that report say under ["finding"/"diagnosis"/"impression"/etc.]?
A. ....
Q. That report does not show [any defect in the spinal canal, such as would be found if there were a herniated disc], does it?
A. No, it does not.
Q. That [finding/opinion/report] does not support your opinion, does it?
A. No.
Q. In fact, it is inconsistent with your opinion, isn't it?
A. ....

Comment: Sometimes a question like the last one above triggers a long explanation by the doctor. Depending on the doctor and the circumstances, the explanation could rehabilitate him, or could just make him sound like an advocate rather than a fair-minded physician.

14
Medical Bills

I. [§14.1] Preliminary Considerations

II. [§14.2] Admissibility
   A. [§14.3] By Agreement
   B. By Foundational Testimony
      1. [§14.4] Identifying Bills; Plaintiff's Testimony
      2. [§14.5] Necessity of Treatment
      3. [§14.6] Reasonableness of Charges
         a. [§14.7] Billing Doctor
         b. [§14.8] Other Doctor

III. [§14.9] Showing Payment; Collateral Source Rule
   A. [§14.10] By Plaintiff
   B. [§14.11] By Defendant
   C. [§14.12] By Workmen's Compensation Carrier

IV. [§14.13] Covering Notations of Payment

I. [§14.1] PRELIMINARY CONSIDERATIONS

A plaintiff is entitled to recover the reasonable value of all medical services and supplies necessary for the treatment of the injuries caused by the defendant. See generally Johns, CALIFORNIA DAMAGES 81 (1969); 2 Witkin, SUMMARY OF CALIFORNIA LAW 1612 (7th ed, 1960). See also BAJI No 14.10. Medical bills are tangible evidence of the medical expenses the plaintiff can recover as damages. They can be introduced in evidence by agreement (see §14.3) to show the services and supplies the plaintiff received and the charges made, or after a foundation is laid (see §14.2) to corroborate testimony on these matters.

Problems arise in the proof of medical expenses when the plaintiff received treatment from several different doctors, hospitals, and other sources and it is impractical to call a separate witness to testify about each charge or to lay a foundation for each bill. Problems arise in the use of medical bills to prove medical expense when the bills have not been paid or were paid by someone other than the plaintiff (see §14.9), and when the bills contain notations that indicate payment by an insurer (see §14.13). The proof of future medical expenses requires testimony from a medical expert that the plaintiff is reasonably certain to require medical treatment in the future (see generally §6.77) and from the doctor or an economist (see generally §7.9) on the probable cost of future care.

Before trial the plaintiff's attorney should try to obtain accurate and complete bills or receipts for all treatment rendered to the plaintiff including bills from hospitals, doctors, nurses, dentists, physiotherapists, pharmacies, sellers of prosthetic devices, and others. Some doctors send bills directly to insurers, and the lawyer may have to write the doctor to obtain a bill from him. When medical records are subpenaed, the subpena or supporting declaration can specify that statements of charges are also to be produced. See §13.15.

II. [§14.2] ADMISSIBILITY

Medical bills and receipts for medical services and supplies can be received in evidence (a) by agreement of the parties (see §14.3), or (b) on a foundational showing that satisfies relevance (Evid C §§350–352), authentication (Evid C §§1400–1401), best evidence (Evid C §1500), and hearsay (Evid C §1200) requirements. Introduction of the bills alone, however, may not be sufficient to prove medical expense. It must also be shown that the treatment was necessary and the charges reasonable (see §§14.5–14.6), and bills may be excluded if necessity and reasonableness are not shown.

Any party can serve a subpena duces tecum for business records concerning services rendered, supplies furnished, and charges made, on the custodian of records or other qualified witness at each of the hospitals, doctors' offices, pharmacies, etc. at which the plaintiff obtained treatment. See generally §§11.8–11.15 on introducing subpenaed business records. The affidavit (Evid C §1561) or testimony of each custodian lays the foundation for introduction of the bills from his office, although relevance, necessity, and reasonableness must still be shown.

MEDICAL BILLS §14.3

If the plaintiff's attorney offers in evidence the medical bills received by the plaintiff, he can usually have the plaintiff authenticate them by testifying that he received each one from the doctor, hospital, etc., indicated on the bill (by letterhead or signature) for treatment that he received from that source. The plaintiff can usually offer in evidence the original bills he received, although a best evidence objection is rarely made, and copies can often be introduced under an exception to the best evidence rule. Although medical bills are hearsay, they can be admitted in evidence for the limited purpose of corroborating the plaintiff's testimony that he incurred a liability for medical expenses and, if paid, to show that the charges were reasonable. See *PG&E v G. W. Thomas Drayage & Rigging Co.* (1968) 69 C2d 33, 42, 69 CR 561, 567; *Plonley v Reser* (1960) 178 CA2d Supp 935, 937, 3 CR 551, 553.

Relevance can be shown through a plaintiff's or treating doctor's testimony that the bills are for treatment for the injuries allegedly caused by the defendant, not for other conditions. Charges for the treatment of unrelated conditions can be deleted from a bill or covered before it is offered in evidence. See §14.13.

The necessity of the treatment for which the plaintiff was billed can be shown by the treating doctor, or any doctor to whom the extent of the plaintiff's injuries was known or made known. See §14.5. Any doctor familiar with customary medical charges can testify whether the charges for the services rendered the plaintiff were reasonable. See §14.6. It is usually best to have one doctor testify to necessity and reasonableness for all medical bills.

A. [§14.3] *By Agreement*

The easiest way to introduce medical bills in evidence is usually to obtain the agreement of all parties. Judges encourage agreement to avoid the need for time consuming, but routine, foundational testimony. The lawyer who wants to offer medical bills should obtain agreement not only that the bills be received in evidence, but also that the services were necessary and the charges reasonable. Mere receipt of the bills in evidence by agreement or otherwise does not make the bills evidence of the necessity of the treatment or reasonableness of the charges. See *Latky v Wolfe* (1927) 85 CA 332, 346, 259 P 470, 477 (unpaid medical bills not evidence of reasonable value of services). Nor is a stipulation that the hospital bill is a specified amount evidence of its reasonable value. *Gimbel v Laramie* (1960) 181 CA2d 77, 81, 5 CR 88, 91 (recovery for hospital costs not allowed; no proof of reasonable value).

Agreement can be sought before trial by sending copies of the bills to other counsel and asking for a written stipulation or agreement to stipulate at trial. See §§8.21, 8.24 on stipulations for the admission of exhibits. At trial, a lawyer can show the bills to opposing counsel, give him an opportunity to study them, and ask him to stipulate to their admission (or to stipulate to the total amount of the plaintiff's medical expense), along with necessity and reasonableness. Opponents can be asked to point out any bills or items they feel are questionable. Sometimes the proponent can clear up these questions or would be willing to delete an item.

If a pertrial conference is held, the lawyer can request that a paragraph be inserted in the pretrial order providing for admission, and stating that the treatment was necessary and the charges reasonable. See generally §8.23 on using pretrial orders. Anticipating the problems and time involved in proof of bills at trial, some judges will insert in the pretrial order a paragraph such as the following:

The plaintiff shall serve on the defendant [within ...... days of this order/at least ...... days before the date of trial] a copy of a bill or receipt for all claimed medical expenses. Unless the defendant serves an objection to a bill or receipt within .... days after receiving such copy, it may be introduced in evidence at trial without further foundation, and the treatment billed will be deemed to have been necessary and the charge for it reasonable.

A request for admission (CCP §2033) may also be used in advance of trial to secure the admission of medical bills. See generally §8.22.

B. By Foundational Testimony

1. [§14.4] Identifying Bills; Plaintiff's Testimony

While the plaintiff is testifying, he can be shown each medical bill or receipt he received, and he can state who sent it, what services or supplies it covered, and the amount of the charge. This testimony should be sufficient to authenticate the bills. See Evid C §1400. It should also qualify the bills to be received over a hearsay objection (see Evid C §1200) for the limited purpose of corroborating the testimony the plaintiff has given (or could give) on medical treatment and expenses. See *PG&E v G. W. Thomas Drayage & Rigging Co.* (1968) 69 C2d 33, 43, 69 CR 561, 567. Whether the plaintiff received an original typed bill, a carbon copy, or a photocopy, it can be argued that it is "the writing itself" insofar as it is to be used to corroborate his testimony, and is not subject to a best evidence objection. See Evid C §1500.

MEDICAL BILLS §14.4

If no controversy about medical expenses is anticipated, the plaintiff may be asked to identify all his medical bills at once. Otherwise, his lawyer could ask about each bill separately. For example:

Q. Were you hospitalized for your injuries?
A. Yes.
Q. For how many days?
A. ....
Q. I now show you this paper. Can you tell us what it is?
A. Yes. It is a bill from .... Hospital for my treatment.
Q. Please tell us what treatment and charges it shows, and the amounts for each.
A. [First there is a charge of $...... per day for ...... days. There is a charge of $...... for medication./etc.]
Q. What is the total charge by the hospital?
A. $.........

Comment: The lawyer could have this bill marked for identification at this point (see generally §8.8), or offer it in evidence (see §8.14), or simply hold it and offer it along with all other medical bills and receipts after they have been similarly identified.

Q. [Did you pay this bill?/Has this bill been paid?]
A. Yes.

Comment: If the plaintiff paid the bill, he should so testify. If it was paid by a collateral source (see §14.9), he can testify that it has been paid without saying by whom (see §14.10). Testimony that a medical bill has been paid is some evidence that it is reasonable. *Dewhirst v Leopold* (1924) 194 C 424, 433, 229 P 30, 33.

If the bill has not been paid, the plaintiff's lawyer usually would not ask this question. The plaintiff can recover the reasonable value of medical expenses even though he has not paid them.

Q. Were you treated by Dr. ....?
A. Yes.
Q. How often did he treat you?
A. [Once a week for two months and then once every two weeks.]
Q. What did the treatment consist of?
A. [He removed the cast that had been put on in the hospital, then gave me massage and diathermy treatments.]
Q. Did he send you a bill for his services?
A. Yes.
Q. Is this it? [Bill is shown to witness.]
A. Yes.

§14.5 MEDICAL BILLS

Q. [Did you pay it?/Has this bill been paid?]
A. Yes.

Comment: See preceding *Comment* on testimony about payment.

Q. Did Dr. .... prescribe any medication for you or any braces or appliances?
A. Yes. [He gave me a prescription for a painkiller called ...., and for a neck collar.]
Q. Did you obtain [the drugs and the collar]?
A. Yes.
Q. Where?
A. ....
Q. Did you pay for them?
A. Yes.
Q. How much?
A. [$...... for the drugs, and $...... for the collar.]
Q. Can you identify these papers that I now show you?
A. Yes. These are the receipts I got when I paid for [the drugs and the collar].

2. [§14.5] Necessity of Treatment

To be entitled to recover damages for medical expenses, a plaintiff must show or obtain agreement that the expenses relate to treatment made necessary by the injury. *Harris v Los Angeles Transit Lines* (1952) 111 CA2d 593, 598, 245 P2d 35, 37. The expert testimony of a doctor is usually required to show the necessity of the treatment for which the plaintiff was charged. The injured party, as a lay witness, cannot ordinarily testify to necessity. For discussion of a doctor's opinion testimony on the causal connection between the defendant's tort and the personal injuries, see §§6.71–6.74.

The treating doctor might testify as follows on the necessity for the treatment given:

Q. Did you treat [Mr. ..../the plaintiff] for the [injury/condition] you diagnosed?
A. Yes.
Q. Will you describe the nature of that treatment?
A. [A cast was placed on the wrist, etc.]
Q. Was that treatment necessary for [the fracture]?
A. Yes.
Q. Did any part of the treatment you gave him relate to any other condition than [that fractured wrist and its consequences]?
A. No.

Comment: A doctor other than the treating doctor could testify on need for treatment as follows:

Q. Are you familiar with the injuries the plaintiff [suffered/incurred] and the treatment he received?
A. Yes. [I have read the records of the treating doctors and the hospital records on the plaintiff, and he gave me a history of that treatment.]
Q. Please describe the treatment.
A. [He had a fractured wrist which was placed in a cast, etc.]
Q. Is that treatment customary for the injuries plaintiff sustained?
A. Yes.
Q. Was the treatment he was given necessary to cure or relieve the effects of [the fracture]?
A. Yes.

3. [§14.6] Reasonableness of Charges

The injured party must prove that the charges for the treatment were reasonable. *Harris v Los Angeles Transit Lines* (1952) 111 CA2d 593, 598, 254 P2d 35, 37. See also Anno, 12 ALR3d 1347 (1967).

Reasonableness can be shown through the testimony of any doctor familiar with the charges customarily made for such treatment, although the doctor's testimony is not conclusive and the trier of fact may find a different amount on the basis of the evidence. *Harris v Los Angeles Transit Lines, supra.* See also *Caulfield v Market St. Ry. Co.* (1937) 20 CA2d 220, 66 P2d 752 (award was less than amounts plaintiff testified she incurred for treatment). A showing that medical bills were paid is some evidence of reasonable value and is sufficient in the absence of contrary evidence. *Dewhirst v Leopold* (1924) 194 C 424, 433, 229 P 30, 33; see *Rollins v Hedin* (1952) 114 CA2d 488, 250 P2d 728 (stipulation to admission of paid medical bills foreclosed defendants from arguing that reasonableness of charges was not proved).

Even though a medical bill has been received in evidence, unless it is shown that the bill was paid, it is not evidence of reasonable value and it is insufficient to support an award of medical expenses. *Linde v Emmick* (1936) 16 CA2d 676, 684, 61 P2d 338, 342; *Latky v Wolfe* (1927) 85 CA 332, 347, 259 P 470, 477. But application of this rule depends on the circumstances of each case. See, *e.g., Shriver v Silva* (1944) 65 CA2d 753, 767, 151 P2d 528, 535 (award of billed amounts upheld where no objection was made to introduction of bills or to reasonableness of disputed charges until appeal, and amounts appeared reasonable); *Malinson v Black* (1948) 83 CA2d 375, 379, 188 P2d 788, 791 (plaintiff estimated expenses incurred); see *Townsend v Keith* (1917) 34 CA 564, 168 P 402.

a. [§14.7] Billing Doctor

The billing doctor can show the reasonableness of his charges. For example:

Q. What were your charges for the treatment you have just described?
A. [The ...... house calls were $...... each in the total sum of $......, and the ...... office visits were $...... each in the total sum of $.......]
Q. Have you figured the total of your charges?
A. Yes. The total was $.......
Q. Were those charges reasonable for the treatment rendered?
A. Yes, they were.

b. [§14.8] Other Doctor

A doctor other than the billing doctor can testify to the reasonableness of charges by hospitals, treating doctors, etc., when he is familiar with the charges usually made for the services and supplies. The practice is based on the rule that an expert may give an opinion on subjects within his special training, and his testimony may be based on personal knowledge or matters made known to him (*e.g.,* by hypothetical question). See Evid C §801(b); *Zelayeta v Pacific Greyhound Lines, Inc.* (1951) 104 CA2d 716, 724, 232 P2d 572, 577. The testimony regarding reasonable value might be as follows:

Q. [Mr. ..../The plaintiff] was billed for [a neurological examination by a Dr. ....]. Was [such an examination] necessary in this case?
A. Yes.
Q. Why?
A. [The patient complained of headaches and blurred vision. Under these circumstances, he should be examined by a neurologist.]
Q. Please describe [a neurological examination].
A. ....
Q. [How long does the examination take?]
A. [About an hour.]
Q. Do you know what is the standard and customary charge in the community for [a neurological examination]?
A. I do.

MEDICAL BILLS §14.10

Q. What is it?
A. $.........
Q. Was this charge of $...... to [Mr. ..../the plaintiff] reasonable?
A. Yes, it was.

III. [§14.9] SHOWING PAYMENT; COLLATERAL SOURCE RULE

A plaintiff is entitled to recover necessary and reasonable medical expenses even though the bills were not paid or were paid by some collateral source not related to the defendant, as long as the treatment was not given gratuitously and the defendant is not a public entity. See *Mathes v Aggeler & Musser Seed Co.* (1919) 179 C 697, 178 P 713; *Gersick v Shilling* (1950) 97 CA2d 641, 650, 218 P2d 583, 589. On the collateral source rule generally, see *De Cruz v Reid* (1968) 69 C2d 217, 223, 70 CR 550, 554; Johns, CALIFORNIA DAMAGES 83, 154 (1969); 2 Witkin, SUMMARY OF CALIFORNIA LAW 1609, 1612 (7th ed, 1960).

A plaintiff's lawyer can object to any reference by defense counsel to payment by a collateral source. A safer course is to ask the judge in chambers at the outset of the trial that defense counsel be ordered not to question the plaintiff or any witness about payment and not to mention payment by a collateral source. See *Sacramento & San Joaquin Drainage Dist. v Reed* (1963) 215 CA2d 60, 66, 29 CR 847, 851 on the propriety of motions ad limine. If defense counsel argues that he should be permitted to ask about payment, the judge may inquire why he wants to do so, take offers of proof if necessary, and weigh defendant's reasons against the dangers mentioned in Evid C §352.

Defense counsel can show payment by a defense connected source. See §14.11. The defense can also show payment of the same bill by more than one collateral source as evidence that plaintiff was taking unnecessary treatment in order to obtain the additional insurance payments. See *Garfield v Russell* (1967) 251 CA2d 275, 278, 59 CR 379, 381.

A. [§14.10] *By Plaintiff*

A plaintiff may want to show that medical bills have been paid; payment is evidence that the charges were reasonable. See *Dewhirst v Leopold* (1924) 194 C 424, 433, 229 P 30, 33. The plaintiff can also prevent defense counsel from asking about or mentioning a collateral source. See §14.9. However, if the bills were not paid, defense counsel might be permitted to question the plaintiff about nonpayment on the ground that it shows plaintiff's belief that the charges were not reasonable.

B. [§14.11] *By Defendant*

A plaintiff cannot recover medical expenses paid by the defendant, and if the plaintiff offers evidence of these expenses, the defense may show payment by a defendant connected (as distinguished from a collateral) source including defendant's insurance. *Dodds v Bucknum* (1963) 214 CA2d 206, 212, 29 CR 393, 396 (medical bills of plaintiff, a guest passenger, were paid by defendant-host's carrier).

The plaintiff may (1) introduce evidence of the expenses and let defendant show payment from his side; (2) introduce no evidence of the expenses leaving no occasion for the defendant to show payment; or (3) seek agreement that he will prove medical expenses and the defendant will not show payment but that the verdict will be reduced by the amount of expenses paid. Plaintiffs' lawyers sometimes fear that the first approach would give jurors the idea that plaintiff was seeking a double recovery, while defense lawyers may wish to avoid proof of payment when it would reveal that the defendant was insured. Many plaintiffs' lawyers dislike the second approach, feeling that the lower the special damages proved, the lower the general damages the jury is likely to award.

It is a good idea for plaintiff's attorney to raise the question of how defense connected payments are to be handled in chambers at the outset of trial. The judge may help counsel reach agreement on the approach to be used.

C. [§14.12] *By Workmen's Compensation Carrier*

The fact that plaintiff's medical bills were paid by the employer's workmen's compensation insurance carrier is inadmissible (see *Huber v Henry J. Kaiser Co.* (1945) 71 CA2d 278, 285, 162 P2d 693, 696), unless, (1) the employer has intervened in the third party suit as a party plaintiff under Lab C §3852 (evidence of payment is relevant to issue of employer's damages as result of third party's negligence); (2) the defendant pleads contributory negligence of the employer as a pro tanto defense (to extent of compensation benefits) even though the employer has neither intervened in the employee's action nor brought his own action (see *Tate v Superior Court* (1963) 213 CA2d 238, 248, 28 CR 548, 552); and (3) the employer has been joined as a cross-defendant, the defendant contending that the employer's negligence contributed to the injury and that no recovery is allowable for compensation benefits paid by the employer (see *Witt v Jackson* (1961) 57 C2d 57, 72, 17 CR 369, 378 (injured employee's damages reduced by amount of workmen's compensation benefits received)). See generally *De Cruz v Reid* (1968) 69 C2d 217, 70 CR 550.

IV. [§14.13] COVERING NOTATIONS OF PAYMENT

Medical bills are introduced in evidence in the same manner as other exhibits. See §§8.3–8.15. However, if a bill contains a notation indicating that it was paid by someone other than the plaintiff (*e.g.,* an insurer) an attorney can ask, out of hearing of the jury, that the notation be covered or deleted, and the judge will instruct the clerk to do so. Some plaintiff's lawyers make photocopies that do not show the notation of payment. The original bills can then be shown to defense counsel, and the copies can be received in evidence.

15
Photographs

I. [§15.1] Value as Evidence

II. [§15.2] Admissibility
   A. [§15.3] By Agreement
   B. [§15.4] By Authentication
     1. Qualifying Authenticating Witness
       a. [§15.5] Nonphotographers
       b. [§15.6] Professional Photographers
       c. [§15.7] Amateur Photographers
     2. Authenticating Particular Photographs
       a. [§15.8] Scene of Accident
       b. [§15.9] Changed Scene
       c. [§15.10] Accident Reconstructions
       d. [§15.11] Damaged Vehicles
       e. [§15.12] Injured Persons
   C. [§15.13] Objections to Admission
     1. [§15.14] Prejudicial; Unduly Inflammatory
     2. [§15.15] Misrepresentative or Misleading; Credibility versus Admissibility
     3. [§15.16] Cumulative
     4. [§15.17] Irrelevant

III. Presenting to Jury
   A. [§15.18] Prints; Enlargements
   B. [§15.19] Transparencies

I. [§15.1] VALUE AS EVIDENCE

Photographs are an important tool in personal injury cases. They are used primarily to show accident scenes, damage to vehicles, and injuries to the person. Because photographs show so much detail, they substantiate testimony effectively and give variety to evidence. They can be used to advantage in closing arguments, and can often go to the jury room during the jury's deliberation. Photographs can have a great impact on the jury and can enable jurors to understand issues more clearly. For further discussion of uses of photographs, see CALIFORNIA CIVIL PROCEDURE DURING TRIAL §12.18 (Cal CEB 1960) and 3 AM JUR TRIALS 133–183 (1965). Types of photographic evidence range from conventional black and white prints to color prints and slides, and from microphotographs to aerial photographs. On aerial photographs, see §19.4.

While photographs can be used effectively and persuasively, they should not be overused, particularly to show the plaintiff's injuries. The defense attorney can argue that extensive pictures detract attention from a weak case on the liability issue.

II. [§15.2] ADMISSIBILITY

A photograph is a writing (see Evid C §250) and therefore must be authenticated (see §15.4) before it can be received in evidence (Evid C §1401(a)), unless adverse parties agree to its admission without that foundation (see §15.3).

A. [§15.3] *By Agreement*

Lawyers often ask for and obtain advance agreement to the admission of photographs in evidence. This spares the need for authenticating testimony. An adverse lawyer is willing to agree to the admission of photographs that help, or at least do no harm to, his side. He also knows that the foundation for admission may be easily laid, and that many judges resolve doubts about admissibility by receiving photographs "for what they are worth" and letting an objector assert his arguments against their weight or credibility. Photographs received without foundational testimony may be given little weight or attention by jurors. Not objecting avoids being overruled with the implication that the judge, by permitting the exhibit to be received, has endorsed its credibility. On the other hand, an attorney who has photographs to offer in evidence might not seek an agreement to their admission or accept a waiver of authenticating testimony when the testimony would add to the credibility and weight of an important exhibit.

A lawyer can seek agreement before trial to the admission of photographs in evidence by circulating a written stipulation form (see

PHOTOGRAPHS   §15.4

§8.21) with a print of each picture to be received attached. This can be done when authenticating testimony would be difficult, expensive, or disruptive to put on, or when there is no reason to try to "build up" the photographs by bringing in testimony about them. Advance agreement could also be sought at a pretrial or trial setting conference (see generally §8.23) or by a request for admission (see §8.22).

At the trial lawyers may stipulate orally to the receipt of photographs in evidence. After looking at the photographs the adverse party may offer to dispense with authentication, or the lawyer offering the photographs may ask opposing counsel to waive the requirement of authentication. It is done frequently to save time and avoid disruption when there are no important reasons for either side to insist on authenticating testimony. See §8.24 for form of oral stipulation.

B. [§15.4] *By Authentication*

A photograph is authenticated when a witness who has personal knowledge of what is depicted in it testifies that it is a "correct representation." *Berkovitz v American River Gravel Co.* (1923) 191 C 195, 201, 215 P 675, 678; *Adams v San Jose* (1958) 164 CA2d 665, 667, 330 P2d 840, 841; Witkin, CALIFORNIA EVIDENCE §636 (2d ed, 1966). The authenticating witness need not be a photographer (see §15.4) nor are his precise words crucial. Many lawyers ask witnesses whether each photograph is a "fair and accurate representation" of what it is supposed to represent. Appellate decisions have used such phrases as "faithful representation" (*People v Durrant* (1897) 116 C 179, 213, 48 P 75, 83); "reasonable representation of that which it is alleged to portray" (*Anello v Southern Pac. Co.* (1959) 174 CA2d 317, 323, 344 P2d 843, 846); "truly represents what it purports to represent" (*Holland v Kerr* (1953) 116 CA2d 31, 37, 253 P2d 88, 91); and "fairly depicts" (*Barone v Jones* (1947) 77 CA2d 656, 660, 176 P2d 392, 394).

Authenticating testimony is elicited according to the nature of the photograph and the status of the authenticating witness. See §§15.5–15.7. There is no need to ask an authenticating witness who saw the matter depicted in a photograph such questions as: when and by whom was the photograph made; what kind of film, camera, and other equipment was used; what were the shutter speed, lens aperture, and focal length of the lens; were filters or artificial lights used; and how and by whom were the negatives developed and printed? These questions are bypassed when the witness says that the photograph is an accurate representation. It does not matter how that accurate representation was achieved.

Some photographs show scenes or matter never seen by the photographer or any other person. These include X-ray films, photographs taken through electron microscopes, photographs made by cameras tripped by remote control, and even crowd scenes in which the photographer was unaware of an event being recorded on his film. Authentication of these photographs probably should include testimony by the photographer about how the picture was made and the reliability of the technique and equipment used. See, *e.g.,* chap 16 on X-ray films.

When an attorney has a photograph, but there is no witness available to authenticate it, the photograph might authenticate itself. A judge could find that what it depicts is enough evidence that it correctly represents what it purports to represent. These photographs have been termed "silent witnesses" and are considered "substantive" rather than "illustrative" evidence. See Witkin, CALIFORNIA EVIDENCE §637 (2d ed, 1966).

Evidence Code §403 calls for the trial judge to determine only if there is enough evidence to sustain a finding that an offered photograph is authentic. If there is enough, the jury then must decide whether the photograph is authentic on the basis of all the evidence. It must disregard the photograph unless it finds the preliminary fact of authenticity exists. See Official Comment to Evidence Code §1400.

1. Qualifying Authenticating Witness

   a. [§15.5] Nonphotographers

Any witness who can testify from personal knowledge that the photograph correctly represents what it purports to depict can authenticate it. The witness need not have taken the photograph. *Adams v San Jose* (1958) 164 CA2d 665, 667, 330 P2d 840, 841; Witkin, CALIFORNIA EVIDENCE §636 (2d ed, 1966). Photographs are often authenticated by witnesses who had no part in their preparation.

To qualify a nonphotographer witness to authenticate a photograph, the lawyer needs to bring out only that the witness saw firsthand what the photograph shows. His qualifications are the same as those of any lay witness. See §§1.13–1.15. The witness can then testify that the photograph correctly represents what he saw.

An adverse lawyer can challenge a witness's qualifications to authenticate a photograph by showing that the witness did not have personal knowledge of what is depicted in the photograph. See Evid C §702. An adverse lawyer could also bring out that the witness did not have the capacity or opportunity to perceive the scene or matter well enough to testify later that the photograph correctly depicts it, or

PHOTOGRAPHS §15.6

the capacity to remember what it looked like. See Evid C §780. The photograph could sufficiently refresh the witness's memory, however, so that he could truthfully say he now independently remembers what is depicted by the photograph.

b. [§15.6] Professional Photographers

Lawyers frequently employ legal, commercial, and other professional photographers to prepare photographic exhibits for use in litigation. These photographers have the skill and equipment to make photographs that are beyond the abilities of amateurs. Even photographs of ordinary scenes are likely to portray more information with greater accuracy, and their professional appearance and quality will add to their weight as exhibits, which usually justifies the additional cost.

Some legal photographers who specialize in preparing exhibits for courtroom use are keenly aware of such problems as lighting, perspective, distortion, and printing that can cause a photograph to mislead the viewer. They take pains to produce photographs that are accurate and unlikely to be misinterpreted. Good legal photographers can so prepare exhibits as to ease their admission into evidence.

Usually, legal and commercial photographers are not called as witnesses to authenticate photographs they have made. A witness called to give other testimony can usually authenticate them. See §15.5. However, professional photographers are called as witnesses when the lawyer wants to emphasize photographic evidence; the accuracy of the process by which the picture was made is important; the exhibit consists of surveillance photographs; or an adverse photograph is to be discredited.

When a professional photographer is called as a witness, it is customary to bring out his training and experience, ability to make fair and accurate legal photographs, and impartiality. For example:

Q. What is your profession?
A. [Legal/commercial/etc.] photographer.
Q. Do you have your own place of business?
A. Yes, at [give address].
Q. How long have you been a professional photographer?
A. [I've been earning my living at it since ...., 19....... Of course, I've been involved in photography since ...., 19.......]
Q. Have you taken any course work or formal training in photography?
A. ....

Comment: Many professional photographers are essentially self-taught; experience is more important than formal training. Some have taken a course or two at an art or photography school or in college, and occasionally one will have taken engineering courses or other special training, perhaps in the military.

Q. Have you prepared photographs in the past at the request of lawyers for use in lawsuits?
A. I have.
Q. Can you estimate in how many cases you have prepared photographs?
A. Yes. More than ....
Q. Have you prepared these photographs at the request of both plaintiffs' and defendants' lawyers?
A. Yes.

c. [§15.7] Amateur Photographers

Photographs made by amateur photographers can be valuable evidence. A bystander at an accident scene, for example, may have taken pictures that show the positions and condition of vehicles before they are moved and the activities and the injuries of people involved. Snapshots taken of an injured person can show the injuries shortly after the accident and during the early stages of treatment and recovery. These pictures may be used at trial to show matters that could otherwise be brought out only by testimony.

After a lawyer has entered a case, he may have additional photographs made by professional photographers to obtain exhibits of professional quality. See §15.6. Occasionally a lawyer will designate a client, friend, or relative to take pictures in order to save the expense of a professional job, or perhaps to convey the impression that the client needs to save that expense.

Sometimes attorneys themselves take photographs for use in litigation or have them taken by the investigators they employ. A disadvantage of this approach is that jurors might distrust the photograph because of its partisan source, or transfer skepticism about the accuracy or fairness of the photograph to the attorney.

Amateur photographers usually authenticate their own photographs, since they are ordinarily at the trial to testify about the conditions and events they observed when they took the pictures. They are in the best position to say that the photographs correctly depict what they saw when they took them.

If an attorney or an investigator took the pictures, it would be better to have some other witness authenticate them. The attorney does not

PHOTOGRAPHS §15.8

want to have to testify about, or vouch for, his own or his investigator's product.

Although it is technically unnecessary for authentication, jurors are more likely to believe that an amateur's pictures fairly and accurately represent a scene if they are told some of his experience and training in photography and how the pictures were developed and printed.

Q. How long have you been taking pictures, Mr. ....?
A. ...... years.
Q. Do you have any idea how many you have taken over that time?
A. Yes. More than ....
Q. Have you ever had any training in photography?
A. Yes. [I took a course in photography at an evening high school.]

Comment: Some serious amateur photographers are as well equipped, experienced, and skilled as many professionals. They can be questioned further about course work or training, the photography books and magazines they read, whether they do their own darkroom work, whether they have won any prizes in photography contests, and so forth.

2. Authenticating Particular Photographs

   a. [§15.8] Scene of Accident

Photographs are commonly used to show accident sites. They can give the judge and jurors a clear picture of the scene and a better understanding of what the witnesses are talking about. The photographs can also aid witnesses whose recollections of the scene may have faded or changed.

Occasionally, photographs taken at or near the time of the accident and showing the vehicles, objects, and persons involved, will be used to show the accident scene. These photographs are ordinarily authenticated by the photographer. He is likely to be called as a witness anyway, since he usually has personal knowledge of the facts beyond those shown in his photographs, and he is the person best able to explain how long after the accident the pictures were taken and whether the vehicles, objects, or persons had changed positions before they were recorded on film.

Usually, accident scene photographs are made some time after the accident. They show the site of the accident and such details as crosswalks, traffic signs and signals, and other stationary objects. Of course, any change in the "permanent" features of the scene between

§15.8 PHOTOGRAPHS

the time of the accident and the time of the photograph should be explained (see §15.9) as should any attempt to show in the photographs a reconstruction of the events of the accident (see §15.10). Even if the attorney has had accident site photographs made by a professional photographer, the authentication for their admission is usually supplied by some other person. For example:

Q. Are you familiar with the intersection of .... and .... Streets?
A. Yes.
Q. On what occasions have you seen that intersection?
A. ....

Comment: The preceding questions are unnecessary if the witness has already testified that he was at the scene of the accident. A lawyer who wanted to "build up" the exhibit could ask additional questions to establish how well he perceived the scene (*e.g.,* whether he walked around to different viewpoints, revisited the scene, etc.), and how well he remembers the appearance of the scene.

Q. I now show you these photographs marked for identification as [plaintiff's/defendant's] exhibits ...... through .... Can you state briefly what each one shows?
A. [These are different views of that intersection.]
Q. Does each one [correctly/fairly and accurately/etc.] portray that intersection as you observed it?
A. Yes.

Comment: Individual photographs can be authenticated or described one at a time. For example:

Q. What does exhibit ...... show?
A. That is the view of the intersection of .... and .... Streets.
Q. Which direction are we looking in this photograph?
A. [North, along .... Street.]
Q. Can you tell whether it was taken from the middle of the street, or from some other point?
A. [It looks to me like it was taken down the northbound traffic lane near the center line.]

Comment: Many professional photographers label each picture with what it shows and the camera position. For example: "View looking north along Main Street toward its intersection with First Street, made with the camera 3 feet east of the center line of Main Street and 100 feet back from the southerly curb line of First Street." Frequently, lawyers will stipulate to admission of photographs bearing this labeling.

b. [§15.9] Changed Scene

Photographs taken some time after an accident may show changes in the scene. The fact that there are changes does not necessarily render the photograph inadmissible. *Bateman v Doughnut Corp. of America* (1944) 63 CA2d 711, 147 P2d 404. The photograph can still be valuable to show the general configuration of the scene. Adverse attorneys should be ready to object, however, if the changes might confuse the jurors, undue time would be consumed to explain the changes, or a changed matter might be prejudicial. See Evid C §352. Prejudice might result, for example, if the photograph showed a subsequent repair or improvement. See Evid C §1151.

If the photograph does show a change from the scene that existed at the time of the accident, it is usually better to bring this out on direct examination. For example:

Q. Are you familiar with the intersection of .... and .... Streets as it existed on ...., 19......?
A. Yes.
Q. Please look at these photographs marked for identification as [plaintiff's/defendant's] exhibits ...... through .... What do they show?
A. They show that intersection.
Q. Do you see any differences between what is shown in the photographs and what the intersection looked like on ...., 19......?
A. Yes.
Q. What are the differences?
A. [The photographs show signal lights on the corners where there were stop signs on ...., 19.......]
Q. What about markings painted on the pavement?
A. [On ...., 19......, the word "Stop" was painted just in front of the crosswalk at each corner, but that does not appear in these pictures.]
Q. With the exceptions you have mentioned, are these photographs [correct/fair and accurate/etc.] representations of the intersection of .... and .... Streets as it existed on ...., 19 ......?
A. Yes.

c. [§15.10] Accident Reconstructions

The events of an accident can be reconstructed and photographs of the reconstruction taken to illustrate a witness's recollection or a theory of how an accident occurred. Usually a witness to the accident sets up the reconstruction by directing where people and vehicles should be positioned. Photographs of the reconstruction can be received in evidence to illustrate the witness's testimony about, or the party's theory of, how the accident occurred. See *Wilson v San Francisco* (1959) 174 CA2d 273, 344 P2d 828.

The witness who authenticates these photographs is usually the person who observed the accident and directed the reconstruction. For example:

Q. Where were you at about ....m. on ...., 19......?
A. At the intersection of .... and .... Streets.
Q. Did you see an accident occur at that time and place?
A. Yes.
Q. Did you see the vehicles before, during, and after the collision?
A. Yes.
Q. Did you return to that intersection on ...., 19......?
A. Yes.
Q. Who was with you at that time?
A. [You, Mr. ...., Mr. ...., and a photographer whose name I don't remember.]
Q. What did you and the other people do at that time?
A. [Well, Mr. .... got into a .... automobile and Mr. .... into a .... I told them where to place their cars so that they would be in the position that the cars were in just before the accident, at the time of the collision, and when they came to rest. The photographer took a picture each time I signaled him that the cars were in the right position.]
Q. I show you these pictures marked for identification [plaintiff's/defendant's] exhibits ...... through .... What do they show?
A. [They show the intersection and the vehicles as we reconstructed them that day.]
Q. Do these photographs [correctly/fairly and accurately/etc.] represent the scene as you reconstructed it that day?
A. Yes.

Comment: At this point, the witness can be asked to describe the accident, using the photographs to illustrate his testimony. If the camera can be placed in the position the witness occupied when he saw the accident, the witness might testify not only that the pictures show the accident, but also that they show what he saw.

Costs of reconstructing an accident can be high, and the case may be overplayed by such evidence. Accordingly, reconstructions should be, and are, used sparingly.

PHOTOGRAPHS   §15.11

    d. [§15.11] Damaged Vehicles

Photographs showing a vehicle after an accident are used to show points and force of impact and to justify repair bills.

While experienced legal photographers can usually make more accurate and informative pictures of vehicle damage, it is common for the owner of the vehicle, if he also owns a camera, to take pictures sufficient to supply the needed evidence. The following dialogue illustrates how photographs of a vehicle might be authenticated by an owner who is an amateur photographer.

Q. Were you the owner of the 19 ...... [state make and model] automobile involved in the accident on ...., 19......?
A. Yes.
Q. Can you tell us what condition it was in just before the accident?
A. ....
Q. Had it ever been in an accident?
A. ....
Q. Do you have any pictures that show how it looked before the accident?
A. Yes. [Here are some that I took on ...., 19........]

Comment: These photographs could be marked and offered in evidence at this point.

Q. Did you see your car after the accident?
A. Yes.
Q. Where?
A. [First, I saw it in the street just after the collision, then I saw it later in the .... body shop on .... Street.]

Comment: If the witness did not see the car immediately after the accident, before it was moved, the adverse party might claim that some of the damage shown was incurred while towing it in.

Q. Did you take pictures of it at [the garage]?
A. Yes.

Comment: At this point the lawyer might want to show briefly an amateur photographer's background and experience in photography to bolster the claim that the photographs are accurate. See §15.7. The lawyer could also bring out information about the processing and custody of the films and prints. For example:

Q. How many pictures did you take?
A. [I shot a roll of ...... from different angles and with different exposure settings to be sure I got good pictures.]

§15.12   PHOTOGRAPHS

Q. What did you do with the film?
A. [I took it to the drugstore where I take all my film to be developed/ I developed it in my own darkroom that same evening.]

(If film sent out for processing)

Q. Did you get back a set of prints?
A. Yes.

(If developed by the witness)

Q. Did you make prints from the developed negatives?
A. Yes.
Q. Where was that done?
A. [In my darkroom.]
Q. What did you do with the prints?
A. I gave [them/a set] to you.
Q. Are these the prints?
A. Yes.
Q. Do they [correctly/fairly and accurately/etc.] show the condition of your car on ...., 19......?
A. Yes.

e. [§15.12] Injured Persons

Plaintiff's lawyers often ask a professional photographer to photograph visible injuries at various times during treatment and recovery. The treating doctor, the injured person, a friend, or a relative could supply authenticating testimony that the photographs correctly portray the injuries as they appeared when the pictures were taken. See §15.5. The following example illustrates how a commercial or legal photographer might authenticate photographs showing injuries.

Q. What is your profession, Mr. ....?
A. [Commercial/Legal/etc.] photographer.

Comment: In some situations, the witness's training, experience, and skill as a photographer are brought out. See §15.6.

Q. Did you make some photographs in this case at my request?
A. Yes.
Q. Did you make these photographs that I now show you, [that are marked for identification plaintiff's exhibits ...... through ......]?
A. I did.
Q. When and where were they taken?
A. On ...., 19......, in [the emergency room at .... Hospital/the office of Dr. ..../my studio at ..../ etc.].

PHOTOGRAPHS §15.14

Q. What do these photographs show?
A. [They show a man who was introduced to me as Mr. ....]
Q. Do these photographs [correctly/fairly and accurately/etc.] portray his appearance at the time you made them?
A. Yes, they do.

Comment: Additional photographs made at other times can be authenticated in the same way. It is important that the dates the pictures were taken be brought out so that the patient's depicted condition can be related to stages of treatment and recovery as testified to by a doctor, the patient, and other witnesses.

Some photographers may need to be warned against using special films and filters that make bruises, scars, and other injuries look worse than they are. On the other hand, the photographer's goal is to produce pictures that show the injuries as they looked to him when he took the pictures, and this can mean that he must choose a special combination of film, lighting, and filters in order to produce realistic, fair, and accurate photographs.

C. [§15.13] *Objections to Admission*

Objections to admission of a photograph in evidence include insufficient foundation (see §15.4), prejudicial or unduly inflammatory (see §15.14), misleading (see §15.15), cumulative (see §15.16), and irrelevant (see §15.17).

It does not appear that photographs are objectionable as hearsay because they are not "statements." See Evid C §§225, 1200. And most photographs are not subject to the objection that they are not the best evidence. See McBaine, CALIFORNIA EVIDENCE MANUAL §587 (2d ed, 1960). The photograph is a writing (see Evid C §250), but it is offered as secondary evidence of the appearance of a scene, person, or object. A best evidence problem does arise when the photograph is of written material. See Evid C §1500 (precludes evidence other than the writing itself to prove the content of a writing). The photograph must either be introduced under some exception to the best evidence rule (see Evid C §§1501–1566), or the trial judge must be persuaded that it is not offered to prove the content of the writing.

1. [§15.14] Prejudicial; Unduly Inflammatory

If the photograph is gruesome or shocking, the opposing party may object on the ground that its admission would be prejudicial. Evidence Code §352 gives the trial judge discretion to exclude evidence if "its probative value is substantially outweighed by the probability that its

§15.15

admission will . . . create substantial danger of undue prejudice . . . ." See CALIFORNIA TRIAL OBJECTIONS §§28.1–28.4, 33.1–33.4 (Cal CEB 1967). The court enjoys "wide discretion" (*Anello v Southern Pac. Co.* (1959) 174 CA2d 317, 322, 344 P2d 843, 846), and in *Calandri v Ione Unified School Dist.* (1963) 219 CA2d 542, 552, 33 CR 333, 338, in which the trial court had rejected photographs showing the bloody condition of plaintiff's hand following the accident, the appellate court upheld the ruling but stated that a contrary determination would not have been an abuse of discretion. Generally the courts are more likely to admit than to reject photographs having probative value even though they may be gruesome and shocking. See Witkin, CALIFORNIA EVIDENCE §633 (2d ed, 1966). However, the court is more likely to exclude the most inflammatory photographs if given a choice of milder ones.

2. [§15.15] Misrepresentative or Misleading; Credibility versus Admissibility

Photographs can be misleading. Distance is distorted if the picture is taken with the camera close to the ground. Height is exaggerated if the picture is taken with the camera close to the base of the object and shooting upward. Perspective can be affected by the use of wide-angle lenses or the telephoto lenses frequently used for surveillance shots.

If the photograph sought to be introduced in evidence misleads or misrepresents, the trial judge has discretion to exclude it under Evid C §352 if "its probative value is substantially outweighed by the probability that its admission will . . . create substantial danger . . . of misleading the jury." See CALIFORNIA TRIAL OBJECTIONS §§33.1–33.4 (Cal CEB 1967). See also Comment, 8 HASTINGS LJ 310 (1957) (discussion and criticism of refusal to admit misrepresentative photographs); Witkin, CALIFORNIA EVIDENCE §638 (2d ed, 1966).

3. [§15.16] Cumulative

Cumulative evidence is evidence that repeats the substance of evidence already introduced. See generally CALIFORNIA TRIAL OBJECTIONS §§24.1–24.8 (Cal CEB 1967). The judge can exclude cumulative evidence if its probative value is substantially outweighed by the probability that its admission will consume an undue amount of time or create undue prejudice. Evid C §352. If the judge considers photographs cumulative, he may exclude them. *Summers v Burdick*

PHOTOGRAPHS §15.18

(1961) 191 CA2d 464, 471, 13 CR 68, 71. To overcome the objection of cumulative evidence, the party offering the photographs must convince the judge that they differ in a material way from those already admitted.

4. [§15.17] Irrelevant

Only relevant evidence is admissible. Evid C §350. Relevant evidence means evidence that tends to prove or disprove a fact in dispute. Evid C §210; see generally CALIFORNIA TRIAL OBJECTIONS §§17.1–17.5 (Cal CEB 1967). For example, a photograph of an accident scene is relevant when liability is in issue. If liability and property damage are not in issue, a photograph showing a badly damaged automobile might still be relevant to show the severity of impact in substantiation of the personal injuries claimed. A photograph showing scarring before plastic surgery took place is relevant to the issue of damages.

III. PRESENTING TO JURY

A. [§15.18] Prints; Enlargements

Most photographs used in the courtroom are black and white prints. Since large color prints are expensive, transparencies are ordinarily used to show color. See §15.19. Attorneys should try to use only the standard print size (eight by ten inches), since if a number of prints are to be introduced, they are more convenient to handle if they are all the same size.

Prints made with a glossy surface usually show more fine detail, but prints with a dull (mat) surface are easier to mark. Since photographic exhibits get a good deal of handling, they are usually printed on heavy photographic paper. Larger prints can be mounted on cardboard to keep them from buckling or bending.

Almost all prints are enlargements ("projection prints") made from smaller negatives, although a few (even some eight by ten prints) are "contact printed" from negatives of the same size. There is no difference in the authentication needed for enlargements and contact prints. However, if the print is more than eight by ten, it is sometimes helpful to have a witness testify that no inaccuracies or distortions were introduced by the projection printing process.

After a print has been received in evidence it can be passed to the judge and from juror to juror. When lawyers want jurors to look at a photograph while a witness is testifying about it, a large print (24 by 30 inches or larger) can be tacked on a blackboard or wall. Or a number (*e.g.,* 16) of identical prints can be made from the same negative; then, with the judge's permission, one photograph can be introduced, and separate copies given to each juror, the judge, and the opposing counsel to examine during testimony. See §§8.16–8.17.

Photographs that are introduced in evidence on the basis of foundational testimony are handled much like other exhibits. See generally §§8.3–8.15.

B. [§15.19] *Transparencies*

Color slides, or transparencies, are a common form of photographic exhibit. They are viewed by transmitted light, through the use of either a hand viewer or a slide projector. Transparencies are usually small (1 by 1½ inches (35 mm.) or 2¼ by 2¼ inches) and little can be distinguished in them unless they are seen through a viewer or projected on a screen or white wall. Lawyers usually prefer that they be projected, because they can then be viewed by the entire courtroom at the same time and because projection in a darkened courtroom heightens the impact of the presentation. A lawyer who wants to project transparencies, however, must check to be sure that the courtroom is equipped for projection. See §17.26. In addition, the proponent of the transparencies may wish to offer a small lighted viewer for the jurors to use in the jury room.

The admissibility of transparencies should be decided before they are projected for viewing by the jury. This may mean projecting the slide and taking authenticating testimony outside the jury's presence or providing a hand viewer so that opposing counsel, the judge, and the witness can see the slide before it is projected.

The exhibit to be marked and introduced is the miniature transparency, but the trier of fact can only become aware of the evidence it embodies when it is projected or "enlarged" by a viewer. The projector, screen, and viewer are not exhibits and need not be introduced in evidence. They are merely aids to perceiving the evidence. See §8.18.

16
X-Ray Films

I. [§16.1] Value as Evidence

II. ADMISSIBILITY

  A. [§16.2] By Agreement
  B. [§16.3] By Authentication
    1. Laying Foundation
      a. [§16.4] Identity of Patient; Date Film Taken
      b. [§16.5] Interpretation
      c. [§16.6] Nature and Validity of X-Ray Process
      d. [§16.7] Filmmaking Procedure
      e. [§16.8] Dependability of Equipment
    2. [§16.9] Choosing Authenticating Witness
      a. [§16.10] Doctor Who Made Films
      b. [§16.11] X-Ray Technician
      c. [§16.12] Doctor Who Ordered Films
    3. Authenticating Particular Films
      a. [§16.13] Normal Person
      b. [§16.14] Soft-Tissue Injuries
  C. [§16.15] As Aid to Testimony
  D. [§16.16] X-Ray Report
  E. [§16.17] Films in Hospital Records

III. Presenting to Jury

  A. [§16.18] Viewing Box
  B. [§16.19] Stereoscopic Films
  C. [§16.20] Positive Prints and Enlargements
  D. [§16.21] Cineradiography

IV [§16.22] Sending Films to Jury Room

I. [§16.1] VALUE AS EVIDENCE

Doctors perform X-ray examinations, or have them performed, when they suspect internal injury or abnormality. Radiation (the "X ray") is passed through a part of the patient's body to a film, which is exposed by the radiation as a photographic negative is exposed by light. X-ray films depict internal anatomy and conditions as white or gray shadows on the black film, with dense structures, such as bones, showing as whiter shadows than less dense structures, such as soft tissues. (Positive prints can be made from these negatives (see §16.22).) Other terms for X-ray films that lawyers may encounter include "radiographs," "roentgenograms," "skiagrams," "X-ray plates," and "X rays."

X-ray films are generally used in the courtroom as tangible exhibits to support a doctor's testimony, or to permit a medical witness to testify more clearly and understandably. They refresh the witness's memory and give him something to look at and point to as he conveys medical information.

Some films show internal conditions that are clear even to judges and jurors. These include obvious bone fractures or misalignments, metal plates and surgical nails in place, protruding discs and other defects outlined by radiopaque dyes, and certain foreign objects in the body. Sometimes jurors can recognize abnormalities depicted in the plaintiff's X-ray films if they can also see comparison films that show the same structures in a normal person. See §16.13. X-ray films of the plaintiff made over a period of time can also show healing.

Many X-ray films used by medical witnesses to illustrate testimony are received in evidence but not shown to the jury. Laymen have difficulty seeing even obvious abnormalities in X-ray films, and if they are shown the films, there is always the danger that they might misinterpret them and arrive at conclusions contrary to the credible medical testimony.

II. ADMISSIBILITY

A. [§16.2] *By Agreement*

X-ray films are not admitted into evidence by stipulation as readily as photographs. See §15.2. The lawyer who wants to introduce X-ray films must usually call a medical witness to interpret them to the trier of fact anyway (see §16.5), and the same witness can usually supply authenticating testimony (see §§16.4–16.8). Adverse attorneys are wary about agreeing to the admission of X-ray films since they themselves cannot easily identify what and whom they show. Thus,

X-RAY FILMS §16.3

the reasons for agreeing to the admission of photographs (see §15.3) are often outweighed by other considerations when X-ray films are involved.

A lawyer who wants to obtain agreement to the admission of X-ray films by means of a written stipulation (see §8.21 for a form) is faced with the problem of how to let the other attorneys see the films they are being asked to agree on. Prints or duplicates that might be circulated with the stipulation form are not commonly made from X-ray films; although it can be done (see §16.20), doctors prefer to analyze originals. Lawyers are understandably reluctant to let originals out of their doctors' custody, and adverse attorneys are equally reluctant to stipulate to the admission of films until their own doctors have had a chance to study the originals.

If a pretrial conference is held, agreement to the admission of designated X-ray films can sometimes be obtained and incorporated into the pretrial order. The conference provides an opportunity for all the attorneys to see the films while the proponent retains control of them. The films can be made a part of the court record at that time, or they can be marked so that adverse attorneys are assured that the films offered at trial are the same as those they agreed to if the proponent wishes to retain them for his medical witnesses to study before trial. Each film or set of films agreed on should be designated in the pretrial order (see §8.23 for form) with a description such as:

1. One X-ray film showing .... 's right shoulder, taken on ...., 19......, and marked plaintiff's exhibit ....

An attorney might agree to admission of an X-ray film into evidence for use by medical experts but not be willing to agree in advance that the film can be viewed by jurors. Although viewing by jurors is a matter within the court's discretion, the following clause might be inserted in the written stipulation or pretrial order:

This agreement permits the use of these X-ray films by witnesses for all parties, but not the passing or other display of the films to the jury.

At trial, adverse lawyers who are satisfied that films accurately represent the plaintiff may offer to stipulate to their admission without authenticating testimony. See §8.24. The proponent may decline the offer if he believes that authenticating testimony will add to the weight given the exhibits or the testimony derived from them.

B. [§16.3] *By Authentication*

An X-ray film, like a photograph, is a writing. See Evid C §250.

Unless adverse parties waive the objection, a writing must be authenticated before it can be received in evidence. Evid C §1401. See generally §8.11.

Unlike a photograph, an X-ray film usually cannot be authenticated merely by a witness testifying that it is a "correct" or "fair and accurate" representation of what it purports to depict. X-ray films portray the inside of the body, which no one has seen unless surgery was performed.

The fairness and accuracy of the depiction in an X-ray film depend on (1) the validity, reliability, and trustworthiness of the X-ray process; (2) the dependability of the equipment used to make the particular film; (3) the procedure by which the film was made and developed; and (4) the skill, training, and experience of the person who operated the equipment to make the film. See Anno, 5 ALR3d 303, 307 (1966); Comment, *Photographic Evidence—Is There a Recognized Basis for Admissibility,* 8 HASTINGS LJ 310, 312 (1957). These indications of the correctness of what is depicted are rarely questioned, however, and there is usually little, if any, testimony given on them. See §§16.6–16.8. Authenticating testimony more often concentrates on identifying the person and body area shown and the date the film was taken (see §16.4) and on interpreting what pathology, if any, is shown (see §16.5).

The relevance of some X-ray films offered in evidence can be challenged by objection, especially if they depict a person other than the plaintiff or were made before or long after the accident. X-ray films are not necessarily irrelevant, however, because they are taken several years after the injury. *Wilburn v U.S. Gypsum Co.* (1936) 16 CA2d 111, 60 P2d 188. Judges rarely exclude X-ray films as inflammatory or prejudicial. Compare §15.14 (inflammatory photographs). A judge is more likely to exclude X-ray films, or at least to keep them from being passed or displayed to jurors, on the ground that their probative value is outweighed by the danger of confusing or misleading the jury (Evid C §352).

1. Laying Foundation

   a. [§16.4] Identity of Patient; Date Film Taken

Of prime importance in authenticating an X-ray film is identifying the person it depicts and the time it was made. The doctor, nurse, or technician who conducted the X-ray examination or made the film can testify when the film was made and of whom. This witness can also trace the custody of the film from the time it was made to the courtroom. A doctor who had his patient X-rayed by someone else

X-RAY FILMS §16.5

can usually testify to circumstances that show with reasonable certainty that the film depicts his patient at a particular time.

Markings on the film itself may also be sufficient evidence of the subject's name and of the date the film was taken. See *Kimball v Northern Elec. Co.* (1911) 159 C 225, 230, 113 P 156, 159. The usual practice in making X rays is to place a name plate against the X-ray film when it is being made, thereby eliminating the danger of a mixup.

b. [§16.5] Interpretation

X-ray films are not usually admitted in evidence unless an expert medical witness interprets and explains them. This is because a trier of fact cannot be expected to understand what is shown in the films without expert assistance. Interpretation is usually viewed as a requirement for admission that is separate from authentication, although a doctor's identification of the body area shown in a film is part of a showing that the film is what it is claimed to be.

Usually, any licensed physician is considered qualified to interpret an X-ray film, although in extreme cases a radiologist may be necessary. See *Lamb v Moore* (1960) 178 CA2d 819, 824, 3 CR 507, 511. The relative weight given to a physician's or radiologist's interpretation is a question for the jury. *Sim v Weeks* (1935) 7 CA2d 28, 36, 45 P2d 350, 354.

X-ray technicians and nurses are generally not qualified to interpret films even though they can authenticate them. See *Lamb v Moore, supra.* Dentists, osteopaths, and chiropractors are generally qualified to interpret X-ray films related to their fields of knowledge.

In eliciting testimony interpreting an X-ray film, the lawyer should make certain that the doctor expresses what he sees in the films in terms that can be understood by the trier of fact. For example:

Q. Have you previously had an opportunity to study these films?
A. Yes. [I read them in my office on ...., 19......, and I reviewed them again this morning.]
Q. What area of the body is pictured in these films?
A. ....
Q. And in what direction are we looking when we look at these films?
A. These are [antero-posterior] views.
Q. And that means we are looking from the [front straight toward the back] of the patient, is that correct?
A. Yes.
Q. Does this film show a normal [shoulder joint]?
A. [No. There is a fracture line here through the cap of the humerus.]

Comment: The lawyer would continue to elicit testimony about the injury or condition shown in the film.

c. [§16.6] Nature and Validity of X-Ray Process

While the relevancy and accuracy of what is pictured in an X-ray film depend on the validity of the X-ray process, *i.e.*, its reliability and trustworthiness to portray internal anatomy, there is usually no need for an authenticating witness to testify about validity. Courts have taken judicial notice of this scientific advancement. *Reynolds v Struble* (1933) 128 CA 716, 725, 18 P2d 690, 694.

An attorney who wants his witness to say a few words about the validity of the X-ray process might bring out testimony that X-ray examination is a common diagnostic procedure; doctors generally rely on X-ray films in making diagnoses and prescribing treatment; followup surgery usually confirms what was shown in the X-ray films; and while some films may be badly made or ambiguous in what they show, there is no real doubt in the medical profession about the reliability and trustworthiness of the X-ray process.

d. [§16.7] Filmmaking Procedure

A statement by the authenticating witness about the procedure followed in making the particular X-ray films rarely does much to authenticate them. Judges and jurors assume that a proper, or standard, procedure was followed unless there is a dispute over what the films show and an attorney opposing admission inquires into the procedure.

A plaintiff's attorney can ask the witness to describe the procedure when he wants to show any discomfort or danger to which his client was subjected by being examined.

e. [§16.8] Dependability of Equipment

Testimony about the dependability of the equipment used to make X-ray films is rarely introduced. Judges and jurors assume that dependable equipment was used unless an adverse party claims that some shadow in a film was a defect produced by the equipment rather than a representation of the patient's anatomy or condition. When testimony about the equipment is elicited, the witness usually states that it is standard equipment for the use to which it was put, appeared to work properly, was periodically inspected and serviced, and so forth. The fact that the film looked to a doctor like a properly made film, or showed what he expected it to show, is also evidence that the equipment was working properly.

X-RAY FILMS §16.10

2. [§16.9] Choosing Authenticating Witness

A lawyer who wants to lay a foundation for admission of X-ray films in evidence should first decide whom to use as an authenticating witness. Since X-ray films are almost invariably interpreted and explained to the trier of fact by a doctor (see §16.5), it is usually convenient to have the same doctor supply authenticating testimony.

Treating and examining physicians are most frequently called on to authenticate and interpret X-ray films. A doctor's general qualifications to testify as a medical expert are usually sufficient to enable him to testify about X-ray examinations and to authenticate and interpret films. A medical witness's qualifications are usually brought out when he takes the stand. Any special experience or training in X-ray examination and interpretation can be elicited when the films are discussed.

Radiologists to whom patients are sent by treating and examining doctors for X-ray examinations and film preparation are generally not called to testify about X-ray films unless some matter of authentication or interpretation of the films is in dispute and the case is important enough to warrant the expense of an additional expert witness. If called, their qualifications are elicited in the same way as those of other medical specialists. See §§6.5–6.26.

X-ray technicians and nurses can also authenticate films they have taken, but they cannot interpret them. See §16.16. Therefore, technicians and nurses generally are not called as witnesses unless (a) there is some dispute about the identity of the person shown, the date the film was taken, or the X-ray procedure, technique, or equipment; or (b) the lawyer feels that the technician's or nurse's testimony would add to the weight of the exhibit.

a. [§16.10] Doctor Who Made Films

A physician who has taken the X-ray films himself is qualified to authenticate them. See Anno, 5 ALR3d 303, 341 (1966). He need not be a specialist in X-ray matters, *i.e.*, a roentgenologist or radiologist. Ordinarily, the foundational questions can be kept to a minimum when the physician who took the films is on the stand and has been qualified as a doctor of medicine. For example:

Q. Doctor, have you examined [Mr. ..../the plaintiff] in this case?
A. Yes, in my office on ...., 19.......
Q. Did you take any X-ray films of him?
A. Yes, I took three films of his [back].

Q. I show you three films [marked exhibits ...... through ...... for identification]. Can you identify them?
A. Yes, these are the three I took.

Comment: If opposing counsel wishes more proof of identity, the doctor can testify regarding the markings on the films. For example:

Q. How do you know they are of Mr. ....?
A. The markings on the films bear his name and the date on which I took them.

Comment: At this point the lawyer can formally offer the films in evidence (see §8.14), and when they have been received and marked in evidence (see §8.15), the doctor can interpret them. See §16.5.

b. [§16.11] X-Ray Technician

An X-ray technician can authenticate the X-ray films he has taken at the request of a doctor. See Anno, 5 ALR3d 303, 342 (1966). He might be examined as follows:

Q. What is your occupation?
A. X-ray technician.
Q. Where do you work?
A. In the X-ray department at .... Hospital.
Q. What has been your training and experience as an X-ray technician?
A. ....
Q. Did you take X-ray films of [Mr. ..../the plaintiff]?
A. Yes.
Q. Why did you take them?
A. Dr. .... asked me to do so.
Q. When did you take them?
A. On ...., 19.......
Q. Where did you take them?
A. At .... Hospital.
Q. I show you two X-ray films [marked exhibits ...... and ......]. Can you identify them?
A. Yes, they are the films I made of Mr. .... on that date.
Q. How do you know they are of Mr. ....?
A. They have the markings I put on them, giving the subject's name and the date they were taken.

Comment: The lawyer could offer the films in evidence at this point (see §§8.14–8.15) or wait until a doctor is on the stand to interpret them.

c. [§16.12] Doctor Who Ordered Films

A doctor who orders an X-ray examination performed by another doctor or an X-ray specialist may authenticate the films. See *Simpson v Steinhoff* (1933) 131 CA 660, 663, 21 P2d 960, 961; Anno, 5 ALR3d 303, 344 (1966). The same rule applies to dentists, osteopaths, and chiropractors. The foundational facts must show the doctor's connection with the films. For example:

Q. When did you examine [Mr. ..../the plaintiff]?
A. On ...., 19.......
Q. Did you have an X-ray examination made of him?
A. Yes. I sent him to .... Hospital for X-ray films to be made of [describe part of body] on ...., 19.......
Q. Were films made as directed by you?
A. Yes.
Q. Did you see them?
A. Yes. On ...., 19......, I saw the films at the hospital.
Q. Who had taken them?
A. ...., an X-ray technician at the hospital.
Q. I show you two X-ray films [marked exhibits ...... and ...... for identification]. Can you identify them?
A. Yes, they are the films I saw.

Comment: The lawyer can offer the films in evidence at this point (see §§8.14–8.15) or wait until the doctor has interpreted them (see §16.5).

3. Authenticating Particular Films

a. [§16.13] Normal Person

A party seeking to show an injured person's abnormality by using X-ray films may offer in evidence films of a normal person for illustration and comparison. *Bruce v Western Pipe & Steel Co.* (1917) 177 C 25, 27, 169 P 660, 661; *DeMartini v McDonnell* (1936) 14 CA2d 405; 58 P2d 170. After the films of the plaintiff have been introduced in evidence, films of the normal person may be offered as follows:

Q. Doctor, you have testified that the X-ray films taken of [Mr. ..../the plaintiff] show a [recently healed fracture of the pelvis with a considerable defect now present in that bone]. How does [Mr. ....'s/plaintiff's] injured [pelvis] differ now from that of a normal [pelvis]?
A. Perhaps the clearest way to demonstrate the difference is to show you an X ray of the normal [pelvis bone] of a person of the

§16.14 X-RAY FILMS

same sex and approximate size and age as [Mr. ..../the plaintiff].

Q. Do you have such a film here?

A. Yes, I have a film of another patient, also a [man], about the same size, weight, and age as [Mr. ..../the plaintiff].

Q. How does that film of a normal [pelvis] compare to [Mr. ....'s/ plaintiff's]?

A. Here you will see that the normal [pelvis], unlike [Mr. ....'s/ plaintiff's], is [describe differences].

b. [§16.14] Soft-Tissue Injuries

In cases of injuries to soft tissue, which do not show on X-ray films, defense counsel may emphasize that the films show no injuries. The jury might be pursuaded that the injuries are not serious. To offset this possibility, counsel for the plaintiff should have his medical witness (or even a defense doctor on cross-examination) use various colored grease pencils to draw the nerves, muscles, and ligaments on the films during his testimony. He can then demonstrate to the jury by use of the films that there has been an injury to those tissues. For example:

Q. Doctor, please take the X-ray films to the viewing box and use them to help describe the injury for the jury.

A. All right. This is the first X-ray we took of the cervical spine or neck.

Q. From what position was it taken?

A. It is a lateral or side view.

Q. Would you write on it "side view" with the colored crayon so that the jury can see what we are looking at? Now, Doctor, you testified earlier that there was a herniated disc between the fourth and fifth cervical vertebrae. Is that correct?

A. Yes, that is correct.

Q. Doctor, do those vertebrae show on this X-ray film?

A. Yes, they do.

Q. Please take the blue crayon and outline them for us and label them C4 and C5.

A. All right. They are these two bones, these two vertebrae right here. [Doctor draws edges on film or overlay.]

Q. Now would you take the red crayon and mark the area where the disc would appear?

A. Yes. It is this area between the vertebrae. It would be like a rubber tire lying on its side separating the vertebrae. [Doctor draws on film or overlay.]

X-RAY FILMS §16.16

Q. Is there any particular significance in the appearance of the vertebrae at the level of C4 and C5 and the area that you have drawn?
A. Yes, there is.
Q. Could you explain that to us?
A. Yes. If you will look closely at the film, you will notice that the space that I have drawn in red where the disc is between C4 and C5 is narrower than at the other levels of the spine. For instance, the space between what we'll call C3 and C4 is wider. [Doctor illustrates.]
Q. What is the significance of the narrowing of this disc space?
A. It shows that the disc separating the two vertebrae, has decreased in size like a tire with the air let out of it. While it is not completely diagnostic, it leads me to believe that there is trouble in this area.

Comment: Each film that the doctor feels is diagnostic is gone through in order and on each one the doctor draws the bony tissue, the disc, the nerves emanating from the spinal cord, and the impingement on the nerve root caused by the disc herniation.

C. [§16.15] As Aid to Testimony

If admission of an X-ray film is disputed, it may help to have the authenticating doctor also testify that the film will aid him in formulating and illustrating his testimony and in testifying more clearly, fully, and accurately. The doctor's statements may forestall a judge's inclination to exclude the X-ray film on the ground that its probative value is outweighed by the danger of undue prejudice, consumption of time, or misleading jurors (Evid C §352). Further, the judge might permit the doctor to look at, testify from, and point to the film as an aid to testifying, even though he otherwise excludes the film from admission. See §8.34.

D. [§16.16] X-Ray Report

When a doctor refers his patient to a radiologist or other doctor for an X-ray examination, the referring doctor often receives not only films of his patient, but also a report from the other doctor that describes the procedure and interprets the films. An attorney who wants to offer one of these X-ray reports in evidence must be prepared to meet objections that it is hearsay, not the best evidence, and not authenticated.

If the patient's condition, or what the films show, is in dispute, it may be worthwhile to ask the doctor who made the report to testify about the filmmaking procedure and his interpretation of the films.

The witness can use the report to refresh his memory, or as past recollection recorded. If it does not seem worthwhile to call the doctor who made the report, the lawyer might seek the agreement of other counsel to admission of the report in lieu of that doctor's testimony.

A medical witness who has based an opinion, in part, on a report received from another doctor can testify about that report, and perhaps even read its contents into evidence — not as independent proof, but for the limited purpose of showing the basis for his own opinion. See Evid C §§801(b), 802; *Kelley v Bailey* (1961) 189 CA2d 728, 737, 11 CR 448, 454. See also §§6.56–6.63.

An X-ray report can often be received in evidence as part of a hospital record or a business record of the clinic or doctor's office in which it was prepared (see §13.39).

E. [§16.17] Films in Hospital Records

A patient admitted to a hospital is often sent to the hospital's radiology department for X-ray examination. The treating physician orders particular films, the radiology department conducts the X-ray procedures, and often the radiologist prepares a report interpreting the films. These films and reports are made part of the patient's hospital record, although the films themselves are often filed separately from the rest of the report, and can be received in evidence on the same basis as hospital records generally. See §13.39.

Frequently X-ray films are presented in court as part of subpenaed hospital or doctor's office records. If the parties do not stipulate that the films may be admitted in evidence, the doctor who ordered them taken or the person taking them may have to be brought in to make the authentication. The opposing party, however, does not ordinarily raise an objection to the subpenaed films' authenticity. The proponent generally puts a doctor on the stand to identify the films by means of the markings and then to interpret them.

Q. I show you two X-ray films in the records of [............... Hospital/clinic/doctor's office], [marked exhibits ...... and ...... for identification]. What do the markings show?
A. The markings show that these films were taken of the plaintiff on ...., 19........
Q. Have you examined the [hospital's/clinic's/doctor's] records?
A. Yes.
Q. Do they indicate who ordered the films?
A. Yes, Dr. ....
Q. Do they show who took them?
A. Yes, ..., an X-ray technician.

Q. What do the films show?
A. This film, marked exhibit ...... shows a [describe nature of injury].

III. PRESENTING TO JURY

A. [§16.18] *Viewing Box*

Many courtrooms have a viewing box for the presentation of X-ray films. While some boxes are fixed in position near the witness stand, which limits their visibility to some jurors, newer courtrooms have portable boxes to permit maximum visibility. Counsel having films to present should ascertain in advance the availability of a viewing box, and if none is provided, his medical witness can probably obtain one.

B. [§16.19] *Stereoscopic Films*

Ordinary X-ray films have only height and width so that they present a flat view of the subject. Stereoscopic X-ray films provide depth by taking two film views of the subject from slightly different angles. The viewer then gets a three-dimensional effect of seeing a solid object rather than a flat surface. This process is especially useful to show a fracture of the skull or pelvis, conditions in the chest or spinal column, and objects lodged in body joints. A special viewing machine must be used for stereoscopic viewing in the courtroom. See 44 MICH L REV 773, 783 (1946).

To lay a proper foundation for introduction of the films in evidence, counsel must bring out their stereoscopic nature.

Q. I show you an X-ray film marked exhibit ...... for identification. Did you take this film of the plaintiff on ...., 19......?
A. Yes, at .... Hospital.
Q. Is it an ordinary X-ray film?
A. No, it is stereoscopic.
Q. What is a stereoscopic X-ray film?
A. It is a film that shows depth as well as height and width.
Q. How is it made?
A. ....
Q. How is the stereoscopic film viewed?
A. ....

C. [§16.20] *Positive Prints and Enlargements*

If a lawyer anticipates that jurors may have difficulty following a doctor's interpretation of X-ray films, he should consider having positive prints made from the film. Positive prints can show bones and dense structures as black and grey shadows against a white background. During medical testimony a set of prints may be passed from juror to juror, prints may be made for each juror, or enlargements may be made for all to view simultaneously.

Some lawyers are critical of X-ray prints because they do not pick up many fine points shown on the X-ray films and because the printing process may distort what is on the films. However, prints do present some abnormalities more clearly than films, and counsel should discuss with his medical witness the usefulness of prints in the particular case.

To lay a proper foundation for introduction of prints, the X-ray film must first be authenticated (see §§16.3–16.8). The medical witness should then be asked about the positive print made of the film.

Q. Did you order a positive print of this X-ray film?
A. Yes.
Q. I show you this photograph [marked exhibit .... for identification]. Is it a print of the X-ray film that is exhibit ......?
A. Yes.
Q. Is it a correct representation of the film?
A. Yes.

Comment: If enlargements have been made of positive prints, the lawyer should determine if they correctly represent the X-ray films (*Sim v Weeks* (1935) 7 CA2d 28, 40, 45 P2d 350, 356). See also §15.18.

Q. Is this positive print a contact print or an enlargement of the X-ray film?
A. An enlargement.
Q. What is an enlargement?
A. It is a print larger than the negative from which it was made.
Q. Does this enlarged print correctly show the film?
A. Yes, it does.
Q. Does the fact that it is an enlargement distort or alter the film in any way?
A. No.
Proponent. Your Honor, I offer these prints in evidence as [plaintiff's/defendant's] exhibits ...... through ....

Comment: If the enlargement does distort or alter the film, the medical witness should point out and explain the distortion or alteration and demonstrate how to view the enlarged print without being misled.

This procedure will help to obtain a favorable ruling on admissibility of the print if opposing counsel later asserts that the print is misleading.

D. [§16.21] *Cineradiography*

Motion pictures can be taken of X-ray images shown on a fluoroscope. They are useful in the detection of defects by injecting radiopaque dyes, and, in cases involving injuries to moving parts of the body, such as joints, they show the effects of the injuries on function. It is necessary to lay the foundation for the motion pictures. See chap 17.

IV. [§16.22] SENDING FILMS TO JURY ROOM

The jury may take X-ray films into the jury room for viewing if the trial judge allows it (CCP §612), and no instruction is needed to limit their use to illustrative evidence only (see *Sinz v Owens* (1949) 33 C2d 749, 759, 205 P2d 3, 9). Many judges believe that the jury should be restricted to the testimony of the experts regarding the films and will not permit the jury to take the films into the jury room for viewing because they may be unable to read them properly. See CALIFORNIA CIVIL PROCEDURE DURING TRIAL §§12.30–12.33 (Cal CEB 1960). Since there is a good possibility that the jury may be misled in viewing X-ray films without the help of expert testimony, lawyers might be well-advised not to request that films be sent to the jury room during deliberations. See generally §8.19.

17

Motion Pictures

I. **Value as Evidence**

    A. [§17.1] Visual Impact
    B. [§17.2] Common Uses

II. **[§17.3] Dangers**

III. **[§17.4] Admissibility**

    A. [§17.5] Relevance
    B. [§17.6] Authentication
        1. [§17.7] Qualifying Authenticating Witness
            a. [§17.8] Professional Cinematographer
            b. [§17.9] Amateur Cinematographer
        2. [§17.10] Equipment and Lighting
        3. [§17.11] Developing and Printing
        4. [§17.12] Editing
        5. [§17.13] Custody
        6. [§17.14] Projection
        7. [§17.15] Accuracy
    C. [§17.16] Challenging Authentication

IV. **Particular Motion Pictures**

    A. [§17.17] Surveillance
        1. [§17.18] Authentication
        2. [§17.19] Cross-Examination
        3. [§17.20] Setting up Plaintiff
        4. [§17.21] Rehabilitation
    B. [§17.22] Reenactment of Event
    C. [§17.23] Experiments
    D. [§17.24] Normal Activity Before Injury
    E. [§17.25] Activity After Injury

V. Presenting to Jury

A. [§17.26] Equipment and Facilities In Courtroom
B. [§17.27] Strategy

VI. [§17.28] Sending Films to Jury Room

I. VALUE AS EVIDENCE

A. [§17.1] Visual Impact

Motion pictures, if used sparingly, can add a sense of reality, clarity, and drama to the evidence that contrasts favorably with the tedium of testimony, resulting in a greater impact on the jury. Not subject to faulty observation, fading memory, or failing words, they often are more accurate than eyewitness testimony and can give a different focus and an expanded scope to the events portrayed to the jury.

B. [§17.2] Common Uses

Assuming they are not edited, motion pictures show events as they occurred. Normally, the crucial issues of causality are not filmed "live." Thus, motion pictures are most often used to impeach a plaintiff's claim of physical disability (see §§17.17–17.20) and in other situations where planning is possible. For example, motion pictures can show experiments filmed before trial, thus avoiding the pitfalls of a live performance in the courtroom. See §17.23. They can portray a reconstructed accident scene that helps the jury to visualize the actual event accurately in context (see §17.22), and they can show the difficulties experienced by a severely injured plaintiff in performing normal activities.

II. [§17.3] DANGERS

The dramatic effect of motion pictures in the courtroom and their powerful impact on juries have led some courts to adopt a cautious attitude toward their admission in evidence. Jurors can be persuaded to give them more weight than they deserve, and they can overreact, particularly to films of plaintiff's activities, on the issue of extent of disability. Courts are concerned that motion pictures may have a misleading effect, and have pointed to use of telescopic lenses, ingenious stage settings, skillful editing and direction, special camera

MOTION PICTURES §17.5

angles, speeded up reproduction, and selective filming of activities as means by which deception can take place. *Harmon v San Joaquin Light & Power Corp.* (1940) 37 CA2d 169, 174, 98 P2d 1064, 1067; Witkin, CALIFORNIA EVIDENCE §§639–640 (2d ed, 1966).

III. [§17.4] ADMISSIBILITY

Motion pictures are admissible in evidence (*Heiman v Market St. Ry.* (1937) 21 CA2d 311, 315, 69 P2d 178, 180) on a showing of relevance and authentication. They do not violate the hearsay or best evidence rules. See Anno, 62 ALR2d 686, 689 (1958).

The admission of motion pictures can sometimes be obtained by consent through a pretrial order or stipulation. See generally §§8.20–8.24. However, an agreement is not usually sought before trial because of the surprise element and special value of pictures—particularly the frequently used surveillance movies.

The trial court has discretionary power to admit or reject motion pictures (Evid C §352; *Deward v Clough* (1966) 245 CA2d 439, 449, 54 CR 68, 75), and they should be received with caution (*Harmon v San Joaquin Light & Power Corp.* (1940) 37 CA2d 169, 174, 98 P2d 1064, 1067). The admonition of caution, however, is not always observed. See *Greeneich v Southern Pac. Co.* (1961) 189 CA2d 100, 107, 11 CR 235, 239, in which the court upheld, two to one, the admission of sound motion pictures showing a train approaching and crossing an intersection in the daytime with its whistle blowing when the issue was whether the decedent could hear the train when the accident occurred at an unlighted intersection on a foggy night. (For criticism of this case, see Comment, 47 IOWA L REV 1138 (1962).)

A. [§17.5] *Relevance*

Motion pictures, like other evidence, must be relevant to be admissible (Evid C §350), *i.e.,* they must tend to prove or disprove a fact in dispute (Evid C §210). See CALIFORNIA TRIAL OBJECTIONS §§17.1–17.2 (Cal CEB 1967). Relevance is seldom an issue since motion pictures are offered to prove or disprove facts clearly in issue, *e.g.,* pictures taken at the time of the accident showing the actual occurrence or after the accident but showing the scene as it existed at the time of the accident, pictures of plaintiff's activities tending either to confirm or deny his claim of disability, and pictures taken of the reconstructed accident scene.

B. [§17.6] *Authentication*

Motion pictures, like photographs and X-ray films, are writings (see Evid C §250; §15.5) and therefore must be authenticated (Evid C §1400) to be received in evidence (Evid C §1401(a)).

Authentication is established when a witness who has personal knowledge of the scenes depicted in the motion pictures testifies that they are a true representation of those scenes. See Evid C §1400; *Heiman v Market St. Ry.* (1937) 21 CA2d 311, 315, 69 P2d 178, 180; Witkin, CALIFORNIA EVIDENCE §639 (2d ed, 1966).

While moving pictures have been likened to photographs in that they are a series of single pictures (*Heiman v Market St. Ry., supra*), they generally require additional authentication because of the greater possibility of falsification (*Harmon v San Joaquin Light & Power Corp.* (1940) 37 CA2d 169, 174, 98 P2d 1064, 1067; Witkin, EVIDENCE §639). The proponent of films should be prepared to present evidence on (1) the conditions surrounding the taking of the pictures; (2) the qualifications of the camera operator; (3) the type of camera, film, lens, and lighting used; (4) the developing and printing of the films; (5) any alterations, editing, splicing, etc.; (6) the custody of the film; (7) the speed of projection compared to camera speed; (8) the distance from projector to screen; and (9) the accuracy of the films. For foundational dialogues, see §§17.7–17.15 and CALIFORNIA CIVIL PROCEDURE DURING TRIAL §12.20 (Cal CEB 1960).

Motion pictures are usually shown first to the trial judge and opposing counsel out of the presence of the jury. Authenticating testimony can also be heard in chambers if opposing counsel objects to admission of the film. See Evid C §402.

1. [§17.7] Qualifying Authenticating Witness

The person who took the pictures is often called as the authenticating witness because of the courts' cautious attitude toward receiving motion pictures in evidence. Others can testify that the pictures truly represent the events they saw, but only the cameraman can give testimony on the technical facts of the filmmaking, which are crucial to the court's acceptance or rejection of the films. Further, the jurors are likely to give greater weight to pictures authenticated by the person taking them, and the adverse party will be limited accordingly in attacking the validity and credibility of the films.

Before showing the pictures to the jury, the proponent should put the cinematographer on the stand to make the authentication, beginning with his qualifications and experience. Amateur cinematog-

MOTION PICTURES §17.9

raphers can be qualified, but it is better to have an expert take and authenticate the pictures.

a. [§17.8] Professional Cinematographer

The following dialogue shows how a professional cinematographer might be qualified:

Q. What is your occupation?
A. I am a professional [photographer/cinematographer].
Q. How long have you been in that business?
A. ...... years.
Q. Where do you work?
A. [I have my own studio at ....]
Q. Do you take motion pictures as part of your business?
A. Yes.
Q. What training have you had in taking motion pictures?
A. [I have taken courses in filmmaking at .... School and received on-the-job training as an assistant with ....]
Q. What experience have you had in taking motion pictures?
A. [I have been making films since 19....... I have taken, developed, printed, and edited thousands of feet of film, and have put together more than ...... films.]
Q. Did you take motion pictures of the intersection at .... and .... Streets in this city on ...., 19......?
A. Yes.
Q. How many feet of film did you take?
A. I took [a total of 400 feet, 250 on the afternoon of ...., 19......, and 150 the next morning].

Comment: For detailed testimony describing varying circumstances in which particular types of pictures were taken, see §§17.18, 17.25.

Q. Did you bring those pictures with you to court today?
A. Yes.
Q. Are these all the pictures you took on those days?
A. Yes.

Comment: The lawyer may have the film marked for identification and then proceed with evidence on the technical aspects of taking the films. See §§17.10–17.15.

b. [§17.9] Amateur Cinematographer

Sometimes films taken by an amateur cinematographer are the only ones available or the value of the case does not warrant the expense of having an expert take additional films. The qualifying testimony should show whatever qualifications the amateur has, including years and variety of experience, courses taken in photography, and the photography publications he reads. For example:

Q. Have you had any training in photography or filmmaking?
A. Yes. [I took a course in photography at .... that included filmmaking.]
Q. How long have you been taking motion pictures?
A. ...... years.
Q. Do you know how many feet of film you have taken in that time?
A. Yes. More than ....
Q. What types of motion pictures have you taken?
A. [Many different types. I frequently make films of athletic events, public gatherings, and so on.]
Q. Do you read any publications on photography and taking motion pictures?
A. Yes. [I subscribe to and read .... and ....]

Comment: Since some "amateurs" have extensive skill, equipment, and experience, they can be questioned further about doing their own darkroom work, any prizes in photography contests, etc.

    2. [§17.10] Equipment and Lighting

The cinematographer can next be questioned regarding the equipment used in taking the moving pictures, including the type of camera, settings, speed, lenses, and film. For example:

Q. What type of camera did you use to take the pictures?
A. It was a ...., [8/16] millimeter motion picture camera.
Q. Had you used that particular camera before?
A. Yes. [I have had it for ...... years. It is an excellent camera for this kind of assignment.]
Q. What lenses did you use in taking the pictures?
A. A telescopic lens for closeups and a standard lens for everything else.
Q. What type of film did you use?
A. .... film. It's correct for that camera and the particular pictures taken.
Q. In taking the pictures, what camera speed did you use?
A. ...... frames per second except for slow motion pictures at ...... per second.

Comment: If the camera was locked and sealed at the proper speed

MOTION PICTURES §17.13

setting during the filming, that should be brought out in the direct examination.

When lighting is important, the following questions may be asked:

Q. What lens opening did you use?
A. ....
Q. Why?
A. I used a light meter to determine the light conditions, and it indicated the opening I selected.
Q. What was the weather like?
A. Cloudy, but bright.

3. [§17.11] Developing and Printing

Authenticating testimony should briefly cover the development and printing process used on the exposed films. Ordinarily, the cinematographer uses a film processing company rather than doing it himself.

Q. Who developed the film?
A. I sent it to .... Company, which does the developing and printing of all my films, and they returned it to me a short time later.

4. [§17.12] Editing

The proponent should usually avoid having any alterations made of the film, including editing or splicing, to prevent any loss of confidence on the part of the jury in the film's reliability. Any changes should be fully explained. For example:

Q. Has there been any editing, splicing, or alteration of any kind made in this film?
A. ....
(If the answer is yes, continue)
Q. What are those changes?
A. ....
Q. Why were they made?
A. ....

5. [§17.13] Custody

Counsel should show that, except for processing, the films were in the custody of the cinematographer from the time of exposure until they were brought to the courtroom to demonstrate that the films were not altered by anyone.

Q. Where were the films kept after being exposed?
A. [I kept them locked away in my desk until today except for developing and viewing.]

6. [§17.14] Projection

The cinematographer should name the type of projector being used and testify that he will show the films on the projector at the same rate of speed at which they were taken. For example:

Q. What projector are you going to use to show the films?
A. A .... It is a standard projector for the camera used.
Q. At what speed will you show the pictures?
A. I will show them at the normal speed, which is ...... frames per second. The pictures were taken at that speed.

7. [§17.15] Accuracy

The authenticity of motion pictures cannot be established until a witness testifies that the films are a true representation of the scenes depicted. Usually the cinematographer is the authenticating witness and can give the necessary testimony, since he personally observed the scenes he was filming.

Q. Have you viewed the film?
A. Yes.
Q. Is it a fair and accurate representation of what you were filming?
A. Yes.
Counsel. Your Honor, at this time we offer the film in evidence as [plaintiff's/defendant's] exhibit next in order and ask permission to show it to the jury.

Comment: The adverse party may ask to cross-examine the authenticating witness on foundation and to see the film before it is shown to the jury.

C. [§17.16] *Challenging Authentication*

Because of the overwhelming influence motion pictures can have on a jury, it is important to determine any misleading aspects and to search out any flaws in the making of the films. Even if the challenging party cannot prevent admission of the films in evidence, he can still raise doubts about the film's accuracy.

The cross-examiner should attempt to establish the cinematographer's lack of expertise in the use of the camera. Bias can be brought out by showing that he (1) took the pictures at the request of the opposition's lawyer; (2) was paid by that lawyer; (3) looked for pictures favorable to the party paying him; and (4) did, or would, avoid taking unfavorable pictures. Lack of proper care and maintenance of the camera might be shown and doubt cast on the speed of the camera at the time of shooting. Editing or splicing must be inquired into to search out any alterations and distortions. Where lighting is important, the type of lighting used in taking the pictures must be brought out. For example, in a personal injury action for damages from a fall on a poorly lighted stairway, pictures showing a well lighted stairway would be prejudicial and misleading. Gaps in custody of the films might be shown, leaving the jury with a suspicion that they were altered or distorted.

Surveillance films require close scrutiny of their preparation and content because of the possibility that unfair tactics were used. The party opposing their admission should make every effort to diminish the importance of the films in the jurors' minds. The authenticating witness should be questioned about circumstances surrounding the filmed events and whether the events were manipulated to entrap the person filmed. See §§17.17–17.21 on surveillance films.

IV. PARTICULAR MOTION PICTURES

A. [§17.17] Surveillance

Probably the most common use of motion pictures in personal injury work is surveillance of the injured plaintiff to show performance of activities in excess of what he admits he can do. Surveillance films are used not only to show the extent of disability but also to discredit the plaintiff. By use of interrogatories plaintiff's counsel may ascertain whether and by whom motion pictures have been taken. The cinematographer's deposition can then be taken, and the films may be seen if the witness used them to refresh his recollection before the deposition. See Evid C §771. See generally §1.39. If the interrogatories reveal that pictures were taken, but they are not shown at trial, plaintiff's lawyer can suggest in final argument that they must have been favorable to his client.

In a significant number of cases, the motion pictures are obtained only after the cinematographer has set up the activities the plaintiff unwittingly performs. He may flatten a tire on the plaintiff's car, arrange for heavy objects to be delivered to his doorstep or driveway, engage him to perform labor in exchange for payment, and so forth. After thus creating the situation, the cinematographer can surreptitiously take pictures from a previously selected and prepared vantage point.

1. [§17.18] Authentication

Authentication of surveillance pictures is substantially the same as for other motion pictures. See §§17.6–17.15. In addition, the authenticating witness should testify that plaintiff is the person in the film; state the dates, places, and times the films were taken; and describe the activities observed. For example:

Q. Did you take motion pictures of Mr. ...., the plaintiff in this case?
A. Yes.
Q. Do you see the subject of those pictures here in court now?
A. Yes.
Q. Will you kindly point him out to the jury?
A. [Witness points to the plaintiff.]
Proponent. Let the record show the witness has pointed to the plaintiff.
Q. At whose request did you take the pictures?
A. My employer, ..., requested that I take undercover surveillance motion pictures of the plaintiff.
Q. Did you receive any other instructions?
A. Yes, I was to get films representative of his physical activities.
Q. Did you get them?
A. Yes, I took 350 feet of film.
Q. On what dates, places, and times did you take the pictures?
A. On ...., 19......, at 7 a.m., I went to his house on .... Street and took 150 feet of film of his activities.
Q. What was he doing?
A. He was changing a flat tire on a car parked in front of his house.
Q. Did he have any help from anyone?
A. No. He did it all by himself.
Q. Describe his activities in changing the tire.
A. He performed all of the usual activities, including getting the spare tire out of the trunk; lifting it and carrying it to the side of the car; taking the flat tire off with a lug wrench; lifting the flat tire, carrying it around to the trunk, and placing it inside; and putting the spare on.
Q. Did he do any bending or stooping?
A. Yes. On several occasions he bent over to lift up a tire and also to get the spare tire out of the trunk and the flat tire into the trunk. He worked at the wheel in a stooped position for several minutes while using the lug wrench.
Q. Did you see any actions or expressions of pain by the plaintiff during or after the tire change?

MOTION PICTURES §17.19

A. No.
Q. Did he appear to you to be favoring his [back] at any time?
A. No. He did not.
Q. When was the next occasion for you to take pictures?
A. The next and last time was the following day at his place of work at ....
Q. What were his activities at that time?
A. He was in a junkyard handling various pieces of metal. Between the hours of 8 a.m. and 11 a.m., I took 200 feet of film of him unloading and loading several trucks. He handled auto fenders and bumpers.

2. [§17.19] Cross-Examination

Before the surveillance films are shown in the courtroom, plaintiff's attorney will have determined in the judge's chambers whether or not he can keep the pictures out. If he does not think that the films can be excluded, it is advisable to save his cross-examination of the authenticating witness until after the films are shown to the jury and use his "big guns" when they may be badly needed. It is at this point that the jury, having just viewed the movies, is inclined to be suspicious of the extent of plaintiff's claimed disability and possibly of the very integrity of the plaintiff. If some of the jurors overreacted, this is the time to restore the balance by raising doubts about the cinematographer's expertise, equipment, or bias; the quality and accuracy of the pictures; and the possibility of entrapment or other behavior that may cause resentment against the intrusion on the plaintiff's privacy. For example:

Q. You do not consider yourself to be an expert cinematographer, do you?
A. ....
Q. You have never attended any courses or otherwise had any exposure to expert training in the use of motion picture cameras, have you?
A. ....
Q. You testified that the camera speed was 16 frames per second during the taking of the pictures. How do you know that?
A. The speed setting was 16 frames per second.
Q. Did you check the setting before taking the pictures?
A. Yes.
Q. The setting can be altered by accident, can't it?

§17.19   MOTION PICTURES

A. Yes, but on that camera the setting of 16 frames per second is locked in place.
Q. It is possible for someone to undo the lock and change the setting, isn't it?
A. Yes.
Q. It is also possible for the lock to loosen and the setting to change accidentally, isn't it?
A. Yes.
Q. In that event, the pictures would be taken at an incorrect speed, wouldn't they?
A. Yes. [But they weren't in this case.]
Q. Your firm was hired to take pictures of the plaintiff for use in this case by the defendant, isn't that correct?
A. Yes.
Q. Then you wanted pictures that were as favorable to the defendant as possible, didn't you?
A. ....

Comment: The answers to this line of questioning may not be favorable, but the basic point will have been made to the jury.

Q. At the same time, you wouldn't want to take pictures favorable to the plaintiff, would you?
A. ....
Q. So you watched and waited for evidence favoring the people paying you, isn't that right?
A. ....
Q. Was this the only day your firm had plaintiff under surveillance?
A. ....
Q. How many hours did you watch his activities?
A. ....
Q. In all those hours of observing the plaintiff, you've got on film only [five minutes] of physical activities that you thought could help your client?
A. ....
Q. Are you familiar with the practice of tires being deliberately flattened in order that pictures can be taken?
A. ....
Q. You've done it yourself, haven't you?
A. ....

Comment: The answer is not likely to be in the affirmative, even though ruses are often used to obtain motion pictures of physical activities.

MOTION PICTURES §17.20

Q. Did you in any way flatten the tire yourself or cause it to become flat?
A. ....
Q. Did anyone you know do it?
A. ....

Comment: If the answer to either of the last two questions is yes, the cross-examiner can exploit the admission of the unlawful activity. In view of the unlikelihood of an admission, the lawyer may wish an investigation made of the tire to reveal evidence of tampering. Any suspicious activity reported by the plaintiff should be looked into.

Q. Are you aware that for the rest of the day the plaintiff was in considerable pain and couldn't go to work until the following day?
A. No.

Comment: The lawyer may also wish to bring out the cinematographer's unawareness of the plaintiff's having been under sedation for pain during the activities or the use of an artificial appliance, such as a back support, holding the back rigid to avoid pain.

3. [§17.20] Setting up Plaintiff

If the plaintiff's attorney has not learned of the motion pictures through discovery, the defense should attempt on cross-examination of plaintiff to elicit testimony flatly contradictory to the films before showing them to the jury. Without this preparation, the pictures will have less impact on the jury and may even aid the plaintiff if the jury is not convinced that he is a gross exaggerator or an outright liar. See 4 DEFENSE LJ 131, 137 (1958).

Without revealing that he has a film, the defense lawyer should ask the plaintiff specifically whether he can perform certain activities. After plaintiff has denied any ability to perform those activities, the motion pictures can be presented to best advantage, clearly revealing plaintiff as an untrustworthy witness. For example, the defense lawyer may have a film showing the plaintiff bowling on several occasions after the injury. He may have cause to believe plaintiff will deny bowling since he has denied it to the doctors and in his deposition. The cross-examination might proceed as follows:

Q. You used to bowl before you got hurt, didn't you?
A. I certainly did, and now I can't do it.
Q. Why can't you bowl since the injury?
A. My back hurts too much.
Q. Have you tried it?

A. Yes, on one occasion I tried it, and I had to stop because of the pain.
Q. Is it your testimony that you have tried to bowl only one time since the injury because it hurt too much?
A. Yes.

Comment: The pictures showing successive bowling episodes will be much more effective than if the questions had not been asked. Too close questioning may produce an accurate answer and reduce the effect of the film, but more likely the witness will continue to deny the activities.

It is advisable for the defense to have pictures of plaintiff's activities on successive days to avoid his claiming increased disability from the activities pictured on only one day. It is not uncommon for a plaintiff to claim that on the day following the activities shown in the film, his condition was so bad that bed rest was required.

4. [§17.21] Rehabilitation

After the films have been shown and the authenticating witness cross-examined, the plaintiff's lawyer must consider rehabilitating the plaintiff in the eyes of the jury. The plaintiff may be able to mitigate the pictures' effect by testifying to the infrequency with which he performs the pictured activities because of the pain it produces, how he has to treat himself after the activities (*e.g.,* use of pain pills and bed rest), how the work shown was not as difficult as it looked in the pictures, the number of rest periods (not photographed) he took during the work, that he was wearing a back support and was under sedation for pain at the time, or any entrapment by the cinematographer. See *Harmon v San Joaquin Light & Power Corp.* (1940) 37 CA2d 169, 174, 98 P2d 1064, 1067.

One of the most effective ways to rehabilitate the plaintiff is to have a doctor testify that the pictured activities are not inconsistent with the plaintiff's complaints or the doctor's own findings. To the inexpert viewer the pictures often appear to show considerable activity in excess of what the plaintiff admitted he could do. The medical witness can often discern whether plaintiff guarded himself in his movements to avoid extremes of motion that produce pain; lifted with his back straight; was wearing a brace, support, or other artificial appliance; or was otherwise restricted in ways that laymen might not observe.

MOTION PICTURES §17.23

B. [§17.22] *Reenactment of Event*

Motion pictures can be used for clarity or special effect in reenacting an event in issue. Courts are expecially cautious in their attitude toward these films, however, because of the inherent dangers of inaccuracy and misleading the jury. For examples of those dangers, see *Greeneich v Southern Pac. Co.* (1961) 189 CA2d 100, 11 CR 235; Wigmore, EVIDENCE §798 (2d ed, 1923). Special care must be taken to make the reenactment as nearly like the real event as possible to avoid a ruling against admission, particularly when actors are used rather than the actual parties involved.

Authenticating testimony is substantially the same as for a reconstructed scene in photographs. See §15.10. The authenticating witness is usually the person who observed the event and directed the reconstruction. His testimony should show that the reenactment and the actual event are substantially the same. The cinematographer can be brought in to authenticate the technical procedures of the filming. See §§17.6–17.15.

C. [§17.23] *Experiments*

Motion pictures of experiments made out of court are admissible in evidence if they are relevant and properly authenticated (*People v Freeman* (1951) 107 CA2d 44, 54, 236 P2d 396, 402), and the conditions of the experiment are substantially the same as those from which the dispute arose (*Andrews v Barker Bros.* (1968) 267 CA2d 530, 537, 73 CR 284, 289). They avoid the danger of performing an experiment that fails in the courtroom, since the experiment can be done out of court until it works as it should and then filmed for presentation in court. The film is shown first to the judge, who has considerable discretion to admit or exclude the evidence.

The experiment should be performed by an expert who must keep full records to have before him at trial. The expert and the cinematographer will be the authenticating witnesses unless the expert makes the film himself. For a detailed description of motion pictures of experiments, see Weinstein, *The Movie Is the Thing,* 2 Prac Law 68 (Feb. 1956).

The expert should first be questioned about his qualifications. Then, as part of his testimony in connection with the issues in dispute, he can authenticate the motion pictures and explain the experiment shown in the film.

§17.23 MOTION PICTURES

Q. Did you conduct an experiment in connection with the matters about which you have been testifying?
A. Yes.
Q. Did you take motion pictures of the experiment?
A. Yes.
Q. Did you bring the film with you today?
A. Yes.

Comment: At this point the lawyer can have the reels of film in metal containers marked for identification.

Q. Did you take the pictures?
A. Yes.
Q. When did you take them?
A. On ...., 19......, in my laboratory.
Q. Were you able to make the film and conduct the experiment at the same time?
A. Yes. First I set up the experiment. Then I focused the camera on the area where the experiment was to take place, started the camera, and walked over and conducted the experiment.

Comment: The witness should then authenticate the pictures including the type of camera, film, speed, accuracy, etc. See §§17.10–17.15.

Q. Please describe the experiment to be shown in the film.
A. It consists of ....
Q. Does the film fairly and accurately portray the experiment you conducted?
A. Yes.

Comment: The film can be offered in evidence at this point and if voir dire examination is not requested, the proponent can ask that the film be shown. The witness should be asked to describe what the film shows.

Q. As the film is shown, would you please describe what is happening in it?
A. ....

Comment: The proponent can let the witness proceed to narrate the action (see §1.9 on narrative answers), or he can ask specific questions as the film progresses. For example:

Q. What are we seeing now?
A. The materials and apparatus I set up to use in the experiment.
Q. Who is the person entering and going to the table?

MOTION PICTURES §17.26

A. That's me coming in to make the experiment.
Q. What are you doing with the materials?
A. I am ....

Comment: The description continues in question and answer form and can be concluded as follows:

Q. What is happening now?
A. The experiment is finished, and I am leaving the area to turn off the camera.

D. [§17.24] *Normal Activity Before Injury*

If motion pictures of the plaintiff's normal activity before the injury are available, the contrast between his limited ability after the accident and his prior healthy condition can be graphically presented. If plaintiff had a disability before the accident from a congenital condition or injury, defense counsel could use films taken before the accident to show little or no change following the accident.

E. [§17.25] *Activity After Injury*

The plaintiff's lawyer may have motion pictures made of the plaintiff's activities after injury to supplement testimony regarding the disability. *Lehmuth v Long Beach Unified School Dist.* (1960) 53 C2d 544, 555, 2 CR 279, 286 (films of plaintiff still in hospital four months after accident). The everyday problems of a person using a prosthetic device can be demonstrated better in a film than by his testimony. The jury is likely to be impressed by motion pictures of the plaintiff's activities in his home, on the street, and at work. Similarly, pictures taken of a plaintiff in the hospital with a tracheal tube for breathing, unconsciously flailing his arms and body, etc., will dramatize his condition. It is within the court's discretion to determine whether the pictures are inflammatory. *Lehmuth v Long Beach Unified School Dist., supra.*

V. PRESENTING TO JURY

A. [§17.26] *Equipment and Facilities in Courtroom*

To take full advantage of motion picture evidence, the lawyer must make every effort to ensure a smooth showing in court. Counsel should check to be sure that the courtroom can be equipped for projection.
  (1) Dark shades are necessary to control the lighting.
  (2) The layout must be suitable for setting up the projector and

screen; the screen should be placed so that the jury and judge may view the pictures without having to move.

(3) There must be an electrical outlet within range of the projector's location, or counsel should ask for or supply an extension cord.

In addition to checking the courtroom, counsel should make sure that the equipment is in good operating order and the projectionist is experienced in using it. The projectionist should make several "dry runs" of the screening before trial to avoid annoying adjustments and delays that can reduce the dramatic effect and lessen the weight of the evidence.

B. [§17.27] *Strategy*

Counsel should carefully choose the time to run the motion pictures, aiming for the most persuasive point in the trial. In the case of surveillance pictures, the defense ordinarily reserves them for the last to close its case with its strongest (or, at least, most dramatic) evidence. The jury is often left with a vivid impression of plaintiff's lack of disability and skepticism about his truthfulness.

The plaintiff's lawyer should also show pictures of his client's limitations as close to the end of trial as possible to produce the greatest effect. If the defense has presented evidence raising some doubt about the extent of disability, pictures may be used on rebuttal to help overcome the doubt. If the jury is inclined to find for the plaintiff, the pictures can have considerable weight on the amount of damages awarded.

VI. [§17.28] SENDING FILMS TO JURY ROOM

Motion pictures are exhibits and therefore may be taken into the jury room during deliberations if the court considers it proper. CCP §612. If the jury asks to see the films again, however, the usual practice is to rerun the pictures in the courtroom in the presence of the judge and counsel. This avoids the problem of who would run the projector in the jury room. It is doubtful that a juror would be permitted to operate the projector, as he might try to exert some influence concerning the content of the film. A technician would not be permitted to show the pictures in the jury room, as he might overhear remarks by the jurors.

18

Models

I. [§18.1] Value as Evidence

II. [§18.2] Dangers

III. [§18.3] Scale Models
    A. [§18.4] Admissibility
    B. [§18.5] Authentication
        1. [§18.6] By Model Maker
        2. [§18.7] By Expert

IV. [§18.8] Nonscale Models
    A. [§18.9] Admissibility
    B. Authentication
        1. [§18.10] For Admission in Evidence
        2. [§18.11] For Illustration

V. [§18.12] Skeletons

VI. [§18.13] Duplicates

VII. [§18.14] Presenting to Jury

VIII. [§18.15] Sending Models to Jury Room

I. [§18.1] VALUE AS EVIDENCE

A model is a three-dimensional representation, generally prepared in miniature, to demonstrate a place, object, or idea. Lawyers often use models as visual aids to the court or jury in understanding complicated matters in issue. In a trial involving intricate machinery, models of the machines can illustrate testimony that would otherwise be difficult to understand. Models can be made to depict the scene of an accident and to reenact the events leading up to the accident. They are used to give the trier of fact a three-dimensional "picture" of scenes and objects that would be less successfully described in words or through two-dimensional pictures or drawings. See *People v Kynette* (1940) 15 C2d 731, 755, 104 P2d 794, 807 (models are "pictorial communications" of qualified witness used instead of, or in addition to, some other method of communication). Models often inform and interest jurors more than testimony, and leave a greater and more lasting impression.

Models can be obtained from firms or individuals specializing in making legal models and other demonstrative materials; amateur model makers; stock model sources, such as manufacturers and distributors; and toy departments and novelty stores. For a discussion of the preparation and procurement of various types of models used in lawsuits, see 3 AM JUR TRIALS 377 (1965).

II. [§18.2] DANGERS

Since models have a strong appeal to jurors, they may be given greater weight than they deserve. This is particularly dangerous if the models are inaccurate or misleading. They are not originals and may give the jurors an incorrect impression of what they represent.

On the other hand, too extensive use of models may give jurors the impression that the case is being exaggerated or may engender sympathy for the side that does not appear to have the funds for elaborate visual aids. When many models are presented, the jury may become confused or miss the significance of the more important ones. Moreover, the cost may exceed their value to the case. Therefore, the attorney should use only those models that are most relevant and accurate.

III. [§18.3] SCALE MODELS

Many useful models are prepared to scale, *i.e.*, the model bears an arbitrary, fixed ratio in size to the actual object or place. When certain facts, like dimensions, distances, or lines of sight are in dispute, the model should be made to scale to gain admission in evidence over objection. Even if scale is not crucial to admission, a scale model will impress the jury more strongly and deprive the adverse party of a basis for objection or for attacking its probative value.

A. [§18.4] Admissibility

Scale models are material objects that are admissible in evidence when relevant and properly authenticated. See *Church v Headrick & Brown* (1950) 101 CA2d 396, 415, 225 P2d 558, 568; Witkin, CALIFORNIA EVIDENCE §642 (2d ed, 1966). They are the pictorial communications of a qualified witness. *People v Kynette* (1940) 15 C2d 731, 755, 104 P2d 794, 807. A model purporting to be to scale should conform in all important degrees to the original. Otherwise it may be excluded by the trial judge or given less weight by the jury. The trial judge can exclude a scale model for improper foundation or for misleading or prejudicial effect. See *San Mateo v Christen* (1937) 22 CA2d 375, 378, 71 P2d 88, 89, in which the court stated that it is common knowledge that even scale models can be very misleading because of the disparity in size between the model and the original (small model of 23 acres of land).

Many scale models are not offered in evidence but used simply to illustrate testimony or to aid a witness in testifying. See Anno, 69 ALR2d 424, 433 (1960). See also §8.34. Models not marked for identification or offered in evidence can be withdrawn at the conclusion of the trial; models received in evidence become part of the record, and it may be more difficult to obtain a stipulation and order that they be returned at the end of the trial. See §8.6.

Though made out of court, a model is not a statement, and therefore the hearsay rule does not apply. See Evid C §1200. Further, it is subject to cross-examination through the witness who authenticates it. Although a model may be a writing (see §18.5), it is not evidence of a writing, and therefore the best evidence rule does not apply. See Evid C §1500.

B. [§18.5] Authentication

Models are "writings" (see Evid C §250) and therefore must be authenticated before they may be received in evidence. Evid C §1401(a). Authentication of a scale model is made when a competent witness testifies that the model is identical to the subject depicted except for its size, which bears a fixed ratio to that of the subject. He can then testify that the model is a fair and accurate representation of the subject.

1. [§18.6] By Model Maker

If the model maker is called as a witness to testify to the accuracy of the scale model, the trial court will be more inclined to permit its

§18.7   MODELS

use as illustrative testimony or to admit it in evidence, and the jury will be more likely to give it full weight. The following is a sample authentication of a model built by a design architect.

Q. What is your occupation?
A. Design architect.
Q. What education and experience have you had in design architecture?
A. ....
Q. Do you have a specialty?
A. Yes, I design machinery for use in industry.
Q. How long have you practiced your specialty?
A. ...... years.
Q. Are you familiar with the type of machine involved in this case?
A. Yes. I made a careful study and drawing of it. [Also, I obtained the design specifications from the manufacturer.]
Q. Did you then make a model of it?
A. Yes.
Q. Is this the model you prepared?
A. Yes.
Q. Is it to scale?
A. Yes, the scale between the model and the original is [one-quarter inch] to [one foot] throughout.
Q. What do you mean by a scale of that proportion?
A. It means that [one-quarter inch] on the model equals [one foot] on the original.
Q. Is this model a fair and accurate scale model of the original?
A. Yes.

Comment: The model may now be marked for identification (if it is to be used only to illustrate the witness's testimony on the issues) or offered in evidence as an exhibit.

2. [§18.7] By Expert

Some model makers tend to be hesitant and unconvincing witnesses, and lawyers feel that the authenticating testimony of an engineer or surveyor will give greater prestige and status to the model. These experts are ordinarily engaged to plan the making of the model, including studying and measuring the original, reviewing the manufacturer's specifications, and directing the model maker in its preparation. The expert's qualifying testimony might be as follows:

Q. What is your occupation?
A. Design architect.

MODELS §18.8

Q. What is a design architect?
A. One who designs machinery for use in industry.
Q. How long have you been a design architect?
A. ...... years.
Q. What is your educational background and your experience in design architecture?
A. ....
Q. Are you familiar with [describe original]?
A. Yes.
Q. Did you examine it and make measurements at my request?
A. Yes.
Q. Did you have a scale model made of that ....?
A. Yes.
Q. By whom?
A. Mr. ....
Q. What instructions did you give him?
A. I gave him a copy of the measurements I had made as well as the manufacturer's specifications and instructed him to prepare a model with a fixed scale of ...... to ....
Q. Is this the model?
A. Yes.
Q. Have you checked it for accuracy?
A. Yes. I checked it against the measurements I made on the original.
Q. What was the result?
A. The model is accurate to within a tolerance of plus or minus ...... percent.
Q. Was it prepared to the scale you requested?
A. Yes. It has the scale of ...... to ....
Q. What does that scale mean?
A. .... on the model equals .... on the original.
Q. Is this scale model a fair and accurate representation of the original?
A. It is.

IV. [§18.8] NONSCALE MODELS

Nonscale models are used whenever possible because they are less costly and more easily obtained than scale models. Use of nonscale models is warranted particularly when accuracy of dimension is not crucial and only a rough approximation is needed. They may be obtained at a lower cost from amateur model makers or toy and novelty stores than from legal or commercial model makers.

A. [§18.9] Admissibility

Rules for admitting nonscale models are substantially the same as those for scale models (see §18.4) with the exception of accuracy. A model not purporting to be to scale need not conform in all degrees of scale to the original. The nonscale model may be substantially the same as the original or, at the other extreme, only a stylization of it, unless the inaccuracy produces a misleading effect. See Anno, 69 ALR2d 424, 439 (1960).

Like scale models, nonscale models are admissible in evidence on a showing of relevancy and authentication. See *Church v Headrick & Brown* (1950) 101 CA2d 396, 415, 225 P2d 558, 568; Witkin, CALIFORNIA EVIDENCE §642 (2d ed, 1966). Admission is within the trial court's discretion. *San Mateo v Christen* (1937) 22 CA2d 375, 378, 71 P2d 88, 89.

B. Authentication

1. [§18.10] For Admission in Evidence

Authentication of a nonscale model for introduction in evidence is made when a competent witness testifies that the model is a fair and correct representation of the original. Any lay person familiar with the original can qualify as a competent witness.

Q. Are you familiar with the intersection of .... and .... Streets?
A. Yes.
Q. How have you become familiar with it?
A. I have worked in a store there for ...... years.
Q. I show you a model marked exhibit ...... for identification. Can you identify what it purports to show?
A. Yes. It shows the intersection at .... and .... Streets.
Q. Is it a fair and correct representation of that intersection?
A. Yes.

2. [§18.11] For Illustration

If the nonscale model is offered not as evidence but as illustrative material to assist in understanding a witness's testimony, the foundation need only show that its use will assist the witness and help the court or jury to understand the testimony. The foundation need not include testimony that the model is a fair and accurate representation. See Anno, 69 ALR2d 424, 433 (1960) for the propriety of illustrative

MODELS §18.12

use without admitting the model in evidence. The authentication can be made as follows:

Q. Are you familiar with [the operation of ailerons on a DC6 aircraft]?
A. Yes.
Q. Can you explain the operation in words?
A. Perhaps, but it would be difficult without a model.
Q. I show you this model of a [DC6 aircraft]. Does it purport to be a scale reproduction of the original?
A. No.
Q. Would use of this model help you to illustrate your testimony to the jury?
A. Yes.
Q. Using this model, would you please explain to the jury how the [aileron] operates?
A. Yes. ....

V. [§18.12] SKELETONS

Doctors can use a human skeleton to assist them in making their testimony clearer and more specific. The skeleton may be of the entire body or of a part and may be of real bones or plastic. Admissibility is discretionary with the trial court, and it is helpful to show that use of the skeleton will aid the jury in some manner. See *Dameron v Ansbro* (1918) 39 CA 289, 298, 178 P 874, 879.

Some judges will not permit the use of skeletons (see CALIFORNIA CIVIL PROCEDURE DURING TRIAL §12.22 (Cal CEB 1969)), apparently out of fear that they will be used for dramatic effect or emotional appeal rather than for clarification of expert testimony. Accordingly, the foundation must clearly demonstrate the need for use of the skeleton in presenting the doctor's testimony to the jury in an understandable manner. The doctor is the qualifying witness, and the qualifying questions for admission of the skeleton are asked after the doctor has already been qualified as a medical witness.

Q. Doctor, I show you this object and ask that you tell us what it is.
A. It is a [plastic model of the] human skeleton.
Q. Is the model a fair and accurate representation of a human skeleton?
A. Yes.
Q. Particularly in regard to the [state parts of body involved in case, such as shoulder joints, cervical spine, etc.], is it a fair and accurate representation?
A. Yes.

Q. Would it help you in explaining [Mr. ....'s/the plaintiff's] injury and disability to use and refer to this exhibit?
A. Yes.
Q. In what way?
A. It is the only way I can demonstrate clearly to the jury [the difference in movement between a normal scapula and that of the plaintiff].
Q. Do you have any other reason for use of the [skeleton/model]?
A. Yes. [Give any other reason.]

Comment: Frequently the model will include only a portion of the skeleton. A model of the lumbar area of the back might be introduced as follows:

Q. Doctor, I hand you this model and ask you to describe it, please.
A. It is a plastic model of a portion of the back showing the five lumbar vertebrae and the discs between the vertebral bodies.
Q. Is this model a fair and accurate representation of the bony structure of the lumbar part of the back?
A. It is.

Comment: At this point, the lawyer could offer the model in evidence. See generally §8.14. It is more common, however, just to let the doctor use it while he testifies, without offering it or having it marked.

Q. Doctor, will you please point out on the model the fourth and fifth lumbar vertebrae?
A. Yes. I am pointing to the fourth and now the fifth.

VI. [§18.13] DUPLICATES

Occasionally a material object in issue is unavailable because it cannot be located or was destroyed before its importance was known. If there are duplicates of the object available, one of them may be used as evidence of the original, thereby avoiding the cost, delay, and difficulties of having a model made. When proof is offered that the duplicate is identical to the original, it is admissible in evidence. In *Smith v McClary* (1938) 28 CA2d 468, 471, 82 P2d 712, 713, a lid, not the original, to a 100-pound malt can was admitted on proof that it was identical even though no foundation had been laid regarding the unavailability of the original lid. It has also been held proper to admit in evidence an elastic stocking necessitated by injury even though it was not the one actually worn by the plaintiff. *Johnston v Peairs* (1931) 117 CA 208, 217, 3 P2d 617, 620.

Qualifying testimony for the admission in evidence of a duplicate must be by a witness familiar enough with the actual object to identify it as a duplicate of the original object. Unavailability of the original object should also be shown. A foundation for introduction of the duplicate lid in *Smith v McClary, supra,* might be as follows:

Q. Are you employed at the .... plant?
A. Yes. I've worked there ...... years.
Q. Are you familiar with the lids used on the 100-pound cans of malt?
A. Yes.
Q. I show you a lid. Can you identify it?
A. Yes. It is a lid of the type used to close the malt cans.
Q. Do the lids vary in size, shape, or any other way?
A. No, they are identical. One can be interchanged with the other.
Q. Do you know where the lid is that was on the can in question in this case?
A. No. They are all alike and unless it was set aside, there is no way to tell which one was used.

VII. [§18.14] PRESENTING TO JURY

The model should be small enough to fit through the doors of the courtroom or constructed so that it can be disassembled outside and reassembled inside. The trial court may be inclined to exclude a very large model if already hesitant about admitting it. If, however, the model is very small, the jury may not be able to see it very well while the expert is using it to illustrate a point. In these situations, the jurors can come forward to view the model during a recess, or it can be passed among them. The ideal model is small enough not to be cumbersome or pretentious but large enough to be viewed clearly from the jury box during testimony.

The lawyer should check the courtroom before trial to see where the model can best be placed considering its size and shape. If necessary, he should arrange to have a table or other platform brought in for the presentation. The model should be placed so that the jury and judge can view it clearly without having to move.

If the model has moving parts or must be disassembled during testimony, the lawyer and witness should make themselves familiar with its operation to facilitate a smooth presentation. They should make several "dry runs" to minimize mishaps that can reduce the effect and lessen the weight of the witness's testimony.

VIII. [§18.15] SENDING MODELS TO JURY ROOM

Models ordinarily are not taken into the jury room during deliberations, because they are most often offered as illustrations of testimony rather than evidence. However, the trial judge can permit the jury to take in any exhibits he considers proper. See CCP §612.

However, if a model were taken into the jury room, the jurors might perform experiments and arrive at explanations other than those testified to by the experts. Accordingly, counsel should consider that risk if opposing counsel, or the jurors, request that the model go into the jury room.

19
Maps and Diagrams

I. Kinds; Sources

    A. [§19.1] Accident Scenes
        1. [§19.2] Stock Maps
        2. [§19.3] Custom-Made Diagrams
        3. [§19.4] Aerial Photographs
        4. [§19.5] Police Accident Report Diagrams
        5. [§19.6] Other Sources
    B. [§19.7] Medical Drawings

II. Admissibility

    A. Requirements
        1. [§19.8] Authentication
        2. [§19.9] Relevance; Changes in Scene
    B. [§19.10] By Agreement
    C. Foundation for Custom-Made Accident Scene Diagram
        1. [§19.11] Qualifying Mapmaker
        2. [§19.12] Identifying Diagram
        3. [§19.13] Source of Data; Scale; Accuracy
        4. [§19.14] Reconstruction of Conditions
    D. [§19.15] Judicial Notice of Official Maps
    E. [§19.16] To Aid or Illustrate Testimony

III. [§19.17] Presenting to Jury

IV. Use by Witnesses

    A. [§19.18] Using Prepared Accident Scene Diagram
    B. [§19.19] Preparing Diagram During Testimony

I. KINDS; SOURCES

A. [§19.1] Accident Scenes

A map, diagram, drawing, or sketch of the place where an accident occurred can be used to aid witnesses and jurors in most personal injury trials. In slip and fall cases, diagrams demonstrate, in a way that oral testimony could not, the physical conditions that existed at the time and place of the accident. In construction cases and safe place to work cases, scale diagrams show heights and distances graphically. In motor vehicle accident cases a diagram can help witnesses identify key locations, such as a driver's position when he first saw the other vehicle, its location at that time, the point of impact, and the point where the vehicles came to rest. It may be a detailed diagram of all relevant features of the scene or a skeletal diagram or outline on which the witness sketches the details as he testifies.

An attorney who intends to introduce a diagram of the accident scene can display it and point to it while making his opening statement. If he has no diagram it can still be helpful to sketch the scene on a large sheet of paper or the courtroom chalkboard. If admitted in evidence as an exhibit, a scale diagram can be used as evidence of the facts that are represented in it (*e.g.*, in a motor vehicle case, the location and measurement of the road, lanes, shoulders, divider strips, and traffic controls).

1. *[§19.2] Stock Maps*

The least expensive maps are those kept in stock by government offices or commercial companies. If a map of a relatively large area is needed (*e.g.*, in an aircraft collision case) the lawyer often buys one prepared by the U.S. Coast and Geodetic Survey or by a commercial cartographic company. United States Coast Guard maps and charts are useful in maritime cases.

The stock maps used most frequently in motor vehicle accident cases are prepared by the Division of Highways of the California Department of Public Works. Because they are inexpensive, lawyers often use them rather than, or as a supplement to, expensive custom-made diagrams (see §19.3).

Highway Division maps can be obtained from the district office serving the location where the accident occurred (Los Angeles, San Francisco, San Diego, San Bernardino, Bishop, San Luis Obispo, Fresno, Stockton, Marysville, Redding, or Eureka). Maps of highway bridges can be obtained from the Bridge Division of the Department of Public Works at Sacramento. In some cities, the city engineer has detailed maps that can be used in litigation.

MAPS AND DIAGRAMS   §19.4

A danger in using Highway Division or other official maps is that, although they purport to show the road "as built," they may not incorporate changes made during construction. For example, construction personnel do not always place fenceposts in the precise location shown on a diagram, and confusion could result in court if an investigating police officer recorded the location of skid marks by reference to the posts. In addition, the map may not show improvements or changes made after the original construction was completed, or it may show improvements added after the accident occurred. The lawyer must check stock maps carefully to see that they correctly represent the scene on the date of the accident. See §19.22.

2. [§19.3] Custom-Made Diagrams

Normally the safest and most useful diagram of an accident scene is one drawn by an engineer, draftsman, architect, surveyor, or other person who has the professional skill to prepare an accurate representation. Often there are no accurate stock maps in sufficient detail available for trial use, and the lawyer must have one specially prepared. If the case rests on fixing precise locations (*e.g.,* many divider-line or intersection cases), the cost of a custom-made diagram is often warranted. See §§19.11–19.15 on laying a foundation for admission of these diagrams.

3. [§19.4] Aerial Photographs

Aerial photographs are being used increasingly in motor vehicle cases as photo-diagrams to show the court and jury a roadway or intersection and its surrounding terrain. They are also useful in attractive nuisance and other negligence cases. Many lawyers believe that aerial photographs are substantially more effective than drawn diagrams. They have a definite dramatic effect on jurors who see an actual representation of the scene: the road, trees, signs, etc., in exact size, without any interpretation by mapmakers or artists. On photographs generally, see chap 15.

The scale of an aerial photograph can often be determined by comparing the length of an object (*e.g.,* an automobile) shown in the photograph with its known or measured length. Or, distances on the ground can be measured and marked before the photograph is taken. For example, in one freeway collision case, distances from an identifiable place were measured in 100-foot increments and marked with large white paper strips, easily seen from the air and in the photographs. The point of impact, determined by the police officer (see §4.53), was also identified in this manner. The result was an effective pictorial representation that required little explanation and was easily authenticated.

4. [§19.5] Police Accident Report Diagrams

The police officer who investigates a motor vehicle accident usually includes a diagram of the scene in his accident report. A diagram is included with the sample accident report found in §4.3.

The police accident report diagram is normally prepared shortly after the accident, and its particular value is that it is often the only temporary diagram available. It can be valuable to establish the location of skid and gouge marks, vehicles and victims, traffic control devices, and markings.

The police officer's diagram is seldom to scale and lacks the accuracy of a custom-made diagram. In addition, the ability of police officers to prepare accurate and useful diagrams, even not to scale, varies considerably. Some are carefully done, but others are prepared so rapidly or casually that they are of little use to the lawyer.

5. [§19.6] Other Sources

If the issues of the case make it infeasible to go to the expense of a custom-made diagram, the lawyer may use one drawn by a witness, a member of his staff, or even himself. However, these lay persons are seldom skilled enough to prepare accurate and reliable diagrams, and their rough drawings may be accorded little weight. See *People v Jones* (1962) 205 CA2d 460, 467, 23 CR 418, 423 (maps drawn by attorney excluded). A private investigator may be able to prepare an accurate diagram, but one drawn by an engineer or surveyor ordinarily has a greater aura of impartiality.

In some cases diagrams made by witnesses at depositions can be used effectively by having photographic enlargements made before trial.

B. [§19.7] *Medical Drawings*

Medical drawings and diagrams can be effectively used to amplify, illustrate, and explain medical testimony. They can show the location, nature, and effect of injuries or the manner in which surgical or other medical procedures were performed. Often they demonstrate things that cannot be shown effectively, or at all, on X-ray films or photographs; in other cases they supplement them. They are of particular value when used comparatively—one drawing showing a normal condition and the other showing the abnormal.

MAPS AND DIAGRAMS   §19.8

Stock anatomical charts of normal anatomy and some abnormal conditions are prepared commercially (often in color) and are relatively inexpensive. Large black and white outline drawings can also be obtained from publishers of medical-legal materials, and a doctor can sketch on these outlines to illustrate his testimony. The doctor could also draw on a transparent overlay that is placed on the drawing of normal anatomy, leaving the original drawing unmarked, and isolating one witness's illustrations from those of others who use separate overlays.

Drawings by medical artists normally range in cost from $50 to $75 each, and are often ordered before trial when the subject is an intricate one that a medical witness would have difficulty drawing extemporaneously or quickly. In interviewing the doctor before trial, the lawyer must determine whether drawings or diagrams might be useful. He must also judge how effective the doctor will be in illustrating his testimony. This can be done during a pretrial interview by asking the doctor to illustrate what he says. The lawyer can often tell, from this trial run, whether the illustration is necessary and, if so, whether the doctor finds it easy to sketch as he testifies and whether his sketching makes his testimony more effective. If the witness finds sketching awkward or feels unequipped to make his own diagram, the lawyer should consider obtaining the necessary drawings from a medical artist; then the doctor can merely refer to the drawing to amplify his testimony.

An illustration from a medical text can be projected on a screen or photographed and an enlargement used in court. (Although many lawyers use enlargements of book pages, this may be a violation of the publisher's copyright unless permission is obtained.) The lawyer can ask the doctor before trial about the medical illustrations on which he relies or in which he has confidence. Under these circumstances the medical witness may feel more at ease using the enlarged illustration and, as a result, be more convincing to the jury. A photographic enlargement might cost less than $10. A book page can be projected on a screen or wall by an opaque or "overhead" projector.

II. ADMISSIBILITY

A. Requirements

1. [§19.8] Authentication

A map or diagram is a writing (see Evid C §250), and unless the parties agree to its admission (see §19.10), it must be authenticated before it can be received in evidence. See Evid C §§1400–1401.

Authenticating a map or diagram usually means introducing evidence that it is a correct (or at least helpful and not misleading) representation of what it purports to depict. See generally §8.11. See also §15.4 on authenticating photographs.

A custom-made scale diagram is often authenticated by the person who prepared it. He can testify to his own qualifications, the measurements he made, and his efforts to ensure its accuracy and its relevance to the date of the accident. See, *e.g., People v Jones* (1962) 205 CA2d 460, 467, 23 CR 418, 423. For sample testimony, see §§19.11–19.14.

Many diagrams can be authenticated by a person familiar with the matter depicted even though he did not draw it. For example, a doctor can testify whether a medical drawing is a correct and helpful representation of the anatomy or condition involved in the case. See §19.16.

The admission of maps and diagrams in evidence has also been justified on the ground that they are the "pictorial communications" or nonverbal testimony of a qualified witness. See *People v Kynette* (1940) 15 C2d 731, 755, 104 P2d 794, 807.

2. [§19.9] Relevance; Changes in Scene

A lawyer who wants to offer a map or diagram in evidence should be prepared to show that it is relevant, *i.e.,* that it has a tendency in reason to prove or disprove a disputed fact of consequence in the case, and that its probative value is not outweighed by the probability that its admission would be unduly time consuming or create a substantial danger of undue prejudice, confusing the issues, or misleading the jury. See Evid C §§210, 350–352. See generally §8.10.

Maps and diagrams of vehicle accident scenes give rise to a particular relevance problem; namely, whether they correctly depict the scene in all significant aspects as it existed at the time of the accident. The stock maps of roadways and intersections that can be obtained from the California Department of Public Works or a city engineer (see §19.2) were usually drawn before the road was built and may not reflect changes made during or after construction. The lawyer should also be alert to ensure that the map he obtains does not show modifications made after the date of the accident.

Custom-made diagrams, on the other hand, are often prepared long after an accident occurred. The lawyer may have come into the case late, and many lawyers, to save the expense of the custom-made diagram, do not order one drawn until it seems certain the case will be tried. (A lawyer retained soon after the accident can send a mapmaker to the scene to make measurements at once, but ask him not to draw the map until trial is imminent.) If there was a time lapse between the

MAPS AND DIAGRAMS §19.11

accident and the mapmaker's survey of the scene, he should be prepared to testify to the steps he took to ensure that his diagram depicts the scene as it existed on the date of the accident. See §19.14. He should be particularly alert to the possibility of changes in traffic control signals and markings. The road may have deteriorated between the times of the accident and the survey, or a bad condition may have been repaired.

A diagram may be excluded if it contains irrelevant marks. See *Martin v Leatham* (1937) 22 CA2d 442, 447, 71 P2d 336, 339 (marks from previous trial). Other evidence may render a diagram cumulative. See §15.16 on cumulative photographs. Similarly, a diagram may be excluded as unnecessarily inflammatory for showing, *e.g.*, the location on the highway of severed limbs. See §15.14 on inflammatory photographs.

Medical drawings should help a witness to give his testimony and jurors to understand it, but should not be unnecessarily gruesome. It is worth noting, however, that medical drawings are often preferred to photographs for the very reason that they are less likely to be inflammatory.

B. [§19.10] *By Agreement*

Accident scene maps and diagrams can often be received in evidence by stipulation. Counsel may even agree to share the cost of obtaining or preparing a single map for all parties to use. Agreement to the admission of a map can be sought in advance of trial so that the lawyer is spared the need to locate, prepare, or subpena an authenticating witness. For a general discussion of the admission of exhibits by agreement, with forms for written and oral stipulations, pretrial orders, and requests for admission, see §§8.20–8.24.

Medical drawings and diagrams that illustrate concepts (*e.g.*, vehicle stopping distances and range of vision under varied light conditions) are usually not shown to opponents before trial to preserve an element of surprise. Nor are adverse counsel as likely to stipulate to their admission.

C. *Foundation for Custom-Made Accident Scene Diagram*

1. [§19.11] Qualifying Mapmaker

Any person with a basic grasp of measurement, geometry, and drawing can prepare a scale diagram. The greater his training and experience, however, the more likely are jurors to accept his drawing as accurate. Thus, in an important case in which accuracy is essential,

§19.12   MAPS AND DIAGRAMS

the lawyer might prefer to have a diagram prepared by a surveyor or civil engineer. Many private investigators and legal services, however, are capable of preparing accurate and useful maps.

A lawyer who must or wants to lay a foundation for the admission of a custom-made diagram usually begins by showing the qualifications of the mapmaker. For example:

Q. What is your name and occupation?
A. ....
Q. Where do you [carry on that business/practice your profession/etc.]?
A. ....
Q. How long have you been a [private investigator/civil engineer/surveyor/etc.]?
A. ...... years.
Q. Are you licensed as a .... in California?
A. Yes.
Q. Please summarize for us your academic training [in mapmaking/in your field].
A. ....
Q. Have you had [training/experience] in the investigation of motor vehicle accidents?
A. Yes. [Summarizes training or experience.]
Q. Have you, as part of the practice of your [business/profession] prepared diagrams of vehicle accident scenes?
A. I have.
Q. About how many have you prepared?
A. ....
Q. Have your diagrams been used in court?
A. They have.
Q. Have you prepared diagrams for attorneys representing [plaintiffs] in lawsuits as well as [defendants]?
A. Yes.

Comment: An engineer or surveyor could also be asked about diagrams prepared for public and private agencies or employers.

2. [§19.12] Identifying Diagram

Q. Did you [at my request] prepare a diagram for use in this case?
A. I did.
Q. Is this that diagram?
A. Yes.
Q. Is this your name [here at the bottom]?

MAPS AND DIAGRAMS §19.14

A. Yes.
Q. What location does this diagram show?
A. [The intersection of .... and .... Streets.]

Comment: The diagram could be marked for identification at this point (see §8.8), although many lawyers prefer to wait until it is offered in evidence.

3. [§19.13] Source of Data; Scale; Accuracy

Q. Did you personally visit [this intersection]?
A. Yes.
Q. When?
A. ...., 19.......
Q. Tell us briefly what you did at the scene?
A. [I made a series of measurements and wrote them down. I made a rough sketch of the intersection and marked on it the things I saw and their precise locations/etc.]
Q. When did you actually draw this diagram?
A. ...., 19.......

Comment: If the diagram purports to be to scale, the lawyer should ask about it.

Q. Is this diagram to scale?
A. Yes.
Q. What is the scale?
A. [One inch] on the diagram equals [...... feet] at the scene.
Q. Is this diagram a [correct/fair and accurate] representation of [that intersection] as it existed on ...., 19......?
A. It is.

Comment: The diagram could be offered in evidence at this point. See generally §8.14. If, however, the date the measurements were made is at all remote from the date of the accident, or there is any question that changes occurred between those dates, the lawyer may seek further testimony before offering the diagram (see, *e.g.*, §19.14).

4. [§19.14] Reconstruction of Conditions

Any witness who saw the scene at or near the time of the accident can testify that certain aspects are correctly represented on the diagram. For example, a witness could testify that there was a stop sign at the corner as shown in the diagram. In addition, the person who made the map can describe his efforts to ensure its relevance to conditions on the accident date. The diagram in the police accident report (see §19.5) may provide clues to changes. Or he may check his diagram against those on file with the highway division or city engineer and records of repairs or road modifications. For example:

Q. On what date did you prepare this diagram?
A. ....
Q. About how long after the accident was that?
A. ....
Q. Did you make any inquiry to determine whether your diagram accurately represents the [intersection of .... and .... on ...., 19......]?
A Yes, I did.
Q. What did you do?
A. I visited the [Traffic Signalling Department of the Department of Highways/City Engineering Department] and checked their maps and plans for this vicinity.
Q. What did you do with them?
A. I compared my diagram with the maps and plans of the area on file there.
Q. Does your diagram correctly represent [the conditions/the width of the road/the location of the stop sign/etc.] on ...., 19......?
A. ....

Comment: This testimony may invite a hearsay objection, because the witness has based his testimony on the correctness of the diagram as a representation of the scene on the accident date on what was told him by departmental engineers, and what he saw in their maps. In response, it could be argued that the mapmaker has been qualified as an expert on that subject, and he can base his opinion on accuracy on matter, whether or not admissible, that may reasonably be relied on by experts. See Evid C §801(b). See generally §1.26.

D. [§19.15] *Judicial Notice of Official Maps*

Maps issued by federal or state agencies were judicially noticed before the adoption of the Evidence Code. See *Union Transp. Co. v Sacramento* (1954) 42 C2d 235, 239, 267 P2d 10, 12. In *Wagner v Inglewood* (1921) 53 CA 356, 200 P 60, they are described as "official acts" of the government. It can therefore be argued that official maps are "official acts" within the meaning of Evid C §§452(c) and 453, which permit or require a court to take judicial notice of them. See §§20.4–20.5. See also *People v Watts* (1926) 198 C 776, 790, 247 P 884, 889 (map from files of county surveyor); *Foley v Northern*

MAPS AND DIAGRAMS §19.17

Cal. Power Co. (1913) 165 C 103, 107, 130 P 1183, 1185 (map of addition to town used as diagram of accident scene).

If the lawyer proposes that an official map be admitted in evidence, he may ask the court to take judicial notice of its contents and admit it in evidence as an exhibit. Otherwise he authenticates it as he would any other diagram. See §19.8.

E. [§19.16] *To Aid or Illustrate Testimony*

Many diagrams are used at trial, not to prove the facts they depict, but to help a witness testify or to illustrate his testimony. They may be received in evidence generally or for that purpose, or merely marked for identification. See generally §8.34.

If the lawyer wishes to use a diagram or drawing to aid testimony, he can often have a witness authenticate it for that purpose. For example, a doctor who has already described his own qualifications could testify:

Q. Doctor, I show you this large drawing, and I ask you if you recognize what it portrays?
A. Yes, I do.
Q. What is it?
A. That is a drawing of [the human cervical spine].
Q. Doctor, does this drawing truly and correctly depict [schematically] the appearance of [a human cervical spine]?
A. Yes, it does.

Comment: At this point the diagram could be offered in evidence as an exhibit. If there were an objection to its use as evidence, the lawyer could ask a further question to qualify it to be used to aid testimony. For example:

Q. Would the use of this diagram help you to testify about [Mr. ....'s/plaintiff's alleged] injuries?
A. It would.
Q. And [in your opinion] would this diagram help jurors to understand your testimony?
A. It would.

III. [§19.17] PRESENTING TO JURY

In most cases a single diagram is prepared that is large enough for the jury, the judge, and opposing counsel to see clearly when it is placed on an easel or tacked to a bulletin board. Witnesses then verbally describe the locations on it, pointing to the pertinent part of the

§19.18   MAPS AND DIAGRAMS

map or diagram as they speak. Although an admitted diagram may be passed to the jurors (see generally §8.16), ordinarily their view is clear enough that it is not necessary to do so. Maps and diagrams may also be sent to the jury room. See CCP §612; *Balasco v Chick* (1948) 84 CA2d 802, 809, 192 P2d 76, 80. See generally §8.19.

IV. USE BY WITNESSES

A. [§19.18] *Using Prepared Accident Scene Diagram*

A witness may point to a prepared and previously admitted diagram as he testifies to explain and illustrate what he is saying. For example, a witness may use a diagram of the scene to indicate where he was standing or where a car was when he first saw it; a doctor may use a diagram to explain the location and nature of an injury; and an engineer may use one to show how a piece of equipment was constructed and how it was operated. The witness may add to the diagram, drawing directly on it or on an acetate overlay. A diagram can also be received in evidence after the witness has given his testimony, as an illustration of that testimony. See *Balasco v Chick* (1948) 84 CA2d 802, 809, 192 P2d 76, 80. Sometimes the diagram is not admitted in evidence at all, but merely marked for identification.

A diagram that has been received in evidence can be used by any witness to illustrate, extend, and explain his testimony. For example, in a typical vehicle accident case:

Q. Will you come down to the diagram and show us the position of your car when it came to a stop after the accident?
A. [Witness goes to diagram.]

Comment: The lawyer must see that his witness takes a position that does not block the view of the judge, jurors, or other counsel.

Q. Do you understand this diagram? .... Street is here, running north and south, and .... Street is here, running east and west. If it will help you to look at the photographs that are plaintiff's exhibits A through G, you may do so.
A. No, that is not necessary. I understand the diagram.
Q. Then would you show us where you came to a stop after the impact?
A. [Witness points.] It was here.
Q. This card is a scale replica of a passenger car like yours. Would you place it against the diagram and draw around it to leave an outline of your car's position?

MAPS AND DIAGRAMS   §19.19

A. [Witness does so.]
Q. [Mr. Smith,] would you mark your outline, [S-1], please?
A. [The witness does so.]
Q. Now, is it your testimony that this position you have marked as [S-1] is the location of your car when it came to a stop right after the impact?
A. Yes, it is.
Q. What was your course of travel just before you came to this point of rest?
A. I was driving north on .... Street when I first saw the other car. I put on my brakes and swerved in this direction [pointing].
Q. Would you mark that course of travel by drawing broken lines on the diagram?
A. [Witness does so.]
Q. Now mark that [S-2].
A. [Witness does so.]
Q. And now mark an X at the spot when you began to apply your brakes, and mark it [S-3].
A. [The witness does so.]

Comment: The witness's marks on the diagram are an extension or illustration of his testimony. If the diagram has not already been received as an exhibit, it could be offered at this point.

B. [§19.19] *Preparing Diagram During Testimony*

A witness can be asked to make a drawing on blank paper or on a chalkboard as he testifies. The drawing should be received in evidence as an extension or illustration of his testimony. (A drawing on a chalkboard can be photographed for later use.) For example, a medical expert might illustrate his testimony as follows:

Q. Doctor, you have spoken about the pelvis and the fracture of the pelvis and the sacrum. Would you be able to make a rough drawing showing the pelvis and the sacrum and the fracture site?
A. Yes.
Q. Would it be helpful to an understanding of your testimony if you made such a drawing?
A. Yes, it would.
Q. Would you [go to the chalkboard and] draw the pelvis and sacrum for us and show us where the fracture site is?
A. [Doctor makes drawing and explains what it illustrates.]

PART III
Judicial Notice

20
Judicial Notice

I. Value

    A. [§20.1] Advantages and Disadvantages
    B. [§20.2] Evaluating Precedent

II. Matter Noticed

    A. Mandatory and Permissive Notice
        1. [§20.3] Mandatory
        2. [§20.4] Permissive
        3. [§20.5] Permissive Notice Made Mandatory
    B. Decisional Law as Authority
        1. [§20.6] Matters Outside Evid C §§451–452
        2. [§20.7] Matters Within Evid C §§451–452
    C. Matters of Law
        1. [§20.8] Federal and State Law: Chart
        2. [§20.9] Foreign Law
    D. [§20.10] Word Meanings
    E. Facts and Propositions
        1. [§20.11] Evidence Code Distinctions
        2. [§20.12] Facts Noticed Before Evidence Code: Examples

III. Procedures To Obtain Notice

    A. [§20.13] Necessity of Making Request
    B. When To Make Request
        1. [§20.14] On Demurrer: Form
        2. [§20.15] To Support Motion Before Trial
        3. [§20.16] During Pretrial Proceedings
        4. [§20.17] At Commencement of Trial
        5. [§20.18] In Open Court

§20.1   JUDICIAL NOTICE

      6. [§20.19] When Presenting Jury Instructions
      7. [§20.20] After Trial
   C. [§20.21] Notifying Parties
      1. [§20.22] Informal Oral or Written Notice
      2. [§20.23] In Pleadings: Form
      3. [§20.24] By Notice of Motion
   D. [§20.25] Providing Opportunity To Be Heard
   E. [§20.26] Furnishing Information to Judge
      1. [§20.27] General Reference Books and Services
      2. [§20.28] Books Published by Public Authority
      3. [§20.29] Dictionaries
      4. [§20.30] Maps; Atlases; Gazetteers
      5. [§20.31] Calendars; Almanacs
      6. Case Reports
         a. [§20.32] Published in Jurisdiction
         b. [§20.33] Unofficial Reports; Advance Sheets
      7. [§20.34] Statutes; Ordinances
      8. [§20.35] Rules; Regulations; Orders
         a. [§20.36] California Administrative Code
         b. [§20.37] Federal Register
      9. [§20.38] Miscellaneous "Official Acts"
     10. [§20.39] Court Files and Records
     11. [§20.40] Rules of Court
     12. [§20.41] Mortality Tables
     13. [§20.42] Government Documents: List of Depositories
     14. [§20.43] Legislative History
     15. [§20.44] Weather Bureau Reports
     16. [§20.45] Census Statistics
     17. [§20.46] Cost of Living Indexes
     18. [§20.47] Expert Testimony
   F. [§20.48] Informing Jury of Matter Noticed

I. VALUE

A. [§20.1] Advantages and Disadvantages

Evidence Code §§451–452 define the matters of law and fact that are judicially noticed; if judicial notice is taken of them it is not necessary to offer testimony or other evidence to prove them.

The procedures for judicial notice are not widely employed. Counsel often stipulate to the matter, or a witness is needed for other testimony, and it is as easy to prove it by his testimony as to request the court to notice it judicially. Tactical considerations may influence the lawyer not to request judicial notice. He may not wish to tip his hand

JUDICIAL NOTICE §20.2

by giving his opponent the notification of the request for judicial notice that is required in certain cases. See §20.21.

Judicially noticed facts are usually accepted without question by jurors. However, sometimes greater emphasis can be given a fact by having a witness testify about it. For example, although the court will usually take judicial notice of the decreased purchasing power of the dollar (*Kircher v Atchison, T. & S.F. Ry.* (1948) 32 C2d 176, 187, 195 P2d 427, 434), it is usually more persuasive to have an economist testify about how that fact affects plaintiff's economic loss. In addition, lawyers sometimes fear that jurors will misunderstand the meaning and significance of a matter judicially noticed; they prefer to hammer the point home by having a witness explain it.

If the matter is one within Evid C §§451–452, and there is no tactical advantage in avoiding judicial notice, the lawyer can often accomplish his purpose more quickly and economically by asking the court to take judicial notice. Delays and expense in producing witnesses or documentary evidence can be avoided. With the court's permission, the jury may be told that a matter has been noticed judicially and is therefore established; this often serves to clarify the proceedings for the jurors. Furthermore, the value of judicial notice before trial (on demurrers, motions for summary judgment, motions for change of venue at a pretrial conference, etc.) is often overlooked, and lawyers lose a good opportunity to limit or clarify issues.

B. [§20.2] *Evaluating Precedent*

The Evidence Code, which became effective on January 1, 1967, has enlarged the scope of matters that a court is required (Evid C §451) or permitted (Evid C §452) to notice. In addition, their provisions standardize the procedure for obtaining judicial notice. See §§20.13–20.25. Decisions in cases tried before the effective date of the Evidence Code remain precedent when statutory language in effect at the time of the opinion was carried over into the code. Even when the language is new, preexisting cases may offer guidance on how the courts will rule on questions arising under the code. Whether precedent or not, however, judicial notice cases should be read carefully because indexing and headnoting of court statements in them are sometimes misleading. Headnoters and indexers tend to show as "judicial notice" decision statements that begin "It is common knowledge that . . . ." But in many cases the appellate court is not reviewing the trial court's action in taking, or refusing to take, judicial notice; it is merely stating the grounds on which it finds that the decision of the trial court or the jury verdict is not subject to reversal.

§20.3   JUDICIAL NOTICE

Sometimes the matter that is described as being "of common knowledge" could not be so described in another fact situation. The lawyer must not assume that a trial judge must notice a fact just because an appellate court noticed it.

II. MATTER NOTICED

A. Mandatory and Permissive Notice

1. [§20.3] Mandatory

Evidence Code §451 lists matters of which judicial notice "shall be taken." The trial court commits error if it does not notice these matters, whether or not counsel requests it. If counsel fails to request it, however, an appellate court may find that the court's error was "invited" and thus does not constitute grounds for reversal. Official Comment to Evidence Code §451.

2. [§20.4] Permissive

Matters that a court is permitted but not required to notice judicially are listed in Evid C §452. Notice of these matters may be taken at the request of counsel or by the court on its own motion. When there is any duplication between Evid C §§451 and 452, the mandatory provisions of Evid C §451 control. Evid C §452.

3. [§20.5] Permissive Notice Made Mandatory

The court's permissive authority under Evid C §452 becomes mandatory if the lawyer proposing judicial notice fulfills the requirements of Evid C §453. He must (a) request the court to take judicial notice, (b) give each adverse party sufficient notification of the request, and (c) furnish the court with "sufficient information" that the matter is one covered by Evid C §452 and that the tenor of the matter is as he claims it to be. For means of giving this notice, see §20.21; for types of information used to support requests for notice, see §§20.27–20.47.

B. Decisional Law as Authority

1. [§20.6] Matters Outside Evid C §§451–452

Although authority for judicial notice of matters other than those listed in Evid C §§451 and 452 may be found in case decisions (see Evid C §§450, 160), it is unclear whether the procedural requirements of Evid C §453 (*e.g.*, making a request for notice, notifying adverse parties, and providing opportunity to be heard) apply when notice is taken under the case authority. See CALIFORNIA EVIDENCE

JUDICIAL NOTICE   §20.10

CODE MANUAL 378 (Cal CEB 1966). The prudent lawyer will comply with these statutory requirements.

2. [§20.7] Matters Within Evid C §§451–452

The categories of "facts and propositions" mentioned in Evid C §§451(f) and 452(g)–(h) are carefully defined (see §20.11), but a question often arises whether a particular fact or proposition is "indisputable," "universally known," or of "common knowledge within the territorial jurisdiction of the courts" within the wording of those sections. Lawyers must use discretion in citing case authority to the effect that a specific fact is subject to judicial notice. See §20.2.

C. *Matters of Law*

1. [§20.8] Federal and State Law: Chart

The following chart shows the various types of law that "shall" (Evid C §451) or "may" (Evid C §452) be noticed. Items in the "may" category can, of course, become the subject of mandatory notice if the lawyer proposing notice satisfies the requirements of Evid C §453. See §20.5. The chart should be used as a guide only; the precise wording of the pertinent code section should be consulted in all cases. (See pp 472–473 for chart.)

2. [§20.9] Foreign Law

Evidence Code §452(f) provides that the "law" of foreign nations, foreign public entities, and international organizations may be noticed by the courts. "Law" is defined in Evid C §160 as including constitutional, statutory, and decisional law.

See Evid C §200 for definition of "public entity."

D. [§20.10] *Word Meanings*

The court "shall" take judicial notice of the "true signification of all English words and phrases and all legal expressions." Evid C §451(e). This restates the matter covered in former CCP §1875(1) but eliminates any doubt that the court must notice the meaning of these words, phrases, and expressions. Official Comment to Evidence Code §451. English vernacular language (*People v Thompson* (1931) 119 CA 310, 6 P2d 301) and idioms unique to particular industries (*Hines v Miller* (1898) 122 C 517, 55 P 401) were subject to judicial notice before adoption of the Evidence Code, and they will probably fall within the scope of Evid C §451(e).

	California	United States	Any "State"*	Any Public Entity in U.S.†
Constitutional Law (see §20.34)	Shall Evid C §451(a)	Shall Evid C §451(a)	May Evid C §452(a)	
Court Decisions (see §§20.32–20.33)	Shall Evid C §451(a)	Shall Evid C §451(a)	May Evid C §452(a)	
Statutes (see §20.34)	Shall Evid C §451(a) "public statutory law"	Shall Evid C §451(a) "public statutory law"	May Evid C §452(a) "statutory law"	
Treaties (see §20.34)		Shall Evid C §§451(a), 230	‡	
Resolutions of Legislature (see §20.34)	May Evid C §452(a)	May Evid C §452(a)		
Private Acts of Legislature (see §20.34)	May Evid C §452(a)	May Evid C §452(a)		
Charters of Cities, Counties, and Cities and Counties (see §20.34)	Shall Evid C §451(a) Cal Const art XI, §§7½, 8			
"Legislative Enactments" (see §20.34)	May			
Legislative Journals, Records, Hearings, and Reports (see §20.42)	Evid C §452(b) May Evid C §452(c)	May Evid C §452(b) May Evid C §452(c)	May Evid C §452(b) May Evid C §452(c)	May Evid C §452(b)
Court Records and Files (see §20.39)	May Evid C §452(d) "any court"	May Evid C §452(d) "any court of record"	May Evid C §452(d) "any court of record"	

	California	United States	Any "State"*	Any Public Entity in U.S.†
Court Rules: (see §20.40) Adopted by Judicial Council	Shall Evid C §451(c)			
Approved by U.S. Supreme Court		Shall Evid C §451(d)		
Other	May Evid C §452(e) "any court"	May Evid C §452(e) "any court of record"	May Evid C §452(e) "any court of record"	
Rules, Regulations, Standards In California Administrative Code or Register or in files of Secretary of State (see §20.36)	Shall Evid C §451(b)			
In Federal Register (see §20.37)		Shall Evid C §451(b)		
Other Regulations (see §20.35 for specific examples)	May Evid C §452(b)	May Evid C §452(b)	May Evid C §452(b)	May Evid C §452(b)
"Official Acts" of Legislative, Executive, and Judicial Departments (see §20.38 for specific examples)	May Evid C §452(c)	May Evid C §452(c)	May Evid C §452(c)	
Rules for Members of Bar (see §20.40)	Shall Evid C §451(c)			

* "State" includes states, districts, commonwealths, territories, or insular possessions of the United States. Evid C §220.
† "Public Entity" includes nations, states, cities, counties, cities and counties, districts, public authorities, public agencies, or any other political subdivision or public corporation within the United States or in a foreign nation, unless further qualified. Evid C §200.
‡ Probably not subject to judicial notice. See Official Comment to Evidence Code §452.

Abbreviations and foreign words may be noticed under the permissive provisions of Evid C §452(g) (facts and propositions of common knowledge) or Evid C §452(h) (facts and propositions that are capable of accurate determination).

E. Facts and Propositions

1. [§20.11] Evidence Code Distinctions

Courts must notice "facts and propositions of generalized knowledge that are so universally known that they cannot reasonably be the subject of dispute." Evid C §451(f). These facts need not be known by every man on the street, but they must be known to persons of average intelligence and knowledge. Official Comment to Evidence Code §451.

Courts may notice "facts and propositions that are not reasonably subject to dispute and are capable of immediate and accurate determination by resort to sources of reasonably indisputable accuracy." Evid C §452(h). These are indisputable facts that can be verified immediately by reference to books, documents, expert testimony, etc.

Courts may also notice "facts and propositions that are of such common knowledge within the territorial jurisdiction of the court that they cannot reasonably be the subject of dispute." Evid C §452(g). "Territorial jurisdiction" means the county in which the superior court is located or the judicial district in which the municipal court or justice court is located. The matter noticed need not be something physically located within the jurisdiction, but knowledge of the fact must exist within the jurisdiction. Official Comment to Evidence Code §452.

In *Daar v Yellow Cab Co.* (1967) 67 C2d 695, 716, 63 CR 724, 739, the Supreme Court refused to take judicial notice under Evid C §452(g) of the manner in which Los Angeles cab fares are computed or of passengers' practices of asking cabs to wait, tipping the driver, or tipping him in scrip. These matters were not "of such common knowledge that they cannot reasonably be the subject of dispute."

See §§20.27–20.47 for authority used to support requests for judicial notice of facts.

2. [§20.12] Facts Noticed Before Evidence Code: Examples

The following are examples of the types of fact that were judicially noticed before the adoption of the Evidence Code. The matters listed are not inclusive but are merely a guide to how the courts are likely to apply Evid C §§451(f) and 452(g)–(h) in the future. They are not segregated into "required" and "permitted" categories of notice as these distinctions did not exist before the Evidence Code was enacted.

JUDICIAL NOTICE   §20.12

   a. Alcohol—effects on human behavior (*In re Merkle* (1960) 182 CA2d 46, 50, 5 CR 745, 747)
   b. Alcohol—blood test methods and characteristics (compare *People v Conterno* (1959) 170 CA2d Supp 817, 823, 339 P2d 968, 972, with *King v Ludlow* (1958) 156 CA2d 620, 332 P2d 345 (refusal to notice that .15 percent blood alcohol rendered person under influence))
   c. Automobiles—stopping distances (see *Berton v Cochran* (1947) 81 CA2d 776, 781, 185 P2d 349, 352)
   d. Automobiles—traction effect on control (see *People v Grier* (1964) 226 CA2d 360, 363, 38 CR 11, 12)
   e. Batteries—inability to develop fire (*Markulics v Maico Co.* (1946) 74 CA2d 66, 69, 168 P2d 35, 36)
   f. Cities—location (*People v Ford* (1965) 234 CA2d 480, 496, 44 CR 556, 565)
   g. Coastlines within states (*Boone v Kingsbury* (1928) 206 C 148, 185, 273 P 797, 813)
   h. County officers—identity (*In re Spiers* (1936) 15 CA2d 487, 491, 59 P2d 838, 840)
   i. Dates of year, days of week
   j. Distances (*Warnock v Kraft* (1938) 30 CA2d 1, 3, 85 P2d 505, 506)
   k. District within city (*People v Hosney* (1962) 204 CA2d 584, 587, 22 CR 397, 399)
   l. Gasoline—inflammability (*Varas v Barco Mfg. Co.* (1962) 205 CA2d 246, 262, 22 CR 737, 746)
   m. Highways—location (*People v Kutz* (1960) 187 CA2d 431, 434, 9 CR 626, 628)
   n. Hospitals—existence of county hospital (*Marin v Dufficy* (1956) 144 CA2d 30, 34, 300 P2d 721, 723)
   o. Inflation—decrease in purchasing power (*Kircher v Atchison, T. & S.F. Ry.* (1948) 32 C2d 176, 187, 195 P2d 427, 434; *Chadek v Spira* (1956) 146 CA2d 360, 368, 303 P2d 879, 885)
   p. Life expectancy (*Risley v Lenwell* (1954) 129 CA2d 608, 651, 277 P2d 897, 925)
   q. Narcotics—effects on human behavior (*People v Victor* (1965) 62 C2d 280, 301, 42 CR 199, 212; *People v Jones* (1962) 200 CA2d 805, 812, 19 CR 787, 792)
   r. Population statistics (*People v Wong Wang* (1891) 92 C 277, 280, 28 P 270, 271)
   s. Proximity of cities and counties (*Kantz v Zurich Gen. Acc. & Liab. Ins. Co.* (1931) 212 C 576, 582, 300 P 34, 37)
   t. Smoke—qualities (*McAllister v Workmen's Compensation Appeals Bd.* (1968) 69 C2d 408, 414, 71 CR 697, 700)
   u. Street addresses (*People v Hosney, supra*)
   v. Streets—location (*People v Kutz, supra*)
   w. Sunrise and sunset—times (*Fouch v Werner* (1929) 99 CA 557, 562, 279 P 183, 185)

x. Topography—mountainous nature of county (*Mogle v Moore* (1940) 16 C2d 1, 4, 104 P2d 785, 786; *Vela v Huberty* (1934) 1 C2d 466, 467, 35 P2d 531, 532)

III. PROCEDURES TO OBTAIN NOTICE

A. [§20.13] *Necessity of Making Request*

Although there is no statutory requirement that a lawyer request the court to take judicial notice of a matter that it is required to notice under Evid C §451, the lawyer should nevertheless make a request to preclude any argument on appeal that his failure to do so "invited" the court's error. See §20.3. In addition, he should provide the court with a copy of the decision, statute, or other item that he wishes to have noticed; he does this not merely as a courtesy to the court but to minimize the possibility of an erroneous ruling.

If the matter is not one that is required to be noticed under Evid C §451, it is essential that the lawyer be prepared to show that (1) it is properly the subject of notice under Evid C §452 or other legal authority and (2) its tenor is as he contends it to be. The court is not required to notice the matter unless the lawyer presents "sufficient information to enable [the court] to take judicial notice of the matter." Evid C §453(b); see §20.5.

The trial judge has considerable latitude in deciding the trustworthiness of the sources of information offered by a party proposing judicial notice (Official Comment to Evidence Code §454), and counsel's statements, if unsupported by books, documents, or other authority, may be insufficient to permit the court to grant the request. If an appellate court determines that judicial notice was justified under Evid C §453, it will uphold the trial court's decision to take notice without regard to the information supplied by the proponent. On the other hand, it will affirm the trial court's decision not to take judicial notice unless it finds that the information supplied by the appealing proponent was so persuasive that a reasonable judge could not deny the request. Official Comment to Evidence Code §453.

B. When To Make Request

1. [§20.14] On Demurrer: Form

Despite the usual rule that a court does not look outside the pleadings on a demurrer, it does take judicial notice of matters that render a complaint defective in ruling on a general demurrer under CCP §430(6) (*i.e.,* one for failure to "state facts sufficient to constitute a cause of action"). The judge may consider matter judicially noticed

JUDICIAL NOTICE §20.16

in construing the pleadings. See *Contractor's Safety Ass'n v California Compensation Ins. Co.* (1957) 48 C2d 71, 75, 307 P2d 626, 628.

If the attorney waits to make his request for judicial notice at the hearing on the demurrer, opposing counsel may argue that he has not had sufficient time to meet it. See §20.25. It is better practice to make the request when points and authorities are submitted to the court before the hearing. The following form may be attached to the points and authorities to make the request.

This court is .... to take judicial notice of ....
             permitted/required   (E.g.) files of a court
.... under Evidence Code section ....
of record of a state of the United States   451/
.... Attached hereto as Exhibit A is ....
452   (E.g.) a certified copy of the judgment
....
in Case No. .... of the .... Court of the State of ....
and .... requests this Court to take judicial notice of the
     plaintiff/defendant
existence and tenor of this ....
                                       (E.g.) judgment

Comment: The attorney should then add case citations supporting the taking of judicial notice. See 2 Witkin, CALIFORNIA PROCEDURE 1185 at §208 (1954).

2. [§20.15] To Support Motion Before Trial

A request that the court take judicial notice may also be made to support a motion for summary judgment, a motion for change of venue, etc. The request may be made, and the supporting information provided, in an affidavit accompanying the motion. It may also be made in points and authorities, as is done in requesting judicial notice on a demurrer (see §20.14).

3. [§20.16] During Pretrial Proceedings

Particular issues of fact or law can be clarified, modified, or eliminated before trial by requesting a pretrial conference. While the attorney can make the request at the conference, it often saves time and eliminates any claim of insufficient notice, if he gives notice to the opposing party and the court that at a pretrial conference scheduled for a certain day, he will ask the court to take judicial notice of a specific matter of law or fact. He accompanies this notice with a memorandum of law showing that the court is authorized to take judicial notice of the matter; supporting information can be attached as exhibits. The judge's ruling is then incorporated in his pretrial order.

See generally CAL RULES OF CT 208–218; CALIFORNIA PRETRIAL AND SETTLEMENT PROCEDURES (Cal CEB 1963); CALIFORNIA PRETRIAL AND SETTLEMENT SUPPLEMENT (Cal CEB 1967).

4. [§20.17] At Commencement of Trial

When counsel are assigned to a trial department, the court often calls them into chambers to discuss settlement, answer any questions on procedure, and inquire whether any particular problems are present that should be discussed before trial begins. In other courts counsel take the initiative and request a conference. A request for judicial notice is appropriate at this time. The proponent should come prepared with his authorities, *e.g.,* as part of his trial brief. For example, in an aircraft collision case:

Proponent. Your Honor, may we see you for a short conference in chambers?

Court. Yes.

Proponent. And may I ask that the reporter accompany us?

(The judge, counsel, and reporter adjourn to chambers.)

Proponent. Your Honor, I intend early in the trial to introduce some official records concerning the flight of the aircraft that crashed in this case. I have copies of these records and they contain various abbreviations that are widely used by pilots and air control officers, but will probably be unfamiliar to the jurors. The records will be introduced through the custodian, but she is unfamiliar with these meanings. I ask the court to take judicial notice of the meanings of these abbreviations under Evidence Code section 452 to facilitate the jury's understanding of the entries. The meanings are found in several books on aviation that I have with me; I have marked the passages for your convenience.

I also request that the court take judicial notice under Evidence Code section 451 of Federal Aviation Rule ......, which states .... I have here a photographic copy of pages ...... through ...... of the ...., 19......, Federal Register on which this rule appears.

Comment: Opposing counsel may object that the matter is one that is not subject to judicial notice or that the tenor of the matter is not what the proponent claims it is. He offers his authority and arguments at this time. He may also argue that while the subject is one in which judicial notice may be taken, the proponent has not shown the appli-

JUDICIAL NOTICE §20.21

cability of the matter to his case. In this situation the court may announce that it will not take judicial notice, or that it will take judicial notice and instruct the jury on the matter only after the evidence shows that it is proper to do so on the facts of the particular case.

5. [§20.18] In Open Court

A matter may be so apparently indisputable that counsel would feel entitled to request the court to notice it without retiring to the judge's chambers. For instance, a witness may testify that his car was traveling so many miles per hour and counsel may wish to convert this to feet per second.

Proponent. Your Honor, may we approach the bench?
Court. Yes.
Proponent. I ask the court to take judicial notice of the conversion of miles per hour into feet per second. A vehicle traveling ...... miles per hour is traveling .... feet per second. I have a California Highway Patrol conversion table if you wish to see it.

6. [§20.19] When Presenting Jury Instructions

Requests for judicial notice are frequently made by attorneys as they argue in favor of jury instructions that they are proposing for use in the case. They prepare the instructions assuming that the matter of fact or law will be judicially noticed, and if the judge agrees that notice is proper, he gives the instruction in the proposed form or in a modified form.

7. [§20.20] After Trial

A request for judicial notice may be made after trial in connection with a post-trial motion, such as a motion for new trial, etc. (Official Comment to Evidence Code §458), and in appellate proceedings (Evid C §459).

C. [§20.21] *Notifying Parties*

A lawyer need not give notice to the adverse party of any matter of which he intends to request the court to take judicial notice, when it is a matter that the court "must" notice under Evid C §451. See §20.3. However, if he intends, under Evid C §453, to require the court to notice a matter that it is "permitted" to notice under Evid C §452 (see §§20.4–20.5), he must make the request in a manner that apprises each adverse party of the matter sought to be noticed. He must also give them "sufficient" notice to prepare to meet it. See Evid C §453.

If the court finds that sufficient notice was not given, and thus the adverse party was deprived of sufficient time to prepare, it will decline to take judicial notice of the matter. Official Comment to Evidence Code §453. What is sufficient time will depend on the matter that the lawyer wants the court to notice judicially. For instance, little time is required to meet a request for judicial notice of a reported case of a sister state; substantially more time might be required to meet a request for notice of a foreign statute when there may be questions about the authenticity of the proponent's version, the accuracy of the translation, or the interpretation of certain words or legal phrases.

1. [§20.22] Informal Oral or Written Notice

A lawyer may give opposing counsel oral notice of intent to request judicial notice in court or in chambers. If notice is given in this way, however, counsel should protect his record by having a reporter present to record what is said. Counsel may also merely write opposing counsel of his intent to request judicial notice. His letter would serve as evidence of the notice if any question arises later.

2. [§20.23] In Pleadings: Form

Notice of a request for judicial notice can be made in the pleadings by alleging the matter sought to be noticed. For instance, a complaint might include the following allegation:

At all times mentioned herein, there was in full force and effect in .... a .... found at ....
   (E.g.) the State of Washington   *(E.g.)* statute   *(E.g.)* Revised Code of
............................., which provided as follows:..................................
Washington section ....

Comment: This allegation is followed by an allegation showing how the matter sought to be noticed is pertinent to the issues of the case.

3. [§20.24] By Notice of Motion

A request for judicial notice can be included in the points and authorities or other memorandum accompanying a notice of motion.

D. [§20.25] *Providing Opportunity To Be Heard*

If the matter that counsel seeks to have noticed is one that the court is permitted to notice under Evid C §452, or is required to notice under Evid C §451(f) (see §20.3), and the matter "is of substantial

JUDICIAL NOTICE §20.27

consequence to the determination of the action," the court must give each party an opportunity to present information of "(1) the propriety of taking judicial notice of the matter and (2) the tenor of the matter to be noticed." This must be done before the court takes the case under submission or, in a jury trial, instructs the jury. Evid C §455(a). See §20.6 on matters outside Evid C §§451–452.

Moreover, if the judge resorts to any source of information not received in open court in determining the matter, the information and its source must be inserted in the record and the parties given "reasonable opportunity to meet such information." Evid C §455(b).

E. [§20.26] Furnishing Information to Judge

Evidence Code §454(a) provides that "any source of pertinent information, including the advice of persons learned in the subject matter," may be used to determine "the propriety of taking judicial notice of a matter, or the tenor thereof." The judge may look beyond information furnished by the parties, although when foreign law is in question, and the court "resorts to the advice of persons learned in the subject matter," the advice must either be in writing or be received in open court. Evid C §454(b).

For discussion of the types of law and fact that may be judicially noticed, see §§20.8–20.12.

1. [§20.27] General Reference Books and Services

Encyclopedias, textbooks, treatises, almanacs, journals, etc., of a general nature or on specialized subjects (*e.g.*, medical, economic, and scientific) are used to show that a fact is indisputable and therefore subject to judicial notice. See §20.11. But to the extent that the book presents opinion on disputable facts it is insufficient authority for notice.

The lawyer with a research problem should never overlook the valuable assistance that may be available in reference departments of the larger libraries. Too often the lawyer turns away when a library employee without sufficient reference experience reports that material is unavailable. Whenever possible the lawyer should learn the name of the reference librarian and should not give up his search until that librarian or an assistant with reference experience has been consulted.

Most public libraries have bibliographies that are useful to the lawyer who seeks encyclopedias and other reference sources on specialized subjects. A valuable publication found in most library reference rooms is the American Library Association's GUIDE TO REFERENCE BOOKS (8th ed, 1967).

See generally CALIFORNIA LAW OFFICE HANDBOOK chap 5 (Cal CEB 1962).

2. [§20.28] Books Published by Public Authority

A book, whether on legal or other subjects, that purports to be printed or published by public authority, "is presumed to have been so printed or published." Evid C §644. While the presumption is of little value with respect to California or federal law, which the court is required to notice (Evid C §451(a)), it can be of substantial help to the lawyer who requests judicial notice of a fact (see §§20.11–20.12) or of out-of-state law (see §20.8). A book printed or published by public authority is usually given more credence than one printed privately.

Whenever possible, a lawyer who wishes to take advantage of this presumption to obtain judicial notice of out-of-state law supports his request with official reports or statutes and does not rely on unofficial publications.

3. [§20.29] Dictionaries

English language dictionaries are commonly used to support judicial notice of word meanings. Legal, medical, occupational, idiomatic, and slang dictionaries can also be used. When these sources are not helpful, language experts are used. Legal dictionaries and books of words and phrases are helpful in leading the lawyer to definitions in reported cases.

4. [§20.30] Maps; Atlases; Gazetteers

Maps published in atlases, gazetteers, encyclopedias, and other reference sources can be used to support requests for judicial notice. Maps issued by government authority are probably "official acts" of the executive department and thus may be noticed within the meaning of Evid C §452(c). See *Wagner v Inglewood* (1921) 53 CA 356, 200 P 60. Maps of the U.S. Coast and Geodetic Survey and the U.S. Geological Survey are used (*Union Transp. Co. v Sacramento* (1954) 42 C2d 235, 239, 267 P2d 10, 12), as are maps issued by California agencies, such as the Division of Highways of the California Department of Public Works. Maps made by private individuals are generally not recognized as authority (*South Shore Land Co. v Petersen* (1964)

226 CA2d 725, 746, 38 CR 392, 403), but maps published by recognized cartographic firms are often considered sufficiently authoritative to permit judicial notice. See chap 19 on maps and diagrams.

5. [§20.31] Calendars; Almanacs

Individual calendars are frequently used to show the day or date in any year. Calendar books and almanacs are helpful for past years.

6. Case Reports

a. [§20.32] Published in Jurisdiction

There is a rebuttable presumption that a book containing reports of cases of the "state or nation" where it was published (whether or not it is published by public authority) is correct. Evid C §645. "State" is defined to include any state, district, commonwealth, territory, or insular possession of the United States. Evid C §220. This presumption affects the burden of producing evidence (Evid C §§604, 630), and whenever possible the lawyer should take advantage of it and use case reports that are published in the jurisdiction where the case was adjudicated.

b. [§20.33] Unofficial Reports; Advance Sheets

It is preferable to cite from bound volumes of the official reports. The bound volumes of California Appellate Reports, unlike unofficial reports (*e.g.,* the California Reporter or Pacific Reporter), normally exclude court of appeal opinions on which the California Supreme Court has granted a hearing, since they are a nullity (*Ponce v Marr* (1956) 47 C2d 159, 161, 301 P2d 837, 839) and are not cited or referred to as precedent.

If unofficial reports of court of appeal cases are used, or if the case is so recent that advance sheets must be used, the lawyer should be prepared to satisfy the judge that a hearing has not been granted and to indicate when the time for granting a hearing expired.

7. [§20.34] Statutes; Ordinances

When he can, the lawyer should take advantage of the Evid C §644 presumption and show the judge statute and ordinance books that have been published by public authority. See §20.28. (The wording of Evid C §645 on the presumption of correctness is limited to case reports (see §20.32) and does not extend to statute books, codes, ordinance books, etc.) It is less cumbersome to furnish the judge a book of unannotated statutes, *e.g.,* the United States Code, rather than the United States Code Annotated. Municipal ordinances are not often found in bound volumes; certified copies of ordinances can be obtained from the jurisdiction in question.

8. [§20.35] Rules; Regulations; Orders

The court is required to notice items that are printed in the California Administrative Code or its supplement, the California Administrative Register, or similar federal items required by 44 USC §307 to be printed in the Federal Register. Evid C §451(b); see §20.3. Although a court must take judicial notice of these matters, even without a request, counsel can avoid error and delay by making a request and having available the pertinent issue or a photocopy of the item.

If the item is not found in the California Administrative Code or Register or the Federal Register, it is advisable to obtain a certified copy from the custodian. See *People v Haugh* (1963) 216 CA2d 603, 606, 31 CR 74, 75. See also §20.42 on government documents.

a. [§20.36] California Administrative Code

The following are some of the matters in the California Administrative Code that are of interest to a personal injury lawyer.

1. Safety orders (Title 8; see *Alber v Owens* (1967) 66 C2d 790, 794, 59 CR 117, 120; *Socket v Gottlieb* (1960) 187 CA2d 760, 768, 9 CR 831, 836)
2. Motor vehicle regulations: lights, brakes, seat belts, glass, ambulances, school buses, explosives, loading, etc. (Title 13)
3. Hospital regulations: licensing, reports, records, construction, biologics, etc. (Title 17)
4. Food and drug regulations (Title 17)
5. Fire and panic safety regulations (Title 19)
6. Building standards (Title 24)

b. [§20.37] Federal Register

The Federal Register contains the rules, regulations, orders, general standards, etc., of most government departments and agencies. Among others, these include the Interstate Commerce Commission, Federal Highway Administration, Federal Aviation Administration, Federal Railroad Administration, U.S. Coast Guard, Veterans Administration, Food and Drug Administration, Public Health Service, and Federal Trade Commission.

Evidence Code §451(b) does not refer to the Code of Federal Regulations (CFR), which is an official codification of matters printed in the Federal Register. While 44 USC §311(e) suggests that items

JUDICIAL NOTICE   §20.39

printed in CFR are subject to judicial notice, it is not certain whether this provision requires a state court to take judicial notice of them. See Official Comment to Evidence Code §451. Therefore, it is better practice when requesting judicial notice in California state courts to furnish the judge with a copy of the Federal Register rather than CFR.

9. [§20.38] Miscellaneous "Official Acts"

The "official acts" reference of Evid C §452(c) is largely a catchall for the miscellaneous acts of federal and state government, of which the following are examples.

   a. Attorney general opinions (see *Los Angeles v State Dep't of Pub. Health* (1958) 158 CA2d 425, 431, 322 P2d 968, 971)
   b. PUC decisions and orders (*Pellandini v Pacific Limestone Prods., Inc.* (1966) 245 CA2d 774, 776, 54 CR 290, 291)
   c. Proceedings of the California Unemployment Insurance Appeals Board (*Pratt v Local 683, Film Technicians* (1968) 260 CA2d 545, 562, 67 CR 483, 494)
   d. Proceedings before the Social Security Administration
   e. Proceedings in railroad employees' compensation cases under the Federal Employers' Liability Act (45 USC §51)
   f. Proceedings in cases of injury on navigable waters under the Longshoremen's and Harbor Workers' Compensation Act (33 USC §§901–950)
   g. Proceedings relating to compensation claims of federal government employees (5 USC §§8101–8193)
   h. Records of "a state department" (see Official Comment to Evidence Code §452; *Adoption of McDonnell* (1947) 77 CA2d 805, 808, 176 P2d 778, 780)

Often an administrative proceeding is not reported or, if it is reported, the agency objects to releasing it. If the item is available, counsel should obtain a certified copy for use in requesting judicial notice. "Official acts" in the nature of surveys, maps, reports, etc. (see §20.30), are often available in printed form or as leaflets that clearly show their sources; it is not necessary to have these copies certified.

10. [§20.39] Court Files and Records

Certified copies are used to support requests for judicial notice of documents in court files and records. *Chas. L. Harney, Inc. v California* (1963) 217 CA2d 77, 86, 31 CR 524, 529; see *Stafford v Ware* (1960) 187 CA2d 227, 233, 9 CR 706, 710. However, if the files are in the same court in which counsel's case is being tried, the clerk, on request, usually transmits the file or document to the judge.

11. [§20.40] Rules of Court

A looseleaf volume of the California Rules of Court, amended through 1969, can be ordered from: State of California, Documents Section, Office of General Services, P.O. Box 20191, Sacramento, 95820. It is not possible to place a standing order for supplements, but subscribers are notified when they are published (usually in January and July).

Court rules are also found in the annotated and unannotated codes published commercially in California (West's, Deering's, Standard California Codes, etc.) and new rules are published in the official reports. Rules of conduct for members of the bar are included in West's Bus & P C following §6068.

Court rules approved by the United States Supreme Court for itself and the eleven courts of appeals, and the Rules of Practice in Admiralty and Maritime Cases, are published as they are promulgated or amended in bound copies of the United States Reports; they are also found at the end of 28 USC and 28 USCA.

Local rules of court are often adopted by individual superior and municipal courts to supplement the rules adopted by the California Judicial Council. Similarly, United States District Courts in California have their own local rules. Many of these local rules appear in volume 1A of McKinney's Digest; certain of them are also found in a volume that can be purchased from the Los Angeles Daily Journal.

The lawyer who anticipates any objection to his request for judicial notice, or who seeks to obtain judicial notice of a rule that does not appear in an official publication (*e.g.,* a local rule) can obtain a certified copy from the clerk of the court in question.

12. [§20.41] Mortality Tables

The court may take judicial notice of mortality tables, whether published by the government or by private insurance companies. *Risley v Lenwell* (1954) 129 CA2d 608, 651, 277 P2d 897, 925; *Foerster v Direito* (1946) 75 CA2d 323, 333, 170 P2d 986, 992. The tables vary slightly and a lawyer compares them and picks the one most advantageous to his position; a plaintiff's lawyer normally prefers the most recent tables. If the adverse attorney prefers to have another table used, he should make his request when the court is asked to take judicial notice. *Risley v Lenwell, supra.*

JUDICIAL NOTICE §20.42

The courts also take judicial notice that the tables are merely probable averages and that any individual may live longer, or die earlier, than the period shown on the table. *Temple v De Mirjian* (1942) 51 CA2d 559, 566, 125 P2d 544, 548 (jury can find life will exceed that on table); see also BAJI No 14.69 for an instruction on life expectancy.

The fifth edition of BAJI (1969) provides a mortality table based on 1968 statistics on page 545. Certified copies of government tables can be obtained by writing: Office of Information, National Center for Health Statistics, U.S. DHEW, PHS, HS&MHA, Washington, D.C. 20201. Official government vital statistics, compiled by the Department of Health, Education, and Welfare, can be found in the government documents section of public and university libraries. See §20.42.

Major life insurance companies also provide up-to-date mortality tables on request. For example, the Metropolitan Life Insurance Company publishes statistical bulletins that contain general mortality tables and also tables that show specific causes of death. These bulletins are sent to lawyers, free of charge. Requests should be addressed to: Metropolitan Life Insurance Co., 1 Madison Avenue, New York, N.Y. 10010.

See §20.1 on tactical considerations; a lawyer may use an economist to explain and relate matters of which the court takes judicial notice with respect to damages, such as normal life expectancies as shown on mortality tables. In the ordinary case, an economist is not used, and the lawyer simply submits an instruction like BAJI No 14.69 or asks the court to take judicial notice of a mortality table preliminary to drafting jury instructions on damages.

13. [§20.42] Government Documents: List of Depositories

California libraries that currently receive federal and California state documents are shown on the following list. "Selective" depositories receive only those documents that they specify. Those shown as "complete" libraries purport to receive all documents; they undoubtedly have the most extensive collections available, but they are not "complete" collections in the literal sense.

§20.42 JUDICIAL NOTICE

	United States Complete	United States Selective	California Complete	California Selective
Alhambra Public Library				x
Anaheim Public Library		x		x
Arcata: Humboldt State College Library		x		x
Auburn-Placer County Free Library				x
Bakersfield: Kern County Library		x		x
Belmont: San Mateo County Library				x
Berkeley Public Library				x
Berkeley: University of California Law Library		x		
University of California Library	x		x	
Chico State College Library	*			x
Chula Vista Public Library				x
Claremont: Pomona College Library		x		x
Colusa County Free Library				x
Culver City Library		x		
Davis: University of California Library		x	x	
Dominguez Hills: California State College Library				x
Downey City Library		x		
El Centro Public Library				x
Escondido Public Library				x
Fresno County Free Library		x	x	
Fresno State College Library		x		x
Fullerton Free Public Library		x		x
Fullerton: California State College Library				x
Gardena Library		x		
Glendale Public Library				x
Goleta (see Santa Barbara)				
Hayward Public Library				x
Hayward: California State College Library		x		x
Independence: Inyo County Free Library				x
Inglewood Public Library		x		
Irvine: University of California Library		x		x

*Complete on microprint from 1967.

JUDICIAL NOTICE §20.42

	United States		California	
	Complete	Selective	Complete	Selective
La Jolla: University of California Library	x			x
Lancaster Library		x		
Long Beach Public Library		x		x
Long Beach: California State College Library		x		x
Los Angeles County Law Library		x		
Los Angeles Public Library		x	x	
Los Angeles: California State College Library		x		x
Loyola University Library		x		
Occidental College Library		x		x
Pepperdine College Library			x	
University of California Library		x	x	
University of California School of Law Library		x		
University of Southern California Library		x		x
Lynwood Library		x		
Marysville: Yuba College Library		x		
Mendocino County (see Ukiah-Mendocino)				
Menlo Park: U.S. Geological Survey Library		x		
Modesto: Stanislaus County Free Library				x
Montebello Library		x		
Monterey: U.S. Naval Postgraduate School Library		x		
Monterey Park: Bruggemeyer Memorial Library		x		
Napa City-County Public Library				x
Newhall Library		x		
Northridge: San Fernando Valley State College Library		x		x
Oakland Public Library		x	x	
Oakland: Mills College Library		x		x
Oceanside Public Library				x
Orange: Orange County Public Library		x		x

§20.42 JUDICIAL NOTICE

	United States		California	
	Complete	Selective	Complete	Selective
Palo Alto City Library				x
Palo Alto (see Stanford)				
Pasadena Public Library		x		x
Pasadena: California Institute of Technology Library		x		
Placer County (see Auburn-Placer)				
Pleasant Hill: Contra Costa County Free Library		x		x
Pomona Public Library		x		x
Pomona: California State Polytechnic College Library				x
Quincy: Plumas County Free Library				x
Redding: Shasta County Free Library		x		x
Redlands: A. K. Smiley Public Library				x
University of Redlands Library		x		
Redwood City Public Library		x		x
Reseda: West Valley Regional Branch Library		x		
Richmond Public Library		x		x
Riverside Public Library		x		x
Riverside: University of California Library		x		x
Rohnert Park: Sonoma State College Library				x
Sacramento City-County Library		x		x
Sacramento County Law Library		x		
Sacramento State College Library				x
Sacramento: California State Library	x		x	
Salinas: Monterey County Library				x
San Bernardino County Free Library		x		x
San Bernardino State College Library				x
San Diego County Library		x		x
San Diego Public Library	x		x	
San Diego State College Library		x	x	
San Diego: University of San Diego Law Library (see also La Jolla)		x		
San Francisco Public Library	x		x	
San Francisco State College, Social Science and Business Library		x		

JUDICIAL NOTICE §20.42

	United States Complete	United States Selective	California Complete	California Selective
San Francisco: Mechanics Institute Library		x		
University of California Medical Center Library				x
University of San Francisco Library		x		
San Jose Public Library				x
San Jose State College Library		x		x
San Jose: Santa Clara County Free Library				x
San Leandro Community Library Center		x		
San Luis Obispo County Free Library				x
San Luis Obispo: California State Polytechnic College Library				x
Santa Ana Public Library		x		x
Santa Barbara Public Library				x
Santa Barbara: University of California Library		x		x
Santa Clara: University of Santa Clara Library		x		x
Santa Cruz: University of California Library		x		x
Santa Monica Public Library				x
Santa Rosa-Sonoma County Free Library		x		x
Stanford University Libraries	x		x	
Stockton Public Library		x		x
Stockton: University of Pacific Library				x
Thousand Oaks: California Lutheran College Library		x		
Turlock: Stanislaus State College Library		x		x
Ukiah-Mendocino County Library				x
Vallejo Public Library				x
Ventura City-County Library				x
Visalia: Tulare County Free Library		x		x
Walnut: Mount San Antonio College Library		x		
West Covina Library		x		
Whittier College Library		x		x

14. [§20.43] Legislative History

Federal legislative history (*i.e.,* legislative journals, reports, etc.) is obtained at libraries that are depositories for U.S. government documents. Except for recent California statutes, of which compilations are available from the California State Library in Sacramento, there is little legislative history for California bills and statutes. The state depositories may have legislative history for recent California statutes. See §20.42 for list of depositories of federal and state documents.

Inquiries or calls to the California State Library may prove productive, but postal inquiries or telephone calls to the Library of Congress are normally not satisfactory. However, if a lawyer has someone in Washington who can visit the library, he will be directed to the information he seeks.

The declaration or affidavit of an individual legislator as to his intention, motive, or opinion regarding a piece of legislation is not acceptable to support a request for judicial notice. *Bragg v Auburn* (1967) 253 CA2d 50, 54, 61 CR 284, 288.

15. [§20.44] Weather Bureau Reports

It is probable that weather reports of the U.S. Weather Bureau are "official acts" that may be judicially noticed (Evid C §452(c)); they are commonly the subject of judicial notice.

The National Weather Record Center, Ashville, North Carolina 28801, has weather information on temperature, wind, humidity, rainfall, etc. They are on a three-hour basis for all major population centers in California. It also has more precise hourly information from stations at military and commercial airports. If the location in question is not near any of these stations, reports on a 24-hour basis of rainfall and temperature may be all that is available from the center.

The Weather Record Center supplies certified copies of its reports at a minimal charge, but the request should be made early enough to assure receipt of the information by the time it is needed. If the lawyer is pressed for time he can often obtain this same information from the Weather Bureau, Climatological Office, 50 Fulton Street, San Francisco, California 94102 (telephone 621–1612).

See also §20.42 on government documents.

16. [§20.45] Census Statistics

Census statistics issued by the U.S. Department of Commerce have been judicially noticed. It should be argued that census returns

JUDICIAL NOTICE §20.48

and other population statistics compiled by a federal or state agency are "official acts" that may be noticed under Evid C §452(c). See §20.42 on government documents.

17. [§20.46] Cost of Living Indexes

Plaintiffs' lawyers often argue for increased damage awards on the ground that inflation is decreasing purchasing power; courts have taken judicial notice of this fact (see §20.12). Copies of the Consumer Price Index are available without charge from the Bureau of Labor Statistics of the U.S. Labor Department. There are two offices in California, one at 450 Golden Gate Avenue, San Francisco 94102, and the other at 300 North Los Angeles Street, Los Angeles 90012.

Indexes are available for the United States as a whole and for San Francisco, Los Angeles, and San Diego. For other cities, a single "U.S. City Average" is available. On request, the bureau also furnishes a description of the index telling how it is compiled and how it can be used. A lawyer may make individual requests for information or, if he wishes, he can have his name put on a mailing list to receive all indexes as they are published.

See §20.1 on tactical considerations; lawyers may prefer to offer expert testimony on cost of living increases to impress jurors with the fact of inflation.

18. [§20.47] Expert Testimony

A request for judicial notice may be supported by the advice of "persons learned in the subject matter." Evid C §454. The usual practice is for parties to produce their own experts, but §454 permits appointment by the court when it is desirable to have one not identified with any party. Official Comment to Evidence Code §454. On expert testimony generally, see §§1.19–1.30.

F. [§20.48] *Informing Jury of Matter Noticed*

The attorney's efforts in obtaining judicial notice are of little or no consequence unless the jury is informed that judicial notice has been taken and the matter is considered proved.

The Evidence Code provides that, "If a matter judicially noticed is a matter which would otherwise have been for determination by the jury, the trial court may, and upon request shall, instruct the jury to accept as a fact the matter so noticed." Evid C §457. This section does not say when the court shall instruct the jury that judicial notice is taken of the fact. Traditionally, these explanations are made in jury instructions at the close of the evidence, but it is often helpful to inform the jurors before that time. If judicial notice is requested and taken of a matter in pretrial proceedings, a lawyer can refer to it and explain its significance in his opening statement. If it is requested and taken during trial, the court can at that time be requested to instruct the jury in accordance with Evid C §457. The court's explanation during the taking of evidence often serves to increase the jurors' comprehension of the evidence.

References Cited in Text

AMERICAN JURISPRUDENCE, PROOF OF FACTS. San Francisco, Bancroft Whitney, 1959–1969. 23 vols (general index and medical glossary)
AMERICAN JURISPRUDENCE, TRIALS. San Francisco, Bancroft Whitney, 1964–1969. 16 vols (index)
CALIFORNIA CIVIL APPELLATE PRACTICE (Cal CEB 1966)
CALIFORNIA CIVIL PROCEDURE DURING TRIAL (Cal CEB 1960)
1, 2 CALIFORNIA CIVIL PROCEDURE FORMS MANUAL (Cal CEB 1967)
CALIFORNIA EVIDENCE CODE MANUAL (Cal CEB 1966)
CALIFORNIA JURY INSTRUCTIONS, CIVIL. 5th ed. St. Paul, West Publishing Co., 1969. 640 pp
CALIFORNIA LAW OFFICE HANDBOOK (Cal CEB 1962)
CALIFORNIA PRETRIAL AND SETTLEMENT PROCEDURES (Cal CEB 1963) (1967 supplement)
CALIFORNIA TRIAL OBJECTIONS (Cal CEB 1967)
Houts, Marshall. LAWYERS' GUIDE TO MEDICAL PROOF. Albany, N.Y., Matthew Bender, 1966. (miscellaneous paging)
Johns, Leland M. CALIFORNIA DAMAGES, LAW AND PROOF. Los Angeles, Parker & Sons, 1969. 382 pp
Louisell, David W. MODERN CALIFORNIA DISCOVERY. Berkeley, Berkeley Press, 1963. 462 pp (1968 supplement)
McBaine, James P. CALIFORNIA EVIDENCE MANUAL. 2d ed. St. Paul, West Publishing Co., 1960. 727 pp
REVIEW OF SELECTED 1969 CODE LEGISLATION (Cal CEB 1969)
Robb, Dean A., Harry M. Philo & Richard M. Goodman. LAWYERS DESK REFERENCE. Rochester, N.Y., Lawyers Co-operative Publishing Co., 1968. 1078 pp
Wigmore, John Henry. EVIDENCE. 2d ed. Boston, Little, Brown, 1923. 5 vols
Winchell, Constance M. GUIDE TO REFERENCE BOOKS. 8th ed. Chicago, American Library Ass'n, 1967. 741 pp
Witkin, B. E. CALIFORNIA EVIDENCE. 2d ed. San Francisco, Bancroft Whitney, 1966. 1323 pp (1969 supplement)
———. CALIFORNIA PROCEDURE. San Francisco, B. E. Witkin, 1954. 3 vols (1967 supplement)
———. SUMMARY OF CALIFORNIA LAW. 7th ed. San Francisco, Bender-Moss, 1960. 4 vols (1965 supplement)

Table of Statutes, Rules, and Instructions

California

CONSTITUTION
Art XI, §7½
 §20.8
Art XI, §8
 §20.8

ADMINISTRATIVE CODE
Title 8
 §§5.66, 20.36
Title 13
 §20.36
Title 17
 §20.36
Title 19
 §20.36
Title 24
 §20.36

BUSINESS AND PROFESSIONS CODE
§5501
 §5.41
§6068
 §20.40
§6704
 §5.41

§6736
 §5.41
§6787
 §5.41

CIVIL CODE
§3283
 §6.77
§3333
 §6.71

CODE OF CIVIL PROCEDURE
§283
 §§1.1, 8.20–8.21, 8.24, 9.10, 11.2, 13.13
§376
 §6.34
§377
 §6.34
§430(6)
 §20.14
§607
 §1.45
§607(b)
 §1.45
§610
 §8.35

CCP

§612
§§8.19, 10.21, 16.22, 17.28, 18.15, 19.17
§774
§1.45
§1235
§§10.6–10.7
§1875(1)
§20.10
§1952
§8.6
§1952.2
§8.6
§1985
§§9.7–9.8, 11.9–11.10
§1985.1
§1.2
§1987
§11.9
§1987(c)
§11.8
§1987.5
§§9.8, 11.9–11.10, 13.15
§1989
§4.13
§2015.5
§§9.8, 11.7, 11.10, 11.12, 13.15
§2016
§5.33
§2016(d)
§§10.7, 10.23
§2016(d)(1)
§§10.4–10.5, 10.7, 10.22
§2016(d)(2)
§§10.7, 10.17
§2016(d)(2)–(3)
§10.22
§2016(d)(3)
§10.15
§2016(d)(3)(ii)
§10.16

§2016(d)(4)
§§10.19–10.20
§2016(e)
§10.18
§2016(f)
§10.8
§2016(g)
§1.34
§2017(a)(4)
§10.19
§2017(b)
§10.19
§2019(e)
§§10.4, 10.18
§2019(f)(1)
§10.4
§2021(c)
§10.18
§2021(c)(1)
§10.18
§2021(c)(2)
§10.18
§2030(b)
§10.22
§2031
§10.25
§2032(a)
§10.25
§2032(b)(1)
§10.25
§2033
§§8.22, 10.24, 14.3
§2034(c)
§10.24

EVIDENCE CODE
§140
§§8.1–8.2, 8.35–8.36
§160
§§20.6, 20.9
§170
§1.15

STATUTES, RULES, AND INSTRUCTIONS Evid C

§200
  §§20.8–20.9
§210
  §§1.13, 1.22, 6.41, 8.10
  8.36, 11.4, 13.7, 15.17
  17.5, 19.9
§220
  §§20.8, 20.32
§225
  §§2.7, 8.13, 15.13
§230
  §20.8
§240(a)
  §10.15
§240(b)
  §10.15
§250
  §§1.32, 8.1, 8.11, 8.25, 11.5,
  13.8, 15.2, 15.13, 16.3,
  17.6, 18.5, 19.8
§350
  §§8.10, 8.36, 11.4, 13.7,
  15.17, 17.5
§§350–352
  §§14.2, 19.9
§352
  §§1.13, 1.28, 2.3, 2.6, 3.16,
  6.57, 8.7, 8.10, 8.19, 8.35–
  8.36, 11.4, 13.7, 15.9, 15.14–
  15.16, 16.3, 16.15, 17.4
§352(b)
  §2.13
§353
  §8.20
§355
  §§2.3, 2.13, 6.35, 6.56
§§400–401
  §8.9
§402
  §§8.9, 17.6
§403
  §§1.15, 15.4
§405
  §1.21
§413
  §1.43
§450
  §20.6
§451
  §§4.55, 20.2–20.4, 20.6, 20.8,
  20.13–20.14, 20.17, 20.21
§§451–452
  §§20.1, 20.25
§451(a)
  §§20.8, 20.28
§451(b)
  §§20.8, 20.35, 20.37
§451(c)
  §20.8
§451(d)
  §20.8
§451(e)
  §20.10
§451(f)
  §§20.7, 20.11–20.12, 20.25
§451(g)
  §§20.10–20.11
§451(h)
  §§20.10–20.11
§452
  §§20.2–20.3, 20.5–20.6, 20.8,
  20.13–20.14, 20.17, 20.21,
  20.25
§452(a)
  §20.8
§452(b)
  §20.8
§452(c)
  §§19.15, 20.8, 20.30, 20.38,
  20.44–20.45
§452(d)
  §§2.6, 20.8
§452(e)
  §20.8
§452(f)
  §20.9
§452(g)–(h)
  §§20.7, 20.12

§453
  §§2.6, 19.15, 20.5–20.6, 20.8, 20.13, 20.21
§453(b)
  §20.13
§454
  §20.47
§454(a)
  §20.26
§454(b)
  §20.26
§455(a)
  §20.25
§455(b)
  §20.25
§457
  §20.48
§459
  §20.20
§604
  §20.32
§630
  §20.32
§644
  §§20.28, 20.34
§645
  §§20.32, 20.34
§§700–701
  §1.14
§701
  §10.15
§702
  §§1.15, 3.19, 6.2, 6.41, 6.52, 15.5
§702(a)
  §1.15
§702(b)
  §1.15
§720
  §§1.19–1.20, 5.37, 6.5
§720(a)
  §5.36
§720(b)
  §§1.19, 5.36
§§721–722
  §§2.1, 2.14
§721(a)
  §1.20
§721(a)(1)
  §2.15
§721(a)(2)
  §2.17
§721(a)(3)
  §§1.27, 2.18
§721(b)
  §§2.19, 5.64
§721(b)(1)
  §2.19
§722(b)
  §§2.16, 5.27, 6.31
§723
  §5.28
§762
  §1.43
§764
  §1.10
§765
  §§1.9, 1.41
§767
  §§1.10, 1.41, 1.43, 2.1
§768
  §§8.7, 8.28, 8.33
§§768–769
  §10.7
§§768–770
  §2.9
§768(a)
  §10.7
§768(b)
  §§2.11, 10.7
§769
  §10.7
§770
  §§2.9–2.10
§770(a)
  §2.10
§770(b)
  §2.9
§771
  §§1.31, 1.34, 1.38–1.39, 6.28, 8.7, 8.26, 10.3–10.5, 17.17

STATUTES, RULES, AND INSTRUCTIONS

§771(a)
§§1.32, 1.38, 5.33
§771(b)
§§1.35, 1.38, 10.4
§771(c)
§1.38
§772(c)
§1.43
§773
§1.41
§773(a)
§3.2
§774
§1.43
§776
§§3.2, 10.5, 10.13, 10.17
§778
§2.9
§780
§§2.1, 15.5
§780(c)
§§1.15, 2.4
§780(d)
§§1.15, 2.4
§780(e)
§§1.17, 2.5
§780(f)
§2.2
§780(h)
§§2.7, 2.10
§780(i)
§§2.10, 2.13
§785
§§1.13, 1.22, 2.1, 4.59, 10.6, 10.10
§786
§2.5
§787
§2.5
§788
§§2.5–2.6
§790
§§1.13, 1.17
§791
§§1.44, 9.17, 10.10

§791(a)
§§10.9–10.10
§791(b)
§§1.44, 10.9–10.10
§800
§§1.13, 1.16, 1.26, 3.19, 4.36, 4.40, 5.58, 6.57, 7.1, 9.12
§801
§§1.19, 1.24, 5.61–5.62, 6.2, 6.35, 6.66
§§801–802
§§1.15, 6.65
§801(a)
§§2.17, 4.49, 5.22, 5.58, 6.64, 6.69, 6.73, 6.76
§801(b)
§§1.19, 1.26, 1.28, 5.58, 5.63, 6.35, 6.52, 6.65, 6.69, 6.76, 13.41, 14.8, 16.16, 19.14
§802
§§1.18–1.20, 1.22, 1.27, 1.29, 5.36, 6.2, 6.35, 6.41, 6.56–6.57, 6.67, 13.20, 13.35, 13.41, 16.16
§§802–803
§12.6
§803
§§1.27, 2.18, 13.35, 13.41
§804
§6.35
§804(a)
§6.56
§805
§5.58
§870
§1.17
§§952–954
§6.3
§§994–995
§6.4
§996
§§6.4, 13.11
§§1014–1015
§6.4
§1016
§§6.4, 13.11

Evid C

§1100
  §1.17
§1105
  §3.17
§1151
  §§2.13, 15.9
§1152
  §2.3
§1155
  §§2.2, 2.13, 3.16, 4.47
§§1156–1157
  §13.6
§1158
  §§13.3–13.4
§1200
  §§2.19, 4.15, 4.22, 4.42, 6.33, 6.56, 8.13, 9.9, 9.12, 11.7, 14.2, 14.4, 15.13, 18.4
§1200(a)
  §13.10
§1220
  §§4.42–4.43, 6.34, 13.26
§§1220–1221
  §3.16
§§1220–1252
  §4.42
§1221
  §§4.42, 4.44
§1222
  §3.16
§1224
  §§3.16, 4.45
§§1226–1227
  §§6.34, 13.26
§1227
  §4.42
§1230
  §§4.42, 4.45
§1235
  §§2.7, 2.12, 4.42
§1236
  §1.44
§1237
  §§1.31, 4.23, 8.25–8.27, 8.32, 10.11–10.13

§1237(a)
  §8.25
§1237(a)(2)
  §§4.23, 8.29
§1237(a)(3)
  §8.31
§1237(b)
  §§8.32, 10.11–10.12
§1240
  §§4.25, 4.42, 4.45–4.46, 6.34
§1240(a)
  §4.46
§1240(b)
  §4.46
§1242
  §§4.42, 6.34
§1250
  §§6.34, 6.37, 7.1, 7.7, 13.25
§§1251–1252
  §§6.34, 6.39
§1252
  §§6.34, 6.37, 7.1, 7.7, 13.25
§1270
  §§11.1, 12.3, 13.10
§§1270–1271
  §9.12
§§1270–1272
  §§13.35, 13.40
§1271
  §§9.7, 9.12, 11.7, 11.9, 12.1, 13.10, 13.19
§1271(a)–(c)
  §11.21
§1271(c)
  §§11.17–11.18, 12.1
§1271(d)
  §§9.12, 11.21
§1280
  §§9.7, 9.12, 12.1
§1280(c)
  §9.12
§1282
  §12.8
§1283
  §12.8

STATUTES, RULES, AND INSTRUCTIONS   Health & S C

§1284
    §12.9
§1324
    §2.5
§1400
    §§8.9, 8.11, 11.5, 14.4, 17.6
§§1400–1401
    §§13.8, 14.2, 19.8
§1400(b)
    §9.13
§1401
    §§8.11, 9.13, 11.5, 12.9, 16.3
§1401(a)
    §§15.2, 17.6, 18.5
§1413
    §9.13
§1453
    §12.9
§1500
    §§8.12, 9.14, 10.18, 11.6,
    14.2, 14.4, 15.13, 18.4
§§1501–1566
    §15.13
§§1506–1508
    §12.1
§1530
    §§9.13–9.14
§§1530–1564
    §12.1
§1530(a)
    §9.13
§1530(a)(2)
    §9.13
§1531
    §9.14
§1550
    §11.6
§1560
    §§11.6, 11.8, 11.11, 11.16,
    12.3–12.4, 13.10, 13.14,
    13.18
§§1560–1561
    §13.17
§§1560–1562
    §§11.7, 13.9–13.10, 13.35,
    13.40

§§1560–1564
    §12.3
§§1560–1566
    §§11.8, 11.11, 13.14
§1560(a)
    §11.1
§1560(b)
    §§11.14–11.15
§1560(c)
    §11.11
§1560(d)
    §11.13
§1561
    §§9.12, 11.5, 11.8, 11.12,
    11.16, 11.19, 12.3, 13.8,
    13.10, 13.14, 14.2
§§1561–1562
    §11.15
§1562
    §§11.8, 13.9, 13.14
§1564
    §§9.7, 11.6, 11.9, 11.11,
    11.14–11.16, 13.18
§1565
    §11.15

GOVERNMENT CODE
§68092.5
    §6.4
§68097.1
    §4.12
§68097.2
    §§4.14, 9.7
§68097.3
    §§4.13–4.14
§68097.4
    §4.14
§68097.5
    §4.12
§68097.9
    §4.12
§68097.55
    §4.12

HEALTH AND SAFETY CODE
§10577
    §12.7

503

Lab C   STATUTES, RULES, AND INSTRUCTIONS

LABOR CODE
§3852
   §14.12
§6400
   §5.66

PENAL CODE
§1016
   §4.48

VEHICLE CODE
§2408
   §4.19
§2412
   §4.19
§10012
   §9.3
§17150
   §4.45
§20008
   §9.11
§20012
   §9.4
§20013
   §§9.9–9.12, 9.15–9.16
§40834
   §4.48

CALIFORNIA RULES OF COURT
208–218
   §20.16
214(a)(1)(ii)
   §8.23
243
   §8.6
531
   §8.6

CALIFORNIA JURY INSTRUCTIONS, CIVIL (BAJI)
1.02
   §1.1
2.05
   §2.13

2.06
   §§10.4, 10.21
2.20
   §2.1
2.21
   §10.7
2.24
   §2.6
2.25
   §2.7
2.28
   §2.3
2.40
   §2.15
2.40–2.41
   §1.23
2.41
   §2.15
2.42
   §1.28
2.43
   §§6.35, 6.56
14.10
   §6.77
14.11–14.12
   §3.30
14.12
   §6.77
14.13
   §§3.25, 6.77
14.29
   §20.41
14.65
   §3.22
14.69
   §7.10
14.70
   §7.10

STATUTES, RULES, AND INSTRUCTIONS

United States

UNITED STATES CODE
Title 5
§§8101–8193
  §20.38
Title 28
  §20.40
Title 33
§§901–950
  §20.38

Title 44
§307
  §20.35
§311(e)
  §20.37
Title 45
§51
  §20.38

Index

ACCIDENT REPORT. *See*
Police Accident Report

ADMISSIONS
Adoptive admissions, §4.44
Guilty plea, §4.48
Nolo contendere plea, §4.48
Party's admissions, questions to police officer re, §4.43
Plaintiff's testimony re defendant's admissions, §3.16

ARREST
Police officer as witness, no testimony re arrests, §4.41

ATTORNEYS
Attorney-client privilege, medical experts, §6.3
Direct examination
  Conducting, §§1.5-1.8
  Preparing witness, §§1.1-1.4

BEST EVIDENCE RULE.
See Evidence

BIAS
Impeachment of witnesses, grounds for, §2.2

BIBLIOGRAPHY
Depositions, §10.2
Impeachment of witness, §2.1
Preparation and examination of witnesses, §1.1

BURDEN OF PROOF
Business records, §11.3
Witness capacity, §1.14

BUSINESS RECORDS
Admission in evidence, §§11.2-11.15
Agreement for admission, §11.2
Authentication, §11.5
Best evidence rule, §11.6
Burden of proof, §11.3
Copy of records delivered with custodian's affidavit pursuant to subpena duces tecum, §§11.8-11.13
Custodian's
  Affidavit, §§11.8-11.13
  Declaration, *form,* §11.12
  Testimony
    Checklist for when required, §11.14
    Clause requiring personal attendance of custodian with original records, sample, §11.15
Definition, §11.1
Hearsay, §11.7
Hospital and medical records, §§13.10, 13.34

507

INDEX

BUSINESS RECORDS— *cont.*
Laying foundation for admission, §§11.3–11.7
Official records as, §§12.1, 12.3
Opening and offering copy in evidence, §11.13
Relevancy, §11.4
Request for opening records, samples, §11.13
Stipulation for admission, example, §11.2
Subpena duces tecum, §§11.8–11.15
  Clause requiring personal attendance of custodian with original records, sample, §11.15
  Declaration for, *form*, §11.10
  Issuance, §11.9
  Notice describing procedure for compliance, *form*, §11.11
  Service of, §11.9
Trial uses, §11.1
Wage record used to show earnings loss, §§11.16–11.22
  Content of record, §11.22
  Hearsay rule exception, when, §11.19
  Identifying
    Record and mode of preparation, sample questions-answers, §11.18
    Witness, sample questions-answers, §11.17
  Record made in regular course of business, sample question-answer, §11.19
  Subpenas duces tecum, §11.16
  Time of preparation at or near time of act, condition, or event; sample question, §11.20
  Trustworthiness, §11.21

CALIFORNIA HIGHWAY PATROL VEHICLE ACCIDENT REPORT. *See* Police Accident Report

CHARTS. *See* Tables

CHECKLISTS
Business records, when custodian's testimony required for admission of records in evidence, §11.14
Economists and statisticians as appraisers of impaired earning capacity, checklist of qualifications, §7.11
Exhibits, offering in evidence, §8.3
Impaired earning capacity, checklist for plaintiff's testimony, §3.31
Police officer interviewed
  Evaluating officer as witness, §4.10
  Questions, §4.9
Technical experts, checklist for
  Determining appropriate specialty, §§5.3–5.7
    Buildings, §5.6
    Carrier accidents, §5.4
    Chemicals, §5.7
    Construction sites, §5.6
    Drugs, §5.7
    Explosions, §5.7
    Fall, §5.5
    Foods, §5.7
    Premises, §5.6
    Slip, §5.5
    Vehicle accidents, §5.4
  Qualifications, sample questions-answers re particular items, §§5.39–5.57
Writings as past recollection recorded, checklist for laying foundation, §8.27

INDEX

CITATIONS
Police officer as witness, no testimony re, §4.41

COLLATERAL SOURCE RULE
Medical payments, §14.9
Wages and benefits, §§3.32, 7.8

COSTS
Technical experts, §5.27

CROSS-EXAMINATION
Depositions, use during, §§10.5, 10.7, 10.13
Expert witness, opinion testimony
  Hypothetical questions, §§1.30, 2.18
  Reasons and bases for testimony, §1.27
Leading questions, §1.41
Model, cross-examination of authenticating witness re, §18.4
Motion pictures
  Challenging authentication, §17.16
  Surveillance films, sample questions, §17.19
Objections, §1.41
Plaintiff, cross-examination of, advantages and disadvantages, §3.2
Preparation of witness for, §1.40
Prior felony conviction brought out on, §2.6
Refreshing memory, §1.31
Tactics against, §§1.40–1.42

DECLARATIONS
Business records, declaration for subpena duces tecum, *form*, §11.10
Hospital and medical records, declaration for subpena duces tecum, *form*, §13.15
Police accident report
  Request for copy and declaration, *form*, §9.4
  Subpena duces tecum, declaration for issuance of, *form*, §9.8

DEFINITIONS
Business records, §11.1
Demonstration, §§8.1, 8.36
Deposition, §§10.2, 10.11
Evidence, §8.1
Exhibit, §8.1
Experiment, §8.36
Expert witness, §1.19
Impeachment of witness, §2.1
Law, judicial notice, §20.9
Lay witness, §1.13
Medical history, §6.32
Model, §18.1
Official record, §12.1
Pain, §3.25
Perceive, §1.15
Personal knowledge, §1.15
Photograph, §15.2
Physical examination and findings, §6.40
Qualification of lay witness, §§1.13–1.14
Rebuttal, §1.45
Refreshing memory, §1.31
Relevant evidence, §15.17
Writing, §1.32
X-ray film, §16.1

DEMONSTRATIONS
Discussion of, §8.36
Exhibits distinguished from, §8.1
Experiments, §8.36
Meaning of, §§8.1, 8.36
Sample questions, §8.36
Value, §8.2

DEMURRER
Judicial notice request, made on demurrer, *form*, §20.14

INDEX

DEPOSITIONS
Bibliography, §10.2
Cross-examination, use of depositions during, §§10.5, 10.7, 10.13
Definition, §§10.2, 10.11
Impeachment of adverse witness by, §§10.5, 10.7, 10.10
Interrogatories compared, §10.22
Jury, availability to jury during deliberations, §10.21
Objections to admission, §10.18
  Stipulations reserving objections, §10.17
  Waiver, §§10.17–10.18
Past recollection recorded, depositions by, §10.11
  Adverse witness, §10.13
  Own witness, sample questions, §10.12
Police officer's, §4.11
Presentation at trial, §10.20
Prior consistent statements
  Adverse witness, §10.10
  Own witness, sample questions, §10.9
Prior inconsistent statements
  Adverse witness, sample questions, §10.7
  Own witness, §10.6
  When deponent becomes own witness, §10.8
Refreshing memory by, §10.3
  Adverse witness, §10.5
  Own witness
    Sample questions, §10.4
    Showing prior inconsistent statement, §10.6
Signing of, §§10.4, 10.18
Substitute testimony, deposition as, §10.14
  In interests of justice, §10.16
  When
    Deposition is of adverse party, agent, or witness, §10.17

Substitute testimony—*cont.*
  When—*cont.*
    Witness unavailable, §10.15
Substitution of parties, §10.19
Supplemental proceedings, §10.19
Unavailable witness, §10.14
Uses at trial, §§10.3–10.17
Waiver of
  Objections to admission, §§10.17–10.18
  Signing requirement, §10.18

DIAGNOSIS
Hospital and medical records, sample questions and answers, §13.36
Medical history, diagnostic importance of, §6.36
Medical opinion testimony, diagnosis: nature and extent of injuries, §6.68
  Admissibility, §6.69
  Relating diagnoses to injuries, sample questions, §6.70
Special diagnostic procedures, §§6.51–6.53
  Admissibility of testimony, §6.52
  Extent of testimony, §6.53

DIAGRAMS AND MAPS
Accident scenes, §§19.1–19.6, 19.9–19.14, 19.18–19.19
Admissibility, §§19.8–19.16
Aerial photographs, §19.4
Agreement for admission, §19.10
Aid to testimony, sample questions re using diagram as, §19.16
Authentication, §19.8
Changes in scene, §19.9
Custom-made diagrams, §19.3
  Accuracy, sample questions, §19.13
  Authentication, §19.8

510

INDEX

DIAGRAMS AND MAPS— *cont.*
Custom-made diagrams—*cont.*
 Foundation for accident scene diagram, §§19.11–19.14
 Hearsay testimony, when, §19.14
 Identifying diagram, sample questions, §19.12
 Qualifying mapmaker, sample questions, §19.11
 Reconstruction of conditions, sample questions, §19.14
 Scale, sample questions, §19.13
 Source of data, sample questions, §19.13
 When prepared, §§19.9, 19.13–19.14
Highway Division maps, §19.2
Judicial notice, §§19.15, 20.30
Jury, presenting to, §19.17
Kinds, §§19.1–19.7
Medical drawings, §§19.7–19.10
Official maps, judicial notice, §19.15
Police accident report diagrams, §§4.26, 19.5
 Police officer as witness, questions when using diagram, §4.26
Relevance, §19.9
Requirements for admissibility, §§19.8–19.9
Sources, other, §19.6
Stipulation for admission, §19.10
Stock maps, §§19.2, 19.9
Technical experts, §§19.11, 19.18
Witnesses and prepared accident scene diagram, sample testimony
 Preparing diagram during testimony, §19.19
 Using diagram, §19.18

DISCOVERY
See also Depositions; Interrogatories
Motions for production and inspection and for examination by physicians, §10.25
Request for
 Admission, §10.24
  Exhibits, request for admission, *form*, §8.22
  Medical bills, §14.3
  Production of writing used to refresh memory, §1.39
Technical experts, §5.33
Value of discovery documents, §10.1

DOCUMENTARY EVIDENCE
See Exhibits; Past Recollection Recorded; Refreshing Memory; Statements

DUPLICATES
Exhibits, §8.5
Foundation for introduction of, sample questions, §18.13

EARNINGS
Economists and statisticians as appraisers of impaired earning capacity, §§7.9–7.12
Judicial notice of life expectancy and present cash value of future loss, §§7.10, 20.12(p), 20.41
Plaintiff's testimony re
 Impairment of earning capacity, §§3.30–3.32
  Checklist, §3.31
  Loss of earnings, sample questions, §3.32

511

INDEX

EARNINGS—*cont.*
Wage record used to show earnings loss, §§11.16–11.22
  Content of record, §11.22
  Hearsay rule exception, when, §11.19
  Identifying
    Record and mode of preparation, sample questions-answers, §11.18
    Witness, sample questions-answers, §11.17
  Record made in regular course of business, sample question-answer, §11.19
  Subpena duces tecum, §11.16
  Time of preparation at or near time of act, condition, or event; sample question, §11.20
  Trustworthiness, §11.21

ENGINEERS. *See* Technical Experts

EVIDENCE
  See also specific headings (Business Records; Demonstrations; etc.)
Best evidence rule
  Business records, §11.6
  Exhibits, exception, §8.12
  Hospital and medical records, exception, §13.9
  Medical bills, §14.2
  Photographs, §15.13
  Police accident report, §9.14
Cumulative evidence, photographs, when, §15.16
Definition, §8.1
Real evidence, meaning of, §8.1
Rebuttal, §1.45
Relevant evidence
  Business records, §11.4
  Credibility of witness, evidence re, §1.13
  Definition, §15.17

Relevant evidence—*cont.*
  Diagrams and maps, §19.9
  Exhibits, §8.10
  Hospital and medical records, §13.7
  Medical bills, §14.2
  Motion pictures, §17.5
  Photographs, when, §15.17

EXHIBITS
  See also specific headings (Business Records; Demonstrations; Diagrams and Maps; etc.)
Agreement for admission, §§8.20–8.24
Authentication, §8.11
Best evidence exception, §8.12
Bringing to court, §8.4
Custody, §8.6
Demonstrations distinguished from, §8.1
Duplicates, §8.5
Hearsay exception, §8.13
Hospital and medical records, §13.6
Procedures for securing admission as exhibit, §§13.13–13.19
Indexes for, §8.5
Inspection by adverse counsel, §8.7
Jury
  Jury room, sending exhibits to, §8.19
  Presenting to, §§8.16–8.18
    Explaining, §8.17
    Interpreting, §8.17
    Passing to jurors, §8.16
    Reading, §8.17
    Viewing aids, §8.18
  Viewing scenes and objects outside courtroom, §8.35
Keeping track of, §8.5
Laying foundation, §§8.9–8.13
Marking
  For identification, §8.8

INDEX

EXHIBITS—*cont.*
Marking—*cont.*
 In evidence, §8.15
Meaning of, §8.1
Medical experts, doctors' use of, §6.27
Offering in evidence, §§8.3–8.18
 Checklist, §8.3
 Formal offer, §8.14
Police accident report, admission as, §§9.9–9.15
Pretrial order for admission, *form*, §8.23
Receiving in evidence, §8.15
Release to owner; stipulation, order and receipt for release, *form*, §8.6
Relevance, §8.10
Request for admission, *form*, §8.22
Stipulations
 Admission of exhibits
  Oral stipulation, sample, §8.24
  Written stipulation, *form*, §8.21
 Release to owner, *form*, §8.6
Terminology, §8.1
Uses, §8.2
 Things not in evidence used to help witnesses testify, §8.34
Value, §8.2
When to use, §8.4
Writings as past recollection recorded. *See* Past Recollection Recorded

EXPERIMENTS
Definition, §8.36
Discussion of, §8.36

EXPERT WITNESSES
 See also Medical Experts; Technical Experts
Definition, §1.19

Hypothetical questions, §§1.28, 2.18
 Cross-examination, examples, §1.30
 Direct examination, examples, §1.29
 Objections, §1.28
 Impeachment of, §§2.14–2.19
 Fees and court appearances, §2.16
 Qualifications, §2.15
 Reasons and bases for opinion, §2.18
 Sample questions
  Fees and court appearances, §2.16
  Qualifications, §2.15
  Technical and medical publications, use of, §2.19
 Subject of testimony, §2.17
 Technical and medical publications, use of, §2.19
Judicial notice, expert testimony, §20.47
Leading questions, §1.12
Models, sample questions, §18.7
Opinion testimony, §§1.24–1.27
 Basic discussion, §1.24
 Basis, §1.26
  Stating of, §1.27
 Hypothetical questions. *See* Hypothetical above
 Police officer, §§4.53–4.58
 Stating reasons and bases, §1.27
 Subjects, §1.25
Police officer as, §§4.49–4.58
 Attacking qualifications of, sample voir dire, §4.52
 Decision whether to use officer, §4.50
 Influence of narcotics, opinion re, §4.58
 Loading of truck, questions re, §4.55
 Point of impact, sample testimony, §4.53

513

INDEX

EXPERT WITNESSES—
cont.
Police officer as—*cont.*
Special qualifications, sample testimony, §4.51
Speed
Before collision, §4.57
Safe speed under conditions, §4.56
Subjects of expert testimony, §§4.53–4.58
Vehicle's mechanical condition, opinion re, §4.54
Special qualifications, §§1.19–1.23
Arguing comparative qualifications, §1.23
Offers to concede, example of
Offer, §1.22
Response, §1.22
Police officer, sample testimony, §4.51
Reasons for showing, §1.20
Sufficiency of showing, §1.21
Waiver of testimony re, §1.22

FEES
Expert witness, evidence re fees to impeach, §2.16
Medical experts, §§6.4, 6.31
Medical-legal examiner's fees, sample questions re, §6.31
Police accident report, copy of, §9.3
Subpena to police officers, deposit of fees, §§4.14–4.15
Clause showing deposit of fees, *form,* §4.15
Technical experts, §5.27

FELONY
Impeachment of witness by evidence of prior felony conviction, §2.6

GROUNDS
Impeachment of witnesses, §§2.2–2.13

GUILTY PLEA
Admissible admission, police officer as witness, §4.48

HEARSAY
Business records, when, §11.7
Diagrams, hearsay testimony, §19.14
Exceptions, §4.42
Adoptive admissions, §4.44
Business records, when, §11.7
Driver's statement to show liability of employer or owner, §4.45
Exhibits, §8.13
Medical history, when, §6.34
Party's admissions, §4.43
Public record, absence of, §12.9
Spontaneous statements, §4.46
Vital statistics, §12.7
Wage records, when, §11.19
Hospital and medical records, §13.10
Medical bills, §14.2
Medical history, §6.34
Police accident report, hearsay and exceptions, §§4.5, 4.21, 4.34, 4.42–4.46, 9.12

HOSPITAL AND MEDICAL RECORDS
Admissibility, §§13.6–13.12
Authentication, §13.8
Authorization for medical information, *form,* §13.5
Best evidence, §13.9
Business records, as, §§13.10, 13.34
Causation, medical opinions, §13.37
Circumstances of accident, §13.26

514

INDEX

HOSPITAL AND MEDICAL RECORDS—*cont.*
Contents, §13.2
Cover sheet, §§13.21–13.23
Covering up objectionable items and entries, §13.12
Data and diagnostic summary, §§13.21–13.23
Deletion of objectionable items and entries, §13.12
Delivery of subpenaed copy with custodian's affidavit, §§13.14–13.17
　Encouraging delivery of copy, §13.16
　Offering records in evidence, §13.17
　Supporting declaration, *form*, §13.15
Diagnosis, medical opinions, sample questions and answers, §13.36
Doctors'
　Orders, sample questions, §13.32
　Progress notes, §13.33
Electrographic reports, §13.30
Exhibits, §13.6
　Procedures for securing admission as, §§13.13–13.19
Family medical history, §13.27
Final summary, §13.24
Foundational requirements for admissibility, §§13.7–13.11
　Foundational testimony if record not received in evidence by agreement or on affidavit, §13.19
Hearsay, §13.10
Impeachment, use of record
　Confronting
　　Adverse expert with contradictory matter, sample questions, §13.47

Impeachment, use of record—*cont.*
　Confronting—*cont.*
　　Witness, prior inconsistent statement, sample questions, §13.43
　Prior inconsistent statement, §§13.42–13.46
　　Absence of complaints, sample questions, §13.46
　　Confronting witness, sample questions, §13.43
　　Forgotten statement, sample questions, §13.44
　　Statement of preaccident health, sample questions, §13.45
Insurance coverage, §13.23
Laboratory reports, sample questions, §13.30
Letters
　In records, §13.40
　Requesting medical records, *form*, §13.4
Medical history, §§13.25–13.27
　Sample questions, §13.25
Medical opinions, §§13.35–13.38
Medication sheet, sample questions, §13.32
Narrative summary, §13.24
Nurses' notes, §13.34
Objections, §§13.6, 13.12
Obtaining copy of client's record before suit, §§13.3–13.5
Offering records in evidence, §13.17
Operation report, sample questions, §13.31
Opinion testimony basis, use of record to show, sample questions-answers, §13.41
Other extraneous matter, §13.40
Particular entries: admissibility, interpretation, §§13.20–13.40

515

INDEX

HOSPITAL AND MEDICAL RECORDS—*cont.*
Past medical history, §13.27
Personal attendance of custodian with original records, §13.18
Personal data, §13.22
Physical examination reports, sample questions, §13.28
Physician-patient privilege, §13.11
Procedures for securing admission as exhibit, §§13.13–13.19
Prognosis, medical opinions, §13.38
Refreshing memory, sample questions, §6.28
Relevance, §13.7
Stipulation, example, §13.13
Subpena duces tecum, §§13.14–13.18
Trial uses, §13.1
Trustworthiness, §13.10
Use by doctor, §§6.27–6.28
Vital signs chart, §13.29
X-ray
  Films, §§13.39, 16.17
    Sample questions, §16.17
  Reports, §§13.39, 16.16

HYPOTHETICAL QUESTIONS. *See* Questions

IMPEACHMENT OF WITNESSES
Bias as grounds, §2.2
Bibliography, §2.1
Character for veracity bad, §2.5
Contradictory facts, §2.13
Definition, §2.1
Deposition used to impeach adverse witness, §§10.5, 10.7, 10.10
Expert witnesses, §§2.14–2.19
  Fees and court appearances, §2.16

Expert witnesses—*cont.*
  Medical experts, §13.47
  Qualifications, §2.15
  Reasons and bases for opinion, §2.18
  Sample questions, §§2.15–2.16, 2.19
  Subject of testimony, §2.17
  Technical and medical publications, use of, §2.19
Grounds for, §§2.2–2.13
Hospital and medical records used to impeach
Confronting
  Adverse expert with contradictory matter, sample questions, §13.47
  Witness, prior inconsistent statement, sample questions, §13.43
Prior inconsistent statement, §§13.42–13.46
  Absence of complaints, sample questions, §13.46
  Confronting witness, sample questions, §13.43
  Forgotten statement, sample questions, §13.44
  Statement of preaccident health, sample questions, §13.45
Interests as grounds, §2.2
Introducing otherwise inadmissible matter, §2.13
Leading questions, §2.1
Method, §2.1
Motive as grounds, §2.2
Perception and recollection faulty, §2.4
Police accident report as means of, §9.16
Police officer, §4.59
Prior felony conviction, §2.6
Prior inconsistent statement, §§2.7–2.12
  Confronting witness with statement, §2.10

INDEX

IMPEACHMENT OF WITNESSES — *cont.*
Prior inconsistent statement — *cont.*
  Introducing extrinsic evidence, §2.12
  Not confronting witness with statement, §2.9
  Pinning down testimony, §2.8
  Pressing for admission, §2.11
Prior settlement with adversary, §2.3
Sample questions
  Character for veracity, §2.5
  Fees and court appearances of expert witness, §2.16
  Perception and recollection, §2.4
  Prior felony conviction, §2.6
  Prior inconsistent statement, §§2.8, 2.10–2.12
  Prior settlement, §2.3
  Qualifications of expert witness, §2.15
  Technical and medical publications, used to impeach expert witness, §2.19

INSTRUCTIONS TO JURY
Judicial notice request, made when presenting jury instructions, §20.19

INSURANCE
Hospital and medical records, insurance coverage, §13.23
Plaintiff's testimony of defendant's admission re, §3.16
Police officer as witness, parties' statements re liability insurance, §4.47

INTERROGATORIES
Advantages and disadvantages, §10.22
Depositions compared, §10.22
Restrictions, §10.23
Uses, §10.22
  Restrictions, §10.23

INTOXICATION
Police officer as witness, questions re driver's intoxication, §4.36

JUDICIAL NOTICE
Advance sheets, case report, §20.33
Advantages, §20.1
Almanacs, §20.31
Atlases, §20.30
Books published by public authority, §20.28
Calendars, §20.31
California Administrative Code, §20.36
Case reports
  Advance sheets, §20.33
  Published in jurisdiction, §20.32
  Unofficial reports, §20.33
Census statistics, §20.45
Cost of living indexes, §20.46
Court files and records, §20.39
Decisional law as authority, matters
  Outside Evid C §§451–452, §20.6
  Within Evid C §§451–452, §20.7
Depositories, list of, §20.42
Dictionaries, §20.29
Disadvantages of, §20.1
Expert testimony, §20.47
Facts and propositions
  Evidence Code distinctions, §20.11
  Examples of facts noticed before Evidence Code adopted, §20.12
Federal and state law, chart of, §20.8
Federal Register, §20.37

INDEX

JUDICIAL NOTICE—*cont.*
Foreign law, §§20.9, 20.26
Gazetteers, §20.30
General reference books and services, §20.27
Government documents, §20.42
Indexing and headnoting of court statements in judicial notice cases are sometimes misleading, §20.2
Information furnished to judge, §§20.26–20.47
Jury, informing jury of matter noticed, §20.48
Legislative history, §20.43
Life expectancy and present cash value of future loss, §§7.10, 20.12(p), 20.41
Mandatory, §20.3
   Permissive notice made mandatory, §20.5
Maps, §§19.15, 20.30
Matter noticed, §§20.3–20.12
Mortality tables, §20.41
Notifying parties of request, §§20.21–20.24
   By notice of motion, §20.24
   In pleadings, *form*, §20.23
   Informal oral or written notice, §20.22
   "Official acts," miscellaneous, §20.38
Official records, §12.4
Opportunity to be heard, providing for, §20.25
Orders, §§20.35–20.37
Ordinances, §20.34
Permissive, §20.4
   Made mandatory, §20.5
Precedent, §20.2
Presumption re
   Books published by public authority, §20.28
   Case reports published in jurisdiction, §§20.32, 20.34

Procedures to obtain notice, §§20.13–20.48
Record of prior felony conviction to impeach witness, §2.6
Regulations, §§20.35–20.37
Request
   Necessity of making, §20.13
   Notice of. *See* Notifying above
   When to make
     After trial, §20.20
     At commencement of trial, §20.17
     During pretrial proceedings, §20.16
     In open court, §20.18
     On demurrer, *form*, §20.14
     To support motion before trial, §20.15
     When presenting jury instructions, §20.19
Rules, §§20.35–20.37
Rules of Court, §20.40
Statutes, §20.34
Truck loading regulations, §§4.55, 20.36(2)
Unofficial case reports, §20.33
Value of, §§20.1–20.2
Weather Bureau reports, §20.44
Word meanings, §20.10
X-ray films, nature and validity of process, §16.6

JURY
   See also Instructions to Jury
Depositions, availability to jury during deliberations, §10.21
Diagrams and maps, presenting to, §19.17
Exhibits
   Jury room, sending exhibits to, §8.19
   Presenting to, §§8.16–8.18
   Explaining, §8.17

INDEX

JURY—*cont.*
Exhibits—*cont.*
  Presenting to—*cont.*
    Interpreting, §8.17
    Passing to jurors, §8.16
    Reading, §8.17
    Viewing aids, §8.18
    Viewing scenes and objects outside courtroom, §8.35
  Judicial notice, informing jury of matter noticed, §20.48
  Models
    Presenting to jury, §18.14
    Sending models to jury room, §18.15
  Motion pictures
    Presenting to jury, §§17.26–17.27
    Sending to jury room, §17.28
  Photographs, presenting to, §§15.18–15.19
  Technical expert, sufficiency of qualifications to gain jurors' confidence, §5.37
  X-ray films
    Clause restricting viewing by, sample, §16.2
    Jury room, sending films to, §16.22
    Presenting to, §§16.18–16.21

LAY WITNESSES. *See* Witnesses

LEADING QUESTIONS. *See* Questions

LETTERS
Hospital and medical records
  Letters in records, §13.40
  Requesting medical records, *form*, §13.4

LISTS
Depositories, §20.42
Opinion testimony, list of subjects for
  Expert witness, §1.25
  Lay witness, §1.17

MAPS. *See* Diagrams and Maps

MEDICAL BILLS
Admissibility, §§14.2–14.8
Agreement for admission, §14.3
Best evidence, §14.2
Billing doctor, sample questions re reasonableness of charges, §14.7
Collateral source rule, §14.9
Defendant's payment of bills, showing of, §14.11
Foundational testimony, §§14.4–14.8
Hearsay, §14.2
Identifying bills, sample questions, §14.4
Necessity of treatment, sample questions, §14.5
Other doctor, sample questions re reasonableness of charges, §14.8
Payment
  Covering notations of, §14.3
  Showing of, §§14.9–14.12
Plaintiff's
  Foundational testimony, sample, §14.4
  Payment of bills, showing of, §14.10
Preliminary considerations, §14.1
Pretrial order re admission, §14.3
Proof of medical expenses, §14.1
Reasonableness of charges, §§14.6–14.8
Relevance, §14.2
Request for admission, §14.3
Service of copy of, §14.3
Stipulation, §14.3
Workmen's compensation carrier's payment of, §14.12

INDEX

MEDICAL EXPERTS
See also Medical History; Physical Examinations
Attorney-client privilege, §6.3
Content of testimony, §6.2
Drawings, §§19.7–19.10
Exhibits, doctor's use of, §6.27
Family physician, sample questions for, §6.30
Fees, §§6.4, 6.31
  Medical-legal examiner's fees, sample questions, §6.31
Licensed doctors, §6.6
Malpractice cases, §§6.1, 6.6
Medical-legal examiner, sample questions for, §6.31
Nondoctors, §6.7
Opinion testimony
  Admissibility of, §§6.64–6.67
    Cause of injuries, §6.73
    Diagnosis, §6.69
    Prognosis, §6.76
  Bases
    Improper, §6.66
    Procedures for showing bases and reasons, sample questions, §6.67
    Proper, §6.65
  Cause of injuries, §6.71
    Admissibility, §6.73
    Form of testimony, sample questions, §6.74
    Value of causation testimony, §6.72
  Diagnosis: nature and extent of injuries, §6.68
    Admissibility, §6.69
    Relating diagnoses to injuries, sample questions, §6.70
  Procedures for showing bases and reasons, sample questions, §6.67
  Prognosis: continuing, permanent, and future injuries, §6.75
    Admissibility, §6.76

Opinion testimony—*cont.*
  Prognosis—*cont.*
    Continuing conditions, sample questions, §6.78
    Future conditions, sample questions, §6.79
    Permanency, sample questions, §6.78
    Reasonable medical certainty, §6.77
  Referring doctor's opinion, reports from other examiners, §§6.56–6.57
  Outside consultant, determining whether to call, §6.55
Patient-litigant exception to physician-patient privilege, §6.4
Personal physician, sample questions for, §6.30
Physician-patient privilege, §6.4
Privileges, §§6.3–6.4
Professional relationship, occasion for seeing patient, §§6.29–6.31
Qualifications, §§6.5–6.26
Questions
  General, §6.8
  Particular items, §§6.10–6.26
  Sample questions re
    Authorship, §6.24
    Degrees, §6.13
    Education, §6.13
    General practice, §6.17
    Hospital staff memberships, §6.23
    Internship, §6.14
    Lecturing, §6.22
    License, §6.12
    Medical literature, familiarity with, §6.25
    Medical society memberships, §6.21
    Military service, §6.15
    Name, §6.11

INDEX

MEDICAL EXPERTS—*cont.*
Questions—*cont.*
  Sample questions re—*cont.*
    Nature of practice, §§6.17–6.20
    Office address, §6.11
    Orthopedic surgery; training, experience, board certification, §§6.18–6.20
    Private practice, entry and duration, §6.16
    Profession, §6.11
    Residency, §6.14
    Specialty, §6.18
    Teaching, §6.22
  Specific, §6.9
Reasons for calling, §6.1
Records, medical and hospital
  Impeachment of adverse expert, confronting with contradictory matter, §13.47
  Refreshing memory, sample questions, §6.28
  Use by doctor, §§6.27–6.28
Referring doctor and reports from other examiners, §§6.54–6.63
Refreshing memory, §6.28
Reports, doctor's use of, §§6.27–6.28
Sequence of testimony, §6.2
Sufficiency, §§6.6–6.7
X-ray films, §§16.9, 16.16

MEDICAL HISTORY
Admissibility, §§6.33–6.35
Circumstances of accident, §6.38
  Hospital and medical records, §13.26
  Sample questions, §6.38
Definition, §6.32
Diagnostic importance, sample questions, §6.36
Discussion of, §6.32
Hearsay rule exceptions, §6.34
Hospital and medical records, medical history
  Circumstances of accident, §13.26
  Past and family history, §13.27
  Sample questions, §13.25
  Statement of preaccident health, use of record to impeach, §13.45
Nature of, sample questions, §6.36
Opinion basis, admissible solely to show, §6.35
Preaccident history, sample questions, §6.39
Use of hospital and medical record to impeach statement of preaccident health, sample questions, §13.45
Subjective signs, sample questions, §6.37
Symptoms, sample questions, §6.37

MEDICAL RECORDS. *See* Hospital and Medical Records

MODELS
Admissibility of
  Nonscale models, §18.9
  Scale models, §18.4
Authentication of
  Nonscale models, authentication for
    Admission in evidence, §18.10
    Illustration, §18.11
  Scale models, §18.5
    Expert as witness, sample questions, §18.7
    Model maker as witness, sample questions, §18.6
Cross-examination, §18.4
Dangers in using, §18.2

MODELS—*cont.*
Duplicates, sample questions for foundation for introduction of, §18.13
Expert as witness, sample questions, §18.7
Jury
  Presenting to, §18.14
  Sending models to jury room, §18.15
Model maker, sample questions, §18.6
Nonscale models, §§18.8–18.11
Scale models, §§18.3–18.7
Skeletons, sample questions re, §18.12
Value as evidence, §18.1

MOTION AD LIMINE
Collateral source, §14.9
Subsequent marriage, §3.5

MOTION PICTURES
Accuracy, sample questions, §17.15
Activity
  After injury, §17.25
  Normal activity before injury, §17.24
Admissibility, §§17.4–17.16
Authentication, §§17.6–17.15
  Challenging authentication, §17.16
  Surveillance films, §17.18
Cinematographer as authenticating witness, sample questions when
  Amateur, §17.9
  Professional, §17.8
Custody of film, sample questions, §17.13
Dangers of using, §17.3
Developing, sample questions, §17.11
Editing, sample questions, §17.12
Equipment
  In courtroom, §17.26

Equipment—*cont.*
  Sample questions re, §17.10
Experiments, sample questions, §17.23
Jury
  Presenting to, §§17.26–17.27
    In courtroom; equipment and facilities, §17.26
    Strategy, §17.27
  Sending films to jury room, §17.28
Lighting, sample questions, §17.10
Printing, sample questions, §17.11
Projection, sample questions, §17.14
Reenactment of event, §17.22
Relevance, §17.5
Surveillance films, §17.17
  Authentication, sample questions, §17.18
  Cross-examination, sample questions, §17.19
  Presentation strategy, §17.27
  Rehabilitation, §17.21
  Setting up plaintiff, sample questions, §17.20
Uses, §17.2
Value as evidence, §§17.1–17.2
Visual impact, §17.1

MOTOR VEHICLES
Damage to, questions to police officer re, §4.31
Driver, questions to police officer witness re
  Identity, §4.34
  Injuries, §4.35
  Intoxication, §4.36
  Possession of license, §4.33
Identity, questions to police officer re, §4.29
Loading of truck, police officer's expert testimony re, §4.55

INDEX

MOTOR VEHICLES—*cont.*
Mechanical condition, §4.32
   Police officer's expert testimony re, §4.54
Photograph of damaged vehicle, sample questions for authentication, §15.11
Plaintiff's testimony re, §3.11
Point of rest, questions to police officer re, §4.30

NARCOTICS
Police officer's expert testimony re influence of, §4.58

NOLO CONTENDERE
Plea not admissible, police officer as witness, §4.48

NURSES
As witness, §7.3
Hospital and medical records, nurses' notes, §13.34
Nursing services by family members, sample questions, §7.5

OBJECTIONS
Cross-examination, §1.41
Depositions, objections to admission of, §10.18
   Stipulations reserving objections, §10.17
   Waiver, §§10.17–10.18
Hospital and medical records, §§13.6, 13.12
Hypothetical questions for expert witness, §1.28
Personal knowledge of witness, showing required when objections to testimony, §1.15
Photographs, objections to admission, §§15.13–15.17
Police accident report, objections to admission, §§9.11–9.14

Questions calling for narrative answers, §1.9

OFFICIAL RECORDS.
See Records

OPINION TESTIMONY
Expert opinion testimony, §§1.24–1.27
Bases, §1.26
   Stating of, §1.27
Basic discussion, §1.24
Hypothetical questions, §§1.28, 2.18
   Cross-examination, examples, §1.30
   Direct examination, examples, §1.29
   Objections, §1.28
Medical. *See* Medical below
Police officer's opinion re
   Influence of narcotics, §4.58
   Loading of truck, §4.55
   Point of impact, sample testimony, §4.53
   Safe speed under conditions, §4.56
   Speed before collision, §4.57
   Subjects of expert testimony, §§4.53–4.58
   Vehicle's mechanical condition, §4.54
Reasons and bases for opinion
   Impeachment, examination re reasons, §2.18
   Procedures for showing bases and reasons for medical opinion testimony, sample questions, §6.67
   Stating of, §1.27
Subject matter, §1.25
   Police officer's expert testimony, §§4.53–4.58

523

INDEX

OPINION TESTIMONY—*cont.*
  Hospital and medical record used to show basis for opinion testimony, sample questions and answers, §13.41
  Lay opinion testimony, §§1.16–1.18, 7.1, 7.3
    Basic discussion, §1.16
    Foundation, §1.18
    Subject matter, §1.17
  Medical history admissible solely to show basis of opinion, §6.35
  Medical opinion testimony
    Admissibility of, §§6.64–6.67
      Cause of injuries, §6.73
      Diagnosis, §6.69
      Prognosis, §6.76
    Bases
      Improper, §6.66
      Procedures for showing bases and reasons, sample questions, §6.67
      Proper, §6.65
    Cause of injuries, §6.71
      Admissibility, §6.73
      Form of testimony, sample questions, §6.74
      Value of causation testimony, §6.72
    Diagnosis: nature and extent of injuries, §6.68
      Admissibility, §6.69
      Relating diagnoses to injuries, sample questions, §6.70
    Procedures for showing bases and reasons, sample questions, §6.67
    Prognosis: continuing, permanent, and future injuries, §6.75
      Admissibility, §6.76
      Continuing conditions, sample questions, §6.78

Medical opinion testimony—*cont.*
  Prognosis—*cont.*
      Future conditions, sample questions, §6.79
      Permanency, sample questions, §6.78
      Reasonable medical certainty, §6.77
    Referring doctor's opinion, reports from other examiners, §§6.56–6.57
  Technical experts
    Admissibility, §5.58
    Analyses as bases, §5.62
    Bases of opinions, stating of, §§5.60–5.66
    Books as bases, §5.64
    Community standards as bases, §5.65
    Elicitation of, §§5.58–5.68
    Expressing opinion, sample questions-answers, §5.67
    Facts in evidence as bases, §5.61
    Industry standards as bases, sample questions and answers, §5.65
    Official regulatory standards as bases, §5.66
    Other literature as bases, §5.64
    Perception of expert as bases, §5.62
    Reasons for opinion, sample question-answer for stating of, §5.68
    Special qualifications of expert as bases, sample questions-answers, §5.63
    Statutory standards as bases, §5.66
    Subject of opinion, sample question-answer for showing of, §5.59
    Sufficiency of expert's qualifications to permit admission, §5.36

INDEX

OPINION TESTIMONY— *cont.*
Technical experts—*cont.*
Tests as bases, sample questions-answers, §5.62
Treatises as bases, §5.64

ORDERS
Exhibits
Pretrial order for admission, *form,* §8.23
Release to owner; stipulation, order and receipt for release, *form,* §8.6

PARTIES
See also Plaintiff's Testimony
Adverse party's rights re writings used for
Past recollection recorded, sample questions, §8.33
Refreshing memory, §1.38
References to and addressing parties during direct examination, §1.8
Statements to police officer, admissibility, §§4.42–4.48

PAST RECOLLECTION RECORDED
Depositions used as, §10.11
Adverse witness, §10.13
Own witness, sample questions, §10.12
Distinguished from refreshing memory, §§1.31, 8.26, 10.11
Interrogatories, use of, §10.22
Police accident report as means of, §§4.1, 4.23, 4.26, 9.2, 9.6, 9.9
Writings as, §§8.25–8.33
Adverse parties' rights, sample questions, §8.33

Writings as—*cont.*
Distinguished from writings used to refresh memory, §§1.31, 8.26
Laying foundation, §§8.27–8.31
Another's writings, §§8.29–8.31
Checklist, §8.27
Declarant's testimony, §8.30
Witness's writing, sample questions, §8.28
Writer's testimony, sample, §8.31
Reading into evidence, §8.32
X-ray film report, §16.16

PHOTOGRAPHS
Accident reconstructions, sample questions for authentication, §15.10
Admissibility, §§15.2–15.17
Aerial photographs, §19.4
Agreement for admission, §15.3
Amateur photographers as authenticating witnesses, sample questions, §15.7
Authentication, §§15.2, 15.4
Definition, §15.4
Enlarged prints, §15.18
Particular photographs, §§15.8–15.12
Qualifying authenticating witness, §§15.5–15.7
Transparencies, §15.19
Best evidence rule, §15.13
Changed scene, authentication, sample questions, §15.9
Credibility versus admissibility, §15.15
Cumulative evidence, when, §15.16
Damaged vehicles, sample questions for authentication, §15.11
Definitions
Authentication, §15.4
Photograph, §15.2

525

PHOTOGRAPHS — *cont.*
Enlargements, §15.18
Injured persons, sample questions for authentication, §15.12
Irrelevant photos inadmissible, §15.17
Jury, presenting to, §§15.18–15.19
Misrepresentative or misleading photos, §15.15
Nonphotographers as authenticating witnesses, §15.5
Objections to admission, §§15.13–15.17
Prejudicial photos, §15.14
Pretrial, §15.3
Prints, §15.18
Professional photographers as witnesses, sample questions, §15.6
Relevant evidence, when, §15.17
Scene of accident, sample questions for authentication, §15.8
Stipulation to receive in evidence, §15.3
Transparencies, §15.19
Unduly inflammatory photos, §15.14
Value as evidence, §15.1

PHYSICAL EXAMINATIONS
Admissibility of testimony re, §6.41
Character of, sample questions, §6.43
Clinical tests, sample questions, §6.48
Definition, §6.40
Failure to make observation or test, explanation re, §6.50
Findings
  Absence of, sample questions re, §6.49
  As injuries, §6.47

Findings — *cont.*
  Connecting findings to injuries, sample questions, §6.46
  Definition, §6.40
  Negative findings, sample questions re, §6.49
General appearance, sample questions, §6.44
Hospital and medical records, sample questions re physical examination reports, §13.28
Injuries, sample questions re explanation of, §6.45
Manipulations, sample questions re, §6.48
Medical terms, sample questions re explanation of, §6.45
Mental status, sample questions, §6.44
Motion for examination by physicians, §10.25
Reports from other examiners, §§6.54–6.63
  Admissibility
    Extent of showing, §6.57
    To show basis of referring doctor's opinions, §6.56
  Contents, sample questions, §6.63
  Determining whether to call outside consultant, §6.55
  Identity of
    Results and report, sample questions, §6.61
    Tester or examiner, sample questions, §6.58
  Reasons for test or examination, sample questions, §6.60
  Referral as customary medical practice, sample questions, §6.59

INDEX

**PHYSICAL EXAMINA-
TIONS** — *cont.*
Reports from other examiners — *cont.*
  Reliability of tester or examiner, sample questions, §6.58
  Return of results and report, sample questions, §6.61
  Witness's reliance, sample questions, §6.62
Scope, §6.40
Special diagnostic procedures, §§6.51–6.53
  Admissibility of testimony, §6.52
  Extent of testimony, §6.53
  Specific questions re, use of, §6.42
  Type of, sample questions, §6.43

PLAINTIFF'S TESTIMONY
Accidents of plaintiff other than current one, §3.18
Admissions of defendant, §3.16
Age, sample questions, §3.4
Birthplace, sample questions, §3.4
Checklist for impaired earning capacity, §3.31
Chronology of accident, §§3.13–3.15
Clothing worn at time of accident, §3.9
Conduct of plaintiff and defendant before impact, §3.13
Cross-examination, §3.2
Custom, §3.17
Description of injuries and treatment, sample questions and answers, §3.24
Destination, §3.10
Direct examination, §3.1
Disability generally, §§3.26–3.28

Earnings
  Earning capacity impaired, §§3.30–3.32
  Loss of earnings, sample questions, §3.32
Extent of, §§3.1–3.2
Family status, sample questions, §3.5
Financial status, sample questions, §3.7
Habit, §3.17
Health before accident, §§3.20–3.22
  Good health, §3.20
  Predisposition to injury, sample questions, §3.22
  Prior conditions, sample questions, §3.21
    Aggravation of, sample questions, §3.22
Housewife's injury, §3.28
Impact, §3.14
  Conditions after impact, §3.15
  Conduct of plaintiff and defendant before impact, §3.13
Injury testimony, §§3.19–3.29
Insurance, defendant's admission re, §3.16
Liability testimony, §§3.8–3.18
Mechanics of injury, §3.23
Medical bills, §14.4
Mental suffering, §3.29
Name, sample questions, §3.4
Normal life, impairment of, §§3.26–3.28
Occupation, sample questions, §3.6
Pain, sample questions-answers, §3.25
Personal background, §§3.3–3.7
Physical condition and appearance of plaintiff before accident, §3.9
Presence of plaintiff throughout trial, §3.3

527

INDEX

**PLAINTIFF'S TESTI-
MONY**—*cont.*
Purpose at time of accident,
§3.10
Residence, sample questions,
§3.4
Route, §3.10
Scene of accident, §3.12
Time of day, §3.12
Vehicle, §3.11
Weather, §3.12
Work
  Need to return to work, sample
  questions re, §3.7
  Work history, sample questions, §3.6
Worker's injury, §3.27

POLICE ACCIDENT REPORT
Admission as exhibit, §§9.9-9.15
Authentication, §9.13
California Highway Patrol Vehicle
  Accident Report
  Code for interpreting, §4.4
  Sample, §4.3
Contents, §9.1
Diagrams, §§4.26, 19.5
Fee for copy, §9.3
Hearsay and exceptions, §§4.5,
  4.21, 4.34, 4.42-4.46,
  9.12
Impeachment of witness by,
  §9.16
Investigative use, obtaining report for, §9.3
  Authorization, *form,* §9.5
  Request and declaration,
  form, §9.4
Objections to admission, §§9.11-
  9.14
Offering report in evidence,
  §9.15
Past recollection recorded, use
  of report, §§4.1, 4.23,
  4.26, 9.2, 9.6, 9.9
  Sample questions, §4.23

Prior statement of witness,
  using report to show
  Prior consistent statement,
  §9.17
  Prior inconsistent statement,
  §9.16
Privilege, §9.11
Refreshing memory, use of report, §§4.1, 4.21-4.22,
  4.26, 9.2, 9.6, 9.9,
  9.17
  Sample questions re report,
  §§1.36, 4.22
Review of, §§4.2-4.4
Stipulation for admission, §§9.9-
  9.10
Subpenas duces tecum, §§4.21,
  9.7
  Declaration for, *form,*
  §9.8
  Trial use, obtaining report for,
  §§9.6-9.8
Uses, §9.2
  As aid to testimony, §§4.1,
  4.21-4.23, 9.2
Value, §§9.1-9.2

POLICE OFFICERS
  See also Police Accident
  Report; Subpenas
Activities and observations at
  accident scene, sample
  testimony, §§4.24-4.41
Aiding victims, §4.25
Attendance at trial, §§4.12-
  4.15
  See also Subpenas
Debris, questions re, §4.37
Deposition of, §4.11
Diagrams, use of, §§4.26, 19.5
  Questions re, §19.4
Drivers; passengers; pedestrians;
  questions re, §§4.33-
  4.36
Eliciting unfavorable opinion on
  direct examination,
  sample testimony, §4.59

INDEX

POLICE OFFICERS — *cont.*
Expert witness, officer as, §§4.49–4.58
  Attacking qualifications of, sample voir dire, §4.52
  Decision whether to use officer, §4.50
  Influence of narcotics, opinion re, §4.58
  Loading of truck, questions re, §4.55
  Point of impact, sample testimony, §4.53
  Special qualifications, sample testimony, §4.51
  Speed
    Before collision, §4.57
    Safe speed under conditions, §4.56
  Subjects of expert testimony, §§4.53–4.58
  Vehicle's mechanical condition, opinion re, §4.54
Identification of, §4.5
Impartiality of, sample questions re, §4.19
Impeachment of, §4.59
Interviews with officer
  Arranging time and place, §4.7
  Checklists
    Evaluating officer as witness, §4.10
    Questions, §4.9
  Compensation, §4.8
  Courthouse interview, §4.16
  Evaluation of officer as witness, §4.10
  Purpose, §4.6
Intoxication of driver, questions re, §4.36
Investigative
  Background, sample questions re, §4.18
  Procedure, sample questions re, §4.20

Past recollection recorded, §§4.1, 4.23
  Sample questions, §4.23
Police background, sample questions re, §4.18
Preparation as witness, §§4.1–4.16
Qualifications as witness, §§4.17–4.20
Refreshing memory, §§4.1, 4.21–4.22, 4.26
  Sample questions, §§1.36, 4.22
Reimbursement of police agency, §4.14
Remuneration for
  Investigative interview, none, §4.8
  Trial, §4.14
Roadway, questions re, §§4.26–4.28
Skid marks, questions re, §§4.37, 4.53
Statements of parties and witnesses, §§4.42–4.48
Time of arrival at accident scene, questions re, §4.24
Traffic, questions re
  Clearing traffic, §4.25
  Traffic controls, §4.38
Value as witness, §4.1
Visibility, questions re, §4.40
Weather, questions re, §4.39

PRESUMPTIONS
Books published by public authority, judicial notice, §20.28
Case reports published in jurisdiction, §§20.32, 20.34

PRETRIAL
Exhibits, pretrial order for admission, *form,* §8.23
Judicial notice request, made during pretrial proceedings, §20.16

INDEX

PRETRIAL—*cont.*
Medical bills, pretrial order re, §14.3
Photographs, §15.3

PRIOR STATEMENTS.
See Statements

PRIVILEGES
Physician-patient privilege, hospital and medical records, §13.11
Police accident report, §9.11

PROGNOSIS
Hospital and medical records, sample questions and answers, §13.38
Medical opinion testimony re continuing, permanent, and future injuries, §6.75
  Admissibility, §6.76
  Continuing conditions, sample questions, §6.78
  Future conditions, sample questions, §6.79
  Permanency, sample questions, §6.78
  Reasonable medical certainty, §6.77

QUESTIONS
Answering questions on direct examination, how to, §1.3
Hypothetical questions, expert witness, §1.28
  Cross-examination, examples, §1.30
  Direct examination, examples, §1.29
  Impeachment of witness, use of hypotheticals, §2.18
  Objections to use, §1.28
Leading questions
  Cross-examination, §1.41

Leading questions—*cont.*
  Expert witnesses, §1.12
  Foundational matters, §1.11
  Impeachment of witness, use of, §2.1
  Preliminary matters, §1.11
  Purpose of, §1.10
  Refreshing memory during testimony, examples, §1.37
  Narrative answers, use of questions calling for, §1.9
  Phrasing questions for direct examination, §1.6
  Technical experts, determining form of questions for examination of, §5.35

RADIOGRAPHS. *See* X-Ray Films

REBUTTAL
Discussion of, §1.45
Showing prior consistent statements, §1.44

RECORDS
See also Business Records; Hospital and Medical Records
Missing person records, §12.8
Official records
  Absence of, §12.9
  Admissibility, §§12.1–12.5
  Agreement for admission, §12.2
  As business records, §§12.1, 12.3
  Custodian's affidavit, admissibility by, §12.3
  Definition, §12.1
  Foundational testimony, §12.5
  Independent evidence of trustworthiness, §12.4
  Judicial notice, §12.4
  Particular records, §§12.6–12.8

INDEX

RECORDS—*cont.*
Official records—*cont.*
  Show of trustworthiness, admissibility by, §12.4
  Subpena duces tecum, §12.3
  Presumed death, findings of, §12.8
School records, laying foundation for plaintiff's public school record, §12.6
Vital statistics, §12.7
Wage record. *See* Business Records

REFRESHING MEMORY
Adverse party's rights, §§1.38, 6.28
Basic discussion, §1.31
Before testimony, §§1.33–1.34
  Suggestion, use of, §1.34
  Writings, §1.33
Cross-examination, §1.31
Definition, §1.31
Depositions, use of, §10.3
  Adverse witness, §10.5
  Own witness
    Sample questions, §10.4
    Showing prior inconsistent statement, §10.6
During testimony, §§1.35–1.37
  Leading questions, examples, §1.37
  Writing
    Carried to stand, examples, §1.36
    Handed to witness, examples, §1.35
Interrogatories, use of, §10.22
Medical experts, doctors, §6.28
Past recollection recorded, distinguished from, §§1.31, 8.26, 10.11
Police accident report as means of, §§4.1, 4.21–4.22, 4.26, 9.2, 9.6, 9.9, 9.17
Sample questions re report, §§1.36, 4.22

Writings
  Adverse party's rights re, §1.38
  Before testimony, §1.33
  During testimony
    Carried to stand, examples, §1.36
    Handed to witness, examples, §1.35
  Request for production as discovery device, §1.39
  Types of, §1.32
X-rays, use of
  Film, §16.1
  Report on film, §16.16

RELEASE
Exhibits; stipulation, order and receipt for release, *form*, §8.6

RELEVANCY. *See* Evidence

REPORTS
Accident report. *See* Police Accident Report
Electrographic reports, §13.30
Laboratory reports, sample questions, §13.30
Medical reports
  Doctor's use of, §6.27
    Refreshing memory, §6.28
  From other examiners, §§6.54–6.63
    Admissibility to show basis of referring doctor's opinions, §6.56
    Contents, sample questions, §6.63
    Extent of showing, §6.57
    Identity of results and report, sample questions re, §6.61
    Identity of tester or examiner, sample questions re, §6.58

531

REPORTS—*cont.*
Medical reports—*cont.*
From other examiners—*cont.*
Reasons for test or examination, sample questions re, §6.60
Referral as customary medical practice, sample questions re, §6.59
Reliability of tester or examiner, sample questions re, §6.58
Return of results and report, sample questions re, §6.61
Witness's reliance, sample questions, §6.62
Operation report, sample questions, §13.31
Physical examination reports, sample questions, §13.28
X-ray films, report on, §16.16
Hospital and medical records, §13.39

REQUESTS
Admission, request for, §10.24
Exhibits, request for admission, *form,* §8.22
Medical bills, §14.3
Police accident report, request for copy, *form,* §9.4

RES GESTAE. *See* Spontaneous Statements

RESIDENCE
Plaintiff's testimony re, sample questions, §3.4

ROADWAY
Police officer as witness, questions re
Contour, §4.27
Diagram, §4.26
Layout, §4.27
Obstructions, §4.28

Police officer as witness—*cont.*
Surface, §4.27

ROENTGENOGRAMS. *See* X-Ray Films

SEMANTICS
Direct examination, §1.7

SERVICE
Business records, service of
Declaration or affidavit, §11.10
Notice describing procedure for compliance, §11.11
Subpena duces tecum, §11.9
Hospital and medical records, service of subpena duces tecum, §§13.14–13.15
Medical bills, copy of, §14.3

SETTLEMENTS
Prior settlement, impeachment of witness by evidence of, §2.3

SIGNATURES
Depositions, §§10.4, 10.18

SKELETONS
Sample questions re, §18.12

SKIAGRAMS. *See* X-Ray Films

SKID MARKS
Questions to police officer as
Expert witness, point of impact, §4.53
Witness, §4.37

SPEED
Police officer's expert testimony re
Safe speed under conditions, §4.56
Speed before collision, §4.57

INDEX

SPEED—*cont.*
Testimony re, §1.17
 Caveat, §1.4
 Police officer's. *See* Police above

SPONTANEOUS STATEMENTS
Hearsay exception, §4.46
Questions to police officer witness re, §4.46

STATEMENTS
 See also Spontaneous Statements
Parties' and witnesses' statements to police officer, §§4.42–4.48
 Adoptive admissions, §4.44
 Driver's statement to show liability of employer or owner, §4.45
 Guilty plea, §4.48
 Hearsay exceptions, §§4.42–4.46
 Liability insurance, statements re, §4.47
 Nolo contendere plea, §4.48
 Party's admissions, §4.43
 Spontaneous statements, §4.46
Prior consistent statements
 Depositions, use of
  Adverse witness, §10.10
  Own witness, sample questions, §10.9
 Interrogatories, used to show, §10.22
 Police accident report, used to show, §9.17
 Showing on redirect examination, examples, §1.44
Prior inconsistent statements, impeachment of witness by, §§2.7–2.12
 Deposition, use of
  Adverse witness, sample questions, §10.7

Prior inconsistent statements—*cont.*
 Deposition, use of—*cont.*
  Own witness, §10.6
  When deponent becomes own witness, §10.8
 Hospital and medical records used to impeach, §§13.42–13.46
  Absence of complaints, sample questions re, §13.46
  Confronting witness, sample questions, §13.43
  Forgotten statement, sample questions, §13.44
  Statement of preaccident health, sample questions, §13.45
 Interrogatories, used to show, §10.22
 Police accident report, sample use of, §9.16

STIPULATIONS
Business records, example, §11.2
Depositions, stipulations reserving objections, §10.17
Diagrams and maps, §19.10
Exhibits
 Admission of exhibits
  Oral stipulation, sample, §8.24
  Written stipulation, *form*, §8.21
 Release to owner; stipulation, order and receipt for release, *form*, §8.6
Hospital and medical records, example, §13.13
Medical bills, §14.3
Photographs, receipt in evidence, §15.3
Police accident report, stipulation for admission of, §§9.9–9.10

533

INDEX

STIPULATIONS—*cont.*
Witness, stipulation not to call, §1.1
X-ray films, stipulation for admission, §16.2

SUBPENAS
See also Subpenas Duces Tecum
Police officer's attendance at trial, subpena compelling
  Deposit of fees, §4.14
    Clause in subpena showing deposit of fees, *form,* §4.15
  Range of, §4.13
  Use of, §4.12

SUBPENAS DUCES TECUM
Business records, §§11.8–11.15
  Clause requiring personal attendance of custodian with original records, *sample,* §11.15
  Declaration for, *form,* §11.10
  Issuance, §11.9
  Notice describing procedure for compliance, *form,* §11.11
  Service of, §11.9
Hospital and medical records, §§13.14–13.18
  Declaration for subpena duces tecum, *form,* §13.15
  Service, §§13.14–13.15
Official records, §12.3
Police accident report, §§4.21, 9.7
  Declaration for issuance of subpenas duces tecum, *form,* §9.8
Wage records, §11.16

SUPPLEMENTAL PROCEEDINGS
Depositions, §10.19

TABLES
Judicial notice, chart of federal and state law, §20.8

TECHNICAL EXPERTS
Ceramic engineers, §5.8
Chemical engineers, §5.9
Chemists, §5.10
Civil engineers, §5.11
Climatologists, §5.12
Costs, §5.27
Credibility, §5.24
Descriptions of specialties, §§5.8–5.21
Determination of appropriate specialty, checklists, §§5.3–5.7
  Buildings, §5.6
  Carrier accidents, §5.4
  Chemicals, §5.7
  Construction sites, §5.6
  Drugs, §5.7
  Explosions, §5.7
  Fall, §5.5
  Foods, §5.7
  Premises, §5.6
  Slip, §5.5
  Vehicle accidents, §5.4
Diagrams, §§19.11, 19.18
Discovery considerations, §5.33
Electrical engineers, §5.13
Examples in personal injury cases, §5.2
Fees, §5.27
Health chemistry engineers, §5.14
Hypothesis of, testing of, §5.34
Industrial engineers, §5.15
Juror's confidence, sufficiency of experts' qualifications to gain, §5.37
Knowledge of subject
  Criteria for selecting expert, §5.23
  Qualifications, sample questions re subject in issue, §5.57

INDEX

TECHNICAL EXPERTS— *cont.*
Locality of trial, §5.26
Locating expert through
  Articles, §5.32
  Books, §5.32
  Client, §5.30
  Court decisions, §5.29
  Other lawyers, §5.29
  Research services, §5.32
  Universities, §5.31
Manner of expression, §5.25
Mechanical engineers, §5.16
Metallurgical engineers, §5.17
Meteorologists, §5.12
More than one expert, use of, §5.28
Nonprofessional experts, §5.18
Offers to concede qualifications, handling of, §5.38
Opinion testimony
  Admissibility, §5.58
  Analyses as bases, §5.62
  Bases of opinions, stating of, §§5.60–5.66
  Books as bases, §5.64
  Community standards as bases, §5.65
  Elicitation of, §§5.58–5.68
  Expressing opinion, sample questions and answers, §5.67
  Facts in evidence as bases, §5.61
  Industry standards as bases, sample questions and answers, §5.65
  Official regulatory standards as bases, §5.66
  Other literature as bases, §5.64
  Perceptions of expert as bases, §5.62
  Reasons for opinion, sample question-answer for stating of, §5.68

Opinion testimony—*cont.*
  Special qualifications of expert as bases, sample questions and answers, §5.63
  Statutory standards as bases, §5.66
  Subject of opinion, sample question-answer for showing of, §5.59
  Sufficiency of qualifications of expert to permit admission of, §5.36
  Tests as bases, sample questions-answers, §5.62
  Treatises as bases, §5.64
Personality, §5.25
Pharmacologists, §5.19
Physicists, §5.20
Preparation for examination of, §§5.33–5.35
Qualifications, checklist and sample questions and answers re particular items, §§5.39–5.57
  Address, §5.40
  Authorship, §5.54
  Consultation experience in other cases, §5.56
  Education and degrees
    Nonprofessionals, §5.43
    Professionals, §5.42
  Employee of defendant company, present employment, §5.46
  Knowledge of subject in issue, §5.57
  Lecturing, §5.53
  Licenses, §5.41
  Military service, §5.51
  Name, §5.40
  Nonprofessionals
    Education and degrees, §5.43
    Present employment, §5.47
    Specialization, §5.49
  Occupation, §5.40

INDEX

TECHNICAL EXPERTS — *cont.*
Qualifications — *cont.*
Officer of research or consulting firm, present employer, §5.45
Patents, §5.55
Present employment, §§5.44–5.47
Previous employment, §5.50
Professional societies, §5.52
Professionals
Education and degrees, §5.42
Specialization, §5.48
Professor, present employment, §5.44
Registration, §5.41
Specialization
Nonprofessional, §5.49
Professional, §5.48
Teaching, §5.53
Questions, determining form of, §5.35
Reasons for using, §5.1
Selection of, criteria for, §§5.22–5.28
Sufficiency of qualifications to
Gain jurors' confidence, §5.37
Permit admission of opinion testimony, §5.36
Toxicologists, §5.21
Trial use, before and at, §5.1
When to employ, §5.33

TIME
Caveat re testimony on, §1.4
Plaintiff's testimony re, §3.12
Police officer's time of arrival at accident scene, questions re, §4.24

TRAFFIC CONTROLS
Police officer as witness, question re, §4.38

WAGE RECORDS. *See* Business Records

WAIVER
Depositions, waiver of
Objections to admission, §§10.17–10.18
Signing requirement, §10.18
Expert witness, waiver of testimony re special qualifications, §1.22

WEATHER
Judicial notice of Weather Bureau reports, §20.44
Plaintiff's testimony re, §3.12
Police officer as witness, questions re, §4.39

WITNESSES
See also Cross-examination; Depositions; Expert Witnesses; Impeachment of Witnesses; Interrogatories; Medical Experts; Opinion Testimony; Past Recollection Recorded; Plaintiff's Testimony; Police Officers; Questions; Refreshing Memory; Technical Experts
Acquaintances, sample questions, §7.7
Answering questions, how to, §1.3
Appraisers of impaired earning capacity, §§7.9–7.12
Attendance, §1.2
Behavior, §1.2
Bibliography, §§1.1, 2.1
Bystanders at accident scene, §7.2
Capacity, §1.14
Competency, §1.14
Credibility, §1.13
Definitions
Lay witness, §1.13
Perceive, §1.15

INDEX

WITNESSES—*cont.*
Definitions—*cont.*
  Personal knowledge, §1.15
  Qualification of lay witness, §§1.13–1.14
Diagram of accident scene, sample testimony re
  Preparing diagram during testimony, §19.19
  Using prepared diagram, §19.18
Distance, testimony re, §1.17
  Caveat, §1.4
Dress, §1.2
Economists as appraisers of impaired earning capacity, §§7.9–7.12
  Basis of testimony, §7.10
  Checklist for qualifications, §7.11
  Topics of testimony, §7.12
Employer, sample questions, §7.8
Family members, §§7.4–7.5
Fellow workers, §7.6
Medical personnel, §7.3
Motion pictures, cinematographer as authenticating witness, sample questions when
  Amateur, §17.9
  Professional, §17.8
Narrative answers, §1.9
Neighbors, sample questions, §7.7
Nurses, §7.3
Other witnesses on damages, §§7.1–7.12
Personal knowledge, §1.15
Personnel manager, sample questions, §7.8
Photographs, qualifying authenticating witness
  Amateur photographer, sample questions, §15.7
  Nonphotographer, §15.5
  Professional photographer, sample questions, §15.6
Phrasing questions for, §1.6
Preparation of, §§1.1–1.4

Qualifications, §§1.13–1.15
Rebuttal, §1.45
  Showing prior consistent statements, §1.44
Redirect examination
  Limitations, §1.43
  Purposes, §1.43
  Showing prior consistent statements, examples, §1.44
References to and addressing witnesses during direct examination, §1.8
Statements to police officer, admissibility, §4.42
Statisticians as appraisers of impaired earning capacity, §§7.9–7.12
  Basis of testimony, §7.10
  Checklist for qualifications, §7.11
  Topics of testimony, §7.12
Stipulations, when to use, §1.1
Style and sequence of direct examination, §1.5
Supervisors, §7.6
Testimony on damages and injuries, scope of, §7.1
Wage record witness, sample questions-answers for identifying, §11.17
Writings of, as past recollection recorded, sample questions, §8.28
X-ray films, authenticating witnesses
  Choosing of, §16.9
  Doctor, sample questions for doctor who
    Made films, §16.10
    Ordered films, §16.12
  X-ray technician, sample questions for, §16.11

WRITINGS. *See* Past Recollection Recorded; Refreshing Memory

X-RAY FILMS
Admissibility, §§16.2–16.17
Agreement for admission, §16.2
As aid to testimony, §16.15
Authentication, §16.3
    Laying foundation, §§16.4–16.8
    Particular films, §§16.13–16.14
    Witnesses, §§16.9–16.12
Cineradiography, §16.21
Date film taken, §16.4
Dependability of equipment, §16.8
Description of, sample, §16.2
Enlargements, sample questions, §16.20
Exclusions, when, reasons for, §16.3
Filmmaking procedure, testimony re, §16.7
Hospital and medical records, films in, §§13.39, 16.17
    Sample questions, §16.17
Identity of patient, §16.4
Interpretation of, sample questions, §16.5
Judicial notice, §16.6
Jury
    Clause restricting viewing by, sample, §16.2
    Jury room, sending films to, §16.22
    Presenting to, §§16.18–16.21
Laying foundation for, §§16.4–16.8
Medical experts, §§16.9, 16.16
Nature of process, §16.6
Normal person's X-ray used, sample questions re, §16.13
Past recollection recorded, use of report on film, §16.16
Positive prints, sample questions, §16.20
Reasons for, §16.1
Refreshing memory, §§16.1, 16.16
Report, §16.16
    Hospital and medical records, §§13.39, 16.16
Soft-tissue injuries, sample questions re, §16.14
Stereoscopic films, sample questions re, §16.19
Stipulation for admission, §16.2
Synonymous terms, §16.1
Validity of process, §16.6
Value as evidence, §16.1
Viewing box for presentation, §16.18
Witnesses for authenticating
    Choosing of, §16.9
    Doctor, sample questions for doctor who
        Made films, §16.10
        Ordered films, §16.12
    X-ray technician, sample questions for, §16.11